Lecture Notes in Computer Science 4339

Commenced Publication in 1973
Founding and Former Series Editors:
Gerhard Goos, Juris Hartmanis, and Jan van Leeuwen

Eduard Ayguadé Gerald Baumgartner
J. Ramanujam P. Sadayappan (Eds.)

Languages and Compilers for Parallel Computing

18th International Workshop, LCPC 2005
Hawthorne, NY, USA, October 20-22, 2005
Revised Selected Papers

Volume Editors

Eduard Ayguadé
Computer Architecture Department
Universitat Politécnica de Catalunya
08034 Barcelona, Catalunya, Spain
E-mail: eduard@cepba.upc.es

Gerald Baumgartner
Department of Computer Science
Louisiana State University
Baton Rouge, LA 70803, USA
E-mail: gb@csc.lsu.edu

J. Ramanujam
Department of Electrical and Computer Engineering
Louisiana State University
Baton Rouge, LA 70803, USA
E-mail: jxr@ece.lsu.edu

P. Sadayappan
Department of Computer Science and Engineering
The Ohio State University
Columbus, OH 43210, USA
E-mail: saday@cis.ohio-state.edu

Library of Congress Control Number: 2006939009

CR Subject Classification (1998): D.3, D.1.3, F.1.2, B.2.1, C.2.4, C.2, E.1, D.4

LNCS Sublibrary: SL 1 – Theoretical Computer Science and General Issues

ISSN 0302-9743
ISBN-10 3-540-69329-7 Springer Berlin Heidelberg New York
ISBN-13 978-3-540-69329-1 Springer Berlin Heidelberg New York

Springer is a part of Springer Science+Business Media

springer.com

Printed in Germany

Typesetting: Camera-ready by author, data conversion by Scientific Publishing Services, Chennai, India
Printed on acid-free paper SPIN: 11967729 06/3142 5 4 3 2 1 0

Preface

The 18th International Workshop on Languages and Compilers for High-Performance Computing was scheduled to be held in New Orleans, Louisiana, in October 2005. Unfortunately, because of the devastation caused by Hurricane Katrina the meeting needed to be moved. It was held in Hawthorne, New York, thanks to help from IBM. The workshop is an annual forum for leading research groups to present their current research activities and the latest results, covering languages, compiler techniques, runtime environments, and compiler-related performance evaluation for parallel and high-performance computing. Sixty-five researchers from Canada, France, Japan, Korea, P.R. China, Spain, Switzerland, Taiwan, UK, and the USA attended the workshop.

Thirty-four research papers (26 regular papers and eight short papers) were presented at the workshop. These papers were reviewed by the Program Committee; external reviewers were used as needed. The authors then received additional comments during the workshop. The revisions after the workshop are now assembled into these final proceedings.

We thank Siddhartha Chatterjee from the IBM T.J. Watson Research Center for his keynote talk titled "The Changing Landscape of Parallel Computing." The workshop included a special session titled "High-Productivity Languages for HPC: Compiler Challenges" consisting of invited talks on the three languages being developed by the DARPA High-Productivity Computing Systems (HPCS) vendors. The talks were given by Steve Dietz (from Cray on the language Chapel), Vivek Sarkar (from IBM on the language X10), and David Chase (from Sun on the language Fortress). Frederica Darema gave a presentation during the workshop banquet about the proposed Dynamic Data-Driven Applications Systems (DDDAS) program at the US National Science Foundation.

The workshop was sponsored by the US National Science Foundation and by International Business Machines Corporation. Their generous contribution is greatly appreciated. We appreciate the assistance offered by the staff in the Department of Computer Science and Engineering at the Ohio State University and thank Alex Ramirez of Universitat Politécnica de Catalunya (Spain) for generous help with the paper submission and review software. Our special thanks go to the LCPC 2005 Program Committee and the external reviewers for their efforts in reviewing the submissions. Advice and suggestions from both the Steering Committee and the Program Committee are much appreciated. Finally, we wish to thank all the authors and participants for their contributions and lively discussions, which made the workshop a success.

November 2006

Eduard Ayguadé, Gerald Baumgartner,
J. (Ram) Ramanujam, P. (Saday) Sadayappan

Preface

Organization

Committees

General/Program Co-chairs:

Eduard Ayguadé
(Universitat Politècnica de Catalunya, Spain)
Gerald Baumgartner
(Louisiana State University, USA)
J. (Ram) Ramanujam
(Louisiana State University, USA)
P. (Saday) Sadayappan
(The Ohio State University, USA)

Program Committee:

Nancy Amato
(Texas A&M University, USA)
Gheorghe Almási
(IBM Thomas J. Watson Research Center, USA)
Eduard Ayguadé
(Universitat Politècnica de Catalunya, Spain)
Gerald Baumgartner
(Louisiana State University, USA)
Calin Cascaval
(IBM Thomas J. Watson Research Center, USA)
Rudolf Eigenmann
(Purdue University, USA)
Zhiyuan Li
(Purdue University, USA)
Sam Midkiff
(Purdue University, USA)
J. (Ram) Ramanujam
(Louisiana State University, USA)
Lawrence Rauchwerger
(Texas A&M University, USA)
P. (Saday) Sadayappan
(The Ohio State University, USA)
Bjarne Stoustrup
(Texas A&M University, USA)
Peng Wu
(IBM Thomas J. Watson Research Center, USA)

Local Organizing Committee:	Gheorghe Almási (IBM Thomas J. Watson Research Center, USA)
	Calin Cascaval (IBM Thomas J. Watson Research Center, USA)
	Peng Wu (IBM Thomas J. Watson Research Center, USA)
Steering Committee:	Utpal Banerjee (Intel Corporation, USA)
	David Gelernter (Yale University, USA)
	Alex Nicolau (University of California, Irvine, USA)
	David Padua (University of Illinois at Urbana-Champaign, USA)

Sponsors

National Science Foundation, USA
International Business Machines Corporation

Table of Contents

Revisiting Graph Coloring Register Allocation: A Study of the Chaitin-Briggs and Callahan-Koblenz Algorithms

Keith D. Cooper, Anshuman Dasgupta, and Jason Eckhardt

Department of Computer Science, Rice University
{keith, anshuman, jle}@cs.rice.edu

Abstract. Techniques for global register allocation via graph coloring have been extensively studied and widely implemented in compiler frameworks. This paper examines a particular variant – the Callahan Koblenz allocator – and compares it to the Chaitin-Briggs graph coloring register allocator. Both algorithms were published in the 1990's, yet the academic literature does not contain an assessment of the Callahan-Koblenz allocator. This paper evaluates and contrasts the allocation decisions made by both algorithms. In particular, we focus on two key differences between the allocators:

Spill code: The Callahan-Koblenz allocator attempts to minimize the effect of spill code by using program structure to guide allocation and spill code placement. We evaluate the impact of this strategy on allocated code.

Copy elimination: Effective register-to-register copy removal is important for producing good code. The allocators use different techniques to eliminate these copies. We compare the mechanisms and provide insights into the relative performance of the contrasting techniques.

The Callahan-Koblenz allocator may potentially insert extra branches as part of the allocation process. We also measure the performance overhead due to these branches.

1 Introduction

While processor speed has increased dramatically in the last 20 years, main memory speeds have struggled to keep up. To address this disparity, current computer architectures contain several levels of smaller but faster storage in between main memory and the processor. Consequently, modern compilers must ensure that frequently used values in a program are stored in the higher echelons of this memory hierarchy. In particular, registers are the fastest storage locations and compilers run a register allocation phase to map values in the program to registers available on the target architecture. This phase is critical in producing a speedy program. However, it is prohibitively expensive to optimally conduct global register allocation since the problem is NP-complete [18]. As a

E. Ayguadé et al. (Eds.): LCPC 2005, LNCS 4339, pp. 1–16, 2007.

result, allocation is usually performed by a heuristic driven algorithm. Our paper will focus on two such algorithms – the Chaitin-Briggs allocator [5] and the Callahan-Koblenz hierarchical allocator [6] – that map the register allocation problem to a graph coloring problem. Both algorithms construct and color an interference graph that represents correctness constraints. As can be expected, optimal coloring of the interference graph is also NP-complete and the allocators resort to heuristics to color the graph.

The major difference in the two allocators lies in their consideration of program structure. After constructing the interference graph, Chaitin-Briggs does not consider the control flow of the program. In contrast, the Callahan-Koblenz algorithm constructs a hierarchy of tiles to capture loops and conditional control flow in the program. This tile representation of the program is then used to guide allocation and spill decisions. We shall analyze the impact of these locality-based decisions on the quality of generated code. Another key difference in the two allocators lies in their register-to-register copy removal techniques. The removal of unnecessary register copies is an integral part of both algorithms. While the Chaitin-Briggs algorithm conducts copy coalescing to eliminate redundant copies, Callahan-Koblenz uses a *preferencing* technique which is a mechanism that influences the way certain nodes are colored. We shall compare the effectiveness of the two techniques on various benchmarks.

The Chaitin-Briggs allocator has been investigated extensively, and is implemented in practically every industrial and research compiler. In contrast, while the original Callahan-Koblenz article presents a fascinating approach and makes compelling arguments about its functionality, the authors did not present an experimental evaluation. In particular, they described a relatively high-level description of the algorithm and did not provide a comparison to a high-quality baseline allocator. If the Citeseer literature database is any indication, there has been wide interest in the Callahan-Koblenz article – it has been cited almost as frequently as the well-known Briggs paper [5]. However, even after more than a decade since its publication, there still has been no evaluation published in the literature. This is unfortunate since industrial practitioners, in particular, are necessarily conservative about implementing unproven or poorly-understood algorithms in their compilers. This is especially true in the case of the Callahan-Koblenz algorithm, which, as will be seen in the following sections, is significantly more complicated than the proven, easy to implement Chaitin-Briggs allocator. This paper intends to address this gap in the literature and to provide researchers and practitioners with empirical data about the performance of this intriguing algorithm. Because Callahan-Koblenz is considered an extension to graph-coloring techniques, we used Chaitin-Briggs – a well-understood graph coloring algorithm – as the baseline of comparison.

2 Graph Coloring Register Allocation

Register allocators typically take an intermediate representation of a program as input. This representation does not impose any architectural limitations on the number of registers – values are contained in locations known as virtual registers. It is the allocator's responsibility to map the theoretically unlimited virtual registers into a finite number of machine (or physical) registers. Moreover, while conducting this mapping, it needs to maintain the semantics of the program. Graph coloring register allocators construct an interference graph that represents these safety constraints. Program values are represented by nodes in the interference graph and edges between nodes imply that those values cannot share a physical register. Values that cannot share a physical register are said to *interfere* with each other. Both the Chaitin-Briggs and Callahan-Koblenz allocators construct such an interference graph for each procedure in the program and then attempt to color it. However, the two graph coloring algorithms use significantly different techniques to construct and color their interference graphs and to spill registers. To understand and highlight the impact of these differences in allocation decisions, we present a summary of the algorithms in the next two sections.

2.1 Chaitin-Briggs Allocator

As the name suggests, the Chaitin-Briggs allocator ("CB") is based on Chaitin's classical graph coloring allocator. In describing their algorithm, Briggs et al. identify several major phases in their allocator. Our implementation faithfully follows the implementation described in the paper except we do not need to discover and number live ranges (Briggs et. al call this the "Renumber" phase) since this information is already available in the static single assignment form (SSA) based representation we use. The major phases, as depicted in Figure 1 and described in [5] are:

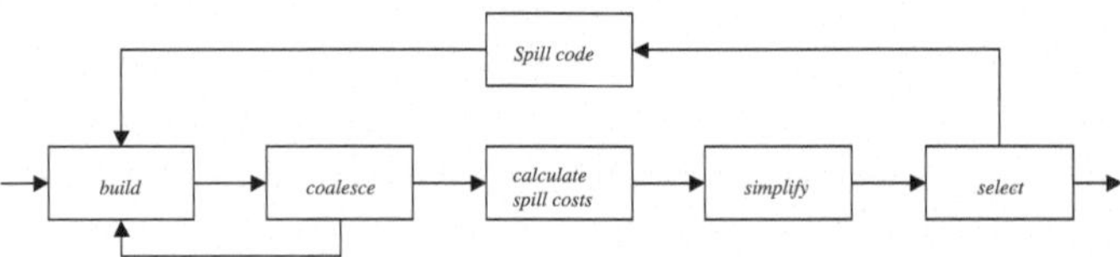

Fig. 1. Overview of the Chaitin-Briggs allocator

Build the Interference Graph: Identify interferences by constructing live ranges and marking interferences between these ranges.
Coalesce: Remove register-to-register copies if the source and the destination registers do not interfere. The build and coalesce phases are repeated until no more coalescing can be conducted. We will provide a detailed analysis of the effects of coalescing in Section 4.2.
Calculate Spill costs and Simplify: These phases calculate spill costs for every node in the interference graph and then order the nodes by pushing them on a stack after removing these nodes from the graph. The Simplify phase first removes all trivially colorable nodes – i.e. nodes that have fewer neighbors than

the number of available physical registers. If it reaches the point where no such node remains in the graph, then this phase consults the spill heuristic, chooses the node with the lowest spill cost, and pushes that node onto the stack. The process is repeated until the graph is empty and all nodes have been placed on the stack.

Select: The allocator tries to color the graph by repeatedly popping a node from the stack, inserting it into the graph, and attempting to assign it a color. If all colors have already been exhausted by its neighbors, then the node is marked for spilling and left uncolored.

Spill code insertion: If any nodes were marked for spilling by the previous phase, then the graph was not successfully colored. As a result, spill code is inserted for those nodes and the allocator is restarted on the modified program. The Briggs allocator marks nodes to be spilled at a later stage than Chaitin's algorithm. The authors call this procedure optimistic coloring since the algorithm defers the spilling of a node in the hope that the node will become colorable.

2.2 Callahan-Koblenz Allocator

The Callahan-Koblenz allocator ("CK") extends Chaitin's allocator by directly incorporating program structure into the allocation process. By doing so, the allocator can decide *which* variables to spill, as well as determine *where* to place the spill code. In contrast to the "spill everywhere" approach of Chaitin, Callahan-Koblenz has the potential to place spills in less frequently executed portions of the program.

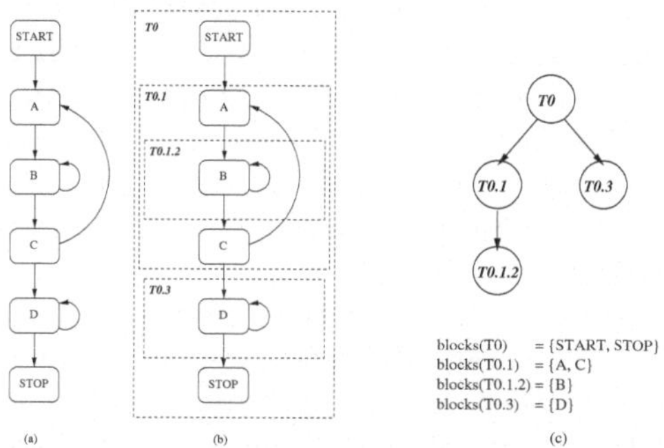

Fig. 2. Example tile tree: (a) CFG; (b) tiles overlaid on CFG; (c) the tile tree

Callahan-Koblenz represents the hierarchical program structure with a *tile tree*. Roughly, each tile in the tree represents a region of code such as a loop or conditional and each pair of tiles in the tree must either be disjoint or properly nested, one within the other. Such a tree structure isolates the high- and low-frequency code regions and provides a basis for the allocator's overall operation and spill placement decisions. Figure 2 shows an example control-flow graph and its corresponding tile tree, where the set $blocks(T)$ represents all basic blocks which belong to tile T, but not to any subtiles of T. Each tile boundary represents an implicit split-point of all values live at that boundary. One of the strengths of Callahan-Koblenz lies in the ability to allocate each portion of a live range between the tile boundaries independently. These split-points also become the locations where any necessary spill code for global values will be placed. Figure 3 depicts the overall structure of the Callahan-Koblenz allocator. Once a tile tree has been constructed, two major passes are made over the tile tree.

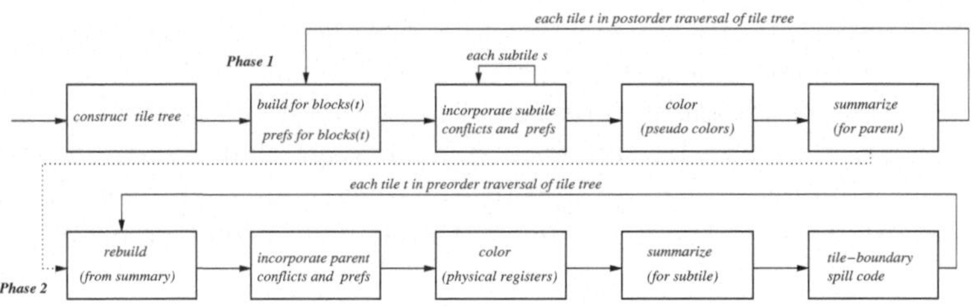

Fig. 3. The Callahan-Koblenz Allocator

Phase 1 (bottom-up): Each tile T is visited in postorder and processed independently with the goal of producing a preliminary allocation. The overall processing of each tile is similar to a Chaitin-Briggs allocator, but includes extra bookkeeping between tiles, and does not perform coalescing.
Build and preferences: Build the interference graph much like Chaitin-Briggs, but restricting attention to $blocks(T)$. Moreover, unlike the standard builder, interferences are not constructed for any variable which is live across, but not referenced in the subtree rooted at T.[1] Preferences (such as for the source and destinations of copy instructions) are also setup at this time.
Incorporate subtile summaries: All subtiles of T will have already been processed, and a compact summary of their allocations stored. This information is incorporated into T's interference graph.
Color: Coloring operates similarly to the Chaitin-Briggs allocator except that color choice may be influenced by preferences and that color may potentially be propagated to other nodes. Except for nodes which must receive a particular physical register, colors assigned in this phase are "pseudo colors" in the sense that they will be re-colored with a physical register in the second phase.
Summarize: After T is processed, a compressed representation of its' interference graph and allocation is constructed and passed up to the parent tile. Included in the summary are all tile-global variables allocated to registers, all tile-globals allocated to memory, and *tile summary variables*. Each TSV corresponds to a set of tile-local variables that were allocated the same color, so that the local allocation is represented in a very compact form.

[1] Such live ranges, which we abbreviate "LBNR", are similar to the "delayed bindings" of [15], or the "inactive" live ranges of [3].

Phase 2 (top-down): Each tile T is visited in preorder with the goal of providing the final assignment of physical registers. Spill code is introduced at tile boundaries to reconcile differences in each tile's allocation.
Rebuild: Reconstruct the interference graph for T from its summary information.
Incorporate parent summaries: Conflicts for LBNRs that were excluded in the first phase are now added to the graph for consideration, if they received a register in the parent.
Color: A final coloring is performed, binding pseudo-colors to physical registers. As before, coloring decisions are influenced by any preferences.
Summarize: Save T's allocation and preference information to be passed down to its subtiles.
Spill code: Spill code is introduced at the tile boundaries, which may not be the same tile where a particular spill decision was made.

3 Experimental Setup

For our experimental setup, we used the LLVM compiler infrastructure [14]. We ran the allocators on an Intel Pentium 4 machine with 1 GB of main memory running Redhat Linux 9.0. The Pentium 4 processor has 7 allocatable integer registers and 8 allocatable floating point registers. We selected benchmarks that performed mostly integer computations, since the current LLVM x86 backend has limited support for global floating-point register allocation. That is, LLVM is generally unable to allocate floating-point values across basic blocks due to complications in handling the stack-based FP register file of x86. As a result, the allocators were evaluated on programs from the SPEC 2000 integer benchmarks and one program from the Mediabench suite: `epic`.

4 Evaluating the Allocators

In evaluating the allocators, we posed and answered two major questions. Since a critical goal of the CK algorithm is to minimize dynamic memory references generated by spill code, the primary question that needs to be addressed is to what extent it improves on the "spill everywhere" approach of Chaitin. Second, the CK allocator might place extra operations on tile boundaries while stitching subtiles back together. We wish to measure this overhead and determine whether it is tolerable. To this end, our evaluation process consisted of running both allocators on a number of benchmarks and comparing two key features of the register-allocated output: the spill instructions emitted and the register-to-register copies eliminated. We measured both the number of static spills and copies emitted as well as the number of these instructions executed on test inputs. We also measured the execution time of the allocated code on these inputs.

While evaluating the allocators, it is tempting to focus solely on the runtime of the allocated program. However, this might prove to be misleading on certain environments due to three issues. First, some architectures (the x86 included) use sophisticated techniques to minimize memory latency. Thus, even if the allocation algorithm allocates more virtual registers to physical registers and reduces the amount of spill code in the program, this improvement might not be reflected in a decrease in execution time. Second, the effects of cache hits and misses on spill code is unpredictable and might affect the runtime of the code. In the degenerate case, code with more spill code might benefit from random cache effects and execute faster than code with fewer spill instructions. The allocators we evaluated do not optimize for cache effects while emitting spill code – as a result, the impact of cache on allocated code is purely accidental and we would like to factor these effects out. Lastly, the evaluated allocators might produce starkly different allocations for rarely executed procedures of a benchmark. This difference might not be reflected in the execution time of the entire program. However, it is sometimes instructive to examine the contrasting allocations of these procedures. Keeping these considerations in mind, we decided on spill code and register copies eliminated as our two major evaluation metrics. An analysis of the spills and copies in the code will give us a relatively architecture-independent understanding of both allocators. In our comparisons, we used both the dynamic as well as the static versions of these metrics.

4.1 Comparing the Spill Code Emitted by Both Allocators

A graph coloring allocator typically uses heuristics to color the interference graph using the same number of colors as available physical registers, k. However, the coloring will be unsuccessful if the graph is not k-colorable, or if the heuristics fail to color a k-colorable graph. At this point, most allocators modify the program and repeat the coloring process. After an unsuccessful coloring effort, Chaitin-Briggs and Callahan-Koblenz relegate uncolorable nodes to memory and rebuild the interference graph. This process of placing a live range in memory instead of a register, known as *spilling*, reduces the length of the live range and, in general, makes the modified graph more colorable. Since the spilled range must now be fetched from memory, the allocator tries to reduce the number of these memory accesses (*spills*) executed at runtime. Callahan-Koblenz and Chaitin-Briggs use heuristic techniques to identify candidates for spilling . Though their heuristics share a general goal – to make the graph more colorable and to minimize the amount of spill code – they differ in their formulations.

Spill code insertion strategy in Chaitin-Briggs: In the Briggs allocator, the spill heuristic is computed by counting the load and store instructions required if the live range were to be spilled. Specifically, if d_i is the loop depth of instruction i, the spill cost for a node is estimated to be:

$$SpillCost = LoadsCost + StoresCost \text{ where } LoadsCost = LoadWeight * \sum_{l \in SpillLoads} 10^{d_l}$$

$StoresCost$ is calculated in a similar manner. For our experiments, the weights for load and store costs were set to 1. If a spill is required, the node with the lowest ratio of spill cost to the number of interference edges is selected for spilling.

Once a live range is spilled in Chaitin-Briggs, it is loaded before a use and stored after a definition throughout the function.

Spill code insertion strategy in Callahan-Koblenz: A more fine-grained spill strategy is used by the CK allocator. We give a brief overview here, but consult [6] for a more detailed discussion. Because live ranges can be split at tile-boundaries, the allocator may choose to place a variable v in different locations for each tile that it crosses. For example, v may be allocated to a register within tile t, while being relegated to memory in the parent or a subtile. The following set of equations forms the cornerstone of this strategy:

$$LocalWeight_t(v) = \sum_{b \in blocks(t)} P(b) \cdot Ref_b(v)$$

where t is a tile, $P(x)$ denotes the probability of executing a block or taking a control flow edge and $Ref_b(v)$ is the number of references to v within b. Assuming that allocating a register to variable v in t is profitable (see below) during the bottom-up phase, $LocalWeight_t(v)$ is analogous to Chaitin-Briggs' *SpillCost* heuristic and is used, along with the degree of the node corresponding to v, in a similar fashion. However, this cost is computed based only on blocks that occur strictly within tile t, as opposed to the whole function. Moreover, the reference count of block b is weighted by the probability of b being executed. Note that for the purposes of this work, we use a static estimate of $P(b)$ rather than actual profile data to ensure a fair comparison of the spill heuristics for both allocators. If b is a block, we set $P(b) = 10^{depth(b)}$. If e is an edge emanating from a block b, $P(e)$ is computed as the reciprocal of the number of outgoing edges of b.

$$Weight_t(v) = \sum_{s \in subtiles(t)} (Reg_s(v) - Mem_s(v)) + LocalWeight_t(v)$$

Overall decisions regarding whether or not a variable should be spilled are based on $Weight_t(v)$. It is computed as a combination of $LocalWeight_t(v)$ and various penalty costs that may arise from making certain allocation decisions with respect to the parent or children of t. It may happen that the penalty outweighs the benefit of allocating v to a register, indicating that the allocator should force v into memory.

$$Transfer_t(v) = \sum_{e \in E(t)} P(e) \cdot Live_e(v), \quad where\ E(t) = EntryEdges(t) \cup ExitEdges(t).$$

$$Reg_t(v) = \begin{cases} 0, & if\ InReg_t(v) = false \\ \min(Transfer_t(v), Weight_t(v)), & if\ InReg_t(v) = true \end{cases}$$

$$Mem_t(v) = \begin{cases} 0, & if\ InReg_t(v) = true \\ Transfer_t(v), & if\ InReg_t(v) = false \end{cases}$$

where $InReg_t(v)$ is a boolean predicate which is true if v received a register in tile t, and false otherwise. $Live_e(v)$ is a predicate that indicates if variable v is live along edge e.

Table 1. Dynamic spill operations for SPECInt2000 and `epic` (billions)

Benchmark	CB	CK					% imp.	
		M	M_{TB}	$M + M_{TB}$	C_{TB}	All		(w/C_{TB})
gzip	96.82	51.01	6.09	57.10	0.99	58.09	41.02	40.00
vpr	10.77	8.96	1.12	10.08	0.00	10.08	6.41	6.41
crafty	71.21	55.10	5.07	60.17	0.44	60.61	15.50	14.89
parser	51.54	27.66	1.05	28.71	1.12	29.83	44.30	42.12
eon	36.10	36.30	0.28	36.58	0.00	36.58	-1.33	-1.33
gap	53.02	43.45	4.29	47.74	0.55	48.29	9.96	8.93
bzip2	103.00	72.14	17.80	89.94	2.14	92.08	12.68	10.60
twolf	53.70	31.81	11.96	43.77	1.32	45.09	18.49	16.03
epic	8.78	4.50	6.85	11.35	0.44	11.79	-29.27	-34.23
MEAN IMPROVEMENTS							**20.52**	**19.07**

$Transfer_t(v)$, $Reg_t(v)$, and $Mem_t(v)$ represent the various penalty costs. The first corresponds to the cost due to tile-boundary spills, while the remaining two account for any penalties due to a tile and its parent choosing different locations for the same live range. If v is allocated to a register in tile t, $Reg_t(v)$ is the penalty of allocating v to memory in the parent of t. Likewise, if v is allocated to memory in tile t, then $Mem_t(v)$ is the penalty of allocating v to a register in the parent of t.

Analysis of Spill Code Inserted: Table 1 shows the dynamic spill behavior of each benchmark for CB and CK. The column marked *CB* is the number of dynamic memory operations executed by the CB-compiled version of each benchmark. The CK results are broken down into the three types of spill operations that can occur. Column M is the number of dynamic memory operations executed within tile boundaries (e.g., loops). Column M_{TB} and C_{TB} are the number of dynamic memory and register-to-register copy operations executed on tile boundaries, respectively. The two additional CK columns represent the sum of all dynamic memory operations ($M + M_{TB}$) and the sum of all dynamic spill operations (memory operations or copies). It is useful to isolate the different types of spills for CK in order to see the effects of tiling more directly. Finally, the last two columns show the percent improvement of CK over CB. In the first case, only memory operations are considered, whereas memory and copy operations are considered in the second case. This distinction was made to show how prevalent any remaining tile-boundary register-register copies were (indicating success or failure of inter-tile preferencing), and what overall impact they had on the improvements. Overall, the benchmarks allocated with CK executed significantly fewer dynamic spill operations than those allocated by CB— up to 44% fewer on `parser`. On average, 20.52% fewer spill operations were executed for CK than for CB. On the other hand, there were two losses for CK. One slight loss in `eon`, and one significant 29.27% loss in `epic` (more on this later).

We examined some of the benchmarks in detail at the assembly language level to understand choices made by each allocator, and why CK performed relatively well compared to CB. Consider the code in Figure 4a, which is a typical scenario present in many of the benchmarks. Here there are two live ranges x and t

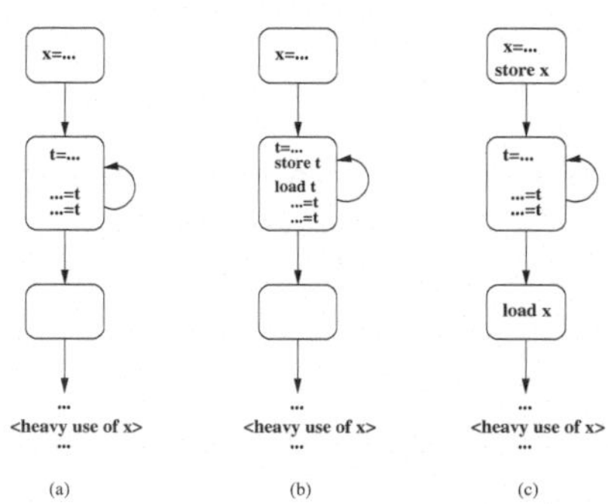

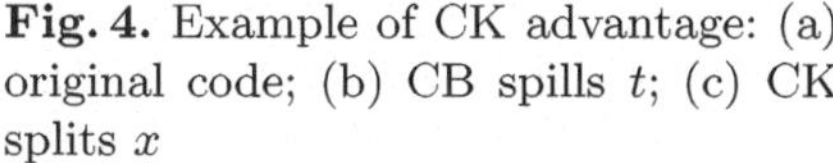

Fig. 4. Example of CK advantage: (a) original code; (b) CB spills t; (c) CK splits x

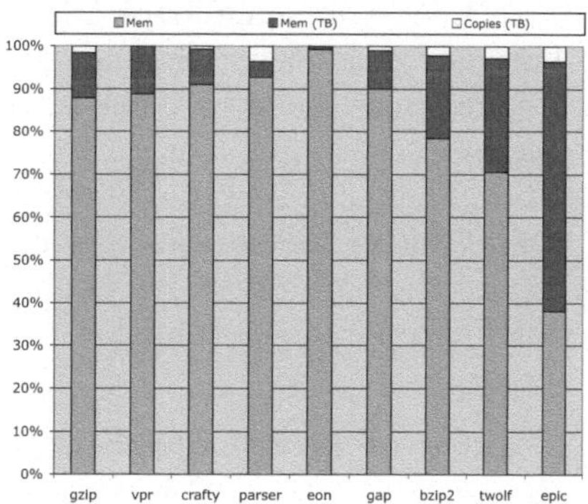

Fig. 5. Dynamic Spill Operation Types by Percentage. `TB` indicates operations on tile boundaries.

competing for one register, where x is referenced once early, and heavily in some distant part of the program. There are a only few references to t in a small portion of the program, but they occur in a loop, making them frequently executed. Let us assume the total number of references to x exceeds those of t. In the standard CB scheme, since the spill cost is calculated based on the references throughout the program, then x would get a color and t would be spilled (as in Figure 4b). But from the perspective of t, spilling t is a poor choice, since x is never even referenced in the loop. On the other hand, the opposite choice (giving t the color) is bad too as the many references to x will now be through memory. Because CB must spill a live range entirely, one of two poor choices must be made. As mentioned earlier, CK can consider each live range in fragments, over regions of the program. Here CK splits x before and after the loop, so that the loop portion and non-loop portions are allocated independently. This allows the result seen in Figure 4c, where t gets the register *and* x gets the register (but x is allocated to memory within the loop where it has no references). Notice also that there is a tradeoff in making such a split. A store and a load operation must be placed at loop entry and exit to make the split, which is clearly profitable here.

Returning to the loss in the `epic` benchmark, it is useful to examine the breakdown of spill operation types for CK. The graph in Figure 5 shows the percentage of total spill operations represented by each type. Looking at the `epic` bar, it is evident that something went wrong with CK's heuristics. That is, more than half of all the dynamic spill operations are memory operations on the tile boundaries. Without looking at the code, this would seem indicate that CK did not calculate trade-offs between intra- and inter-tile spilling appropriately.

In fact, on examining the assembly code, we found just that behavior. One routine dominating execution time contains a number of triply-nested loops. In one such nest, there is heavy register pressure in the inner loop, little pressure in the middle loop, and medium pressure in the outermost loop and non-loop code. There are also a number of global values live across the entire loop nest, with references in some loops and not others. Unfortunately, for some of these globals, the constituent fragments within each loop were alternately allocated to registers and memory. That is, the outermost loop allocated g to a register, the next deeper loop allocated g to memory, and the inner loop allocated it to a register. Thus, at every tile boundary there are memory operations to transfer g in and out of memory as appropriate. It turns out that these tile-transfers dominate the spill operation count, as seen in the graph. It would have been better to keep g in the same location across more than one tile boundary.

4.2 Inter-register Copy Elimination and Its Impact on Allocation

Prior research has demonstrated that the removal of register-to-register copies improves code quality [10,11]. Therefore, the efficacy of the copy coalescing phase is critical to the performance of the allocators. An effective copy removal strategy becomes even more imperative for register allocation in a SSA-based intermediate representation such as LLVM. While converting from SSA form to executable code, ϕ-functions are replaced by register-to-register copies [4]. In both implemented allocators, we ran an initial pass that merged the live ranges created by the ϕ-node elimination process. This transformation, specified by Briggs in [3], ensures that the input to the two allocators remained consistent. The two-address nature of x86 code and copies generated due to procedure-calling conventions also present many opportunities for copy removal. Since the two allocators implement different copy-removal mechanisms, we shall compare this feature in more detail in the next two paragraphs.

Coalescing and Biased Coloring: The Chaitin-Briggs allocator uses two complementary mechanisms – coalescing and biased coloring – to remove register copies in the code. After building the graph, if the allocator encounters a register copy, it coalesces the source and destination live ranges if they do not interfere. This algorithm is called *aggressive coalescing* because it combines nodes without examining the resulting node's degree. After coalescing, the algorithm rebuilds the interference graph and repeats the coalesce-rebuild process until no more copies can be eliminated. In Chaitin-Briggs, coalescing is intentionally constrained – to retain flexibility during coloring, it only examines copies between two virtual registers. To eliminate copies between physical and virtual registers, Chaitin-Briggs adds the color associated with the physical register to a list of colors desired by the virtual register and attempts to assign this color to the register during the *biased coloring* phase. Biased coloring is, in spirit, very similar to preferencing in the CK allocator. However, unlike in Callahan-Koblenz, biased coloring plays only a secondary role in Chaitin-Briggs since coalescing is powerful enough to eliminate most copies.

Preferencing: Preferencing refers to the notion that it may be attractive to assign the same color to multiple variables By making the coloring algorithm sensitive to such preferences, the likelihood of choosing the desired color for a node is increased. Copy removal in the CK allocator is performed by preferencing the source variable S and destination variable D of a copy together by adding each to the others *preference list.* The preference-guided color assignment algorithm then attempts to give the same color to S and D. If the attempt is successful (the preference was *satisfied*), then the resulting copy is redundant and can be trivially removed. Similarly, if either S or D is a physical register, such as a copy generated to implement subroutine linkage conventions, we setup a *local preference.* This is different than the previous case in that a variable is preferenced to a specific physical register. During color assignment, when a node receives a color, the color is propagated to all the nodes on its preference list as their local preference. If a node has a local preference, then the coloring mechanism will first attempt to assign that register before resorting to using another register. Furthermore, it will try to avoid giving a node a color that is preferred by uncolored neighbors.

In addition to copy removal, preferencing is used to influence the colors that different parts of a global live range receive. Recall that tile boundaries are implicit split-points for variables live at that boundary. Because tiles are processed independently, it is important to pass around information about these variables (in the form of preferences) so that each tile attempts to place the same global into the same register. These preferences, of course, are not generated in response to copy instructions. However, if they are not satisfied, then copy operations will be inserted at the boundary to resolve the differing allocations.

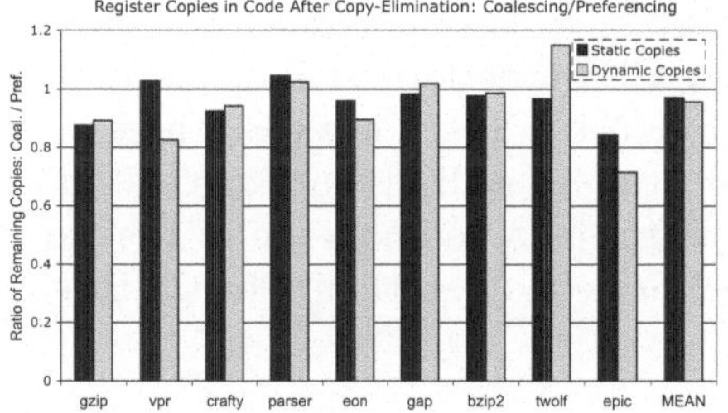

Fig. 6. Aggressive Coalescing & Biased Coloring vs. Preferencing

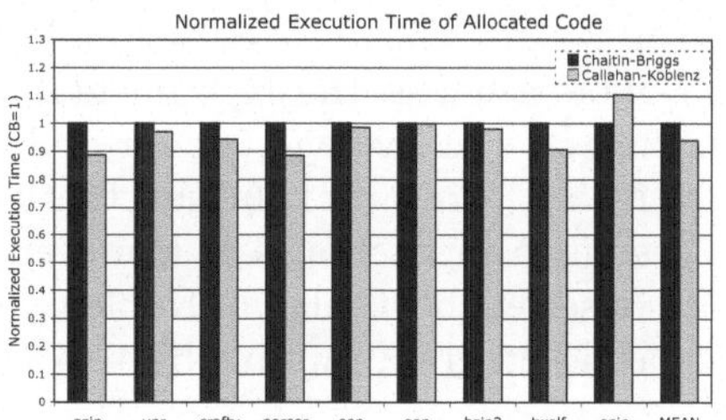

Fig. 7. Runtime of Allocated Code

Experimental Evaluation: In comparing the copy-removal mechanisms, we wanted to ensure that our measurements would not be hampered by the inconsistent namespaces created by both allocators. Therefore, we modified CB and CK to operate on the same structure – we constructed a single tile for the entire program and provided this tile as input to the allocators. The results of our experiments are displayed in Figure 6 – it shows the number of copies remaining in the code after copy-removal was conducted. Our experiments show that overall, coalescing used in conjunction with biased coloring performs better and removes 3.6% more copies on average than preferencing. This translates into a 4.5% decrease in copies executed at runtime. We were, however, surprised by how closely the two algorithms performed. In stark contrast to coalescing which is executed each time the interference graph is rebuilt, preferencing can remove copies only while coloring the graph. We conclude that the careful mechanisms built into preferencing allow it to be competitive with a much more aggressive technique.

4.3 Control-Flow Overhead of Tiling and Execution Time Differences

To maintain the structural properties of the tile tree during construction, the tile tree builder may have to insert extra blocks at tile boundaries. Typically these blocks fall through to their successor and, therefore, do not result in any additional branches in the final program. However, there are cases when inserting blocks results in unavoidable branches. We measured the control-flow overhead incurred due to these branches. On average, Callahan-Koblenz inserted 5.8% more branch instructions in the code. However, the increase in executed branches was comparatively lower: 1.4% over all benchmarks. This difference between static and dynamic branches indicates that the branches placed at tile boundaries are infrequently executed.

We built three versions of each benchmark and compared their execution times – executables were created by running the Chaitin-Briggs allocator, the Callahan-Koblenz allocator, and the default linear-scan allocator that shipped with LLVM. Both CB and CK perform better than the linear-scan allocator, recording improvements on average of 5.4% and 10.6% respectively. The comparison between Callahan-Koblenz and Chaitin-Briggs is summarized in Figure 7. As can be seen from the experimental results, CK outperforms CB on most of the benchmarks – on average, it improved performance by 6.1% over CB. These gains were mainly a result of the substantial reduction in spill instructions executed, as described in Section 4.1. However, on `epic`, as a consequence of the extra spills inserted by Callahan-Koblenz, it performed worse than Chaitin-Briggs, increasing program runtime by 10.4%.

5 Conclusion

We have evaluated the Callahan-Koblenz allocator on three major criteria: the amount of spill code inserted, the register-to-register copies eliminated, and the overhead incurred due to tile construction. As seen in Section 4.1, CK was able to significantly reduce the number of spill instructions when compared to Chaitin-Briggs. This reduction can be attributed, in part, to being able to independently allocate different parts of one live range. Secondly, tile local variables are given precedence over LBNRs in that we prefer to spill a LBNR over a tile local. This strategy is often beneficial, since unreferenced variables are typically long lived and thus conflict with many variables in the same region. The CK results emphasize that the spill-everywhere approach of Chaitin-Briggs can potentially degrade performance. We were initially concerned that copy coalescing, a more aggressive technique, might significantly outperform preferencing. However, our results indicate that preferencing is reasonably competitive with coalescing. Our experiments showed that, on average, Callahan-Koblenz emitted fewer spill instructions and produced faster running code than Chaitin-Briggs. However, we reiterate that these experiments were not designed to determine which allocator is better. Rather, our primary goal was to provide an understanding of the CK allocator by using another graph coloring technique as a point of reference. To that end, we did not consider adding improvements in the Chaitin-Briggs spilling strategy as suggested in various research publications. Specifically, modifications proposed by Bergner [1], Simpson [9] and Briggs [3] would reduce the number of spills produced by the allocator. In future research, we intend to devise techniques for improving the quality of spill code in both allocators.

6 Related Work

Though early computer science literature alludes to graph coloring approaches to register allocation, Chaitin et al. presented the first paper comprehensively describing a graph coloring register allocator [8,7]. Subsequently, a number of improvements have been proposed for Chaitin's Yorktown allocator: Bernstein et. al. augmented the allocator's coloring strategy by choosing the best of three heuristics [2]. They also presented a technique that attempted to reduce the amount spill code inserted by Chaitin's allocator. Bergner and his colleagues noted that spilling can be improved for live ranges that have a small region of overlap [1]. They called their technique interference graph spilling. Our paper focuses on the refinement of Chaitin's allocator by Briggs et. al [5]. By adding deferred spilling, Briggs and his colleagues were able to significantly improve allocation, registering a reduction of spill costs up to 40% in their test suite.

To improve on the Yorktown allocator, some researchers incorporated program structure into their allocation algorithms. Norris et. al. [17] designed an allocator that operates on the program dependence graph and attempted to carefully place spill code. They compared their results to a Chaitin-style allocator and reported up to a 3.7% decrease in spill code. Knobe and Zadeck [12] describe a structure-based allocator using the notion of a *control tree*, which is vaguely similar to a tile tree. This allocator is similar to Callahan-Koblenz in that it can split live ranges around control tree nodes, it can spill inside of conditionals, and its *pruning* of *wedges* is not unlike CK's handling of LBNRs; however, no empirical evaluation of the technique is presented. Lueh's "Fusion" allocator also leverages program structure and appears to improve performance over Chaitin-style allocation by an average of 8.4% on the SPEC92 benchmarks [16]. A recent article suggests that with a careful relaxation of the ordering of the coloring stack, more preferences can be satisfied [13]. The hierarchical allocator evaluated in this paper was designed by Callahan and Koblenz and published in 1991 [6]. Since then, we know of one other attempt to implement the CK allocator by Wu [19]. However, the implementation deviates significantly from the published algorithm. The author reserves registers to accommodate machine operands for spilling which significantly cripples the algorithm while the published Callahan and Koblenz paper clearly states that the hierarchical allocator does not reserve registers. There are several other major differences from the published algorithm including ignoring the degree of a node while spilling and not maintaining information during the bottom-up walk of the tree.

Acknowledgements

This work would have proved much more difficult without the enthusiastic help of Tim Harvey, Brian Koblenz, David Callahan, Michael Berg, and the LLVM group at the University of Illinois. Our colleagues in the compiler groups at Rice provided interesting discussions and helpful criticism. To these people go our heartfelt thanks. This work has been supported by the Los Alamos Computer Science Institute, by Texas Instruments, and by the National Science Foundation through grant number 0331654.

References

1. Peter Bergner, Peter Dahl, David Engebretsen, and Matthew T. O'Keefe. Spill Code Minimization via Interference Region Spilling. In *SIGPLAN Conference on Programming Language Design and Implementation*, pages 287–295, 1997.
2. David Bernstein, Dina Q. Goldin, Martin C. Golumbic, Hugo Krawczyk, Yishay Mansour, Itai Nahshon, and Ron Y. Pinter. Spill Code Minimization Techniques for Optimizing Compilers. In *SIGPLAN Conference on Programming Language Design and Implementation*, pages 258–263, 1989.
3. Preston Briggs. Register Allocation via Graph Coloring. Technical Report TR92-183, Rice University, 24, 1992.
4. Preston Briggs, Keith D. Cooper, Timothy J. Harvey, and L. Taylor Simpson. Practical Improvements to the Construction and Destruction of Static Single Assignment Form. *Software – Practice and Experience*, 28(8):859–881, 1998.
5. Preston Briggs, Keith D. Cooper, and Linda Torczon. Improvements to Graph Coloring Register Allocation. *ACM Transactions on Programming Languages and Systems*, 16(3):428–455, May 1994.
6. D. Callahan and B. Koblenz. Register Allocation via Hierarchical Graph Coloring. *SIGPLAN*, 26(6):192–203, June 1991.
7. G.J. Chaitin. Register Allocation and Spilling via Graph Coloring. In *SIGPLAN82*, 1982.
8. G.J. Chaitin, M.A. Auslander, A.K. Chandra, J. Cocke, M.E. Hopkins, and P.W. Markstein. Register Allocation via Coloring. *Computer Languages*, 6:45–57, January 1981.
9. K. D. Cooper and L.T. Simpson. Live range Splitting in a Graph Coloring Register Allocator. In *Proceedings of the International Compiler Construction Conference*, March 1998.
10. Lal George and Andrew W. Appel. Iterated register coalescing. *ACM Trans. Program. Lang. Syst.*, 18(3):300–324, 1996.
11. Suhyun Kim, Soo-Mook Moon, Jinpyo Park, and Kemal Ebciolu. Unroll-based register coalescing. In *ICS '00: Proceedings of the 14th international conference on Supercomputing*, pages 296–305, New York, NY, USA, 2000. ACM Press.
12. Kathleen Knobe and Kenneth Zadeck. Register Allocation Using Control Trees. Technical Report CS-92-13, Brown University, Department of Computer Science, March 1992.
13. Akira Koseki, Hideaki Komatsu, and Toshio Nakatani. Preference-directed graph coloring. In *Proceedings of the ACM SIGPLAN 2002 Conference on Programming language design and implementation*, pages 33–44. ACM Press, 2002.

14. Chris Lattner and Vikram Adve. LLVM: A Compilation Framework for Lifelong Program Analysis and Transformation. In *Proceedings of the 2004 International Symposium on Code Generation and Optimization (CGO'04)*, Mar 2004.
15. P. Geoffrey Lowney, Stefan M. Freudenberger, Thomas J. Karzes, W. D. Lichtenstein, Robert P. Nix, John S. O'Donnell, and John C. Ruttenberg. The Multiflow Trace Scheduling Compiler. *The Journal of Supercomputing*, 7(1-2):51–142, 1993.
16. Guei-Yuan Lueh, Thomas Gross, and Ali-Reza Adl-Tabatabai. Fusion-based register allocation. *ACM Transactions on Programming Languages and Systems*, 22(3):431–470, 2000.
17. Cindy Norris and Lori L. Pollock. Register Allocation over the Program Dependence Graph. In *SIGPLAN Conference on Programming Language Design and Implementation*, pages 266–277, 1994.
18. Ravi Sethi. Complete Register Allocation Problems. In *Proceedings of the fifth annual ACM symposium on Theory of computing*, pages 182–195. ACM, Apr 1973.
19. Q. Wu. Register Allocation via Hierarchical Graph Coloring. Master's thesis, Michigan Technological University, 1996.

Register Pressure in Software-Pipelined Loop Nests: Fast Computation and Impact on Architecture Design

Alban Douillet and Guang R. Gao

Department of Electrical and Computer Engineering
University of Delaware, Newark, DE 19716-3130
{douillet,ggao}@capsl.udel.edu

Abstract. Recently the Single-dimension Software Pipelining (SSP) technique was proposed to software pipeline loop nests at an arbitrary loop level [18,19,20]. However, SSP schedules require a high number of rotating registers, and may become infeasible if register needs exceed the number of available registers. It is therefore desirable to design a method to compute the register pressure quickly (without actually performing the register allocation) as an early measure of the feasibility of an SSP schedule. Such a method can also be instrumental to provide a valuable feedback to processor architects in their register files design decision, as far as the needs of loop nests are concerned.

This paper presents a method that computes quickly the minimum number of rotating registers required by an SSP schedule. The results have demonstrated that the method is always accurate and is 3 to 4 orders of magnitude faster on average than the register allocator. Also, experiments suggest that 64 floating-point rotating registers are in general enough to accommodate the needs of the loop nests used in scientific computations.

1 Introduction

Software pipelining [1,4,9,10,13] is an efficient and important method to schedule loops by overlapping the execution of successive iterations. The most popular technique, modulo-scheduling (MS) [3,8,10,12,16,21], only addresses single loops or the innermost loop of a loop nest. Traditional approaches to schedule loop nests mainly focus on scheduling the innermost loop and extending the schedule toward the outer levels by hierarchical reduction [10,14]. An alternative way is to perform MS after loop transformations [2]. A new resource-constrained scheduling technique named Single-dimensional Software-Pipelining (SSP) [18,19,20] does not restrain itself to the innermost loop and can software pipeline any given loop in a loop nest. If the innermost level is chosen, SSP is proven to be equivalent to MS. Experimental results have shown that SSP often outperforms MS, and is fully compatible with the wide array of loop optimizations and transformations used for MS. The technique can currently be applied to any source imperfect loop nests with no conditional statements or function calls and with run-time constant trip counts.

In the SSP compilation process, shown in Figure 1, registers are allocated after the one-dimensional (1-D) schedule is computed. However, both phases are time-consuming (the register allocation problem is NP-complete [18], even for single loops [16]). Therefore, it is preferable to detect early if the register allocator is bound to fail

E. Ayguadé et al. (Eds.): LCPC 2005, LNCS 4339, pp. 17–31, 2007.

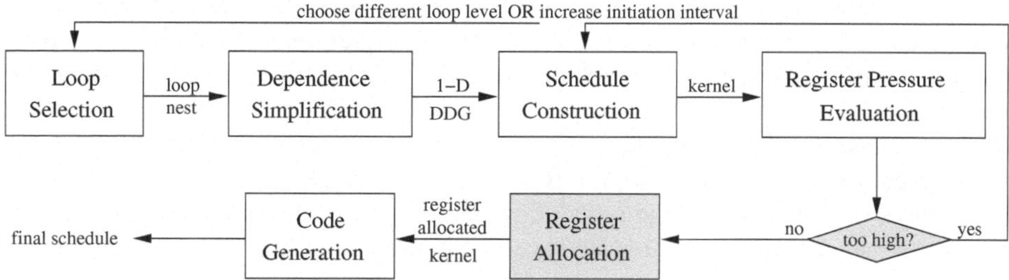

Fig. 1. SSP Compilation Flow

because of a too high register pressure. The scheduler can then compute a different, but more favorable schedule. We propose in this paper a fast evaluation method to measure the rotating register pressure, named $MaxLive$, of any kernel computed by the SSP scheduler. It is defined as the maximum number of lifetimes at any time during the execution of the loop nest scheduled with SSP. It is a theoretical lower bound that may not be achievable. Only loop variants, allocated to rotating registers, are considered. Loop invariants are assumed to be allocated to static registers. When unspecified, 'register' will always refer to 'rotating register'. Any register spilling technique is assumed to have been applied earlier to the 1-D schedule and is not the subject of the paper.

Such an evaluation method is important and has many uses. (1) First, it allows the compiler to avoid running the expensive register allocator when it is bound to fail. A new 1-D schedule with lower requirements can then be computed by increasing the initiation interval or choosing another loop level, for instance. (2) Second, because the register pressure is a direct function of the 1-D schedule , the method can be used to compare the register pressure of 1-D schedules computed by different SSP scheduling methods. (3) Third, the computed register pressure can also be used to measure the effectiveness of any register allocator. (4) Last, the method provides a valuable feedback to processor architects in their register files design decision, as far as the needs of loop nests are concerned. Other questions can then be answered. Is the register pressure the same for both floating-point (FP) and integer (INT) registers? Are the register files of the target architectures balanced enough to efficiently handle the register pressure? Can we anticipate the final register pressure or the number of registers allocated by a specific register allocator?

Several issues specific to SSP must be handled. First, the final schedule is composed of more than one repeating pattern. Second, some lifetimes are stretched to honor resource constraints. Last, the initiation rate of the lifetimes is irregular. In this paper, we propose a method to compute the rotating register pressure of any given 1-D schedule. The method is fast: it approximates $MaxLive$ by skipping the initialization and conclusion phases of the final schedule and considers a unique outermost loop iteration, or outermost iteration for short. A second method, comprehensive, accurate, but very slow, is used as reference. For clarity and space reasons, the second method is not presented in the paper, but is accessible in [5] instead. We will refer to them as the fast method and the comprehensive method, respectively.

It is the first time a method to compute the register pressure of an SSP schedule is proposed. With single loops, where MS is used, the traditional technique is to count the number of lifetimes in the kernel, also named $MaxLive$ [17]. Our method can be seen as its natural extension to handle the more complex issues specific to the multidimensional case, presented in section 3.2. $MaxLive$ was the chosen method to evaluate the efficiency of register allocators in [6,11]. Other work [15] considered the theoretical register pressure during the scheduling phase by counting the number of buffers required for each functional units. However the number of buffers did not take into account that some buffers could be reused. The register pressure was also studied for non software-pipelined schedules, such as the concept of $FatCover$ in [7]. Llosa et al. [11] used $MaxLive$ to measure the register pressure of floating-point benchmarks. Their results also show that a FP register file of 64 registers would accommodate most of the register pressure and limit accesses to memory in the case of MS scheduled loops. The results were later confirmed in [22].

The methods presented in this paper were implemented in the Open64/ORC 2.1 compiler on an Itanium workstation. The experiments were conducted on a set of 125 loop nests of various depths. The experiments lead to several conclusions. (1) The fast method is at least 3 orders of magnitude faster than the register allocator and could therefore be used in a compiler framework to quickly determine the feasibility of an SSP schedule. (2) Most of the loop nests of depth 3 or less require less than 96 INT registers and about half of the loop nests of depth 4 or higher cannot be scheduled because of a too high INT register pressure. (3) The FP register pressure never exceeds 47 registers and therefore more than half of the FP register file is never used, showing an imbalance in the usage of the register files between INT and FP. (4) If half of the FP register file is used for INT values instead, then 76% of the loop nests of depth 5 could be software-pipelined with SSP.

The paper is organized as follows. Section 2 briefly introduces the SSP method. Section 3 defines some notations and conventions used in the paper, formulates the problem and explains in details the issues to tackle. Our solution is then described in Section 4. Experiments and results are presented in Section 5 before concluding in Section 6.

2 Single-Dimension Software Pipelining

2.1 Overview

Single-dimension Software Pipelining (SSP) [18,19,20] is a resource-constrained scheduling method to software pipeline perfect and imperfect loop nests with constant trip counts at run-time. Unlike traditional innermost-loop-centric approaches [10,14,16], SSP does not necessarily software pipeline the innermost loop of a loop nest, but directly software pipelines the loop level estimated to be the most profitable. The enclosing loops of the selected loop, if any, are untouched. If the innermost loop level is chosen, SSP is equivalent to MS applied to single loops. SSP retains the simplicity of MS, and yet may achieve significantly higher performance [19].

Figure 2(a) shows an example of a double loop nest. In Figure 2(b), the innermost loop is modulo scheduled, whereas, in Figure 2(c), the outermost loop is software

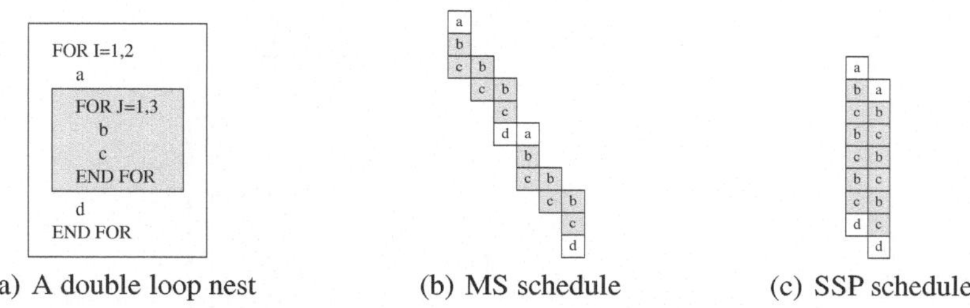

(a) A double loop nest (b) MS schedule (c) SSP schedule

Fig. 2. Simple SSP software pipelining example

pipelined using SSP. Note that, although the two outermost iterations are running in parallel, the innermost loop is running sequentially within each outermost iteration. In our example the SSP schedule is shorter by 2 cycles.

SSP proceeds in several steps to produce the final schedule [18,19,20]. First, the most profitable loop level is chosen for scheduling based on instruction-level parallelism or other criterion. Second, multi-dimensional dependences are simplified into a 1-dimensional problem from which a 1-D schedule is computed, represented by a kernel. Registers are then allocated to the loop variants in the kernel. Last, the 1-D schedule is mapped back to the multi-dimensional iteration space and the final schedule is generated as an assembly code.

Because the enclosing loops to the selected loop are untouched, they are ignored from our point of view and we will always see the chosen loop as the outermost loop of the loop nest. The loops are then referred as L_1, L_2, . . ., L_n from the outermost level to the innermost level where n is the depth of the loop nest.

2.2 From the Kernel to the Final Schedule

The final schedule is exclusively made of multiple copies of the kernel, with sometimes variations or truncations. As such, one only needs to consider the kernel when counting the lifetimes in the final schedule. A kernel is composed of S stages. Each stage takes T cycles to execute. Zero or more operations are scheduled in each modulo-cycle of each stage with the restriction that operations from different levels must be scheduled into different stages.

Figure 3(b) shows the kernel of the triple loop nest from Figure 3(a). There are 5 stages a, b, c, d , and e. The outermost loop is made of all the $S = S_1 = 5$ stages, the middle loop of $S_2 = 3$ stages (b, c, d), and the innermost loop of $S_n = 2$ stages (c, d). Each stage is made of $T = 2$ modulo-cycles and some stages have empty schedule slots.

A more generic kernel is shown in Figure 3(c). The indexes of the first and last stage of loop level i are noted f_i and l_i respectively. The number of stages at level i is noted $S_i = l_i - f_i + 1$. The total number of stages is noted S and is equal to S_1. All the stages have the same initiation interval T. In Figure 3(b), $f_1 = 0$, $f_2 = 1$, $f_3 = 2$, $l_3 = 3$, $l_2 = 3$, $l_1 = 4$, and $T = 2$.

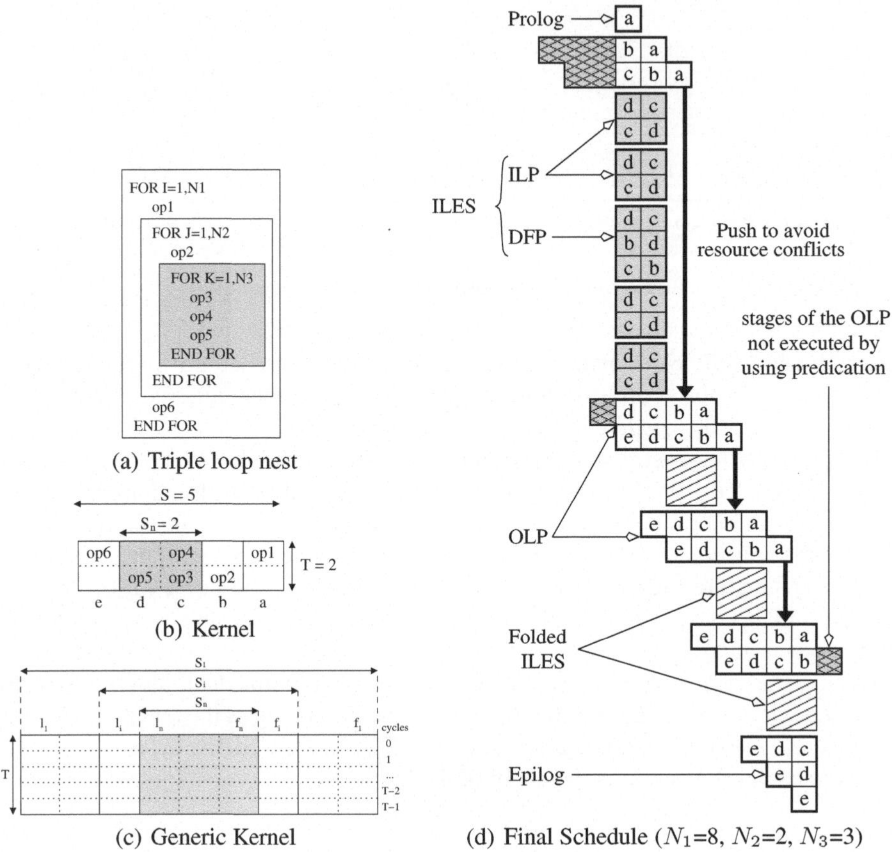

(a) Triple loop nest

(b) Kernel

(c) Generic Kernel

(d) Final Schedule (N_1=8, N_2=2, N_3=3)

Fig. 3. A More Complex Example

Figure 3(d) shows the final schedule of our example. The stages are symbolized by their letters for clarity purposes. We assume that the trip counts for each loop are $N_1 = 8$, $N_2 = 2$, and $N_3 = 3$ (stage b appears only twice in each column, and stages c and d appear three times after each instance of stage b). A column represents the execution of a single outermost iteration (8 total). Both inner loops are represented only for the first two outermost iterations. Afterwards, they are symbolized by a dashed box. Because of resource constraints, only a group of $S_n = 2$ outermost iterations can fully be executed in parallel [20,19]. The other outermost iterations are delayed and pushed later in the schedule, as illustrated by the thick vertical arrow.

Because of the delays and the repetitive nature of the schedule, the final schedule can be decomposed into five different patterns: the prolog, the outermost loop pattern (OLP), the innermost loop pattern (ILP), the draining and filling pattern[1] (DFP), and the epilog. The ILP and DFP form the Inner Loop Execution Segment (ILES). Each pattern can be fully derived from the kernel. The ILP and DFP are obtained by cyclicly

[1] Also called *transition code* in [20].

considering S_n consecutive stages among the S_i stages of the kernel for loop level i [19]. Predication is used in the OLP to truncate unnecessary stages.

3 Problem Formulation and Lifetimes Classification

3.1 Lifetimes Notations and Conventions

The distance in terms of outermost iterations between the definition and the use of a loop variant is called the $omega$ value of the use. The maximum $omega$ value of all the uses of a loop variant represents the number of live-in values required for the variant. Similarly, if live-out values are required from a loop variant, we note $alpha$ the number of values. Those notations are consistent with Rau's conventions [17]. A loop variant is statically defined only once per loop level.

The time period when an instance of a loop variant v is live is called the *scalar lifetime*, or *lifetime* for simplicity, of that instance. In our examples, as shown in Figure 4(a), a circle represents the start of a lifetime, a cross the end, and a dash a non-killing use of the variable. At any given cycle c of the final schedule, the number of lifetimes is called the $FatCover$ at cycle c. $MaxLive$ is the maximum of all the $FatCovers$.

In order for the operations to be interruptible and restartable in a VLIW machine and to avoid dependencies between operations scheduled in the same cycle, a lifetime is started at the beginning of the cycle of the defining operation and is killed at the end of the cycle of the killing operation. This convention matches Rau's convention about scalar lifetimes in [17]. A register cannot be used and defined in the same cycle, except if it is by the same operation, as shown in Figure 4(b) and 4(c). We assume that the intermediate representation follows the same conventions. A loop variant can be redefined by the same operation like in Figure 4(c). In the latter case, the operation will be considered only as a use of the variant for the purpose of our algorithms.

3.2 Problem Formulation and Issues

The problem can be formulated as follows: *given a loop nest and a SSP schedule for it, evaluate the rotating register pressure* $MaxLive$ *of the final schedule.*

The problem presents several issues. First, the lifetimes do not exhibit regular patterns like with modulo scheduling. Successive instances of the same lifetime do not reappear every T cycles: because of the push operations, some delays are encountered. For the same reason, some lifetimes appear to be *stretched* until the stalled outermost iterations they belong to resume their execution. Examples can be seen in Figure 5.

Second, the number of lifetimes in the same stage and modulo-cycle may vary, depending on the position of the stage in the final schedule. For instance, Figure 4(d) shows a part of the final schedule presented in Figure 3(d). The loop variant is defined in the first instance of stage d and used in stage c. The same loop variant is defined again in the second instance of d but never used. However, the register required for the definition must be accounted for during the only cycle where the second instance of the loop variant is live. Symmetrically, a value may be defined each iteration and never used until the last iteration, where the value is used in the enclosing loop (Figure 4(e)).

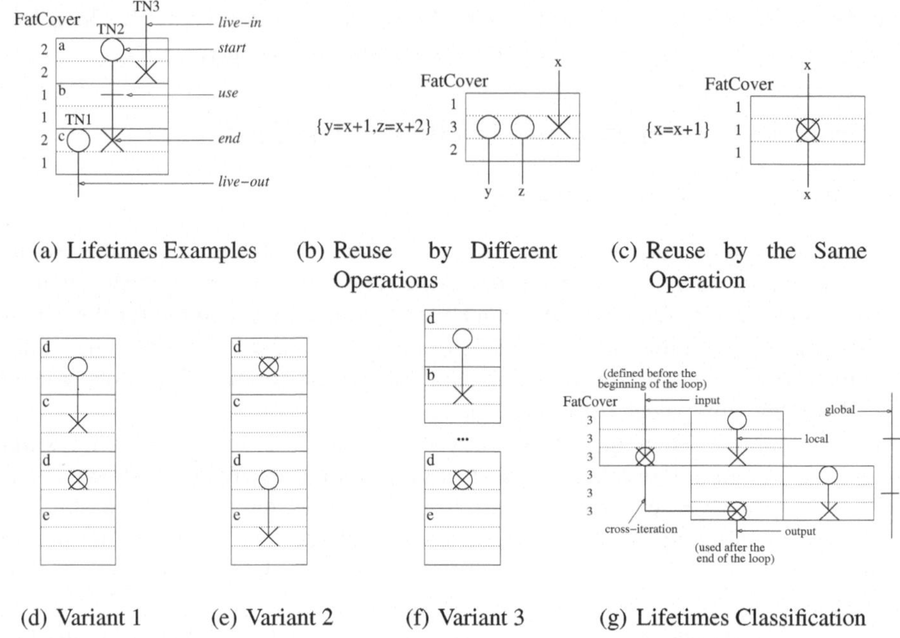

(a) Lifetimes Examples (b) Reuse by Different Operations (c) Reuse by the Same Operation

(d) Variant 1 (e) Variant 2 (f) Variant 3 (g) Lifetimes Classification

Fig. 4. Lifetimes Notations, Situations, and Classification

Similarly, whether the stage belongs to the last instance of the enclosing loop also influences the number of local lifetimes. In Figure 4(f), the last instance of the loop variant is used at the beginning of the enclosing loop. If it is the last iteration of the enclosing loop, then the value is never used and the local lifetime is reduced to a single cycle. We refer to those two situations as $first$ and $last$.

Finally, the method must be fast in order to be used as a tool by the register allocator and the scheduler to help detect infeasible solutions early.

3.3 Lifetimes Classification

For the purpose of the algorithms described in this paper, lifetimes are classified into 5 categories, illustrated in Figure 4(g). Global lifetimes covers the whole execution of the loop nest. This is typical of loop invariants and those lifetimes are not considered by our algorithm. Output lifetimes hold values computed within the loop nest that will be used outside. The number of parallel live-out values of the same loop variant is equal to the $alpha$ value of the variant. Input lifetimes start before the beginning of the loop and terminates before the end. The number of parallel live-in values of the same loop variant is the maximum of all the $omega$ values of the variant among all its uses. Cross-iteration lifetimes cross outermost iterations. By construction, a sequence of cross-iteration lifetimes start with input lifetimes. Every other lifetime is said to be local to the current outermost iteration.

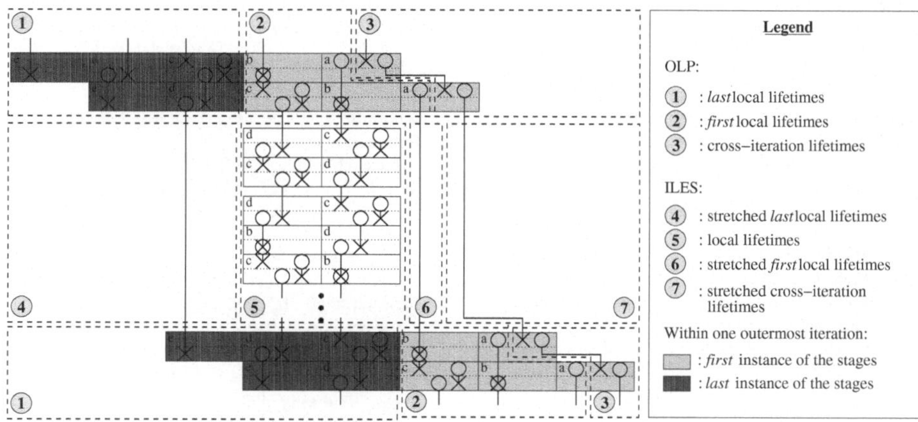

Fig. 5. Register Pressure Computation Overview

4 Register Pressure Computation

This section presents the details of our solution. We make the assumption that the maximum register pressure will appear in the steady phase (OLP and ILES) of the final schedule. Therefore, input and output lifetimes are ignored and only local and cross-iteration lifetimes are considered. Experiments in Section 5.1 will show that this assumption is always correct.

A snapshot of our final schedule during the steady phase is shown in Figure 5. The lifetimes can be partitioned into 7 groups, shown in the legend. To compute the maximum register pressure of the final schedule, we count the number of lifetimes in each of the seven groups. Cross-iteration lifetimes are counted by analyzing the definition and uses of each cross-iteration loop variant. Local lifetimes are counted for each single stage of the kernel for both situations: first or last in the current outermost iteration. The exact algorithms are available in [5]. An overview is given in the next subsections.

4.1 Cross-Iteration Lifetimes

Because the outermost loop level is the only level actually software pipelined, only variants defined in the outermost level can have a cross-iteration lifetime. The first step consists of identifying the cross-iteration variants. They are defined in the stages appearing in the outermost loop only and show at least one use with an omega value greater than 0. Then, for each variant, the stage and modulo-cycle of the definition and of the last use are computed and noted S_{def}, c_{def}, S_{kill}, and c_{kill}, respectively. The definition of each variant is unique and therefore easily found. Because cross-iteration lifetimes span several outermost iterations, the last use of a such lifetimes must be searched among each of the spanned iterations. The stage index of the last use is computed by adding the omega value of the use to its stage index.

Afterward, the number of cross-iteration variants lifetimes at modulo-cycle c in the OLP is then given by $LT_{cross}(c)$, shown in Figure 8. $S_{kill}(v) - S_{def}(v) + 1$ represents

```
COMPUTE_CROSS_ITERATION_LT():
  civs ← ∅ // cross-iteration variants set
  ovs ← set of the variants defined in the outermost loop

  // Identify the cross-iteration variants
  for each operation op in the schedule
    for each source operand src of op
      if omega(op, src) > 0 and src ∈ ovs then
        civs ← civs ∪ {src}
        initialize S_def, c_def, S_kill, c_kill for src to −1

  // Collect the parameters for each cross-iteration variant
  for each stage s from l_1 to f_1, backwards
    for each cycle c from T − 1 to 0, backwards
      for each operation op in s at cycle c
        for each source operand src of op in civs
          if S_kill(src) = s + omega(op, src) then
            S_kill(src) unchanged
            c_kill(src) ← max(c_kill(src), c)
          else if S_kill(src) < s + omega(op, src) then
            S_kill(src) ← s + omega(op, src)
            c_kill(src) ← c
        for each result operand res of op in civs
          c_def(res) ← c
          S_def(res) ← s
```

```
COMPUTE_LOCAL_LT():
  // Start recursive analysis from the outermost level
  ∀(s, c, p) ∈ [f_1, l_1]X[0, T]X{first, last}
    LT_local(s, c, p) ← −1,     Visit_Level(1, ∅)

  // Initialize first with last value if first uninitialized
  for each stage s from f_1 to l_1
    for each cycle c from 0 to T
      if LT_local(s, c, first) = −1 then
        LT_local(s, c, first) ← LT_local(s, c, last)

VISIT_LEVEL(level level, live set live):
  // Count the local lifetimes for loop level 'level'
  for each stage s from l_level to f_level, backwards
    for each cycle c from T to 0, backwards
      live ← live ∪ DEF(s, c) ∪ USE(s, c)
      if LT_local(s, c, last) = −1 then
        LT_local(s, c, last) ← |live|
      else
        old ← LT_local(s, c, first)
        LT_local(s, c, first) ← max(old, |live|)
      live ← (live − DEF(s, c)) ∪ USE(s, c)
  // Recursive call for the inner levels
  if level < n and s = f_level+1 then
    Visit_Level(level + 1, live)
```

Fig. 6. Fast Method Algorithms

the length in stages of the lifetime of v. The two other δ terms are adjustment factors to take into account the exact modulo-cycle the variant is defined or killed in the stage. Figure 7(a) shows an example of a cross-iteration lifetime. The lifetime starts at $S_{def} = 1$, corresponding to stage b, and $c_{def} = 2$, and stops $omega = 3$ iterations later in stage $S_{kill} = 0 + omega$ at modulo-cycle $c_{kill} = 0$. Then the number of cross-iteration lifetimes for that variant is equal to 2, 1, and 2 at modulo-cycle 0, 1, and 2 respectively.

4.2 Local Lifetimes

The computation of the local lifetimes is done by using traditional backwards data-flow liveness analysis on the control-flow graph (CFG) of the loop nest where each loop level is executed only once. A generic example for a loop nest of depth 3 is shown in Figure 7(b). The final schedule is partitioned into $2 * n - 1$ blocks of stages. For each level but the innermost, there are two blocks. The first is made of the stages exclusively belonging to the loop level and executed before the ILP, and the second of the stages exclusively belonging to the same level but executed after. The innermost level has only one block made of the S_n innermost stages. The separations correspond to the separations between stages of different levels in the kernel and the order in which the stages are visited is the order of the stages in the kernel. The figure shows the stage indexes for each block. Stages visited as $first$ are represented in light gray whereas stages visited as $last$ are in dark gray.

4.3 Register Pressure

The OLP is composed of S_n kernels, each made of all the S stages. The register pressure is the sum of the cross-iteration and local lifetimes for each stage. The distinction

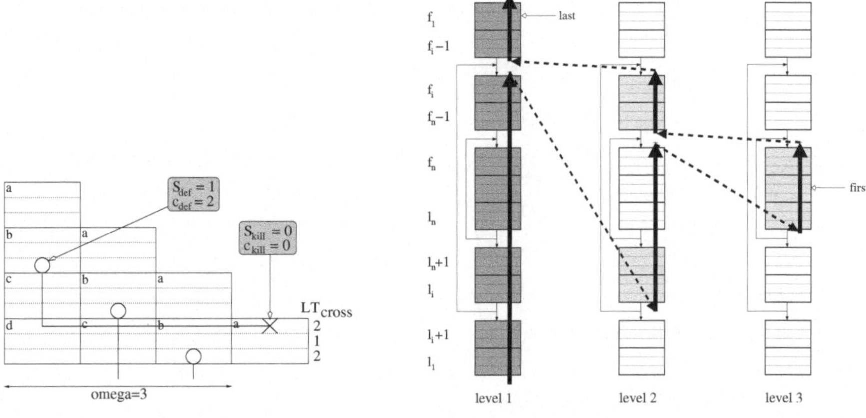

(a) Cross-iteration Lifetimes Example (b) Local Lifetime Computation Order

Fig. 7. Lifetimes Computation

between first and last instance of the local lifetimes must be made, leading to $S - n$ different cases. We then obtain the formula for LT_{olp} shown in Figure 8. The first term counts all the cross-iteration lifetimes. The second is the maximum number of local lifetimes among the S_n possible instances of kernel in the OLP.

The formula for the ILP and DFP is LR_{iles}. The first three terms correspond to the three types of stretched lifetimes shown in Figure 5: 7, 4, and 6 in that order. Their number is fixed for the entire execution of the ILES and equal to the number of lifetimes live at the exit of the OLP. The fourth term of the formula corresponds to the local lifetimes of the ILES (5). $MaxLive$ is then the maximum between between the maximum register pressure of the OLP and the maximum register pressure of the ILES patterns.

Although it is possible to modify the algorithms and formulas to make the $MaxLive$ computation incremental, it is not believed that our method is fast enough to help guide the instruction scheduler.

5 Experiments

The algorithms were implemented in the ORC 2.1 compiler and tested on an 1.4GHz Itanium2 machine with 1GB RAM running Linux. The benchmarks are SSP-amenable loop nests extracted from the Livermore Loops, the NPB 2.2 benchmarks and the SPEC2000 FP benchmark suite. A total of 127 loop nests were considered. When all the different depths are tested, 328 different test cases were available. There were 127, 102, 60, 30, and 9 loop nests of depth 1, 2, 3, 4, and 5, respectively.

The main results are summarized here and explained in details in the next subsections. (1) The fast method is 1 to 2 orders of magnitude faster than the comprehensive method, and 3 to 4 orders of magnitude faster than the register allocator. (2) Despite the approximations made by the fast method, its computed $MaxLive$ is identical to $MaxLive$ computed by the comprehensive method. No rule of thumb could be

$$
\begin{aligned}
LT_{cross}(c) &= \sum_{v \in civs} ((S_{kill}(v) - S_{def}(v) + 1) + \delta_{def}(c, v) + \delta_{kill}(c, v)) \\
&\quad \text{where} \begin{cases} \delta_{def}(c, v) = -1 \text{ if } c < c_{def}(v), 0 \text{ otherwise} \\ \delta_{kill}(c, v) = -1 \text{ if } c > c_{kill}(v), 0 \text{ otherwise} \end{cases} \\
LT_{iles}(c) &= LT_{cross}(T) + \sum_{s=l_n}^{l_1} LT_{local}(s, T, last) + \sum_{s=f_1}^{f_n - 2} LR_{local}(s, T, first) \\
&\quad + \max_{l \in [2,n]} \left(\max_{i_0 \in [0, S_l - 1]} \left(\sum_{i=0}^{S_n - 1} LT_{local}(f_l + (i_0 + i)\% S_l, c, first) \right) \right) \\
LT_{olp}(c) &= LT_{cross}(c) + \max_{i \in [1, S_n]} \left(\sum_{s=l_n - i}^{l_1} LT_{local}(s, c, last) + \sum_{s=f_1}^{l_n - 1 - i} LT_{local}(s, c, first) \right) \\
FatCover_{olp} &= \max_{\forall c \in [0, T-1]} (LT_{olp}(c)) \\
FatCover_{iles} &= \max_{\forall c \in [0, T-1]} (LT_{iles}(c)) \\
MaxLive &= max(FatCover_{iles}, FatCover_{olp})
\end{aligned}
$$

Fig. 8. Register Pressure Computation Formulas

deduced to predict $MaxLive$ by only considering the 1-D schedule parameters such as kernel length, number of loop variants, and others. Rotating Register pressure increases quickly for integer values as the loop nest gets deeper and about half of the loop nests of depth 4 or 5 show a $MaxLive$ higher than the size of the INT register file. (3) The floating-point rotating register pressure remains about constant as the depth of the loop nests increases, and never exceeds 47 registers. Consequently, the floating-point rotating register file could be reduced from 96 to 64 registers. The extra 32 registers could be added to the integer register file instead.

5.1 Compilation Time

The time measurements are presented in Figure 9(a) where the loop nests have been sorted first by increasing depth, delimited by tics on the horizontal axis, then by increasing kernel length. Note the logarithmic scale for the vertical axis. The comprehensive and fast methods take up to 3.18 and 0.04 seconds respectively, with an average of 0.16 and 0.005 seconds. The running time of each method is directly related to the kernel length. The shape of the graph confirms the quadratic running time of the fast method and the influence of the depth of the loop nest. The fast method is 22.9 times faster than the comprehensive method, with a maximum of 217.8. As the loop nest gets deeper, the speedup becomes exponentially more significant.

The running time of the fast method and the register allocator from [18] are compared in Figure 9(d). On average, the fast method is 3 orders of magnitude faster than the register allocator with a maximum of 20000. As the loop nest gets deeper, i.e. as the $MaxLive$ increases and the need for a quick method to evaluate the register pressure a priori becomes stronger, the speedup increases, making the fast method a valid tool to detect infeasible schedules before the register allocator.

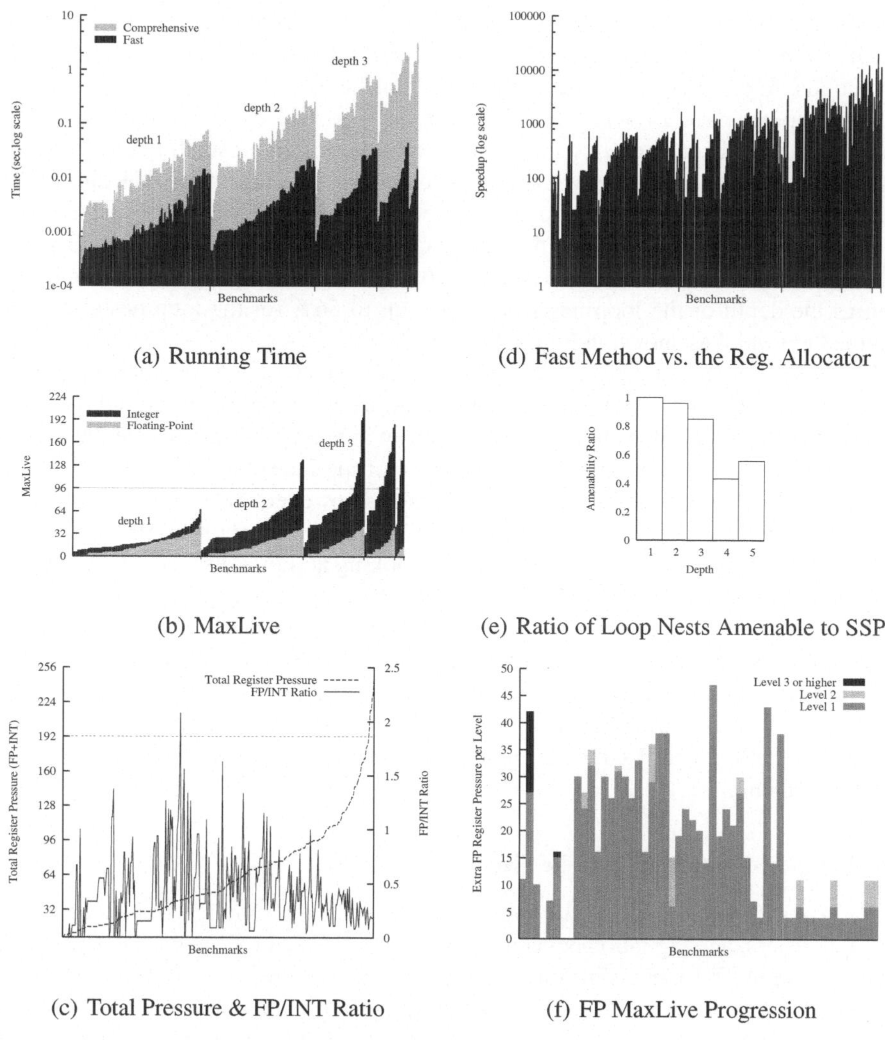

(a) Running Time

(d) Fast Method vs. the Reg. Allocator

(b) MaxLive

(e) Ratio of Loop Nests Amenable to SSP

(c) Total Pressure & FP/INT Ratio

(f) FP MaxLive Progression

Fig. 9. Experimental Results

Although the fast method does not take into account live-in and live-out lifetimes, the computed $MaxLive$ was identical for the two other methods in all the benchmarks tested. $MaxLive$ is indeed less likely to appear in the prolog and epilog.

5.2 MaxLive

The computed $MaxLive$ is a optimistic lower bound on the actual register pressure. It does not take into account that a value held in one register at cycle c must remain in the same register at cycle $c + 1$ or that the use of rotating registers reserves a group of consecutive registers at each cycle, even if some of them are not currently used.

The actual register allocation solution computed by an optimal register allocator may allocate more registers than $MaxLive$. However, with the addition of register copy instructions, $MaxLive$ registers can always be reached

The computed $MaxLive$ is shown in Figure 9(b) for INT and FP loop variants. The benchmarks have been sorted by increasing depth, indicated by small tics on the horizontal axis, and by increasing $MaxLive$. The average $MaxLive$ for INT and FP are 47.2 and 15.0 respectively with a maximum of 213 and 47. If we only consider rotating registers, the 96 hard limit on the number of available FP registers in the Itanium architecture is never reached. However the 96 limit for INT registers is reached more often as the depth of the loop nests increases, up to 56% for the loop nests software pipelined at level 4 as shown in Figure 9(e).

INT $MaxLive$ increases faster than FP $MaxLive$. INT $MaxLive$ indeed increases as the nest gets deeper because more inner iterations are running in parallel. It is particularly true for INT values that are used as array indexes. If an array index is defined in the outermost loop, then there is one instance of the index for each concurrent outermost iteration in the final schedule. For FP values however, this is not the case. They are typically defined in the innermost loop only and have very short lifetimes.

We also tried to approximate $MaxLive$ by looking at the 1-D schedule parameters. However no rule of thumb could be derived by looking at one parameter such as S, S_n, the length of the kernel or the number of loop variants. The $MaxLive$ was also compared to the actual number of registers allocated by the register allocator. Unlike in MS where the number of registers allocated rarely exceeds $MaxLive$+1 [17], the difference with SSP varies between 0% and 77%. Such results are explained by the higher complexity of SSP schedules compared to MS and because $MaxLive$ is not a tight lower bound.

5.3 Floating-Point Register File Size

Figure 9(c) shows the total register pressure, defined as the sum of $MaxLive$ for INT and FP registers, and the ratio between $MaxLive$ for FP and INT registers. The benchmarks are sorted by increasing ratio. The total register pressure rarely exceeds 192 registers, the size of the rotating register file in the Itanium architecture. Although FP $MaxLive$ can be twice higher than INT $MaxLive$, the FP/INT ratio remains lower than 0.5 when the total register pressure is greater than 96.

Figure 9(f) shows FP $MaxLive$ as the same loop nest is scheduled at deeper levels. FP $MaxLive$ does not or barely increases as a same loop nest is scheduled at a deeper level. The maximum FP $MaxLive$ never exceeds 47 registers.

Several conclusions, that may be useful for future designs of architectures with the same number of functional units and superscalar degree than the Itanium architecture, can be drawn from these remarks. First, the INT register file may benefit from a smaller FP register file with a ratio of 2 for 1. The FP register size can either be decreased to save important chip real estate, or the INT register file increased to allow more SSP loops to be register allocated. Second, for the set of benchmarks used in our experiments, the optimal size for the FP register file would be 64. It would not prevent any other loop nests from being register allocated while giving extra registers to the INT register file. If a size of 64 and a INT/FP ratio of 2 are chosen, the feasibility ratio for loop nests of depth 4 and 5 would jump from 43% and 56% to 77% and 67%, respectively. The FP/INT ratio chosen for the Itanium architecture is not incorrect, but was chosen with MS loops in mind, which exhibits a lower INT $MaxLive$.

6 Conclusion

Single-dimension Software Pipelining (SSP) software pipelines a loop nest at an arbitrary level. However the register pressure is too high for half of the loop nests of depth 4 or more. It is therefore necessary to know the register pressure early in the compilation process to avoid calling the register allocator when it is bound to fail. The results of the evaluation could also be used to evaluate the efficiency of any SSP register allocator. We proposed in this paper a methodology that quickly computes the rotating register pressure of an SSP schedule

Results showed that our method is accurate and at least 3 orders of magnitude faster than the register allocator on average, making it a valid tool to detect infeasible schedules early. From a hardware co-design point of view, experimental results suggest that SSP schedules would benefit from a smaller floating-point rotating register file of 64 registers and a twice as large integer rotating register file.

Acknowledgments

We would like to acknowledge Dr. Hongbo Rong for his enthusiastic moral and technical support during the course of this work, and Jean-Christophe Beyler and the anonymous reviewers for their insightful comments. This work was supported in part by the Defense Advanced Research Projects Agency (DARPA) under contract No.NBCH30904, by NSF grants No.0103723 and No.0429781, and by DOE grant No.DE-FC02-OIER25503.

References

1. A. Aiken, A. Nicolau, and S. Novack. Resource-constrained software pipelining. *IEEE Transactions on Parallel and Distributed Systems*, 6(12):1248–1270, Dec. 1995.
2. S. Carr, C. Ding, and P. Sweany. Improving software pipelining with unroll-and-jam. In *Proc. 29th Annual Hawaii Int'l Conf. on System Sciences*, pages 183–192, 1996.
3. A. Dani, V. Ramanan, and R. Govindarajan. Register-sensitive software pipelining. In *Proc. of 12th Int'l Par. Processing Symp./9th Int'l Symp. on Par. and Dist. Systems*, 1998.
4. A. Darte, R. Schreiber, B. R. Rau, and F. Vivien. Constructing and exploiting linear schedules with prescribed parallelism. *ACM Trans. on Design Automation of Electronic Systems*, 2001.
5. A. Douillet and G. R. Gao. Register pressure in software-pipelined loop nests: Fast computation and impact on architecture design. CAPSL TM 58, Univ. of Delaware, Newark, Delaware, 2005. In ftp://ftp.capsl.udel.edu/pub/doc/memos.
6. A. Eichenberger, E. Davidson, and S. Abraham. Minimum register requirements for a modulo schedule. In *Proc. of the 27th int'l symp. on Microarchitecture*, pages 75–84, 1994.
7. L. J. Hendren, G. R. Gao, E. R. Altman, and C. Mukerji. A register allocation framework based on hierarchical cyclic interval graphs. In *Proc. of the 4th Int'l Conf. on Compiler Construction*, pages 176–191. Springer-Verlag, 1992.

8. R. Huff. Lifetime-sensitive modulo scheduling. In *Proc. of the conf. on Programming language design and implementation*, pages 258–267. ACM Press, 1993.
9. S. Jain. Circular scheduling: A new technique to perform software pipelining. In *Proc. of the Conf, on Programming Language Design and Implementation*, pages 219–228, 1991.
10. M. Lam. Software pipelining: An effective scheduling technique for VLIW machines. In *Proc. of the conf. on Programming language design and implementation*, 1988.
11. J. Llosa, E. Ayguadé;, and M. Valero. Quantitative evaluation of register pressure on software pipelined loops. *International Journal of Parallel Programming*, 26(2):121–142, 1998.
12. J. Llosa, A. González, E. Ayguadé, and M. Valero. Swing modulo scheduling: A lifetime sensitive approach. In *Proc. Conf. on Par. Arch. and Compil. Tech.*, pages 80–86, 1996.
13. S.-M. Moon and K. Ebcioğlu. Parallelizing nonnumerical code with selective scheduling and software pipelining. *ACM Trans. on Prog. Lang. and Systems*, 19(6):853–898, 1997.
14. K. Muthukumar and G. Doshi. Software pipelining of nested loops. In *Proc. of the Int'l Conf. on Compiler Construction*, volume 2027, pages 165–181. LNCS, 2001.
15. Q. Ning and G. R. Gao. A novel framework of register allocation for software pipelining. In *Proc. of the symp. on Principles of programming languages*, pages 29–42, 1993.
16. B. R. Rau. Iterative modulo scheduling: an algorithm for software pipelining loops. In *Proc. of the int'l symp. on Microarchitecture*, pages 63–74, 1994.
17. B. R. Rau, M. Lee, P. P. Tirumalai, and M. S. Schlansker. Register allocation for software pipelined loops. In *Proc. of the conf. on Prog. lang. design and impl.*, pages 283–299, 1992.
18. H. Rong, A. Douillet, and G. R. Gao. Register allocation for software pipelined multi-dimensional loops. In *Proc. of the conf. on Prog. lang. design and impl.*, 2005.
19. H. Rong, A. Douillet, R. Govindarajan, and G. R. Gao. Code generation for single-dimension software pipelining of multi-dimensional loops. In *Proc. of Int. Symp. on Code Generation and Optimization*, page 175, 2004.
20. H. Rong, Z. Tang, R. Govindarajan, A. Douillet, and G. R. Gao. Single-dimension software pipelining for multi-dimensional loops. In *Proc. of Int. Symp. on Code Generation and Optimization*, pages 163–174, 2004.
21. J. Ruttenberg, G. R. Gao, A. Stoutchinin, and W. Lichtenstein. Software pipelining showdown: optimal vs. heuristic methods in a production compiler. In *Proc. of the conf. on Prog. lang. design and impl.*, pages 1–11, 1996.
22. J. Zalamea, J. Llosa, E. Ayguadé, and M. Valero. Two-level hierarchical register file organization for vliw processors. In *Proc. of the symp. on Microarch.*, pages 137–146, 2000.

Manipulating MAXLIVE for Spill-Free Register Allocation

Shashi Deepa Arcot, Henry Gordon Dietz, and Sarojini Priyadarshini Rajachidambaram

Electrical and Computer Engineering Department, University of Kentucky
sarco0@engr.uky.edu, hankd@engr.uky.edu, rspriya@uky.edu

Abstract. This paper explores new compilation methods, including Genetic Algorithms (GAs) and a new adaptation of Sethi-Ullman numbering, to aggressively restructure basic block code and allocate registers so that the number of registers used does not exceed the number available. Although the approach applies to a wide range of target architectures, it is investigated primarily for *nanocontrollers*, which have a combination of properties that make avoiding spills particularly difficult, but mandatory.

1 Introduction

The problem of efficiently allocating registers for temporary values is an old problem, but also is a topic of ongoing research. In large part, the importance of register allocation has been increasing because:

- Although both logic and memory speeds have been exponentially improving, the exponents are different. Main memory was once faster than processor logic for simple operations such as integer addition, but modern processors can perform hundreds to thousands of integer additions in the time taken to make one random address access to main memory.
- Registers play a key role in implementing instruction-level parallelism (ILP). Superscalar (multiple issue) execution logic may require many operands each clock cycle. As compared to multi-port caches and main memory interfaces, it is relatively straightforward to construct multi-port register files. Registers also facilitate pipelined execution.
- A variety of automatic coding mechanisms tend to generate much larger basic blocks with more complex dependence patterns than are commonly found in hand-written code. For example, many compilers now use loop unrolling or unraveling; similar code sequences also are generated automatically by tools like ATLAS[14].

While all three of the above increase the importance of register allocation, the first two primarily increase the benefit in using a good allocation, while the third essentially implements a qualitative change in the register allocation problem itself. In the general case, optimal allocation of registers is known to require more than polynomial time, but it is only with the common use of huge basic blocks that the theoretical complexity has

E. Ayguadé et al. (Eds.): LCPC 2005, LNCS 4339, pp. 32–46, 2007.

become a serious practical constraint on basic block algorithms. Thus, register allocation has become critical at the same time that the known optimal solutions have become intractable.

Beyond the needs of conventional computing systems, we have recently become focused on finding ways to bring programmable intelligence to nanofabricated and MEMS devices; these very simple computing elements are called *nanocontrollers*[7]. For the specific problem of allocating registers for nanocontroller programs, the second of the above issues does not apply, but first and third are exceptionally severe. There literally is no main memory in a nanocontroller system; thus, using memory to hold values that could not be allocated to registers is not an option. Further, because nanocontrollers provide only a single type of instruction which operates on one bit at a time, basic blocks often contain thousands of instructions. These basic blocks are not the result of unrolling, but of bit-level logic optimization using the ternary 1-of-2 multiplexor operation. The dependence structure within a block is correspondingly more complex than that generated by unrolling loops involving traditional binary operations. In summary, nanocontroller register allocation is a much harder problem than conventional register allocation, but a good solution also may be adapted to handle microcontrollers and future generations of conventional processors. The two solutions described in this paper both are very general, and are effective for *very large* basic blocks using any combination of unary, binary, and ternary operations.

Section 2 reviews some of the traditional approaches and issues involving register allocation. Our first and more conservative approach, which uses a Genetic Algorithm (GA) to reorder instructions, is detailed in Section 3. An extreme, but amazingly effective, approach combining aspects of Sethi-Ullman numbering with a Genetic Algorithm is described in Section 4. Brief conclusions are given in Section 5.

2 Traditional Approaches to Register Allocation

The term "register allocation" commonly is applied to a wide range of slightly different problems involving making efficient use of registers. The maximum number of values (or variables) that must temporally coexist in a program is called MAXLIVE. If MAXLIVE exceeds the number of registers available, values must be swapped between temporary memory locations and registers. Methods aimed at reducing the cost of spill/reload code include algorithms based on shortest path [9,4,10] and various methods for coloring a live-range interference graph [3,4,8]. However, spill/reload only are eliminated if MAXLIVE does not exceed the number of available registers, in which case optimal register assignment is straightforward.

Reordering and other alterations of the computation can change MAXLIVE. Sethi-Ullman Numbering [13], henceforth referred to as SUN, efficiently determines how to order evaluation of a binary operation expression tree so that MAXLIVE and the number of instructions used for the computation both are provably minimal. The SUN algorithm proceeds in two distinct phases with $O(m)$ complexity for m instructions. First, each node is labeled with a number, according to a set of rules, such that the label corresponds to the minimum number of registers required to evaluate the subtree rooted at that point without any stores (i.e., without register spill/reload). These labels are then used to order node evaluation, allocate registers, and emit instructions. Common Subexpression Elimination (CSE) greatly reduces the number of instructions that need to be executed and is nearly universally used in modern compilers, but generates Directed Acyclic Graphs (DAGs) that are incompatible with the original SUN algorithm; a multitude of attempts to extend SUN to handle DAGs have failed to produce an algorithm that is both fast and effective[1].

For nanocontrollers and some microcontrollers, even a single spill renders a program unusable because there is no place to spill to. Thus, minimizing the number of instructions only is relevant if the code is spill free. Put another way, even increasing the number of instructions to be executed is highly desirable if it makes the difference between being spill-free and being unusable. Although Genetic Algorithm (GA) [8] and Genetic Programming (GP)[5] have been applied to register allocation problems before, this paper uses GA technology directly to reduce MAXLIVE so that spill-free code can be produced.

3 Genetic Algorithm for Reordering to Minimize MAXLIVE

Given that reordering the instruction sequence can significantly change MAXLIVE, it seems appropriate to investigate methods that can reasonably efficiently find a good instruction order. Even with good pruning, it is not practical to use exhaustive search for reordering basic blocks containing thousands of instructions. However, simulated evolutionary processes are very effective for many conceptually similar problems, so we created a Genetic Algorithm (GA) for reordering.

3.1 Structure of the GA

The use of a GA to generate code is commonly referred to as Genetic Programming (GP)[12], however, neither the data structures standardly used with GP nor with traditional GA systems is efficient in solving the instruction rescheduling problem. Despite that, the overall structure of the GA used for rescheduling to minimize MAXLIVE, as shown in Algorithm 1, is relatively conventional. An island model is used in order to allow subdivisions of the population to converge to different solutions in relative isolation, thus making the system somewhat more robust. A non-generational steady-state formulation is used primarily to simplify the coding and reduce execution overhead.

Fundamentally, the problem in making the GA efficient is one of maintaining good adjacency properties through mutation and crossover operations; a new schedule should have many properties in common with its parent(s). In the particular case of instruction scheduling, it also is important to consider only valid schedules, e.g., only schedules in which no instruction is scheduled before an instruction that produces one of its inputs. Even using simplifications such and earliest and latest slot markings for instructions, checking validity of a schedule is relatively expensive. Discovering that a schedule is not valid also wastes the effort of creating and checking that schedule. Thus, the preferred solution is to generate only valid schedules.

This is done by using an unusual genome representation which we have recently used for several types of scheduling GAs: rather than representing an instruction schedule directly, a schedule is represented by giving each instruction an integer "scheduling

Algorithm 1. Steady-State Island GA For Scheduling

Repeat the following until the allotted time or number of trials has elapsed:

1. If the population is not yet full, create a new valid, but randomly-ordered, instruction schedule; goto step 5
2. Pick a number of population members at random and identify the two selected members with the worst and best metrics (a form of tournament selection); an island model may be enforced at this stage by biasing selections to stay within the same static subdivision of the population
3. If random choice selects mutation or if the two schedules selected are duplicates, perform mutation by replacing the poorest-metric selected member with a new schedule created by mutation of the other selected member; goto step 5
4. By default perform crossover by picking an additional population member at random, sorting the three selected members by metric value, and replacing the poorest-metric one with the crossover product of the other two
5. Evaluate the metric for the newly-created population member
6. Determine if the newly-created population member is a new best and mark it accordingly; it is the new best if it is the only member of the population or if a symmetric "better than" comparison function finds its metric to be better than that of the previous best schedule

priority." The schedule is generated using these priorities to break ties in an otherwise conventional list scheduling procedure. The schedule is created by starting with the first instruction slot and working toward the last, at each slot updating the set of schedulable instructions and then inserting the highest priority schedulable instruction in that slot. Clearly, only valid schedules are produced in this way. Further, most adjacency properties are inherited from parent(s) even though the actual schedules may differ in what appear to be complex ways; changes in priorities may rearrange, spread, insert, or delete subsequences of instructions, but before/after relationships between instructions with priorities that were not changed by mutation or crossover are most often preserved. It also is trivial to compute a MAXLIVE-based metric while generating the schedule.

The mutation and crossover operations are straightforward. Mutation replaces some priorities with random values, whereas crossover mixes priorities from two parents. Interestingly, as a schedule is being assembled for evaluation, it is easy to tag each instruction with the number of live values at its position in the schedule, and hence to know which instructions are involved in subsequences requiring MAXLIVE registers. Thus, we can bias the mutation and crossover operations to change priorities for instructions in those regions, significantly improving the speed of convergence.

3.2 Experimental Procedure

In order to determine just how well the reordering GA works, we constructed a test framework which we have used for all the data presented in this paper.

A simple program is used to generate pseudo-random BitC programs containing a single basic block each. BitC is a simple C dialect designed from programming nanocontrollers[7]; it differs from C primarily in that it allows bit precisions to be specified for each variable and incorporates some additional operators, such as binary minimum and maximum (`?<` and `?>`). The base BitC compiler which we earlier developed for our research in nanocontrollers, `bitcc`, converts each variable-precision word-level operation into a multitude of single-bit operations implemented using the only operation provided by nanocontrollers, the ITE (If-The-Else) 1-of-2 multiplexor function. The operations are then optimized by a variant of BDD (Binary Decision Diagram) logic minimization methods[2,11], yielding better code than simple bit-slice formulations would, but producing very complex DAG structures. In the `bitcc` output used for the current study, storage of final values into registers is done by separate explicit store operations.

An ITE+store to SITE (Store-If-Then-Else) converter was constructed specially for this research. This program removes the explicit stores, combining them with ITEs in an optimal way. Thus, sets of operations like `temp=(i?t:e); s=temp;` are converted into `s=(i?t:e);`. The SITE-only DAG, which incorporates a reference sequential order, is then coded as a set of C data structures and output to `dag.h`. This "pre-cooked" set of data structures makes it much easier to perform register allocation experiments by avoiding the need to integrate the algorithm under test with the rest of the compiler. Using this approach, the GA reordering code is just over 300 lines of C code and the SUN-based GA described in Section 4is just under 600 lines of C code.

A variety of shell scripts and filters were developed to run tests and collect data. Relatively simple cases occur very often in randomly-generated code, for example, when a later store into a variable overwrites the value stored by a more complex computation very little code results. Thus, our methodology includes a filtering step that removes all cases with MAXLIVE naturally less than 3. Additionally, filters are applied to remove statistically redundant cases. Our scripts allow large numbers of test cases to be executed serially or in parallel on cluster supercomputers.

The results presented in scatter plots in this paper cover 32,912 representative test cases obtained by filtering millions of random basic blocks as described above. They were processed using KASY0 (Kentucky ASYmmetric Zero), a 128-node 2GHz Athlon XP cluster supercomputer. All the GAs were given the same fast-running parameters: population size of 50, subdivided among 4 islands, with crossover 3 times more likely than mutation, and a limit of evaluating only 1,000 individuals.

3.3 Results

At the outset, in early 2004, we had hoped that reordering instructions would be sufficient to dramatically reduce MAXLIVE, but experimental results are mixed.

For relatively modest basic block sizes, such as those commonly arising from handwritten code in languages like C for targets like IA32, the GA reordering does well. However, ternary instructions and larger basic blocks tend to yield not just larger, but also more complex DAG structures. Our preliminary tests showed that, for the large ternary instruction basic blocks common in nanocontroller code, GA reordering reduced MAXLIVE significantly in absolute terms, but not enough to make a qualitative difference for our nanocontroller compilation problem. These (unpublished) early observations are echoed in the more extensive data presented here.

The GA reordering of instructions does not change the total number of instructions which must be executed (assuming no register spill/reload operations are needed), nor

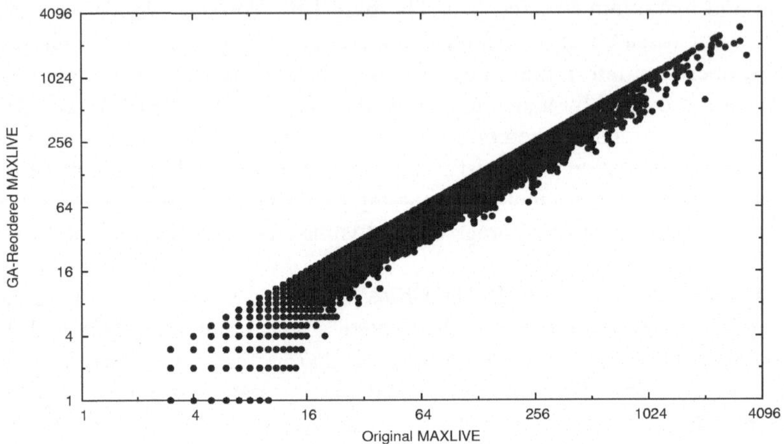

Fig. 1. GA-Reordered Vs. Original MAXLIVE

does it alter the underlying DAG structure. Thus, the only relevant issue is the reduction in MAXLIVE, which is shown in the scatter-plot of Figure 1. Note that both axes in this graph are logarithmically scaled. As observed in preliminary experiments, although MAXLIVE is reduced more in absolute terms for the larger cases, the relative reduction for relatively small cases is significantly larger than for larger cases. The average reduction over all 32,912 cases is approximately 18%. Thus, while these results clearly confirm that GA reordering is well worth applying, it alone is not sufficient for nanocontroller targets – which are expected to provide only about 64 registers.

4 SUN with GA-Reenabling of CSEs

Given that even GA reordering of instructions is not sufficient to make big blocks spill free, it is necessary to consider techniques that trade execution of more instructions for a more dramatic reduction in MAXLIVE.

The approach is based on the SUN algorithm, but makes considerable extensions to it. The first extension is the generalization of SUN to manage up to three operands per instruction. This modification is required because the SUN algorithm as originally presented assumes each single-instruction operation takes precisely two source operands, yet the only instruction supported by current nanocontroller designs takes three source operands and different operand counts may be useful for other types of specialized processors.

As suggested earlier, the lack of register-memory instructions requires only a minor adjustment to the SUN algorithm, but three other issues are more difficult to resolve. There have been many attempts to extend SUN to handle optimal register allocation and instruction scheduling for DAGS. Although, under certain restricted conditions, DAGs can be handled using a modified SUN algorithm, the optimality of the solution is a casualty in every reasonably efficient scheme. The fact that DAGs for nanocontroller programs are exceptionally large and complex makes the algorithm's execution time significant and yields a very small fraction of the DAG for which special-case extensions of SUN can be applied. Our solution is to convert the DAG to a tree by logically replicating every common subexpression in every place from which it is referenced. This solution may seem extreme, but the DAG generally has an inherently higher MAXLIVE than a tree; given the extreme pressure to fit in a limited register file, it is natural to focus first on minimizing MAXLIVE and only secondarily to attempt to retrieve some of the benefits of common subexpression elimination.

4.1 Generalization of SUN Labeling for Ternary Instructions

The labeling method used in the original SUN algorithm is focused on binary operations: instructions with two input operands. Unary operations are trivially labeled using the rule that any operation node *n* with only one input operand is labeled with $L(n) = 1$. It is not trivial to extend SUN labeling to three or more input operands. However, digital nanocontrollers as currently proposed have an instruction set consisting of only a single instruction which happens to take three input operands. Three-input operations, generally involving multiplexor-like functionality used to simulate enable masking, also have become common in multimedia instruction set extensions to many modern processors[6].

The labeling of three-input operation trees is significantly more complex than that of two-input operation trees because the number of possible relationships between subtree labels grows exponentially as the number of inputs per operator increases. To each node *n*, the label $L(n)$ is assigned as:

1. If *n* is a leaf, $L(n) = 0$;
2. If *n* has descendants with labels l_1, l_2, and l_3 sorted into order such that $l_1 >= l_2 >= l_3$,
   (a) If $l_1 > l_2 > l_3$, $L(n) = l_1$;
   (b) If $l_1 > l_2 == l_3 == 0$, $L(n) = l_1$;
   (c) If $l_1 > l_2 == l_3 != 0$ and $l_1 - l_2 == 1$, $L(n) = l_1 + 1$;
   (d) If $l_1 > l_2 == l_3 != 0$ and $l_1 - l_2 > 1$, $L(n) = l_1$;
   (e) If $l_1 == l_2 > l_3$, $L(n) = l_1 + 1$;
   (f) If $l_1 == l_2 == l_3 != 0$, $L(n) = l_1 + 2$;
   (g) If $l_1 == l_2 == l_3 == 0$, $L(n) = 1$;

Rule 1 reflects the now-common simplifying fact that modern processors avoid using memory operands directly. For example, leaf nanocontroller operations always can be labeled with L(n) = 0 because there literally is no way for an instruction to reference data other than making a register reference. Constants are referenced from pre-allocated registers; given bit-wide data paths and operations, only the constants 0 and 1 are possible, so hardwiring just two pre-allocated registers suffices. Nanocontrollers have only registers in which to store data, so in fact all user-defined variables become preallocated registers. Nanocontrollers even perform input/output (I/O) operations using pre-allocated registers that are really I/O channels; for example, register 6 might be a "global OR" output signal and register 7 might be an analog zero-crossing detector input. Data can be directly used from a pre-allocated register identically to how it would be used from any other register; no load instruction in needed (or even exists for nanocontrollers).

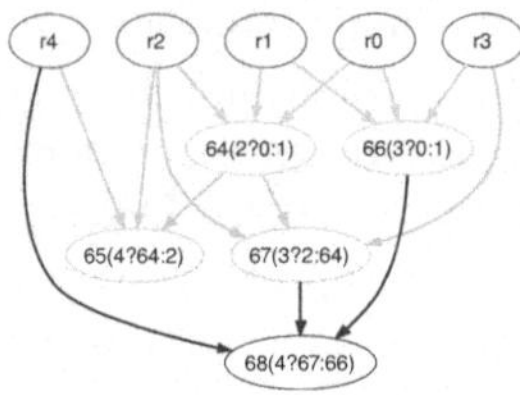

Fig. 2. Simple ITE DAG

Rule 2 reflects register needs for non-leaf nodes. As complex as this rule is, the complexity is significantly reduced by the fact that it is expressed in terms of the labels of the three input subtrees in an order that is sorted by label. Thus, l_1, l_2, and $l_3$are the descendant labels in decreasing label order, not subtree position order. The complexity of this rule is still high primarily because equal labels and labels of 0 are both special cases. However, in practice, the complexity of the rule has little impact on the feasibility of the technique. It also is useful to note that the ternary node case also handles both binary and unary node labellings by allowing the missing descendants to be treated as if they had 0 labels.

4.2 Tree Generation

At the time the SUN algorithm was proposed, it was quite natural to use trees as the intermediate form. However, coding styles have significantly changed, so that various compiler optimizations yielding DAGs are now essentially mandatory. For nanocontroller programs, these DAGs are particularly large and complex thanks to treatment of each bit position separately and target hardware support for only one type of instruction (which corresponds to a 1-of-2 multiplexor).

As stated earlier, nanocontroller programs generate optimized DAGs which are large and complex. Each SITE that is generated is a node in the DAG. The root node(s) of every DAG corresponds to a SITE that is a final store into a variable. All the interior nodes correspond to the temporary SITEs which represent the ITE operations. By convention, our tools number these starting at 64, the default number of physical nanocontroller registers available. The leaf nodes are the ITEs 0 and 1 or the ITEs that correspond to the initially defined user-variables – nodes numbered less than 64. Trees are generated by conceptually converting all the DAGs to trees in such a way that each node is replicated at every point that it is referenced.

To demonstrate the treatment of a DAG as a tree, consider the simple example DAG shown in Figure 2. Ternary nodes tend to yield more complex DAGs than do binary nodes.

Although the SUN algorithms cannot operate on a DAG, it is easy to treat the DAG as a tree. Logically, the transformation is simply that, whenever a node has more than one exit arc, the node is replicated to make one copy per exit arc. As a node is thus replicated, any entry arcs must also be replicated to point at the copies. This in turn makes the nodes behind those entry arcs have multiple exit arcs, thus requiring them to be replicated in the same fashion. The result of this transformation is shown in Figure 3.

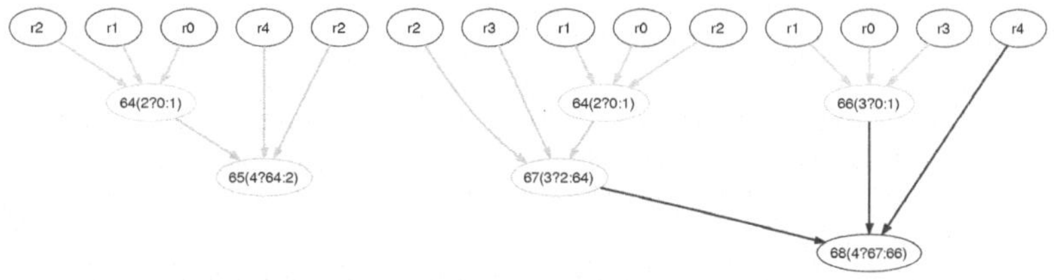

Fig. 3. Trees Derived From Simple ITE DAG

A subtle point in this transformation is the fact that a single DAG becomes multiple trees. Even if the original DAG had unconnected components, the default sequential order (as listed above) can yield a default execution order. For our purposes, the SUN algorithm will provide the order within each tree, but ordering across trees must be provided in another way. The solution used in this paper is to order the tree walks in the same order as the nodes without exit arcs were originally ordered. Thus, in Figure 3, the tree ending in 65 (right) would be evaluated before the one ending in 68 (left).

Of course, the transformation to create a tree does not merely enable SUN analysis, but also provides a key relationship between nodes that are the roots of common subexpressions in the DAG. We can use the rules of our modified SUN to label tree nodes for walking, thus implying a walk order, but then not actually duplicate the common subexpression nodes. This is the core idea behind the SUN-based GA: to use a Genetic Algorithm (GA) to selectively re-enable CSE (Common Subexpression Elimination); where MAXLIVE will not be too adversely affected using the walk order determined using the tree, do not replicate the common subexpression node.

4.3 GA Optimization of Subexpression Instantiation

It should not be surprising that the basic steady-state island GA structure of Algorithm 1 also serves well for the SUN-based GA. The details are surprisingly straightforward, as outlined in Algorithm 2.

Whereas the GA-reordering algorithm described in Section 3 required a fairly complex data structure, our SUN-based GA for selective reinstantiation of CSEs can effectively use a very conventional bit-sequence genome. Each genome is a bit vector with one bit for each potential CSE; a 1 means instantiate (i.e., the CSE is enabled), a 0 means duplicate to make a tree.

To evaluate the merit of a genome, the DAG is recursively walked as a sequence of trees (as per Section 3). The walk uses the labels and ordering of operand evaluation created by treating the DAG as a tree and applying the rules in Section 4.1. As each node is visited, it is allocated a register if needed. Nodes representing enabled CSEs are walked only the first time they are encountered. After the value of a non-CSE node has been used, the register allocated to it is freed. The register allocated to an enabled CSE node is freed only after no reference to that CSE remains, which is determined by decrementing a reference count associated with that node. The value of MAXLIVE and number of instructions that would be generated by the walk are both tracked during the evaluation; as noted in Algorithm 2, the recursive walk can be aborted early if MAXLIVE

Algorithm 2. SUN-Based GA Procedure Overview

1. Use the tree interpretation (Section 4.2) of the DAG to label nodes as described in Section 4.1. Note that interpreting the DAG as a tree does not require literally duplicating nodes; no node copies are made in our coding. The labeling can even take advantage of the fact that CSEs need only be traversed once to be labeled, because additional traversals would yield the same labels.
2. Apply the steady-state island GA (Algorithm 1),with the following adjustments:
   (a) The initial population is loaded with both the tree (no CSEs instantiated) and original DAG (all CSEs instantiated) as members in addition to random members.
   (b) As the search progresses, the evaluation of any population member can be truncated when its value of MAXLIVE reaches a "terrible" level that can be specified as input to the GA and also can be dynamically updated as better MAXLIVE values are encountered in the search.

becomes too large. The metric favors generating fewer instructions once the MAXLIVE constraint has been met.

The mutation and crossover operations are very standard GA bit-genome operations. The only notable difference is that random choices are made for each bit position in crossover, rather than using the even more common subsequence interchange. The randomly generated (initial) population members are created using a two-step process that first selects a random target "loading" and then randomly turns on bit positions to achieve that loading; this yields a better coverage of the full range of CSE enable densities.

Overall, the SUN-based GA is a very standard GA that has an unusual merit evaluation process.

4.4 Results

Testing the SUN-based GA for selectively enabling common subexpression elimination immediately revealed that the concept of allowing some redundant evaluation was able to dramatically reduce MAXLIVE. In fact, the reduction possible for large blocks is nothing short of shocking, with nearly every nanocontroller test case collapsing to a form using approximately a dozen temporary registers despite initially having a MAXLIVE of hundreds or even thousands.

In order to expose the general relationship between enabling CSEs and increasing MAXLIVE, a series of experiments were conducted using our SUN-based GA to optimize a moderately complex nanocontroller basic block for various target MAXLIVE values. This basic block, with all possible common subexpressions eliminated, consists of 3,041 ternary SITE instructions and yields a MAXLIVE of 561 in its default ordering. In this particular case, our GA reordering the instructions is able to reduce MAXLIVE only slightly, to 553. However, disabling all CSEs results in a pure tree which, using our modified SUN algorithm requires only 12 registers. Unfortunately, the pure tree contains 23,819 SITEs – nearly 8 times as many instructions.

Figure 4 shows how the number of enabled CSEs varies with the MAXLIVE target using our SUN-based GA. All of the CSE counts plotted are for the coding yielding

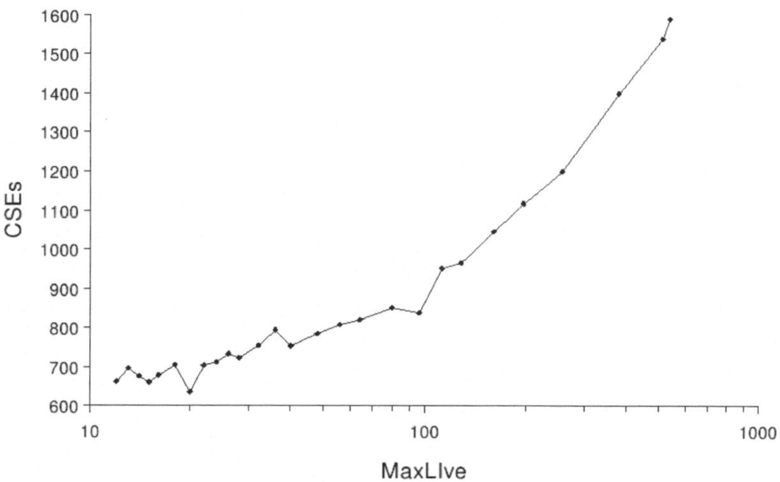

Fig. 4. Enabled CSEs Vs. MAXLIVE For A Nanocontroller Basic Block

the lowest number of SITEs for the given MAXLIVE target. Surprisingly, the SUN-based GA was able to achieve a MAXLIVE of 12 with 662 CSEs enabled. However, the impact of enabling these 662 CSEs on reducing the number of SITEs is minimal; because some CSEs are nested and the subtree sizes saved by enabling a CSE vary widely, the relationship between the number of CSEs enabled and the total number of SITEs remaining is not direct.

Figure 5 shows how the total number of SITEs varies with the MAXLIVE target for the same test case used in Figure 4. Note that in both figures, MAXLIVE is plotted on the X axis using a log scale. Clearly, although large reductions in MAXLIVE are possible, they come at a high price in additional instructions to be executed. The decrease in MAXLIVE is approximately linear with the increase in SITEs. However, the slope is favorable; as the number of additional instructions increases by nearly an order of magnitude, close to two orders of magnitude reduction in MAXLIVE is realized.

The search space is sufficiently large so that exhaustive evaluation of any but the smallest examples is impractical; ignoring the ordering problem, any problem with k potential CSEs has 2^kdifferent code structures to evaluate. For basic blocks of nanocontroller code, k commonly exceeds 1,000 – as it does in this example. Thus, we do not have known optimal solutions for typical problems and cannot make specific claims about the absolute quality of the SUN-based GA results. For Figures 4 and 5, the search was constrained to take approximately one minute to optimize for each target MAXLIVE (running compiled C code on a 1.4GHz Athlon XP system under Linux), and this restriction has no doubt contributed to the noise level visible in the curves for this one test case.

In addition to the detailed study of how a specific DAG's processing changes with different target values for MAXLIVE, it is useful to examine the statistical behavior of the algorithm over a large set of cases. For this purpose, we used the exact same cases that we employed to evaluate the GA for reordering instructions (Section 3.3). This

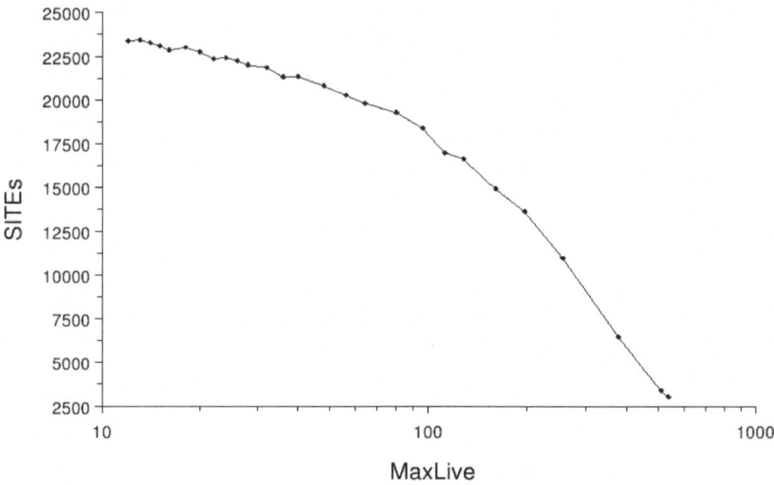

Fig. 5. Number Of SITEs Vs. MAXLIVE For A Nanocontroller Basic Block

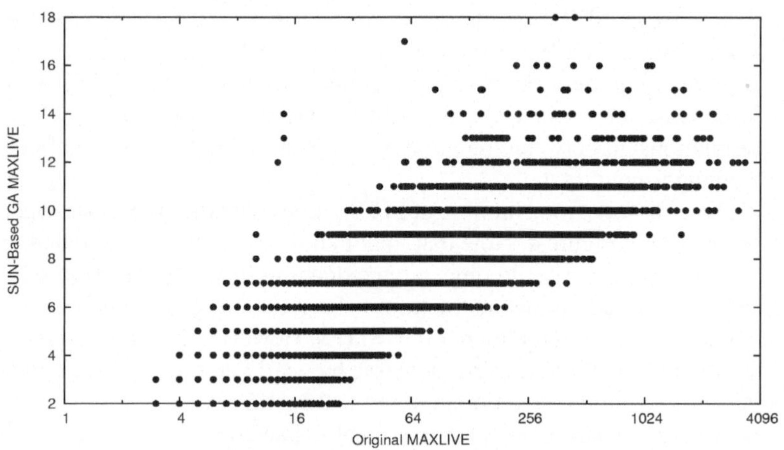

Fig. 6. SUN-Based GA Vs. Original MAXLIVE

enables direct comparison of the two approaches, as well as statistical evaluation of each independently.

Perhaps the most important statistic is how well MAXLIVE can be reduced by the SUN-based GA. Figure 9 shows that the performance in this respect is nothing short of amazing; none of the 32,912 test cases needed more than 18 registers – well within our nominal nanocontroller goal of fitting within 64 registers. Note the logarithmic scale in the X axis of this graph. Even a DAG having a default-order MAXLIVE of 3,409 still fit in 18 registers – more precisely, that case fit in just 12 registers!

Of course, there has to be a catch, and there is. As Figure 9 clearly shows, making MAXLIVE as small as possible often requires executing many more instructions than the

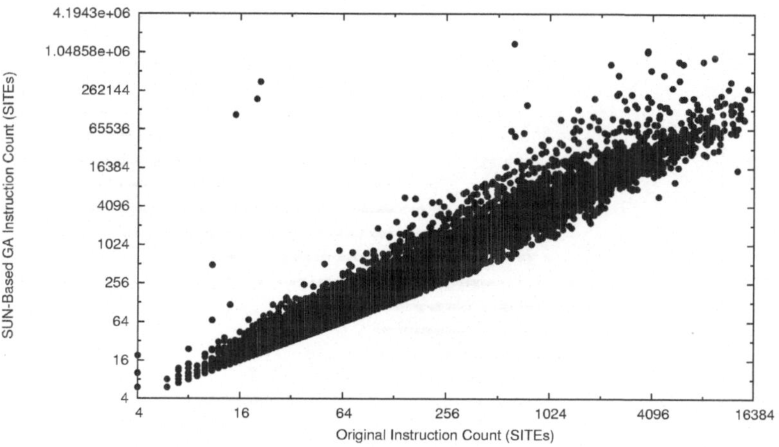

Fig. 7. SUN-Based GA Vs. Original Instruction Counts (SITEs)

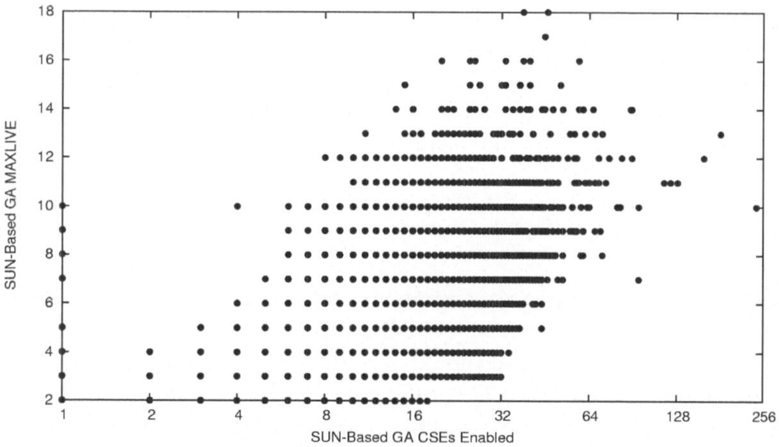

Fig. 8. SUN-Based GA MAXLIVE Vs. CSEs Enabled

original DAG would have required. Note that both axes in this graph are logarithmic, but the largest original block had 15,309 instructions (SITEs) while the largest produced by SUN-based GA had 1,431,548. On average, there was a factor of 8X expansion in code size to obtain the lowest possible MAXLIVE. As dramatic as this tradeoff is, such a code size expansion can be acceptable if it is the difference between being able to use the code and not being able to; even on desktop processors, the penalty for accessing main memory may be high enough to occasionally warrant executing 8X more instructions. Further, recall from Figure 5 that the SUN-based GA is able to efficiently target a specific MAXLIVE target, so it is not necessary to suffer code expansion beyond that needed to reach the target MAXLIVE value.

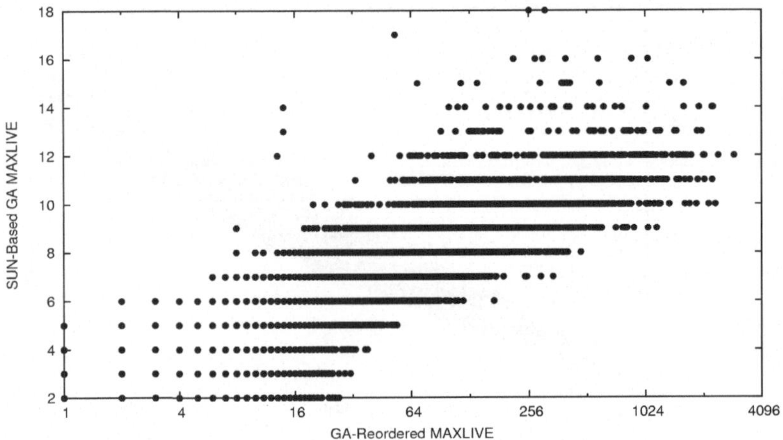

Fig. 9. SUN-Based GA Vs. GA-Reordered MAXLIVE

Given that the SUN-based GA approach selectively enables CSEs, one might expect that the number of CSEs enabled is essentially zero in order to achieve the minimum MAXLIVE value, but Figure 8 shows that is not the case. A modest reduction in the number of instructions generated is generally possible, without adversely affecting MAXLIVE, by carefully selecting to enable some CSEs.

5 Conclusion

This paper has presented two very aggressive methods for attempting to force an extremely complex block to meet a very small MAXLIVE constraint. One technique, GA reordering, clearly works well and should be widely applied; there is no major penalty. The other technique, SUN-based GA, offers amazing reductions in MAXLIVE, but at the expense of significant code expansion. Figure 9 shows that the SUN-based GA is able to handle extremely complex blocks exponentially better than GA reordering.

If the goal is simply to be spill free, the lowest-cost method that results in a viable MAXLIVE should be used. Often, GA reordering will suffice. When it does not, the SUN-based GA should be used with an explicit cut-off value equal to the number of registers available. Adapting these methods to achieve goals more complex than just freedom from spills, such as simultaneously optimizing pipeline performance or minimizing power consumption, is future work.

References

1. A. V. Aho, S. C. Johnson, and J. D. Ullman. Code generation for expressions with common subexpressions. *J. ACM*, 24(1):146–160, 1977.
2. R. E. Bryant. Graph-based algorithms for boolean function manipulation. *IEEE Transactions on Computers*, C35(8), 1986.

3. G. J. Chaitin. Register allocation & spilling via graph coloring. *Proceedings of the 1982 SIGPLAN Symposium on Compiler Construction*, 1982.
4. C-H. Chi and H. G. Dietz. Register allocation for gaas computer systems. *IEEE Proceedings of the 21st Hawaii International Conference on Systems Sciences, Architecture Track*, 1, January 1988.
5. Keith D. Cooper, Philip J. Schielke, and Devika Subramanian. Optimizing for reduced code space using genetic algorithms. In *LCTES99: Proceedings of the ACM SIGPLAN 1999 workshop on Languages, compilers, and tools for embedded systems*, pages 1–9, New York, NY, USA, 1999. ACM Press.
6. H. G. Dietz and R. J. Fisher. Compiling for simd within a register. *Languages and Compilers for Parallel Computing, edited by S. Chatterjee, J,. F. Prins, L. Carter, J. Ferrante, Z. Li, D. Sehr, and P-C Yew, Springer-Verlag, New York, New York*, 1999.
7. Henry G. Dietz, Shashi D. Arcot, and Sujana Gorantla. Much ado about almost nothing: Compilation for nanocontrollers. *Languages and Compilers for Parallel Computing, Lecture Notes in Computer Science*, 2958:466–480, January 2004.
8. R. Filho and G. Lorena. A constructive genetic algorithm for graph coloring, 1997.
9. L. P. Horwitz, R. M. Karp, R. E. Miller, and S. Winograd. Index register allocation. *Journal of the ACM (JACM), http://portal.acm.org/citation.cfm?doid=321*, 13, January 1966.
10. David Padua Jia Guo, Maria Jesus Garzaran. The power of belady's algorithm in register allocation for long basic blocks. *Languages and Compilers for Parallel Computing, http://parasol.tamu.edu/lcpc03/informal-proceedings/Papers/35.pdf*, 2003.
11. K. Karplus. Representing boolean functions with if-then-else dags. *Technical Report UCSC-CRL-88-28, University of California at Santa Cruz*, November 1988.
12. John R. Koza. *Genetic Programming*. MIT Press, Cambridge, MA, 1992.
13. R. Sethi and J. D. Ullman. The generation of optimal code for arithmetic expressions. *Journal of the ACM, http://doi.acm.org/10.1145/321607.321620*, 17(4), 1970.
14. R. Whaley and J. Dongarra. Automatically tuned linear algebra software. *Technical Report UT CS-97-366, University of Tenessee*, 1997.

Optimizing Packet Accesses for a Domain Specific Language on Network Processors

Tao Liu[1,2], Xiao-Feng Li[3], Lixia Liu[3], Chengyong Wu[1], and Roy Ju[4]

[1] Institute of Computing Technology, Chinese Academy of Sciences, Beijing, China
{liutao, cwu}@ict.ac.cn
[2] Graduate School of Chinese Academy of Sciences, Beijing, China
[3] Intel China Research Center Ltd., Beijing, China
{xiao.feng.li, lixia.liu}@intel.com
[4] Microprocessor Technology Labs, Intel Corporation, Santa Clara, CA, USA

Abstract. Programming network processors remains a challenging task since their birth until recently when high-level programming environments for them are emerging. By employing domain specific languages for packet processing, the new environments try to hide hardware details from the programmers and enhance both the programmability of the systems and the portability of the applications. A frequent issue for the new environments to be widely adopted is their relatively low achievable performance compared to low-level, hand-tuned programming. In this paper we present two techniques, Packet Access Combining (PAC) and Compiler-Generated Packet Caching (CGPC), to optimize packet accesses, which are shown as the performance bottleneck in such new environments for packet processing applications. PAC merges multiple packet accesses into a single wider access; CGPC implements an automatic packet data caching mechanism without a hardware cache. Both techniques focus on reducing long memory latency and expensive memory traffic, and they also reduce instruction counts significantly. We have implemented the proposed techniques in a high level programming environment for network processor named Shangri-La. Our evaluation with standard NPF benchmarks shows that for the evaluated applications the two techniques can reduce the memory traffic by 90% and improve the packet throughput by 5.8 times, on average.

1 Introduction

Network processors (NPs) have been proposed as a key building block of modern network processing systems. To meet the challenging performance and programmability requirements of network applications, network processors typically incorporate some unconventional, irregular architectural features, e.g. multiple heterogeneous processing cores with hardware multithreading, exposed multi-level memory hierarchy, and banked register files, etc. [9, 11]. Effective utilization of these features is critical to the performance of NP-based systems. However, the state-of-the-art of programming with NPs is still at a low level, often assembly language, which requires extensive knowledge of both the applications and the architectural details of the target system. A low-level programming task is tedious, time-consuming, and error-prone. It is difficult to port an application across different network processors even within the

E. Ayguadé et al. (Eds.): LCPC 2005, LNCS 4339 , pp. 47 – 61, 2007.

same family. A high-level programming environment is hence desirable to facilitate the packet processing application development on NPs. The key to the success of such a programming environment is not only its ease of programming, but also its ability to deliver high performance.

Packet processing systems typically store packets in a packet buffer in DRAM, which usually has a large capacity but a long access latency compared to other memory levels. Since there are a large number of packet accesses in network applications, DRAM bandwidth needs to be high enough to sustain maximal packet processing throughput. Although the DRAM access latency can be partially hidden using multithreading, the bandwidth problem remains critical. Actually, DRAM bandwidth has been considered as the bottleneck of network application performance in some prior studies [1, 8, 12]. Our approach is to optimize the packet accesses automatically in a compiler, which reduces both the packet access count and the aggregate access size, so that the total access time and bandwidth requirement are effectively reduced.

In this paper, we present two techniques used for packet access optimizations. The first one is *Packet Access Combining (PAC)*, which reduces the number of packet accesses by merging several access requests into one; and the second technique is *Compiler-Generated Packet Caching (CGPC)*, which implements an automatic packet data caching mechanism to minimize the number of accesses to the packet buffer in DRAM as well as reduce the instruction count.

We implemented the proposed optimizations in Shangri-la [3], which is a programming environment for network processors, and targets the Intel IXP family [11]. Shangri-La encompasses a domain-specific programming language designed for packet processing named *Baker* [2], a compiler that automatically restructures and optimizes the applications written in Baker, and a runtime system that performs resource management and dynamic adaptation at runtime. The compiler consists of three components: a profiler, a pipeline compiler, and an aggregate compiler. The profiler extracts runtime characteristics by simulating the application with test packet traces. The pipeline compiler is responsible for pipeline construction (partition application into a sequence of staged aggregates, where an aggregate includes the code running on one processing element) and data structure mapping. The aggregate compiler takes aggregate definitions and memory mappings from the pipeline compiler and generates optimized code for each of the target processing cores. It also performs machine dependent and independent optimizations, as well as domain-specific transformations to maximize the throughput of the aggregates. The work presented here is implemented in the pipeline compiler and the aggregate compiler.

Our experiments are performed on Intel IXP2400, which contains eight Microengines (MEs) for data plane processing and one XScale core for control plane processing. IXP2400 has four types of memory levels: local memory, scratchpad, SRAM and DRAM. Experimental results show that our approach can reduce the memory traffic by 90% and improve the throughput by a factor of 5.8X, on average.

The rest of the paper is organized as follows. Section 2 introduces the related features of the Baker language. Section 3 and Section 4 describe Packet Access Combining and Compiler-Generated Packet Caching, respectively. Section 5 presents the experimental results. Section 6 reviews related work. Section 7 concludes the paper.

2 Baker Language and Packet Access Characteristics

Baker is a domain-specific programming language for packet processing on highly concurrent hardware. It presents a data-flow programming model and hides the architecture details of the target processors. Baker provides domain-specific constructs, such as *Packet Processing Functions (PPFs)* and *Communication Channels (CCs)*, to ease the design and implementation of packet processing applications, as well as enable effective and efficient compile-time parallelization and optimizations.

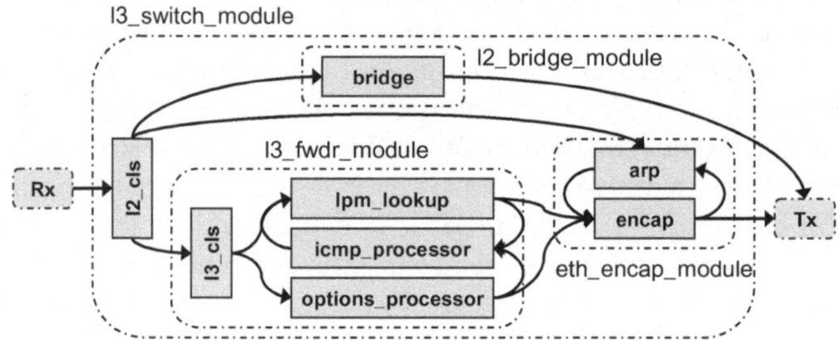

Fig. 1. The packet flow graph of Layer 3 Switch Baker program (L3-Switch): bridges Ethernet packets and switches IPv4 packets

Baker programs are organized as data flow graphs (referred to as *packet flow graphs*) with the nodes representing *Packet Processing Functions* and the arcs representing *Communication Channels*, as shown in **Fig. 1**. A PPF can have its private data, functions and channel endpoints, and performs the actual packet processing. CCs are logically asynchronous and unidirectional queues, and can be created by wiring the input and output endpoints of PPFs. Baker also provides *module* as a way to encapsulate PPFs, shared data and configuration functions. *Rx* and *Tx* are native modules provided by system vendors which can be used as a device driver to receive and transmit packets with external interfaces, respectively.

```
protocol ether {
  dst : 48;
  src : 48;
  type : 16;
  demux{ 14 };
};
```

```
protocol ipv4 {
  ver : 4;
  length : 4;
  ...
  ttl: 8;
  prot: 8;
  checksum: 16;
  ...
  demux{length << 2};
};
```

```
void A.process(ether_packet_t* pkt){
  ipv4_packet_t* p;
  mac_addr_t mac;
  mac = pkt->dst;
  ...
  if(fwd){
    p = packet_decap(pkt);
    channel_put(l3_fwdr_chnl,p);
  }
}
```

Fig. 2. Protocol construct and packet primitives in Baker

The format of the packet header of any protocol can be specified using the *protocol* construct, as illustrated in **Fig. 2**. These definitions introduce new types called *ether_packet_t* and *ipv4_packet_t*, which are processed as built-in types to support operations on Ethernet and IPv4 packet headers, respectively. To access the packet fields of a particular protocol header, programmers must specify a pointer to packet and the field name of corresponding protocol construct. The pointers to packets are referred as *packet handles*. As illustrated in **Fig. 2**, *pkt* is a packet handle to *ether_packet_t*, thus *pkt->dst* represents the *dst* field of Ethernet header. We called the reference to a packet field as a *packet access*.

Baker provides an encapsulation mechanism to layer different packet protocols. The *packet_encap/packet_decap* primitive is to add or remove a protocol header to or from the current packet. As illustrated in **Fig. 2**, *p = packet_decap(pkt)* will remove the Ethernet header from the *pkt* packet so as to convert it to an IPv4 packet.

Besides packet accesses and packet encapsulations, Baker also provides other primitives to ease the manipulations of packets. For example, *channel_get* and *channel_put* are for receiving and transmitting packets through a channel, respectively.

These primitives constitute a packet abstraction model which provides a very convenient way for programmers to write network applications without concerning the underlying implementations. To keep the portability, all packet primitives are implemented as intrinsic functions in the runtime system. The Baker primitives implemented in the runtime system are briefly described below.

The *packet handle* actually points to *metadata* in SRAM, which is data that is associated with a packet but does not come directly from an external source. The metadata is useful to store the packet-associated information generated by one PPF and pass it to another PPF to be processed. For example, the output port is likely part of metadata. The pointers (*head pointer* and *tail pointer*) in the metadata point to the actual packet data in DRAM, as illustrated in **Fig. 3**.

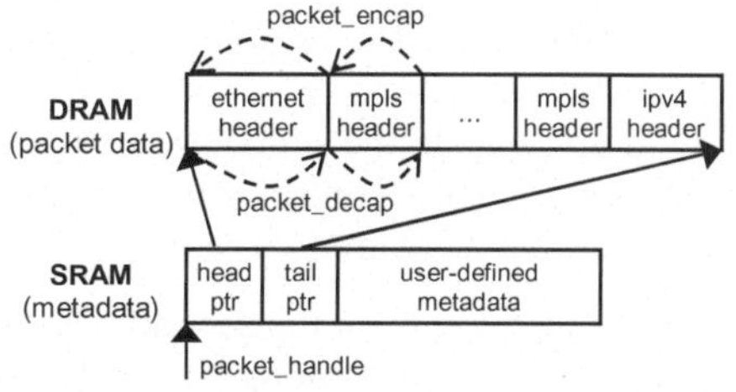

Fig. 3. The layout of packet data and metadata

Packet encapsulations are implemented as intrinsic calls: *packet_encap/packet_decap(packet_handle, size)*. The *size* is the number of bytes to add to or remove from the head. As the example in **Fig. 2**, *p = packet_decap(pkt)* will be converted to *packet_decap(pkt,14)*. The *14* is the length of Ethernet header, which can be determined by the *demux* field in the protocol construct. The implementation of this intrinsic simply increases the *head pointer* in the metadata by 14 bytes.

Packet accesses (packet reads and writes) are implemented as intrinsic calls: *packet_read/packet_write(packet_handle,offset,size,data)*. For example, *data=p->ttl* and *p->ttl=data* can be converted to *packet_read(p,64,8,data)* and *packet_write (p,64,8,data)*, respectively. The size of *8* means that this packet access will retrieve or modify a bit field which is 8-bit wide, and the offset of *64* specifies that the distance to the beginning of the current protocol header is 64 bits. The fourth parameter, *data*, is the input or output data to be read from or written to as specified by programmers. The two intrinsic calls, referred to as *packet access intrinsics* will access DRAM to retrieve or modify packet data. They resolve the DRAM address by the value of *head pointer* plus the offset parameter.

In the Intel IXP2xxx network processors, DRAM can only be accessed in multiples of 8 bytes starting on any 8-byte boundary. Although *packet_read* and *packet_write* intrinsics can specify arbitrary offset and size, the runtime system must take care of address alignment and access granularity. For example, write accesses smaller than 8-byte cause read-modify-write operations to merge data, and the runtime system will generate a mask to select which bytes to be written into DRAM. In a read-modify-write operation it will cause two DRAM accesses.

3 Packet Access Combining

In general, a *packet_read* intrinsic has one DRAM access (for packet data) and one SRAM access (for packet metadata) and dozens of other instructions. A *packet_write* doubles the cost. In a Baker program, each of the packet accesses may operate on only a few bits of the packet header. However, since each DRAM access operates at an 8-byte granularity, a naive code generation that translates a packet access into an intrinsic call can cause a significant waste of DRAM bandwidth and incur unnecessary execution time due to the long DRAM access latency.

The idea of PAC optimization is based on the observation that many packet reads (writes) access contiguous locations. It is possible for the compiler to automatically merge several packet reads (writes) into one, so that only one *packet_read* (*packet_write*) intrinsic is issued to load (store) all of the needed data at once. Thus the DRAM access count can be reduced.

PAC optimization should not change the semantics of the original program, so the application of PAC must comply with control and data dependence requirements. When combining two packet reads, there are two requirements that must be satisfied:

1. *Dominance*: The first read must dominate the second read in flow graph;
2. There are no intervening packet writes along the path from the first read to the second read altering the packet data that the second read will use.

Correspondingly, the requirements of combing two packet writes are:

1. *Control Equivalence*: The first packet write dominates the second and the second post-dominates the first.
2. There are no intervening packet reads (writes) along the path from the first write to the second write using (altering) the packet data of the second write.

The conditions for combining more than two packet reads (writes) can be derived from the requirements above since the compiler can always merge the first two packet reads (writes) into one and then merge this new one with the third read (write). The compiler can follow this process iteratively till all of the reads (writes) that satisfy the conditions are combined.

Fig. 4 gives an example of PAC optimization. **Fig. 4.a** is the flow graph before a PAC optimization. The packet accesses are represented as packet access intrinsic calls. There are two packet reads and two packet writes accessing nearby but different fields of IPv4 header. PAC wants to merge the two reads into a single read, and the two writes into a single write. The flow graph after combining is shown in **Fig. 4.b**. The benefit of PAC is clear: two packet access intrinsic calls were removed. To formalize the solution of the combining problem, we develop a bit-field dataflow analysis on these packet accesses.

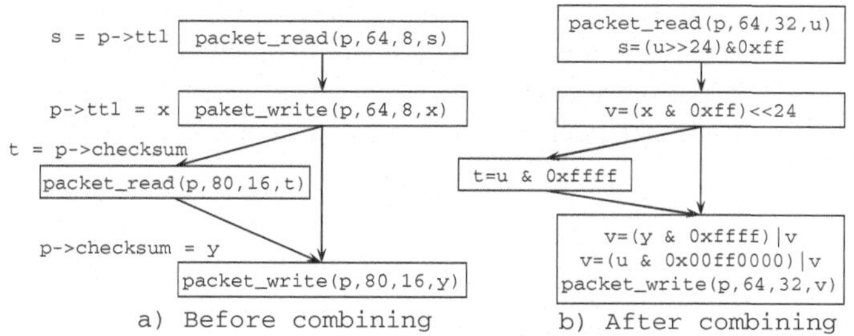

Fig. 4. An example of PAC

3.1 Algorithm

According to the requirements described above, only those packet accesses that satisfy the following conditions can be combined: First, all accesses must be of the same type (read or write), and operate on the same packet. Second, the offsets and sizes of all accesses must be known at compile-time. Third, the size of the combined access must be within the burst size of a single DRAM access. Last, there shouldn't be any violation of control and data dependence due to combining these accesses.

Packet access combining can be performed in the following four steps:

1. Collect the candidate packet access information
We first traverse a program function to collect the necessary information for each packet access, including the packet handle, offset and size. This information will be used in the succeeding steps.

2. Compute the dominance relations
As discussed above, these packet accesses to be combined must satisfy the dominance relationship (control dependence). Because one basic block (BB) can only have one branch or call instruction, these packet access calls must be in different BBs. Hence, the dominance relationship of packet accesses can be represented as dominate tree of BBs.

3. Perform a packet field live analysis
We perform a data-flow analysis on packet fields of packet accesses. In the analysis, a packet read can be considered as a use to a bit-field of packet buffer, and a packet write can be considered as a definition. To uniquely identify each packet access and describe the bits information of them, a triplet *{bb,ph,pf}* was introduced to represent *packet access info* during the iterative dataflow analysis. The *bb* depicts the basic block that the packet access resides in. The *ph* (packet handle) indicates which packet instance it will access. The *pf* (packet field) is a bit vector each bit of which represents a bit in the packet buffer. The corresponding bits that the packet access will read or

modify are set to valid while other bits are set to invalid. If the *packet access info* is propagated across a *packet_encap* or *packet_decap* call, its *pf* must shift corresponding bits because the current *head pointer* has been changed. The dataflow analysis of packet reads is a backward dataflow problem. Its corresponding flow equations are specified as **Fig. 5**. $PF_{rev\_in}(BB_i)$ and $PF_{rev\_out}(BB_i)$ are the sets of reversed input and output packet accesses information of BB_i, respectively. After the bitwise dataflow analysis, PF_{rev_in} of each BB contains all possible packet accesses which can be propagated to the exit of this BB. We said a packet access *s* is *live* at BB_i if $s \in PF_{rev\_in}(BB_i)$ and the valid bits in s.pf has not been changed with respect to its original BB (s.bb). A packet access live at a given program point indicates that it can be combined with another packet access resided at this point without violating any data dependence.

$$PF_{rev\_in}(BB_i) = \bigcup_{BB_j \in Succ(BB_i)} PF_{rev\_out}(BB_j) \qquad Gen(BB_i) = \begin{cases} \{(i, s.ph, s.pf)\} & \text{if } BB_i \text{ has packet access "}s\text{"} \\ \phi & \text{otherwise} \end{cases}$$

$$PF_{rev\_out}(BB_i) = Cap(BB_i, Kill(BB_i, PF_{rev\_in}(BB_i) \cup Gen(BB_i)))$$

$$Kill(BB_i, set) = \begin{cases} \{(x.bb, x.ph, (\sim s.pf) \& x.pf) \mid x.ph = s.ph, \forall x \in set\} \cup \{x \mid x.ph \neq s.ph, \forall x \in set\} \\ \qquad \text{if } BB_i \text{ has packet write "}s\text{"} \\ set \qquad \text{otherwise} \end{cases}$$

$$Cap(BB_i, set) = \begin{cases} \{(x.bb, x.ph, x.pf >> bits) \mid \forall x \in set\} & \text{if } BB_i \text{ has packet\_encap(bits)} \\ \{(x.bb, x.ph, x.pf << bits) \mid \forall x \in set\} & \text{if } BB_i \text{ has packet\_decap(bits)} \\ set & \text{otherwise} \end{cases}$$

Fig. 5. Data-flow equations of packet field live analysis for packet reads

4. Finalize the combining

For each packet access, the candidates can be selected by taking a bitwise OR operation on the current packet access's *pf* field and those of all live packet accesses at this point. If the bit width of combined result does not exceed the width limit of DRAM instructions, the corresponding live packet access is a candidate. We use the *combining density* to describe data reuse characteristics as defined in Eq. (**1**). In this equation *field_len1* and *field_len2* are the valid bit widths of the *pf* fields in the current packet access and candidate packet access, respectively. *combined_len* is the valid bit width after the combination. For example, if the two packet accesses are to the same packet field, the value of combining density equals the width of the packet field. If the packet fields are adjacent, the value is zero, and so on. We will first combine the packet accesses whose combining density is higher.

$$\text{CombiningDensity} = \text{field\_len1} + \text{field\_len2} - \text{combined\_len}\,. \qquad (1)$$

After the combination, the offset and size of current packet access are adjusted to retrieve all needed packet data and the redundant packet access is eliminated. The cached packet data can be kept in registers.

The algorithm of PAC can be easily extended to handle more complex cases. For example, it can combine two packet writes even if they are to non-adjacent fields of a packet. By using a dominator packet read to cache the data of the gap between two packet writes, we can combine the two packet writes with the cached gap into a wide write. Furthermore, it can combine packet writes located in basic blocks that are not control equivalent. It may still be worth combining if we can reduce the number of packet writes on the critical path. To maintain correctness, compensation packet writes must be generated in the corresponding exits to cold paths.

4 Compiler-Generated Packet Caching

By default, for each packet access our compiler will generate a packet access intrinsic call which is implemented in the runtime system. This approach, though allows the flexibility of changing the implementation of the packet buffer without modifying the compiler, will incur significant performance overhead. In fact, we may not need to invoke the intrinsic call to load the packet data for every reference in the program. If we preload all needed packet data into a cache, the subsequent packet accesses can be replaced by cache accesses. Actually, packet data accesses exhibit good spatial locality w.r.t. different fields in the same packet [15]. Based on this observation, we propose a new approach to implement packet accesses, named *Compiler-Generated Packet Caching (CGPC)*. CGPC tries to identify the critical path of the packet flow in a network application based on profiling information and optimize all packet accesses along the path. If there are multiple accesses to the same packet in the critical path, the related packet data will be buffered in the fastest level of memory (e.g., the local memory in IXP2400), and those accesses that can be resolved statically will be replaced by the accesses to the buffered data. For those accesses that can only be resolved at run time, efficient code sequence will be generated to calculate the offset and alignment and perform the access. Actually, CGPC can be considered as an extreme situation of PAC that it tries to combine all the packet accesses in a thread into only one packet read at the thread entrance and one packet write at the thread exit.

4.1 Algorithm

CGPC is performed in two steps. First, an inter-procedure analysis, referred to as *Packet Flow Analysis*, is to identify the critical path in the packet flow graph and calculate associated information of each packet access and *packet_encap/decap*. Second, a compiler generates the instructions for each packet access and *packet_encap/decap* based on the packet flow analysis information.

4.1.1 Packet Flow Analysis

The information needed by the packet flow analysis is collected by a profiler. By utilizing user-supplied packet traces, the profiler simulates the execution of network applications at a high-level Intermediate Representation (IR) in the compiler. After the simulation, the profiling information, such as execution frequency and access statistics, is available. The pseudo code of the algorithm for the packet flow analysis is presented in **Fig. 6**. `Flow_Anaysis` is a recursive function which starts the analysis from the endpoint of the channel coming out of the *Rx* module. The cached packet data should be preloaded at the entry of the packet flow, but the preload width can not be determined until the analysis is finished. During the analysis, the value of the current *head pointer* is tracked and updated whenever encountering a *packet_ encap/decap*.

However, different intrinsic calls and control structures complicate this process. If a *packet_encap/decap* sits inside a loop with an unknown loop count, inside an if-branch, or inside a circle of the packet flow graph, we may not be able to track a constant value of *head pointer* statically.

```
Process_Instrinsic_Call(currCall){
  if(currCall is packet_encap/decap){
    if(is_in_loop){
      set unresolved flag;
      set currCall dynamic;}
    else{
      Increase/Decrease currOfst;
      set currCall eliminable;}
  }
  if(currCall is packet_read/write){
    if(access offset is variable||unresolved)
      set currCall dynamic;
    else{
      set currCall static;
      calculate absolute offset and size;}
    update preload & writeback range;
  }
  if(currCall is channel_put){
    if(send packet to Tx or Xcale){
      set packet_is_over;
      if(cache has been written) writeback cache;
    }
    if(send packet to ME){
      if(cache has been written) writeback cache;
      callee=Get_End_Func(currChannel);
      Flow_Analysis(callee->first_Stmt);
    }
  }
  if(currCall is packet_drop)
    set packet_is_over;
  ...... // other cases
}
```

```
Flow_Analysis(currStmt){
  switch(currStmt){
    case Intrinsic_Call:
     {Process_Intrinsic_Call(Intrinsic_Call);
      break;}
    case Call:
     {callee=Get_Callee(Call);
      if(callee has been analysed) break;
      else{
        Flow_Analysis(callee->first_Stmt);}
      break;}
    case Loop:
     {set is_in_loop flag;
      estimate loop count by profiler;
      Flow_Analysis(Loop body);
      if(not in outer loop) reset is_in_loop flag;
      break;}
    case If:
      {Flow_Analysis(if condition);
       Flow_Analysis(then branch);
       then_ofst=currOfst;
       Flow_Analysis(else branch);
       else_ofst=currOfst;
       if(then_ofst==else_ofst) break;
       if(packet_is_over in then/else branch)
         set currOfst to else_ofst/then_ofst;
       else
         set unresolved flag; break;}
    ...... // other cases
    default:
      {Flow_Analysis(kid nodes of currStmt);}
}}
```

Fig. 6. The algorithm of packet flow analysis

For each packet access, if the *head pointer* is not resolved as a compile-time constant or its offset parameter is a variable, it will be marked as *dynamic*. They need a compiler to generate code to compute the offset and alignment at runtime so as to access the cached data. Other packet accesses will be marked as *static* and will have their offsets and alignments calculated at compile-time. Since the offsets of static packet accesses are known at compile-time, we can use the absolute offset in the cache to access packet data across different protocol layers. As a result, some *packet_encap/decaps* become redundant if they are used only to provide the encapsulation protection for static packet accesses. These *packet_encap/decaps* are marked as *eliminable*, which means they can be removed safely. Other *packet_encap/decaps* are marked as *dynamic* which will be used in generating code for dynamic packet accesses. When packets flow to the *Tx* module or heterogeneous cores (e.g., XScale), the packet flow path is ended and the cached packet data should be written back to DRAM if it has been modified. If we use a processor-local memory (e.g., local memory in ME) as a cache and packets flow across different cores (e.g., MEs), the cached data should be written back to DRAM when it comes out of one processing core and reloaded when it enters another core.

Fig. 7 illustrates the critical packet flow path of L3-Switch. The *head pointer* can always be determined statically along this path. All packet accesses are resolved except one in the *lpm_lookup* PPF, which is used to verify the checksum of IPv4 header. Its offset is a variable and this access is executed ten times for every processed packet. We need to insert code to compute its offset at runtime.

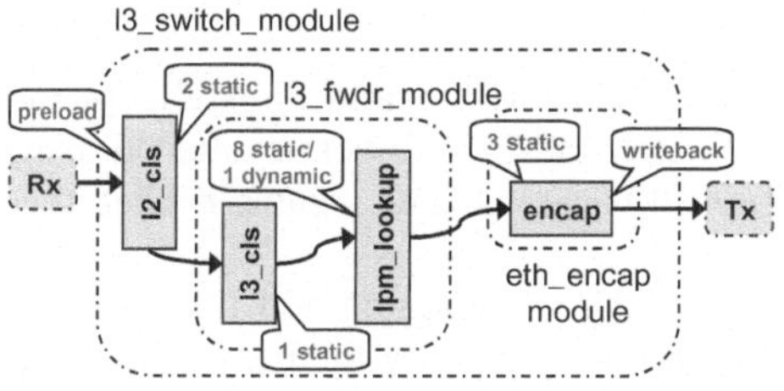

Fig. 7. The critical path of L3-Switch

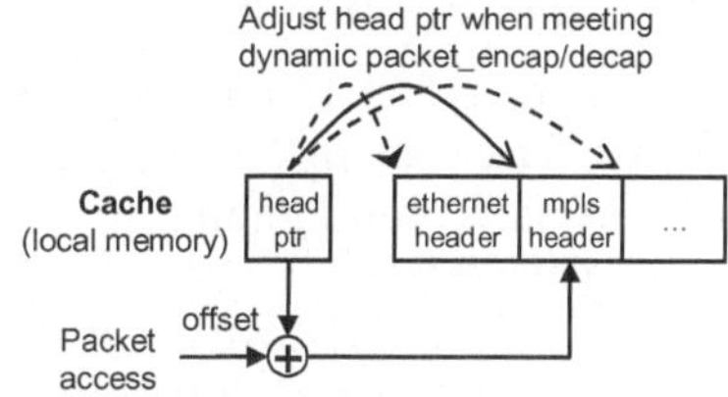

Fig. 8. Dynamic offset and alignment resolution

4.1.2 Compiler-Generated Packet Accesses

After the packet flow analysis, the flags (as shown in **Fig. 6**) and necessary information are annotated on each packet access and *packet_encap/decap*. In the code generator, the actual code is generated according to the flags and the information. If the packet access is static, the cache can be accessed directly with a constant offset and size provided by the packet flow analysis. An unaligned access can be effectively optimized to a wide access followed by some shift instructions. As for a dynamic access, the offset and alignment must be calculated at runtime. Our solution is illustrated in **Fig. 8**. We use a variable to track the value of *head pointer* and initialize it when the compiler preloads the cache. When a packet flows across a dynamic *packet_encap/decap*, additional instructions are executed to update its value at runtime. We can then use the variable of *head pointer* to generate code for the dynamic packet access. The absolute offset of a dynamic packet access in cache can be determined by adding the original offset to the current *head pointer*. A check is performed on the absolute offset. If the offset within the cache, it can directly access the cached data. Otherwise, it will fall through to invoke the original intrinsic call.

After the optimization, a DRAM access is performed only when preloading and writing back the cache. An unaligned DRAM access will cause a much higher cost than the aligned one. For example, an unaligned write would need a write-after-read operation to keep the unwritten section intact, which needs to be implemented in two DRAM accesses. Instead, our compiler implements all preload and write back operations at the aligned boundaries. All intermediate packet accesses' offsets are adjusted according to the alignment. As a result, our implementation properly aligns all DRAM accesses. Although this approach may waste some cache space to hold unused data, it avoids the write-after-read operations on DRAM and reduces the alignment instructions.

5 Evaluations

We have evaluated the proposed optimizations with representative workloads on real network processors. In this section, we will present the hardware evaluation environment, benchmarks, and experimental results.

5.1 Benchmark Applications

We use three typical network applications, L3-Switch, MPLS and Firewall, for our evaluation. They are all written in Baker. L3-Switch and MPLS were evaluated using the NPF standard configurations [16, 17]. Firewall was evaluated using a packet trace internally developed.

Layer 3 Switch (L3-Switch) [16] implements Ethernet bridging and IPv4 routing. For each packet received, it performs table lookups to determine the next hop, decrements the Time-To-Live (TTL), and updates the checksum for the packet header.

Multi-Protocol Label Switch (MPLS) [17] attaches one or more labels in the head of each packet and routes the packet based on the label rather than the destination address. By using the label as an index into a forwarding table, the routing process can be accomplished more quickly.

Firewall sits between a private network and its Internet connection, protecting the internal network against attacks. The firewall takes actions, such as passing or dropping a packet, based on an ordered list of user-defined rules. These rules specify the actions to take when the fields of incoming packets (e.g. source and destination IPs, source and destination ports, protocol etc.) match certain patterns.

5.2 Experimental Environment

Our evaluations were conducted on a RadiSys ENP-2611 evaluation board, which contains an Intel IXP2400 network processor running MontaVista Linux on the XScale core. IXP2400 consists of eight multi-threaded MicroEngines (MEs) for traffic processing, an Intel XScale core for control plane processing, 8MB SRAM, and 64MB DRAM [10]. An IXIA packet generator with two 1Gbps optical ports was used to generate packet traffics and collect statistics. When the ports are used in full duplex mode, the peak input rate is 2Gbps.

The memory hierarchy of IXP2400 consists of four different memory levels: local memory, Scratchpad, SRAM, and DRAM, with increasing capacities and access latencies. **Table 1** lists their access parameters. There is no hardware cache; any access

Table 1. The parameters of different levels of memories in IXP 2400 (Unit B stands for Bytes)

Memory Type	Size	Access time (Cycles)	Start Address Alignment	Min Length	Max Length
Local Memory	2560B	3	4B boundary	4B	4B
Scratchpad	16KB	60	4B boundary	4B	64B
SRAM	256MB	90	4B boundary	4B	64B
DRAM	2GB	120	8B boundary	8B	128B

to the memory units is carried out explicitly with specific instructions for respective memory types.

For all configurations in our evaluation, six MEs with each ME having eight thread contexts all ran the same code from the critical path of an application. The other two MEs were dedicated to receive (Rx) and transmit (Tx) module, respectively. The cold path and control plane code of the application were mapped to XScale.

5.3 Packet Access Count and Aggregate Access Size

We compared the number of packet-related DRAM accesses and the packet forwarding rates for the three applications, with and without the proposed optimizations. The BASE configuration enables only typical scalar optimizations. We evaluated these two optimizations on top of BASE separately. PAC enables the packet access combining. Procedure inlining was performed to expose more opportunities for combining. CGPC represents the compiler-generated packet caching. Since CGPC can be considered as an aggressive version of PAC, we have not evaluated the combined effect.

Table 2. Memory access statistics (per packet) and instruction counts

		DRAM Access Count	Aggregate Access Size (Bytes)	Instruction Count[1]
L3-Switch	BASE	29	696	2033
	PAC	13	200	1190
	CGPC	2	72	770
MPLS	BASE	16	384	1851
	PAC	9	212	1428
	CGPC	2	48	1495
Firewall	BASE	24.2	580	1742
	PAC	4.4	140	572
	CGPC	1	32	375

Table 2 shows the DRAM access count and aggregate access size per packet and the instruction count for each benchmark application. We can see that PAC can reduce the DRAM access dramatically. CGPC has the lowest number of DRAM accesses and reduces the aggregate access size by 90% on average (L3-Switch: 89.7%, MPLS: 87.5%, Firewall: 94.5%). Taking L3-Switch as an example, its packet accesses are marked in **Fig. 7**. There are 9 static packet reads, 5 static unaligned packet writes, and 1 dynamic packet read on the critical path. The dynamic packet read is caused by a checksum checking, which iterates through the packet header in a unit of 2-byte. PAC merges the static packet accesses but cannot catch the dynamic one. CGPC can deal with all of the packet accesses, thus only need DRAM accesses in the preload and

[1] The instruction count is an approximate number of the instructions actually executed in MicroEngines for one packet processing. It includes critical path code and packet accesses. A packet read takes about 50 instructions and a packet write takes about 100 instructions.

write back operations. MPLS presents a challenge to our techniques initially. It pushes, swaps, and pops MPLS labels dynamically, which may include an arbitrary number of MPLS headers and our techniques can not determine the cache layout statically. However, the results demonstrate that CGPC remain effective for this dynamic situation. Overall, PAC and CGPC not only reduce the memory traffic, but also reduce the number of executed instructions.

5.4 Forwarding Rate

The forwarding rates of three applications on the minimum sized 64-byte packets are presented in **Fig. 9**. The numbers of MEs to execute the applications are plotted on the X-axis and the achieved forwarding rates are plotted on the Y-axis. To obtain the full benefits of PAC, we unrolled the checksum checking loop in L3-Switch before applying PAC to convert the dynamic packet read to static. PAC reduces the packet processing time by removing considerable DRAM accesses and instructions. As a result, it gets a higher forwarding rate. CGPC provides a higher performance impact than PAC because it has no excessive DRAM accesses and the solution for resolving the offset and alignment is effective. Compared to BASE, CGPC improves the throughput by 5.8 times on average (L3-Switch: 7.6; MPLS: 3.9; Firewall: 5.9).

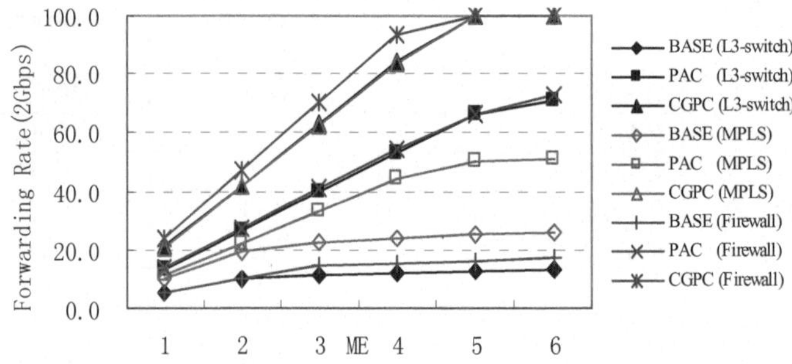

Fig. 9. Performance of L3-Switch, MPLS and Firewall

In the BASE configuration, all three applications get their memory bus saturated when the number of MEs increases. However, PAC provides good scalability by relieving the contention of DRAM bandwidth. Compared to PAC, CGPC generates fewer instructions and DRAM accesses so that it obtains nearly perfect scalability and reaches the full line rate quickly. The result shows the system performance is largely determined by both the instruction count and DRAM bandwidth. We also applied these optimizations on SRAM accesses without as apparent benefits as DRAM accesses. It is because IXP2400 has only one DRAM controller but two independent SRAM controllers.

6 Related Work

Several high-level programming languages, such as microC [11] and picocode [9], have been introduced with their corresponding NPs. But they are all extended to expose hardware details and their performances heavily rely on the use of such features. A number of domain-specific languages, such as Click [13], NesC [7], etc., have been developed to ease programming, and they are more hardware-independent and include special constructs to express the tasks in packet processing applications. But they do not focus on efficient compilation.

Mudigonda et al. [15] analysed the characteristics of packet data and application data accesses. They exhibit the spatial locality of packet data accesses and temporal locality of application data accesses. They use a cache to improve the hit rate of application data structures. Iyer et al. [12] studied a cache-based memory hierarchy of packet buffer. Hasan et al. [8] proposed several techniques to exploit row locality (i.e. successive accesses falling within the same DRAM rows) of DRAM accesses. But their techniques needed hardware support and focused on the input- and output-side of packet processing, which can be implemented in our *Rx* and *Tx* modules. Sherwood et al. [18] designed a pipelined memory subsystem to improving the throughput in accessing application data structures.

Davidson and Jinturkar [6] described a memory coalescing algorithm for general purpose processors similar to packet access combining. This algorithm replaced narrow array access with double-word accesses in unrolled loops. It performed a profitability and safety analysis on programs, and generated alignment and alias checks at runtime if necessary. But Packet Access Combining works on a whole procedure and focuses on packet accesses. It utilizes some domain knowledge and does not need a complex alias analysis. Thus, PAC is always profitable when it can be applied.

There are several techniques which can be used to improve packet accesses. McKee et al. [14] designed a separate stream buffer to improve the performance of stream accesses. Chen et al. [4] described a hardware-based prefetching mechanism to hide memory latency.

7 Conclusion

Performance and flexibility are two major but sometime conflicting requirements to packet-processing systems and the programming environments associated with them. High level programming environments with domain specific languages can satisfy the flexibility requirement. However, how to utilize hardware features effectively to achieve high performance with automatic compiler supports in such programming environments requires more explorations. In this paper, we address one major type of memory accesses in network applications – accesses to packet data structures, which constitute a significant portion of the total memory accesses. We propose two compilation techniques to reduce the latencies of packet accesses and the contention of DRAM bandwidth.

Packet access combining tries to reduce the number of packet accesses by utilizing wide memory references and code motion. It does not incur extra memory space compared with caching. Furthermore, it is hardware-independent and always beneficial when applied. Compiler-generated packet caching can be viewed as compiler-controlled caching. It buffers the packet data to be referenced and replace all of the packet accesses on the critical path with accesses to a buffer in cache. Through a profiling-based program analysis, it minimizes the required cache size and the number of cache misses.

We performed experiments on a real packet processing platform with three representative network applications, L3-Switch, MPLS and Firewall. The experimental results demonstrate that the efficiency of packet accesses is critical to the system performance, and our techniques can reduce the number of packet accesses and the total memory bandwidth requirements significantly.

References

1. W. Bux, W. E. Denzel, T. Engbersen, A. Herkersdorf, and R. P. Luijten. "Technologies and building blocks for fast packet forwarding." *IEEE Communications Magazine*, pp. 70-77, January 2001.
2. M. Chen, E. Johnson, R. Ju. "Compilation system for throughput-driven multi-core processors." In *Proc. of Micro-37*, Portland, Oregon, December 2004.
3. M. Chen, X. Li, R. Lian, J. Lin, L. Liu, T. Liu, and R. Ju. "Shangri-la: Achieving high performance from compiled network applications while enabling ease of programming." In *Proc. of ACM SIGPLAN PLDI*, Chicago, Illinois, USA, June 2005.
4. T. Chen and J. Baer. "Effective Hardware-based Data Prefetching for High-performance Processors." *IEEE Transactions on Computers*, 44(5), May 1995.
5. T. Chiueh and P. Pradhan. "High-performance IP routing table lookup using CPU caching." In *IEEE Infocom'99*, New York, NY, March 1999.
6. J. W. Davidson and S. Jinturkar. "Memory Access Coalescing: A Technique for Eliminating Redundant Memory Accesses." In *Proc. of ACM SIGPLAN PLDI*, pp. 186-195, June 1994.
7. D. Gay, P. Levis, R. von Behren, M. Welsh, E. Brewer, and D. Culler. "The nesC Language: A Holistic Approach to Networked Embedded Systems." In *Proc. of ACM SIGPLAN PLDI*, June 2003.
8. J. Hasan, S. Chandra, and T. Vijaykumar. "Efficient Use of Memory Bandwidth to Improve Network Processor Throughput." In *ISCA*, 2003.
9. IBM PowerNP Network Processors, http://www-3.ibm.com/chips/techlib/techlib.nsf/products/IBM_PowerNP_NP4GS3.
10. Intel Corporation. *Intel IXP2400 Network Processor: Hardware Reference Manual*. 2002.
11. Intel IXP family of Network processors, http://www.intel.com/design/network/products/npfamily/index.htm.
12. S. Iyer, R. R. Kompella, and N. McKeown. "Analysis of a memory architecture for fast packet buffers." In *Proc. IEEE Workshop High Performance Switching and Routing (HPSR)*, 2001.
13. E. Kohler, R. Morris, B. Chen, J. Jannotti, and M. F. Kaashoek. "The Click Modular Router." *Transactions on Computer Systems*, 2000.
14. S. McKee, R. Klenke, K. Wright, W. Wulf, M. Salinas, J. Aylor, and A. Batson. "Smarter Memory: Improving Bandwidth for Streamed References." *IEEE Computer*, July 1998.
15. J. Mudigonda, H. Vin, and R. Yavatkar. "A Case for Data Caching in Network Processors." Under Review. http://www.cs.utexas.edu/users/vin/pub/pdf/mudigonda04case.pdf
16. Network Processing Forum. "IP Forwarding Application Level Benchmark." http://www.npforum.org/techinfo/ipforwarding_bm.pdf.
17. Network Processing Forum. "MPLS Forwarding Application Level Benchmark and Annex." http://www.npforum.org/techinfo/MPLSBenchmark.pdf.
18. T. Sherwood, G. Varghese, and B. Calder. "A Pipelined Memory Architecture for High Throughput Network Processors." In *30th International Symposium on Computer Architecture*, June 2003.

Array Replication to Increase Parallelism in Applications Mapped to Configurable Architectures

Heidi E. Ziegler, Priyadarshini L. Malusare, and Pedro C. Diniz

University of Southern California / Information Sciences Institute
4676 Admiralty Way, Suite 1001
Marina del Rey, California, 90292
{ziegler,priya,pedro}@isi.edu

Abstract. Configurable architectures, with multiple independent on-chip RAM modules, offer the unique opportunity to exploit inherent parallel memory accesses in a sequential program by not only tailoring the number and configuration of the modules in the resulting hardware design but also the accesses to them. In this paper we explore the possibility of array replication for loop computations that is beyond the reach of traditional privatization and parallelization analyses. We present a compiler analysis that identifies portions of array variables that can be temporarily replicated within the execution of a given loop iteration, enabling the concurrent execution of statements or even non-perfectly nested loops. For configurable architectures where array replication is essentially free in terms of execution time, this replication enables not only parallel execution but also reduces or even eliminates memory contention. We present preliminary experiments applying the proposed technique to hardware designs for commercially available FPGA devices.

1 Introduction

Emerging computing architectures now have multiple computing cores and multiple memory modules such as discrete and programmable register files as well as RAM blocks. For example, field-programmable gate arrays (FPGAs) allow designers to define an arbitrary set of registers and customize the topology of internal RAM blocks [12] to suit the data and computational needs of the computation. Other programmable architectures simply allow for the arrangement of registers and fine-grain functional units to create tailored pipelined architectures [5]. Overall these flexible architectures provide ample opportunities to exploit data parallelism as well as coarse and fine-grain parallelism.

Unfortunately, mapping sequential applications to these architectures is a difficult task. Programmers must explicitly manage the mapping and organization of arrays among the rich set of storage resources, configurable register sets and on and off-chip memories, if they are to fully exploit the architectural benefits of configurable devices. The wide range of design choices faced by the programmer makes it desirable to develop automated analysis and mapping tools that

E. Ayguadé et al. (Eds.): LCPC 2005, LNCS 4339, pp. 62–75, 2007.

can navigate certain characteristics of the design space, in particular, the data dependences found in common sequential imperative programs.

In this paper we focus on *array privatization* and *array replication* techniques to enable compilers to uncover parallelism opportunities in sequential computations that are traditionally impeded by both *anti* and *output-dependences.* We focus on array privatization not across loop iterations but within the same loop iteration. It focuses on the analysis of non-perfectly nested loops by determining *anti-dependences* between a sequence of nested loops in a *control loop.*

When two computations, that execute serially, access the same array location, reading its previous value and then writing a new value into the location, this gives rise to an *anti-dependence* between them. Similarly when two computation use the same location to store consecutive values that are otherwise independent creates an *output-dependence.* These dependences can be eliminated by creating a copy of the array, that each computation freely accesses. Each computation uses a distinct memory location to write and read a value, and in the absence of *true-dependences* between these loops nest, they can execute concurrently within the same iteration of the *control loop.*

This concurrent execution, however, raises the issue of memory contention when two or more concurrently executing loop nests access the same array region, *i.e.,* the loops exhibit *input-dependences.* To overcome this memory contention, we take advantage of the flexibility of memory mapping in configurable architectures by creating copies of shared array variables. By accessing the array copies, the parallel loop nests can therefore execute concurrently due to the absence of *anti-dependences* but also be contention-free. When the original computation exhibits *loop-carried true-dependences* (*i.e.,* values written in a given iteration that are read in a later iteration of a loop), the transformed code must update the array copies (not necessarily all of them) when the concurrent execution terminates to ensure that subsequent computations proceed with the correct values.

This transformation explores a space-time tradeoff. In order to eliminate *anti-, output-* and *input-dependences*, the implementation requires additional memory space. In addition, some execution time overhead is incurred in updating the copies to enforce the original program data dependences. The analysis abstractions, in cooperation with estimates of memory space usage, allow for an effective algorithm to manage this tradeoff and adjust, possibly dynamically, the performance of the implementation in response to available resources.

In this paper we evaluate the replication and privatization transformations when mapping a set of computations to a configurable computing device, a Xilinx Virtex™ FPGA. We simulate the transformed code as a concurrently executing hardware design, thereby revealing the effects on performance and the corresponding cost of storage.

This paper makes the following specific contributions:

– Describes the application of *array replication* and *array privatization* transformations to take advantage of the flexibility of configurable architectures.

– Extends existing array data-flow analysis to identify opportunities for concurrent execution of entire loops when arrays are replicated and temporarily privatized.
– Presents experimental results of our array replication algorithm when applied to a sample set of image processing computations for specific mappings to an FPGA device.

Preliminary results reveal that a modest increase of storage for private and replicated data leads to hardware designs that exhibit respectable execution time speedups, making this approach feasible when storage space is not a limiting factor in the design.

With the increase in VLSI device capacity and the emergence of computing architectures that have multiple computing units on the same die and a very rich set of configurable storage structures, the placement and layout of data will become increasingly important if applications are to fully exploit the true potential of internal data bandwidth and computational units.

This paper is structured as follows. Section 2 illustrates a motivating example for array replication. Section 3 describes the compiler analyses and a data replication algorithm. In section 4 we present preliminary experimental results of the application of the proposed analyses to a set of multimedia computations targeting an FPGA configurable device. We discuss related work in section 5 and then conclude in section 6.

2 Example

We now present an example showing how array replication (or copying) eliminates *anti-* and *output-dependences* thereby enabling concurrent execution of loops. This example also illustrates the elimination of *input-dependences* (*i.e.,* when two loops access arrays that are stored in the same memory module) that reduces memory contention introduced by concurrency. The computation is illustrated in figure 1 and consists of an outer `i` loop with three loop nests, `L1`, `L2` and `L3` nested within. Each of these three loop nests access a two-dimensional array variable `A` using affine subexpressions. The first two loop nests `L1` and `L2` read two consecutive rows of the array whereas the third loop nest `L3` writes the array row read by the first loop nest in the same iteration of `i` and in iteration `i+1` by the second loop nest.

Within loop `i`, one cannot execute loops `L1` and `L2` concurrently with loop `L3`, since there is an *anti-dependence* between `L3` and the other loops. Iterations of the `i` loop also cannot be executed concurrently given the *loop-carried true-dependence* between `L3` and `L2`. As such, privatization of `A` is therefore not possible either [11].

A way to enable concurrent execution of all loop nests during the execution of each iteration of the `i` loop is to create a copy of array `A` named `A_3`, which `L3` can update locally while loops `L1` and `L2` read from the original array `A`. We call this transformation where the array is being replicated with respect to the loop nest that writes it, a *partial replication.* At the end of concurrent

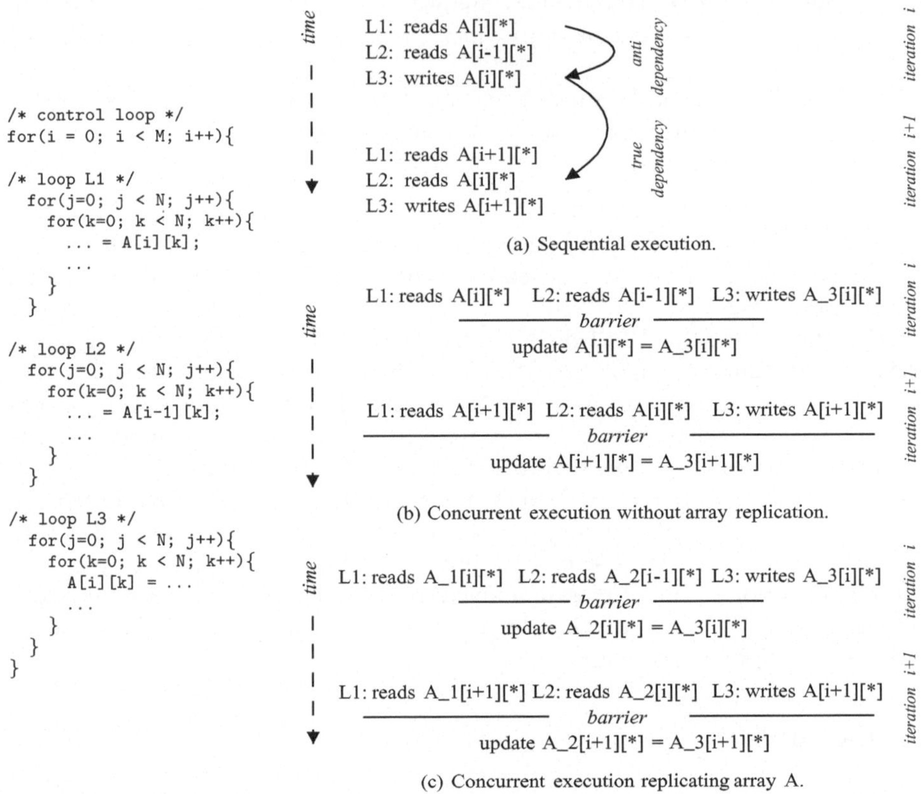

Fig. 1. Example computation and illustrative sequential and concurrent execution

execution of loops L1 through L3 within one iteration of the i loop, we insert a synchronization *barrier* and then update the original array A with the new values generated by loop L3. This concurrent execution is illustrated in figure 1(b) and the corresponding parallel code is depicted in figure 2(a).

Due to the concurrent execution of the three loop nests, there is now memory contention on array A by the loops L1 and L2. In an architecture with memory modules with a limited number of memory ports and in the absence of careful scheduling of read operations the execution of each loop will possibly stall for data. To alleviate the memory contention, we further replicate array A and assign these new arrays A_1 and A_2 to two memories that can be accessed in parallel by loops L1 and L2. In this extended replication transformation, called *full replication*, we create copies that are local to the loops that both read and write the arrays.[1] We trade decreased execution time for increased array storage.

[1] There are additional degrees of replication with respect to the loops that read a given array. Furthermore, this need to replicate to reduce memory access contention interacts with other transformations such as custom data-layout enabled by loop unrolling as described in [9].

```
for(i = 0; i < M; i++){ /* control loop */

  begin par
  {
    for (j=0; j < N; j++){ /* loop L1 */
      for (k=0; k < N; k++){
        ... = A[i][k];
        ...;
      }
    }
  }

  {
    for (j=0; j < N; j++){ /* loop L2 */
      for (k=0; k < N; k++){
        ... = A[i-1][k];
        ...;
      }
    }
  }

  {
    for (j=0; j < N; j++){ /* loop L3 */
      for (k=0; k < N; k++){
        A_3[j][k] = ...;
        ...;
      }
    }
  }
  end par
  /* update original A */
  for (k=0; k < N; k++){
    A[i][k] = A_3[i][k];
  }
}
```

(a) Transformed code with partial replication

```
for(i = 0; i < M; i++){ /* control loop */

  begin par
  {
    for (j=0; j < N; j++){ /* loop L1 */
      for (k=0; k < N; k++){
        ... = A_1[i][k];
        ...;
      }
    }
  }

  {
    for (j=0; j < N; j++){ /* loop L2 */
      for (k=0; k < N; k++){
        ... = A_2[i-1][k];
        ...;
      }
    }
  }

  {
    for (j=0; j < N; j++){ /* loop L3 */
      for (k=0; k < N; k++){
        A_3[j][k] = ...;
        ...;
      }
    }
  }
  end par
  /* update A_2 */
  for (k=0; k < N; k++){
    A_2[i][k] = A_3[i][k];
  }
}
```

(b) Transformed code with full replication

Fig. 2. Transformed example computation

In addition, the implementation must update the arrays to ensure data consistency. While updating complete arrays is a safe and conservative approach, in actuality, only array elements that correspond to *loop-carried true-dependences* need to be updated. In our example and given that the array section written by L3 is read only by L2 in the next iteration of the i loop, the implementation only needs to update the array A_2 associated with L2 and not A_1 associated with L1. In other words the definition of the array row written by L3 reaches L2 but not L1. Figure 2(b) depicts the transformed code after the replication of these arrays and the corresponding concurrent execution is illustrated in figure 1(c).

While the inclusion of a copy operation is likely to decrease performance benefits of such transformations in a classical architecture, in the context of configurable architectures, it has little if any impact on overall execution time. When the implementation of the computation in L3 has to issue a write operation to a specific memory module with a configurable number of read and write ports, one can specify a multi-port write operation to occur synchronously to many memory modules without any performance penalty.

This example illustrates the kind of computation the array privatization and replication analysis described in this paper is designed to handle. First, we focus on non-perfectly nested loops with intra-iteration *anti-dependences* and *true-dependences* to recognize computations that can execute concurrently by the introduction of one copy to the loop nest that modifies sections of an array. These values must then be copied back into the original array or other copies at the end of the execution of the parallel code region. Second, we introduce array copies to eliminate memory contention during the concurrent execution of multiple loop nests, thereby eliminating memory contention by exploiting the memory bandwidth available in architectures with configurable storage units.

3 Compiler Analysis

We now describe the compiler analysis and basic abstractions used to determine the opportunities for array replication with the goal of executing loop nests concurrently while reducing memory contention caused by accessing shared arrays. In this section we focus on imperfectly nested loops that manipulate array references. Whereas our analysis can be very precise for arrays that have affine array access functions, it can also handle, with loss of precision, references that are very irregular, *i.e.*, array-based indirect accesses.

3.1 Basic Abstractions and Auxiliary Functions

This analysis focuses on imperfectly nested loops where the outermost loops i_1 through i_k in the nest are perfectly nested. The i_k loop in the nest has a loop body that consists of a sequence of loop nests, each of which is a perfectly nested loop as well. We name the i_k as the *control loop* and build a control-flow-graph CFG corresponding to its body where each node corresponds to a loop nest. For the example in section 2, the CFG is a linear sequence of loop nests `L1` through `L3`, with loop `i` as the *control loop*. The corresponding CFG and dependences between the nodes are illustrated in figure 3.

For each loop nest, corresponding to a node n_k in the CFG, we define the *upwards-exposed read* and *write* regions for a given array `A` denoted by $\mathtt{ER(A, n_k)}$ and $\mathtt{WR(A, n_k)}$ respectively. The accessed array region is described by a set of linear inequalities. Given that each loop nest may be enclosed by a *control loop*, the corresponding dimension in the linear inequality will consist of symbolic information. A simple, yet effective implementation restriction is to limit the analysis to loops with single-induction variable affine subexpressions making the presence of index variables of the control loop simple. Figure 3 depicts the CFG of the control loop for the example in section 2, along with the relevant exposed-read and write region abstractions for the array `A`.

Using these abstractions, the compiler can compute data dependences between nodes of the CFG uncovering *anti-*, *input-*, *output-* and *true-dependences* by determining if the intersection between $\mathtt{ER(A, n_i)}$ and $\mathtt{WR(A, n_j)}$ between nodes n_i and n_j corresponding to the same array are non-empty. For instance, an *anti-dependence* exists between loops n_i and n_j due to array variables `A` iff

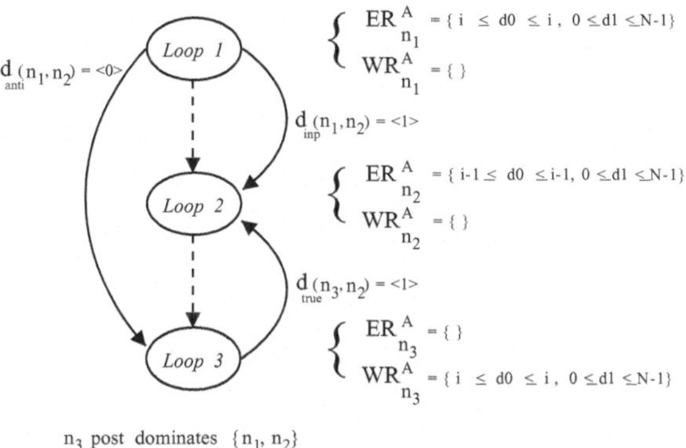

Fig. 3. Control flow graph and dependence information for the example code

$\{\mathtt{WR(A,n_i)} \cap \mathtt{ER(A,n_j)}\ with\ i > j\} \neq \emptyset$. In some cases the intersection will yield symbolic variables corresponding to the loops of the nest and the dependence test must conservatively assume dependence. In addition, we also define a dependence distance for each dependence type. For the example in section 2, there is a *loop-carried true-dependence* on the control loop `i` with a distance of 1 between the nodes corresponding to the loops `L2` and `L3` since `L3` writes the ith row of the array `A` which is read by `L2` on the subsequent iteration of `i`.

3.2 Algorithm for Detecting Replication

Using the abstractions for data accesses, `ER` and `WR`, as well as the δ data dependence distance information, we now describe a compiler algorithm that determines opportunities for parallel execution of the loop nests that make up the body of the control loop. The algorithm also determines which arrays can be replicated to mitigate memory contention resulting from concurrent execution.

The algorithm, shown in figure 4, is structured into 5 main steps. In the first step the algorithm extracts the control loop `i` and the CFG corresponding to the enclosed loops. In the second step, for each node n_k, the algorithm computes `ER` and `WR` for each array variable `A`. In step three, the algorithm computes the dependence distances between every pair of nodes. In step four, the algorithm determines the opportunities for concurrent execution of the nodes within the same iteration of the `i` loop. The basic idea of this step is to identify a straight-line sequence of nodes such that the last node of the sequence exhibits an *anti-dependence* with the other nodes but there are no *true-* or *output-dependences* for that same iteration.[2] The set of nodes that meet this data dependence and control dependence criteria are gathered in a *parallel region* corresponding to the new node named `parallel(`n_k`)`. The compiler creates an array copy corresponding to this parallel node in order to eliminate *anti-dependences* and inserts

[2] Extending this simple algorithm to regions of the CFG with control-flow leads to several code generation complications.

```
Step 1. Extract control loops and coarse-grain control flow graph
        extract control loops i_0,...,i_k and CFG;

Step 2. Determine exposed read and write information for each loop
        for all nodes n_i ∈ CFG
          for all arrays A n_i manipulates
            compute ER(A, n_i) and WR(A, n_i);

Step 3. Compute dependence types and distances
        for all pairs of nodes (n_i,n_j) ∈ CFG
          compute δ_type(n_i, n_j) <,=,> ⟨x⟩ where x is distance

Step 4. Identify parallel regions
        for all nodes n_k ∈ CFG s.t. WR(A, n_k) ≠ ∅ do
          if(numPreds(n_k) > 1) then
            parallel(n_k) = ∅;
            continue;
          R = {n_k};
          n = preds(n_k);
          while (n ≠ entry OR numSuccs(n) = 1) do
            if ((n_i ∉ R) AND (ER(A, n_i) ≠ ∅) AND (δ_true(n_i, n_k) = ⟨0⟩)) then
              R = R + {n_i}
            end if;
          end while;
          parallel(n_k) = R;
          insert fork before firstNode(parallel(n_k));
          insert join barrier after lastNode(parallel(n_k));
          end for;
        end for;

Step 5. Reduce contention by replicating arrays
        for all parallel regions of CFG do
          // Partial Replication case
          insert update array variable A for WR(A, n_k);
          if (FullReplication) then
            selectNumberCopies(parallel(n_k));
            for all n_j ∈ parallel(n_k) do
              update copy of A that has δ_true(n_j, n_k) > ⟨0⟩;
              for all arrays B replicate array for which δ_input(n_i, n_j) = ⟨0⟩;
            end for all;
          end if;
        end for;
```

Fig. 4. Parallelism detection and replication algorithm

synchronization code at the beginning and end of the parallel region so that values in the original array are updated with the value generated by n_k.

In step five, the algorithm identifies which array should be replicated for each parallel region. In this step the algorithm must decide how many copies to insert for each array variable and which copies need to be updated due to *true-dependences* across iterations of the control loop. In its simplest form, *partial replication*, there is a single copy for each parallel region that corresponds to a single node writing to an array variable. In the *full replication* variation, the algorithm generates one copy per each node that reads the array variable as well. Rather then updating all array copies, the algorithm only updates copies using the reaching definitions across loop iterations which is captured by loop-carried dependence information [13]. To this effect the algorithm determines which nodes, and for each array variable, exhibit a *loop-carried true dependence*, at the control-loop level. The particular value of the dependence distance of the control loop indicates the number of iterations across which the values need to be updated in the original array location or copies. For the shortest distance of 1, the values must be updated at the end of the current iteration to be used in the subsequent iteration. However, if the distance is longer, one can delay the update and overlap it with the execution of another iteration thereby hiding its cost.

In this description we have statically determined which nodes of the CFG and therefore which loop nests operate on copies of the array using an external function, `selectCopies(parallel(n_k))`. We foresee a more sophisticated algorithm, possibly dynamic, in which the need to replicate is selected at run-time depending on execution conditions.

3.3 Granularity of Replication

The algorithm described above can be augmented to allow the compiler to uncover opportunities for fine-grain replication by observing the order (in terms of array dimensions) in which multiple loop nests access the same array variables. In the example in figure 1 during parallel execution all loop nests access shared arrays in the same order, therefore array replication can occur at the finest granularity of an element.[3] Then concurrently executing loop nests only require 1 element of replicated data in the array copy. As soon as a loop nest has finished processing a given element, another element of the array can be copied. In addition the updates for copies can also proceed at a finer granularity as long as the iterations of the various concurrent loops execute synchronously. A similar analysis approach has been developed in the context of choosing the granularity of multiple communicating computations executing in a pipelined fashion [13].

In addition to requiring less storage space, at an increase in synchronization cost, this strategy also allows for the updates of copies to be executed concurrently with the parallel execution of the loop nests with the proper synchronization. This strategy reduces the execution time overhead of copy updating and substantially reduces the storage overhead.

The presence of irregular data access patterns, *i.e.,* non-affine does not pose a fundamental problem for the analysis outlined here. Rather then being able to determine exactly the array sections that need to be replicated in the case of a finer-grain synchronization, the analysis settles for replication at the next computational level at which the irregular data access pattern has been absorbed in a specific array dimension.

4 Experimental Results

We now describe the experimental methodology and results for the manual application of the analysis and program transformations to a set of kernels.

[3] The finest granularity may not be the best choice as additional execution time overhead might not be amortized over the small data size.

4.1 Methodology

We applied the analysis algorithm described in section 3 and evaluated the benefits and drawbacks using 3 synthetic kernels `hist`, `bic` and `lcd`.

The `hist` kernel is composed of 3 nested loops inside a single control loop with a total of 15 lines of C code. Each of the inner loop nests in `hist` manipulates 3 distinct array variables exhibiting anti-dependences among the last loop nest and the first two nests. There is a true dependence between the first and second loop nests preventing them from being executed concurrently even when anti-dependences are removed by replication. Nevertheless, the second and third loop nests can be executed concurrently.

The `bic` kernel is composed of 4 loop nests inside a single control loop with a total of 50 lines of C code. Each of the inner loop nests manipulates 4 array variables. This kernel exhibits intra-iteration anti-dependences among the four loop nests and an output dependence between the last two nests. Replicating a single array variable, however, will enable the concurrent execution of the first three loop nests.

The `lcd` kernel is composed of 3 loop nests inside a single control loop with a total of 20 lines of C code. Each of the inner loop nests manipulates 2 array variables. This kernel exhibits only intra-iteration anti-dependences among the last loop nest and the first two loop nests allowing the three loop nests to be executed concurrently via replication of a single array variable.

After we apply the analysis outline in section 3, we manually translate each of these kernels into behavioral VHDL and simulate the execution of the control loop using the Monet™ [7] behavioral synthesis tool. From this simulation, we obtain the execution time of each loop nest, in clock cycles at a given frequency, assuming each loop nest executes sequentially. Using the number of clock cycles obtained via the Monet simulation, we then use a simple discrete event simulator to determine the parallel execution time when one or more of the arrays have been replicated, thereby allowing for concurrent execution as well as reduced memory contention. This simulator allows us to determine the waiting time of each loop nest in the control loop as well as the overall percentage of time the execution spends stalled for memory operations. In our experiments we did not consider software pipelining execution techniques as they further increase the memory contention thereby skewing the replication results to be even more favorable to the application of the technique presented here. In these results we assume that every RAM is dual ported, with a one read and one write port that can be accessed in parallel and assigned the latency of every read and write operation to be 3 clock cycles.

4.2 Results

We now describe the results in terms of execution time reduction due to parallelism and the impact on memory space usage for each kernel. The *original* version is simply the kernel executing in a sequential fashion without any replication or parallel execution. The *partial replication* version corresponds to the introduction of array copies for eliminating anti-dependences. In this version parallel loops may still access shared data. Finally, the *full replication* version includes copies of the array variables to decrease memory contention.

Table 1 summarizes the results in terms of execution time for each kernel and each analysis variation. For the *partial* and *full replication* versions, we have included the cost of performing the update operations after the parallel regions execute. The table indicates the amount of time each transformed kernel spends doing computation (comp. columns), updating the copies if any (update columns), stalling for memory (stall columns) and the overall percentage reduction (red. columns) of the total execution time taking into account the copy operations which execute sequentially after the parallel region executes.

Table 1. Execution time results (cycles in thousands)

Kernel	*Original Code*					*Partial Replication*					*Full Replication*				
	comp.	update	total	stall	red. %	comp.	update	total	stall	red. %	comp.	update	total	stall	red. %
`hist`	1.86	0	1.86	0	–	1.29	0.07	1.36	0	26.9	1.29	0.07	1.36	0	26.9
`bic`	131.1	0	131.1	0	–	77.8	4.11	81.9	36.9	37.5	65.55	4.11	69.66	0	46.8
`lcd`	61.44	0	61.44	0	–	49.15	4.10	53.25	24.58	13.3	24.57	4.10	28.68	0	53.3

As can be seen, there is a sharp decrease in the execution time in the *partial replication* code versions due to parallel execution ranging from 13% to 37%. This reduction simply reflects the concurrent execution of loop nests as revealed by comparing the values in the comp. columns for the *original* and *partial replication* versions. The results for the *partial replication* versions also reveal the opportunity to reduce execution time since the *stall time* values are substantial in the case of `bic` and `lcd`. For `hist` there is no stall time in the *partial replication* version given that only two loop nests execute concurrently and one of them updates a local copy. By aggressively replicating data in the *full replication* versions, the execution time is subsequently reduced leading to overall speedups between 1.37 and 2.1 over the original code version.

Table 2 depicts the space requirements for each code version. For each kernel and respective code version, we describe the number and size (in terms of number of array elements) the code uses along with the total space in bytes and percentage increase over the *original* code version.

Reflecting the opportunity for replication, the space requirements increase monotonically between the *partial* and *full replication* code versions. In the case of the `lcd` and `hist` kernels there is a substantial increase in memory usage close to 100%. While this increase may seem extreme, we note that these figures are biased by the fact that we do not take into account other kernel data structures. This effect is apparent in the `bic` kernel where due to the fact that this kernel manipulates a larger number of arrays that are not replicated, the percentage increase of space requirements is much smaller.

Table 2. Space requirements results

Kernel	*Original Code*			*Partial Replication*			*Full Replication*		
	Array Info	Total Size (KBytes)	Incr. (%)	Array Info	Total Size (KBytes)	Incr. (%)	Array Info	Total Size (KBytes)	Incr. (%)
`hist`	1 × (64 *by* 64) 3 × (64)	17.15	—	2 × (64 *by* 64) 3 × (64)	33.56	95.5	2 × (64 *by* 64) 3 × (64)	33.56	95.5
`bic`	6 × (64 *by* 64)	98, 30	—	7 × (64 *by* 64)	114.7	16.7	10 × (64 *by* 64)	163.8	66.7
`lcd`	2 × (64 *by* 64)	32.77	—	3 × (64 *by* 64)	49.15	50.0	4 × (64 *by* 64)	65.54	100.0

4.3 Discussion

These preliminary results indicate that the execution overhead of updating array copies can be negligible, allowing full exploitation of the concurrent execution performance benefits. The results also reveal that memory contention, even with a small number of concurrent tasks can be substantial. In this scenario, the fully replicated variation allows for the elimination of memory contention, and further improve execution performance. Overall fully replicated code versions achieve speedups between 1.4 and 2.1 with a maximum increase in memory usage by a factor of 2.

Although there are other execution techniques, such as pipelining, these results reveal that using replication techniques a compiler can eliminate anti-dependences enabling substantial increases in execution speed at modest increases in memory space requirements. This experience reveals that replication can be a valuable technique for parallel performance when memory space is not at a premium.

5 Related Work

In this section we discuss related work in the areas of array data-flow analysis, privatization, storage reuse and replication.

Array Privatization/Renaming and Data-flow Analysis. Array privatization determines that a variable assigned within the loop is used only in the same iteration in which it is assigned [4,6]. Renaming is designed to allow for concurrent operations that have output and anti-dependences but where there is no flow of values between statements of a loop nest. It has been used mainly for scalar variables as for arrays the additional memory costs make it very unprofitable for traditional high-end architectures. Array data-flow analysis [3,10] focuses on data dependence analysis that is used to determine the privatization requirements as well as the conditions for parallelization.
Replication for Shared Memory Multiprocessor Systems. Many compilers targeting shared memory systems replicate data to enable concurrent read accesses [1] and further [8] investigates adaptive replication in order to reduce synchronization overheads that may ultimately degrade performance.

Memory Parallelism. There have been many approaches to improve memory parallelism. In particular, for FPGAs, [9] introduces a novel data and code transformation called *custom data layout*. After applying scalar replacement to reduce the number of memory accesses, this transformation is applied to partition the remaining array accesses across available memories.

The approach described in this paper differs from these efforts in many respects. First, and unlike traditional privatization analyses, we relax the conditions for privatization allowing anti-dependences both within the same iteration as well as across iterations of the control loop. Array renaming is the technique used in our first transformation to expose concurrency across multiple loop nests[2]. We augment this transformation with replication (or copying) to increase the memory bandwidth and hence eliminate contention. Despite the similarities our combined renaming and replication transformations allow for values to flow across iterations of the control loop whereas simple renaming has been used within the same loop nest. Second, data layout techniques typically work in combination with loop-based transformations such as loop unrolling to expose more parallel accesses when the unrolled body reveals references with data access patterns that are disjoint in space. The transformations described here are clearly orthogonal to these two approaches. Lastly, the approach described here is geared towards non-perfectly nested loops where an outermost control loop or loops need to be executed sequentially due to true loop-carried dependences but each loop nested within can execute concurrently.

The approach described here takes advantage of the fact that configurable architectures can mitigate several sources of replication overhead typically not possible in traditional computing architectures. First, the number and connectivity of memory units can be tailored to the exact number of array copies. Second, the spatial nature of the execution in configurable architecture allows the execution of the copy/update operations without substantially instruction overhead. Furthermore it is possible to perform a single write operation to multiple memories simultaneously thereby updating more than one array copy.

6 Conclusion

Configurable architectures offer the potential for customized storage structures. This flexibility enables the application of low overhead data replication and privatization techniques to mitigate or even eliminate memory contention issues in concurrent loop execution where shared data are accessed. In this paper we have presented a simple array data-flow analysis algorithm to uncover the opportunities for array replication and temporary privatization in computations expressed as non-perfectly nested loops. The experimental results, for a set of kernels targeted to commercially available FPGA devices, reveal that a modest increase in storage for private and replicated data leads to hardware designs that exhibit small speedups. These results make this approach feasible when chip capacity for data storage is available.

References

1. F. Allen, M. Burke, R. Cytron, J. Ferrante, W. Hsieh, and V. Sarkar. A Framework for Determining Useful Parallelism. In *Proc. Intl. Conf. Supercomputing*, ACM, pages 207–215, 1988.
2. R. Allen and K. Kennedy. Automatic Translation of Fortran Programs to Vector Form. 9(4):491–542, 1987.
3. V. Balasundaram and K. Kennedy. A technique for summarizing data access and its use in parallelism enhancing transformations. In *Proc. ACM Conf. Programming Languages Design and Implementation*, pages 41–53, 1989.
4. R. Eigenmann, J. Hoeflinger, Z. Li, and D. Padua. Experience in the AutomaticParallelization of four Perfect Benchmark Programs. In *Proc. 4th Workshop Languages and Compilers for Parallel Computing*, LNCS. Springer-Verlag, 1991.
5. S. Goldstein, H. Schmit, M. Moe, M. Budiu, S. Cadambi, R. Taylor, and R. Laufer. PipeRench: a coprocessor for streaming multimedia acceleration. In *Proc. 26th Intl. Symp. Comp. Arch.*, pages 28–39, 1999.
6. Z. Li. Array privatization for parallel execution of loops. In *Proc. ACM Intl. Conf. Supercomputing*, 1992.
7. Mentor Graphics Inc. *Monet*^{TM}, 1999.
8. M. Rinard and P. Diniz. Eliminating Synchronization Bottlenecks in object-based Programs using Adaptive Replication. In *Proc. Intl. Conf. Supercomputing*, ACM, pages 83–92, 1999.
9. B. So, M. Hall, and H. Ziegler. Custom Data Layout for Memory Parallelism. In *Proc. Intl. Symp. Code Gen. Opt.*, pages 291–302, March 2004.
10. C.-W. Tseng. Compiler optimizations for eliminating barrier synchronization. In *Proc. Fifth Symp. Principles and Practice of Parallel Programming*, volume 30(8) of *ACM SIGPLAN Notices*, pages 144–155, 1995.
11. P. Tu and D. Padua. Automatic Array Privatization. In *Proc. 6th Workshop Languages and Compilers for Parallel Computing*, LNCS. Springer-Verlag, 1993.
12. Xilinx Inc. *Virtex-II Pro*^{TM} *Platform FPGAs: introduction and overview*, DS083-1(v2.4.1) edition, March 2003.
13. H. Ziegler, M. Hall, and P. Diniz. Compiler-generated Communication for Pipelined FPGA applications. In *Proc. 40th Design Automation Conference*, June 2003.

Generation of Control and Data Flow Graphs from Scheduled and Pipelined Assembly Code

David C. Zaretsky[1], Gaurav Mittal[1], Robert Dick[1], and Prith Banerjee[2]

[1] Department of Electrical Engineering and Computer Science, Northwestern University
2145 N. Sheridan Road, Evanston, IL 60208-3118
{dcz, mittal, dickrp}@ece.northwestern.edu
[2] College of Engineering, University of Illinois at Chicago
851 South Morgan Street, Chicago, IL 60607-7043
prith@uic.edu

Abstract. High-level synthesis tools generally convert abstract designs described in a high-level language into a control and data flow graph (CDFG), which is then optimized and mapped to hardware. However, there has been little work on generating CDFGs from highly pipelined software binaries, which complicate the problem of determining data flow propagation and dependencies. This paper presents a methodology for generating CDFGs from highly pipelined and scheduled assembly code that correctly represents the data dependencies and propagation of data through the program control flow. This process consists of three stages: generating a control flow graph, linearizing the assembly code, and generating the data flow graph. The proposed methodology was implemented in the FREEDOM compiler and tested on 8 highly pipelined software binaries. Results indicate that data dependencies were correctly identified in the designs, allowing the compiler to perform complex optimizations to reduce clock cycles.

1 Introduction

Traditionally, the high-level synthesis problem is one of transforming an abstract, timing-independent specification of an application into a detailed hardware design. High-level synthesis tools generally convert the abstract design into a control and data flow graph (CDFG) that is composed of nodes representing inputs, outputs, and operations. The CDFG is a fundamental component of most compilers, where most optimizations and design decisions are performed to improve frequency, power, timing, and area. Building a CDFG consists of a two-step process: building the control flow graph (CFG), which represents the path of control in the design, and building the data flow graph (DFG), which represents the data dependencies in the design. However, when high-level language constructs are not readily available, such as in the case where legacy code for an application on an older processor is to be migrated to a new processor architecture, a more interesting problem presents itself, known as *binary translation*. Much research has been performed on CDFG generation from software binaries and assembly code. However, there has been very little work on generating complete CDFGs from scheduled or pipelined software binaries. Data

E. Ayguadé et al. (Eds.): LCPC 2005, LNCS 4339 , pp. 76–90, 2007.

dependency analysis of such binaries is more challenging than that of sequential binaries or high-level language applications.

When translating assembly codes from digital signal processors (DSPs), it is common to encounter highly pipelined software binaries that have been optimized manually or by a compiler. Consider the Texas Instrument C6000 DSP assembly code for the *vectorsum* function in Figure 1. In this architecture, branch operations contain 5 delay slots and loads contain 4 delay slots. The `||` symbol indicates the instruction is executed in parallel with the previous instruction and the `[ ]` symbol indicates the operation is predicated on an operand. Clearly, the *vectorsum* code is highly pipelined; each branch instruction is executed in consecutive iterations of the loop. Moreover, the dependencies of the ADD instruction in the loop body change with each iteration of the loop: A6 is dependent on the load at instruction 0x0004 in the first iteration of the loop, A6 is dependent on the load at instruction 0x000C in the second iteration of the loop, etc. Generating a CDFG to represent this pipelined structure is very challenging. In doing so, one must consider the varying data dependencies and also ensure that each branch is executed at its proper time and place. Branch instructions that fall within the delay slots of other branch instructions complicate the structure of the control flow graph. For instance, when the predicate condition, A1, on the branch instruction in the loop body is *false*, the previous branch instructions that were encountered during the execution sequence will continue to propagate and execute. This may occur within the loop, or possibly after exiting the loop. More complex software pipelines may contain branch instructions with various targets, producing multiple exit points in a CDFG block.

```
0x0000 VECTORSUM:      ZERO  A7
0x0004                 LDW   *A4++, A6      ; 4 delay slots
0x0008         ||      B     LOOP           ; 5 delay slots
0x000C                 LDW   *A4++, A6
0x0010         ||      B     LOOP
0x0014                 LDW   *A4++, A6
0x0018         ||      B     LOOP
0x001C                 LDW   *A4++, A6
0x0020         ||      B     LOOP
0x0024                 LDW   *A4++, A6
0x0028         ||      B     LOOP
0x002C         ||      SUB   A1, 4, A1
0x0030 LOOP:           ADD   A6, A7, A7
0x0034         || [A1] LDW   *A4++, A6
0x0038         || [A1] SUB   A1, 1, A1
0x003C         || [A1] B     LOOP           ; branches executes here
0x0040                 STW   A7, *A5
0x0044                 NOP   4
```

Fig. 1. TI C6000 assembly code for a pipelined *vectorsum* procedure

In this paper, we present a methodology for generating CDFGs from scheduled and pipelined assembly code. This process consists of three stages: generating a control flow graph, linearizing the assembly code, and generating the data flow graph. We use the methods described by Cooper et al. [6] for generating a CFG from scheduled assembly code. In addition, we extend their work to support more complex architectures that employ parallel instruction sets and dynamic branching. We also present a linearization process, in which pipelined structures are serialized into linear assembly. This allows for proper data dependency analysis when constructing data flow graphs. This methodology was incorporated in the FREEDOM compiler, which translates DSP assembly code into hardware descriptions for FPGAs. The techniques described in this paper were briefly discussed in previous work [11,19]; here we present a more refined and elegant approach in greater detail.

The remainder of this paper is structured as follows: Section 2 discusses related work in the area of CDFG generation from assembly code. Section 3 provides an overview of the FREEDOM compiler infrastructure and its intermediate language architecture. Section 4 describes our method of generating a CDFG from scheduled and pipelined assembly code in detail. Finally, Sections 5 and 6 present experimental results and conclusions, respectively.

2 Related Work

There has been a great deal of fundamental research and study of binary translation and decompilation. Cifuentes et al. [3,4,5] described methods for converting assembly or binary code from one processor's instruction set architecture (ISA) to another, as well as decompilation of software binaries to high-level languages. Kruegel et al. [9] described a technique for decompilation of obfuscated binaries. Stitt and Vahid [16,17] reported work on hardware-software partitioning of software binaries. Levine and Schmidt [10] proposed a hybrid architecture called HASTE, in which instructions from an embedded processor are dynamically compiled onto a reconfigurable computational fabric using a hardware compilation unit. Ye et al. [18] developed a similar compiler system for the CHIMAERA architecture.

Control and data flow analysis is essential to binary translation. Cifuentes et al. [5] described methods of control and data flow analysis in translating assembly to a high-level language. Kastner and Wilhelm [8] reported work on generating CFGs from assembly code. Decker and Kastner [7] described a method of reconstructing a CFG from predicated assembly code. Amme et al. [1] presented work on a memory aliasing technique, in which data dependency analysis is computed on memory operations using a value-based analysis and modified version of the GCD test [2].

There has been very little work on generating CDFGs from highly pipelined software binaries in which branch instructions appear in the delay slots of other branch instructions. The most comprehensive work on building CFGs from pipelined assembly code was reported by Cooper et al. [6]. However, their method does not consider the complexities of modern processor architectures that utilize instruction-level parallelism and dynamic branching techniques. In this paper, we address these issues and present methods to handle CDFG generation from software binaries that feature these sophisticated scheduling techniques.

3 Overview of the FREEDOM Compiler

This section provides a brief overview of the FREEDOM compiler infrastructure, as shown in Figure 2. The compiler was designed to have a common entry point for all assembly languages. Towards this effort, the front-end uses a description of the source processor's ISA in order to configure the assembly language parser. The ISA specifications are written in SLED from the New Jersey Machine-Code toolkit [14,15]. The parser generates a virtual assembly representation called the Machine Language Syntax Tree (MST), which has a syntax similar to the MIPS ISA. The MST is generic enough to encapsulate most ISAs, including those that support predicated and parallel instruction sets. All MST instructions are three-operand, predicated instructions in the format: *[pred] op src1 src2 dst.* A CDFG is generated from the MST, where optimizations, scheduling, and resource binding are preformed. The CDFG is then translated into a high-level Hardware Description Language (HDL) that models processes, concurrency, and finite state machines. Additional optimizations and customizations are performed on the HDL for the target architecture. This information is acquired via the Architecture Description Language (ADL) files. The HDL is translated directly to RTL VHDL and Verilog to be mapped onto FPGAs, and a testbench is generated to verify that the output is correct.

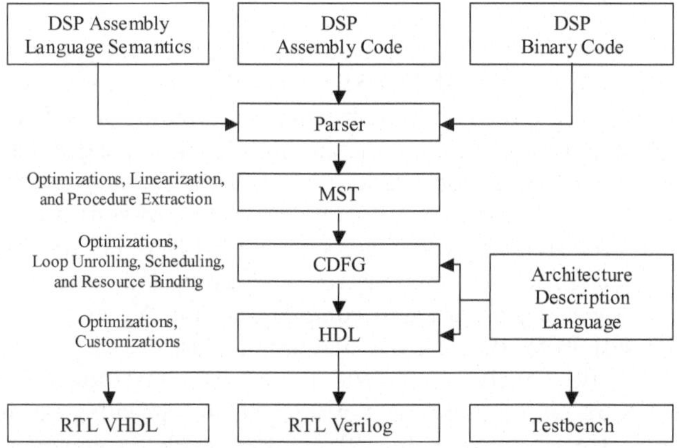

Fig. 2. Overview of the FREEDOM compiler infrastructure

The fixed number of physical registers on a processor necessitates advanced register reuse algorithms in compilers. These optimizations often introduce false dependencies based on register names, resulting in difficulties when determining data dependencies for scheduled or pipelined binaries and parallel instruction sets. To resolve these discrepancies, each MST instruction is assigned a timestep, specifying a linear instruction order, and an operation *delay*, equivalent to the number of execution cycles. Each cycle begins with an integer-based *timestep, T*. Each instruction n in a parallel instruction set is assigned the timestep $T_n = T + (0.01 * n)$. Assembly instructions may be translated into more than one MST instruction. Each instruction m

in an expanded instruction set is assigned the timestep $T_m = T_n + (0.0001 * m)$. The write-back time for the instruction, or the cycle in which the result is valid, is defined as $wb = timestep + delay$. If an operation delay is zero, the resulting data is valid instantaneously. However, an operation with delay greater than zero has its write-back time rounded down to the nearest whole number, or *floor(timestep)*, resulting in valid data at the *beginning* of the write-back cycle.

Figure 3 illustrates how the instruction timestep and delay are used to determine data dependencies in the MST. In the first instruction, the MULT operation has one delay slot, and the resulting value in register A4 is not valid until the beginning of cycle 3. In cycle 2, the result of the LD instruction is not valid until the beginning of cycle 7, and the result of the ADD instruction is not valid until the beginning of cycle 3. Consequently, the ADD instruction in cycle 3 is dependant upon the result of the MULT operation in cycle 1 and the result of the ADD operation in cycle 2. Likewise, the first three instructions are dependant upon the same source register, A4.

TIMESTEP	PC	OP	DELAY	SRC1	SRC2	DST
1.0000	0X0020	MULT	(2)	$A4,	2,	$A4
2.0000	0X0024	LD	(5)	*($A4),		$A2
2.0100	0X0028	ADD	(1)	$A4,	4,	$A2
3.0000	0X002c	ADD	(1)	$A4,	$A2,	$A3

Fig. 3. MST instructions containing timesteps and delays for determining data dependencies

4 Building a Control and Data Flow Graph

This section presents our methodology for generating a CDFG from scheduled and pipelined assembly code. This process consists of three stages: generating a control flow graph, linearizing the assembly code, and generating a data flow graph.

4.1 Generating a Control Flow Graph

Cooper et al. [6] presented a three-step process for building a CFG from scheduled assembly code, which was used as the first stage in the proposed work. The first step of their algorithm partitions the code at labels (entry points) into a set of basic blocks. During this process, they assume all entry points are complete, and no branch targets an instruction without a label. The second step adds edges between basic blocks in the CFG to represent the normal flow of control. Here, they only consider non-pipelined branch instructions, or those that do not appear within the delay slots of other branch instructions. Pipelined branches are handled in the third step using an iterative algorithm that simulates the flow of control for the program by propagating branch and counter information from block to block. Their method is shown to terminate in linear time for CFGs containing only branches with explicit targets. Figure 4 illustrates the CFG generated for the *vectorsum* procedure in Figure 1.

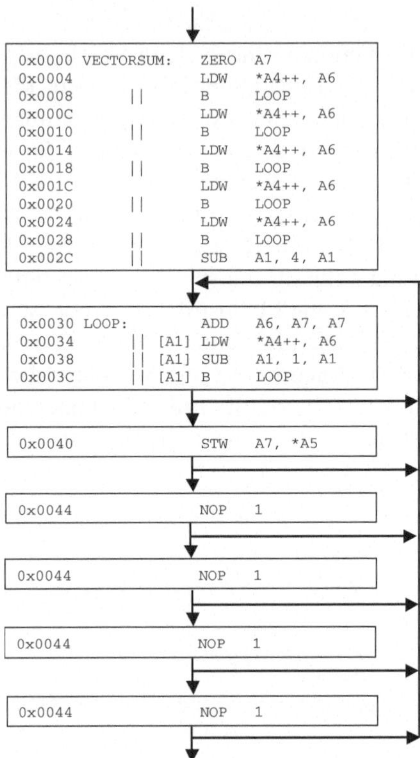

Fig. 4. Control flow graph for *vectorsum*

In practice, the assumptions made in their work pose some difficulties in generating CFGs for some modern processor architectures. For instance, they assume all labels and branch targets are well defined. However, some disassemblers limit the labels to a procedure level only and refrain from including them locally within procedure bounds. In some architectures, registers may be used in branch targets, as in the case of a long jump where a static PC value is loaded into the register prior to the branch instruction. To handle these situations, we introduce a pre-processing step that determines all static branch targets and adds the respective labels to the instructions. Some architectures may also support dynamic branch targets, in which the destination value may be passed to a register as a function parameter, such as with procedure prologues and epilogues. In these situations, we take an optimistic approach by assuming the dynamic branch operation is a procedure call. The branch is temporarily treated as a NOP instruction when building the initial CFG to allow the control flow to propagate through. We rely on post-processing steps, such as alias analysis and procedure extraction to determine the possible destinations [12]. The CFG is then regenerated with the newly identified destination values.

Many of today's processor architectures utilize instruction-level parallelism to achieve higher performances, which complicates generation of CFGs. For instance, a branch destination may have a target within a parallel set of instructions. This would break up the control flow at intermediate points within a basic block, creating erroneous data dependencies. In Figure 5, the ADD, SUB, and SRL instructions are scheduled in parallel. However, if the predicated branch is taken, the ADD instruction is not executed. Consequently, the entry label on the SUB instruction partitions the control flow in the middle of the parallel set, placing the latter two instructions in a separate basic block. This forces the A7 operand in the SRL instruction to use the resulting value from the ADD instruction in the previous block. To account for such discrepancies, we introduce a procedure that checks for entry points (labels) within a parallel set of instructions. If such an entry point exists, the instructions falling below the entry point are replicated and added to the top portion of the parallel set. Figure 6 shows the MST code after instruction replication. The SUB and SRL instructions have been replicated and a branch operation has been added to jump over the replicated code segment. We rely on subsequent optimizations in the CDFG, such as code-hoisting [13], to eliminate superfluous operations.

```
0x0800          [A1] B      L1
0x0804               NOP    5
0x0808               ADD    A4, A7, A7
0x080C  L1:  ||      SUB    A4, 1, A4
0x0810       ||      SRL  A4, A7, A8
0x0814  L2:          ...
```

Fig. 5. Branch target inside a parallel instruction set

```
10.0000  0x0800    [A1] GOTO (6) L1
11.0000  0x0804         NOP  (5) 5
16.0000  0x0808         ADD  (1) $A4, $A7, $A7
16.0100  0x080C         SUB  (1) $A4, 1, $A4     ; replicated SUB
16.0200  0x0810         SRL  (1) $A4, $A7, $A8   ; replicated SRL
16.0300  0x0810         GOTO (0) L2              ; added 'branch-over'
17.0000  0x080C  L1:    SUB  (1) $A4, 1, $A4
17.0100  0x0810         SRL  (1) $A4, $A7, $A8
18.0000  0x0814  L2:    ...
```

Fig. 6. MST representation with instruction replication

4.2 Event-Triggered Operations

In the previous section, a methodology for generating a CFG from pipelined assembly code was presented. The CFG represents the flow of control in the program via edges connecting basic blocks in the graph. However, the CFG does not inherently contain any information regarding propagation delay. In translating pipelined or scheduled assembly code from one architecture to another, it is essential that the compiler capture the propagation delay and data dependencies correctly. Failure to do so may result in false data dependencies, incorrect data value propagation, and possibly an ill-terminated or non-terminating program. Referring back to the *vectorsum* procedure in

Figure 1, we find that the main loop body will execute an unknown number of times until the predicate condition on the branch instruction is *false*, namely, when $A1 = 0$. At that point, the loop will continue to iterate for 5 more cycles until the branches within the pipeline have completed. During this time, data is still computed and propagated through the loop. Should the compiler not consider the propagation delay on the branch instructions, the loop may terminate early, producing erroneous data. Similarly, failure to consider the propagation delay in the pipelined load instructions will also result in erroneous data.

As a solution, we introduce the concept of an *event-triggered* operation, composed of a *trigger* and an *execute* stage. An event *trigger* is analogous to the read stage in a pipelined architecture, where the instruction is fetched and register values are read; an event *execute* is analogous to the write-back stage in the pipeline, during which the values are written to the destination register or memory. The event triggering and execution stages are offset by the delay of the operation.

An operation event is encapsulated in the MST language using a virtual shift register with a precision *d*, corresponding to the number of delay cycles for the operation. Virtual registers are temporary operands created by the compiler that do not exist within the framework of the source architecture's physical registers. In practice, this results in the addition of a very small shift register since most ISAs generally have no more than 4-6 delay slots in any given multi-cycle instruction. When a pipelined instruction is encountered during the normal flow of the program, an event is triggered by assigning a '1' to the highest bit (d-1) in the shift register. In each successive cycle, a shift-right logical operation is performed on the register. The event is executed after *d* cycles, when a '1' appears in the zero bit of the shift register.

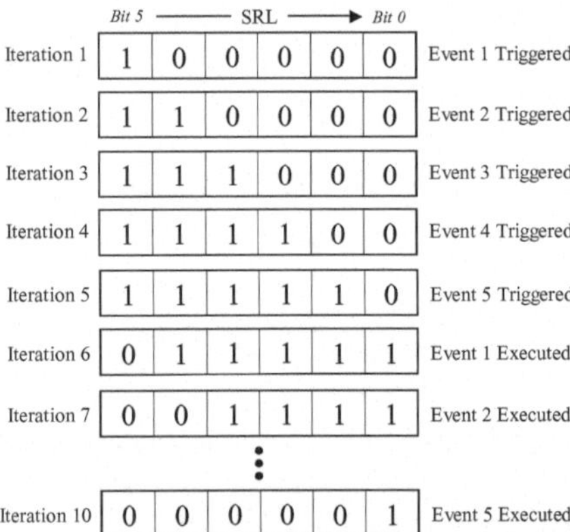

Fig. 7. Event-triggering for a pipelined branch operation in a loop body

Figure 7 illustrates the event triggering for the branch operation in the loop body of the *vectorsum* procedure, which has an operation delay of 6 cycles. In the first iteration of the loop, an event is triggered when the branch instruction is encountered by setting the high bit of shift register. In each subsequent cycle, the register is shifted right while a new event is triggered. After six iterations, event 1 is executed and the branch to LOOP is taken. This is followed by subsequent event executions through the tenth iteration of the loop, until the pipeline in the shift register has been cleared.

The technique described here is utilized in the linearization process for pipelined operations as discussed in the following sections.

4.3 Linearizing Pipelined Operations

This section describes the linearization process for pipelined operations. The concept of this process is to serialize the pipelined assembly instructions into linear assembly, such that the each pipelined instruction has a well-defined data flow path. The process for linearizing computational operations (arithmetic, logical, memory, etc.) and branch operations are described independently, as they function differently in pipeline architectures. The linearization process assumes that the CFG is complete, i.e., no edges will be inserted between blocks in the future. Consequently, if new edges are added in the future, data propagation and data dependencies are not guaranteed to be correct. To ensure its completeness, we force the algorithm to cover all possible control paths when generating the CFG. This is accomplished in a preprocessing pass that ensures all branch instructions in the program are predicated. A constant predicate of '1', whose condition always resolves to *true*, is added to all non-predicated branch instructions. This forces the branch to be treated as a conditional, and allows the control flow to propagate to the fall-through block. Subsequent optimizations, such as dead-code elimination [13], will remove any resulting extraneous operations.

4.3.1 Linearizing Computational Operations

In the linearization process for computational operations, multi-cycle instructions are serialized into a well-defined data flow path along the pipeline. In order to accomplish this task, virtual registers are introduced to break multi-cycle instructions into a sequence of multiple *single-cycle* instructions. Each instruction in the sequence is guarded by a predicate on an event-triggering register, as described above. Should the program encounter the instruction through a path outside the normal pipeline data flow path, the predicate will prevent the operation from executing.

The linearization process works as follows: For an instruction with n delay slots, the original instruction is modified to write to a temporary virtual register R_n, and the delay of the instruction is changed to a single cycle. In each of the subsequent $n-1$ cycles, the value is propagated through virtual registers along the pipelined data flow path by assigning $R_{n-1} \leftarrow R_n$, $R_{n-2} \leftarrow R_{n-1}$, …, $R_0 \leftarrow R_1$ in sequence, where R_0 is the original register name. Each of these instructions is predicated on its respective cycle bit of the shift register: $P[n-1]$ through $P[0]$. If the end of a basic block is reached, the linearization is propagated to the successor blocks. This approach assumes that no two instructions are scheduled such that both have the same destination register and write-back stages in the same cycle. This is a fair assumption, since compilers generally do not produce code resulting in race conditions. If two or more identical instructions have intersecting pipeline paths, redundant instructions may be avoided by tracking the timesteps to which they have been written. We rely on optimizations, such as copy and constant propagation [13], to remove any extraneous operations.

```
              :                          :
12.000  0x000C             MOVE(0) 1, $P1[4]    ; LD event cycle 1
12.001  0x000C             SRL(1) $P1, 1, $P1
12.002  0x000C  [$P1[4]]   LD(1) *mem($A4), $A6_4
              :                          :
13.000  0x000C             SRL(1) $P1, 1, $P1   ; LD event cycle 2
13.001  0x000C  [$P1[3]]   MOVE(1) $A6_4, $A6_3
              :                          :
14.000  0x000C             SRL(1) $P1, 1, $P1   ; LD event cycle 3
14.001  0x000C  [$P1[2]]   MOVE(1) $A6_3, $A6_2
              :                          :
15.000  0x000C             SRL(1) $P1, 1, $P1   ; LD event cycle 4
15.001  0x000C  [$P1[1]]   MOVE(1) $A6_2, $A6_1
              :                          :
16.000  0x000C  LOOP:      SRL(1) $P1, 1, $P1  ; LD event cycle 5
16.001  0x0014             OR(0) $P1[0], $P2[0], $MP0
16.002  0x001C             OR(0) $MP0, $P3[0], $MP1
16.003  0x0024             OR(0) $MP1, $P4[0], $MP2
16.004  0x0034             OR(0) $MP2, $P5[0], $MP3
16.005  0x000C  [$MP3]     MOVE(1) $A6_1, $A6  ; intersecting LDs 1-5
              :                          :
```

Fig. 8. Linearization of pipelined load (LD) instruction in the *vectorsum* procedure

Figure 8 illustrates the linearization process in the MST for the first pipelined LD instruction in the *vectorsum* example of Figure 1. In timestep 12, an event is triggered for the LD instruction by posting a '1' to the high bit in the virtual shift register *P1*. Additionally, the LD instruction is modified to write to virtual register *A6_4*, and the operation delay is changed from 5 cycles to 1 cycle. In the subsequent cycles, *A6_4* is written to *A6_3*, *A6_3* is written to *A6_2*, and *A6_2* is written to *A6_1*, at which point the linearization is propagated to the *LOOP* block. *A6_1* is finally written to the physical register *A6* in timestep 16. Each of these move instructions is guarded by a predicate on a *P1* bit, which is right-shifted in each cycle along the same control path. The same methodology is applied to each LD instruction in program. Although the propagation instructions may read and write to the same register in parallel, the one-cycle delay on each instruction enforces the correct data dependencies.

It is interesting to note that the pipelined LD instructions have intersecting paths. As an example, all five LD instructions will have their 5th cycles intersect in the same timestep (16), where *A6* ← *A6_1*. To avoid extraneous instructions, the propagation instructions are merged by OR-ing their predicates, as shown in the figure.

4.3.2 Linearizing Branch Operations

Unlike computational instructions, branch instructions do not propagate data. Rather, they trigger a change in control flow after a certain number of delay cycles. In linearizing branch operations, only the *event* is propagated through the CFG, as described above. At each branch execution point in the CFG, which can only be the end of a basic block, a copy of the branch instruction is inserted. The branch instruction is predicated on the event shift-register. Similar to the process above, if two or more of the same branch instruction have intersecting paths, redundant instructions may be eliminated by tracking the timesteps to which the instructions have been written. Two or more of the same branch instruction that execute at the same point can be merged by OR-ing their predicates. The original branch instructions are replaced with NOP instructions in order to maintain the correct instruction flow. Figure 10 illustrates the linearization process for pipelined branch operations.

```
                 :              :
11.000  0x0008          MOVE(0) 1, $P1[5]     ; branch event cycle 1
11.001  0x0008          SRL(1)  $P1, 1, $P1
11.002  0x0008          NOP(1)  1             ; branch replaced with NOP
                 :              :
12.000  0x0008          SRL(1) $P1, 1, $P1    ; branch event cycle 2
                 :              :
13.000  0x0008          SRL(1) $P1, 1, $P1    ; branch event cycle 3
                 :              :
14.000  0x0008          SRL(1) $P1, 1, $P1    ; branch event cycle 4
                 :              :
15.000  0x0008          SRL(1) $P1, 1, $P1    ; branch event cycle 5
                 :              :
16.000  0x0008  LOOP:   SRL(1) $P1, 1, $P1    ; branch event cycle 6
16.008  0x0008          OR(0) $P1[0], $P2[0], $MP0
16.009  0x0010          OR(0) $MP0, $P3[0], $MP1
16.010  0x0018          OR(0) $MP1, $P4[0], $MP2
16.011  0x0020          OR(0) $MP2, $P5[0], $MP3
16.012  0x0028          OR(0) $MP3, $P6[0], $MP4
16.013  0x003C  [$MP4]  GOTO(0)  LOOP   ; intersection branches 1-6
                 :              :
```

Fig. 9. Linearization of a pipelined branch instruction in the *vectorsum* procedure

4.3.3 The Linearization Algorithm

Figure 9 presents our algorithm for linearizing pipelined operations. The procedure has the same general organization as the algorithm presented by Cooper et al. [6] for generating CFGs. The algorithm initially creates a *worklist* of *instruction counters* for each basic block in the CFG in lines 1-3, and then iterates through the worklist in lines 4-25. An instruction counter is particular to a block, and holds a list of pending instructions and a counter representing the remaining clock cycles before each instruction is executed. To prevent redundant iterations over blocks, in lines 8-9, the algorithm checks that the block has not seen any of the pending instruction counters before continuing. The algorithm then iterates over the block by *whole timesteps* in lines 10-20. The instructions in each timestep are iterated through in lines 11-17, as the algorithm searches in line 12 for previously unvisited pipelined instructions to add to the instruction counter. Lines 13-15 add a counter for the branch instructions with cycle delays greater than zero; the original branch instruction is replaced with a NOP instruction to maintain the correct program flow. Lines 16-17 add counters for all multi-cycle instructions whose write-back time falls outside the block. Unique *event* instructions are inserted for each pending instruction in lines 18-20, as described above; those that have completed are removed from the instruction counter list. After iterating over the instructions within each timestep, the pending instruction counters are decremented in line 21. At the conclusion of the iteration over timesteps in the block, lines 22-26 propagate all pending counters to new instruction counters for each successor block edge; the new instruction counters are added to the worklist. The algorithm terminates once no new instruction counters are encountered by any block and the worklist is empty. The algorithm runs in $O(n)$ time, where n is the number of instructions in the program, assuming a small, constant number of outgoing edges between blocks.

```
Linearize_Pipelined_Operations( CFG )
1  worklist = empty list of InstrCounters
2  for each basic block in CFG do
3    add InstrCounter(block) to worklist
4  while worklist->size() > 0 do
5    instr_counter = worklist->front()
6    remove instr_counter from worklist
7    block = instr_counter->block
8    if block has seen all live counters in instr_counter then
9      continue
10   for each whole timestep ts in block do
11     for each instruction i in timestep ts do
12       if i has not been seen by instr_counter then
13         if i is a branch instruction and i->delay > 0 then
14           add {i:i->delay} to instr_counter
15           replace branch instruction i with NOP instruction
16         else if (i->timestep + i->delay) > block->max_time
17           add {i:i->delay} to instr_counter
18       for each counter c in instr_counter do
19         insert a unique event instruction for c in timestep ts
20         if c = 0 then remove c from instr_counter
21     instr_counter->DecrementCounters()
22   if instr_counter has live counters
23     for each successor s of block do
24       target_instr_counter = InstrCounter(s)
25       add unique live counters to target_instr_counter
26       add target_instr_counter to worklist
```

Fig. 10. Linearization algorithm for pipelined operations

4.4 Generating the Control and Data Flow Graph

In the previous sections we described how to build a CFG and break data dependencies in pipelined and scheduled assembly code. In this section we combine the two techniques to generate the complete CDFG. The procedure is described in Figure 12, which takes a list of assembly instructions as input and returns a CDFG. The procedure begins with a preprocessing step to ensure that all branch instructions in the program are predicated as described in the previous section. The algorithm constructs the CFG using Cooper's algorithm, and then linearizes the pipelined operations as described above. The data flow graph is then generated from the newly serialized instructions, based on the data dependency analysis technique described in Section 3. The procedure concludes by implementing single static-variable assignment (SSA) [13], which is a method of breaking data dependencies by ensuring that every assignment in the CDFG has a unique variable name.

Traditionally, a *Φ-function* is used in SSA to join multiple assignments to a variable, stemming from different paths in the CFG. The number of arguments to the *Φ-function* is equal to the number of definitions of the variable from each point in the CFG. This method often causes a significant bottleneck when handling numerous data paths. Interestingly, once the pipelined operations in the CDFG have been linearized, the *Φ-function* becomes superfluous, as only the latest definition of a variable will reach the end of the block and propagate through the control flow. Those instructions with multi-cycle delays that originally crossed basic block boundaries have since been serialized into multiple single-cycle instructions. As a result, the latest definition of each SSA variable may be assigned back to its original variable name at the end of the block, thus eliminating the need for the *Φ-function*. Optimizations, such as copy propagation and dead-code elimination [13], will remove extraneous assignment operations created by this process.

```
Generate_CDFG( instr_list )
 Predicate_Pipelined_Instrs( CFG )
 CFG = Generate_Ctrl_Flow_Graph( instr_list )
 Linearize_Pipelined_Operations( CFG )
 CDFG = Generate_Data_Flow_Graph( CFG )
 Generate_SSA( CDFG )
 return CDFG
```

Fig. 11. Procedure for generating a CDFG

5 Experimental Results

The correctness of the methodology presented in this paper was verified using the FREEDOM compiler [11,19] on 8 highly pipelined benchmarks in the Texas Instruments C6000 DSP assembly language. The FREEDOM compiler generated CDFGs and RTL code targeting the Xilinx Virtex II FPGA. Each benchmark was simulated using Mentor Graphic's ModelSim to verify bit-true accuracy and obtain cycle counts.

There has been little work reported on translating highly pipelined software binaries to RTL code for FPGAs. This makes comparison with other approaches difficult. However, it is interesting to consider the impact and effectiveness of this algorithm in a high-level synthesis tool. Table 1 shows comparisons in cycle counts for the TI C6000 DSP and the Virtex II FPGA, generated by the FREEDOM compiler. Also shown is the number of pipelined operations in each benchmark and the number of instructions inserted during the linearization process to demonstrate the impact on code size when using this approach.

Results indicate the FREEDOM compiler successfully generated the correct CDFGs from the pipelined assembly code, allowing complex optimizations and scheduling to significantly reduce clock cycles in the FPGA design. On average, approximately 9 instructions were added for each pipelined operation and there was a 27% increase in code size during the linearization process. *Please note that these values reflect the size of the design before CDFG optimizations, which will further reduce implementation complexity. A detailed evaluation of the performance and optimizations of the FREEDOM compiler has been presented in other work [11,19].*

Table 1. Experimental results on pipelined benchmarks using the FREEDOM compiler

Benchmark	DSP Cycles	FPGA Cycles	# Pipelined Instructions	# Added Instructions
memmove	125747	2516	33	352 (24.7%)
memcpy	69615	2004	14	136 (52.3%)
divi	282301	16127	17	141 (27.3%)
mpyd	1329176	39669	26	269 (14.0%)
remi	260148	16888	13	130 (34.6%)
dsp_fir_gen	30851	685	49	683 (43.1%)
lms_filter	33537580	773288	147	967 (13.7%)
noise_canceller_fir	8239397	163778	21	105 (5.3%)

6 Conclusions

This paper presents a methodology for correctly representing the data dependencies and data propagation when generating CDFGs from highly pipelined and scheduled assembly code. This process consists of three stages: generating a control flow graph, linearizing the assembly code, and generating the data flow graph. We use a known method for generating the control flow graph from scheduled assembly code and describe further techniques for handling more complex architectures that employ parallel instruction sets and dynamic branching. We present a linearization process, in which pipelined structures are serialized into linear assembly. This allows for proper data dependency analysis when generating the data flow graph.

The work was verified in the FREEDOM compiler on 8 highly pipelined software binaries for the TI C6000 DSP, targeting the Xilinx Virtex II FPGA. Results indicate that data dependencies were correctly identified, enabling the compiler to perform complex optimizations and scheduling to reduce clock cycles in the designs.

References

1. Amme W, Braun P, Thomasset F, and Zehendner E (2000) Data Dependence Analysis of Assembly Code. International Journal of Parallel Programming, vol. 28, issue 5.
2. Banerjee U (1988) Dependence Analysis for Supercomputers. Kluwer Academic Publishers, Norwell, MA.

3. Cifuentes C and Gough K (1993) A Methodology for Decomposition. Proceedings for XIX Conferencia Latinoamericana de Informatica. Buenos Aires, Argentina, pp 257-266.
4. Cifuentas C and Malhotra V (1996) Binary Translation: Static, Dynamic, Retargetable? Proceedings for the International Conference On Software Maintenance (ICSM). Monterey, CA, pp 340-349.
5. Cifuentes C, Simon D, and Fraboulet A (1998) Assembly to High-Level Language Translation. Proceedings of the International Conference on Software Maintenance (ICSM). Washington, DC, pp 228-237.
6. Cooper K, Harvey T, and Waterman T (2002) Building a Control-Flow Graph from Scheduled Assembly Code. Technical Report 02-399. Department of Computer Science, Rice University, Houston, TX.
7. Decker B and Kästner D (2003) Reconstructing Control Flow from Predicated Assembly Code. Proceedings of the 7th International Workshop on Software and Compilers for Embedded Systems (SCOPES). Vienna, Austria, pp 81-100.
8. Kästner D and Wilhelm S (2002) Generic Control Flow Reconstruction from Assembly Code. Proceedings of the Joint Conference on Languages, Compilers and Tools for Embedded Systems (LCTES), vol. 37, issue 7, pp 46-55.
9. Kruegel C, Robertson W, Valeur F, and Vigna G (2004) Static Disassembly of Obfuscated Binaries. Proceedings of USENIX Security 2004. San Diego, CA, pp 255-270.
10. Levine B and Schmidt H (2003) Efficient Application Representation for HASTE: Hybrid Architectures with a Single Executable. Proceedings of the 11th Annual IEEE Symposium on Field-Programmable Custom Computing Machines. Napa, CA, pp 101-107.
11. Mittal G, Zaretsky D, Tang X, and Banerjee P (2004) Automatic Translation of Software Binaries onto FPGAs. Proceedings of the 41st Annual Conference on Design Automation. San Diego, CA, pp 389-394.
12. Mittal G, Zaretsky D, Memik G, and Banerjee P (2005) Automatic Extraction of Function Bodies from Software Binaries. Proceedings for the IEEE/ACM Asia and South Pacific Design Automation Conference (ASPDAC). Beijing, China.
13. Muchnick S (1997) Advanced Compiler Design Implementation. Morgan Kaufmann Publishers, San Francisco, CA.
14. Ramsey N and Fernandez M (1995) New Jersey Machine-Code Toolkit. Proceedings of the 1995 USENIX Technical Conference. New Orleans, LA, pp 289-302.
15. Ramsey N and Fernandez M (1997) Specifying Representations of Machine Instructions. ACM Transactions on Programming Languages and Systems (TOPLAS), vol. 19, issue 3. New York, NY, pp 492-524.
16. Stitt G and Vahid F (2003) Dynamic Hardware/Software Partitioning: A First Approach. Proceedings of the Design Automation Conference. Anaheim, CA, pp 250-255.
17. Stitt G and Vahid F (2002) Hardware/Software Partitioning of Software Binaries. Proceedings of the International Conference of Computer Aided Design (ICCAD). Santa Clara, CA, pp 164-170.
18. Ye Z, Moshovos A, Hauck S, and Banerjee P (2000) CHIMAERA: A High-Performance Architecture with a Tightly-Coupled Reconfigurable Functional Unit. Proceedings of the 27th International Symposium on Computer Architecture. Vancouver, Canada pp 225-235.
19. Zaretsky D, Mittal G, Tang X, and Banerjee P (2004) Overview of the FREEDOM Compiler for Mapping DSP Software to FPGAs. Proceedings of the 12th Annual IEEE Symposium on Field-Programmable Custom Computing Machines. Napa, CA, pp 37-46.

Applying Data Copy to Improve Memory Performance of General Array Computations

Qing Yi

Department of Computer Science, University of Texas at San Antonio*

Abstract. Data copy is an important compiler optimization which dynamically rearranges the layout of arrays by copying their elements into local buffers. Traditionally, array copy is considered expensive and has been applied only to the working sets of fully blocked computations. This paper presents an algorithm which automatically applies data copy to optimize the performance of general computations independent of blocking. The algorithm automatically decides where to insert copy operations and which regions of arrays to copy. In addition, when specialized, it is equivalent to a general scalar replacement algorithm on arbitrary array computations. The algorithm is fully implemented and has been applied to optimize several scientific kernels. The results show that the algorithm is highly effective and that data copy can significantly improve the performance of scientific computations, both when combined with blocking and when applied alone without blocking.

1 Introduction

Most scientific applications operate on large multi-dimensional arrays that cannot fit in the caches of modern computers. Such computations typically include sequences of loop nests, with each loop selectively accessing elements of arrays. When a loop accesses a non-continuous collection of array elements, that is, when the array elements accessed together close in time are far from each other in the memory, the loop demonstrates poor spatial locality and additionally could incur conflict misses in the cache.

Data copy is an important compiler optimization that can dynamically rearrange the layout of arrays. At the beginning of each computation phase, the transformation can choose to copy a subset of array elements into local buffers. All the relevant array accesses within the computation phase can then be changed to instead operate on the local buffers. At the end of the computation phase, if the selected elements are modified, the local buffers are copied back to the original arrays. Because the local buffers store working sets of computations continuously, data copy optimization can significantly improve the spatial locality of computations.

Data copy was first proposed by Lam, Rothberg and Wolf [9] to reduce cache conflict misses for blocked computations. As an example, Figure 1(a) shows a

* The work was developed when the author was under employment by Lawrence Livermore National Laboratory, Livermore, CA, 94550.

E. Ayguadé et al. (Eds.): LCPC 2005, LNCS 4339, pp. 91–105, 2007.

```
int _j,_k,_i,j,k,i;
double alpha, *A, *B, *C;
......
for (_j=0; _j<n; _j+=16)
  for (_k=0; _k<l; _k+=16)
l_i:for (_i=0; _i<m; _i+=16)
l_j:  for (j=_j; j<min(n,_j+15); ++j)
l_k:    for (k=_k; k<min(l,_k+15); ++k)
l_i:      for (i=_i; i<min(m,_i+15); ++i)
          {
s:          C[i+j*m] = c[i+j*m] +
                alpha * A[i+k*m]*B[k+j*l];
          }
```

(a) without array copy

```
int _j,_k,_i,j,k,i, _bi,_bk,_v0,_v1;
double alpha, *A, *B, *C;
......
for (_j=0; _j<n; _j+=16)
  for (_k=0; _k<l; _k+=16)
l_i:for (_i=0; _i<m; _i+=16) {
      _bi = min(m-_i,16);   _bk = min(l-_k,16);
      _v0 = 0;
      for (_v1=_k; _v1<_k+_bk; ++_v1)
        for (_v2=_i; _v2<_i+_bi; ++_v2)
          A_buf[_v0++] = A[_v1*m+_v2];
l_j:  for (j=_j; j<min(n,_j + 15); ++j) {
        _v0 = 0;
        for (_v1=_i; _v1<_i+_bi; ++_v1)
          C_buf[_v0++] = C[j*m+_v1];
l_k:    for (k=_k; k<_k+_bk; ++k) {
          B_buf = B[j*l+k];
l_i:      for (i=_i; i<min(m,_i+15); ++i)
s:          C_buf[i-_i] = c_buf[i-_i] +
                  alpha*B_buf*A_buf[(k-_k)*_bi+i-_i];
        }
        _v0 = 0;
        for (_v1=j*m+_i; _v1<min(m,_i+16); ++_v1)
          C[_v1] = C_buf[_v0++];
      }
    }
```

(b) with array copy

Fig. 1. Example: blocked matrix multiplication

code fragment (written in C) that performs matrix multiplication, $C = C + alpha * A * B$, where $alpha$ is a scaling factor, and A,B,C are $m * l$, $l * n$ and $m*n$ matrices respectively (each stored in a linearized single-dimensional array). The computation in Figure 1(a) is fully blocked in all loop dimensions, where A,B and C are each partitioned into $16*16$ sub-matrices, and each computation phase (enumerated by the inner loops l_j, l_k and l_i) multiplies a pair of sub-matrices. Because the working set of each computation phase is small enough to fit in the cache of most memory systems, the loop structure in (a) is likely to perform well on modern computers.

The computation in Figure 1(a), however, is not guaranteed to have good memory performance. Because the working set of each computation block is not stored continuously in the memory, each memory access may bring useless elements into cache, resulting in poor spatial locality. Further, when non-continuous array elements are brought into cache, their addresses may conflict with each other, resulting in premature evictions of useful elements. To resolve such problems, compilers could apply data copy transformation, which copies all elements accessed within the computation phase into continuous buffers.

This paper presents a new data copy algorithm for optimizing the performance of general array computations. Figure 1(b) shows the result of transformation after automatically applying our algorithm to the code in (a). Here all elements accessed by the inner loops are copied into separate buffers. Specifically, elements in array B are copied into a scalar variable B_buf, elements in C are copied into a single-dimensional buffer C_buf, and elements in A are copied into a two-dimensional buffer A_buf. The buffer sizes are 1 for B_buf, $\_bi$ for C_buf, and $\_bi * \_bk$ for A_buf respectively, where $\_bi$ and $\_bk$ are the iteration numbers of loops l_i and l_k respectively. The loop body has been accordingly changed to access elements from the local buffers. Since elements in C_buf are modified, these elements are copied back to the original matrix C at the end. As shown in Section 4, the code in (b) can significantly outperform the code in (a) in many cases.

The algorithm in this paper significantly improves previous research [9,13], which treats array copy as an auxiliary optimization for blocking. Previous formulations would have optimized Figure 1(a) by performing all copy operations at the beginning and end of each computation block, i.e., the location that matrix A is copied in Figure 1(b). Our algorithm is much more flexible in that it treats data copy as a stand-alone optimization. Based on heuristics to reduce both buffer size and the overall copy cost, our algorithm automatically decides where to insert copy operations and which regions of the arrays to copy. The transformed code can use buffers at various levels, corresponding to the different levels of caches in modern computers. Our algorithm can also be specialized to perform scalar replacement optimization, which relocates array elements to scalar variables.

The algorithm in this paper is fully implemented and has been applied to optimize several kernels both combined with blocking and without blocking. Our results show that the algorithm is highly effective and that array copy can significantly improve the performance of scientific computations, both when combined with blocking and when applied separately without blocking.

2 Related Work

Lam, Rothberg and Wolf [9] first proposed applying array copy to reduce cache conflict misses in blocked computations. A few years later, Temam, Granston and Jalby [13] investigated different strategies for applying array copy after blocking and presented an effective strategy that selectively copy arrays based on compile-time cost-benefit analysis. Both Lam et al and Temum et al assumed that the blocked computations access arrays only through regular affine expression subscripts, where data copy can always be safely applied. They both consider data copy as an auxiliary optimization for blocking, where copy operations are inserted only at the beginning and end of blocked computations. Since then, very little work has been published to further investigate applying data copy to optimize array computations in scientific applications.

The data copy algorithm in this paper extends previous work in two aspects. First, our algorithm can optimize computations even if they contain regions of code that access arrays through non-affine expression subscripts. Second, our algorithm includes heuristics both to automatically select arrays to copy and to automatically identify different locations to insert copy operations. Thus our algorithm can be applied to optimize general computations independent of blocking.

Besides array copy, many data layout optimizations have been proposed to improve the memory system performance of regular array operations [11,12,3]. These optimizations statically reorganize the layout of arrays to reduce cache conflict misses and to improve spatial locality. They are effective when computations access arrays in a consistent fashion throughout an entire application. However, when computations include different phases, a single memory layout may not be sufficient. This paper does not attempt to globally restructure the layout of data structures. Instead, we dynamically rearrange array elements accessed in each computation phase when beneficial.

Despite being considered expensive, dynamic data layout transformations have been widely applied in optimizing irregular applications [6,7,10], where the structures of the input data are unknown until runtime. Because arrays in irregular applications are accessed through indirect pointers (or index arrays), current compiler technology cannot automate the optimization. In contrast, the data copy transformation in this paper is applied automatically to optimize regular array computations.

The algorithm presented in this paper is similar to the scalar-replacement algorithm by Carr and Kennedy [5] in many respects. Their algorithm aggressively promotes array elements into scalar variables so that these elements can later be allocated to registers. Our algorithm can similarly be configured to perform scalar replacement through restrictions on the size of array regions being copied. Our algorithm is more general than the algorithm by Carr and Kennedy in that we apply data copy to dynamically rearrange the layout of arrays in addition to performing scalar replacement.

3 Applying Data Copy

Figure 2 presents our algorithm for applying data copy to arbitrary array computations. This algorithm takes a code fragment C, partitions the array references in C into groups where each group can be safely copied into a single buffer, performs profitability analysis on each group of array references, and finally applies transformations when beneficial. Section 3.1 describes each step of the algorithm. Section 3.2 then describes the profitability analysis in more detail.

3.1 Data Copy Algorithm

As shown in Figure 2, given an input code fragment C, the algorithm includes the following steps.

Step (1) Construct a dependence graph R, where each node of R is a memory reference in the original code C, and each edge from reference r_1 to r_2 indicates that r_1 and r_2 may access the same memory location (i.e., r_2 and r_1 depend on

```
Apply-data-copy(C)
(1) R = construct-dependence-graph(C)
      nodes(R): memory references in C;  edges(R): dependences between references
      ∀e ∈ edges(R), dep(e): dependence relation;  precise(e): whether dep(e) is precise
(2) Construct a DAG R' from R
      order = evaluate-reference-order(C);  nodes(R') = nodes(R)
      for (each edge e : r1 → r2 in R)
        if (order(r1) < order(r2)) then  add e : r1 → r2 to R'
        else if (order(r1) > order(r2)) then  add reverse(e) : r2 → r1 to R'
(3) groups = apply-typed-fusion(R')
      BadEdges = {e ∈ edges(R') | not precise(e)}
      ∀r ∈ nodes(R),  type(r) = array-name(r)
(4) Profitability-analysis(R,groups)
    for (each refs ∈ groups), compute
      init-stmt(refs) and save-stmt(refs): start and ending points of computation
      cp-region(refs): elements to be copied to local buffer
      shift-buf(refs): offset to shift local buffer
      init-region(refs): elements to be copied before starting
(5) For (each refs ∈ groups), perform array copy transformation
(5.1) buf = create-buffer(cp-region(refs))
(5.2) if (!cover-modify(init-stmt(refs), save-stmt(refs),refs))
        init = copy-init(buf,init-region(refs));  insert-before(init-stmt(refs), init)
      if (is-modified(refs) or shift-buf(refs) ≠ 0)
        save = copy-save(buf,cp-region(refs),shift-buf(refs));
        insert-after(save-stmt(refs), save)
(5.3) for (each r ∈ refs)
        r_buf = buffer-access(r,buf,cp-region(refs));  replace-ref(r, r_buf)
```

Fig. 2. Algorithm for applying array copy

each other), and r_1 is evaluated before r_2. Each edge e from r_1 to r_2 is annotated with two attributes: *dep*(e), the dependence relation that must be satisfied between iterations of loops surrounding r_1 and r_2; and *precise*(e), whether the dependence relation *dep*(e) is precisely determined by the dependence analysis algorithm (i.e., whether both r_1 and r_2 contain only affine expression subscripts). Only when *precise*(e) is true, r_1 and r_2 are guaranteed to refer to the same memory location when *dep*(e) is satisfied, and the elements accessed by r_1 and r_2 can be copied into a single buffer.

The dependence graph R can be constructed using well-studied dependence analysis techniques [1,14,4]. The only difference here is that nodes in R are memory references rather than statements, and that a pair of references may depend on each other even if neither modifies the memory (that is, input dependences are considered together with the true, output and anti dependences).

Step (2) Prepare for Step (3) by converting the dependence graph R into a DAG (directed acyclic graph) R'. First, define a function *order* which assigns a unique integer number to each memory reference and thus imposes a linear order on all memory references. Specifically, $\forall r_1, r_2 \in nodes(R)$, if $order(r_1) <$

$order(r_2)$, then r_1 appears before r_2 in C in static evaluation order; that is, r_1 is traversed before r_2 when we statically interpret the statements in C, assuming all loop bodies and conditional branches (both true and false branches) are entered exactly once.

Copy all the nodes and edges from R into R'. Ensure R' is acyclic by enforcing that every edge e from r_1 to r_2 in R' satisfies the condition $order(r_1) < order(r_2)$. Specifically, $\forall e : r_1 \rightarrow r_2$ in the original graph R, if $order(r_1) < order(r_2)$, copy e into R'. Otherwise, if $order(r_1) > order(r_2)$, reverse $dep(e)$ and then add the reversed dependence from r_2 to r_1 into R'. Finally, if $r_1 == r_2$, the edge is simply ignored because it does not affect the partitioning of memory references.

Step (3) Partition the memory references in R' into separate groups by applying the typed-fusion algorithm by Kennedy and McKinley [8], originally developed for performing loop fusion optimizations. The input to the original typed-fusion algorithm is a loop dependence graph, where each node of the graph is a loop, and each edge from node x to y indicates that there are dependences from statements inside loop x to statements inside loop y. An edge from x to y is annotated as a *bad edge* if the dependence relations between x and y prevent them from being legally fused. Additionally, each node in the loop dependence graph is assigned a type so that loops of different types are never fused. For each given type of loops (e.g., parallel or serial loops), the typed-fusion algorithm aggressively clusters nodes of the given type that are not connected by fusion-preventing *bad* paths. In order for the algorithm to work correctly, it is required that the input dependence graph must be acyclic (i.e., a DAG).

To adapt the typed-fusion algorithm for partitioning memory references, we use the DAG R' (computed in Step (2)) as input to the algorithm. Here *bad edges* are defined to include each edge $e \in R'$ such that $precise(e)$ is false, so that memory references connected by imprecise dependence paths are never placed into the same group. The names of arrays are used to represent types of memory references, and all non-array memory references are assigned a unique *dummy* type, which is never used as input to the fusion algorithm. Therefore no data copy transformation is applied to non-array memory references.

After applying the typed-fusion algorithm to the dependence DAG R', the result is a collection of clustered groups, where each group $refs$ includes a collection of array references that can be safely relocated to a single buffer. Based on the correctness proof of the original typed-fusion algorithm, it is guaranteed that no references in $refs$ are connected to each other by *imprecise* dependence paths.

Step (4) Use profitability analysis (described in Section 3.2) to further filter and configure the groups of array references to be copied. For each group of memory references $refs$, this step computes the following attributes.

- init-stmt($refs$) The starting point of a computation phase to apply data copy. When applying the transformation, the initialization operations should be inserted before this statement.

- save-stmt($refs$) The ending point of the computation phase. If the local buffer needs to be saved, the necessary operations should be inserted after this statement.
- cp-region($refs$) The region of array elements to be relocated to the local buffer.
- shift-buf($refs$) The offset to shift the local buffer between consecutive iterations of the current computation phase. Since accessing the local buffer is cheaper than operating on the original array, when appropriate, the local buffer can be shifted to reduce the overhead of copying from the original array. For more details, see Section 3.2.
- init-region($refs$) The region of array elements to be copied into the local buffer before init-stmt($refs$). Specifically, *init-region($refs$)* equals to *cp-region($refs$)* if the local buffer cannot be shifted (that is, *shift-buf($refs$)* = 0); otherwise, *init-region($refs$)* contains the elements accessed by $refs$ at the first iteration of the computation phase.

The above attributes are used by Step (5) to perform data copy transformations. As example, Figure 3 presents the configuration of these attributes when applying data copy to the matrix multiplication code in Figure 1(a). The evaluation of these attributes is described in more detail in Figure 4 and in Section 3.2.

Step (5) For each group of array references $refs$ to be copied, perform the transformation by allocating a local buffer, inserting operations to copy data between buffer and the original array, and replacing array references in $refs$ with the corresponding buffer accesses.

First, step (5.1) invokes function *create-buffer* to allocate a local buffer from the heap. The allocation is placed at the outermost location where the size of the buffer can be correctly evaluated. Deallocation of the buffer is also automatically inserted if necessary.

Then, step (5.2) inserts operations to copy data between the local buffer and the original array. Unless each iteration of the computation phase modifies all elements accessed by $refs$ before reading them (*cover-modify(init-stmt($refs$),save-stmt($refs$),$refs$)* is true), operations are inserted before *init-stmt($refs$)* to copy elements from the original array to the local buffer. Similarly, if the computation phase modifies elements accessed by $refs$, or if the local buffer needs to be shifted (*shift-buf($refs$)* $\neq 0$) between consecutive iterations of the computation phase, the necessary operations are inserted after *save-stmt($refs$)*.

Finally, step (5.3) replaces each array reference in $refs$ with the corresponding buffer access.

3.2 Profitability Analysis

This section describes Step (4) of the data copy algorithm in Figure 2. As shown in Figure 4, this step uses heuristics to determine whether a data copy transformation is beneficial and how to perform the transformation to ensure profitability. For each group of memory references $refs$ to be copied, it includes the following sub-steps.

references: $\{A[i + k * m]\}$ init-stmt: l_j save-stmt: l_j cp-region and init-region start: $\_i + \_k * m$ copy: $(0, min(m - \_i, 16), 1)$, $(0, min(l - \_k, 16), m)$ shift-buf: 0	references: $\{B[k + j * l]\}$ init-stmt: l_i save-stmt: l_i cp-region and init-region start: $k + j * l$ copy: () shift-buf: 0	references: $\{C[i + j * m]\}$ init-stmt: l_k save-stmt: l_k cp-region and init-region start: $\_i + j * m$ copy: $(0, min(m - \_i, 16), 1)$ shift-buf: 0

Fig. 3. Array copy configurations for Figure 1(a)

Step (4.1) To reduce the overhead of performing data copy, make sure that each array element accessed by $refs$ needs to be copied at most twice: initially copied from the original array to the local buffer, and finally copied back from local buffer to original array.

First, invoke function *split-disconnected-refs(refs,R)* to separate array references in $refs$ that are not connected by dependence paths in R. Disconnected memory references are removed from $refs$ and added into the overall collection (*groups*) of array reference groups.

To ensure that each array element is copied at most twice, find *inroot* = common-loop($refs$), the innermost loop that surrounds all array references in $refs$. For each reference $r_2 \notin refs$, if r_2 is connected with references in $refs$ by dependence edges, and if $\exists r_1 \in refs$ such that $l_{r_1 r_2}$ is the innermost loop surrounding both r_1 and r_2, then the required copy operations must be inserted between r_1 and r_2 and inside loop $l_{r_1 r_2}$. If $l_{r_1 r_2}$ is nested at a deeper loop level within *inroot*, the copy operations inside $l_{r_1 r_2}$ will be evaluated multiple times at each iteration of *inroot* (the current computation phase). To avoid such situation, split $refs$ so that r_1 is placed into a separate group. After this step, all copy operations can be safely inserted immediately inside *inroot*.

Using Figure 1(a) as example, when applying steps (1)-(3) of the algorithm in Figure 2, Figure 3 presents the resulting three array reference groups. Since no splitting is necessary, this step merely set *inroot* to loop l_i for all reference groups.

Step (4.2) Decide the outermost loop, *cproot*, where copy operations can be safely inserted; that is, it is safe to relocate all elements accessed by $refs$ at each iteration of *cproot*. A single iteration of *cproot* therefore comprises the computation phase of the current copy transformation.

First, invoke function *copy-loop(inroot,refs,R)* to find the outermost loop, *outroot*, that contains all references in $refs$ but does not contain any reference r such that (i) r is outside *inroot*, and (ii) r and $refs$ may depend on each other within *outroot*. If *outroot* == *inroot*, copy operations must be inserted inside *inroot* (*cproot* = *inroot*). Otherwise, since no reference $r \notin refs$ can interfere with the memory accessed by $refs$ throughout the execution of *outroot*, it is safe to insert copy operations outside *outroot*. So *cproot* should be the loop immediately enclosing *outroot*.

```
Profitability-analysis(R,groups)
for (each refs ∈ groups)
(4.1) Ensure each element is copied at most twice:
      split-disconnected-refs(refs, R);  inroot = common-loop(refs)
      cut = {r1∈refs | ∃r2∉refs s.t. dep(r2,refs)≠∅ and common-loop(r1,r2) is
          inside inroot }
      if (cut ≠ ∅) split(refs,cut);  groups∪ = {cut};  inroot = common-loop(refs)
(4.2) Compute outermost loop level to perform copy:
      outroot = copy-loop(inroot,refs,R)
      if (outroot == inroot) cproot = inroot
      else cproot = loop-immediately-outside(outroot)
(4.3) Impose size limit on the local buffer
      split-disconnected-refs(refs,R(cproot));
      cut={r∈refs | is-too-big(array-region(r,cproot))}
      if (cut == refs) cproot = loop-immediately-inside(cproot);  repeat step (4.3)
      else split(refs,cut);  groups∪ = {cut};  go back to step (4.1)
(4.4) Ensure profitability of copy transformation
      reuse = {l | l ∈ loops-between(cproot, inroot) and carry-temporal-reuse(refs,l)}
      if (reuse ≠ ∅) cproot = loop-immediately-outside(outermost-loop(reuse))
      else if (|refs| ≤ 3)  groups− = {refs};   continue
(4.5) configure copy transformation
      cp-region(refs) = array-region(refs,cproot)
      shift-buf(refs) = array-region-shift(refs,cproot)
      if (shift-buf(refs) ≠ 0 and cproot ≠ inroot and cproot ≠loop-immediately-
         outside(outroot))
        init-stmt(refs) = cproot;  init-region(refs)=init-array-region(refs,cproot)
        save-stmt(refs)=last-stmt(refs,loop-body(cproot))
      else
        init-stmt(refs)=first-stmt(refs,loop-body(cproot));  init-region(refs)=
         cp-region(refs)
        shift-buf(refs)=0;  save-stmt(refs)=last-stmt(refs,loop-body(cproot))
```

Fig. 4. Profitability analysis of array copy

Using Figure 1(a) as example, since no dependence interference exists, we have *outroot* $= l_j$ for all three array reference groups in Figure 3. Consequently we would have *cproot* $= l_{\_i}$ for all reference groups.

Step (4.3) Impose a size limit on the local buffer. The size limit is dependent on various features of the computer architecture and is given to the data copy algorithm as a configuration parameter. In our prototype implementation, the size limit is imposed by restricting the dimensionality of local buffers using command-line options (see Section 4).

First, invoke function *split-disconnected-refs(refs,R(cproot))* to separate references that are disconnected from each other in the dependence graph of *cproot*. Next, find each reference r in $refs$ such that at each iteration of *cproot*, the elements accessed by r exceed the buffer size limit. If the collection of references that access too many elements includes everything in $refs$ (*cut* $== refs$), lower *cproot* to be the loop immediately inside and repeat step (4.3). Otherwise, since only a subset of references in $refs$ are causing the problem, split $refs$ by removing such references, then restart from step (4.1).

Using Figure 1(a) as example, after Step (4.2), we have *cproot* $= l\_i$ for all reference groups in Figure 3. Since each reference group has a single array reference, and each array reference accesses at most $16 * 16$ elements at each iteration of loop l_i, the local buffer for each reference group has two dimensions. If only single-dimensional buffers are allowed, this step would reset *cproot* $= l_j$ for all reference groups. Similarly, if only scalar replacement is allowed, we would have $cproot(\{B[k + j * l]\}) = l_k$, and $cproot(\{A[i + k * m]\}) = cproot(\{C[i + j * m]\}) = l_i$.

Step (4.4) Evaluate the benefit of applying data copy and refrain from applying the transformation (by removing $refs$ from *groups*) if the benefit does not outweigh the cost.

First, find all the loops between *cproot* and *inroot* that carry temporal reuses of $refs$; that is, these loops do not increase the overall size of elements accessed by $refs$. Collect these loops into a set *reuse* in Figure 4.

If *reuse* is not empty, it is profitable to perform array copy because the local buffer will be reused many times. Find the outermost loop l in *reuse* such that all the other loops between *cproot* and l merely increase the buffer size without introducing any memory reuse. Reduce buffer size by lowering *cproot* to be the loop immediately enclosing l.

If *reuse* is empty, the copied elements are reused at most a few times ($\leq$ the number of elements in $refs$). If the number of elements in $refs$ is less than 3, the copy overhead is likely to outweigh the benefit of reuse. In this case, remove $refs$ from the groups of references to be optimized.

Using Figure 1(a) as example, suppose that *cproot* $= l\_i$ for all reference groups in Figure 3 before entering this step. After this step, we would have *reuse* $= \{l_j\}$, $\{l_k\}$ and $\{l_i\}$ for reference groups $\{A[i + k * m]\}$, $\{C[i + j * m]\}$ and $\{B[k + j * l]\}$ respectively. Consequently, $cproot(\{C[i + j * m]\})$ and $cproot(\{B[k + j * l]\}$ would be reset to l_j and l_k respectively, resulting in the data copy transformation shown in Figure 1(b).

Step (4.5) Suppose it is beneficial to apply data copy at each iteration of loop *cproot*. Compute necessary configurations to determine where to insert copy operations and what to copy.

First, invoke function *array-region(refs,cproot)* to summarize all the array elements accessed by $refs$ at each iteration of *cproot*. The result includes the starting address of the array to be copied and a sequence of tuples, (i_1, n_1, s_1), (i_2, n_2, s_2), ..., (i_m, n_m, s_m), where in each $(i_j, n_j, s_j)(j = 1, ..., m)$, i_j specifies the current array dimension to be copied, n_j specifies the number of elements to be copied at dimension i_j, and s_j specifies the incremental stride at dimension i_j. This formulation allows multiple copy specifications for each array dimension, thus allowing linearized arrays (e.g., the arrays in Figure 1(a)) to be correctly

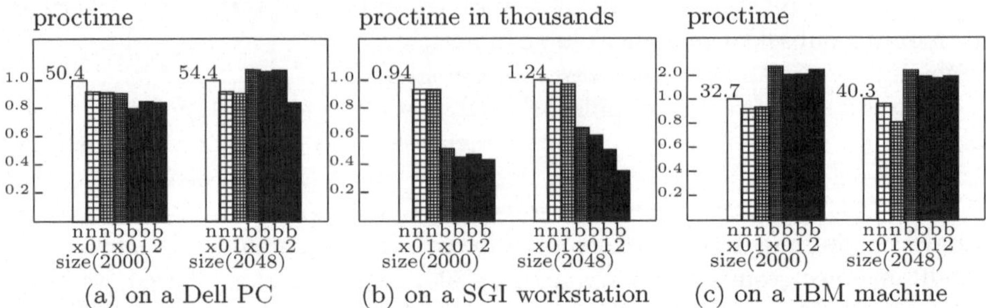

(a) on a Dell PC (b) on a SGI workstation (c) on a IBM machine

Fig. 5. Performance of dgemm (nx:original non-blocked version; n0:optimized with 0-dimensional data copy; n1:optimized with 1-dimensional data copy; bx:optimized with loop blocking; b0:optimized with blocking and 0-dimensional data copy; b1:optimized with blocking and 1-dimensional data copy; b2:optimized with blocking and 2-dimensional data copy)

copied. Given the the sequence $(i_1, n_1, s_1)(i_2, n_2, s_2)...(i_m, n_m, s_m)$, the size of the buffer is $n_1 * n_2 * ... * n_m$.

After computing *cp-region(refs)*, invoke function *array-region-shift(refs,cproot)* to compute the intersection of *cp-region* between consecutive iterations of *cproot*. If the overlapping region is not empty (shift-buf($refs$) $\neq 0$), it is more efficient to shift the local buffer rather than re-initiating the entire buffer from the original array. Shifting the local buffer is safe if *cproot* does not contain other references that interfere with $refs$ (*cproot* $\neq$ *inroot* and *cproot* is not the loop enclosing *outroot*).

If shifting the local buffer is necessary, the local buffer should be initialized before entering *cproot*. Thus *init-stmt*($refs$) = *cproot*. The initialization should copy elements accessed by $refs$ at the first iteration of *cproot*, so *init-region*($refs$) = *init-array-region*($refs$, *cproot*). The buffer needs to be shifted and re-initialized at the end of each iteration of *cproot*, so *save-stmt*($refs$) is the last statement in the loop body of *cproot*.

If shifting of local buffer is not necessary, we configure the transformation to always initialize the entire buffer in the loop body of *cproot* before the first statement that contains a reference in $refs$. Similarly, if necessary, the entire buffer should be restored back to the original array after the last statement that contains a reference in $refs$.

The configurations for applying array copy to Figure 1(a) is shown in Figure 3. Based on these configurations, applying Step (5) of Figure 2 to the code in Figure 1(a) would result in the optimized code in Figure 1(b).

4 Experimental Results

We have implemented our data copy algorithm within the loop transformation framework by Yi, Kennedy and Adve [15], which has been integrated as a C/C++ source-to-source translator within ROSE, a C/C++ compiler

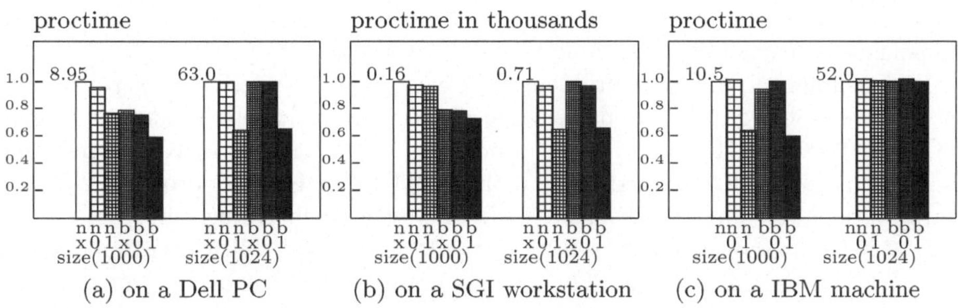

(a) on a Dell PC (b) on a SGI workstation (c) on a IBM machine

Fig. 6. Performance of dgetrf (nx:original non-blocked version; n0:optimized with 0-dimensional data copy; n1:optimized with 1-dimensional data copy; bx:optimized with loop blocking; b0:optimized with blocking and 0-dimensional data copy; b1:optimized with blocking and 1-dimensional data copy)

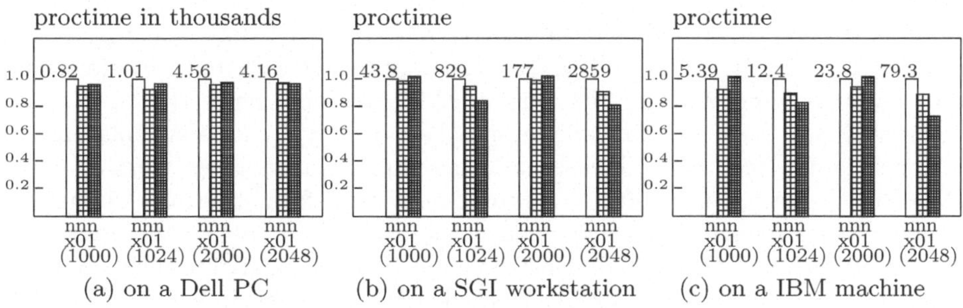

(a) on a Dell PC (b) on a SGI workstation (c) on a IBM machine

Fig. 7. Performance of tomcatv using mesh sizes 1000, 1024, 2000 and 2048 (nx:original version; n0:optimized with 0-dimensional data copy; n1:optimized with 1-dimensional data copy)

infrastructure at LLNL [17]. This section presents the result of applying our algorithm to optimize three kernels, *dgemm* (matrix multiplication), *dgetrf* (matrix LU factorization with partial pivoting), and *tomcatv* (mesh generation with Thompson solver). All kernels are written in C. Both *dgemm* and *dgetrf* are transcribed from the corresponding non-blocked Fortran kernels in the LAPACK library [2], and *tomcatv* is transcribed from the Fortran kernel in SPEC95. When applying optimizations to these transcribed C codes, the dependence analysis in ROSE assumed that no arrays are aliased.

Data copy is applied to optimize all kernels. In addition, blocking is applied to *dgemm* and *dgetrf* to investigate the combination of blocking and data copy (the result of applying blocking to *tomcatv* is not shown because it was not beneficial). For each blocked version, different block sizes were experimented and the version with the best performance is presented. When performing data copy transformation, the optimizer is configured by command-line options to restrict the dimensionality of required buffers — if the buffer dimension is restricted to be m (denoted as *m-dimensional copy*), the optimizer would only perform data copy to arrays that require at most m dimensional buffers. When the buffer dimension is restricted to be 0, only scalar replacement is performed.

For each kernel, different problem sizes were experimented. The performance of each version was measured on three different machine architectures: a Dell PC with two 2.2GHz Intel XEON processors (each with a 512KB cache) and 2GB memory; a SGI workstation with a 195 MHz R10000 processor, 32KB 2-way associative first-level cache, 1MB 4-way associative second-level cache, and 256MB memory; and a single 8-way P655+ node (with 16GB memory) on a IBM terascale machine. The kernels were compiled using *gcc* on the Dell PC and vendor-provided compilers on the SGI work station and IBM machine. All versions were compiled using -O3 option, which instructs the compilers to perform aggressive backend optimizations. The processor time (*proctime*) spent executing each version is presented.

Figure 5 presents the performance of *dgemm* using two matrix sizes, 2000^2 and 2048^2. Seven versions are measured for each matrix size, including the original non-blocked version (version nx), versions optimized with data copy optimizations only (versions $n0$ and $n1$), the version optimized with only blocking(version bx, shown in Figure 1(a)) and the versions optimized with both blocking and data copy (versions $b0$,$b1$ and $b2$, version $b2$ is shown in Figure 1(b)[1]).

From Figure 5, we see that 0-dimensional array copy (i.e., scalar replacement) is beneficial for *dgemm* in all cases, and the improvements range from 3%-12%. When using matrix size 2000^2, additional copy transformations do not further improve performance. However, when using matrix size 2048^2, the additional data copy, especially the two dimensional copy of array A, significantly improves the performance (over 40% for the blocked versions on the Dell PC and on the SGI workstation). Here the 2048^2 matrices have incurred much more cache conflict misses, which are subsequently eliminated when the accessed elements are copied into local buffers. The optimizations did not improve the performance as much on the IBM machine due to the heavy integer operation overhead introduced by the optimizations, which will be further investigated.

Figure 6 presents the performance of $dgetrf$ (matrix LU factorization with partial pivoting) using two matrix sizes, 1000^2 and 1024^2. Six versions are measured for each matrix size, including the original non-blocked version (version nx), versions optimized with data copy only (versions $n0$ and $n1$), the version optimized with blocking only (version bx), and versions optimized with both blocking and copy optimizations (versions $b0$ and $b1$). Because $dgetrf$ can be blocked only in the column direction (for details, see Yi et al [16]), at most a single dimension of the matrix needs to be copied. Thus there is no $b2$ version for $dgetrf$.

From Figure 6, we see that 0-dimensional array copy (scalar replacement) is not profitable for $dgetrf$ on the Dell PC and incurs a slight overhead on the IBM machine due to increased register pressure. The 1-dimensional copy transformation, however, significantly improves performance in most cases by

[1] The $b1$ and $b0$ versions are different from version $b2$ in that array A is not copied in $b1$, and only array B is copied in $b0$.

20%-40% except when using 1000^2 matrix on the SGI workstation and when using 1024^2 matrix on the IBM machine. Here because the original arrays were accessed with a large stride, applying data copy have provided much better spatial locality. Again, the versions using 1024^2 matrix have performed much worse than using 1000^2 matrix due to conflict misses in memory systems.

Figure 7 presents the performance of *tomcatv* (mesh generation with Thompson solver) using four mesh sizes, 1000^2, 1024^2, 2000^2 and 2048^2. Because blocking is generally not profitable for *tomcatv*, array copy is the only optimization applied. Three versions are measured for each mesh size, denoted using nx (the original version), $n0$ (optimized with 0-dimensional data copy), and $n1$ (optimized with 1-dimensional data copy). In *tomcatv*, as each element is accessed within the inner loop, the four neighboring elements are also accessed. The local buffer therefore serves as a small shifting window through the entire mesh.

From Figure 7, we see that 0-dimensional array copy (scalar replacement) is profitable for *tomcatv* in almost all cases (ranging from 0.5% to 12%). The 1-dimensional copy transformation significantly improves performance by 11%-19% when using 1024^2 and 2048^2 meshes on the SGI workstation and on the IBM machine, but slightly slows down performance by 0.5%-8% in other cases. Here again, when using 1024^2 and 2048^2 meshes, the extra benefit of applying array copy comes from the reduction of conflict misses in the memory system.

In summary, the experimental results indicate that selectively applying data copy to optimize array computations can significantly improve the performance of scientific applications, especially when array elements are accessed in large strides and when conflict misses become a factor in the memory performance. The performance measurements also indicate that data copy does not need to be applied together with blocking to be effective. In fact, data copy optimization was able to significantly improve performance for all three kernels without blocking. Finally, even when data copy is not beneficial, the overhead is not overly significant, and only small slow downs (.5%-8%) in performance are observed for all kernels.

5 Conclusion

This paper presents a general algorithm for applying data copy to optimize arbitrary array computations. The algorithm is fully implemented and has been applied to automatically optimize several scientific computation kernels on different platforms. The results indicate that the algorithm is highly effective and that array copy can significantly improve the performance of scientific computations, both when combined with blocking and when applied alone without blocking.

References

1. R. Allen and K. Kennedy. *Optimizing Compilers for Modern Architectures.* Morgan Kaufmann, San Francisco, October 2001.
2. E. Anderson, Z. Bai, C. Bischof, S. Blackford, J. Demmel, J. Dongarra, J. D. Croz, A. Greenbaum, S. Hammarling, A. McKenney, and D. Sorensen. *LAPACK Users' Guide.* The Society for Industrial and Applied Mathematics, 1999.

3. J. Anderson, S. Amarasinghe, and M. Lam. Data and computation transformation for multiprocessors. In *ACM Symposium on Principles and Practices of Parallel Programming*, Santa Barbara, July 1995.
4. U. Banerjee. *Dependence Analysis for Supercomputing.* Kluwer Academic Publishers, Boston, 1988.
5. S. Carr and K. Kennedy. Scalar replacement in the presence of conditional control flow. *Software — Practice and Experience*, 24(1):51–77, Jan. 1994.
6. C. Ding and K. Kennedy. Improving cache performance in dynamic applications through data and computation reorganization at run time. In *ACM SIGPLAN Conference on Programming Language Design and Implementation*, Gorgia, May 1999.
7. H. Han and C.-W. Tseng. Improving locality for adaptive irregular scientific codes. Technical Report CS-TR-4039, Dept. of Computer Science, University of Maryland, September 1999.
8. K. Kennedy and K. S. McKinley. Typed fusion with applications to parallel and sequential code generation. Technical Report TR93-208, Dept. of Computer Science, Rice University, Aug. 1993. (also available as CRPC-TR94370).
9. M. Lam, E. Rothberg, and M. E. Wolf. The cache performance and optimizations of blocked algorithms. In *Proceedings of the Fourth International Conference on Architectural Support for Programming Languages and Operating Systems (ASPLOS-IV)*, Santa Clara, Apr. 1991.
10. J. Mellor-Crummy, D. Whalley, and K. Kennedy. Improving Memory Hierarchy Performance For Irregular Applications. In *Proceedings of the 13th ACM-SIGARCH International Conference on Supercomputing*, Phodes, Greece, 1999.
11. M. O'Boyle and P. Knijnenburg. Integrating loop and data transformations for global optimisation. In *International Conference on Parallel Architectures and Compilation Techniques*, Paris, France, Oct 1998.
12. G. Rivera and C.-W. Tseng. Data transformations for eliminating conflict misses. In *ACM SIGPLAN Conference on Programming Language Design and Implementation*, Montreal, Canada, June 1998.
13. O. Temam, E. Granston, and W. Jalby. To copy or not to copy: A compile-time technique for assessing when data copying should be used to eliminate cache conflicts. In *Proceedings of Supercomputing '93*, Portland, OR, Nov. 1993.
14. M. J. Wolfe. *Optimizing Supercompilers for Supercomputers.* The MIT Press, Cambridge, 1989.
15. Q. Yi, K. Kennedy, and V. Adve. Transforming complex loop nests for locality. *The Journal Of Supercomputing*, 27:219–264, 2004.
16. Q. Yi, K. kennedy, H. You, K. Seymour, and J. Dongarra. Automatic blocking of qr and lu factorizations for locality. In *The Second ACM SIGPLAN Workshop on Memory System Performance*, Washington, DC, USA, June 2004.
17. Q. Yi and D. Quinlan. Applying loop optimizations to object-oriented abstractions through general classification of array semantics. In *The 17th International Workshop on Languages and Compilers for Parallel Computing*, West Lafayette, Indiana, USA, Sep 2004.

A Cache-Conscious Profitability Model for Empirical Tuning of Loop Fusion*

Apan Qasem and Ken Kennedy

Department of Computer Science
Rice University
Houston, TX
{qasem,ken}@cs.rice.edu

Abstract. Loop fusion is recognized as an effective program transformation for improving memory hierarchy performance. However, unconstrained loop fusion can lead to poor performance because of increased register pressure and cache conflict misses. The complex interaction between different levels of the memory hierarchy with the input program makes it very difficult to always make the right choice in fusing loops. In this paper, we present a cache-conscious analytical model for profitable loop fusion to be used with a constrained weighted fusion algorithm. We then extend the model to show its effectiveness in the context of an empirical tuning framework. A preliminary evaluation of the model is presented using hand experiments on four applications.

1 Introduction

Loop fusion is recognized as an effective program transformation for improving memory hierarchy performance of applications. Fusion improves data locality by merging loops that access the same data. Although fusion is a useful transformation it is not always profitable. Previous research has shown that unconstrained application of fusion may sometime lead to performance loss [4,10].

Consider the code in Fig 1. In the first loop nest we compute values for array `b`. These same values are then used in the second loop nest. We can exploit this locality in array `b` by performing a two-level fusion operation. In the fused loop nest shown in Fig 1(b) the two references to array `b` are close enough to be put into a register. Thus as a result of fusion we can potentially save NM memory operations. However, there is also an outer loop reuse in array `a` for the references to `a(i,j-1)` and `a(i,j-2)` in loop nest l_1 that we need to consider. In the unfused version the same memory locations in array `a` are touched in every iteration of the outer loop. In the fused version, although we do touch the same locations in array `a`, the amount of data that we bring into cache between reuses has increased. In the fused version, we will be accessing locations in arrays `b`, `c` and `d` before we get to the reused reference of `a`. If the intermediate data between

* This material is based on work supported by the Department of Energy under Contract Nos. 03891-001-99-4G, 74837-001-03 49, 86192-001-04 49, and 12783-001-05 49 from the Los Alamos National Laboratory.

E. Ayguadé et al. (Eds.): LCPC 2005, LNCS 4339, pp. 106–120, 2007.

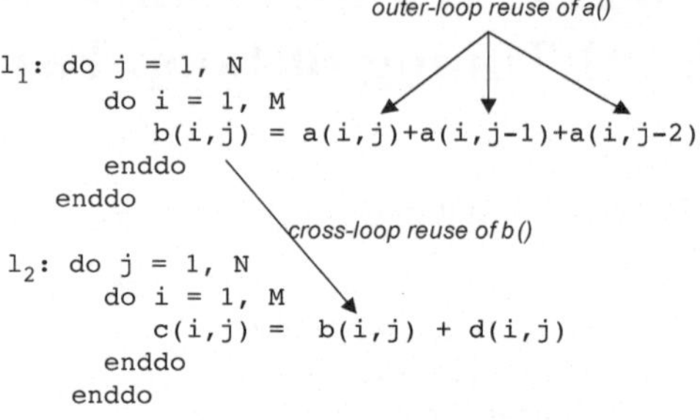

(a) code before fusion

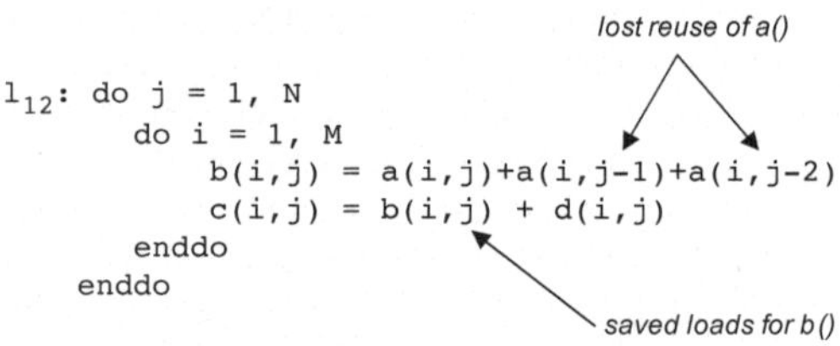

(b) code after two-level fusion

Fig. 1. Example of non-profitable fusion

reuses is larger than the cache capacity then we will incur 2NM cache misses due to the references to a. Moreover, by bringing in data from different arrays between reuses we also increase the likelihood of conflict misses. The occurrence of conflict misses in the loop nest can be even more damaging to performance because it can lead to lost spatial locality in both arrays c and d. Thus for the code in Fig 1 fusion will not yield an overall profit. (Many readers will observe that these issues can be ameliorated by tiling the loop that results after fusion. Although we do not analyze the interaction of tiling with fusion in the body of this paper, we discuss the subject in the final section.)

Fusion can also degrade memory performance by increasing register pressure for the innermost loop. When fusing loops at the innermost level the register requirements may increase to the point where a large number of register spills occur. The cost of these spills may offset any benefits gained by improved locality in the fused loop. The possibility of exceeding the instruction cache capacity is also a concern when fusing loops with large instruction counts in the innermost loop bodies.

The problem of finding the optimal fusion solution has been shown to be NP-complete [2]. For large applications with many fusible loops finding a good fusion solution involves using good heuristics. In this paper, we present a strategy that combines an architecture sensitive cost model with empirical tuning to perform profitable loop fusion. Our cost model considers the size, associativity and latency of various levels of the cache in determining if it is profitable to fuse a pair of loops. We incorporate this cost model into a constraint-based fusion algorithm. We formulate two constraints for the fusion algorithm to ensure that performance does not degrade as a result of increased pressure on system resources due to fusion. Finally, we use empirical tuning to tune a set of fusion parameters which cannot be measured accurately through static analysis.

In the sections that follow we discuss related work, present our analytical model, demonstrate how it can be used in an empirical tuning system, present a preliminary evaluation of the model and finally discuss our conclusions and future work.

2 Related Work

Fusion has been studied in the literature both as a tool for improving data locality and increasing the granularity of parallelism [8]. In this paper we look at fusion in the context of improving data locality only.

In its general form the task of finding the optimal fusion has been shown to be NP-complete [2]. Several algorithms have been described that use heuristics to find good fusion solutions in reasonable time. Lim and Lam use affine transformations to apply fusion [9]. Gao et. al. use a max-flow-min-cut algorithm to partition loop nests into fusible clusters [5]. Kennedy describes a fast-greedy weighted fusion algorithm that runs in polynomial time [7]. In our work we do not look at algorithms for performing loop fusion but rather focus on establishing suitable profitability constraints for legally fusible loops.

Many researchers have proposed models for performing loop fusion to improve memory performance. Ding and Kennedy have looked at reducing effective bandwidth through loop fusion [4]. Verdoolaege et. al. [14] describe a greedy fusion algorithm for incremental loop fusion at multiple levels. However, their locality models do not consider input dependences or the costs associated with cache misses. Song et. al. [13] present a model that combines loop fusion, loop alignment and array contraction. In their model, the primary profitability consideration is reducing bandwidth through reduced-sized arrays. Although they apply conditions to check for excessive register pressure and cache capacity they do not address the issue of conflict misses.

There are two main differences between our approach and the previous work done in this area. Firstly, unlike previous models our approach uses machine specific information (e.g. cache line size, latency) in combination with reuse distances in determining if fusion is profitable for a pair of loops. Secondly, we extend our model to be used in the context of an empirical framework. To our knowledge fusion has not been applied in this setting.

3 Profitability Model

3.1 Quantifying Reuse in Fusible Loops

Capturing inter-loop nest reuse: To determine if it is profitable to fuse a pair of loops we first need to compute the amount of reuse that is exploited as a result of fusion. Fusion improves locality by merging loops that access the same data. Thus any memory location that is accessed in the first loop nest and then re-accessed in the second loop nest is a candidate for potential reuse. This inter-loop reuse can be captured in a dependence graph through the use of loop-crossing dependence edges. A loop-crossing dependence is defined as follows:

Definition 1. Let l_1 and l_2 be two fusible loop nests where reference r_1 accesses location M in some iteration i in l_1 and reference r_2 accesses location M' in some iteration j in l_2. Then there is a *loop-crossing dependence* from r_1 to r_2 if $M = M'$.

To quantify reuse in fusible loops we start with the dependence graph for single loop nests. Then for each pair of adjacent loop nests we add loop-crossing dependence edges between the two dependence graphs.

Pruning the dependence graph: The extended dependence graph described above is able to identify points of potential reuse in fusible loops. However, in cases where there are multiple inter loop dependences with overlapping thresholds the graph might overestimate the amount of reuse exploited by fusion. To account for such situations we need to *prune* the graph so that the sink of each loop-crossing dependence represents a potential savings in memory operations. We note that if there are multiple loop-crossing dependences emanating from the same source reference then all but one of the loop-crossing dependence edges can be eliminated. The edge that remains is the one that points to the sink reference that has no incoming dependence edge from within the loop nest. Similarly, if there are multiple loop-crossing dependences that have a single reference as their sink we can eliminate all but one of the edges. In this case, the edge that remains is the one that has a source with no dependence edges flowing into it from within the loop nest.

In addition to handling the loop-crossing dependences we also need to prune the dependence graph for each loop nest so that the pruned graph has at most one predecessor for each reference and that predecessor refers to the most recent use of the sink. This pruning is essential for our cost model which assumes one predecessor per sink in order to avoid double counting of cost on particular references. We adopt strategies described by Carr [1] to perform this pruning. The strategy involves eliminating all killed dependences from the graph and in cases of group temporal reuse keeping only those edges that have the smallest dependence threshold.

Hierarchical classification of reuse: Once, we have the pruned dependence graph we need to augment it to include information about reuse distances and memory hierarchy levels. The effects of fusion may not be beneficial across all levels of the memory hierarchy. Fusing a pair of loops may improve locality at some level of cache but actually hurt locality at other levels. Hence, to improve overall memory performance we need to be able to quantify reuse that is exploited at each level of the memory hierarchy.

When considering multiple levels of the memory hierarchy, the reuse classification described in [15] is somewhat inadequate. We introduce a new classification of temporal reuse based on the level at which locality is exploited. We associate with each sink node in the dependence graph a value that expresses the level at which the reuse is exploited. This term is called the *reuse level* of a reference and we define this formally as follows:

Definition 2. Let L_i refer to the memory at level i. Then the *reuse level* of a reference r involved in temporal reuse is the smallest k such that

$$ReuseDistance(r) \leq Capacity(L_k)$$

3.2 Accounting for Conflict Misses

Conflict misses can be a big concern for profitable fusion. When fusing loops we often bring accesses to a number of different arrays within the iterations of a single loop nest. If the array locations overlap in cache then we would have to pay the penalty of increased conflict misses. To account for conflict misses we extend the cache associativity model described by Mark and Hill in [6]. We compute the probability of a cache line being evicted before it is reused based on the size and associativity of the cache and the reuse distance.

Let,

r_1 and r_2 = references to the same cache line
m = reuse distance between r_1 and r_2
s = number of sets in cache
a = associativity

If we assume, each line from m is equally likely to be mapped to any of the sets then (this assumption is revisited in Section 5)

$$Pr[a\ lines\ landing\ in\ line\ occupied\ by\ r_1] = Pr[conflict\ miss\ on\ r1]$$
$$= \sum_{i=a}^{m} \binom{m}{i} \left[\frac{1}{s}\right]^{i} \left[\frac{s-1}{s}\right]^{m-i}$$
$$= 1 - \sum_{i=0}^{a-1} \binom{m}{i} \left[\frac{1}{s}\right]^{i} \left[\frac{s-1}{s}\right]^{m-i}$$

Now, we introduce a tolerance term T that expresses how high a probability of a conflict miss we are willing to accept. We then have,

$$T \geq Pr[conflict\ miss\ on\ r1] = 1 - \sum_{i=0}^{a-1} \binom{m}{i} \left[\frac{1}{s}\right]^{i} \left[\frac{s-1}{s}\right]^{m-i}$$

From this inequality we can derive an upper bound on m for a given value of T.

$$m \leq E(a, s, T)$$

Here, $E(a, s, T)$ is the maximum integral m such that $Pr[conflict\ miss\ on\ r1] \leq T$.

Now, given a tolerance term T and the size and associativity of a cache at level k we can express our formula for *effective cache capacity (ECC)* in the following manner:

$$ECC(L_k) = E(a_k, s_k, T) \tag{1}$$

where, s_k and a_k refer to the size and associativity of the cache at level k.

Based on this model of *effective cache capacity* we now have a new definition for the *reuse level* of a reference.

Definition 3. Let L_i refer to the memory at level i. Then the *reuse level* of a reference r involved in temporal reuse is the smallest k such that

$$ReuseDistance(r) \leq ECC(L_k)$$

3.3 Estimating Profitability

With reuse information and the heuristics for conflict miss in place we are now able to estimate the profitability of fusing a pair of loops. For each loop-crossing dependence in the pruned graph we want to determine how many memory operations are saved as a result of placing the source and the sink within the same iteration of the fused loop.

Let,

l_1 and l_2 = candidate loops for fusion that have the same nesting depth
D = set of loop-crossing true and input dependences between l_1 and l_2
C = set of dependences carried by either l_1 or l_2
$ReuseLevel_{\{pre,post\}}(d)$ = reuse level for d before and after fusion
L_k = cache at the kth level where $0 \leq k \leq L$, L_0 refers to the register level and L_L refers to main memory
$cost(L_k)$ = cost of a miss access to L_k

Then for each $d \in D$ we assign a weight w based on the following condition:

if $ReuseLevel_{pre}(d) > ReuseLevel_{post}(d)$

then

$$w(d) = \sum_{i=ReuseLevel_{post}(d)}^{ReuseLevel_{pre}(d)-1} cost(L_i)$$

else

$$w(d) = 0$$

Then total weight is just

$$\sum_{d \in D} w(d)$$

Computing the number of memory operations saved from loop-crossing dependences is not enough to determine if fusion is profitable. As illustrated in the example in Fig 1 in some cases fusion may destroy locality within loop nests. When fusing two loops the reuse distance of any carried dependence increases if that reuse is also not involved in a loop-crossing dependence. We need to account for all such cases where fusion might lead to loss of potential reuse.

For each $c \in C$ we need to compute the cost based on the following condition:

if $ReuseLevel_{pre}(c) < ReuseLevel_{post}(c)$

then

$$w(c) = \sum_{i=ReuseLevel_{pre}(c)}^{ReuseLevel_{post}(c)-1} cost(L_i)$$

else

$$w(c) = 0$$

Then total cost is

$$\sum_{c \in C} w(c)$$

Hence, the final formula for computing the weight between two fusible loops is:

$$W(l_1 l_2) = \sum_{d \in D} w(d) - \sum_{c \in C} w(c)$$

3.4 Resource Constraints

A detailed analysis of the savings in memory operations does not guarantee beneficial fusion. There are several factors that can affect fusion that are not captured by the model we presented for computing weights. Most of these factors have to do with the resource requirements of the fused loop. If the requirements for a particular resource is higher than what is available to the program then the benefits of improved locality through fusion may not be realized. In this section, we establish a set of constraints that need to be considered by a *constrained weighted fusion* algorithm [3].

(i) **Register Pressure:** If the number of required registers for the fused loop body is more than what is available then we have to pay the price for spill costs. To account for register pressure we enforce the following constraint:

$$Register\ Pressure(Loop_{fused}) \leq Register\ Set\ Size$$

We use the methods presented in [1] to estimate register pressure in a loop body. Information about the number of registers available to the program is collected before compilation.

(ii) **Instruction Cache Capacity:** If the number of instructions in the fused body is large enough to blow out of the instruction cache then we have to pay the penalty of fetching those instructions from memory. Again, this phenomenon should be considered when fusing two loops.

$$Instructions(Loop_{fused}) \leq Capacity(I\text{-}Cache)$$

It should be noted that although data cache capacity is another critical resource requirement for a program we do not include it as a constraint here. When using our cost model with a weighted fusion algorithm the weights of the individual edges account for the data cache miss costs. For this reason we do not consider the total data requirements of the fused loop as a separate constraint.

3.5 Using the Model with a Greedy Fusion Algorithm

The fusion model and the resource constraints that we formulated can be incorporated into a constrained weighted fusion algorithm. We choose the pair-wise greedy fusion algorithm as described by Kennedy and Ding in [3]. In this algorithm fusion is formulated as a graph clustering problem in which the vertices represent loops in the program and the weights represent the amount of benefit obtained by fusing the endpoints. At each step the algorithm picks the heaviest *prime edge* in the graph and fuses its endpoints. After each fusion operation weights are recomputed and the graph is updated with new successor, predecessor and prime edge information.

The chief issue that needs to be considered in incorporating our model with the greedy algorithm is the cost associated with recomputing the weights at every step. Since, we perform a detailed analysis in calculating the benefits of fusing two loops we need to annotate the graph with more information to make the reweighing process more efficient.

We construct the pruned dependence graph with reuse information as described previously. We then group the references within each loop nest and label the subgraphs as *supernodes*. We compute the weights between each pair of fusible loops according to the procedure described in section 3.3 We connect each pair of *supernodes* using these weights. Hence, each pair of supernodes has only one node connecting them that represents the net gain from fusing the two loops.

Now, the pair-wise fusion algorithm can proceed normally on the *supernodes* and the edges between them. After fusing a pair of loops, edge weights between *supernodes* have to be updated and the loop-crossing dependence edges adjusted. For this step, we need to examine each loop-crossing dependence coming into and out of the fused loop nest. The edges within the *supernodes* representing outer loop reuse also have to be examined. We note however, that the number of edges in both cases is bounded above by the number of arrays in the loop. Hence, the complexity of a reweighing operation will be $O(A)$ where A is the number of arrays in the program. Having the complexity of the update operation bounded by the number of arrays ensures that the fast greedy algorithm will be able to maintain its original asymptotic time bound inspite of the more detailed profitability analysis.

3.6 Parameterizing the Model

Even the most detailed analytical models may not produce the optimal fusion solution. Profitable fusion depends on a number of architectural features and it is often difficult to determine *a priori* how these features will interact with the fusion choices. For example, using the model presented in 3.3 we may be able to make a prediction about the possibility of conflict misses but we cannot say how good our prediction is until the program is actually run on the target machine. Similar uncertainties remain in measuring register pressure and cache footprints. Our approach to dealing with these uncertainties is the use of empirical tuning. In this section, we show how the analytical model that we have presented in this paper can be parameterized and used in an empirical tuning framework.

The basic idea behind our algorithm for empirically tuning fusion parameters is this: we identify system resources (e.g. available registers) that impose constraints on fusion choices. We then introduce a *tolerance factor* T which determines how much of a given resource we can use in each tuning step. The relationship between the *tolerance factor* for a given resource R and the *available resource* R' can be expressed as

$$R' = f(T, R) \ s.t. \ R' \leq R$$

For example, in the instance of tuning the register pressure parameter, the function $f()$ is a multiplication of the tolerance factor T with the register set size followed by a ceiling operation on the product. We start off conservatively with a low tolerance factor and increase the value of T at each subsequent iteration. We stop the iterative process either when performance degrades or when we have reached the availability threshold of a particular resource.

Since, at each step we only *relax* some fusion constraint, it is easy to show that the set of fused loops grows monotonically during the tuning process. Because of this property we chose a search strategy that is *sequential* and *orthogonal*. For n resources we have an *n-dimensional* search space where the size of each dimension is the range of tolerance factors for a particular resource. For each dimension we perform a sequential search. When searching in a particular dimension we use reference values for all other dimensions.

Our current search model includes three resources: data cache capacity, instruction cache capacity and register pressure. Although, these three resources are somewhat similar they interact with fusion choices in different ways and hence constitute individual search dimensions. We discuss the tolerance factors and feedback parameters for each of these resources next.

Effective Cache Capacity: We compute the *effective cache capacity* using Eq. 1. Intuitively, Eq. 1 tells us what fraction of the cache we can use so that there is $T\%$ probability of a conflict miss between two accesses to the same memory location. So, in this case we have

$$\textit{Effective D-Cache Capacity} = E(a, s, T)$$

where $E(a, s, T)$ is obtained from Eq. 1.

We start of with a low value for T ($T < 0.02$) and at each step we increment T by 0.05 and measure the number of data cache misses at different levels. We stop the search in this dimension when we reach a T for which the number of cache misses increases.

Register Pressure: For the register pressure constraint we have the following equation for T:

$$\textit{Effective Registers} = \lceil T \times \text{Register Set Size} \rceil \text{ where } 0 \leq T \leq 1$$

Feedback parameters we use here are total loads and cycle count. Both parameters serve as good indicators about the occurrence of register spills.

Table 1. Performance results for `advect3d` (large) for different fusion strategies

Fusion Strategy	Cycles ($\times 10^8$)	L1D Misses ($\times 10^7$)	L2 Misses ($\times 10^6$)	L1 I Misses ($\times 10^5$)	Loads ($\times 10^8$)	Speedup over `no-fuse`
`ccfm`	8.41	4.48	5.13	6.14	3.66	1.17
`simple`	12.30	3.78	5.08	4.31	4.26	0.80
`mips-pro`	9.86	3.76	9.18	6.16	3.06	1.00
`no-fuse`	9.87	3.76	9.19	6.26	3.06	1.00

Table 2. Performance results for `advect3d` (small) for different fusion strategies

Fusion Strategy	Cycle ($\times 10^8$)	L1D Misses ($\times 10^7$)	L2 Misses ($\times 10^6$)	L1 I Misses ($\times 10^5$)	Loads ($\times 10^8$)	Speedup over `no-fuse`
`ccfm`	4.22	1.38	2.29	6.98	1.19	1.08
`simple`	5.70	1.68	2.79	7.80	1.61	0.80
`mips-pro`	5.73	1.68	2.80	7.80	1.61	0.80
`no-fuse`	4.58	1.46	2.49	6.98	1.30	1.00

Instruction Cache Capacity: The instruction cache constraint is dealt separately since we do not compute reuse distances for instruction and we are mainly concerned with capacity misses. So, in this case we have:

$$\textit{Effective I-Cache Capacity} = \lceil T \times \textit{Capacity}(\textit{I-Cache}) \rceil \text{ where } 0 \leq T \leq 1$$

For feedback we measure instruction cache misses directly.

4 Preliminary Evaluation

We are currently in the process of implementing our profitability model in a performance-based empirical tuning framework[12]. The system includes a source-to-source code transformer (`LoopTool`) that is capable of performing a collection of loop optimizations including multi-level fusion. In this section, we present an evaluation of our model using the empirical tuning framework.

We applied our model by hand to a set of benchmarks. We then annotated the source with directives to tell `LoopTool` which loops to fuse. The transformed code was then compiled using the native compiler on the target platform.[1] In order to avoid conflicts with the fusion strategies of the native compiler, programs transformed by `LoopTool` were compiled with the fusion option turned off. All experiments were performed on an SGI R12K machine with a two-level cache hierarchy. Experiments were run on four different programs: `advect3d` an advection kernel for weather modeling, `erlebacher` a differential equation solver, `liv18` a hydrodynamics kernel from Livermore loops and `mgrid`, a multi grid solver from SPEC

[1] Since, we applied the model by hand we do not have numbers for the total tuning time. The measured time for the source-to-source transformation was never more than 15 seconds.

Table 3. Performance results for `erlebacher` for different fusion strategies

Fusion Strategy	Cycle ($\times 10^9$)	L1D Misses ($\times 10^8$)	L2 Misses ($\times 10^7$)	L1 I Misses ($\times 10^4$)	Loads ($\times 10^8$)	Speedup over `no-fuse`
`ccfm`	5.23	2.00	2.72	6.57	4.02	1.08
`simple`	5.68	1.85	3.09	6.77	3.90	0.99
`mips-pro`	5.23	1.70	2.74	9.85	4.52	1.08
`no-fuse`	5.65	2.34	2.92	5.95	4.34	1.00

Table 4. Performance results for `liv18` for different fusion strategies

Fusion Strategy	Cycle ($\times 10^9$)	L1D Misses ($\times 10^8$)	L2 Misses ($\times 10^7$)	L1 I Misses ($\times 10^4$)	Loads ($\times 10^9$)	Speedup over `no-fuse`
`ccfm`	3.77	2.14	2.33	4.52	1.55	1.46
`simple`	3.77	2.14	2.33	4.52	1.55	1.46
`mips-pro`	5.06	2.32	3.33	5.54	0.98	1.09
`no-fuse`	5.51	2.62	4.08	5.13	1.18	1.00

2000. We compare results from applying our strategy (`ccfm`) with three different strategies: the `simple` strategy always fuses loops that share some common data, `mips-pro` is the fusion strategy chosen by the MIPSPro 7.3 compiler and `no-fuse` is the option of applying no fusion at all.

Results from `advect3d` using a $256 \times 256 \times 256$ data set is presented in Table 1. The results show that our strategy is able to achieve a 17% speedup over both `mips-pro` and `no-fuse`. Performance improvement of `ccfm` over `simple` is even more dramatic (46%). For `advect3d`, `ccfm` fuses all loops at the two outer levels but refrains from fusing all the innermost loops because it estimates the register pressure will exceed available resources on the target machine. `simple` fuses all loops at each nesting level and creates a large fused body for the inner loop. As a result, this version of the code incurs many register spills as indicated by the large number of issued loads in column 6 of Table 1. Although `simple` is able to achieve some locality in L1 and L2 cache and also the L1 instruction cache, the cost of register spills for this strategy outweighs its benefits. The peformance of `mips-pro` and `no-fuse` is almost identical in this case. Closer inspection of the generated code revealed that MIPSPro chose not to fuse any loops for `advect3d` because the data set was too large for the stack frame size for the target machine. For this reason, we ran another set of experiments with `advect3d` using a smaller ($128 \times 128 \times 128$) data set. Results from the second set of experiments are shown in Table 2. Again, `ccfm` performs significantly better than both `no-fuse` and `simple`. Although, the performance gains have somewhat diminished due to the smaller data set. The more interesting result from this set of experiments is the performance of the `mips-pro` strategy. `mips-pro` performs as poorly as `simple` in this case. We inspected the code generated by `mips-pro` and discovered that it created two separate fully fused loop nests from the 27 fusible loops in the program. In addition, it performed tiling on each fused loop nest. As it turned out the combination of fusion and tiling was not able to improve locality in the program. This is

Table 5. Performance results for mgrid for different fusion strategies

Fusion Strategy	Cycle ($\times 10^{10}$)	L1D Misses ($\times 10^{8}$)	L2 Misses ($\times 10^{7}$)	L1 I Misses ($\times 10^{5}$)	Loads ($\times 10^{9}$)	Speedup over no-fuse
ccfm	1.05	4.63	6.37	3.39	3.64	1.07
simple	1.02	4.53	6.27	3.31	3.59	1.11
mips-pro	1.02	4.53	6.27	3.26	3.59	1.11
no-fuse	1.13	5.14	6.86	3.74	3.74	1.00

indicated by the increased number of misses at all levels of the cache. These results demonstrate that indiscriminate fusion can indeed lead to performance degradation. Our fusion strategy, although less aggressive, achieves locality at both cache levels while keeping the register spill cost at a moderate level. Hence, we are able to achieve an overall performance improvement across all levels of the memory hierarchy.

Results from our experiments with erlebacher are presented in Table 3. Again ccfm is able to outperform both simple and no-fuse through improved locality in the L2 cache. However, in this case mips-pro does as well as ccfm. For erlebacher, mips-pro fuses loops that our fusion strategy rejects because of lost reuse in the outer loops. However, as was the case with advect3d, the MIPSPro compiler applies tiling to these fused loops and in this case tiling is able to recover some of the lost reuse due to over fusion. Thus there is no significant increase in the number of L2 cache misses for mips-pro.

In Table 4 we present results from liv18. We observe the most significant performance improvement for this kernel. This is not surprising since all the work in liv18 is spent in three fusible loop nests. For liv18, our fusion strategy chooses to fuse all three loops all the way through which is equivalent to the simple strategy. Thus in Table 4 the rows corresponding to ccfm and simple are identical. We notice that fusing all the way through does cause some extra loads. However, this loss is more than offset by the benefits obtained from reduced L2 cache misses. mips-pro does not do too well on liv18. It decided to fuse only two of the three fusible loops in the kernel leaving some unexploited reuse in the third loop nest. It was not totally clear as to why mips-pro decided not to fuse the third loop nest. We speculate that it may have been due to loop alignment issues. The loop nests in liv18 need to be aligned before they can be fused. For LoopTool we use the Omega code generator which inserts guards within fused loop nests after alignment. On the other hand, it appears that MIPSPro prefers to peel off iterations of the loop nest that fall outside the alignment range. It is possible that because of this approach the third loop nest was left unfused. Thus the performance improvement we observe over mips-pro may not be due to an improved profitability model but rather due to a limitation in their implementation of the fusion algorithm.

The final benchmark we look at is mgrid. The experimental results from mgrid are presented in Table 5. In this case, although ccfm achieves better performance than no-fuse it is beaten by both mips-pro and simple. mgrid poses a similar situation as advect3d for our fusion strategy. Because ccfm expects lost reuse in

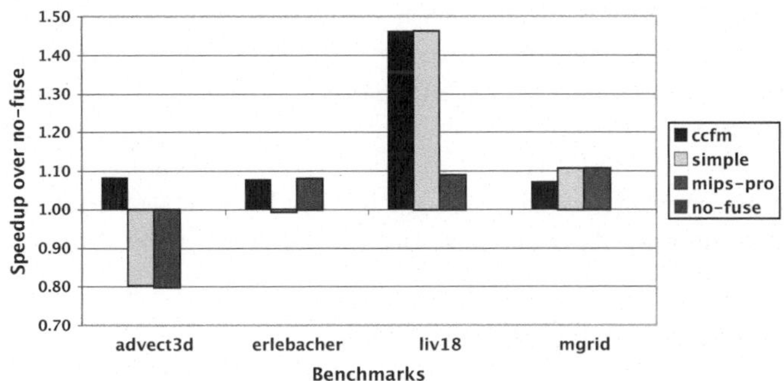

Fig. 2. Performance improvement for different fusion strategies

outer levels it chooses to perform only a two level fusion leaving the innermost loops alone. On the other hand, `mips-pro` decided to fuse all the way through and then apply both tiling and outer loop unrolling to the fused loop nests. This combined transformation strategy improved locality for L2 cache and also reduced the number of loads for the program.

We summarize the results of our experiments in Fig 2. The experimental results presented in this section expose several key aspects for profitable loop fusion. The results show that overly aggressive fusion can indeed lead to performance loss through increased register pressure and lost reuse at outer levels of loop nests. In some cases, this loss can be mitigated by applying transformations such as tiling and unroll-and-jam. However, there are cases when these additional transformations are unable to help improve the overall performance. Thus the interaction between fusion and other transformations, particularly tiling is critical in improving memory performance. To address this issue, we have begun work on a more complex model discussed in the concluding section.

5 Accuracy of the Cache Miss Prediction Model and Its Implications

The cache miss model presented in Section 3.1 makes the assumption that memory accesses between any two reused references are essentially random. Although, this scheme works well when integrated with the rest of our framework it is important to evaluate the accuracy of the model on its own. To validate our model, we performed a series of experiments with a set of synthetic benchmarks and real-world applications [11]. In this section, we provide a brief summary of the experimental results and discuss their implications.

Experimental results from [11] revealed that our model is able to predict an *upper bound* for the conflict miss rate with reasonable accuracy. However, the predicted upper bound for the miss rate can sometimes be significantly greater than the actual miss rate of the program. Although a conservative estimate suffices for profitability estimates of loop fusion it is important to consider its implications on other transformations. A key transformation for improving memory performance in numerical applications is tiling. If we use our conflict miss model with tiling then the *effective cache capacity* would directly determine the tile size for a given loop nest. In that case, a conservative estimate would imply choosing a smaller tile size which in turn may lead to lost reuse in inner loops. Therefore, in such situations we need a cache miss model that is able to predict the cache miss rate more accurately. We are currently working on such a model. Our new model incorporates the effects of tiling and also considers the layout of arrays in memory.

6 Conclusions and Future Work

In this paper, we have presented a model for estimating the profitability of loop fusion and a strategy for parameterizing the model for use in an empirical tuning framework. Preliminary experiments in Section 4 suggest that our strategy can help make the right fusion choices on a set of applications. However, to make a stronger statement about the effectiveness of our approach the model has to be evaluated on a large class of benchmarks and a variety of platforms. Our future plans include a complete implementation of the model in our empirical tuning framework and a more thorough evaluation on a large benchmark suite.

Experimental results from Section 4 also emphasize the need for considering interactions between optimizations for overall improvement in memory performance. In particular, there are complex interactions between tiling and fusion that need to be considered to make fusion profitable. By merging loop bodies fusion can increase the working set size of a loop nest and force the selection of a smaller tile size. A smaller tile size might result in lost reuse in the inner loops. If arrays are not aligned at cache line boundaries (generally the case) then a smaller tile size may result in lost reuse in outer loops as well. In such cases, it may be profitable to tile the two loop nests separately. We are currently working on a profitability model that considers these complex interactions between tiling and fusion to improve overall memory performance. In addition, this model employs a more accurate estimator for *effective cache capacity* that takes the effects of tiling and array allocation strategies into account.

References

1. S. Carr. *Memory-Hierarchy Management.* PhD thesis, Dept. of Computer Science, Rice University, Sept. 1992.
2. A. Darte. On the complexity of loop fusion. In *PACT '99: Proceedings of the 1999 International Conference on Parallel Architectures and Compilation Techniques*, 1999.
3. C. Ding and K. Kennedy. Resource-constrained loop fusion. Technical report, Dept. of Computer Science, Rice University, Oct. 2000.
4. C. Ding and K. Kennedy. Improving effective bandwidth through compiler enhancement of global cache reuse. In *International Parallel and Distributed Processing Symposium*, San Francisco, CA, Apr. 2001. (Best Paper Award.).
5. G. Gao, R. Olsen, V. Sarkar, and R. Thekkath. Collective loop fusion for array contraction. In *Proceedings of the Fifth Workshop on Languages and Compilers for Parallel Computing*, New Haven, CT, Aug. 1992.

6. M. D. Hill and A. J. Smith. Evaluating associativity in cpu caches. *IEEE Trans. Comput.*, 38(12), 1989.
7. K. Kennedy. Fast greedy weighted fusion. In *ICS '00: Proceedings of the 14th international conference on Supercomputing*, 2000.
8. K. Kennedy and K. S. McKinley. Maximizing loop parallelism and improving data locality via loop fusion and distribution. In *Proceedings of the Sixth Workshop on Languages and Compilers for Parallel Computing*, Portland, OR, Aug. 1993.
9. A. Lim and M. Lam. Cache optimizations with affine partitioning. In *Proceedings of the Tenth SIAM Conference on Parallel Processing for Scientific Computing*, Portsmouth, Virginia, Mar. 2001.
10. K. S. McKinley, S. Carr, and C.-W. Tseng. Improving data locality with loop transformations. *ACM Transactions on Programming Languages and Systems*, 18(4):424–453, July 1996.
11. A. Qasem and K. Kennedy. Evaluating a model for cache conflict miss prediction. Technical report, Dept. of Computer Science, Rice University, Oct. 2005.
12. A. Qasem, K. Kennedy, and J. Mellor-Crummey. Automatic tuning of whole applications using direct search and a performance-based transformation system. In *Proceedings of the Los Alamos Computer Science Institute Second Annual Symposium*, Santa Fe, NM, Oct. 2004.
13. Y. Song, R. Xu, C. Wang, and Z. Li. Data locality enhancement by memory reduction. In *Proceedings of the 15th ACM International Conference on Supercomputing*, Sorrento, Italy, June 2001.
14. S. Verdoolaege, M. Bruynooghe, G. Jenssens, and F. Catthoor. Multi-dimensional incremental loop fusion for data locality. In *Proceedings of the IEEE International Conference on Application Specific Systems, Architectures, and Processors*, June 2003.
15. M. E. Wolf and M. Lam. A data locality optimizing algorithm. In *Proceedings of the SIGPLAN '91 Conference on Programming Language Design and Implementation*, Toronto, Canada, June 1991.

Optimizing Matrix Multiplication with a Classifier Learning System*

Xiaoming Li and María Jesús Garzarán

Department of Computer Science
University of Illinois at Urbana-Champaign
{xli15, garzaran}@cs.uiuc.edu
http://polaris.cs.uiuc.edu

Abstract. Compilers have been very successful on automating the process of program optimization, but there is still a significant difference in performance between the code generated by the compiler and the hand-optimized code. Library generators such as ATLAS, SPIRAL, and FFTW address this problem by using empirical search to find the parameter values of certain optimization such as degree of unroll. We have recently developed a generator of sorting routines. Sorting differs from the algorithms implemented by other library generators in that performance of sorting depends not only on the target platform but also on the characteristics of the input data. In our work we used a classifier learning system to generate sorting routines that are capable of adapting to the input data. In this paper we follow a similar approach and use a classifier learning system to generate high performance libraries for matrix-matrix multiplication. Our library generator produces matrix multiplication routines that use recursive layouts and several levels of tiling. Our approach is to use a classifier learning system to search in the space of the different ways to partition the input matrices the one that performs the best. As a result, our system will determine the number of levels of tiling and tile size for each level depending on the target platform and the dimensions of the input matrices.

1 Introduction

Compilers have been very successful on automating the process of program optimization, but there is still a significant difference in performance between the code generated by the compiler and the hand-optimized code. The growing complexity of the architectural features of modern processors makes it very difficult to optimize performance. An approach that some researchers have followed is to use library generators to generate high performance code for some specific problem domains.

Examples of well-known library generators are ATLAS [30], PHiPAC [4], FFTW [11] and SPIRAL [33]. ATLAS and PHiPAC generate linear algebra routines and focus the optimization process on the matrix multiplication routine. During installation, the parameter values of a matrix multiplication implementation, such as tile size and

* This work was supported in part by the National Science Foundation under grant CCR 01-21401 ITR; by DARPA under contract NBCH30390004; and by gifts from INTEL and IBM. This work is not necessarily representative of the positions or policies of the Army or Government.

E. Ayguadé et al. (Eds.): LCPC 2005, LNCS 4339, pp. 121–135, 2007.

amount of loop unrolling, that deliver the best performance are identified using empirical search. This search proceeds by generating different versions of matrix multiplication that only differ in the parameter value that is being sought. An almost exhaustive search is used to find the best parameter values. The other two systems mentioned above, SPIRAL and FFTW, generate signal processing libraries.

Recently we have built a library generator for sorting [17,18]. Sorting is different from the algorithms implemented by the previous library generators in that performance of sorting depends not only on the target platform but also on characteristics of the input data, which are only known at runtime. In the work presented in [18] we used a classifier learning system to generate algorithms capable of adapting to the input data. In the work discussed herein, we follow a similar approach and use a classifier learning system to generate high performance libraries for matrix-matrix multiplication (MMM). Our library generator generates MMM routines that use recursive layouts [7,8] and several levels of tiling. Our approach is to use a classifier learning system to search among all the different ways to partition the input matrices, the one that performs the best. The MMM routine generated with our classifier learning system uses different levels of tiling and tile sizes based on the dimensions of the matrices and the architectural features of the target machine.

ATLAS is a library generator that also produces a MMM routine. The difference between our approach and the one followed by ATLAS is that we use recursive layouts to place the blocks in consecutive memory locations and focus the search on levels of tiling and size of each tile. ATLAS does not search for the number of levels of tiling. In fact, ATLAS only searches for the tile size for a single level of tiling, although a second level of tiling can be implemented [1]. Also, notice that the performance delivered by ATLAS in some platforms is still far from the one delivered by the vendor provided libraries [36], mainly because ATLAS does not take into account all the levels of the memory hierarchy and does not take advantage of some optimizations like prefetching. Our objective is to reduce the performance gap between the hand-optimized code and the automatic generated code by extending the search to consider parameters ignored by ATLAS.

When using a single level of tiling, it has been shown that a model can predict the best value of the tile size almost as well as the empirical search of ATLAS by simply taking into account certain cache parameters [35,36]. However, when tiling for the different levels of the memory hierarchy, the size of the matrices becomes important. If the matrices are not a multiple of the tile sizes, we need to use padding or cleanup code. With padding, the size of the matrices is increased with additional rows or columns of zeros. Arithmetic operations are usually blindly performed on them. With cleanup, additional code (which is usually suboptimal) is executed to multiply the remainder rows or columns. With recursive layouts, padding is the method usually preferred. Given the large sizes of the second and third level of caches of current machines (6 to 8 MB), padding can represent a significant overhead if the tile sizes are computed without taking into account the matrix sizes. On the other hand, choosing the tile sizes based on the matrix sizes and disregarding the cache sizes will result in poor cache utilization. In addition, choosing the number of levels of tiling based on the number of caches of the machine may result in slow-downs. In some platforms it is better to use a single level of tiling because additional levels of tiling introduce additional instructions such as branches that may execute slowly.

We compared the MMM routine generated using a classifier learning system with the MMM routine generated by ATLAS when multiplying matrices of sizes 1000 to 5000. Our preliminary results show that the MMM routine generated using the approach we follow in this paper runs always faster than ATLAS in a Sun UltraSparc III by an average 18%. In the case of Intel Pentium Xeon, our routine is almost always faster than ATLAS by an average 5%. However, ATLAS runs on average 14% faster than our routine in Intel Itanium II. Our experiments also show that padding is important to obtain high performance, and we plan to implement more sophisticated padding strategies to improve the performance of the generated library.

The paper is organized as follows. Section 2 revises some of the compiler optimizations that are applied to MMM. Section 3 presents the partition primitives that will be used by the classifier learning system, which is presented in Section 4. Section 5 presents our experimental setup and preliminary results. Section 6 presents related work, and finally, Section 7 concludes.

2 Matrix-Matrix Multiplication

In this Section we present an overview of an automatic tiling and discuss copying and recursive layouts in the context of matrix-matrix multiplication.

A naïve implementation of matrix-matrix multiplication is shown in Figure 1-(a). Usually this code runs slowly because of the poor utilization of cache memories. A transformation used to increase cache locality is loop tiling. This transformation was first introduced by McKellar and Coffman [19] and discussed in the context of compilers by Abu-Sufah [3] and later by Wolfe [32]. Figure 1-(b) shows the code for a tiled matrix-matrix multiplication using a square tile of size $NB \times NB$. This tile size is a parameter that must be chosen to minimize capacity misses. However, when the matrices are large each row (in a row major layout) can be in a different physical page and then TLB misses can occur. This problem can be avoided if the tile selection considers the number of entries in the TLB in conjunction with the cache size [20]. In any case, to reduce conflict and TLB misses, tiling is usually used in combination with copying [16,28] where the elements of each $NB \times NB$ submatrix are copied into contiguous memory locations.

Tiling has been extensively considered in the literature when applied to a single cache level [9,16,21,25,35]. However, when tiling for a single level of cache, we do not exploit all the cache levels. For example, Figure 2-(a), shows the order in which the submatrices of A, B and C are accessed when executing the code of Figure 1-(b). Each iteration of the outermost loop (j) will traverse the 16 blocks of matrix A. Unfortunately, if matrix A is large, it will not fit in the second level cache. Therefore each j iteration will have to bring all the A blocks back to the second and first cache level. A solution to this problem is to apply another level of tiling [25,34].

Suppose that we apply another level of tiling to the code in Figure 1-(b) by adding three additional loops with the same order JIK. The outer loops would operate on blocks consisting of 2×2 tiles so that the blocks of matrix A will be traversed in the

```
for (j = 0; j < M; j++)
  for (i = 0; i < N; i++)
    for (k = 0; k < K; k++)
      C[i][j]+=A[i][k] * B[k][j]
```

(a) Naïve implementation

```
for (j = 0; j < M; j+ = NB)
  for (i = 0; i < N; i+ = NB)
    for (k = 0; k < K; k = +NB)
      for (jj = 0; jj < j + NB; jj++)
        for (ii = 0; ii < i + NB; ii++)
          for (kk = 0; kk < k + NB; kk++)
            C[ii][jj]+=A[ii][kk] * B[kk][jj]
```

(b) Tiled implementation

Fig. 1. Matrix Multiplication Code

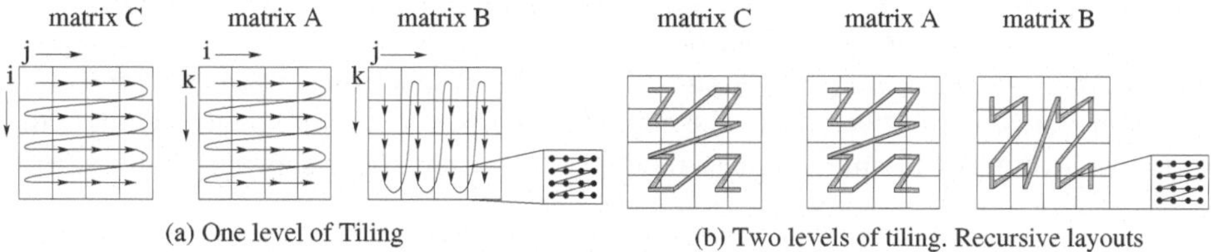

(a) One level of Tiling

(b) Two levels of tiling. Recursive layouts

Fig. 2. Memory layouts for tiled matrix-matrix multiplication. (a)- One level of tiling and block data layout. (b)- Two levels of tiling and recursive layout.

order shown in Figure 2-(b). The blocks of the second level of tiling are no longer consecutive in memory and, as a result, these accesses can result in cache conflicts and TLB misses [22]. To avoid this problem, nonlinear array layout or recursive layouts together with tiling have been used [7,8]. The idea is to copy these blocks into consecutive memory locations. These array layouts are described as based on quadtrees [10] or on space-filling-curves[15,23,27]. Instances of this family are familiar in parallel computing under the names Morton ordering and Hilbert Ordering. The layout shown in Figure 2-(b) for matrix A is known as Z-Morton. These recursive layouts were shown to deliver high performance [7,8], but some considerations need to be taken into account in their implementation:

- These nonlinear layouts can be applied recursively down to the level of individual matrix elements [10]. However, Chatterjee et al. [8] showed that this was counter-productive, and that it is better to follow a recursive layout only until the tile fits in the cache.
- These recursive layouts require that for a matrix of size $M \times N$ and a tile of size $tm \times tn$, the following equations be satisfied: $\frac{M}{tm} = \frac{N}{tn} = 2^d$. Sometimes it is necessary to add padding to the matrix in order to satisfy this equation. The general idea is to select the appropriate tile $tm \times tn$ for the cache of the machine, insert a zero padding and perform the arithmetic operations on the zero padding.

3 Partition Primitives

The library generator used in this study produces a matrix-matrix multiplication (MMM) routine that computes $C = \alpha AB + \beta C$, where A, B and C are matrices of dimensions $M \times K$, $K \times N$ and $M \times N$ respectively. The generated MMM routine uses multilevel tiling and recursive layouts as discussed above. The routine first copies the original matrices from row or column major layout to the recursive layout. Then, it multiplies the matrices and transforms the resulting C matrix back to the row or column major layout. The copy and multiplication procedures are determined by the number of levels of tiling and tile sizes. These values will be selected using empirical search as discussed below. This Section describes the partition primitives which will be used by the search procedure to determine the best number of levels of tiles and tile sizes for the dimensions of the input matrices and target architecture. Before explaining the primitive partitions, we briefly describe the procedures for copying and padding.

We denote the matrix dimensions at level i as M_i, N_i and K_i, where i ranges from 1 to the $number\_of\_levels\_of\_tiling$. If the matrices at level i are partitioned with factors pm_i, pn_i and pk_i, the dimensions of each submatrix in the next recursion level will be $M_{i-1} = \frac{M_i}{pm_i}$, $N_{i-1} = \frac{N_i}{pn_i}$ and $K_{i-1} = \frac{K_i}{pk_i}$ respectively. The partition factors determine how the sub-blocks must be copied from row (or column) major layout to the recursive layout. An example of these recursive layouts has been shown in Figure 2-(b).

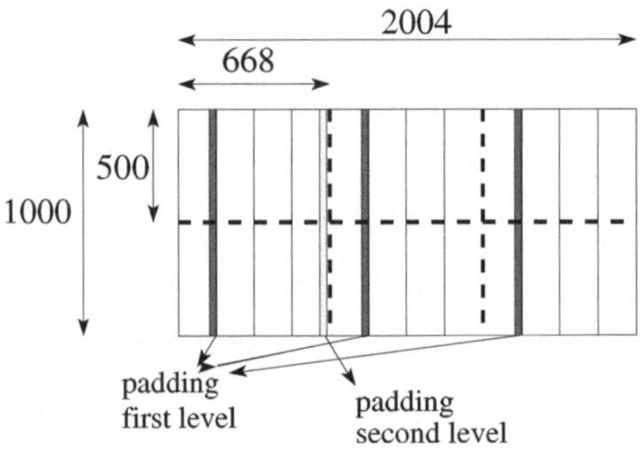

Fig. 3. Example of padding

When the factors in the partition vector are not a divisor of the matrix dimensions we need to use padding. For example suppose A is a matrix of 2000×1000, and we divide it first by (3,2) and then (4,1). Since 3 is not a divisor of 2000, we need to add padding so that we can divide the matrix in exactly 3 pieces. Each resulting submatrix will be of size 667×500. Now, the 667 elements of the X dimension need to be divided by 4. Since 4 is not a divisor of 667, we need to pad each submatrix, and make them to be 668. Thus, we end up with a matrix of size 2004×500. We have 4 additional columns of zeroes which will be blindly multiplied. The example is shown in Figure 3.

Next, we describe the partition primitives that we use in this work.

1. `Partition by Block`(**PB**)
   This primitive specifies the tile or block size. It has three parameters, which are the block size for each M, N and K dimension. So, consider $M = 100, N = 100, K = 40$. If we want tiles of sizes 50, 50, and 20 for the dimensions M, N, and K, respectively, we would specify this as follows `Partition By Block (50,50,20)`.

The `Partition By Block` primitive will compute the partition factors (pm,pn, pk) as follows:

$$pm = \lfloor \frac{m}{bm} \rfloor, pn = \lfloor \frac{n}{bn} \rfloor, pk = \lfloor \frac{k}{bk} \rfloor$$

The `Partition by Block` primitive allows to specify tiles of any size, not only square tiles.

2. `Partition by Size`(PS)
This partition primitive specifies the size of a block and partitions the different dimensions of the matrix until the resulting submatrices are equal or smaller than the size of the specified block. The primitive guarantees that the ratio between the dimensions is kept constant. The primitive allows the specification of the dimensions to be partitioned. It has four parameters. The first three parameters specify if a given dimension M, N and K needs to be partitioned. The fourth parameter specifies the block size. The algorithm used by this primitive is shown below.

```
Input Parameters:
   m,n,k: input matrix dimensions
   muse, nuse, kuse: boolean variables indicating the
                           dimensions to be partitioned
    size: the block size

begin
    maxratio = MIN(m,n,k)/2
    for(ratio=maxratio; ratio ≥ 2;ratio--){
       if(muse) tmpm=⌈m/ratio⌉
       if(nuse) tmpn=⌈n/ratio⌉
       if(kuse) tmpk=⌈k/ratio⌉
       tmpsize=tmpm * tmpk + tmpk * tmpn + tmpm * tmpn
       if(tmpsize ≤ size)
          break;
    }
    if(muse) pm = ratio;
    if(nuse) pn = ratio;
    if(kuse) pk = ratio;
end
```

Notice that most of the previous research on recursive layouts works by dividing each dimension by half. The `Partition by Size` primitive is a generalization of the `divide by half` strategy which can be implemented by setting $muse = nuse = kuse = true$ and $size = \frac{m*k+k*n+m*n}{4}$. In some studies, the recursion is carried down all the way to the individual elements [10,12]. The work in [12] showed that this strategy resulted in minimum number of cache misses. Unfortunately in this case minimizing the number of misses does not necessarily results in better performance, because of the additional instructions that need to be executed. In fact, the work by Chaterjee et al. [7,8] showed that stopping the recursion at tiles of the appropriate size returned better performance. In this paper, when generating the kernel routine for the MMM we will follow the approach of Chatterjee et al.(Section 5).

4 Classifier Learning System

To build a high performance library we need to determine how the input matrices should be partitioned along the M, N and K dimensions. The best partitioning is a function of architectural features such as number of caches and size of each cache and the dimensions of the input matrices. Choosing the correct partition is hard. For some machines, we need to apply a single level of tiling, since the overhead of the additional instructions executed when more levels of tiling are applied results in lower performance. Even when tiling for a single level of cache we need to decide whether to tile for L1 or L2 [2,35]. When tiling for L2 and L3, it is important to take into account the dimensions of the matrices. Since L2 and L3 tend to be large (sometimes 6 or 8 MB), when a dimension of the matrix is not a multiple of the tile size, the amount of padding can be substantial.

We plan to use the partition primitives described in the previous Section as the building blocks to generate a MMM library. By combining the different primitives and selecting different parameter values, the space of the different algorithms that we can generate is very large. As a result, exhaustive search is unfeasible. Our approach is to use a classifier learning system [6,24,31] to search the space of possible algorithms. The main reason to use a classifier learning system is that with this mechanism input characteristics can be used to create a table with the best partitioning parameters. This table can be used at runtime to enable dynamic adaptation.

A classifier system consists of a set of rules. Each rule has two parts, a condition and an action. A condition is a string that encodes certain characteristics of the input, where each element of the string can have three possible values: “0”, “1”, and “*” (don’t care). Similarly, the input characteristics are encoded with a bit string of the same length. If i and c are the input bit string and the condition string respectively, we can define the function $match(i, c)$ as follows:

$$match(i, c) = \begin{cases} true, \ \forall(j) i_j = c_j \vee c_j =' *', wherej = length\_of\_the\_bit\_string \\ false, \ otherwise \end{cases}$$

If there is only one $match(i, c)$ which is $true$, the action corresponding to the condition bit string c is selected. However, for a given input several matches are possible. In this case, we will choose one action among all the rules that match. The mechanism for the selection is explained below (in Section 4.3).

Next we explain how the classifier learning system is tuned for each platform and input

4.1 Representation

Encoding of the Rule Condition. The input characteristic that will determine the parameter values of the partition primitives is the dimension of the matrices. Thus, we will encode possible values of the dimensions of the matrices A, B and C in the condition of the rules.

Action of the Rule. The action part will be a list of the partition primitives `partition by size (PS)` or `partition by block (PB)` with their corresponding parameter values. For example, an action will have the shape `(PS param-list (PB param-list))`, where `param-list` is the list of parameters. This action will return a *single function* that will decompose the input matrices of size $M \times N \times K$ into submatrices of size $M' \times N' \times K'$, that result from applying first the `PS` primitive and them the `PB` primitive.

Notice that each action, even if it contains several partition primitives correspond to a single level of tiling. To apply several levels of tiling, we can recursively invoke the rule set of the classifier system with the size of the resulting submatrices. The recursion will finish when the number of levels of tiling has already reach the maximum number of levels allowed, or when the size of the submatrices is within a predefined range.

4.2 Training

During the training process we generate matrices of different sizes. Given a training input, we have a match rule set, which are the set of rules where the condition matches the bit string that encodes the input characteristics. We use a XCS classifier learning system as the one in [6,31]. In this type of classifier systems, each rule has two attributes. The first attribute is the fitness. The fitness is an estimation of the performance of this rule on the inputs that match the associated condition. The second attribute is the accuracy. The accuracy measures the confidence of the fitness attribute in predicting the correct performance.

In our approach we use a multi-step classifier system, since the output of an invocation can be used as the input for the next invocation. This system works as follows. The first time we invoke the rule set with a training input we have a match rule set. All the actions in the matching rules are the set of strategies that can be used to partition the input matrices. During the training process, all the actions in the matching rules are applied. Thus, given an input of size $M \times \mathbb{N} \times K$, the result will be submatrices of sizes $M_i' \times \mathbb{N}_i' \times K_i'$, where $i = 1..number\_of\_matching\_rules$. Each of the $M_i' \times \mathbb{N}_i' \times K_i'$ generated outputs can be used as the input to the next invocation to the learning classifier system. The system, as explained above, will stop when the maximum level of calls is reached or when the size of the submatrices is within a specified range. At the end, we have many different partition strategies, each of them blocking the matrices with tiles of different sizes, and possibly different levels of tiling. We generate the MMM routine for each partition strategy and measure the execution time. Based on the results obtained, we update the fitness and accuracy of all matching rules used to generate each of the MMM routines. The algorithm is shown in Figure 4.

To generate new conditions and actions, transformations such as mutation and crossover applied in genetic algorithms [13,18] are also used here. MOre details about the XCS classifier learning system that we use in this work can be found in [6,31].

4.3 Runtime

At the end of the training phase we have a tuned rule set. At runtime, the bit string encoding the input characteristics will be used to extract all the rules whose condition matches the input. Among all these rules, the one selected will depend on a function that rewards low execution time and penalizes low accuracy. The runtime overhead includes the computation of the input bit string, and the scan of the rule set to select the best one.

We train the classifier system to learn a set of rules that cover the space of the possible input parameter values, discover the conditions that better divide the input space and tune the actions to learn the best partition scheme based on the input characteristics.

Multi_Step_Classifier_Learning
Inputs:
  M,N,K: dimensions of the input matrices
  l: current level of recursion
Outputs:
  pm_i, pn_i, pk_i, i=[0..max-num-levels]: partition factors
  $exec$: execution time
begin
P= variable that contains the partition factors —pm_i, pn_i, pk_i, i=[0..max-num-levels]
Encode M,N,K into the bit string $\overrightarrow{in}$
$mset = \varnothing$
for each rule r
  $\overrightarrow{rcond}$ = condition of r
  if $match(\overrightarrow{in}, \overrightarrow{rcond})$
    add r to $mset$
while ($mset \neq \varnothing$)
  extract r from $mset$
  act= action part in r
  pm_i, pn_i, pk_i= result of applying act on M, N, K
  Update P with the new pm_i, pn_i, pk_i
  M', N', K'= result of applying pm_i, pn_i, pk_i on M, N, K
  if $notend$ then
    call $Multi\_Step\_Classifier\_Learning$ (M', N', K',$l + 1$)
  else
    Run matrix multiply with M, N, K using P
    Measure execution time $exec$
  Use $exec$ to update $fitness$ and $accuracy$ of r
  return exec
end

Fig. 4. Classifier learning algorithm

5 Experiments

In this section we evaluate our approach of using a classifier learning system to optimize a MMM routine. In Section 5.1 we discuss the environmental setup that we use for the evaluation and in Section 5.2 we present performance results.

5.1 Environmental Setup

We evaluated our approach on three different platforms: Sun UltraSparc III, Intel Itanium 2, and Intel Xeon. Table 1 lists for each platform the main architectural

Table 1. Test Platforms. (1) Intel Xeon has a 8KB trace cache instead of a L1 instruction cache. (2) Intel Itanium2 has a L3 cache of 6MB.

	Sun	Intel	Intel
CPU	UltraSparcIII	Itanium 2	P4 Intel Xeon
Frequency	750MHz	1.5GHz	3GHz
L1d/L1i Cache	64KB/32KB	16KB/16KB	8KB/12KB (1)
L2 Cache	1MB	256KB (2)	512KB
Memory	4GB	8GB	2GB
OS	SunOS5.8	RedHat7.2	RedHat3.2.3
Compiler	Workshop cc 5.0	gcc3.3.2	gcc3.4.1
Options	-native -xO5	-O3	-O3

parameters, the operating system, the compiler and the compiler options used for the experiments.

To generate the MMM library we used the classifier learning system. We trained the classifier with the algorithm of Figure 4. The classifier determines the number of levels of tiling and the tile size for each matrix size. For the implementation of the MMM at the last level of tiling we used the kernel generated by ATLAS. ATLAS generates a MMM routine and uses empirical search to look for the best parameter values of certain compiler transformations such as tile size, loop unrolling and software pipelining [30,35,36]. The kernel in ATLAS produces code for a MMM routine with a single level of tiling and square tiles. Thus, in our MMM library the submatrices in the last level of tiling must also be square. We allow these submatrices to be in the range of 40 - 120, since this range cover most of the different values that ATLAS finds for current platforms [36]. ATLAS generates a single MMM routine and searches for the tile size that obtains the best performance results. In our system, the tile size of the last level is determined by the classifier learning system, but we use ATLAS to search for the rest of the other parameters for each tile size in the range 40 - 120. We limited the maximum number of levels of tiling to be 3, since current architectures have three or less caches, and our experiments showed that increasing the level of tiling beyond 3 resulted in less performance. Apart from this, after we determine the partitioning strategy, we need to copy the tiles to the corresponding recursive layout. In this work we use the Z-Morton layout, although in a longer study we could also search for the best layout. When the matrix is not a multiple of the tiling we insert padding, as shown in Figure 3. Padding can also be necessary to obtain a square tile at the last level of tiling.

To encode the size of the matrices, we used 13 bits per dimension. Since we have 3 dimensions $M \times N \times K$, we used a total of 39 bits. Initially we generated 1000 rules, and we randomly generated the condition and the action part of each rule. For the training we randomly generated matrices whose sizes were between 1000 and 5000. We did not specify any condition to end the training process. Instead, we let the training run for a certain amount of time. In the experiments reported here, we let it run for 1 week.

We compare the MMM routine generated by our classifier learning system with three different approaches:

- L1, where the MMM routine has a single level of tiling.
- L2, where the MMM routine has two levels of tiling.
- ATLAS.

To make a fair comparison with L1 and L2 approaches we used ATLAS to generate the kernel of the MMM routine. In both cases we used the same copying strategy and padding as the one used in the MMM routine generated using the classifier. For the L1 approach we used the tile size that ATLAS found to be the best. For the L2 approach we used the value found by ATLAS for the first level of tiling. For the second level of tiling we chose the size so that $Tile2 = K \times Tile1$. We selected K so that $Tile2$ is multiple of $Tile1$, and smaller than the value that results from resolving the inequality $3{*}Tile2^2 \leq CacheSize$. The exception is Sun UltraSparc III. This machine has a large L2 cache (1 MB) and selecting the $Tile2$ using the previous formula resulted in low performance, since padding represented a large overhead in some cases. We decided to select for the Sun UltraSparc a tile of size 1/3 of the computed value using the previous formulas. Table 2 shows the values used for each $Tile1$ and $Tile2$. In both L1 and L2 we allowed the $Tile1$ to vary within the value reported in the Table and $+/-10$. We varied the size of the $Tile1$ based on the matrix size to minimize the amount of padding.

Table 2. Tile Sizes

	UltraSparcIII	Itanium 2	P4 Intel Xeon
L1_Tile	68	120	60
L2_Tile	380	240	240

For ATLAS we used the code produced by the ATLAS Code Generator using empirical search. ATLAS can also use hand tuned BLAS routines. When ATLAS is installed these hand-coded routines are also executed and evaluated. However, since in this work we are only interested on the comparison on the MMM routine generated by ATLAS, we only used the code generator, without hand-coded code. Notice, that ATLAS can have a L2 Cache Blocking parameter by setting a variable called CacheEdge. For the ATLAS experiments, we set this variable to the appropriate value as reported in [1].

5.2 Experimental Results

Figure 5 presents the performance results of the four MMM routines described in the previous Section: L1, L2, Classifier and ATLAS. For the experiments we multiplied square matrices whose sizes vary from 1000 to 5000, in steps of 100.

The results vary from platform to platform. In the case of the Sun UltraSparc, Classifier is always the best. For this platform L2 is also better than ATLAS and L1. For Itanium 2, the code generated by ATLAS performs better than any of the other routines. Only in a few points the code generated by the Classifier is equal or better. For Intel

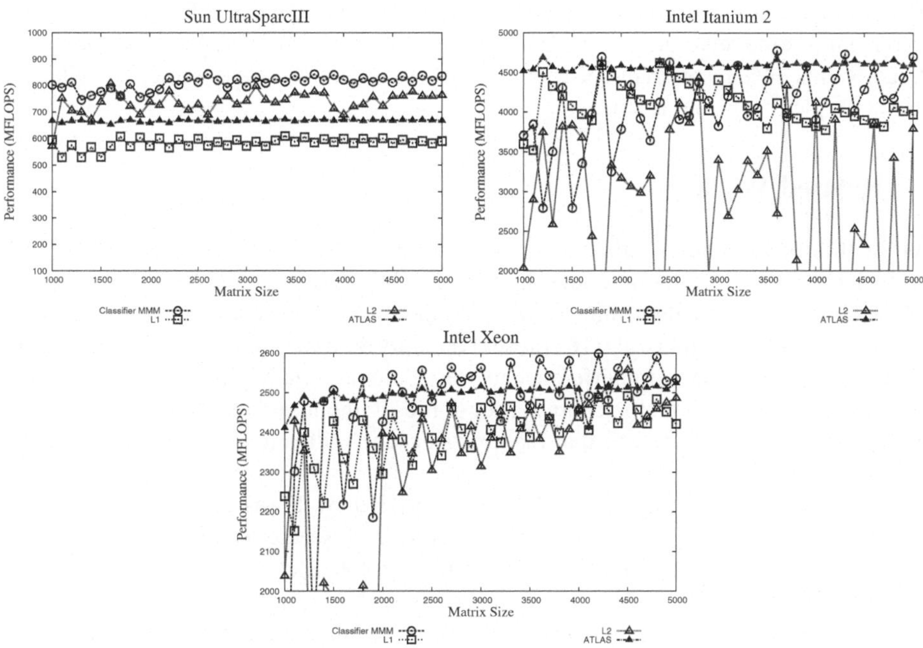

Fig. 5. Performance Results

Xeon, the code generated by the Classifier is usually the fastest, followed by that of ATLAS.

It has been stated [26] that tiling for L1 was enough and that multi-level tiling was not necessary. However, our results for Sun UltraSparc III show that multi-level tiling can improve performance over one level of tiling, since L2 and Classifier are always the best approaches for this platform. For the other two platforms it is not clear if multilevel tiling is better.

The performance results for the Intel platforms Itanium 2 and Xeon shows high variability in performance for the code generated by Classifier, L1 and L2. Since these 3 approaches use padding when the dimensions of the matrices are not multiple of the tile sizes, while ATLAS (whose performance is very stable) uses cleanup code, we think that the variability is due to the fact that the amount of padding changes for the different matrices being multiplied. We need to conduct further experiments to verify this. Also, in the future we plan to study different strategies to pad the matrices more efficiently. For example, we can concentrate all the padding at the end of the matrix, instead of distribute it in each tile, as we have done in the routine in this paper. We will also study the possibility of combining cleanup code with recursive layouts. If we find out that performance is highly dependent on the padding or clean up strategies, we can also search in this space.

Overall, our results, still preliminary, show that the MMM routine generated using the approach we follow in this paper runs always faster than the code generated by

ATLAS in a Sun UltraSparc III by an average of 18%. In the case of an Intel Pentium Xeon, our routine runs almost always faster than ATLAS by an average of 5%. However, ATLAS runs 14% faster than our routine in Intel Itanium II. In the future, we will also add more platforms to this study.

6 Related Work

As mentioned in Section 2 the use of loop tiling to increase cache locality has been extensively studied in the literature. Lam et al. [16], Coleman and McKinley [9] and others have developed algorithms to compute the optimal tile sizes when a single level of tiling is applied. Lam et al. [16] present an algorithm that selects the largest square tile that does not cause self interference misses. Coleman and McKinley [9]'s technique uses the Euclidean G.C.D. to generate a set of tiles without self-interference misses and from those tiles select the one that maximizes cache utilization and minimizes cross-interference misses.

Recursive matrix multiplication has been studied by Frens and Wise [10], Gustavson [14], Chatterjee et al. [8] and Frigo et al [12]. Chaterjee et al [8] shows that recursive layouts can significantly outperform traditional layouts for standard matrix-matrix multiplication. They also show that stopping the recursion when the tile fits into the cache results in better performance because it avoid some of the overheads due to recursive calls. Our approach is different than that of Chaterjee et al. [8]. We use machine learning techniques to search for the appropriate number of levels of tiling and tile sizes based on the dimensions of the input matrices and the architectural platform.

The ATLAS [30] generator uses empirical search to find the optimal tile size for a single level of tiling. However, the ATLAS' search problem is simpler than that of our system because ATLAS only considers the case where the same tile size is used for all the matrix sizes.

Finally, the approach that we present in this paper is also related to the problem of selecting from a set of candidate algorithms the one that performs best for a particular input and system. Systems that follow this approach are described by Li et al. [17,18], Brewer [5] and Thomas et al. [29]. In [17] we used the Winnow algorithm to select from three sequential sorting algorithms the one that performs best for a target system based on the entropy and number of keys of the input data, while in [18] we used a learning classifier system to generate composite sorting algorithms. Brewer [5] and Thomas et al. [29] use a framework for algorithm selection to generate parallel operations that adapt to the input and platform. In particular Thomas et al. [29] describe a general framework that can be easily extended with new operations and different empirical learning approaches.

7 Conclusions

In this paper we have generated a MMM routine using a classifier learning system. The MMM routine generated with our classifier learning system uses different levels of tiling and tile sizes based on the dimensions of the matrices and the architectural features of the machine where it is installed.

We compared the MMM routine generated using a classifier learning system with the MMM routine generated by ATLAS when multiplying matrices of sizes 1000 to 5000. Our preliminary results show that the MMM routine generated using the classifier runs always faster than ATLAS in a Sun UltraSparc III by an average of 18%. In the case of an Intel Pentium Xeon, our routine runs almost always faster than ATLAS by an average of 5%. However, ATLAS runs on average 14% faster than our routine in Intel Itanium II. Our experiments also show that padding is important to obtain high performance, and we plan to implement more sophisticated padding strategies to improve the performance of the generated library.

References

1. ATLAS home page. [Online]. http://math-atlas.sourceforge.net/errata.html#tuneCE.
2. ATLAS home page. [Online]. http://math-atlas.sourceforge.net/faq.html#NB80.
3. W. Abu-Sufah, D. Kuck, and D. Lawrie. On the Performance Enhancememt of Paging Systems through Program Analysis and Transformations. *IEEE Transactions on Computers*, 30(5):341–356, May 1981.
4. J. Bilmes, K. Asanovic, C. Chin, and J. Demmel. Optimizing Matrix Multiply using PHiPAC: A Portable, High-Performance, ANSI C Coding Methodology. In *Proc.of the 11th ACM International Conference on Supercomputing (ICS)*, July 1997.
5. E. A. Brewer. High-level Optimization via Automated Statistical Modeling. In *Proc. of the Symposium on Principles and Practice of Parallel Programming (PPoPP)*, pages 80–91, New York, NY, USA, 1995. ACM Press.
6. M. V. Butz and S. W. Wilson. An Algorithmic Description of XCS. *Lecture Notes in Computer Science*, 1996:253–272, 2001.
7. S. Chatterjee, V. V. Jain, A. R. Lebeck, S. Mundhra, and M. Thottethodi. Nonlinear Array Layouts for Hierarchical Memory Systems. In *International Conference on Supercomputing*, pages 444–453, 1999.
8. S. Chatterjee, A. R. Lebeck, P. K. Patnala, and M. Thotterhodi. Recursive array layouts and fast matrix multiplication. *IEEE Transactions on Parallel and Distributed Systems*, 13:1105–1123, 2002.
9. S. Coleman and K. s. McKinley. Tile Selection Using Cache Organization and Data Layout. In *Proc. of Int. Conference Programming Language Design and Implementation*, pages 279–290, June 1995.
10. J. Frens and D. Wise. Auto-blocking Matrix-Multiplication or Tracking BLAS3 Performance with Source Code. In *Proc. of the Intenational Symp. on Principles and Practice of Parallel programming (PPoPP)*, pages 206–216, June 1997.
11. M. Frigo. A Fast Fourier Transform Compiler. In *Proc. of Programing Language Design and Implementation*, 1999.
12. M. Frigo, C. E. Leiserson, H. Prokop, and S. Ramachandran. Cache-Oblivious Algorithms. In *Proc. of the Intenational Symp. on Foundations of Computer Science (FOCS)*, October 1999.
13. D. Goldberg. *Genetic Algorithms in Search, Optimization, and Machine Learning*. Addison-Wesley, Reading, MA, 1989.
14. F. G. Gustavson. Recursion Leads to Automatic Variable Blocking for Dense Linear-Algebra Algorithms. *IBM Journal of Research and Development*, 41(6):737–755, November 1997.
15. D. Hilbert. Über Stetige Abbildung einer Linie auf ein Flächenstrück. *Mathematische Annalen*, 38:459–60, 1891.

16. M. Lam, E. Rothberg, and M. E. Wolf. The Cache Performance and Optimizations of Blocked Algorithms. In *Proc. of the Int. conf. on Architectural Support for Programming Languages and Operating Systems (ASPLOS)*, pages 63–74, October 1991.
17. X. Li, M. J. Garzarán, and D. Padua. A Dynamically Tuned Sorting Library. In *In Proc. of the Int. Symp. on Code Generation and Optimization*, pages 111–124, 2004.
18. X. Li, M. J. Garzarán, and D. Padua. Optimizing Sorting with Genetic Algorithms. In *In Proc. of the Int. Symp. on Code Generation and Optimization*, pages 99–110, March 2005.
19. A. McKellar and E. Coffman. Organizing Matrices and Matrix Operations for Paged Memory Systems. *In Communications of the ACM*, 12(3):153–165, March 1969.
20. N. Mitchell, K. Hogstedt, L. Carter, and J. Ferrante. Quantifying the Multi-Level Nature of Tiling Interactions. *Int. Journal of Parallel Programming*, 26(6):641–670, June 1998.
21. P. Panda, H. Nakamura, N. Dutt, and A. Nicolau. Augmenting Loop Tiling with Data Alignment for Improved Cache Performance. *IEEE Trans. on Computers*, 48(2):142–149, February 1999.
22. N. Park, B. Hong, and V. Prasanna. Tiling, Block Data Layout, and Memory Hierarchy Performance. *IEEE Trans. on Parallel and Distributed Systems*, 14(7):640–654, July 2003.
23. G. Peano. Sur Une Curbe qui Remplit Toute une Aire Plaine. *Mathematische Annalen*, 36:157–160, 1890.
24. W. S. Pier Luca Lanzi and S. W. Wilson. *Learning Classifier Systems, From Foundations to Applications*. Springer-Verlag, 2000.
25. G. Rivera and C. Tseng. Data Transformations for Eliminating conflict Misses. In *Proc. of Int. Conference Programming Language Design and Implementation*, pages 38–49, June 1998.
26. G. Rivera and C. Tseng. Locality Optimizations for Multi-Level Caches. In *Proc. of IEEE Supercomputing*, November 1999.
27. H. Sagan. *Space-Filling Curves*. Springer-Verlag, 1994.
28. O. Temam, E. Granston, and W. Jalby. To Copy or Not to Copy: A Compile–Time Technique for Assessing When Data Copying Should be Used to Eliminate Cache Conflicts. In *Proc. of the ACM/IEEE Supercomputing Conference*, November 1993.
29. N. Thomas, G. Tanase, O. Tkachyshyn, J. Perdue, N. M. Amato, and L. Rauchwerger. A Framework for Adaptive Algorithm Selection in STAPL. In *Proc. of Symposium on Principles and Practice of Parallel Programming (PPoPP)*, pages 277–288, New York, NY, USA, 2005. ACM Press.
30. R. Whaley, A. Petitet, and J. Dongarra. Automated Empirical Optimizations of Sofware and the ATLAS Project. *Parallel Computing*, 27(1-2):3–35, 2001.
31. S. W. Wilson. Classifier Fitness Based on Accuracy. *Evolutionary Computation*, 3(2):149–175, 1995.
32. M. Wolfe. Iteration Space Tiling for Memory Hierarchies. In *Third SIAM Conference on Parallel Processing for Scientific Computing*, December 1987.
33. J. Xiong, J. Johnson, R. Johnson, and D. Padua. SPL: A Language and a Compiler for DSP Algorithms. In *Proc. of the International Conference on Programming Language Design and Implementation*, pages 298–308, 2001.
34. Q. Yi, V. Adve, and K. Kennedy. Transforming Loops To Recursion for Multi-Level Memory Hierarchies. In *Proc. of the Int. Conf. on Programming Language Design and Implementation (PLDI)*, pages 169–181, June 2000.
35. K. Yotov, X. Li, G. Ren, M. Cibulskis, G. DeJong, M. Garzarán, D. Padua, K. Pingali, P. Stodghill, and P. Wu. A Comparison of Empirical and Model-driven Optimization. In *Proc. of Programing Language Design and Implementation*, pages 63–76, June 2003.
36. K. Yotov, X. Li, G. Ren, M. J. Garzarán, D. Padua, K. Pingali, and P. Stodghill. Is Search Really Necessary to Generate a High Performance Blas? *In Proc. of the IEEE, special issue on Program Generation, Optimization, and Platform Adaptation*, 23:358–386, February 2005.

A Language for the Compact Representation of Multiple Program Versions

Sebastien Donadio[1,2], James Brodman[4], Thomas Roeder[5], Kamen Yotov[5], Denis Barthou[2], Albert Cohen[3], María Jesús Garzarán[4], David Padua[4], and Keshav Pingali[5]

[1] BULL SA
[2] University of Versailles St-Quentin-en-Yvelines
[3] INRIA Futurs
[4] University of Illinois at Urbana-Champaign
[5] Cornell University

Abstract. As processor complexity increases compilers tend to deliver suboptimal performance. Library generators such as ATLAS, FFTW and SPIRALz overcome this issue by empirically searching in the space of possible program versions for the one that performs the best. Empirical search can also be applied by programmers, but because they lack a tool to automate the process, programmers need to manually re-write the application in terms of several parameters whose best value will be determined by the empirical search in the target machine.

In this paper, we present the design of an annotation language, meant to be used either as an intermediate representation within library generators or directly by the programmer. This language that we call *X* represents parameterized programs in a compact and natural way. It provides an powerful optimization framework for high performance computing.

1 Introduction

Processors and machines in general are becoming increasingly complex and it has become extremely difficult even for experts to identify the fastest code sequences and the sequence of transformations that would optimize a given code sequence [6,7,29,30]. Furthermore, the best code for a particular machine is not necessarily the best for other machines, even when architectural differences are minute. Because of this complexity, compilers tend to deliver suboptimal performance and programmers make limited attempts at manual optimization. The result is that, in many cases, applications only use a small fraction of the target machine's power.

Clearly, an optimization methodology must be developed to improve the current situation. Recent studies have shown that a conceptually simple strategy, known as *empirical search*, can be a very effective optimization strategy. Empirical search consists of searching the space of possible program versions, executing each of them on the target machine, and selecting the fastest version.

Empirical search has been studied in the context of compiler transformations [14] and library generators. Thus, ATLAS [27], a linear algebra library generator, searches the space of possible forms of matrix-matrix multiplication routines. The different

E. Ayguadé et al. (Eds.): LCPC 2005, LNCS 4339, pp. 136–151, 2007.

forms vary in the size of tiles, degree of unrolling, and schedule of operations. The SPIRAL [20] and FFTW [10] signal processing library generators search a space consisting of implementations of different formulas representing the transform to be implemented. In the case of library generators, empirical search leads to performance improvements of an order of magnitude over good generic libraries that have not been tuned for a particular machine.

Empirical search can also be applied manually by a programmer. The idea would be for the programmer to write the application in terms of several parameters whose best value for a particular target machine is to be determined by empirical search. The parameters could specify values such as degree of unrolling of a given loop, tile size, etc. Parameters could also be used to represent completely different ways of carrying out a computation or part of a computation by numbering the different strategies and making this number one of the parameters whose value is to be identified.

In this paper we describe an ongoing effort to design and implement a new language, *X*, that could be used by programmers and also serve as an intermediate representation within of library generators. *X* is a language to represent parameterized programs naturally and compactly. Programmers would be able to program in *X* directly. Library generators could be organized as depicted in Figure 1 where it is assumed that functions of the library are designed in a very high level domain specific language which is analyzed, parameterized and translated into *X* programs. The availability of *X* would enable the reuse of a search engine across library generators.

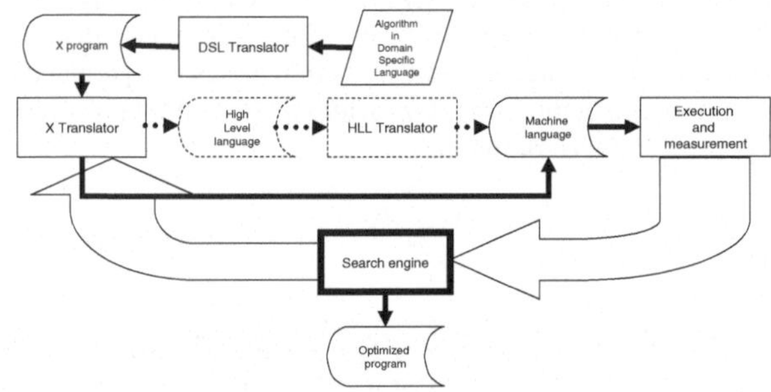

Fig. 1. Programming adaptive library generators

Our objective is to design *X* so that it is easy for the programmer to specify which transformations to apply, and change the order or the values of the transformations. The value of the parameters can be determined using empirical search orchestrated by a search engine which could use the target machine to evaluate the performance of each version of the program or rely on analytical models.

Since many programs spend most of their time executing loops, loop-based optimizations are the main focus of attention of the transformations we propose in this initial version of *X*, although non-loop transformations are also possible.

The output of processing *X* could be machine code, which would give programmers access to low-level optimizations. However, this approach would force the development of an *X* translator for each machine. To make *X* portable, high level language code could be generated so that each version of the code, that is, each point in the search space, would have to be fed to the native compiler. This compiler is in charge of the low-level optimizations such as register allocation and code generation of the executable code. In many occasions, we would like to disable many of the optimizations of the native compiler, but this is not always possible, because disabling all optimizations (-O0) could lead to poor performance. As a result, the transformations represented in *X* may or may not be preserved by the native compiler. The only solution to this problem is the search of the best combination of transformation at the source level that interacts with the low level compiler.

The rest of the paper is organized as follows: Section 2 lists the language requirements to ease the design of multiversion programs; Section 3 analyzes the multiversionning capabilities of macro or multistage languages with respect to these requirements; Section 4 presents the *X* language which combines multistage evaluation with reification and transformation pragmas; Section 5 details the design of the *X* language source-to-source compiler; Section 6 presents promising results on mimicking the code generator for DGEMM (matrix-matrix multiplication) in ATLAS [27]; and Section 7 compares the *X* language with related work and results, before we conclude and sketch future work.

2 Necessary Features of the Language

In this section, we discuss the features that must be exhibited by any language designed specifically for the compact representation of multiple code versions.

1. Elementary transformations. The first features that come to mind are constructs to generate multiple versions of a statement by applying *elementary* transformations to a statement. Elementary transformations are widely used transformations that cannot be conveniently cast in terms of other, simpler transformations. For program optimization, the targets of the transformations are usually compound statements and the transformations typically manipulate the order of execution and the control structure of the components. For sequences of assignment statements, typical elementary transformations are statement reordering, replication, and deletion. Loop transformations include unrolling, interchanging, stripmining, fusion, fission, and scalar replacement. We also consider loop tiling an elementary transformation although in theory it can be represented as a combination of stripmining and interchanging. Some loop scheduling transformations, such as software pipelining, are be considered to be elementary transformations. The reason is that, although scheduling can be represented as a sequence of simpler transformations, it is usually difficult to do so.

   Many of elementary transformations require input parameters, such as the degree of unrolling, tile size, and locations where the loop is to be split in the case of fission. Multiple versions of the initial statement are obtained by varying the values of these parameters.

   Elementary transformations are used in library generators during empirical search. Thus, ATLAS makes use of tiling, unrolling, and loop scheduling; FFTW makes use of scheduling; and SPIRAL applies loop unrolling.

2. Composition of transformations. Usually, the best version of a statement is the result of applying several elementary transformations. Thus, for example, ATLAS applies interchanging, tiling, unrolling and scheduling to the triply nested matrix-matrix multiplication loop during its empirical search for an optimal form of the loop. Therefore, our language should allow the application of multiple transformations to a single statement. An example of composite transformation is *unroll&jam* shown in Figure 2. This transformation can be implemented by applying an outer unroll followed by fusion of the two inner loops. Alternatively, unroll&jam can be implemented by first stripmining the outer loop, then interchanging the inner loop with the newly generated loop, and finally unrolling the innermost loop.

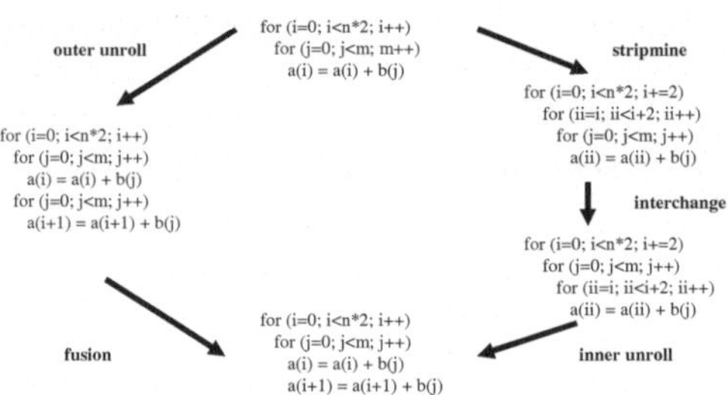

Fig. 2. Unroll & Jam

An important form of transformation composition is *conditional* composition, where a condition is used to select the transformation or the parameter value of a transformation. For example, consider a loop that is to be first stripmined and then the resulting inner loop unrolled. We may want to fully unroll the inner loop but only when the size of the strip is less than a certain threshold and partially unroll otherwise.

3. Procedural Abstraction. For composite transformations, it is convenient to have procedural abstractions to encapsulate new transformations and to avoid having to rewrite sequences of transformations that are applied more than once.
4. A mechanism to define new transformations. This extension mechanism enables the user to add new transformations that cannot be represented as composition of elementary transformations. In particular, programmers should be able to generate application-dependent transformations that take into account the semantics of the computation. The simplest way to represent a transformation is using *transformation rules* which are adequate to represent many transformations. The transformation rules consist of a code template followed by the form resulting after modification by the transformation. For instance, a stripmine transformation with a tile of size 4 could be defined as follows:

```
for (i = 0; i < N; i++) { <body> }
                ->
for (ii = 0; ii < (N/4)*4; ii += 4)
   for (i = ii; i < ii+4; i++) { <body> }

for (i = (N/4)*4; i < N; i++) { <body> };
```

Transforming the top code template into the bottom code is the stripmine transformation, where variable <body> represents the body of the loop to be stripmined.

As the example illustrates, transformation rules are quite convenient. However, since transformations rules are not universal, some transformations must be represented as a program written in, for example, a conventional programming language. In this case, the interface between the source language and the transformation routines must be clearly specified. This interface should contain the abstract syntax tree of the code to be transformed and perhaps other related information such as dependence graphs.

5. A mechanism to name statements. When applying a sequence of transformations, it is often necessary to apply one of the transformations to one of the components of the resulting code. For example, to implement unroll&jam unrolling is applied to the innermost loop resulting from stripmining. Therefore, the ability to name components and subcomponents of statements is necessary to enable the composition of transformations.

3 Macro Language

Perhaps the simplest approach to implement *X* would be to use a macro language. Assuming that the macro language statements are C-like statements preceded by the character `%` and that references to macro language variables are also preceded by `%`, Figure 3 shows an example where the `%for` statement produces the body of a loop unrolled `%d` times. That is, when the `%for` loop is executed, it produces the sequence of assignments: `s=s+a[i+0]; s=s+a[i+1]; ...;s=s+a[i+%d-1]`. In this this example we assumed that `%d` is a sub-multiple of 256 and, for that reason did not include the clean-up code needed to correctly handle the remainder of the `256` iterations of the original loop. Notice that `%d` in Figure 3 will be assigned a value at compile-time, and will usually be assigned several values in successive compilations during an empirical search for the best version of the program.

```
sum=0;
for (i=0;i<256;i+=%d) {
    %for (k=i; k<=i+(%d-1); k++)
        s = s + a[i+%k];
}
```

Fig. 3. Loop unroll using macro statements

An implementation based on macro language would produce a system that relies on generation rather than transformation. Thus, the construct of Figure 3 does not transform an initial loop but *generates* a loop with the body unrolled `%d` times. If the macro language includes procedures, it would be possible to write generation routines that accomplish the same objectives as any transformation. For example, we could conceivably develop an `%unroll-loop` routine that accepts the body of the loop, the index variable, and the degree of unrolling as parameters. These generation routines could be a convenient way to extend the base language with new parameterized statements.

In some cases it is preferable to use the generation approach so that the programmer can produce exactly the transformed code that he desires. For this reason, *X* includes a macro language. However, we have found that the generation approach has two disadvantages:

- The generative approach leads to code that is difficult to develop and understand. If we want to optimize an existing program it will be necessary to modify the original code which may introduce errors. Furthermore, code containing generative statements is difficult to write and read. Therefore, the generative approach has disadvantage even when the parameterized code is to be written from scratch.
- Complexity when composing transformations. Since the programmer is directly manipulating source text, when two or more transformations are applied to a statement, the macro statements can become complicated. For instance, tiling the three loops of the matrix-matrix multiplication code in Figure 4-(a) with square tiles of size `tile` results in the code shown in Figure 4-(b). The variable `%tile` will be instantiated at compile time, so that versions of matrix-matrix multiplication with different tile sizes can be generated by just changing the value of the `%tile` variable. The code in Figure 4-(b) shows the remainder loops when `%tile` is not divisible by `K`, and outlines the additional code that should be written to generate the remainders of `M` and `N`. A programmer who needs to write all this additional code is likely to make mistakes. This problem will be less severe if the macro language contains procedures, but then there would be the need to develop a procedure for each combination of transformations or procedures with a cumbersome parameter list. In any case, tiling can be obtained by composing loop stripmine and loop interchange. Unfortunately, the programmer using macro statements cannot take advantage of this.

```
for (i=0;i<N;i++) {
 for (j=0;j<M;j++) {
  for (k=0;k<K;k++) {
   c[i][j] += a[i][k] * b[k][j];
  }}}
```

(a)

```
for (i=0;i<(N/%tile)*%tile;i+=%tile) {
 for (j=0;j<(M/%tile)*%tile;j+=%tile) {
  for (k=0;k<(K/%tile)*%tile;k+=%tile) {
   for (ii=i;ii<i+%tile;i++) {
    for (jj=j;jj<j+%tile;j++) {
     for (kk=k;kk<k+%tile;kk++) {
      c[ii][jj] += a[ii][kk] * b[kk][jj];
     }}}}
  %if ((K/%tile)*%tile)!=K) {
   for (k=(K/%tile)*%tile;k<K;k++) {
    for (ii=i;ii<i+%tile;i++) {
     for (jj=j;jj<j+%tile;j++) {
      for (kk=k;kk<k+%tile;kk++) {
       c[ii][jj] += a[ii][kk] * b[kk][jj];
      }}}}}}
 %if (((M/%tile)*%tile) != M) {
    ....
 }
%if (((N/%tile)*%tile) != N) {
   ....
}
```

(b)

Fig. 4. (a)-Matrix-matrix multiplication code. (b)-Tiled matrix-matrix multiplication code using macro statements.

4 X Language Using Pragmas

In this Section, we describe the *X* language that we have designed taking into account the features described in Section 2. *X* uses `#pragmas` to name loops or portions of code and to specify the transformations to apply. The syntax of the `#pragmas` used to name loops or code sections has the form:

```
#pragma xlang name <id> { ... }
```

The { } are only necessary when naming a set of statements, but they are not required to name a single statement. These pragmas need to be placed right before the code section to be named. The syntax of the `#pragmas` to specify transformations has the form:

```
#pragma xlang transform keyword <list-input-par> <list-output-par>
```

The original source code only needs to be modified with the name `#pragmas`. The transform `#pragmas` can be in the same file that the source code or in a different one.

```
sum=0;
#pragma xlang name l1
for (i=0;i<256;i++) {
   s = s + a[i];
}
#pragma xlang transform unroll l1 4
```

(a)

```
sum=0;
#pragma xlang name l1
for (i=0;i<256;i+=4) {
   s = s + a[i];
   s = s + a[i+1];
   s = s + a[i+2];
   s = s + a[i+3];
}
```

(b)

Fig. 5. Example in *X* of loop unroll. (a)- Pragmas to name the loop and specify the unroll 4 (b)- Generated code.

In *X*, the `loop unrolling` transformation in Figure 3 is specified as shown in Figure 5. `#pragma xlang name l1` is used to name the loop right after it, while `#pragma xlang transform unroll l1 4` specifies the transformation `unroll l1` 4 times.

The stripmine transformation is specified in *X* with `#pragma xlang transform stripmine l1 4 l3 l1rem` as shown in Figure 6-(a). This transformation will `stripmine` the `l1` loop using a tile size of 4. The generated code is shown in Figure 6-(b). The new loop that results of the `stripmine` transformation is named `l3`. To name the remainder loop, the example uses `l1rem`. Using this postfix notation we can apply the same transformation to `l1` and `l1rem` by simply using `l1*`

```
#pragma xlang name l1
for (i=0;i<N;i++) {
   #pragma xlang name l2
   for (j=0;j<M;j++) {
      c[i] = a[i][j] * b[j];
   }}
#pragma xlang transform stripmine l1 4 l3 l1rem
```

(a)

```
#pragma xlang name l1
for (i=0;i<(N/4)*4;i+=4) {
   #pragma xlang name l3
   for (ii=i;ii<i+4;ii++) {
      #pragma xlang name l2
      for (j=0;j<M;j++) {
         c[ii] = a[ii][j] * b[j];
      }}}
#pragma xlang name l1rem
for (i=(N/4)*4;i<N;i++) {
   #pragma xlang name l2
   for (j=0;j<M;j++) {
      c[ii] = a[ii][j] * b[j];
   }}
```

(b)

Fig. 6. Example in *X* of stripmine.(a)-Pragmas to name loops and specify the stripmine transformation. (b)-Generated code.

Another transformation that *X* includes is array scalarization. The syntax for this transformation is `#pragma xlang transform scalarize-`*`func`* `<array-name> in [<id>]`, where *func* can be `in`, `out`, `-in&out` or `none`. `scalarize -in` is used when copy-in is needed, that is, when the initial values in the array have to

```
sum=0;
#pragma xlang name l1
for (i=0; i<256; i+=2){
   s = s + a[i];
   s = s + a[i+1];
}
#pragma xlang transform scalarize-in a in l1
```

(a)

```
double a0,a1;
sum=0;
#pragma xlang name l1
for (i=0; i<256; i+=2){
   #pragma xlang name l1.loads
   { a0 = a[i];
   a1 = a[i+1]; }
   #pragma xlang name l1.body
   { s = s + a0;
   s = s + a1; }
   }
```

(b)

Fig. 7. Example in *X* of the scalarize-in transformation. (a)-Pragmas for `scalarize-in`. (b)-Code after `scalarize-in` array a in `l1`.

be loaded into the scalar variables. `scalarize-out` is used when copy-out is needed, that is, when the scalar values need to be written back to memory to the corresponding array locations. `scalarize-in&out` is used when both both `in` and `out` are required. `scalarize` is used when nor `in` or `out` are necessary. The programmer must determine which is the appropriate scalarize transformation to apply so that the generated code is correct.

Figure 7-(a) shows an example where the `scalarize-in` transformation is used to scalarize the array a in `l1`. The generated code is shown in Figure 7-(b). The generated code contains the declaration of the new scalar variables `a0` and `a1`, and two new `pragmas` that name certain statements of the generated code. `#pragma xlang name l1.loads` name the statements that load the array values into the scalars. `#pragma xlang name l1.body` name the statements where the array references have been replaced with scalars. Notice that these `#pragmas` are automatically generated after a scalarize transformation is applied, without the programmer specifying anything. In the case of a `scalarize-out` transformation an additional `#pragma` naming `l1.stores` would have been generated. Naming these loop sections allows the programmer to apply new transformations on the generated code. For example, Figure 8-(a) shows an example where the load statements of the copy-in phase have been moved before `l1` and the store statements of the copy-out phase have been moved outside `l1` as shown in Figure 8-(b). In this new example, we have used `#pragma xlang transform lift l1.loads before l1` and `#pragma`

```
for (i=0;i<N;i++) {
 for (j=0;j<M;j++) {
  #pragma xlang name l1
  for (k=0;k<K;k+=2){
   c[i][j] += a[i][k] * b[k][j];
   c[i][j] += a[i][k+1] * b[k+1][j];
  }}}
#pragma xlang transform scalarize-out c in l1
#pragma xlang transform lift l1.loads before l1
#pragma xlang transform lift l1.stores after l1
```

(a)

```
double c0,c1;
for (i=0; i<N; i++) {
 for (j=0; j<M; j++) {
   #pragma xlang name l1.loads
   { c0 = c[i][j]; }
   #pragma xlang name l1
   for (k=0; k<K; k+=2) {
    #pragma xlang name l1.body
    { c0 += a[i][k]*b[k][j];
    c0 += a[i][k+1]*b[k+1][j]; }
   }
   #pragma xlang name l1.stores
   { c[i][j] = c0; }
 }}
```

(b)

Fig. 8. Example in *X* of `scalarize-out` and `lift` transformation. (a)-Pragmas for `scalarize-out` and `lift`. (b)-Generated code.

`xlang transform lift l1.stores after l1`, where the syntax of this transformation is
`#pragma xlang transform lift <statement-id><before | after> <loop-id>`.

X also includes transformations for software pipelining. One difference between the software pipelining and the loop transformations is that software pipelining operates on statements instead of loops. The lower granularity of software pipelining transformations makes them more complex, since the programmer needs to deal with movement of individual statements. The two transformations used for software pipelining are `split` and `shift`. The `split` transformation is not necessarily a software pipelining transformation. It is used to separate atomic instructions. Figure 9 shows how an instruction combining a load and an operation is breaking assignment statements into two statements, one to compute the right hand side and the other to assign the computed value to the left hand side.

```
for (i=0; i<N; i++) {
  for (j=0; j<M; j++) {
    for (k=0; k<K; k++) {
      #pragma xlang name statement st1
      c[i][j] += a[i][k] * b[k][j];
    }}}
#pragma xlang split st1 st2 temp
```

(a)

```
double temp[0..K];
for (i=0; i<N; i++){
  for (j=0; j<M; j++){
    for (k=0; k<K; k++){
      #pragma xlang name statement st1
      temp[k] = a[i][k] * b[k][j];
      #pragma xlang name statement st2
      c[i][j] = c[i][j] + temp[k];
    }}}
```

(b)

Fig. 9. Example split. (a)-Pragmas for `split`. (b)-Generated code.

Figure 10 shows how to software pipeline a loop with the `shift` transformation. We have used `#pragma xlang transform shift l1.1 2`. The first argument `l1.1` corresponds to the first statement of loop `l1` and in general, the `loop.`<n> notation is used to designate the sequence of the first n statements in the body of loop `loop`. In the example, the first statement is shifted with respect to the remaining statements with a latency of 2, given by the second argument. Application of the shift transformation creates a pipeline with multiple stages. The example shows the resulting code, with

```
for (i=0; i<N; i++) {
  for (j=0; j<M; j++) {
    #pragma xlang name l1
    for (k=0; k<K; k++) {
      temp[k] = a[i][k] * b[k][j];
      c[i][j] += temp[k];
    }}}
#pragma shift l1.1 2
```

(a)

```
for (i=0; i<N; i++) {
  for (j=0; j<M; j++) {
    #pragma xlang name l1.prolog
    for (k=0; k<2; k++) {
      temp[k] = a[i][k] * b[k][j];
    }
    #pragma xlang name l1
    for (k=2; k<K; k++) {
      temp[k] = a[i][k] * b[k][j];
      c[i][j] += temp[k-2];
    }
    #pragma xlang name l1.epilog
    for (k=N-1; k<K; k++) {
      c[i][j] += temp[k];
    }}}
#pragma xlang transform fullunroll l1.prolog
#pragma xlang transform fullunroll l1.epilog
```

(b)

Fig. 10. Example shift for software pipeline. (a)-Pragmas for `shift`. (b)-Generated code, including fullunroll.

a prolog and a epilog loop. Notice that these loops can be unrolled using the pragma `fullunroll` as shown in Figure 10-(b).

Defining transformations with respect to existing ones provides a procedural abstraction to the *X* language. We describe them in Section 5.

5 Implementation

In this section, we describe the implementation of the X language translator and present how transformations are encoded.

5.1 X Translation

The X language is translated in two steps. The frontend performs several tasks before passing the result to the backend. First, the frontend parses the annotated C program and builds the associated abstract syntax tree. Next, a tree-walk identifies the loops and transformations specified by the X language directives. The marked loops are then rewritten as series of library calls that represent the loops inside the backend. Also, transformation directives are translated into library calls for performing the appropriate transformations on the annotated loops. After all the annotations of the C program have been translated, the remaining code is transformed using a *multistage* language similar to the language described in Section 3. Our multistage language also resembles 'C [19] which is a generalization of a macro language with arbitrary recursion and where a program may generate another program and execute it, having multiple program levels cooperate and share data possibly at run-time. The final translated program is then ready to be processed by the backend.

In the second step, this program is executed: it reads a separate file describing the optimizations, performs the optimizations and produces the final optimized C code. The macro language is used to manipulate code expressions and to write some optimizations (such as unroll) in a compact way. Partial evaluation of expressions that contain only % variables and constants is done in this step: as presented in Section 3, variable names such as `c_%i` are then expanded into `c_0, c_1, ...` in the resulting code.

Finally, all unoptimized code (not prefixed by pragmas) is printed out without any modification in the final code.

5.2 Defining New Transformations

The definition of transformations in *X* can use pattern rewriting rules and macro code. A pattern rewriting rule contains two patterns: the first pattern is for matching and the second one is for rewriting. When an input code matches the first pattern, the code is rewritten as indicated by the second pattern. If the pattern rewriting rule is not expressive enough, the user has the possibility to define the code using macro code directly. Thus an *X* program could contain both pragmas and macro statements. In fact, it is possible to define a code generator associated with a pattern of code.

In the current implementation, no dependence analysis is integrated yet, so no validity check is performed for the transformation. We envision that, contrary to the compiler, validity checks in X only raise warnings to the user, since the user is assumed to know what he is doing and validity checks may be too conservative.

Procedural abstraction enables the writing of complex transformations from simpler ones. It is an important feature in the definition of transformations. The destination pattern can contain some transform pragmas. For instance, a line such as `#pragma xlang transform fullunroll l1rem` could be added to the destination pattern of stripmine and would fully unroll the remainder loop.

6 Experimental Results

We study in this section a matrix-matrix multiplication and its optimization with *X* language. Starting from a very simple implementation, the goal is to mimic ATLAS by performing the same transformations with the *X*. For this preliminary experiment, the platform used is a NovaScale 4020 server from Bull featuring two 1.3Ghz Itanium 2 (Madison) processors, with a 256KB level 2 cache and a 1.5MB level 3 cache. Quality of compiled code is the key to performance on Itanium because of its explicit parallel assembly and its in-order execution. Scheduling problems cannot be smoothed by hardware mechanisms. All codes (including ATLAS) are compiled using the Intel C compiler (`icc`) version 8.1 with `-O3 -fno-aliases` flags.

6.1 Pragmas for MMM

The initial code for matrix-matrix multiply is a triple-nested loop where the inner loop contains one floating point multiply-add operation. Blocking the code for L2 and L3 cache is key to obtaining high performance. Therefore each loop is tiled three times using *X* pragmas in order to perform the multiplication with blocks fitting into registers

```
#pragma xlang name iloop
for (i = 0; i < NB; i++)
  #pragma xlang name jloop
  for (j = 0; j < NB; j++)
    #pragma xlang name kloop
    for (k = 0; k < NB; k++) {
      c[i][j]=c[i][j]+a[i][k]*b[k][j];
    }
#pragma xlang transform stripmine iloop NU NUloop
#pragma xlang transform stripmine jloop MU MUloop
#pragma xlang transform interchange kloop MUloop
#pragma xlang transform interchange jloop NUloop
#pragma xlang transform interchange kloop NUloop
#pragma xlang transform fullunroll NUloop
#pragma xlang transform fullunroll MUloop
#pragma xlang transform scalarize_in b in kloop
#pragma xlang transform scalarize_in a in kloop
#pragma xlang transform scalarize_in&out c in kloop
#pragma xlang transform lift kloop.loads before kloop
#pragma xlang transform lift kloop.stores after kloop
```

(a)

```
#pragma xlang name iloop
for(i = 0; i < NB; i++){
 #pragma xlang name jloop
 for(j = 0; j < NB; j += 4){
  #pragma xlang name kloop.loads
  {c_0_0 = c[i+0][j+0];
  c_0_1 = c[i+0][j+1];
  c_0_2 = c[i+0][j+2];
  c_0_3 = c[i+0][j+3];
  }
  #pragma xlang name kloop
  for(k = 0; k < NB; k++){
    {a_0 = a[i+0][k];
    a_1 = a[i+0][k];
    a_2 = a[i+0][k];
    a_3 = a[i+0][k];}
    {b_0 = b[k][j+0];
    b_1 = b[k][j+1];
    b_2 = b[k][j+2];
    b_3 = b[k][j+3];}
    {c_0_0=c_0_0+a_0*b_0;
    c_0_1=c_0_1+a_1*b_1;
    c_0_2=c_0_2+a_2*b_2;
    c_0_3=c_0_3+a_3*b_3;}
    ...
  }
  #pragma xlang name kloop.stores
  {c[i+0][j+0] = c_0_0;
  c[i+0][j+1] = c_0_1;
  c[i+0][j+2] = c_0_2;
  c[i+0][j+3] = c_0_3;}
} }
... // Remainder code
```

(b)

Fig. 11. (a) mini-mmm code in X. (b) Code after transformation with $MU = 4$, $NU = 1$.

and the L2 and L3 caches. Figure 11-(a) shows the mini-MMM code tailored for L2 cache, with the pragmas to generate register-blocking.

Note that we do not perform software pipelining because the compiler handles this optimization better than we can at the source level in this case. Likewise, basic block scheduling is correctly handled by the compiler. We have used two `stripmine` and three `interchange` transformations to tile the two nested loops `iloop` and `jloop`. Fig.11-(b) shows a fragment of the resulting code when the values of blocking are 1 for `iloop` and 4 for `jloop`.

For the L2 and L3 tilings, copies of `a`, `b` and `c` are made in order to have all the elements of the submatrices in a contiguous memory block.

6.2 Optimization Tuning

Expressing the optimization is only one step towards high performance code. The other important step consists of finding the right values for the parameters. Many search strategies can be applied, such as the search employed by ATLAS.

For `DGEMM`, we performed an exhaustive search for the appropriate tile sizes around the expected values.Comparison with the naive code shows a speed-up of 80 (for matrices of size 600×600). Figure 12 shows that code optimized with the X language outperforms ATLAS for all matrix sizes when coupling it with a custom memory copy routine called `dcopy`. This routine was automatically produced by a specialized assembly generator, the Xemsys Library Generator [28], using hardware performance counters and static analysis of the assembly code [9].

Coupling our code with the less specialized copy routine of the Intel Math Kernel Library (MKL) yields performance on par with ATLAS on average, and using the plain `memcopy` subroutine of the C library degrades performance slightly. These results are

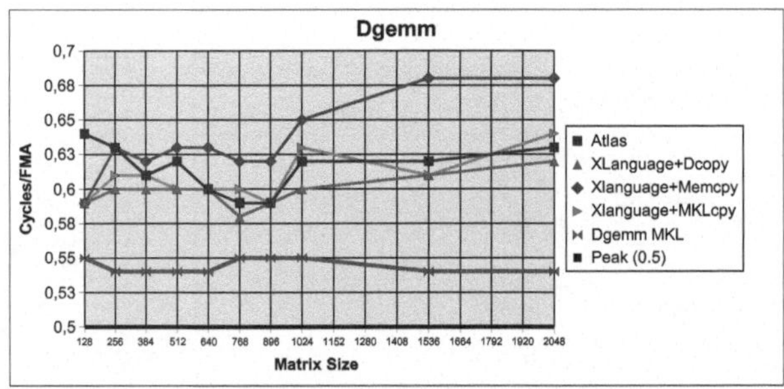

Fig. 12. Preliminary results comparing ATLAS to naive code with pragmas for `DGEMM`

very encouraging. Yet the peak architectural performance for matrix-matrix product on Itanium is 0.5 cycle per fma operation, and the MKL implementation of `dgemm` does achieve 0.55 cycle per fma on average, which is 10% to 15% faster than ATLAS and the X-language implementation. Our future work includes the continuation of our X-language experiment to fully reproduce or outperform the MKL, showing that the added productivity in adaptive library development can translate into added performance as well (with respect to manual designs like ATLAS).

7 Related Work

It is well known that manual optimizations degrade portability: the performance of a C or Fortran code on a given platform does not say much about its performance on different architectures. Several works have successfully addressed this issue, not by improving the compiler, but through the design of application-specific program generators, a.k.a. active libraries [26]. Such generators often rely on feedback-directed optimization to select the best generation strategy [23], but not exclusively [29]. The most popular examples are ATLAS [27] for dense matrix operations and FFTW [10] for the fast Fourier transform. Such generators follow an iterative optimization scheme. Most optimizations performed by these generators are classical loop transformations; some of them involve domain knowledge, from the specialization and interprocedural optimization of library functions [3,8], to application-specific optimizations such as algorithm selection [17]. Recently, the SPIRAL project [21] pioneered the extension of this application-specific approach to a whole domain of programs: digital signal processing. This project is one step forward to bridge the gap between application-specific generators and generic compiler-based approaches, and to improve the portability of application performance.

Beyond application specific generators, iterative optimization techniques prove useful to drive complex transformations in traditional compilers. They use the feedback from real executions of the optimized program to explore the optimization search space using operations research algorithms [15], machine learning [17], and empirical experience [18]. In theory, iterative optimization is fully disconnected from the technical implementation of program optimizations. Yet generative approaches such as multistage evaluation avoid the pattern-matching limitations of syntactic transformation systems, which improves the structure of the search space and the applicability of empirical techniques. Indeed, systematic exploration techniques require a higher degree of flexibility in program manipulation than traditional compiler frameworks [5].

We thus advocate a framework that would allow the domain expert to design and express his own transformations, and to meta-program the search for optimal performance through iterative optimization [4]. This goal is similar to the one of *telescoping languages* [3,13], a compiler approach to reduce the overhead of calling generic library functions and to enable aggressive interprocedural optimizations, by making the semantical information about these libraries available to the compiler. Beyond libraries, similar ideas have been proposed for domain-specific optimizations [16]. These works highlight the increased need for researchers and developers in the field of high-performance computing to meta-program their optimizations in a portable fashion.

Another alternative is *multistage evaluation.* Most programming languages support *macro expansion*, where the macro language allows a limited amount of control (not recursive, in general) on code parts. Yet *multistage evaluation* denotes the syntactic and semantic support allowing a program to generate another program and execute it, having multiple program levels cooperate and share data. *String-based* multistage languages support true recursion and cooperation between levels, but offer no syntactic guarantees on the generated code; the most widely used are the various shell interpreters, and the current version of the *X* language is also of this kind. To increase productivity, *structured* multistage languages enforce syntactic correctness of the generated code: e.g., C++ expression templates [25], ‘C [19] and Jumbo [12]. To further increase productivity and ease debugging, a few multistage languages guarantee that the generated code will not produce any compilation error (syntax, definition and initialization errors, type checking): e.g., MetaML and its successor MetaOCaml [2,24]. The added safety is very valuable to increase the productivity of program generator designers, but the associated constraints may also complicate the meta-programming of specific optimizations [4]. Up to now, the multistage language and meta-programming community has mostly focused on general-purpose transformations like in partial evaluation, specialization and simplification. These transformations are useful, in particular to lower the abstraction penalty, but far from sufficient to adapt a compute-intensive application to a complex architecture. As a matter of fact, research on generative programming and multistage evaluation has not greatly influenced the design of high-performance applications and compilers, most application-specific adaptive libraries being ad-hoc string-based program generators.

The TaskGraph library [1] is closely related with the *X* language. It combines a structured multistage evaluation layer built on top of C++ expression templates, with runtime generation and compilation, and with a transformation toolkit based on SUIF (1.3) [11] and/or ROSE [22]. It is not a language per se, but a set of C++ templates and classes associated with customizable source-to-source transformation capabilities. As such, it should be understood like the underlying infrastructure to build a general-purpose multiversioning language such as *X*. We preferred to redesign our own infrastructure for multistage evaluation and source-to-source transformation, for the sake of simplicity, to avoid the memory and code overhead of C++ templates, and because we do not currently aim for run-time code generation.

8 Conclusions

We presented the design of the *X* language, aimed for application experts who wish to implement adaptive programs without knowledge of compiler internals. The language is designed so that it is easy for the programmer to generate multiversion programs, to specify which transformations to apply on each program part, and to tune the order or the parameters of the transformations. The parameters driving the generation of a specific program version and the application of program transformations can be determined using empirical search orchestrated by a search engine which could use the target machine to evaluate the performance of each version of the program or rely on analytical models.

The *X* language combines the expressive power of multistage languages with a flexible pattern-matching and rewriting language to implement and compose custom program transformations. Also the language is still in its infancy, we presented promising results on mimicking the code generator for DGEMM (matrix-matrix multiplication) in ATLAS [27]. This experiment demonstrates vast amounts of productivity improvements, compared to the manual implementation of an ad-hoc code generator in C, as well as good performance results.

Our future work will include a more thorough experiment with the ongoing design of an active library for adaptive, block-recursive linear algebra computations. For increased productivity, we also plan to provide a more structured multistage sub-language, and to integrate the results of pointer and dependence analyses as indicative feedback to the programmer. Such static analyses should also enable the design of smarter (higher-level) transformation primitives. In the longer term, we also wish to invest in a more robust implementation of the *X* language, based on a run-time compilation framework, like ROSE [22] or TaskGraph [1], and/or using a more abstract code representation in the polytope model [5]. Our main long-term goal is the adoption by application experts with little interest in compiler design and implementation.

References

1. O. Beckmann, A. Houghton, P. H. J. Kelly, and M. Mellor. Run-time code generation in c++ as a foundation for domain-specific optimisation. In *Proceedings of the 2003 Dagstuhl Workshop on Domain-Specific Program Generation*, 2003.
2. C. Calcagno, W. Taha, L. Huang, and X. Leroy. Implementing multi-stage languages using ASTs, Gensym, and reflection. In *ACM SIGPLAN/SIGSOFT Intl. Conf. Generative Programming and Component Engineering (GPCE'03)*, pages 57–76, 2003.
3. A. Chauhan and K. Kennedy. Optimizing strategies for telescoping languages: procedure strength reduction and procedure vectorization. In *ACM Int. Conf. on Supercomputing (ICS'04)*, pages 92–101, June 2001.
4. A. Cohen, S. Donadio, M.-J. Garzaran, D. Padua, and C. Herrmann. In search for a program generator to implement generic transformations for high-performance computing. In *1st MetaOCaml Workshop (associated with GPCE)*, Vancouver, British Columbia, October 2004.
5. A. Cohen, S. Girbal, D. Parello, M. Sigler, O. Temam, and N. Vasilache. Facilitating the search for compositions of program transformations. In *ACM Int. Conf. on Supercomputing (ICS'05)*, Boston, Massachusetts, June 2005. To appear.
6. K. D. Cooper, D. Subramanian, and L. Torczon. Adaptive Optimizing Compilers for the 21st Century. *Journal of Supercomputing*, 23(1):7–22, 2002.
7. K. D. Cooper and T. Waterman. Investigating Adaptive Compilation using the MIPSPro Compiler. In *Proc. of the Symp. of the Los Alamos Computer Science Institute*, October 2003.
8. L. De Rose and D. Padua. Techniques for the translation of matlab programs into fortran 90. *ACM Trans. on Programming Languages and Systems*, 21(2):286–323, 1999.
9. L. Djoudi, D. Barthou, P. Carribault, C. Lemuet, J.-T. Acquaviva, and W. Jalby. A new tool for assembler analysis and optimization on epic architecture. In *Proc. of the Epic Workshop (in conjunction with CGO'05)*, 2005.
10. M. Frigo and S. G. Johnson. FFTW: An adaptive software architecture for the FFT. In *Proc. of the ICASSP Conf.*, volume 3, pages 1381–1384, 1998.
11. M. Hall et al. Maximizing multiprocessor performance with the SUIF compiler. *IEEE Computer*, 29(12):84–89, December 1996.
12. Sam Kamin, Lars Clausen, and Ava Jarvis. Jumbo: run-time code generation for java and its applications. In *ACM Conf. on Code Generation and Optimization (CGO'03)*, pages 48–56, 2003.
13. K. Kennedy. Telescoping languages: A compiler strategy for implementation of high-level domain-specific programming systems. In *Proc. Intl. Parallel and Distributed Processing Symposium (IPIPS'00)*, pages 297–304, 2000.

14. P. Kisubi, P.M.W. Knijnenburg, and M.F.P. O'Boyle. The Effect of Cache Models on Iterative Compilation for Combined Tiling and Unrolling. In *Proc. of the International Conference on Parallel Architectures and Compilation Techniques*, pages 237–246, 2000.
15. T. Kisuki, P. Knijnenburg, M. O'Boyle, and H. Wijshoff. Iterative compilation in program optimization. In *Proc. CPC'10 (Compilers for Parallel Computers)*, pages 35–44, 2000.
16. C. Lengauer, D. Batory, C. Consel, and M. Odersky, editors. *Domain-Specific Program Generation.* Number 3016 in LNCS. Springer-Verlag, 2003.
17. X. Li, M.-J. Garzaran, and D. Padua. A dynamically tuned sorting library. In *ACM Conf. on Code Generation and Optimization (CGO'04)*, pages 111–124, San Jose, CA, March 2004.
18. D. Parello, O. Temam, A. Cohen, and J.-M. Verdun. Towards a systematic, pragmatic and architecture-aware program optimization process for complex processors. In *ACM Supercomputing'04*, page 15, Pittsburgh, Pennsylvania, November 2004.
19. M. Poletto, W. C. Hsieh, D. R. Engler, and M. F. Kaashoek. 'C and tcc: A language and compiler for dynamic code generation. *ACM Trans. on Programming Languages and Systems*, 21(2):324–369, March 1999.
20. M. Puschel, J. Moura, J. Johnson, D. Padua, M. Veloso, B. Singer, J. Xiong, F. Franchetti, A. Gacic, Y. Voronenko, K. Chen, R. W. Johnson, and N. Rizzolo. SPIRAL: Code Generation for DSP Transforms. *Proceedings of the IEEE*, To appear 2005. Special issue on "Program Generation, Optimization, and Adaptation".
21. M. Puschel, B. Singer, J. Xiong, J. M .F. Moura, J. Johnson, D. Padua, M. M. Veloso, , and R. W. Johnson. SPIRAL: A Generator for Platform-Adapted Libraries of Signal Processing Algorithms. *Journal of High Performance Computing and Applications, special issue on Automatic Performance Tuning*, 18(1):21–45, 2004.
22. Markus Schordan and Daniel J. Quinlan. A source-to-source architecture for user-defined optimizations. In *Joint Modular Languages Conference (JMLC'03)*, volume 2789 of *LNCS*, pages 214–223. Springer-Verlag, August 2003.
23. M. D. Smith. Overcoming the challenges to feedback-directed optimization. In *ACM SIGPLAN Workshop on Dynamic and Adaptive Compilation and Optimization*, pages 1–11, 2000. (Keynote Talk).
24. W. Taha. *Multi-Stage Programming: Its Theory and Applications*. PhD thesis, Oregon Graduate Institute of Science and Technology, November 1999.
25. T. Veldhuizen. Using C++ template metaprograms. *C++ Report*, 7(4):36–43, 1995.
26. T. Veldhuizen and D. Gannon. Active libraries: Rethinking the roles of compilers and libraries. In *SIAM Workshop on Object Oriented Methods for Inter-operable Scientific and Engineering Computing*, pages 21–23, October 1998.
27. R. Clint Whaley, Antoine Petitet, and Jack J. Dongarra. Automated Empirical Optimization of Software and the ATLAS Project. *Parallel Computing*, 27(1–2):3–35, 2001. Also available as University of Tennessee LAPACK Working Note #147, UT-CS-00-448, 2000 (`www.netlib.org/lapack/lawns/lawn147.ps`)".
28. Caps entreprise. `http://www.caps-entreprise.com`.
29. K. Yotov, X. Li, G. Ren, M. Cibulskis, G. DeJong, M. Garzarán, D. Padua, K. Pingali, P. Stodghill, and P. Wu. A Comparison of Empirical and Model-driven Optimization. In *Proceedings of the ACM SIGPLAN 2003 Conference on Programming Language Design and Implementation*, pages 63–76. ACM Press, 2003.
30. K. Yotov, X. Li, G. Ren, M. Garzarán, D. Padua, K. Pingali, and P. Stodghill. Is Search Really Necessary to Generate High-Performance BLASs? *Proceedings of the IEEE*, 93(2):358–386, February 2005. Special issue on "Program Generation, Optimization, and Adaptation".

Efficient Computation of May-Happen-in-Parallel Information for Concurrent Java Programs

Rajkishore Barik

IBM India Research Lab
rajbarik@in.ibm.com

Abstract. Modeling of runtime threads in static analysis of concurrent programs plays an important role in both reducing the complexity and improving the precision of the analysis. Modeling based on type based techniques merges all runtime instances of a particular type and thereby introduces inaccuracy in the analysis. Other approaches model individual runtime threads explicitly in the analysis and are of high complexity. In this paper we introduce a thread model that is both context and flow sensitive. Individual thread abstractions are identified based on the context and multiplicity of the creation site. The interaction among these abstract threads are depicted in a tree structure known as Thread Creation Tree (TCT). The TCT structure is subsequently exploited to efficiently compute May-Happen-in-Parallel (MHP) information for the analysis of multi-threaded programs. For concurrent Java programs, our MHP computation algorithm runs 1.77x (on an average) faster than previously reported MHP computation algorithm.

1 Introduction

As concurrent programming is embraced by more and more users, there are several on-going research activities for the last few years in the area of static analysis of concurrent programs. To name a few of these activities: computation of May Happen in Parallel (MHP) information, detection of synchronization anomalies like data races and deadlock, hiding the effect of weak memory models at the programming level, improving the accuracy of data flow analysis, and optimization of concurrent programs.

May Happen in Parallel (MHP) analysis computes pairs of statements that may be executed concurrently in a multi-threaded program. This information can be used in program optimization [9], debugging, program understanding tools, improving the accuracy of data flow approaches, and detecting synchronization anomalies like data races.

Several approaches for computing MHP information for programs have been suggested in the past: B4 analysis by Callahan et al. [3], inter-procedural B4 analysis by Duesterwald et al. [6], non-concurrency analysis by Masticola et al. [14], and data flow analysis based MHP computation for programs with a rendezvous model of concurrency by Naumovich et al. [16]. Most recently [15]

E. Ayguadé et al. (Eds.): LCPC 2005, LNCS 4339, pp. 152–169, 2007.

developed an efficient algorithm for computing MHP information for concurrent Java programs. Their algorithm uses a data flow framework to compute a conservative estimate of MHP information and is shown to be more efficient than reachability analysis based algorithms that determines 'ideal' static MHP information. However, the underlying thread model used in the data flow framework explicitly enumerates all runtime threads during compilation time leading to the complexity of the algorithm bounded by number of runtime threads, i.e., $\Theta((pN)^3)$ complexity, where p is the number of runtime threads and N is the maximum number of statements per runtime thread. Such an explicit enumeration of threads makes the algorithm time consuming, and it is inapplicable to programs with unbounded or large number of runtime threads.

Subsequently, there has been work [13] on aiding a feasible implementation of the MHP algorithm presented by Naumovich et al. [16]. Their main focus is to reduce the size of the program execution graph (PEG) which is the core of MHP algorithm.

1.1 Our Contribution

The main contribution of this paper are:

- We introduce a static model of threads that is flow sensitive and context sensitive; this model is more precise than type based thread disambiguation used in previous approaches [20,18]; yet our model is capable of handling an indefinite number of runtime threads.
- We introduce a thread structure analysis and the concept of the *thread creation tree (TCT)*, which captures the start and join interactions among threads.
- We present an efficient algorithm that computes the MHP information at two levels: first at the thread level, then at the node level. The complexity of our algorithm is $\Theta((kN)^2)$ where k is the number of thread abstractions and N is the maximum number of inter-procedural control flow graph nodes per thread abstraction.

Our results show that our MHP algorithm runs 1.77x faster than MHP algorithm presented by naumovich et al. [16] using our context and flow sensitive thread model.

1.2 Example

Figure 1 shows a sample program that updates a shared object of class `Shared` concurrently. `Main` thread creates two `Task1` threads. These `Task1` threads in turn create various `Task2` threads. Note that modifications of the shared object in `Task2` threads are synchronized. In addition, `Task2` threads join back to `Task1` threads without causing any exception.

For this example, the thread model presented by [15] considers 43 runtime threads explicitly during the static analysis: initial thread starting at `main` method, 2 `Task1` threads, and each `Task1` thread creating 20 `Task2` threads.

Management of such a huge number of runtime threads in the static analysis requires a lot of space and is computationally expensive.

However, the type based thread disambiguation model described in [20,18] considers only 3 thread abstractions during the analysis: initial thread starting at `main` method, one for `Task1` thread and one for `Task2` thread. This kind of modeling seems very efficient but does not produce precise results. To elaborate this: Let us consider the MHP information computation problem. The type based thread modeling concludes that the shared object access in Line 9 of `Main` thread may execute in parallel with the access in Line 24 of `Task1`. This is not always true as the same access in Line 24 for `t2` instance of `Task1` never executes in parallel with Line 9 of `Main` thread (as `t2` is started after Line 9 has finished execution). Additional machinery has to be built into these type based techniques to obtain such precise results.

2 Flow and Context Sensitive Thread Model

2.1 Abstract Thread

An *abstract thread* is a compile time entity that corresponds to a call of the `Thread::start` method in a certain context. Contexts are determined along a symbolic execution of the whole program [18]. In this paper, we use the terms *thread* and *abstract thread* interchangeably; if we refer to *runtime* threads, we note that explicitly.

An abstract thread t_i might correspond to one or multiple runtime threads. In cases where the static analysis can determine that an abstract thread t_i is not started in a loop or recursion (and the creator thread is itself unique), t_i has a unique runtime correspondence, and the predicate $isUnique[t_i]$ holds.

```
1  class Shared { int field=0; }
2  class Main {
3   static Shared s;
4   public static void main(String[] args){
5    s = new Shared();
6    s.field++;
7    Thread t1 = new Task1();
8    t1.start();                      // t1
9    s.field++;
10   Thread t2 = new Task1();
11   t2.start();                      // t2
12   s.field++;
13  }
14 }
15 class Task2 extends Thread {
16  public void run() {
17   synchronized(Main.s){
18      Main.s.field++;
19   }
20  }
21 }
22 class Task1 extends Thread {
23  public void run() {
24   Main.s.field++;
25   Thread[] ta = new Thread[10];
26   for(int i=0;i<10;i++) {
27    ta[i] = new Task2();
28    ta[i].start();                  // t3, t5
29   }
30   for(int i=0;i<10;i++) {
31     ta[i].join();
32   }
33   Main.s.field++;
34   Thread tb= new Thread[10];
35   for(int i=0;i<10;i++) {
36    tb[i] = new Task2();
37    tb[i].start();                  // t4, t6
38   }
39   for(int i=0;i<10;i++) {
40    tb[i].join();
41   }
42  }
43 }
```

Fig. 1. Example program

In the example of Figure 1, our thread model computes 7 different abstract threads: thread corresponding to the `main` method denoted as t_0 , `Task1` thread in Line 8 denoted as t_1, `Task2` thread started in Line 28 of t_1 denoted as t_3, `Task2` thread started in Line 37 of t_1 denoted as t_4, `Task1` thread started in Line 11 denoted as t_2, `Task2` thread started in Line 28 of t_2 denoted as t_5, and `Task2` thread started in Line 37 of t_2 denoted as t_6. The abstract thread t_1 started in line 8 is unique because the creator thread (`main`) is unique, and the start site is not executed in a loop/recursion. The abstract thread t_3 created in line 28, in contrast is not unique, because it is started inside a loop.

3 Program Representation

In this section, we describe other data structures that are necessary for performing MHP analysis on concurrent programs. The thread creation graph (TCG) data structure depicts various start-join interactions among abstract threads and is used to develop an efficient algorithm for MHP.

3.1 Intra-thread Control Flow Graph

The control-flow structure of an abstract thread t_i is represented in an intra-thread control flow graph (ICFG), i.e., $ICFG(t_i)$. $ICFG(t_i) = \langle V(t_i), E(t_i)\rangle$ where $E(t_i)$ denotes the intra-procedural and inter-procedural control flow edges of abstract thread t_i, and $V(t_i)$ comprises of the following types of nodes:

- $USE(t_i)$ refers to the set of shared read access (get/load of shared reference/field/array) nodes in t_i.
- $ASS(t_i)$ refers to the set of shared write access (put/store of shared reference/field/array) nodes in t_i.
- $NEW(t_i)$ refers to the set of allocation nodes in t_i.
- $BEGIN(t_i)$ refers to the set of method entry nodes in t_i.
- $END(t_i)$ refers to the set of method exit nodes in t_i.
- $ENTRY(t_i)$ refers to the unique thread entry node for t_i.
- $EXIT(t_i)$ refers to the unique thread exit node for t_i.
- $CSTART(t_i)$ refers to the set of abstract thread start nodes in t_i.
- $CJOIN(t_i)$ refers to the set of abstract thread join nodes in t_i.
- $CALL(t_i)$ refers to the set of method call nodes in t_i.
- $ACQUIRE(t_i)$ refers to the set of monitor enter nodes in t_i.
- $RELEASE(t_i)$ refers to the set of monitor exit nodes in t_i.

$V(t_i)$ contains two special nodes: $ENTRY(t_i)$ and $EXIT(t_i)$. There is an edge from $ENTRY(t_i)$ to any node at which the thread can be entered, and there is an edge to $EXIT(t_i)$ from any node that can exit the thread.

$E(t_i)$ contains intra-procedural and inter-procedural control flow edges in t_i. The inter-procedural control flow edges do not comprise of subsequent thread creation edges from t_i.

Certain statements need not be represented in the ICFG, e.g., statements that only have a thread-local effect. This includes access nodes (*USE*, *ASS*) that operate on thread local objects (the underlying object model and analysis for determining thread locality is presented in [5,18]

Figure 2 shows the inter-procedural control flow graph for the `main` abstract thread of the example program. Each node in the figure is annotated with the object/field it accesses. $CSTART[t_1]$ and $CSTART[t_2]$ nodes represent the

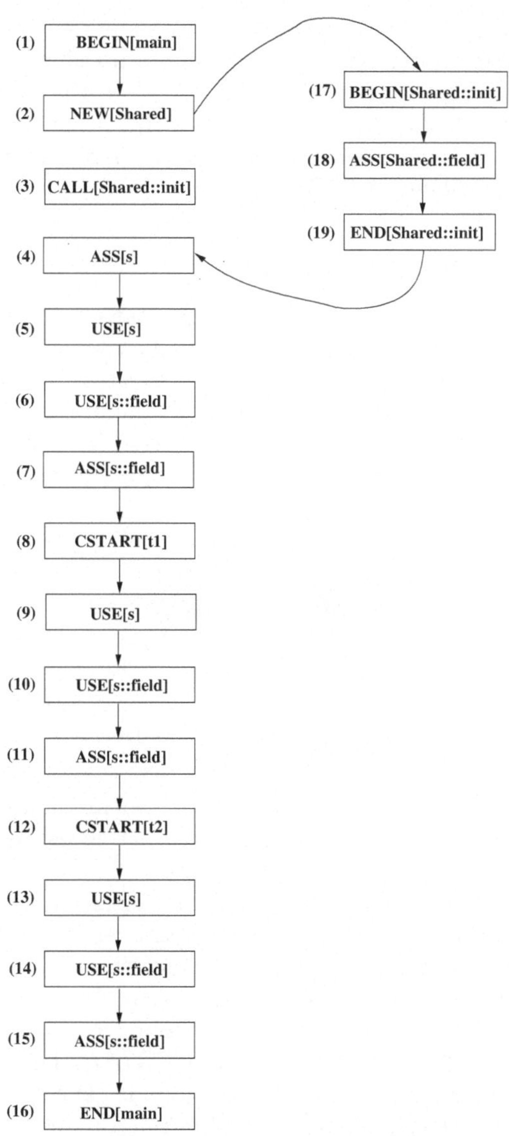

Fig. 2. Inter-procedural control flow graph (ICFG)

invocation of abstract threads t_1 and t_2 respectively. Note that there is no inter-procedural control flow edge connecting the node $CSTART[t_1]$ to $ICFG(t_1)$.

Let the creation node of an abstract thread t_j in t_i is denoted as $CSTART(t_i, t_j)$, i.e., $CSTART(t_i, t_j) \in CSTART(t_i)$. There is no inter-procedural control flow edge from t_i to t_j in $ICFG(t_i)$. Similarly, the join node of an abstract thread t_j in t_i is denoted as $CJOIN(t_i, t_j)$.

3.2 Must-Join

A common pattern in parallel programs is that some threads create subsidiary threads and later join those. We capture this information using the concept of a *must-join* abstract thread. Let $CSTART(t_i, t_j)$ be the node where abstract thread t_j is created in t_i. Let $CJOIN(t_k, t_j) \in V(t_k)$ be the node where abstract thread t_j is joined. t_j is then termed as a *must-join* abstract thread if $t_i = t_k$ and $CJOIN(t_i, t_j)$ *postdom* $CSTART(t_i, t_j)$.

3.3 Thread Creation Tree (TCT)

Threads can be structured according to their start-relationships. The *thread creation tree (TCT)* encodes this information: Abstract threads are represented as nodes, edges encode the start relation. The `main` thread constitutes the root, threads started by the `main` thread are found at the first hierarchy level etc..

The must-join information for each node in the TCT is encoded using a predicate *mjoin*, i.e., $mjoin[t_i] = \texttt{true}$ if t_i is a must-join abstract thread.

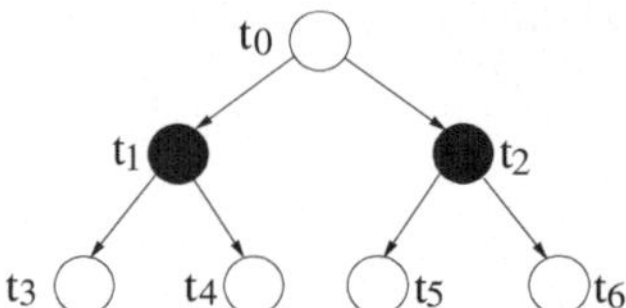

Fig. 3. Thread Creation Tree

The TCT for the program in Figure 1 is given in Figure 3. t_1 and t_2 are colored black as they do not join the main abstract thread t_0, i.e., $mjoin[t_1] = mjoin[t_2] = \texttt{false}$.

The specific case of a mutual thread creation inside a recursion, might lead to an unbounded TCT. We detect this case and resolve it by combining the involved abstract threads. For example, abstract thread t_i creates t_j: Both t_i and t_j have the same static thread type. Since there is recursion involved in the static types of t_i and t_j, the TCT will be unbounded. To handle this, we add only one node to the TCT with ICFG as the ICFG of t_i. The number of runtime instances of the added node in the TCT is not unique. The must-join information of the added node is set based on must-join information of t_i or t_j. In general, if a set of static types are involved in mutual recursion, we create a single node for the same in TCT. The ICFG of this node is created by combining ICFG of all the involved static types (details described in Appendix A).

4 MHP Computation

Given all abstract threads of a program, their ICFGs and the TCT, we compute nodes which may potentially execute in parallel, i.e., MHP information. This computation is performed at two levels: first at the abstract thread level and then at node level. At the abstract thread level, MHP computes pairs of abstract threads that may potentially execute in parallel. This is coarse-grained MHP information. Node level MHP refines this information by considering the individual statements and control-flow structure of threads that are identified as MHP at the thread-level. Since we are doing a compile time approximation of MHP (considering every control flow path), the MHP information we compute is a conservative superset of what actually happens at runtime.

Apart from ordering criteria among threads due to thread start and join, locks are also commonly used to order the execution among threads. We conservatively compute the locks statically using the following manner: In Java, locks are used in a scoped manner. Locks held during an access statement are recorded during the creation of the ICFG and associated with the corresponding node. We define $locks[v_i^m]$ as the set of objects that are locked while executing any node $v_i^m \in V(t_i)$. Nodes that execute in the context of a common unique lock cannot execute concurrently.

Our MHP analysis is based on graph algorithms like reachability and dominance. We write $x \xrightarrow{*} y$ to indicate a directed path from start node x to end node y. A null path is a path whose start node and end node are the same, i.e., a single node. A non-null path from x to y is written as $x \xrightarrow{+} y$. This path definition applies to both ICFG and TCT.

A directed path $t_1 \xrightarrow{*} t_n$ in the TCT is called a *must-join path* if all the nodes that lie on the path from t_1 to t_n are must-join abstract threads, i.e., $mjoin[t_i]$ = `true`, $\forall i = 1, \cdots, n$. For example, the path $t_0 \xrightarrow{+} t_1 \xrightarrow{+} t_3$ in Figure 3 is not a must-join path as $mjoin[t_1]$ = `false`.

The dominance relation between two nodes in the ICFG is represented by *dom*. Further, we denote node dominance as $dom_{v_i^m}[v_i^n]$ that consists of all nodes that lie on all possible directed paths from $v_i^m \in V(t_i)$ to $v_i^n \in V(t_i)$ in $ICFG(t_i)$.

4.1 Thread Level MHP

Thread level MHP computes pairs of abstract threads that may execute in parallel. It exploits the rooted tree structure of the TCT to determine such information.

Let $\|_t$ denote the MHP relation between two abstract threads. The ancestors of an abstract thread t_i in the TCT are represented in a set $anc(t_i)$. *child* and *parent* represent the child and parent relationship in the TCT. Let $yca(t_i, t_j)$ denote the youngest common ancestor of t_i and t_j in TCT. Let $canc(t_i, t_j)$ be

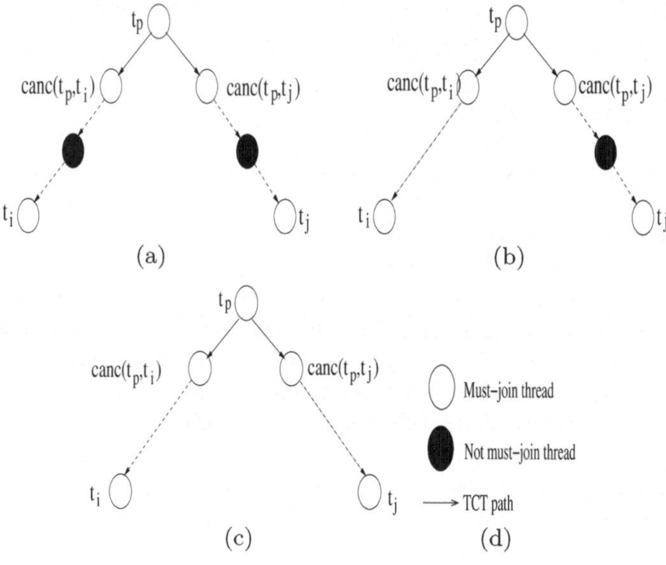

Fig. 4. Thread level MHP

the child of the abstract thread t_i that is either t_j itself or an ancestor of t_j. Mathematically,

$$yca(t_i, t_j) = \left\{ t_k \mid \begin{array}{l} t_k \text{ is the youngest common} \\ \text{ancestor of } t_i \text{ and } t_j \end{array} \right\}$$

$$canc(t_i, t_j) = \begin{cases} t_j, & \text{if } t_j = child(t_i) \\ child(t_i), & \text{if } child(t_i) \in anc(t_j) \\ \text{nil} & \text{otherwise} \end{cases}$$

Computation of thread level MHP is conservative. If an abstract thread t_i is an ancestor of another abstract thread t_j, then we conservatively assume that t_i and t_j run in parallel with each other, i.e., $t_i \|_t t_j$. Further refinement to this MHP information is done in node level MHP in which we consider fine-grained statement level parallelism.

$$t_i \|_t t_j = \text{true} \quad \text{if } t_i \in anc(t_j) \text{ or } t_j \in anc(t_i)$$

Apart from the above conservative case, all other possible cases to determine if any two TCT nodes t_i and t_j may execute in parallel are presented below. For compact representation of the cases we denote the youngest common ancestor of t_i and t_j as t_{yca}, i.e., $t_{yca} = yca(t_i, t_j)$.

- **Case 1:** Let us consider the case where neither the TCT path $canc(t_{yca}, t_i) \xrightarrow{*} t_i$ nor the TCT path $canc(t_{yca}, t_j) \xrightarrow{*} t_j$ is a must-join path. The TCT for this case is shown in Figure 4(a). t_i and t_j may execute in parallel, if at least one of the following conditions holds: (1) their common parent t_{yca} is not unique, or (2) both threads $canc(t_{yca}, t_i)$ and $canc(t_{yca}, t_j)$ may be started in some control-flow in $ICFG(t_{yca})$. This case is mathematically presented in Table 1.

Table 1. Thread Level MHP:Case 1

$$t_i \|_t t_j = \begin{cases} \text{true}, & \text{if } isUnique[t_{yca}] = \text{false} \\ \begin{pmatrix} CSTART(t_{yca}, canc(t_{yca}, t_i)) \xrightarrow{+} CSTART(t_{yca}, canc(t_{yca}, t_j)) \\ \vee \\ CSTART(t_{yca}, canc(t_{yca}, t_j)) \xrightarrow{+} CSTART(t_{yca}, canc(t_{yca}, t_i)) \end{pmatrix} & \text{otherwise} \end{cases}$$

- **Case 2:** Let us consider the case where the TCT path $canc(t_{yca}, t_i) \xrightarrow{*} t_i$ is a must-join path and the TCT path $canc(t_{yca}, t_j) \xrightarrow{*} t_j$ is not a must-join path. This case is shown in Figure 4(b). t_i may execute in parallel with t_j if at least one of the following conditions holds: (1) t_{yca} has multiple runtime instances, (2) there is a control-flow path from $CSTART(t_{yca}, canc(t_{yca}, t_j))$ to $CSTART(t_{yca}, canc(t_{yca}, t_i))$ in $ICFG(t_{yca})$, or (3) there is a control-flow path from $CSTART(t_{yca}, canc(t_{yca}, t_i))$ to $CSTART(t_{yca}, canc(t_{yca}, t_j))$ without $CJOIN(t_{yca}, canc(t_{yca}, t_i))$ in $ICFG(t_{yca})$. This case is mathematically presented in Table 2.

Table 2. Thread Level MHP:Case 2

$$t_i \|_t t_j = \begin{cases} \text{true}, & \text{if } isUnique[t_{yca}] = \text{false} \\ \left(\begin{array}{c} CSTART(t_{yca}, canc(t_{yca}, t_j)) \xrightarrow{+} CSTART(t_{yca}, canc(t_{yca}, t_i)) \\ \vee \\ \left(\begin{array}{c} CSTART(t_{yca}, canc(t_{yca}, t_i)) \xrightarrow{+} CSTART(t_{yca}, canc(t_{yca}, t_j)) \\ \wedge \\ CJOIN(t_{yca}, canc(t_{yca}, t_i)) \notin dom_{CSTART(t_{yca}, canc(t_{yca}, t_i))}[CSTART(t_{yca}, canc(t_{yca}, t_j))] \end{array} \right) \end{array} \right) & \text{otherwise} \end{cases}$$

- **Case 3:** Let us the consider the case where the TCT paths $canc(t_{yca}, t_i) \xrightarrow{*} t_i$ and $canc(t_{yca}, t_j) \xrightarrow{*} t_j$ are must-join paths. This case is shown in Figure 4(c). t_i may execute in parallel with t_j if at least one of the following conditions holds: (1) t_{yca} has multiple runtime instances, (2) there is a control-flow path from the $CSTART(t_{yca}, canc(t_{yca}, t_j))$ to $CSTART(t_{yca}, canc(t_{yca}, t_i))$ without the $CJOIN(t_{yca}, canc(t_{yca}, t_j))$ in $ICFG(t_{yca})$, or (3) there is a control-flow path from $CSTART(t_{yca}, canc(t_{yca}, t_i))$ to $CSTART(t_{yca}, canc(t_{yca}, t_j))$ without the $CJOIN(t_{yca}, canc(t_{yca}, t_i))$ in $ICFG(t_{yca})$. This case is mathematically presented in Table 3.

Consider our example program and its corresponding TCT in Figure 3. t_3 cannot execute in parallel with t_4 because abstract thread t_3 joins t_1 before abstract thread t_4 is started. Similarly t_5 can never run in parallel with t_6. However, all other pairs of abstract threads may run in parallel with each other.

Table 3. Thread Level MHP:Case 3

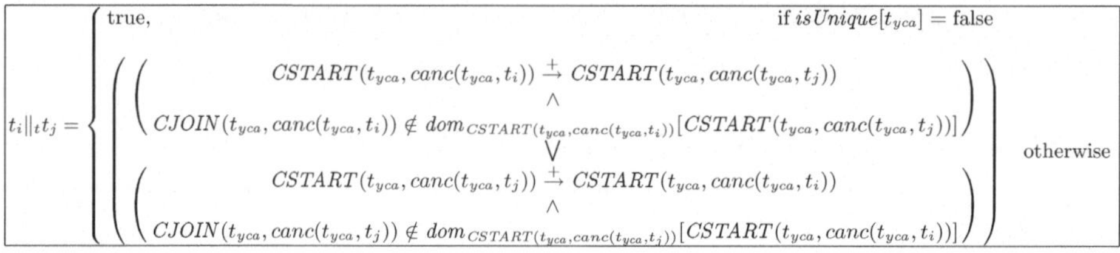

$$t_i \|_t t_j = \begin{cases} \text{true}, & \text{if } isUnique[t_{yca}] = \text{false} \\ \left(\left(\begin{array}{c} CSTART(t_{yca}, canc(t_{yca}, t_i)) \xrightarrow{+} CSTART(t_{yca}, canc(t_{yca}, t_j)) \\ \wedge \\ CJOIN(t_{yca}, canc(t_{yca}, t_i)) \notin dom_{CSTART(t_{yca}, canc(t_{yca}, t_i))}[CSTART(t_{yca}, canc(t_{yca}, t_j))] \end{array} \right) \bigvee \left(\begin{array}{c} CSTART(t_{yca}, canc(t_{yca}, t_j)) \xrightarrow{+} CSTART(t_{yca}, canc(t_{yca}, t_i)) \\ \wedge \\ CJOIN(t_{yca}, canc(t_{yca}, t_j)) \notin dom_{CSTART(t_{yca}, canc(t_{yca}, t_j))}[CSTART(t_{yca}, canc(t_{yca}, t_i))] \end{array} \right) \right) & \text{otherwise} \end{cases}$$

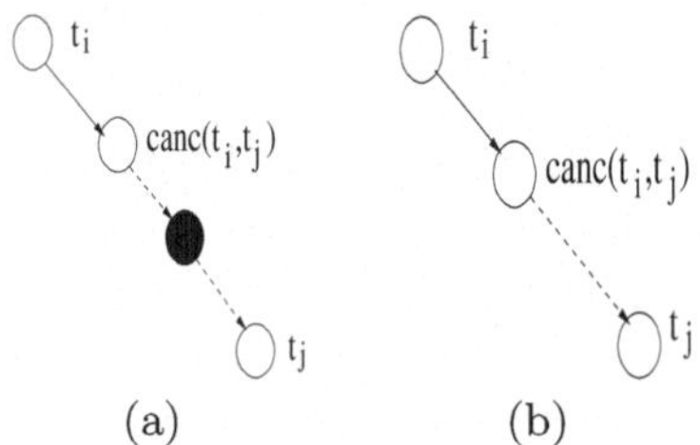

Fig. 5. Node level MHP

4.2 Node Level MHP

Thread level MHP $\|_t$ is a coarse grained approximation of MHP information, because all statements of a thread are subsumed and given the same MHP information. MHP information among statements from threads t_i and t_j can be refined further at the node level in the case where either t_i is an ancestor of t_j or t_j is ancestor of t_i in TCT.

Consider our example program and its corresponding TCT in Figure 3. Thread level MHP computation computes that $t_1 \|_t t_3$. This suggests that all statements of threads t_1 occur in parallel with statements in thread t_3, i.e., $t_1 \|_t t_3$. However, the ICFG nodes corresponding to statement 33 in t_1 will never run in parallel with ICFG nodes corresponding to statement 18 of t_3. This is because the abstract thread t_3 terminates before thread t_1 executes statement 33.

We use the symbol $\|_n$ to denote node level MHP information between two ICFG nodes. Let t_i and t_j be two abstract threads such that $t_i \in anc[t_j]$. All possible cases to determine if any two ICFG nodes v_i^m and v_j^n may execute in parallel are presented below:

- **Case 1:** Let us the consider the case where the TCT path $canc(t_i, t_j) \xrightarrow{*} t_j$ is not a must-join path. This case is shown in Figure 5(a). v_i^m may execute in parallel with v_j^n if at least one of the following conditions holds: (1) t_i has multiple runtime instances, or (2) there is a control-flow path from $CSTART(t_i, canc(t_i, t_j))$ to v_i^m in $ICFG(t_i)$. This case is mathematically presented in Table 4.

Table 4. Node Level MHP:Case 1

$$v_i^m \|_n v_j^n = \begin{cases} \text{true}, & \text{if } \mathit{isUnique}[t_i] = \text{false} \\ \mathit{CSTART}(t_i, \mathit{canc}(t_i, t_j)) \rightarrow v_i^m & \text{otherwise} \end{cases}$$

– **Case 2:** Let us the consider the case where the TCT path $\mathit{canc}(t_i, t_j) \xrightarrow{*} t_j$ is a must-join path. This case is shown in Figure 5(b). v_i^m may execute in parallel with v_j^n if at least one of the following conditions holds: (1) t_i has multiple runtime instances, or (2) there is a control-flow path from $\mathit{CSTART}(t_i, \mathit{canc}(t_i, t_j))$ to v_i^m without the $\mathit{CJOIN}(t_i, \mathit{canc}(t_i, t_j))$ in ICFG (t_i). This case is mathematically presented in Table 5.

Table 5. Node Level MHP:Case 2

$$v_i^m \|_n v_j^n = \begin{cases} \text{true}, & \text{if } \mathit{isUnique}[t_i] = \text{false} \\ \left(\begin{array}{c} \mathit{CSTART}(t_i, \mathit{canc}(t_i, t_j)) \rightarrow v_i^m \\ \wedge \\ \mathit{CJOIN}(t_i, \mathit{canc}(t_i, t_j)) \notin \mathit{dom}_{\mathit{CSTART}(t_i, \mathit{canc}(t_i, t_j))}[v_i^m] \end{array} \right) & \text{otherwise} \end{cases}$$

Table 6. Final MHP computation formula

$$v_i^m \| v_j^n = \begin{cases} (\mathit{locks}[v_i^m] \cap \mathit{locks}[v_j^n]) = \emptyset, & \text{if } t_i = t_j \text{ and } \mathit{isUnique}(t_i) = \text{ false} \\ \left(\begin{array}{c} (\mathit{locks}[v_i^m] \cap \mathit{locks}[v_j^n]) = \emptyset \\ \wedge \\ (t_i \|_t t_j) \wedge (v_i^m \|_n v_j^n) \end{array} \right) & \text{otherwise} \end{cases}$$

To summarize the MHP information based on thread level and node level, let $\|$ denote the generic MHP information between any two nodes $v_i^m \in V(t_i)$ and $v_j^n \in V(t_j)$. Then the condition under which v_i^m may execute in parallel with v_j^n is given in Table 6. Besides the thread and node level MHP relations, the condition also accounts for ordering through common lock protection and concurrency among nodes of abstract threads that are not unique.

The skeleton of the MHP algorithm is provided in Algorithm 1. Step 1 computes the abstract threads and their ICFGs along a symbolic program execution [18]. Step 3 computes *postdom* relation which is necessary to determine if the abstract thread is a must-join abstract thread or not. Step 4 finds out all possible execution paths in the ICFG. Step 5-7 compute node dominance with respect to various CSTART nodes in the abstract thread. Step 8 adds a TCT node along with its must-join information. Step 10 computes all possible must-join chains and also computes youngest common ancestor information for each pair of nodes in TCT. This can be obtained by performing a bottom-up traversal of the TCT. Steps 11-20 compute MHP information between every pair of nodes across all abstract threads using the equation given in Table 6. Since MHP information between a pair of nodes is symmetric, we carefully choose t_j in step 12 so as to reduce the number of comparisons.

Algorithm 1. MHP computation.

1: Perform a symbolic execution over the whole program to identify various abstract threads and their ICFGs.
2: **for** every abstract thread t_i in the program **do**
3:   Compute $postdom(v_i^m)$ for each $v_i^m \in V_i$.
4:   Compute reachability information ($\rightarrow$) for every pair of nodes in V_i.
5:   **for** every child abstract thread t_j created by t_i **do**
6:     Compute $dom_{CSTART(t_i,t_j)}[v_i^m]$ for each $v_i^m \in V_i$.
7:   **end for**
8:   Add appropriate node to TCT.
9: **end for**
10: Compute must-join chains and gather youngest common ancestor information for every pair of nodes in TCT.
11: **for all** abstract thread t_i **do**
12:   **for all** abstract thread t_j **do**
13:     **for all** $v_i^m \in V_i$ **do**
14:       **for all** $v_j^n \in V_j$ **do**
15:         Determine $v_i^m \| v_j^n$ using Table 6.
16:       **end for**
17:     **end for**
18:   **end for**
19: **end for**

4.3 Complexity Analysis

Let k be the total number of abstract threads. Let N be the total number of ICFG nodes per abstract thread. Step 3 can be computed in $\Theta(N^2)$ time using the algorithm suggested by Alstrup et al. [2]. Reachability information in Step 4 can be computed in $\Theta(N^2)$ time using standard depth first search algorithm. Since dominance with respect to a single node is computed in $\Theta(N^2)$ time, steps 2-9 can be executed in a worst case complexity of $\Theta((kN)^2)$. Computation of must-join chain and common parent information in step 10 can be obtained in $\Theta(k^2)$ complexity using a bottom up traversal of TCT. Careful selection of t_j will yield a time complexity of $\Theta((k + \binom{k}{2})N^2)$ for steps 11-21. Hence, the overall worst case time complexity of the algorithm is $\Theta((kN)^2)$. Note that the complexity analysis does not include the cost of computation of abstract threads and their ICFGs.

5 Implementation Details

The abstract threads and their ICFGs are computed by performing a *symbolic execution* over the whole program. The focus of the description here is on the MHP analysis and details of the symbolic execution are discussed in [18].

5.1 Intra-procedural Analysis

During intra-procedural analysis, we obtain a flow-sensitive control flow graph for a method. Each node in this graph corresponds to instructions in the original program/byte-code sequence: *BEGIN* and *END* nodes to indicate begin and end of methods, *USE* and *ASS* nodes for accessing and modifying shared data, *CSTART* and *CJOIN* nodes to indicate child abstract thread start and joins, *ACQUIRE* and *RELEASE* nodes to represent monitor regions, *NEW* nodes to indicate object/array allocations, *CALL* nodes to denote method invocations, and *ENTRY* and *EXIT* nodes to indicate thread entry and exit points (these two nodes can be maintained separately or merged with *BEGIN* and *END* nodes of the `run` method of the thread). While creating *CSTART* nodes, we create new abstract threads. For the `main` thread in Java, we create a special abstract thread.

5.2 Inter-procedural Analysis

The *CALL* nodes of various methods are linked to their polymorphic callee's *BEGIN* nodes. The *END* nodes of the callee's are connected back to the successors of the caller's *CALL* node. In case a method is involved in recursion, we reuse the already computed intra-thread control flow graph nodes and hence do not descend into its call again. This approach can lead to artifact paths in the ICFG that cannot execute in real program execution. However, this does not affect the conservative results of the analysis. In case the target of a *CALL* node is not involved in any shared data access (leads to side effect free calls), we do not descend into it.

The nodes in ICFG are properly annotated with current set of locks. The lock sets are propagated as a stack in a flow sensitive manner along with the symbolic execution. Since the symbolic execution in every method is performed in a depth first order, the lock set of a successor depends both on the lock set of one of the predecessors and on the current node. Lock sets are modified appropriately for *ACQUIRE* and *RELEASE* nodes.

Along with the symbolic execution we gradually update the TCT. Initially TCT contains one node for the abstract thread corresponding to the `main` thread. Then as and when we encounter new *CSTART* nodes at various contexts, we create new abstract threads and add them to TCT.

5.3 Barriers

A barrier synchronization point has the effect of causing all threads to wait at the barrier until every thread has reached it. Barriers can be implemented in various ways in Java [12]. Since it is hard to detect barrier synchronization points using program analysis, we annotate programs at barrier synchronization points. This annotation helps us reduce the MHP pairs as the following way: statements above a barrier point never execute concurrently with the ones below the barrier.

5.4 Limitation

The 2-level MHP algorithm computes MHP information for programs with no synchronization constructs like `wait`, `notify` and `notifyAll`. The presence of such constructs may require the MHP algorithm to enumerate every runtime threads explicitly in the compilation time and thereby making the analysis expensive and inapplicable to unbounded number of threads.

6 Experience

In this section, we report our experience in a Java-IA32 way-ahead compilation environment on a Pentium IV CPU at 2.66GHz running Redhat Linux. Our runtime system is based on GNU libgcj version 2.96 [7]. The numbers we present refer to the overall program including library classes, and excluding native code. The effect of native code for aliasing and object access has been modeled explicitly in the compiler.

We use several multi-threaded benchmark programs [10,24] to evaluate the precision of our analysis. `JGFCrypt`, `JGFSeries`, `JGFSor`, `JGFLUFact`, `JGFSparsematmult`, `JGFMoldyn`, `JGFRaytracer`, and `JGFRaytracer` are multi-threaded benchmarks from Java Grande Forum [10]. Other benchmarks `philo`, `elevator`, `sor` and `tsp` are described in [18].

We compare the running time of our analysis with that of [16] et al. We modified their MHP algorithm to use our context and flow sensitive thread model. We also use the interprocedural control flow graph structure (ICFG) described in Section 3.1 instead of the Program Execution Graph (PEG) that they proposed. To model PEG interactions at thread start and join in ICFG, we keep additional information in ICFG nodes regarding threads started and joined at that node; this helps us propagate the OUT and M information in their MHP algorithm. Abstract threads which do not represent multiple instances of the runtime threads are handled easily by their MHP algorithm. For a non-unique abstract thread, we add additional explicit MHP computation among the nodes of the abstract thread (similar to the way our MHP algorithm computes MHP information for non-unique abstract threads).

Table 7. Running time of our MHP algorithm vs Naumovich et al.

Benchmarks	Naumovich et al. MHP [16] in millisecond	Our 2-level MHP in milliseconds	Speedup
JGFSor	51	27	1.89
JGFSparsematmult	34	9	3.78
JGFSeries	33	11	3.00
JGFLUFact	50	29	1.72
JGFCrypt	163	83	1.96
JGFMoldyn	13415	13119	1.02
JGFMontecarlo	3242	3193	1.02
JGFRaytracer	2176	2034	1.07
philo	34	15	2.43
elevator	248	183	1.36
sor	338	210	1.61
tsp	696	696	1.00
mtrt	4217	3823	1.10

Table 8 reports number of abstract threads and their corresponding number of ICFG nodes. In all the benchmarks, except the `main` thread which is unique, other abstract threads have multiple instances. Table 7 compares the running time of our MHP algorithm as opposed to Naumovich et al. On an average, we show 1.77x speedup on the running time of MHP algorithm.

For larger benchmarks like `JGFMoldyn`, `JGFMontecarlo`, `JGFRayTracer`, and `tsp`, the abstract thread(s) except the `main` thread have higher number of ICFG nodes (Column 2 in Table 8). Since the computation of MHP information for abstract threads having multiple instances is same for both our algorithm and Naumovich et al. algorithm (Note that Naumovich et al. modeled runtime threads and hence did not have multiple instances of a thread; we added extra code to adapt to our thread model), the improvements are not significant. However, for other benchmarks like `JGFSeries` and `JGFSparsematmult`, we obtain large running time benefits.

Table 8. Details about benchmarks

Benchmarks	Num of abstract threads	Num of ICFG nodes in abstract threads
JGFSor	2	48+69
JGFSparsematmult	2	68+20
JGFSeries	2	53+21
JGFLUFact	2	57+57
JGFCrypt	3	52+61+61
JGFMoldyn	2	280+758
JGFMontecarlo	2	520+316
JGFRaytracer	2	387+221
philo	2	17+93
elevator	2	83+142
sor	3	83+77+77
tsp	2	181+398
mtrt	3	85+1022+1022

7 Conclusion

In this paper, we present a new thread model where individual thread abstractions are obtained in a flow and context sensitive manner from the program. The new thread abstraction models runtime threads precisely and yet efficiently during compile time. This thread model can be used in various concurrent program analysis and optimizations to improve the precision of results.

The thread model is subsequently used to compute MHP information efficiently. Splitting the MHP computation based on thread structure level (TCT) and individual thread abstraction's control flow structure level reduces the complexity of the algorithm as opposed to data flow based approach proposed by Naumovich et al. [15]. The TCT structure depicts interaction among threads and can be used to perform various thread structure analysis.

As concurrent programming is embraced by more users (and finds its way into future processor architectures), there will be increased demand on the compiler to produce precise static analysis results. Context and flow sensitive thread abstractions and thread structure analysis described in this paper can provide a solid back-bone for concurrency -aware compilation systems.

Acknowledgments

We thank Christoph v. Praun, Vivek Sarkar and Prof. Thomas Gross for their invaluable comments during early version of the paper. We also thank Matteo Corti and Florian Schneider for their contributions to the compiler infrastructure.

References

1. Alfred V. Aho, Ravi Sethi, and Jeffrey D. Ullman. *Compilers Principles, Techniques, and Tools.* Addison-Wesley publishing company, 1986.
2. Stephen Alstrup, Peter W. Lauridsen, and Mikkel Thorup. Dominators in linear time. *DIKU technical report*, (35), 1996.
3. David Callahan and Jaspal Subhlok. Static analysis of low-level synchronization. In *Workshop on parallel and distributed debugging*, pages 100–111, 1989.
4. Jong-Deok Choi, Manish Gupta, Mauricio J. Serrano, Vugranam C. Sreedhar, and Samuel P. Midkiff. Escape analysis for java. In *Proceedings of the Conference on Object-Oriented Programming Systems, Languages, and Applications (OOPSLA)*, pages 1–19, 1999.
5. JongDeok. Choi, K. Lee, A. Loginov, R. O. Callahan, V. Sarkar, and M. Sridharan. Efficient and precise datarace detection for multithreaded object-oriented programs. In *Proceedings of the ACM SIGPLAN Conference on Programming Language Design and Implementation (PLDI)*, pages 258–269, 2002.
6. Evelyn Duesterwald and Mary Lou Soffa. Concurrency analysis in the presence of procedures using a data-flow framework. In *Proceedings of the Symposium on Testing, Analysis, and Verification*, pages 36–48, 1991.
7. Gnu software, gcj - the gnu compiler for the java programming language. http://gcc.gnu.org/java.
8. James Gosling, Bill Joy, Guy Steele, and Gilad Bracha. *The Java Language Specification.* Sun Microsystems, second edition, 2000.
9. Krinke J. Static slicing of threaded programs. *Proceedings of the ACM SIGPLAN/SIGSOFT Workshop on Program Analysis for Software Tools and Engineering*, pages 35–41, June 1998.
10. Java grande forum, multi-threaded benchmark suite. http://www.epcc.ed.ac.uk/javagrande.
11. Leslie Lamport. How to make a correct multiprocess program execute correctly on a multiprocessor. *IEEE Transactions on Computers*, 46(7):779–782, July 1997.
12. D. Lea. *Concurrent Programming in Java.* Addison-Wesley, second edition, 2000.
13. Lin Li and Clark Verbrugge. A practical mhp information analysis for concurrent java programs. In *The 17th International Workshop on Languages and Compilers for Parallel Computing (LCPC'04)*, 2004.

14. S. P. Masticola and B. G. Ryder. Non-concurrency analysis. In *Proceedings of the Fourth Symposium on on Principles and Practices of Parallel Programming*, pages 129–138, May 1993.
15. G. Naumovich, G. S. Avunin, and L. A. Clarke. An efficient algorithm for computing mhp information for concurrent java programs. In *Proceedings of the 7th European Software Engineering Conference and 7th International Symposium on Foundations of Software Engineering*, pages 338–354, September 1999.
16. Gleb Naumovich and George S. Avrunin. A conservative data flow algorithm for detecting all pairs of statements that may happen in parallel. In *Proceedings of the 6th ACM SIGSOFT international symposium on Foundations of software engineering*, pages 24–34, 1998.
17. Christoph von Praun and Thomas R. Gross. Object race detection. In *Proceedings of Object-Oriented Programming, Systems, Languages, and Applications (OOPSLA'01)*, pages 70–82, October 2001.
18. Christoph von Praun and Thomas R. Gross. Static conflict analysis for multithreaded object-oriented programs. In *In Proceedings of the ACM SIGPLAN 2003 conference on Programming language design and implementation*, pages 115–128, 2003.
19. Martin Rinard. Analysis of multithreaded programs. In *Proceedings of Static Analysis Symposium (SAS'01)*, July 2001.
20. Erik Ruf. Effective synchronization removal for java. In *Proceedings of the ACM SIGPLAN 2000 conference on Programming language design and implementation (PLDI'00)*, pages 208–218, 2000.
21. V. Sarkar. Analysis and optimization of explicitly parallel programs using the parallel program graph representation. In *The 10th International Workshop on Languages and Compilers for Parallel Computing (LCPC'04)*, 1997.
22. V. Sarkar and Simons B. Parallel program graphs and their classification. In *The Proceedings of ACM SIGPLAN-SIGSOFT workshop on Program analysis for software tools and engineering*, 1998.
23. Dennis Shasha and Marc Snir. Efficient and correct execution of parallel programs that share memory. *ACM Transactions on Programming Languages and Systems*, 10(2):282–312, April 1988.
24. Spec jvm98 benchmarks, the standard performance evaluation corporation. http://www.spec.org/osg/jvm98.
25. Zehra Sura, Xing Fang, Chi-Leung Wong, Samuel P. Midkiff, Jaejin Lee, and David Padua. Compiler techniques for high performance sequentially consistent java programs. In *PPoPP '05: Proceedings of the tenth ACM SIGPLAN symposium on Principles and practice of parallel programming*, pages 2–13, New York, NY, USA, 2005. ACM Press.
26. Robert Tarjan. Depth-first search and linear graph algorithms. *SIAM Journal on Computing*, 1(2):146–160, June 1972.
27. R. N. Taylor. Complexity of analyzing the synchronization structure of concurrent programs. *Acta Informatica*, 19:57–84, 1983.

A Appendix – Thread Creation Tree

The thread creation tree described in Section 3.3 precisely depicts the start-join ordering semantics among abstract threads in a program. Since the tree is computed in a context and flow sensitive manner, presence of cyclic thread

```
class A extends Thread {
   void run() {
       Thread b=new B();
       b.start();
   }
}
class B extends Thread {
    void run() {
        Thread c=new C();
        c.start();
    }
}
class C extends Thread {
   void run() {
      Thread a=new A();
      a.start();
  }
}
```

Fig. 6. Recursive program

creation might make the TCT unbounded. Consider the code fragment given Figure 6: Thread A creates Thread B; Thread B creates Thread C; Thread C subsequently creates Thread A. Clearly there is a recursion involved in the creation of various threads. This requires special handling to avoid the recursive invocation of `start` methods.

To handle the above scenario, we perform a strongly connected component search algorithm over the call graph of the whole program to detect all those `start` methods of static thread types that are involved in a recursion. Let $\{s_1, s_2, \cdots, s_n\}$ be the set of all such strongly connected components, where each $s_i = \{x_{i1}, x_{i2}, \cdots, x_{im}\}$. Each x_{ij} denote a static thread type. Subsequently, we compute a conservative inter-procedural control flow graph for each s_i by combining the inter-procedural control flow graph of all x_{ij}. While combining the inter-procedural control flow graphs, `start` method invocations for static thread types in s_i are treated as normal method invocations and are connected via control flow edges.

While performing symbolic execution (described in Section 5), if we encounter a `start` method invocation of a static thread type which belongs to any of the above computed s_i then we create a node in the TCT corresponding to s_i. *isUnique* and *mjoin* predicates for the created TCT node are conservatively set to `false`. ICFG of the created TCT node is set to the inter-procedural control flow graph of s_i.

Evaluating the Impact of Thread Escape Analysis on a Memory Consistency Model-Aware Compiler

Chi-Leung Wong[1], Zehra Sura[2], Xing Fang[3], Kyungwoo Lee[3], Samuel P. Midkiff[3], Jaejin Lee[4], and David Padua[5]

[1] KAI Software Lab, Intel Americas, Inc., Champaign, IL, USA
chi.leung.david.wong@intel.com
[2] IBM Thomas J. Watson Research Center, Yorktown Heights, NY, USA
zsura@us.ibm.com
[3] Purdue University, West Lafayette, IN, USA
{xfang,kwlee,smidkiff}@ecn.purdue.edu
[4] Seoul National University, Seoul, Korea
jlee@cse.snu.ac.kr
[5] Dept. of Computer Science, University of Illinois at Urbana-Champaign, USA
padua@cs.uiuc.edu

Abstract. The widespread popularity of languages allowing explicitly parallel, multi-threaded programming, e.g. Java and C#, have focused attention on the issue of *memory model* design. The Pensieve Project is building a compiler that will enable both language designers to prototype different memory models, and optimizing compilers to adapt to different memory models. Among the key analyses required to implement this system are *thread escape analysis*, i.e. detecting when a referenced object is accessible by more than one thread, *delay set analysis*, and *synchronization analysis*.

In this paper, we evaluate the impact of different escape analysis algorithms on the effectiveness of the Pensieve system when both delay set analysis and synchronization analysis are used. Since both analyses make use of results of escape analyses, their precison and cost is dependent on the precision of the escape analysis algorithm. It is the goal of this paper to provide a quantitative evalution of this impact.

1 Introduction

In shared memory parallel programs, different threads of the program communicate with each other by reading from and writing to shared memory locations. Experience shows that to achieve high performance without extensive analyses, it is necessary to allow memory accesses to follow an order of execution that is non-intuitive one[13]. Memory system behavior observed by different processors constitute the memory model. It is difficult to define a memory model that is both easy to use and implement efficiently. The goal of the Pensieve compiler system is to provide a testbed to evaluate memory models by creating "virtual"

E. Ayguadé et al. (Eds.): LCPC 2005, LNCS 4339, pp. 170–184, 2007.

memory models and to evaluate the overhead of these models in the presence of aggressive compiler analyses and optimizations. Given a program and a memory model specification, the Pensieve compiler will ultimately be able to generate different versions of machine code corresponding to the specified memory model. However, the current version of the Pensieve system only creates a sequentially consistent "virtual" memory model and implements it on the Intel IA32 and PowerPC processors, so the virtual memory model and the target memory models are currently hardwired inside the system. An important issue in the system design is performance — both the compilation time and application time should be minimized. In this paper, we investigate the impact of escape analysis on our Pensieve system. We study how escape analysis affects the cost and precision of other analysis algorithms, which in turn affects both the compilation cost and application performance. In particular, this paper makes the following contributions:

- it describes the Pensieve compilation system;
- it describes the interaction between escape analysis and synchronization/ delay set analyses.
- it presents a quantitative study on the impact of escape analysis on the Pensieve system.

1.1 Memory Models

A memory model[1] specifies the memory system behavior, and can be specified for programming languages as well as hardware. Memory models are necessary because they define the allowable set of outcomes of a parallel program and, as a result, they allow programmers to reason about their programs and compilers to generate valid code. Until recently, memory models were of concern only to expert systems programmers, and computer architects. With the advent of languages like Java and C#, many programmers write multi-threaded programs targeting Internet, database, and GUI applications, in addition to traditional high performance computing applications. Because of this, memory models have become an issue for much of the programmer community and for language and compiler designers. The trade-offs between ease-of-use and performance have become increasingly important.

Sequential Consistency. A well-known memory model is sequential consistency (SC), defined by Lamport[15]. It is often considered to be the simplest and most intuitive memory consistency model [13]. Scheurich and Dubois[19] described a sufficient condition for SC and Gharachorloo et. al.[8] presented the condition in a slightly difference way. The idea of these sufficient conditions is to delay a memory access until all previous ones within the same thread are completed. These conditions impose constraints so that some performance improving optimizations cannot be applied in the hardware . In addition, it constrains

[1] Memory models are often called consistency models in the context of hardware.

compiler optimizations that may reorder memory accesses. The issue of memory models can be illustrated by the busy-wait synchronization example shown in Figure 1(a). Both `x` and `a` are shared variables accessible by two concurrent threads. Thread 1 does some computation and stores the result in `a`, and then uses `x` to inform Thread 2 that a *new* value of `a` is ready to be read. Thread 2 waits for the data by executing a `while` loop that reads `x` and waits for the value to become non-zero, at which time the thread will read the value from `a`. The program shown in Figure 1(a), if executed in a SC environment, achieves the described intention.

Relaxed Consistency Models. Most multiprocessor systems implement consistency models, such as weak ordering and release consistency [4], which impose fewer constraints than SC on the order of shared memory accesses. Where clear, we will refer to these more relaxed models by the acronym RC. RC models allow more instruction reordering, increasing the potential for instruction level parallelism and as a result can potentially deliver better performance. Synchronization primitives, such as *fences*, are used in these systems to force an order on memory operations that is more constrained than that implied by the default consistency model.

The program shown in Figure 1(a), if executed in a RC environment, is not guaranteed to achieve the programmer's intention. This is because, for performance reasons, the compiler or hardware may reorder the two memory operations performed by Thread 1 such that the update of `x` reaches Thread 2 *before* the update of `a`. If this happens, `T2` could read the updated value of `x` (i.e. 1), exit the loop, and then read an *old* value (i.e. 0) of `a`. Therefore, the intention of the programmer is not achieved. In the presence of the `fence` instruction, the memory reording does not happen. Figure 1(b) shows a correct implementation of the busy-wait construct using fences.

Both `x` and `a` are zero initially.

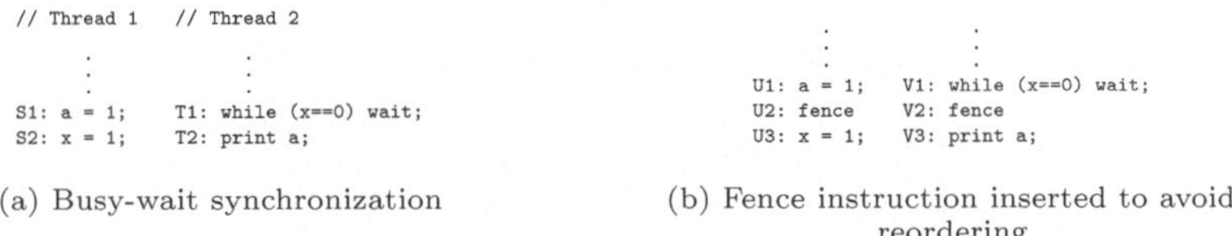

(a) Busy-wait synchronization (b) Fence instruction inserted to avoid reordering

Fig. 1. Memory model issues example

1.2 Enforcing Memory Models

Enforcing a memory model implies enforcing some memory access orders. However, not all orderings specified by the memory model need to be enforced. In fact, only those orderings that may affect the outcome of the program must be enforced. To generate efficient and correct code, a compiler must determine which memory accesses may not be reordered and enforce only those orderings. The orderings that must be enforced are called *delays*. In [20], Shasha and Snir give minimal criteria for which orders must be enforced in order to have a sequential consistent execution of a program. Both [20] and this paper assume that the hardware provides primitives, such as fences, powerful enough to enforce the required orderings. Moreover, some compiler optimizations must be constrained if applying them may violate a delay. In [20], the authors present a delay set analysis (DSA) algorithm to determine the required orderings. DSA requires the thread structure of the programs to determine the delay information.

In Section 2, we describe the Pensieve system design. In Section 3, we describe the escape analysis proposed in [23]. In Section 4 and Section 5, we describe how the escape analysis impact delay set analysis and synchronization analyses respectively. In Section 6, experimental results are presented to evaluate the impact of escape analysis quantitatively. This paper concludes in Section 7.

2 Pensieve Compiler System Design

Our Pensieve Compiler System supports SC on top of two hardware platforms that support more relaxed memory models — the Intel platform and the PowerPC platform, which is an extension of the Jikes RVM infrastructure [7,9]. Figure 2 gives an overview of the Pensieve system.It shows three phases:

1. In the analysis phase, a set of delays is computed. The delays are the ordering constraints to be enforced both by the compiler and the hardware.
2. In the modified code optimization phase, the set of delays identified by the analysis phase is checked before performing an optimization transformation. If a transformation would violate a delay, it is not applied.
3. In the fence insertion and optimization phase, fences are inserted into the program to force the delays to be enforced by the hardware. This phase looks for opportunities to synchronize multiple delays with a single fence instruction. The details of this phase are described in [10,11].

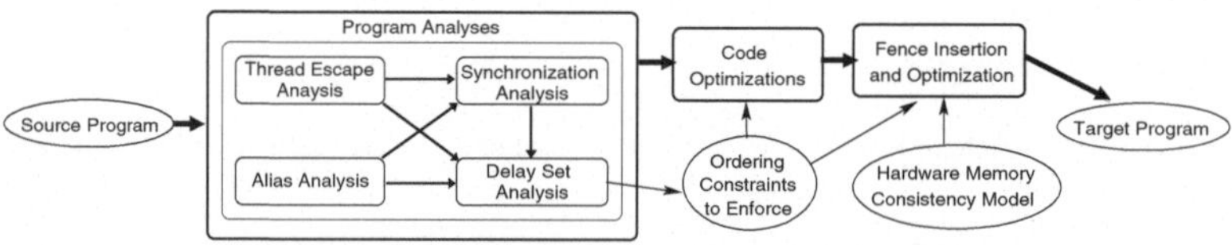

Fig. 2. Overview of the Pensieve system

3 Thread Escape Analysis

Thread escape analysis aims at identifying objects which *may* be accessed by two or more threads. In the Pensieve System environment, the analysis is performed as the application programs are running, so the time to perform escape analysis is a part of the overall execution time. Therefore, an inexpensive and moderately accurate analysis algorithm will be a good choice in our approach. In this project, we balance analysis algorithm performance and accuracy. While we are not aiming at having an escape analysis that is precise for the whole program, the analysis should be precise enough that fences are not unnecessarily inserted into frequently executed methods. In light of this, we chose to design the simplest possible algorithm to minimize the cost of the analysis. In the Pensieve compiler system, we have implemented four escape analysis algorithms:

- a *connectivity* based analysis described in [23]
- a *field* based analysis described in [22]
- Bogda's analysis described in [6]
- Ruf's analysis described in [18]

3.1 Connectivity Based Analysis

The basic characteristics of the algorithm[23] are:

- Analysis of most memory accesses is field insensitive, with accesses in `Runnable` objects being field sensitive.
- More precise context information is constructed for the `run()` method of a `Runnable` class (i.e. `this` is not assumed to escape) than for other methods.
- Objects assumed to be reachable by multiple threads, are marked as escaping only if they are *accessed* by multiple threads.

The analysis is a two-phase analysis. The **bottom-up phase** computes the effect of methods and computes how the methods make arguments escaping. The **top-down phase** computes the context of methods and determines how the caller makes arguments escaping before passing them to their callees. Both phases are done by visiting the strongly connected component (SCC) graph induced by the call graph in (reverse) topological order. The analysis makes use of the union-find data structure to avoid fixed point computations for recursive methods within an SCC.

3.2 Field Based Analysis

The basic characteristics of the algorithm[22] are:

- Analysis of all objects is field sensitive. To avoid an expensive analysis, unlike [18], it merges escaping properties of fields of all objects of the same type. For example, if O_1`.f` $= O_2$ and O_2 is found to be escaping, then for any object O, if O is referened by a field `f`, it is assumed to be escaping.
- Analysis of the `run()` method of a `Runnable`, looks for conditions implying `this` is not escaping, instead of assuming `this` is escaping. .

The analysis is an iterative analysis — the analysis is performed until no escaping properties of variables and fields change. It is a partially context sensitive analysis.

3.3 Bogda's Analysis

Bogda's analysis[6] is a two phase and iterative analysis. The basic characteristics of the algorithm are:

- an object is escaping if any of the following conditions is fulfilled
  - it is reachable via more than one field reference;
  - it is reachable by a static field; or
  - it is reachable by a `Runnable` object.

3.4 Ruf's Analysis

Ruf's analysis[18] is a three phase analysis. Like our connectivity based analysis, it makes use of the union-find data structure to avoid fixed point computations for recursive methods inside an SCC. The basic characteristics of the algorithm are:

- an object is escaping if it is both
  - reachable from static fields or `Runnable` objects;
  - synchronized by more than one thread.

Since the analysis is designed for synchronization removal, we have adapted it for fence insertion. Instead of using the second condition "synchronized by more than one thread", the adapted analysis checks whether an object is "accessed by more than one thread". After the adaptation, the cost of analysis could be increased because there are more object accesses than synchronization operations.

4 Impact of Escape Analysis on Delay Set Analysis

Delay set analysis computes a *delay set*, i.e. a set of ordered pairs of memory access (x, y) such that y must be delayed until x has completed. In [20], Shasha and Snir present an accurate method to find the minimal delay set. In the Pensieve compiler system, we use a much simpler approximate method described in[21]. The analysis in [20] finds cycles in a graph where nodes are shared variable accesses from two or more threads. In our simplified escape analysis, we look for pairs of shared memory accesses (x, y) such that x precedes y; y is aliased to y' in another thread; x is aliased to x' in another thread; and y' precedes x'.

Escape analysis affects both the precision and cost of delay set analysis. The fewer the number of escaping variables, the fewer pairs (x, y) that need to be checked, and the fewer the number of x' and y' accesses. This increases both the speed and the precison of delay set analysis.

5 Impact of Escape Analysis on Synchronization Analysis

Synchronization information helps reduce the number of conflict edges in the graph considered for delay set analysis, and thus improves the precision of delay set analysis[14].

In our analysis, we consider the following Java synchronization primitives:

- `synchronized` blocks, used for lock-based synchronization
- thread `start()` and `join()` calls, used to determine the program thread structure.

Our lock-based synchronization analysis has been described in [22]. It improves the accuracy of our approximate delay set analysis. In essence, we can ignore pairs of nodes (x, y) and (x', y'), as described above, when both are synchronized with the same lock. See [22] for details.

A detailed description of our start-join-based synchronization analysis is given in [21]. The idea is to make use of the Java language semantics of `start()` and `join()`. When a thread is spawned via a thread `start()`, all memory accesses of the creator thread that are initiated before `start()`, complete before the point where the new thead starts. Also, if a thread T invokes a `join()` call to wait for another thread to terminate, then all memory accesses performed by the terminating thread complete before T continues execution after the `join()`.

Escape analysis affects the precision of synchronization analysis. When doing synchronization analysis, we consider only `join()` calls that are matched with some `start()` call. A `join()` is matched with a `start()` only if the objects that they are invoked on do not escape. Matched `join()` calls can reduce the number of pairs (x, y) to be considered. Therefore, when escape information is more precise, more `join()` calls can be matched, so more pairs (x, y) can be ignored.

6 Experimental Results

In this section we present the results of executing benchmark programs compiled with our Pensieve compiler using the four escape analyses described in Section 3. Our goal is to quantitatively evaluate the impact of different escape analysis algorithms.

6.1 Benchmark Programs

Table 1 shows the benchmark programs used in the experiments. These are standard benchmarks from the SPECjvm98, SPECjbb2000 and the Java Grande benchmark suite. There are also some programs taken from the literature, including the concurrent implementation of two data structures, hashmaps and

Table 1. Benchmark Characteristics

Benchmark	Description	Source	# bytecodes
moldyn	Molecular dynamics application	Java Grande Forum Multithreaded Benchmarks[3]	26,913
montecarlo	MonteCarlo simulation	Java Grande Forum Multithreaded Benchmarks[3]	63,452
raytracer	Ray tracing application	Java Grande Forum Multithreaded Benchmarks[3]	33,198
mtrt	Ray tracing application	From the SPECjvm98 benchmark suite[2]	290,260
boundedbuf	Producer-consumer application	Uses Doug Lea's Blocking Queue class[16]	12,050
geneticalgo	Parallel genetic algorithm	Adapted from the sequential version version in [16]	30,147
hashmap	Microbenchmark for concurrent hashmaps	Uses Doug Lea's ConcurrenthashMap class[16]	24,989
seive	Sieve of Erastothenes	From an example in [12]	10,811
disksched	Disk scheduler using an elevator algorithm	From an example in [17]	21,186
jbb	Middle-layer database server application	SPECjbb2000[1]	521,021

queues. These concurrent data structures are expected to be widely used and have been incorporated in the Java standard libraries.

6.2 Target Architectures

The experiments are performed on two platforms — the Intel IA32 platform and the PowerPC platform:

- The Intel platform is a Dell PowerEdge 6600 SMP with 4 Intel 1.5Ghz Xeon processors with 1MB cache each, and 6G system memory.
- The PowerPC platform is an IBM SP 9076-550 with 8 375Mhz processors with 8GB system memory.

6.3 Software Settings

Our compiler system is implemented on top of the Jikes Research Virtual Machine [7,5,9] version 2.3.4. We use the FastAdaptiveSemiSpace configuration with no fences inserted within the virtual machine code. For the experiments reported below, we force the system to use the optimizing compiler. To evaluate the impact of escape analyses, we compare the analysis times of delay set analysis and synchronization analysis. In addition, we compare the precision of delay set analysis and synchronization analysis w.r.t. different escape analyses by comparing the application execution time and the number of fences inserted. In all the graphical plots, the geometrical means are included to summarize data for all the benchmark programs.

There are six escape analyses compared:

- `empty` assumes all memory accesses are escaping accesses.
- `argEscape` assumes all memory locations reachable from some arguments are escaping.
- `connect` is the connectivity based escape analysis algorithm described in Section 3.
- `field-based` is the field based escape analysis algorithm described in Section 3.
- `bogda` is Bogda's escape analysis algorithm described in Section 3.
- `ruf5` is Ruf's escape analysis algorithm described in Section 3.

6.4 Cost of Escape Analysis

Figure 3 presents the time taken using a log scale for performing escape analysis. The times for `empty` and `argEscape` are small because they are very simple. Other than these two trivial analyses, the connectivity based analysis is the fastest because it does not require a fixed-point computation. It takes longer than `empty` and `argEscape` because it is an interprocedural analysis. The analysis times of `field-based` and `bogda` are longer because they are interprocedural iterative analyses that requires a fixed-point computation. On average, the analysis time of `ruf5` is between those of `connect` and `field-based`.

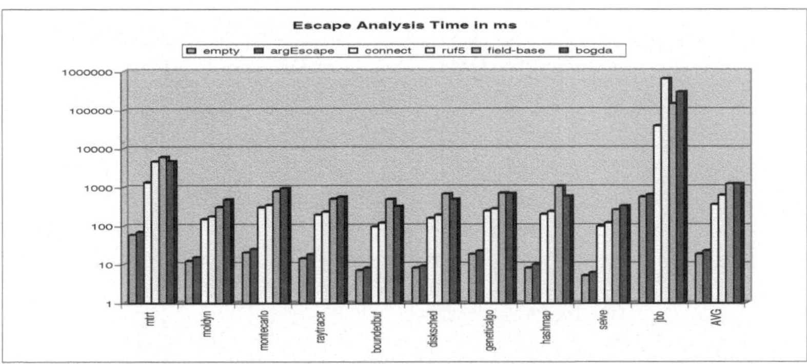

Fig. 3. Escape analysis time in msec

	connect	ruf5	bogda	field-based	argEscape	empty
mtrt	62371	54240	200307	207529	243376	247371
moldyn	11782	297740	297782	298239	308673	309121
montecarlo	22132	3583	4101	7095	31766	31847
raytracer	17768	46960	48967	49116	63153	63539
boundedbuf	2599	4498	4733	4778	6163	6163
disksched	4855	5394	5425	5791	7748	7748
geneticalgo	9574	17126	18282	16877	26952	26952
hashmap	4030	4134	4274	4274	4972	4972
seive	2668	4925	4925	5139	5525	5525
jbb	1872250	916591	832800	836559	1847126	1852503

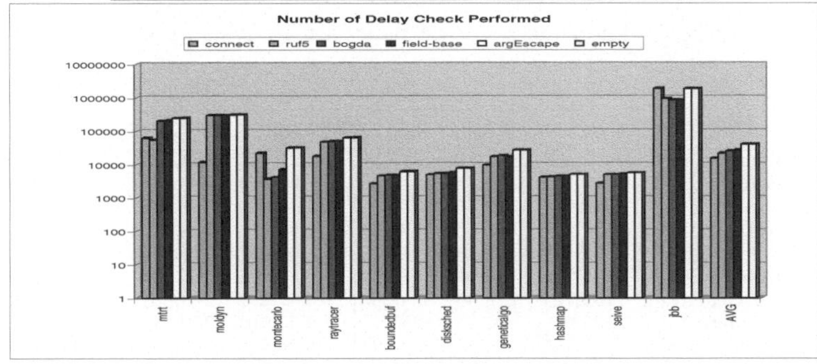

Fig. 4. Number of delay checks

6.5 Impact on the Cost of Delay Set Analysis and Synchronization Analysis

We evaluate the impact of escape analysis on delay set analysis and synchronization analysis separately. In both cases, we measure the time taken to perform these two analyses. In case of delay set analysis, we also measure the number of memory access pairs checked for delays.

Figure 4 shows the number of delay checks for different escape analysis algorithms. Since the value range is huge, it is plotted using a log scale. We can see `connect` analysis lead to fewer checks than other escape analyses for most benchmarks except `mtrt`, `montecarlo` and `jbb`. By comparing `connect` and `field-based` for benchmarks `montecarlo` and `jbb`, we can see that in these benchmarks, being field sensitive is important. On average, `connect` leads to

	connect	ruf5	bogda	field-based	argEscape	empty
mtrt	58.41	56.25	93.52	90.38	104.20	108.35
moldyn	1.90	46.26	47.04	47.26	49.53	49.61
montecarlo	9.53	1.77	1.88	2.27	11.13	10.48
raytracer	2.80	8.14	8.53	8.70	11.05	11.07
boundedbuf	0.42	0.70	0.71	0.69	0.89	1.83
disksched	0.85	1.03	1.03	1.09	1.46	1.46
geneticalgo	1.93	3.59	3.68	3.41	5.25	4.76
hashmap	0.59	0.69	0.72	0.71	0.79	0.83
seive	0.87	1.16	1.19	1.19	1.48	1.30
jbb	304.09	144.76	127.21	127.43	297.69	295.74

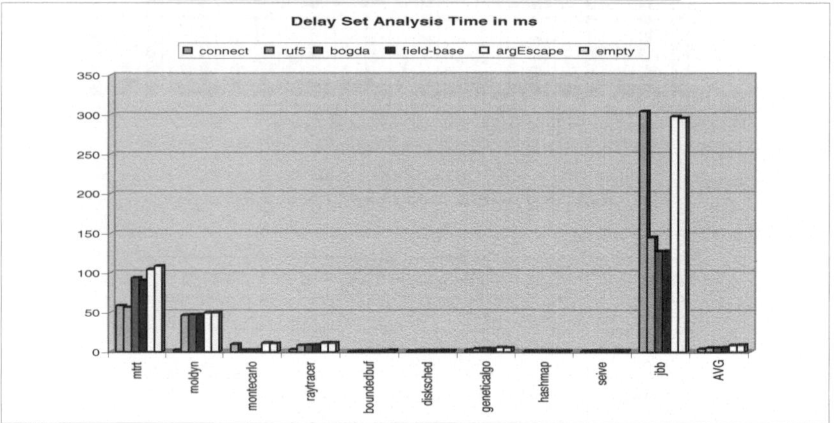

Fig. 5. The time spent on delay set analysis in msec

	field-based	bogda	empty	argEscape	connect	ruf5
mtrt	478.30	829.88	873.38	905.41	841.13	839.60
moldyn	73.85	122.74	133.15	132.14	130.63	132.87
montecarlo	270.28	343.19	359.99	362.02	358.69	349.72
raytracer	134.14	188.00	198.61	200.09	200.85	190.60
boundedbuf	67.57	118.79	117.81	117.04	125.85	123.36
disksched	103.17	160.92	180.60	182.97	165.02	161.78
geneticalgo	159.78	228.40	248.58	247.21	248.88	251.44
hashmap	139.50	237.22	251.10	251.19	252.38	247.33
seive	38.18	74.56	76.94	76.75	76.04	75.48
jbb	56070.55	74231.65	59977.42	58466.61	72130.53	133368.70

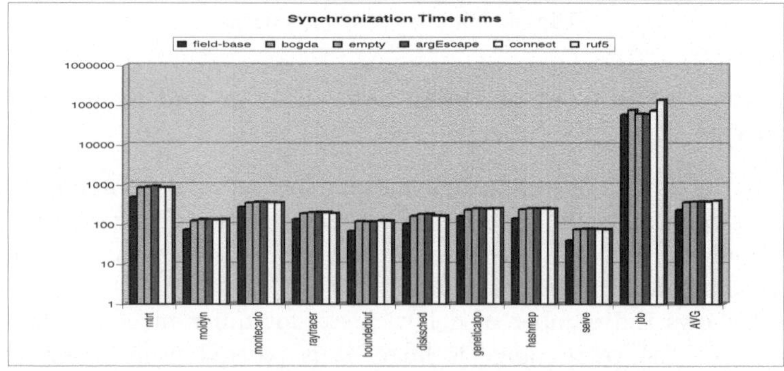

Fig. 6. The time spent on synchronization analysis time in msec

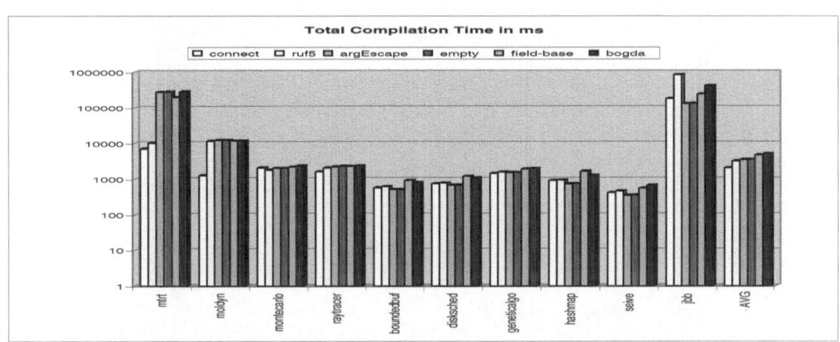

Fig. 7. Total Compilation Time in msec

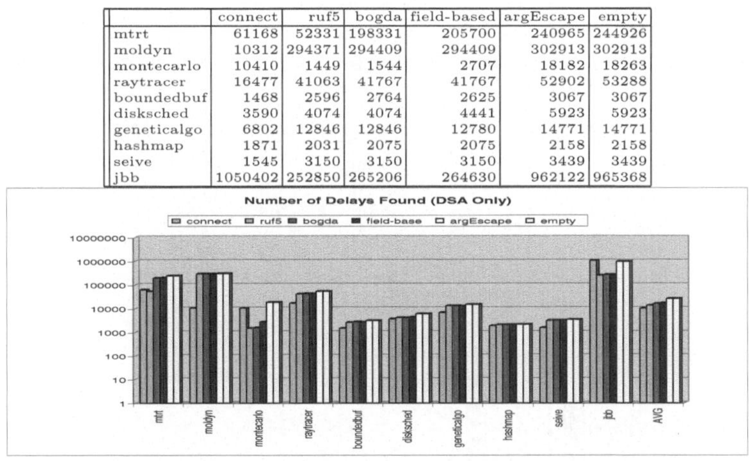

	connect	ruf5	bogda	field-based	argEscape	empty
mtrt	61168	52331	198331	205700	240965	244926
moldyn	10312	294371	294409	294409	302913	302913
montecarlo	10410	1449	1544	2707	18182	18263
raytracer	16477	41063	41767	41767	52902	53288
boundedbuf	1468	2596	2764	2625	3067	3067
disksched	3590	4074	4074	4441	5923	5923
geneticalgo	6802	12846	12846	12780	14771	14771
hashmap	1871	2031	2075	2075	2158	2158
seive	1545	3150	3150	3150	3439	3439
jbb	1050402	252850	265206	264630	962122	965368

Fig. 8. The number of delays found (delay set analysis only)

fewer checks than other escape analyses. A similar pattern is observed for the delay set analysis times shown in Figure 5.

Figure 6 shows the synchronization analysis time. We can see the analysis times for synchronization analysis are similar for `bogda`, `empty`, `argEscape`, `connect` and `ruf5`. We observe that `field-based` leads to faster synchronization analysis on all benchmarks. In our system implementation, `field-based` shares some data structures with synchronization analysis, so synchronization analysis reuses data computed by `field-based`. We expect these data reuses reduce the synchronization analysis time.

The total compilation time is shown in Figure 7. We observe that, on average, `connect` outperforms other non-trivial escape analysis algorithms in this aspect.

	connect	ruf5	bogda	field-based	argEscape	empty
mtrt	61160	52323	197468	204837	239914	243875
moldyn	10312	294324	294362	294362	302866	302866
montecarlo	9846	1406	1501	2664	17618	17699
raytracer	16477	40945	41648	41648	52783	53169
boundedbuf	1468	2596	2764	2625	3067	3067
disksched	3590	4069	4069	4436	5918	5918
geneticalgo	6802	12835	12835	12769	14760	14760
hashmap	1871	2028	2072	2072	2155	2155
seive	1541	3146	3146	3146	3435	3435
jbb	1049689	252753	265108	264532	961432	964669

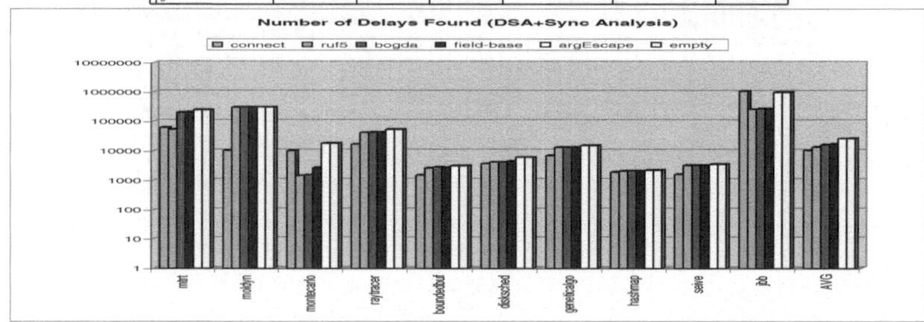

Fig. 9. The number of delays found (delay set analysis + synchronization analysis)

	connect	ruf5	bogda	field-based	argEscape	empty
mtrt	3.80	3.78	23.47	24.26	27.08	27.06
moldyn	74.08	659.89	663.48	660.92	661.80	664.59
montecarlo	119.25	96.52	75.79	93.09	143.04	143.33
raytracer	74.94	798.80	796.49	795.08	801.13	798.53
boundedbuf	1484.75	1467.53	1430.16	1506.80	1443.88	1407.05
disksched	5.83	4.70	4.88	4.86	5.54	5.86
geneticalgo	53.22	59.16	55.91	58.92	57.62	65.74
hashmap	42.07	52.63	50.12	48.45	48.20	55.05
seive	160.79	219.55	220.04	217.83	214.93	215.61
jbb	4346.56	4419.63	4822.99	4746.00	4206.01	4231.55

(a) Application execution time

(b) Slowdown

Fig. 10. Slowdown due to fence instruction insertion (delay set analysis only)

6.6 Impact on Analysis Precision

The analysis precision of delay set analysis and synchronization analysis can be measured in terms of application execution time and number of delays found. In both cases, we can view the precision in the following cases:

- the performance of delay set analysis (without applying synchronization analysis)
- the performance of delay set analysis with refinement of synchronization analysis

	connect	ruf5	bogda	field-based	argEscape	empty
mtrt	3.77	3.80	23.50	24.70	27.08	27.05
moldyn	76.42	664.30	670.10	665.27	663.29	666.33
montecarlo	119.21	95.26	76.88	98.98	147.86	144.56
raytracer	74.91	798.32	795.36	796.14	801.17	802.04
boundedbuf	1496.27	1464.73	1453.98	1491.85	1415.81	1432.90
disksched	4.89	5.87	4.37	4.05	5.75	5.55
geneticalgo	56.76	62.55	63.92	56.26	58.61	57.24
hashmap	51.78	41.29	48.66	59.47	49.31	49.44
seive	161.18	220.07	220.14	220.81	218.31	221.04
jbb	4330.03	4417.78	4803.98	4741.15	4221.02	4215.59

(a) Application execution time

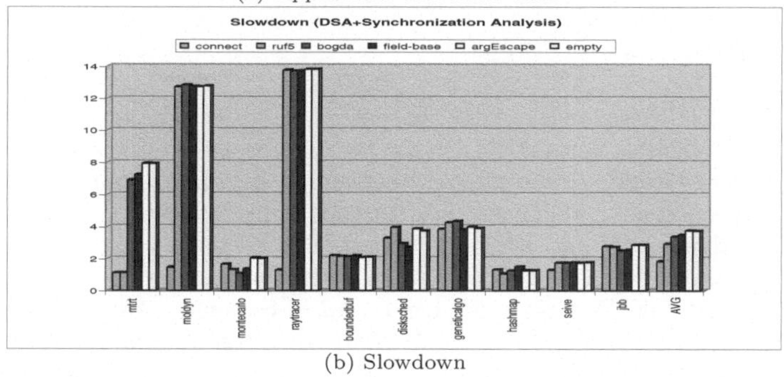

(b) Slowdown

Fig. 11. Slowdown due to fence instruction insertion (delay set analysis + synchronization analysis)

Figure 8 shows the number of delays found when only delay set analysis is applied. We can see that for most benchmarks fewer delays are found when `connect` is applied. Similar to the pattern described in previous section, `connect` does not outperform other escape analyses for benchmarks `mtrt`, `montecarlo` and `jbb`. We can see a similar pattern when both delay set analysis and synchronization analysis are applied, shown in Figure 9.

Finally, the application execution times are reported in Figure 10 (only DSA applied) and Figure 11 (both DSA and synchronization analysis applied). In both settings, we also plot the slowdown graphs in the same figure. We can see the `connect` performs well for most benchmarks except for `montecarlo`, `disksched` and `jbb`. On average, `connect` is the best analysis from slowdown perspective.

7 Conclusions

In this paper, we have presented the Pensieve Compiler System. The system presented in this paper focuses on enforcing SC on the Intel IA32 and PowerPC platforms. We also presented the interactions between our thread escape analyses, synchronization analysis, and delay set analysis implemented in the system. We can see, on average, the connectivity analysis is the best escape analysis algorithms leading to good application performance. From the analysis time perspective, connectivity analysis is much faster than other non-trivial analyses. Ruf's analysis is the second best analysis that lead to good application performance. For some benchmarks, Ruf's analysis outperforms connectivitiy analysis. However, Ruf'a analysis is much slower than connectivity analysis, so we choose to use `connect` as the escape analysis in the Pensieve system.

By comparing with the field based analysis, we can see the importance of being field sensitive for benchmarks like `montecarlo` and `jbb`. The result motivates further works to design a fast and precise escape analysis to be used by delay set analysis and synchronization analysis by enabling field sensitivity for connectivity analysis without increasing the analysis cost significantly.

References

1. SPEC JBB 2000 Benchmark. URL: http://www.specbench.org/jbb2000.
2. SPEC JVM Client98 Suite. URL: http://www.specbench.org/jvm98/jvm98.
3. The Java Grande Forum Multi-threaded Benchmarks. URL: http://www.epcc.ed.ac.uk/javagrande/threads/contents.html.
4. Sarita V. Adve and Kourosh Gharachorloo. Shared memory consistency models: A tutorial. *IEEE Computer*, pages 66–76, December 1996.
5. M. Arnold, S. Fink, D. Grove, M. Hind, and P. Sweeney. Adaptive optimization in the Jalapeño JVM. In *Proc. ACM SIGPLAN Conference on Object-Oriented Programming and Systems, Languages, and Applications (OOPSLA) 2000*, Minneapolis, MN, October 2000.
6. Jeff Bogda and Urs Holzle. Removing unnecessary synchronization in java. In *Proceedings of the 14th ACM SIGPLAN conference on Object-oriented programming, systems, languages, and applications*, pages 35–46. ACM Press, 1999.
7. B. Alpern et. al. The Jalapeño virtual machine. *IBM System Journal*, 39(1), February 2000.
8. Kourosh Gharachorloo et. al. Memory consistency and event ordering in scalable shared-memory multiprocessors. In *Proceedings of The 17th Annual International Symposium on Computer Architecture (ISCA)*, pages 15–26, May 1990.
9. Michael G. Burke et. al. The Jalapeño Dynamic Optimizing Compiler for Java. In *Proceedings of the 1999 ACM Java Grande Conference*, pages 129–141, Palo Alto, CA, USA, Jun 1999.
10. Xing Fang, Jaejin Lee, and Samuel P. Midkiff. Automatic fence insertion for shared memory processing. In *2003 ACM International Conference on Supercomputing*, June 2003.
11. Xing Fang, Jaejin Lee, and Samuel P. Midkiff. An optimizing and retargetable fence insertion algorithm. Technical Report ECE-HPCLab-033002, High Performance Computing Lab, School of Electrical and Computer Engineering, Purdue University, 2003.
12. Stephen Hartley. *Concurrent Programming: the Java Programming Language*. Oxford University Press, 1998.
13. Mark D. Hill. Multiprocessors should support simple memory-consistency models. *IEEE Computer*, August 1998.
14. Arvind Krishnamurthy and Katherine Yelick. Analyses and optimizations for shared address space programs. *Journal of Parallel and Distributed Computing*, 38:139–144, 1996.
15. Leslie Lamport. How to make a multiprocessor computer that correctly executes multiprocess programs. *IEEE Transactions on Computers*, C-28(9):690–691, September 1979.

16. Doug Lea. *Concurrent Programming in Java.* Addison Wesley, 1999. URL: `http://gee.cs.oswego.edu/dl/cpj`.
17. Douglas Lea and Doug Lea. *Concurrent Programming in Java: Design Principles and Patterns.* Addison-Wesley Longman Publishing Co., Inc., Boston, MA, USA, 1996.
18. Erik Ruf. Effective synchronization removal for java. In *Conference on Programming Languages, Design, and Implementation (PLDI)*, 2000.
19. C. Scheurich and M. Dubois. Correct memory operation of cache-based multiprocessors. In *Proc. of the 14th Annual Int'l Symp. on Computer Architecture (ISCA'87)*, pages 234–243, 1987.
20. Dennis Shasha and Marc Snir. Efficient and correct execution of parallel programs that share memory. *ACM Transactions on Programming Languages and Systems*, 10(2):282–312, April 1988.
21. Zehra Sura, Xing Fang, Chi-Leung Wong, Samuel P. Midkiff, Jaejin Lee, and David Padua. Compiler techniques for high performance sequentially consistent java programs. In *Proceedings of the ACM SIGPLAN Symposium on Principles and Practice of Parallel Programming*, Chicago IL, 2005.
22. Zehra N. Sura. *Analyzing Threads for Shared Memory Consistency.* PhD thesis, University of Illinois at Urbana-Champaign, 2004.
23. Chi-Leung Wong. *Thread Escape Analysis for a Memory Consistency Model-aware Compiler.* PhD thesis, University of Illinois at Urbana-Champaign, 2005.

Concurrency Analysis for Parallel Programs with Textually Aligned Barriers

Amir Kamil and Katherine Yelick

Computer Science Division, University of California, Berkeley
{kamil,yelick}@cs.berkeley.edu

Abstract. A fundamental problem in the analysis of parallel programs is to determine when two statements in a program may run concurrently. This analysis is the parallel analog to control flow analysis on serial programs and is useful in detecting parallel programming errors and as a precursor to semantics-preserving code transformations. We consider the problem of analyzing parallel programs that access shared memory and use barrier synchronization, specifically those with textually aligned barriers and single-valued expressions. We present an intermediate graph representation for parallel programs and an efficient interprocedural analysis algorithm that conservatively computes the set of all concurrent statements. We improve the precision of this algorithm by using context-free language reachability to ignore infeasible program paths. We then apply the algorithms to static race detection and show that it can benefit from the concurrency information provided.

1 Introduction

As the rate of scaling of uniprocessor machines slows down, application writers and system vendors alike have been turning to multiprocessor machines for performance. Most major CPU manufacturers have chip products with multiple cores, so that parallelism once hidden within the micro-architecture will now be exposed to the assembly language and, in all likelihood, to application level software. Such systems are modeled after SMP multiprocessors and allow all processors to simultaneously access shared memory. In addition, for large-scale parallel machines there is increasing interest in global address space languages, which give programmers the illusion of a shared memory machine on top of distributed memory machines and clusters. Analysis and optimization of parallel shared memory code is increasingly important in both of these settings.

In this paper we introduce an *interprocedural concurrency analysis* for programs with barrier synchronization, which captures information about the potential concurrency between statements in a program. The analysis is done for the Titanium language [25], a single program, multiple data global address space variation of Java that runs on most parallel and distributed memory machines. We first construct a *concurrency graph* representation of a program, taking advantage of two features of the Titanium language parallel execution model: *textual barrier alignment*, which statically guarantees that all threads reach the same textual sequence of barriers, and *single-valued* expressions, which provably evaluate to the same value on all threads [1]. We then present a simple

E. Ayguadé et al. (Eds.): LCPC 2005, LNCS 4339, pp. 185–199, 2007.

algorithm that uses the concurrency graph to determine the set of all concurrent expressions in a program. This analysis proves too conservative, however, and we improve its precision by performing a context-free language analysis on a modified form of the concurrency graph. We prove the correctness of both analyses and show that their total running times are quadratic in the size of the input program.

Concurrency analysis can be used to improve the quality of other analyses and to enable optimizations. To demonstrate the usefulness of our concurrency analysis, we apply it to data race analysis, which can be used to report potential program errors to application programmers. In related work with Su [16] and in a companion report [17], we tackled the problem of *memory consistency model enforcement*, which can be used to provide a stronger and more intuitive memory model while still allowing the compiler and hardware to reorder memory operations in many instances. We demonstrated that memory model enforcement can have a significant negative impact on optimizations, but that this effect is mitigated when combined with our concurrency analysis. In this paper, we focus on the foundations of the concurrency analysis problem: how it can be performed efficiently and be made accurate enough to effectively increase the precision of both clients on a set of application benchmarks.

2 Titanium Background

Titanium is a dialect of Java, but does not use the Java Virtual Machine model. Instead, the end target is assembly code. For portability, Titanium is first translated into C and then compiled into an executable. In addition to generating C code to run on each processor, the compiler generates calls to a runtime layer based on GASNet [6], a lightweight communication layer that exploits hardware support for direct remote reads and writes when possible. Titanium runs on a wide range of platforms including uniprocessors, shared memory machines, distributed-memory clusters of uniprocessors or SMPs, and a number of specific supercomputer architectures (Cray X1, Cray T3E, SGI Altix, IBM SP, Origin 2000, and NEC SX6). Instead of having dynamically created threads as in Java, Titanium is a *single program, multiple data* (SPMD) language, so the number of threads is fixed at program startup and all threads execute the same code image.

2.1 Textually Aligned Barriers

Like many SPMD languages, Titanium has a *barrier* construct that forces threads to wait at the barrier until all threads have reached it. Aiken and Gay introduced the concept of *structural correctness* to enforce that all threads execute the same number of barriers, and developed a static analysis that determines whether or not a program is structurally correct [1,13]. The following code is not structurally correct:

```
if (Ti.thisProc() % 2 == 0)
  Ti.barrier(); // even ID threads
else
  ; // odd ID threads
```

Titanium provides a stronger guarantee of *textually aligned barriers*: not only do all threads execute the same number of barriers, they also execute the same *textual* sequence of barriers. Thus, both the above structurally incorrect code and the following structurally correct code are erroneous in Titanium:

```
if (Ti.thisProc() % 2 == 0)
  Ti.barrier(); // even ID threads
else
  Ti.barrier(); // odd ID threads
```

The fact that Titanium barriers are textually aligned is central to our concurrency analysis: not only does it guarantee that code before and after each barrier cannot run concurrently, it also guarantees that code immediately following two different barriers cannot execute simultaneously.

Titanium's type system ensures that barriers are textually aligned by making use of *single-valued* expressions [1]. Such expressions provably evaluate to the same value for all threads[1], and include the following:

- compile-time constants
- program arguments
- certain library functions, such as `Ti.numProcs()`, which returns the total number of threads
- expressions that are combinations of the above

Other expressions such as those involving references and method calls can also be single-valued, the details of which can be found in the Titanium reference manual [14].

Barrier alignment can only be violated if different threads take different program paths, and any of those paths contain a barrier. Titanium statically prevents this by requiring path forks, including conditionals, loops, and dynamically dispatched method calls, to be conditioned on single-valued expressions if any of the branches contains a barrier. This guarantees that all threads take the same branch and therefore execute the same barriers. The examples above are erroneous: they each have branches with barriers but `Ti.thisProc() % 2 == 0` is not single-valued, so not all threads take the same branch. If the condition was replaced by the single-valued expression `Ti.numProcs() % 2 == 0`, then both examples would become legal.

In addition to the existing barriers in a program, our concurrency analysis also exploits single-valued expressions to determine which conditional branches can run concurrently. The analysis does not insert any new barriers, and it ignores the lock-based `synchronized` construct of Java, which is rarely used in Titanium programs.

2.2 Intermediate Language

In this paper, we will operate on an *intermediate language* that allows the full semantics of Titanium but is simpler to analyze. In particular, we rewrite dynamic dispatches, `switch` statements, and conditional expressions (`?/:`) as conditional `if ... else ...` statements.

[1] In the case of single-valued expressions of reference type, the result is not the same but is *replicated and coherent*. See the Titanium language reference for details [14].

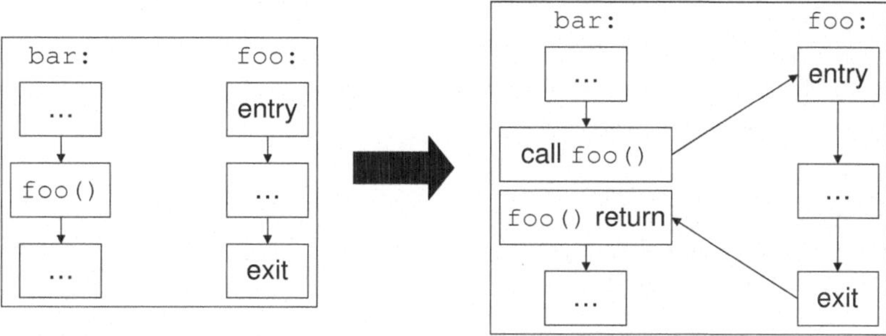

Fig. 1. Construction of the interprocedural control flow graph of a program from the individual method flow graphs

2.3 Control Flow Graphs

The algorithms in this paper are whole-program analyses that operate over a *control flow graph* that represents the flow of execution in a program. Nodes in the graph correspond to expressions in the program, and a directed edge from one expression to another occurs when the target can execute immediately after the source.

The Titanium compiler produces an intraprocedural control flow graph for each method in a program. We modify each of these graphs to model transfer of control between methods by splitting each method invocation node into a call node and a return node. The incoming edges of the original node are attached to the call node, and the outgoing edges to the return node. An edge is added from the call node to the target method's entry node, and from the target method's exit node to the return node. Figure 1 illustrates this procedure. We also add edges to model interprocedural control flow due to exceptions.

3 Concurrency Analysis

Titanium's structural correctness allows us to develop a simple graph-based algorithm for computing concurrent expressions in a program. The algorithm specifically takes advantage of Titanium's textually aligned barriers and single-valued expressions. The following definitions are useful in developing the analysis:

Definition 3.1 (Single Conditional). A *single conditional* is a conditional guarded by a single-valued expression.

Since a single-valued expression provably evaluates to the same result on all threads, every thread is guaranteed to take the same branch of a single conditional. A single conditional thus may contain a barrier, since all threads are guaranteed to execute it, while a non-single conditional may not.

Definition 3.2 (Cross Edge). A *cross edge* in a control flow graph connects the end of the first branch of a conditional to the start of the second branch.

Algorithm 3.3.
ConcurrencyGraph(P : program) : graph
1. Let G be the interprocedural control flow graph of P, as described in §2.3.
2. For each conditional C in P {
3. If C is not a single conditional:
4. Add a cross edge for C in G.
5. } // End for (2).
6. For each barrier B in P:
7. Delete B from G.
8. Return G.

Fig. 2. Algorithm 3.3 computes the concurrency graph of a program by inserting cross edges into its control flow graph and deleting all barriers

Cross edges do not provide any control flow information, since the second branch of a conditional does not execute immediately after the first branch. They are, however, useful for determining concurrency information, as shown in Theorem 3.4.

In order to determine the set of concurrent expressions in a program, we construct a *concurrency graph* G of the program P by inserting cross edges in the interprocedural control flow graph of P for every non-single conditional and deleting all barriers and their adjacent edges. Algorithm 3.3 in Figure 2 illustrates this procedure. The algorithm runs in time $O(n)$, where n is the number of statements and expressions in P, since it takes $O(n)$ time to construct the control flow graph of a program. The control flow graph is very sparse, containing only $O(n)$ edges, since the number of expressions that can execute immediately after a particular expression e is constant. Since at most n cross edges are added to the control flow graph and at most $O(n)$ barriers and adjacent edges are deleted, the resulting graph G is also of size $O(n)$.

The concurrency graph G allows us to determine the set of concurrent expressions using the following theorem:

Theorem 3.4. *Two expressions* a *and* b *in* P *can run concurrently only if one is reachable from the other in the concurrency graph* G.

In order to prove Theorem 3.4, we require the following definition:

Definition 3.5 (Code Phase). For each barrier in a program, its *code phase* is the set of statements that can execute after the barrier but before hitting another barrier, including itself[2].

Figure 3 shows the code phases of an example program. Since each code phase is preceded by a barrier, and each thread must execute the same sequence of barriers, each thread executes the same sequence of code phases. This implies the following:

Lemma 3.6. *Two expressions* a *and* b *in* P *can run concurrently only if they are in the same code phase.*

Using Lemma 3.6, we can prove Theorem 3.4. Details are in [17].

[2] A statement can be in multiple code phases, as is the case for a statement in a method called from multiple contexts.

```
B1: Ti.barrier();
L1: int i = 0;
L2: int j = 1;
L3: if (Ti.thisProc() < 5)
L4:   j += Ti.thisProc();
L5: if (Ti.numProcs() >= 1) {
L6:   i = Ti.numProcs();
B2:   Ti.barrier();
L7:   j += i;
L8: } else { j += 1; }
L9: i = broadcast j from 0;
B3: Ti.barrier();
LA: j += i;
```

Code Phase	Statements
B1	L1, L2, L3, L4, L5, L6, L8, L9
B2	L7, L9
B3	LA

Fig. 3. The set of code phases for an example program

Algorithm 3.7.
ConcurrentExpressions(P : program) : set
1. Let $concur \leftarrow \emptyset$.
2. Let $G \leftarrow$ **ConcurrencyGraph**(P) [Algorithm 3.3].
3. For each access a in P {
4. Do a depth first search on G starting from a.
5. For each expression b reached in the search:
6. Insert (a, b) into $concur$.
7. } // End for (3).
8. Return $concur$.

Fig. 4. Algorithm 3.7 computes the set of all concurrent expressions in a given program

By Theorem 3.4, in order to determine the set of all concurrent expressions, it suffices to compute the pairs of expressions in which one is reachable from the other in the concurrency graph G. This can be done efficiently by performing a depth first search from each expression in G. Algorithm 3.7 in Figure 4 does exactly this. The running time of the algorithm is dominated by the depth first searches, each of which takes $\mathrm{O}(n)$ time, since G has at most n nodes and $\mathrm{O}(n)$ edges. At most n searches occur, so the algorithm runs in time $\mathrm{O}(n^2)$.

4 Feasible Paths

Algorithm 3.7 computes an over-approximation of the set of concurrent expressions. In particular, due to the nature of the interprocedural control flow graph constructed in §2.3, the depth first searches in Algorithm 3.7 can follow *infeasible paths*, paths that cannot structurally occur in practice. Figure 5 illustrates such a path, in which a method is entered from one context and exits into another.

In order to prevent infeasible paths, we follow the procedure outlined by Reps [21]. We label each method call edge and corresponding return edge with matching parentheses, as shown in Figure 5. Each path then corresponds to a string of parentheses

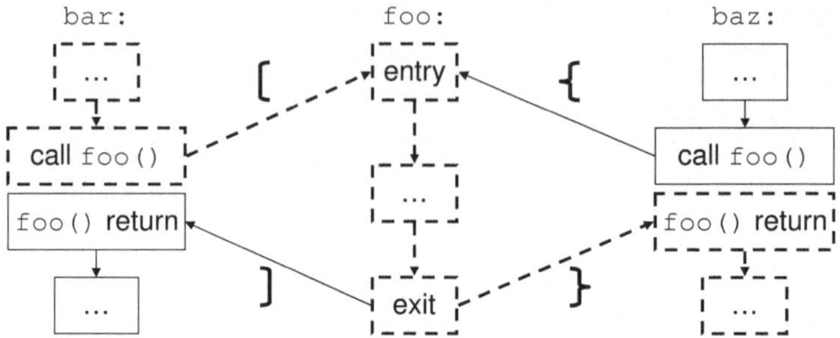

Fig. 5. Interprocedural control flow graph for two calls to the same function. The dashed path is infeasible, since `foo()` returns to a different context than the one from which it was called. The infeasible path corresponds to the unbalanced string "[}".

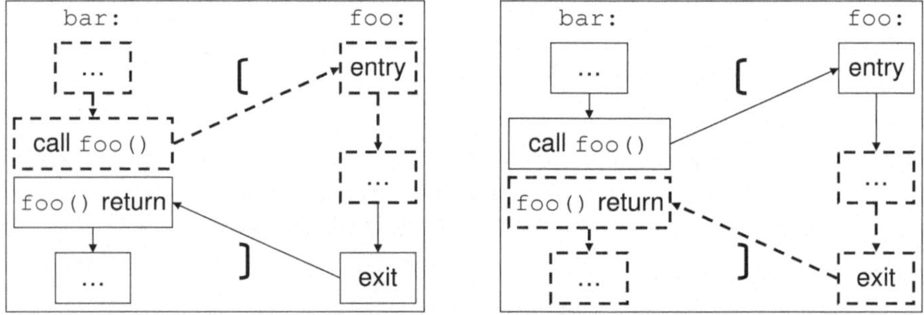

Fig. 6. Feasible paths that correspond to unbalanced strings. The dashed path on the left corresponds to a method call that has not yet returned, and the one on the right corresponds to a path that starts in a method call that returns.

composed of the labels of the edges in the path. A path is then infeasible, if in its corresponding string, an open parenthesis is closed by a non-matching parenthesis.

It is not necessary that a path's string be balanced in order for it to be feasible. In particular, two types of unbalanced strings correspond to feasible paths:

- A path with unclosed parentheses. Such a path corresponds to method calls that have not yet finished, as shown in the left side of Figure 6.
- A path with closing parentheses that follow a balanced prefix. Such a string is allowed since a path may start in the middle of a method call and corresponds to that method call returning, as shown in the right side of Figure 6.

Determining the set of nodes reachable[3] using a feasible path is the equivalent of performing context-free language (CFL) reachability on a graph using the grammar for each pair of matching parentheses ($(_\alpha$ and $)_\alpha$. CFL reachability can be performed

[3] In this section, we make no distinction between *reachable* and *reachable without hitting a barrier*. The latter reduces to the former if all barrier nodes are removed from each control flow graph.

in cubic time for an arbitrary grammar [21]. Algorithm 3.7 takes only quadratic time, however, and we desire a feasibility algorithm that is also quadratic. In order to accomplish this, we develop a specialized algorithm that modifies the concurrency graph G and the standard depth first search instead of using generic CFL reachability.

At first glance, it appears that a method must be revisited in every possible context in which it is called, since the context determines which open parentheses have been seen and therefore which paths can be followed. However, as shown in the companion report, the set of expressions that can be executed in a method call is the same regardless of context [17]. This implies that the set of nodes reachable along a feasible path in a program's control flow graph is also independent of the context of a method call, with two exceptions:

- If a method call can complete, then the nodes after the call are reachable from a point before the call.
- If no context exists, such as in a search that starts from a point within a method f, then all nodes that are reachable following any method call to f are reachable.

The second case above can easily be handled by visiting a node twice: once in *some* context, and again in no context. The first case, however, requires adding bypass edges to the control flow graph.

4.1 Bypass Edges

Recall that the interprocedural control flow graph was constructed by splitting a method call into a call node and a return node. An edge was then added from the call node to the target method's entry, and another from the target's exit to the return node. If the target's exit is reachable (or for our purposes, reachable without hitting a barrier) from the target's entry, then adding a *bypass edge* that connects the call node directly to the return node does not affect the transitive closure of the graph.

Computing whether or not a method's exit is reachable from its entry is not trivial, since it requires knowing whether or not the exits of each of the methods that it calls are reachable from their entries. Algorithm 4.1 in Figure 7 computes this by continually iterating over all the methods in a program, marking those that can complete through an execution path that only calls previously marked methods, until no more methods can be marked. In the first iteration of loop 3, it only marks those methods that can complete without making any calls, or equivalently, those methods that can complete using only a single stack frame. In the second iteration, it only marks those that can complete by only calling methods that don't need to make any calls, or equivalently, those methods that can complete using only two stack frames. In general, a method is marked in the ith iteration if it can complete using i, and no less than i, stack frames[4]. As shown in the companion report, Algorithm 4.1 marks all methods that can complete using any number of stack frames [17].

[4] Note that just because a method only requires a fixed number of stack frames doesn't mean that it can complete. A method may contain an infinite loop, preventing it from completing at all, or barriers along all paths through it, preventing it from completing without executing a barrier. Algorithm 4.1 does not mark such methods.

Algorithm 4.1.
ComputeBypasses(P : program, $G_1, \ldots, G_k$: intraprocedural flow graph) : set
1. Let $change \leftarrow true.$
2. Let $marked \leftarrow \emptyset.$
3. While $change = true$ {
4. $change \leftarrow false.$
5.   Set $visited(u) \leftarrow false$ for all nodes u in $G_1, \ldots, G_k$.
6.   For each method f in P {
7.   If $f \notin marked$ and $CanReach(entry(f), exit(f), G_f, marked)$ {
8. $marked \leftarrow marked \cup \{f\}.$
9. $change \leftarrow true.$
10.   } // End if (7).
11.   } // End for (6).
12. } // End while (3).
13. Return $marked.$

14. Procedure $CanReach(u, v$: vertex, G : graph, $marked$: method set) : boolean:
15.   Set $visited(u) \leftarrow true.$
16.   If $u = v$:
17.   Return $true.$
18.   Else If u is a method call to function g and $g \notin marked$:
19.   Return $false.$
20.   For each edge $(u, w) \in G$ {
21.   If $visited(w) = false$ and $CanReach(w, v, G, marked)$:
22.   Return $true.$
23.   } // End for (20).
24.   Return $false.$

Fig. 7. Algorithm 4.1 uses each method's intraprocedural control flow graph (G_i) to determine if its exit is reachable from its entry

Algorithm 4.1 requires quadratic time to complete in the worst case. Each iteration of loop 3 visits at most n nodes. Only k iterations are necessary, where k is the number of methods in the program, since at least one method is marked in all but the last iteration of the loop. The total running time is thus $O(kn)$ in the worst case. In practice, only a small number of iterations are necessary[5], and the running time is closer to $O(n)$.

After computing the set of methods that can complete, it is straightforward to add bypass edges to the concurrency graph G: for each method call c, if the target of c can complete, add an edge from c to its corresponding method return r. This can be done in time $O(n)$.

4.2 Feasible Search

Once bypass edges have been added to the graph G, a modified depth first search can be used to find feasible paths. A stack of open but not yet closed parenthesis symbols must

[5] Even on the largest example we tried (>45,000 lines of user and library code, 1226 methods), Algorithm 4.1 required only five iterations to converge.

Algorithm 4.2.
FeasibleSearch(v : vertex, G : graph) : set

```
 1. Let visited ← ∅.
 2. Let s ← ∅.
 3. Call FeasibleDFS(v, G, s, visited).
 4. Return visited.

 5. Procedure FeasibleDFS(v : vertex, G : graph, s : stack, visited : set):
 6.   If s = ∅ {
 7.     If no_context_mark(v) return.
 8.     Set no_context_mark(v) ← true.
 9.   } // End if (6).
10.   Else {
11.     If context_mark(v) return.
12.     Set context_mark(v) ← true.
13.   } // End else (10).
14.   visited ← visited ∪ {v}
15.   For each edge (v, u) ∈ G {
16.     Let s' ← s.
17.     If label(v, u) is a close symbol and s' ≠ ∅ {
18.       Let o ← pop(s').
19.       If label(v, u) does not match o:
20.         Skip to next iteration of 15.
21.     } // End if (17).
22.     Else if label(v, u) is an open symbol:
23.       Push label(v, u) onto s'.
24.     Call FeasibleDFS(u, G, s).
25.   } // End for (15).
```

Fig. 8. Algorithm 4.2 computes the set of nodes reachable from the start node through a feasible path

be maintained, and an encountered closing symbol must match the top of this stack, it the stack is nonempty. In addition, as noted above, the modified search must visit each node twice, once in no context and once in *some* context. Algorithm 4.2 in Figure 8 formalizes this procedure, and a proof of correctness is provided in the companion report [17].

Since G contains bypass edges and Algorithm 4.2 visits each node both in some context and in no context, it finds all nodes that can be reachable in a feasible path from the source. Since it visits each node at most twice, it runs in time $\mathrm{O}(n)$.

4.3 Feasible Concurrent Expressions

Putting it all together, we can now modify Algorithm 3.7 to find only concurrent expressions that are feasible. As in Algorithm 3.7, the concurrency graph G must first be constructed. Then the intraprocedural flow graphs of each method must be constructed, Algorithm 4.1 used to find the methods that can complete without hitting a barrier, and

Algorithm 4.3.
FeasibleConcurrentExpressions(P : program) : set

```
Let G ← ConcurrencyGraph(P) [Algorithm 3.3].
For each method f in P {
  Construct the intraprocedural flow graph G_f of f.
  For each barrier B in f {
    Delete B from G_f.
  } // End for (4).
} // End for (2).
Let bypass ← ComputeBypasses(P, G_1, ..., G_k) [Algorithm 4.1].
For each method call and return pair c, r in P {
  If the target f of c, r is in bypass:
    Add an edge (c, r) to G.
} // End for (9).
For each expression a in P {
  Let visited ← FeasibleSearch(a, G) [Algorithm 4.2].
  For each expression b ∈ visited:
    Insert (a, b) into concur.
} // End for (13).
Return concur.
```

Fig. 9. Algorithm 4.3 computes the set of all concurrent expressions that can feasibly occur in a given program

the bypass edges inserted into G. Then Algorithm 4.2 must be used to perform the searches instead of a vanilla depth first search. Algorithm 4.3 in Figure 9 illustrates this procedure.

The setup of Algorithm 4.3 calls Algorithm 4.1, so it takes $O(kn)$ time. The searches each take time $O(n)$, and at most n are done, so the total running time is $O(kn + n^2) = O(n^2)$, quadratic as opposed to the cubic running time of generic CFL reachability.

5 Evaluation

Concurrency information is useful for many program analyses and optimizations. In this paper, we focus on one in particular, static race detection, to evaluate our concurrency analysis. Results for how enforcement of a sequentially consistent memory model can benefit from the analysis are available in a companion report [17].

5.1 Benchmarks

We use the following set of benchmarks for our evaluation:

- **`gas`** [5] (8841 lines): Hyperbolic solver for a gas dynamics problem in computational fluid dynamics.
- **`gsrb`** (1090 lines): Nearest neighbor computation on a regular mesh using red-black Gauss-Seidel operator. This computational kernel is often used within multigrid algorithms or other solvers.

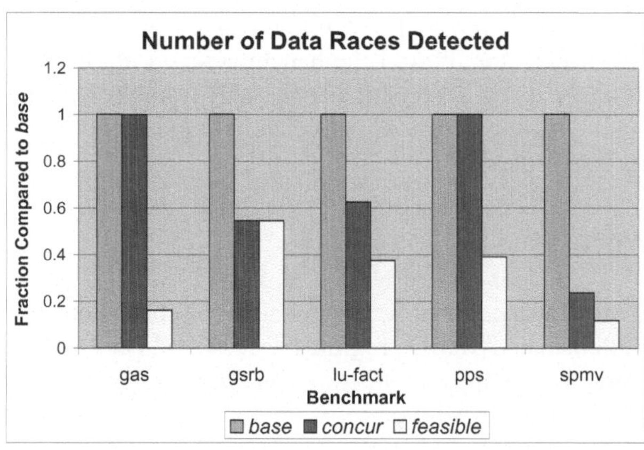

Fig. 10. Fraction of data races detected at compile-time compared to **base** (lower is better)

- **`lu-fact`** (420 lines): Dense linear algebra.
- **`pps`** [4] (3673 lines): Parallel Poisson equation solver using the domain decomposition method in an unbounded domain.
- **`spmv`** (1493 lines): Sparse matrix-vector multiply.

The line counts for the above benchmarks underestimate the amount of code actually analyzed, since all reachable code in the 37,000 line Titanium and Java 1.0 libraries is also processed.

5.2 Static Race Detection

In parallel programs, a *data race* occurs when multiple threads access the same memory location, at least one of the accesses is a write, and the accesses can occur concurrently [19]. Data races often correspond to programming errors and potentially result in nondeterministic runtime behavior. Concurrency analysis can be used to statically detect races at compile-time [11,12], particularly when combined with alias analysis [2].

Using our concurrency analysis and a thread-aware alias analysis, we built a compile-time data race analysis into the Titanium compiler. Static information is generally not enough to determine with certainty that two memory accesses compose a race, so nearly all reported races are false positives. (The correctness of the alias and concurrency analyses ensure that no false negatives occur.) We therefore consider a race detector that reports the fewest races to be the most effective.

Figure 10 compares the effectiveness of three levels of race detection:

- **base:** only alias analysis is used to detect potential races
- **concur:** our basic concurrency analysis (§3) is used to eliminate non-concurrent races
- **feasible:** our feasible paths concurrency analysis (§4) is used to eliminate non-concurrent races

The results show that the addition of concurrency analysis can eliminate most of the races reported by our detector. Two of the benchmarks do not benefit at all from the basic concurrency analysis, but all benefit considerably from the feasible paths analysis. The concurrency analysis should be of significant help to users of our race detector by weeding out many false positives.

6 Related Work

An extensive amount of work on concurrency analysis has been done for both languages with dynamic parallelism and SPMD programs. Duesterwald and Soffa presented a data flow analysis to compute the *happened-before* and *happened-after* relation for program statements [11]. Their analysis is for detecting races in programs based on the Ada rendezvous model [23]. Masticola and Ryder developed a more precise non-concurrency analysis for the same set of programs [18]. The results are used for debugging and optimization. Jeremiassen and Eggers developed a static analysis for barrier synchronization for SPMD programs with non-textual barriers and used the information to reduce false sharing on cache-coherent machines [15]. Their analysis doesn't take advantage of barrier alignment or single-valued expressions, so it isn't as precise as ours.

Others besides Duesterwald and Soffa and Masticola and Ryder have developed tools for race detection. Flanagan and Freund presented a static race detection tool for Java based on type inference and checking [12]. Boyapati and Rinard developed a type system for Java that guarantees that a program is race-free [7]. Tools such as Eraser [22] and TRaDe [9] detect races at runtime instead of statically. Other static and dynamic race detection schemes have also been developed [24,3,10,8,20].

Our work differs from previous work in that we develop an analysis specifically for SPMD programs with textual barriers. This allows our analysis to be both sound and precise. In addition, our analysis takes advantage of single-valued expressions, which no previous analysis does.

We presented a more abstract version of our concurrency analysis and its application to sequential consistency in a previous paper [16]. That analysis was slightly less precise, followed infeasible program paths, and would have been much more difficult to modify to ignore them.

7 Conclusion

In this paper, we made several contributions to the foundation of parallel program analysis, specifically the concurrency analysis problem of determining whether two statements can execute concurrently. We introduced a graph representation of parallel programs with textually aligned barriers and two different concurrency analyses. The first was a basic concurrency analysis that uses barriers and single-valued expressions, and the second a more complex one that only explores those execution paths across function calls that can occur in practice. We experimented with several benchmark programs using a data race detector built on our concurrency analysis. Our experiments showed that the analyses were able to eliminate a large fraction of the false positives reported in all programs. We believe the efficiency and precision of our concurrency analysis make it a very useful tool in analyzing parallel programs with textually aligned barriers.

In addition to aiding in optimizations and helping to detect parallel programming errors, the ability to perform such analyses may affect a language designer's choice of programming model semantics. Simpler programming models, such as those that prohibit races, use synchronous communication, or ensure a strong memory model, may be feasible if accurate analyses can be developed to enable optimizations while ensuring a stronger semantics. Our analysis is one piece of a larger picture on the kinds of parallelism constructs and synchronization operations for which accurate concurrency analyses can be developed.

Acknowledgments

We would like to thank Jimmy Su, who helped us a great deal both in developing the concurrency algorithms and in implementing them. We would also like to thank the Titanium group for their valuable support.

This work was supported in part by the Department of Energy under contracts DE-FC03-01ER25509 and DE-AC02-05CH11231, by the California State Micro program, by Sun Microsystems, and by Microsoft.

References

1. A. Aiken and D. Gay. Barrier inference. In *Principles of Programming Languages*, San Diego, California, January 1998.
2. L. O. Andersen. *Program Analysis and Specialization for the C Programming Language.* PhD thesis, DIKU, University of Copenhagen, May 1994.
3. D. F. Bacon, R. E. Strom, and A. Tarafdar. Guava: a dialect of Java without data races. In *OOPSLA '00: Proceedings of the 15th ACM SIGPLAN conference on Object-oriented programming, systems, languages, and applications*, pages 382–400, New York, NY, USA, 2000. ACM Press.
4. G. T. Balls. *A Finite Difference Domain Decomposition Method Using Local Corrections for the Solution of Poisson's Equation.* PhD thesis, Department of Mechanical Engineering, University of California at Berkeley, 1999.
5. M. Berger and P. Colella. Local adaptive mesh refinement for shock hydrodynamics. *Journal of Computational Physics*, 82(1):64–84, May 1989. Lawrence Livermore Laboratory Report No. UCRL-97196.
6. D. Bonachea. GASNet specification, v1.1. Technical Report UCB/CSD-02-1207, University of California, Berkeley, November 2002.
7. C. Boyapati, R. Lee, and M. Rinard. Ownership types for safe programming: preventing data races and deadlocks. In *OOPSLA '02: Proceedings of the 17th ACM SIGPLAN conference on Object-oriented programming, systems, languages, and applications*, pages 211–230, New York, NY, USA, 2002. ACM Press.
8. G.-I. Cheng, M. Feng, C. E. Leiserson, K. H. Randall, and A. F. Stark. Detecting data races in Cilk programs that use locks. In *SPAA '98: Proceedings of the tenth annual ACM symposium on Parallel algorithms and architectures*, pages 298–309, New York, NY, USA, 1998. ACM Press.

9. M. Christiaens and K. De Bosschere. TRaDe, a topological approach to on-the-fly race detection in Java programs. In *Proceedings of the Java Virtual Machine Research and Technology Symposium (JVM '01)*, April 2001.
10. A. Dinning and E. Schonberg. Detecting access anomalies in programs with critical sections. In *PADD '91: Proceedings of the 1991 ACM/ONR workshop on Parallel and distributed debugging*, pages 85–96, New York, NY, USA, 1991. ACM Press.
11. E. Duesterwald and M. Soffa. Concurrency analysis in the presence of procedures using a data-flow framework. In *Symposium on Testing, analysis, and verification*, Victoria, British Columbia, October 1991.
12. C. Flanagan and S. N. Freund. Type-based race detection for Java. In *PLDI '00: Proceedings of the ACM SIGPLAN 2000 conference on Programming language design and implementation*, pages 219–232, New York, NY, USA, 2000. ACM Press.
13. D. Gay. *Barrier Inference.* PhD thesis, University of California, Berkeley, May 1998.
14. P. N. Hilfinger, D. Bonachea, K. Datta, D. Gay, S. Graham, B. Liblit, G. Pike, J. Su, and K. Yelick. Titanium language reference manual, version 2.19. Technical Report UCB/EECS-2005-15, University of California, Berkeley, November 2005.
15. T. Jeremiassen and S. Eggers. Static analysis of barrier synchronization in explicitly parallel programs. In *Parallel Architectures and Compilation Techniques*, Montreal, Canada, August 1994.
16. A. Kamil, J. Su., and K. Yelick. Making sequential consistency practical in Titanium. In *Supercomputing 2005*, November 2005. To appear.
17. A. Kamil and K. Yelick. Concurrency analysis for parallel programs with textually aligned barriers. Technical Report UCB/EECS-2006-41, EECS Department, University of California, Berkeley, April 18 2006. Available at http://www.eecs.berkeley.edu/Pubs/TechRpts/2006/EECS-2006-41.html.
18. S. Masticola and B. Ryder. Non-concurrency analysis. In *Principles and practice of parallel programming*, San Diego, California, May 1993.
19. R. H. B. Netzer and B. P. Miller. What are race conditions?: Some issues and formalizations. *ACM Lett. Program. Lang. Syst.*, 1(1):74–88, 1992.
20. R. O'Callahan and J.-D. Choi. Hybrid dynamic data race detection. In *PPoPP '03: Proceedings of the ninth ACM SIGPLAN symposium on Principles and practice of parallel programming*, pages 167–178, New York, NY, USA, 2003. ACM Press.
21. T. Reps. Program analysis via graph reachability. In *ILPS '97: Proceedings of the 1997 international symposium on Logic programming*, pages 5–19, Cambridge, MA, USA, 1997. MIT Press.
22. S. Savage, M. Burrows, G. Nelson, P. Sobalvarro, and T. Anderson. Eraser: a dynamic data race detector for multithreaded programs. *ACM Trans. Comput. Syst.*, 15(4):391–411, 1997.
23. United States Department of Defense. Reference manual for the Ada programming language. Technical Report ANSI/MIL-STD-1815A, Washington, D.C., January 1983.
24. C. von Praun and T. R. Gross. Static conflict analysis for multi-threaded object-oriented programs. In *PLDI '03: Proceedings of the ACM SIGPLAN 2003 conference on Programming language design and implementation*, pages 115–128, New York, NY, USA, 2003. ACM Press.
25. K. Yelick, L. Semenzato, G. Pike, C. Miyamoto, B. Liblit, A. Krishnamurthy, P. Hilfinger, S. Graham, D. Gay, P. Colella, and A. Aiken. Titanium: A high-performance Java dialect. In *Workshop on Java for High-Performance Network Computing*, Stanford, California, February 1998.

Titanium Performance and Potential: An NPB Experimental Study

Kaushik Datta[1], Dan Bonachea[1], and Katherine Yelick[1,2]

[1] Computer Science Division, University of California at Berkeley
[2] Lawrence Berkeley National Laboratory
{kdatta,bonachea,yelick}@cs.berkeley.edu

Abstract. Titanium is an explicitly parallel dialect of Java™ designed for high-performance scientific programming. We present an overview of the language features and demonstrate their use in the context of the NAS Parallel Benchmarks, a standard suite of common scientific kernels. We argue that parallel languages like Titanium provide greater expressive power than conventional approaches, enabling much more concise and expressive code that minimizes time to solution. Moreover, we have found that the Titanium implementations of three of the NAS Parallel Benchmarks can match or even exceed the performance of the standard Fortran/MPI implementations at realistic problem sizes and processor scales, while still using far cleaner, shorter and more maintainable code.

1 Introduction

The tension between programmability and performance in software development is nowhere as acute as in the domain of high end parallel computing. The entire motivation for parallelism is high performance, so programmers are reluctant to use languages that give control to compilers or runtime systems. Yet the difficulty of programming large-scale parallel machines is notorious– it limits their marketability, hinders exploration of advanced algorithms, and restricts the set of available programmers. The Titanium language was designed to address these issues, providing programmers with high level program structuring techniques, yet giving them control over key features of parallel performance: data layout, load balancing, identification of parallelism, and synchronization.

Modern parallel architectures can be roughly divided into two categories based on the programming interface exposed by the hardware: shared memory systems where parallel threads of control all share a single logical memory space (and communication is achieved through simple loads and stores), and distributed memory systems where some (but not necessarily all) threads of control have disjoint memory spaces and communicate through explicit communication operations (e.g. message passing). Experience has shown that the shared memory model is often easier to program, but it presents serious scalability challenges to hardware designers. Thus, with a few notable exceptions, distributed memory machines currently dominate the high-end supercomputing market.

E. Ayguadé et al. (Eds.): LCPC 2005, LNCS 4339, pp. 200–214, 2007.

The Partitioned Global Address Space (PGAS) model seeks to combine the advantages of both shared and distributed memory. It offers the programmability advantages of a globally shared address space, but is carefully designed to allow efficient implementation on distributed-memory architectures. Titanium [1], UPC [2] and Co-array Fortran [3] are examples of modern programming languages that provide a global address space memory model, along with an explicitly parallel SPMD control model. PGAS languages typically make the distinction between local and remote memory references explicitly visible to encourage programmers to consider the locality properties of their program, which can have a noticeable performance impact on distributed memory hardware.

A major focus of this paper is to showcase the performance and productivity benefits of the Titanium programming language in the context of the NAS Parallel Benchmarks [4], a set of benchmarks representative of common scientific kernels. We demonstrate by example that scientific programming in PGAS languages like Titanium can provide major productivity improvements over programming with serial languages augmented with a message-passing library. Furthermore, we show evidence that programming models with one-sided communication (such as that used in PGAS languages) can achieve application performance comparable to or better than similar codes written using two-sided message passing, even on distributed memory platforms.

2 Titanium Overview

Titanium [1] is an explicitly parallel, SPMD dialect of Java^{TM} that provides a Partitioned Global Address Space (PGAS) memory model. Titanium supports the creation of complicated data structures and abstractions using the object-oriented class mechanism of Java, augmented with a global address space to allow for the creation of large, distributed shared structures. As Titanium is essentially a superset of Java [5], it inherits all the expressiveness, usability and safety properties of that language.

Titanium notably adds a number of features to standard Java that are designed to support high-performance computing. They include: flexible and efficient multi-dimensional arrays, built-in support for multi-dimensional domain calculus, locality and sharing reference qualifiers, explicitly unordered loop iteration, user-defined immutable classes, operator-overloading, and cross-language support. These features are described in detail later in this paper, as well as in the Titanium language reference [6]. Titanium also adds several other features to Java, including: C++-style templates, user-controlled memory management with explicit memory zones, compile-time checking of barrier synchronization, and library support for synchronization and collective communication.

The current Titanium compiler implementation [7] uses a static compilation strategy - programs are translated to intermediate C code and then compiled to machine code using a vendor-provided C compiler. They are then linked to native runtime libraries which implement communication, garbage collection, and other system-level activities. There is no JVM, no JIT, and no dynamic class loading. Thus, Titanium is extremely portable, and Titanium programs can basically be run unmodified on uniprocessors, shared memory machines and distributed memory machines. The current implementation runs on a large range of platforms, including uniprocessors, shared memory multiprocessors, distributed-memory clusters of uniprocessors or SMPs, and a number of specific supercomputer architectures (Cray X1/T3E, IBM SP, SGI Altix/Origin).

3 The NAS Parallel Benchmarks

The NAS Parallel Benchmarks consist of a set of kernel computations and larger pseudo-applications taken primarily from computational fluid dynamics [4]. They reflect several different types of communication and computation patterns: nearest neighbor computation on a 3-D mesh (MG), FFTs with an all-to-all transpose on a 3-D mesh (FT), and 2-D sparse matrices with indirect array accesses (CG). However, they do not reflect features of some full applications, such as adaptivity, multiple physical models, or dynamic load balancing. Titanium has been demonstrated on these more complete and more general application problems [8, 9].

The original reference implementation of the NAS Parallel Benchmarks is written in serial Fortran with MPI [10]. We use this implementation as the baseline for comparison in this study. MPI represents both the predominant paradigm for large-scale parallel programming and the target of much concern over productivity, since it often requires tedious packing of user level data structures into aggregated messages to achieve acceptable performance.

4 Titanium Features in the Multigrid (MG) Benchmark

4.1 Titanium Arrays

The NAS benchmarks, like many scientific codes, rely heavily on arrays for the main data structures. Titanium extends Java with a powerful multidimensional array abstraction that provides the same kinds of subarray operations available in Fortran 90. Titanium arrays are indexed by *points* and built on sets of points, called *domains*. Points and domains are first-class entities in Titanium – they can be stored in data structures, specified as literals, passed as values to methods and manipulated using their own set of operations. For example, the class A version of the MG benchmark requires a 256^3 grid with a one-deep layer of surrounding ghost cells, resulting in a 258^3 grid. Such a grid can be constructed with the following declaration:

```
double [3d] gridA = new double [[-1,-1,-1]:[256,256,256]];
```

The 3-D Titanium array `gridA` has a rectangular index set that consists of all points $[i, j, k]$ with integer coordinates such that $-1 \leq i, j, k \leq 256$. Titanium calls such an index set a *rectangular domain* with Titanium type `RectDomain`, since all the points lie within a rectangular box. Titanium arrays can only be built over `RectDomains` (i.e. rectangular sets of points), but they may start at an arbitrary base point, as the example with a $[-1, -1, -1]$ base shows. In this example the grid was designed to have space for ghost regions, which are all the points that have either -1 or 256 as a coordinate.

The language also includes powerful array operators that can be used to create alternative views of the data in a given array, without an implied copy of the data. For example, the statement:

```
double [3d] gridAIn = gridA.shrink(1);
```

creates a new array variable `gridAIn` which shares all of its elements with `gridA` that are not ghost cells. This domain is computed by shrinking the index set of `gridA` by one element on all sides. `gridAIn` can subsequently be used to reference the non-ghost elements of `gridA`. The same operation can also be accomplished using the `restrict` method, which provides more generality by allowing the index set of the new array view to include only the elements referenced by a given `RectDomain` expression, e.g.: `gridA.restrict(gridA.domain().shrink(1))`, or a using `RectDomain` literal: `gridA.restrict([[0,0,0]:[255,255,255]])`.

Titanium also adds a looping construct, `foreach`, specifically designed for iterating over the points of a domain. More will be said about `foreach` in section 5.1, but here we demonstrate the use of `foreach` in a simple example, where the point `p` plays the role of a loop index variable:

```
foreach (p in gridAIn.domain()) {
   gridB[p] = applyStencil(gridA, p);
}
```

The `applyStencil` method may safely refer to elements that are one point away from `p`, since the loop is over the interior of a larger array. Note that this one loop concisely expresses iteration over multiple dimensions, corresponding to a multi-level loop nest in other languages. A common class of loop bounds and indexing errors is avoided by having the compiler and runtime system keep track of the iteration boundaries for the multidimensional traversal.

4.2 Stencil Computations Using Point Literals

The stencil operation itself can be written easily using constant offsets. At this point the code becomes dimension-specific, and we show the 2-D case with the stencil application code shown in the loop body (rather than a separate method) for illustration. Because points are first-class entities, we can use named constants that are declared once and re-used throughout the stencil operations in MG. Titanium supports both C-style preprocessor definitions and Java's final variable style constants. The following code applies a 5-point 2-D stencil to each point `p` in `gridAIn`'s domain:

```
final Point<2> NORTH = [0,1], SOUTH = [0,-1],
               EAST  = [1,0], WEST  = [-1,0];

foreach (p in gridAIn.domain()) {
  gridB[p] = S0 * gridAIn[p] +
             S1 * ( gridAIn[p + NORTH] + gridAIn[p + SOUTH] +
                    gridAIn[p + EAST ] + gridAIn[p + WEST ] );
}
```

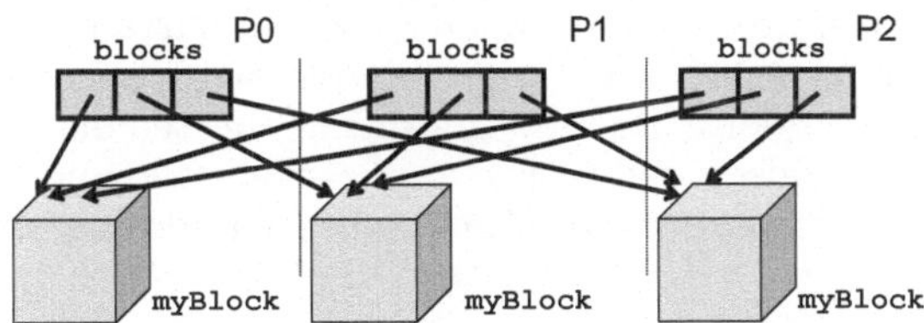

Fig. 1. Distributed data structure built using the `exchange` operation in MG

The full MG code used for benchmarking in section 7 includes a 27-point stencil applied to 3-D arrays, and the Titanium code, like the Fortran code, uses a manually-applied stencil optimization that eliminates redundant common subexpressions, a key optimization for the MG benchmark [11].

4.3 Distributed Arrays

Titanium supports the construction of distributed array data structures using the global address space. Since distributed data structures are built from local pieces rather than declared as a distributed type, Titanium is referred to as a "local view" language [11]. The generality of Titanium's distributed data structures are not fully utilized in the NAS benchmarks, because the data structures are simple distributed arrays, rather than trees, graphs or adaptive structures [8]. Nevertheless, the general pointer-based distribution mechanism combined with the use of arbitrary base indices for arrays provides an elegant and powerful mechanism for shared data.

The following code is a portion of the parallel Titanium code for the MG benchmark. It is run on every processor and creates the `blocks` distributed array that can access any processor's portion of the grid.

```
Point<3> startCell = myBlockPos * numCellsPerBlockSide;
Point<3> endCell = startCell + (numCellsPerBlockSide - [1,1,1]);
double [3d] myBlock = new double[startCell:endCell];

// create distributed array "blocks"
double [1d] single [3d] blocks = new double
  [0:(Ti.numProcs()-1)] single [3d];
blocks.exchange(myBlock);
```

First, each processor computes its start and end indices by performing point arithmetic operations. These indices are used to create the local 3-D array `myBlock`. Then, the pointer-based distributed data structure `blocks` is created using the `exchange` collective. Figure 1 illustrates the resulting data structure for a 3-processor execution.

4.4 Domain Calculus

A common operation in any grid-based code is updating ghost cells according to values stored on other processors or boundary conditions in the problem statement. Ghost cells are a set of array elements surrounding the local grid that cache elements of neighboring grids. Simple array operations can be used to fill in these ghost regions, thereby migrating the tedious business of index calculations and array offsets out of the application code and into the compiler and runtime system. The entire Titanium code for updating one plane of ghost cells is as follows:

```
// use interior as in stencil code
double [3d] myBlockIn = myBlock.shrink(1);
// update overlapping ghost cells of neighboring block
blocks[neighborPos].copy(myBlockIn);
```

The array method `A.copy(B)` copies only those elements in the intersection of the index domains of the two array views in question. Using an aliased array for the interior of the locally owned block (which is also used in the local stencil computation), this code performs copy operations only on ghost values. Communication will be required on some machines, but there is no coordination for two-sided communication, and the copy from local to remote could easily be replaced by a copy from remote to local by swapping the two arrays in the copy expression. The use of the global indexing space in the grids of the distributed data structure (made possible by the arbitrary index bounds feature of Titanium arrays) makes it easy to select and copy the cells in the ghost region, and is also used in the more general case of adaptive meshes.

Similar Titanium code is used for updating the other five planes of ghost cells, except in the case of the boundaries at the end of the problem domain. The MG benchmark requires periodic boundary conditions, and an additional array view operation is needed before the copy to logically translate the array elements to their corresponding elements across the domain:

```
// update neighbor's overlapping ghost cells across periodic boundary
// by logically shifting the local grid to across the domain
blocks[neighborPos].copy(myBlockIn.translate([-256,0,0]));
```

The translate method translates the indices of the array view, creating a new view where the relevant points overlap their corresponding non-ghost cells in the subsequent copy.

4.5 Distinguishing Local Data

The `blocks` distributed array contains all the data necessary for the computation, but one of the pointers in that array references the local block which will be used for the local stencil computations and ghost cell surface updates. Titanium's global address space model allows for fine-grained implicit access to remote data, but well-tuned Titanium applications perform most of their critical path computation on data which is either local or has been copied into local memory. This avoids fine-grained communication costs which can limit scaling on distributed-memory systems with high interconnect latencies. To ensure the compiler statically recognizes the local block of data as residing locally, we declare a reference to this thread's data block using Titanium's *local* type qualifier.The original declaration of `myBlock` should have contained this local qualifier. Below we show an example of a second declaration of such a variable along with a type cast:

```
double [3d] local myBlock2 = (double [3d] local) blocks[Ti.thisProc()];
```

By casting the appropriate grid reference as *local*, the programmer is asking the compiler to use more efficient native pointers to reference this array, potentially eliminating some unnecessary overheads in array access (for example, dynamic checks of whether a given global array access references data that actually resides locally and thus requires no communication). As with all type conversion in Titanium and Java, the cast is dynamically checked to maintain type safety and memory safety. However, the compiler provides a compilation mode which statically disables all the type and bounds checks required by Java semantics to save some computational overhead in production runs of debugged code.

The Titanium optimizer also includes a Local Qualification Inference (LQI) optimization that automatically propagates locality information gleaned from allocation statements and programmer annotations in the application code using a constraint-based inference [12]. LQI can effectively remove serial overheads associated with global pointers, as evidenced by the 81% reduction in the running time of MG on 8 processors of the G5/InfiniBand machine.

4.6 The MG Benchmark Implementation

Figure 2 presents a line count comparison for the Titanium and Fortran/MPI implementations of the benchmarks, breaking down the code in the timed region into categories of communication, computation and declarations. Comments, timer code, and initialization code outside the timed region are omitted.

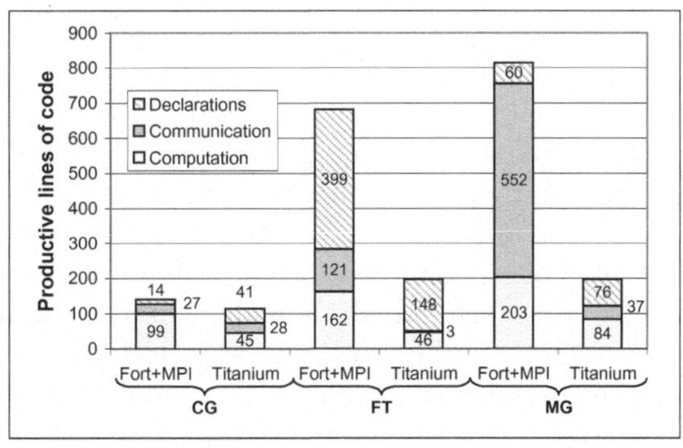

Fig. 2. Timed region line count comparison

The figure shows that MG communication and computation line counts heavily favor Titanium. This discrepancy is mainly due to Titanium's domain calculus and array copy operations, and to a lesser extent, Titanium array features for local stencil computations.

5 Titanium Features in the Conjugate Gradient (CG) Benchmark

5.1 Foreach Loops

As described in section 4.2, Titanium has an unordered loop construct called *foreach* that simplifies iteration over multidimensional arrays and provides performance benefits. If the order of loop execution is irrelevant to a computation, then using a *foreach* loop to traverse the points in a *RectDomain* explicitly allows the compiler to reorder loop iterations to maximize performance– for example by performing automatic cache blocking and tiling optimizations [13, 14]. It also simplifies bounds-checking elimination and array access strength-reduction optimizations.

Another example of the *foreach* loop can be found in the sparse matrix-vector multiplies performed in every iteration of the CG benchmark. The sparse matrix below is stored in CSR (Compressed Sparse Row) format, so the `rowRectDomains` array contains a *RectDomain* for each row of the matrix. Each *RectDomain* then contains its row's first and last indices for arrays `colIdx` and `a`.

```
// the following represents a matrix in CSR format
// all three arrays were previously populated
RectDomain<1> [1d] rowRectDomains; // RectDomains of row indices
int [1d] colIdx;  // column index of nonzeros
double [1d] a;    // nonzero matrix values
...
public void multiply(double [1d] sourceVec, double [1d] destVec) {
  foreach (i in rowRectDomains.domain()) {
    double sum = 0;
    foreach (j in rowRectDomains[i])
      sum += a[j] * sourceVec[colIdx[j]];
    destVec[i] = sum;
} }
```

This calculation uses nested foreach loops that highlight the semantics of *foreach*; namely, that the loop executes the iterations serially in an unspecified order. The outer loop is expressed as a *foreach* because each of the dot products operates on disjoint data, so ordering does not affect the result. The inner loop is also a *foreach*, which indicates that the sum can be done in any order. This allows the compiler to apply associativity and commutativity transformations on the summation. Although these may affect the exact result, it does not affect algorithm correctness for reasonable matrices.

5.2 The CG Benchmark Implementation

Figure 2 illustrates the line count comparison for the timed region of the Fortran+MPI and Titanium implementations of the CG benchmark. In contrast with MG, the amount of code required to implement the timed region of CG in Fortran+MPI is relatively modest, primarily owing to the fact that no application-level packing is required or possible for this communication pattern. Also, MPI's message passing semantics implicitly provide pairwise synchronization between message producers and consumers, so no additional code is required to achieve that synchronization.

6 Titanium Features in the Fourier Transform (FT) Benchmark

6.1 Immutables and Operator Overloading

The Titanium immutable class feature provides language support for defining application-specific primitive types (often called "lightweight" or "value" classes) - allowing the creation of user-defined unboxed objects, analogous to C structs. These provide efficient support for extending the language with new types which are manipulated and passed by value, avoiding pointer-chasing overheads which would otherwise be associated with the use of tiny objects in Java.

One compelling example of the use of immutables is for defining a Complex number class, which is used to represent the complex values in the FT benchmark. Figure 3 compares how one might define a Complex number class using either standard Java Objects versus Titanium immutables.

Java Version

```
public class Complex {
  private double real, imag;
  public Complex(double r, double i)
    { real = r; imag = i; }
  public Complex add(Complex c)
    { ... }
  public Complex multiply(double d)
    { ... }
  ...
}
   /* sample usage */
Complex c = new Complex(7.1, 4.3);
Complex c2 = c.add(c).multiply(14.7);
```

Titanium Version

```
public immutable class Complex {
  public double real, imag;
  public Complex(double r, double i)
    { real = r; imag = i; }
  public Complex op+(Complex c)
    { ... }
  public Complex op*(double d)
    { ... }
  ...
}
   /* sample usage */
Complex c = new Complex(7.1, 4.3);
Complex c2 = (c + c) * 14.7;
```

Fig. 3. Complex numbers in Java and Titanium

In the Java version, each complex number is represented by an Object with two fields corresponding to the real and imaginary components, and methods provide access to the components and mathematical operations on Complex objects. If one were then to define an array of such Complex objects, the resulting in-memory representation would be an array of pointers to tiny objects, each containing the real and imaginary components for one complex number. This representation is wasteful of storage space – imposing the overhead of storing a pointer and an Object header for each complex number, which can easily double the required storage space for each such entity. More importantly for the purposes of scientific computing, such a representation induces poor memory locality and cache behavior for operations over large arrays of such objects. Finally, note the cumbersome method-call syntax which is required for performing operations on the Complex Objects in standard Java.

Titanium allows easy resolution of these performance issues by adding the *immutable* keyword to the class declaration, as shown in the figure. This one-word change declares the Complex type to be a value class, which is passed by value and stored as an unboxed type in the containing context (e.g. on the stack, in an array, or as a field of a larger object). The figure illustrates the framework for a Titanium-based implementation of Complex using immutables and operator overloading, which mirrors the implementation provided in the Titanium standard library (ti.lang.Complex) that is used in the FT benchmark.

Immutable types are not subclasses of java.lang.Object, and induce no overheads for pointers or Object headers. Also they are implicitly final, which means they never pay execution-time overheads for dynamic method call dispatch. An array of Complex immutables is represented in-memory as a single contiguous piece of storage containing all the real and imaginary components, with no pointers or Object overheads. This representation is significantly more compact in storage and efficient in runtime for computationally-intensive algorithms such as FFT.

The figure also demonstrates the use of Titanium's operator overloading, which allows one to define methods corresponding to the syntactic arithmetic operators applied to user classes (the feature is available for any class type, not just immutables). This allows a more natural use of the $+$ and $*$ operators to perform arithmetic on the Complex instances, allowing the client of the Complex class to handle the complex numbers as if they were built-in primitive types.

6.2 Cross-Language Calls

Titanium allows the programmer to make calls to kernels and libraries written in other languages, enabling code reuse and mixed-language applications. This feature allows programmers to take advantage of tested, highly-tuned libraries, and encourages shorter, cleaner, and more modular code. Several of the major Titanium applications make use of this feature to access computational kernels such as vendor-tuned BLAS libraries.

Titanium is implemented as a source-to-source compiler to C, which means that any library offering a C interface is potentially callable from Titanium. To perform cross language integration, programmers simply declare methods using the *native* keyword, and then supply implementations written in C.

The Titanium NAS FT implementation featured in this paper calls the FFTW [15] library to perform the local 1-D FFT computations, thereby leveraging the auto-tuning features and machine-specific optimizations made available in that off-the-shelf FFT kernel implementation. Note that although the FFTW library does offer a 3-D MPI-based parallel FFT solver, our benchmark only uses the serial 1-D FFT kernel – Titanium code is used to create and initialize all the data structures, as well as to orchestrate and perform all the interprocessor communication operations.

6.3 Nonblocking Arraycopy

Titanium's explicitly nonblocking array copy library methods helped in implementing a more efficient 3-D FFT.

The Fortran code performs a bulk-synchronous 3-D FFT, whereby each processor performs two local 1-D FFTs, then all the processors collectively perform an all-to-all communication, followed by another local 1-D FFT. This algorithm has two major performance flaws. First, because each phase is distinct, there is no resulting overlap of computation and communication - while the communication is proceeding, the floating point units on the host CPUs sit idle, and during the computation the network hardware is idle. Secondly, since all the processors send messages to all the other processors during the global transpose, the interconnect can easily get congested and saturate at the bisection bandwidth of the network. This can result in a much slower communication phase than if the same volume of communication were spread out over time during the other phases of the algorithm.

Both these issues can be dealt with using a slight reorganization of the 3-D FFT algorithm employing nonblocking array copy. The new algorithm, implemented in Titanium, first performs a local strided 1-D FFT, followed by a local non-strided 1-D FFT. Then, we begin sending each processor's portion of the grid (slab) as soon as the corresponding rows are computed. By staggering the messages throughout the computation, the network is less likely to become congested and is more effectively utilized.

Moreover, we send these slabs using nonblocking array copy, addressing the other issue with the original algorithm. Nonblocking array copy allows us to inject the message into the network and then continue with the local FFTs, thus overlapping most of the communication costs incurred by the global transpose with the computation of the second FFT pass. Reorganizing the communication in FT to maximize overlap results in a large performance gain, as seen in figure 4.

6.4 The FT Benchmark Implementation

In terms of code size, figure 2 shows that the Titanium implementation of FT is considerably more compact than the Fortran+MPI version. There are three main reasons for this. First, over half the declarations in both versions are dedicated to verifying the checksum, a Complex number that represents the correct "answer" after each iteration. The Titanium code does this a bit more efficiently, thus saving a few lines. Secondly, the Fortran code performs cache blocking for the FFTs and transposes, meaning that it performs them in discrete chunks in order to improve locality on cache-based systems. Moreover, in order to perform the 1-D FFTs, these blocks are copied to and from a separate workspace where the FFT is performed. While this eliminates the need for extra arrays for

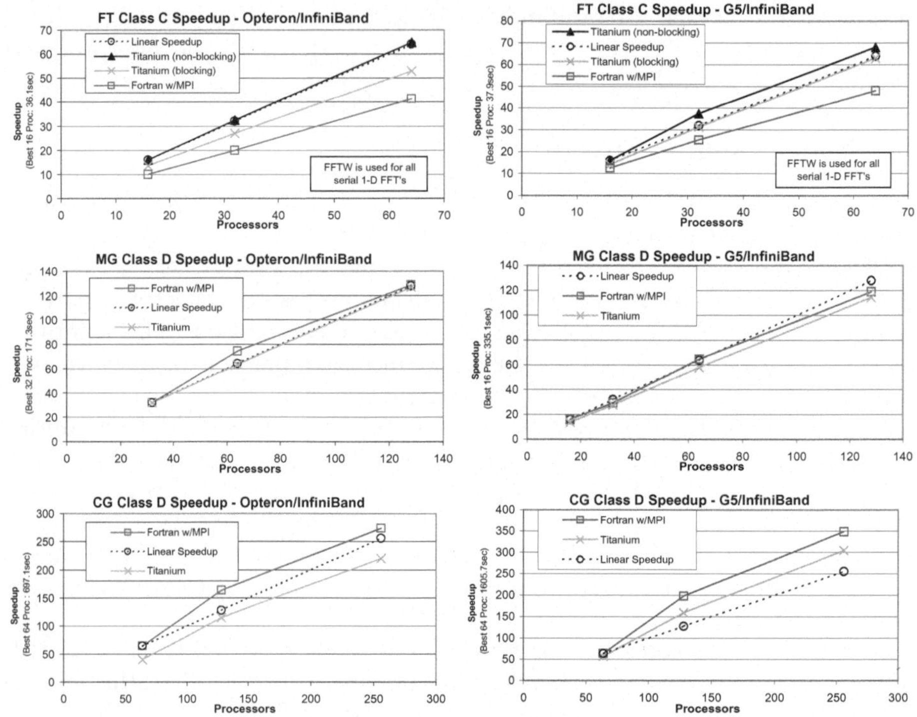

Fig. 4. Performance comparisons for FT, MG, and CG respectively

each 1-D FFT, any performance benefit hinges on how quickly the copies to and from the workspace are done. The Titanium code, on the other hand, allocates several arrays for the 3D FFT, and therefore does not do extra copying. It is consequently shorter code as well. Finally, Titanium's domain calculus operations allow the transposes to be written much more concisely than for Fortran, resulting in a 121 to 3 disparity in lines of communication.

7 Performance Results

7.1 Experimental Methodology

In order to compare performance between languages, we tested the Titanium and Fortran with MPI implementations on an Opteron cluster and a G5 cluster, both with InfiniBand interconnects. For details concerning the input sizes for each problem class, please see the NAS benchmark specification [4].

During data collection, each data point was run consecutively three times, with the minimum being reported. In addition, for a given number of processors, the Fortran and Titanium codes were both run on the same nodes (to ensure consistency). In all cases, performance variability was low, and the results are reproducible.

The actual performance results for all three benchmarks are shown in figure 4. Note that all speedups are measured against the base case of the best time at the lowest number of processors for that graph, and the absolute performance of that case is shown on the y axis. Consequently, the language that has the higher speedup for a given number of processors *actually runs faster* for that case.

7.2 FT Performance

Both implementations of the FT benchmark use the same version of the FFTW library [15] for the local 1-D FFT computations, since it always outperformed the local FFT implementation in the stock Fortran implementation. However, all the communication and other supporting code is written in the language being examined.

As seen at the top of figure 4, the Titanium FT benchmark thoroughly outperforms Fortran, primarily due to two optimizations. First, the Titanium code uses padded arrays to avoid the cache-thrashing that results from having a power-of-two number of elements in the contiguous array dimension. This helps to explain the performance gap between Fortran and the blocking Titanium code.

Secondly, as explained in section 6 the best Titanium implementation also performs nonblocking array copy. This permits us to overlap communication during the global transpose with computation, giving us a second significant improvement over the Fortran code. As a result, the Titanium code performs 36% faster than Fortran on 64 processors of the Opteron/InfiniBand system.

7.3 MG Performance

For the MG benchmark, the Titanium code again uses nonblocking array copy to overlap some of the communication time spent in updating ghost cells. However, the performance benefit is not as great as for FT, since each processor can only overlap two messages at a time, and no computation is done during this time. Nonetheless, the results in figure 4 demonstrate that Titanium performs nearly identically to Fortran for both platforms and for both problem classes.

7.4 CG Performance

The Titanium CG code implements the scalar and vector reductions using point-to-point synchronization. This mechanism scales well, but only provides an advantage at larger numbers of processors. At small processor counts (8 or 16 on the G5), the barrier-based implementation is faster.

The CG performance comparison is shown at the bottom of figure 4. In some cases the CG scaling for both Titanium and Fortran is super-linear due to cache effects. For both platforms, however, Titanium's performance is slightly worse than that of Fortran, by a constant factor of about 10-20%. One reason for this is that point-to-point synchronization is still a work in progress in Titanium. Currently, if a processor needs to signal to a remote processor that it has completed a put operation, it sends two messages. The first is the actual data sent to the remote processor, and the second is an acknowledgment that the data has been sent. This will eventually be implemented as one message in Titanium, and should help bridge the remaining performance gap between the two languages.

8 Related Work

The prior work on parallel languages is too extensive to survey here, so we focus on three current language efforts (ZPL, CAF, and UPC) for which similar studies of the NAS Parallel Benchmarks have been published. All of these studies consider performance as well as expressiveness of the languages, often based on the far-from-perfect line count analysis that appears here.

ZPL is a data parallel language developed at the University of Washington. A case study by Chamberlain, Deitz and Snyder [11] compared implementations of NAS MG across various machines and parallel languages (including MPI/Fortran, ZPL, Co-Array Fortran [3], High Performance Fortran, and Single-Assignment C). They compared the implementations in terms of running time, code complexity and conciseness. Our work extends theirs by providing a similar evaluation of Titanium for MG, but also includes two other NAS benchmarks.

Co-Array Fortran (CAF) is an explicitly parallel, SPMD, global address space extension to Fortran 90 initially developed at Cray Inc [3]. CAF has a built-in distributed data structure abstraction. However, layouts are more restrictive than in a language like ZPL or HPF, since distribution is specified by identifying a co-dimension that is spread over the processors. Titanium's pointer-based layouts can be used to express arbitrary distributions. Communication is more visible in CAF than the other languages, because only statements involving the co-dimension can result in communication. Because CAF is based on F90 arrays, it has various array statements (which are not supported in Titanium) and subarray operations (which are).

Unified Parallel C (UPC) [2] is a parallel extension of ISO C99 that provides a global memory abstraction and communication paradigm similar to Titanium. The Berkeley UPC [16] and Intrepid UPC compilers use the same GASNet communication layer as Titanium, and Berkeley UPC uses a source-to-source compilation strategy analogous to the Berkeley Titanium compiler and Rice CAF compiler. Bell et al [17] reimplemented some of the NAS benchmarks in UPC's one-sided communication paradigm, producing performance improvements of up to 2x over the MPI-Fortran versions.

9 Conclusions

We have shown that Titanium is well-suited to three common yet diverse scientific kernels from both an expressiveness and performance standpoint. However, Titanium applications are not merely limited to the NAS benchmarks, as it supports more general distributed data layouts and irregular parallelism patterns than these problems require. In addition, the use of Java as a base language provides support for strong typing, user-defined classes, inheritance, and dynamic memory management. All of these features help raise the level of abstraction when compared to most serial languages commonly used in parallel computing.

References

[1] Yelick, K., Semenzato, L., Pike, G., Miyamoto, C., Liblit, B., Krishnamurthy, A., Hilfinger, P., Graham, S., Gay, D., Colella, P., Aiken, A.: Titanium: a high-performance Java dialect. In: Proceedings of ACM 1998 Workshop on Java for High-Performance Network Computing. (1998)

[2] UPC Community Forum: UPC specification v1.2. (2005) `http://upc.gwu.edu/documentation.html`.

[3] Numrich, R., Reid, J.: Co-array fortran for parallel programming. In: ACM Fortran Forum 17, 2, 1-31. (1998)

[4] Bailey, D.H., Barszcz, E., Barton, J.T., Browning, D.S., Carter, R.L., Dagum, D., Fatoohi, R.A., Frederickson, P.O., Lasinski, T.A., Schreiber, R.S., Simon, H.D., Venkatakrishnan, V., Weeratunga, S.K.: The NAS Parallel Benchmarks. The International Journal of Supercomputer Applications **5**(3) (1991) 63–73

[5] Gosling, J., Joy, B., Steele, G.: The Java Language Specification. second edn. (2000)

[6] Hilfinger, P., Bonachea, D., Gay, D., Graham, S., Liblit, B., Pike, G., Yelick, K.: Titanium language reference manual. Tech Report UCB/CSD-01-1163, U.C. Berkeley (2001)

[7] Titanium home page. http://titanium.cs.berkeley.edu.

[8] Wen, T., Colella, P.: Adaptive mesh refinement in Titanium. In: 19th International Parallel and Distributed Processing Symposium (IPDPS). (2005)

[9] Givelberg, E., Yelick, K.: Distributed immersed boundary simulation in Titanium (2003)

[10] MPI Forum: MPI: A message-passing interface standard, v1.1. Technical report, University of Tennessee, Knoxville (June 12, 1995) `http://www.mpi-forum.org/docs/mpi-11.ps`.

[11] Chamberlain, B.L., Deitz, S.J., Snyder, L.: A comparative study of the NAS MG benchmark across parallel languages and architectures. In: Supercomputing '00: Proceedings of the 2000 ACM/IEEE conference on Supercomputing. (2000)

[12] Liblit, B., Aiken, A.: Type systems for distributed data structures. In: the 27th ACM SIGPLAN-SIGACT Symposium on Principles of Programming Languages (POPL). (2000)

[13] Pike, G., Hilfinger, P.N.: Better tiling and array contraction for compiling scientific programs. In: Proceedings of the IEEE/ACM SC2002 Conference. (2002)

[14] Pike, G.R.: Reordering and storage optimizations for scientific programs (2002)

[15] Frigo, M., Johnson, S.G.: The design and implementation of FFTW3. Proceedings of the IEEE **93**(2) (2005) 216–231 Special issue on "Program Generation, Optimization, and Platform Adaptation".

[16] The Berkeley UPC Compiler (2002). http://upc.lbl.gov.

[17] Bell, C., Bonachea, D., Nishtala, R., Yelick, K.: Optimizing application performance using one-sided communication. Technical Report to appear, Lawrence Berkeley National Laboratory (2005)

Efficient Search-Space Pruning for Integrated Fusion and Tiling Transformations

Xiaoyang Gao[1], Sriram Krishnamoorthy[1], Swarup Kumar Sahoo[1], Chi-Chung Lam[1], Gerald Baumgartner[2], J. Ramanujam[3], and P. Sadayappan[1]

[1] Department of Computer Science and Engineering
The Ohio State University, Columbus, OH 43210, USA
{gaox,krishnsr,sahoo,clam,saday}@cse.ohio-state.edu
[2] Department of Computer Science
Louisiana State University, Baton Rouge, LA 70803, USA
gb@csc.lsu.edu
[3] Department of Electrical and Computer Engineering and
Center for Computation and Technology
Louisiana State University, Baton Rouge, LA 70803, USA
jxr@ece.lsu.edu

Abstract. Compile-time optimizations involve a number of transformations such as loop permutation, fusion, tiling, array contraction, etc. Determination of the choice of these transformations that minimizes the execution time is a challenging task. We address this problem in the context of tensor contraction expressions involving arrays too large to fit in main memory. Domain-specific features of the computation are exploited to develop an integrated framework that facilitates the exploration of the entire search space of optimizations. In this paper, we discuss the exploration of the space of loop fusion and tiling transformations in order to minimize the disk I/O cost. These two transformations are integrated and pruning strategies are presented that significantly reduce the number of loop structures to be evaluated for subsequent transformations. The evaluation of the framework using representative contraction expressions from quantum chemistry shows a dramatic reduction in the size of the search space using the strategies presented.

1 Introduction

Optimizing compilers incorporate a number of loop transformations such as permutation, tiling, fusion, etc. Considerable work has been done on improving locality and/or parallelism by loop fusion [8,9,10,11,19]. Fusion often creates imperfectly nested loops, which are more complex to tile effectively than perfectly nested loops. Several works have addressed the tiling of imperfectly nested loops [2,20]. Although there has been much progress in developing unified frameworks for modeling a variety of loop transformations [1,2,16], their use has so far been restricted to optimization of indirect performance metrics such as reuse distance, degree of parallelism, etc.

E. Ayguadé et al. (Eds.): LCPC 2005, LNCS 4339, pp. 215–229, 2007.

The development of model-driven optimization strategies that target direct performance metrics remains a difficult task. In this paper, we address the problem in the specific domain of tensor contractions involving tensors too large to fit into physical memory. We use certain properties of the computations in this domain to integrate various transformations and investigate pruning strategies to reduce the search space to be explored.

The large sizes of the tensors involved require the development of *out-of-core* implementations that orchestrate the movement of data between disk and main memory. In this paper, we discuss the integration of loop fusion and tiling transformations with the objective of minimizing disk I/O cost. We first divide the input program into several independent loop nests, then enumerate the set of fusion structures of each loop nest. Then, a generalized tiling approach that significantly reduces the number of loop structures to be explored is presented. It also enables subsequent optimizations of I/O placements and loop permutations. This approach enables an exploration of the entire search space using a realistic performance model, without the need to resort to heuristics and search of a limited subspace of the search space to limit search time.

The rest of this paper is organized as follows. In the next section, we elaborate on the computational context of interest and introduce some preliminary concepts; in addition, an overview of the program synthesis system and the overall approach are given. Section 3 describes a tree partitioning algorithm. In Section 4, we propose a loop structure enumeration algorithm and prove its completeness. The reduction in the space of loop structures to be explored is shown for representative computations in Section 5. Conclusions are provided in Section 6.

2 Background

The work presented in this paper is being developed in the context of the Tensor Contraction Engine (TCE) program synthesis tool [3,4,5,6,14]. The TCE takes as input a high-level specification of a computation expressed as a set of tensor contraction expressions, and transforms it into efficient parallel code. The current prototype of the TCE incorporates several compile-time optimizations which are treated in a decoupled manner, with the transformations being performed in a pre-determined sequence. In [12,13], we presented an integrated approach to determine the tile sizes and I/O placements for a fixed loop structure. Techniques to prune the search space of possible I/O placements, orderings, loop permutations and tiling for given a choice of fusion of tensor contractions were presented in [18]. In this paper, we present a technique to enumerate the various fusion structures and develop an algorithm to significantly reduce the number of loop nests to be evaluated for each fusion structure.

2.1 Computational Context

In the class of computations considered, the final result can be expressed using a collection of multi-dimensional summations of the product of several input arrays. For example, we consider a transformation used in quantum chemistry to transform a set of two-electron integrals from an atomic orbital (AO) basis to a molecular orbital (MO) basis:

$$B(a,b,c,d) = \sum_{p,q,r,s} C1(d,s) \times C2(c,r) \times C3(b,q) \times C4(a,p) \times A(p,q,r,s)$$

Here, all arrays would be initially stored on disk. The indices p, q, r and s have the same range N. The indices a, b, c and d have the same range V. Typical values for N range from 60 to 1300; the value for V is usually between 50 and 1000.

The calculation of B is done in four steps to reduce the number of floating point operations.

$$\begin{aligned}
T1(a,q,r,s) &= \sum_{p} C4(a,p) \times A(p,q,r,s) \\
T2(a,b,r,s) &= \sum_{q} C3(b,q) \times T1(a,q,r,s) \\
T3(a,b,c,s) &= \sum_{r} C2(c,r) \times T2(a,b,r,s) \\
B(a,b,c,d) &= \sum_{s} C1(d,s) \times T3(a,b,c,s)
\end{aligned}$$

The sequence of contractions in this form can be represented by an operation tree as shown in Fig. 1(a). The leaves correspond to the input arrays and the root corresponds to the output array. The intermediate arrays and output array are produced by the tensor contraction of their immediate children. The edges in the operation tree represent the *producer-consumer* relationship between contractions.

Assuming that the available memory space is less than V^4 (which is 3TB for $V = 800$), any one of the arrays A, $T1$, $T2$, $T3$ and B is too large to entirely fit in memory. Therefore, if the computation is implemented as a succession of four independent steps, the intermediates $T1$, $T2$ and $T3$ have to be written to disk after they are produced, and read from disk before they are used in the next step. Furthermore, the amount of disk access volume could be much larger than the total volume of the data on disk. Since none of these arrays can be fully stored in memory, it is not possible to read each element only once from disk. Suitable fusion of the common loops between producing and consuming contractions can reduce the size of the intermediate array, making it feasible to retain it in memory. Henceforth, the term intermediate node will be used to refer to both the intermediate array produced in the corresponding interior node, and the contraction that produces it. The reference shall be clear from the context.

Given a choice of fusion, an intermediate node not fused with its parent divides the operation tree into two parts, both of which can be evaluated independently. Such an intermediate node is called a *cut-point*. A cut-point node is assumed to be resident on disk. A connected operation tree without any interior cut-points

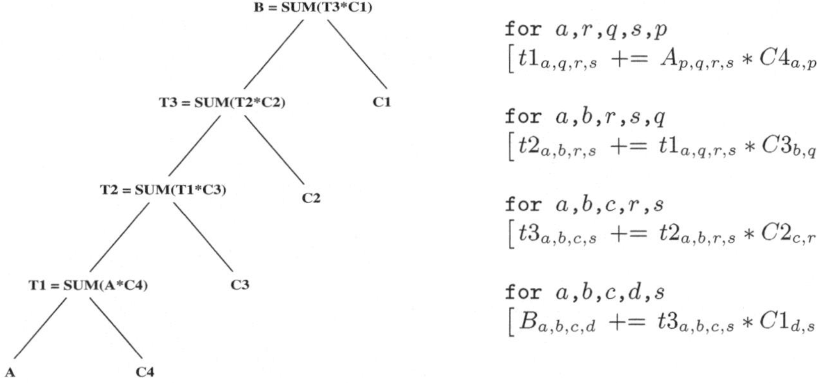

(a) Operation tree for the four-index transform

(b) Corresponding unfused code structure

Fig. 1. Operation tree and unfused code structure for the four-index transform

is called a *fused sub-tree*. The divided operation tree for the four-index transform corresponding to $T1$ being a cut-point is shown in Fig. 2(a). The *loop nesting tree* (LNT) represents the loop structure of a fused sub-tree. Each node in a LNT is labeled by the indices of a set of fully permutable loops appearing together at the same level in the imperfectly nested loop structure. Loops in the children nodes are surrounded by loops in the parent node. Fig. 2(b) shows two possible LNT's for the two fused subtrees in Fig. 2(a), respectively. The corresponding code structure is shown in Fig. 2(c).

2.2 Overall Approach

The program synthesis system takes an operation tree representing a set of tensor contractions as input, and generates an efficient loop structure with explicit disk I/O statements to implement the computation. The optimization process may be viewed in terms of the following steps.

1. Operation Tree Partitioning: In this step, we divide the original operation tree into several fused subtrees by identifying cut-points. The optimal loop structures for the subtrees are independent of each other, and are determined separately.
2. Loop Structures Enumeration: For each fused subtree, we enumerate candidate loop structures to be evaluated, as a set of LNT's.
3. Intra-Tile Loop Placements: For a given LNT, we tile all loops at each node and propagate intra-tile loops to all the nodes below it.
4. Disk I/O Placements and Orderings: We then explore various possible placements and orderings of disk I/O statements for each disk array in a tiled loop structure with a pruning strategy to determine the best placement and ordering.

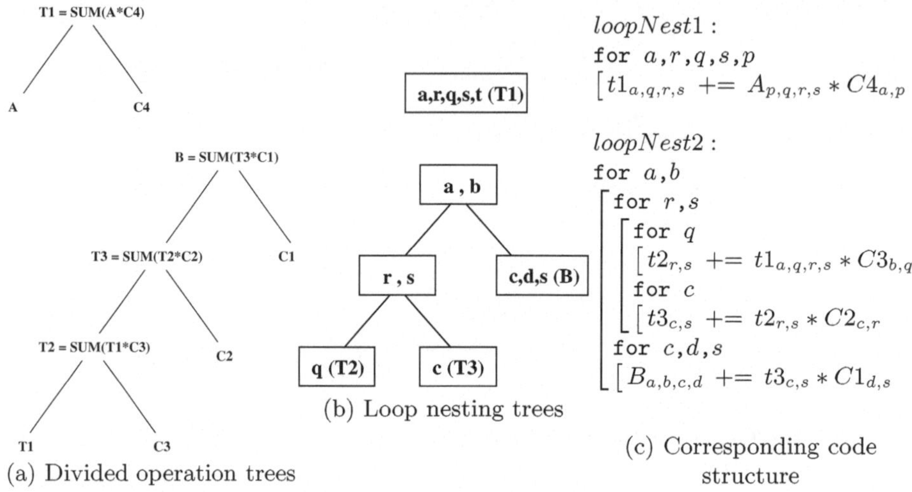

(a) Divided operation trees (b) Loop nesting trees (c) Corresponding code structure

Fig. 2. Representations involved in generation of a fused code structure

5. Tile Size Selection: For each combination of loop transformations and I/O placements, the I/O cost is formulated as a non-linear optimization problem in terms of the tile sizes. The tile sizes that minimize the disk I/O cost are determined using a general-purpose non-linear optimization solver.
6. Code Generation: We calculate the disk access cost for each solution obtained, and generate code for the one with the minimal disk I/O cost.

The possible choices of fused subtrees are first enumerated. This is explained in Section 3. Given a fused sub-tree, the optimal loop structure and the corresponding cost can be determined by the following steps: 1) enumerating all candidate loop structures; 2) enumerating placements and ordering of disk I/O statments; 3) determining the tile size to minimize the disk I/O cost for each combination; and 4) selecting the program structure with the minimal disk I/O cost. The algorithm for enumerating candidate loop structures is discussed in Section 4. The search space of disk I/O placements and orderings, loop permutations and tile sizes is pruned and modeled as a non-linear optimization problem in [18], which is then solved to determine the disk I/O cost. In this paper, we focus on determination of the fused sub-trees and the enumeration of candidate loop nesting trees to be evaluated.

3 Tree Partitioning

In this section, we discuss the procedure to enumerate the set of all fused subtrees to be evaluated. In general, fusing a loop between the producer of an intermediate array and its consumer eliminates the corresponding dimension of the array and reduces the array size. If the array fits in memory after fusion, no disk I/O is required for that array. On the other hand, if the array does not fit in the physical memory after fusion, the disk I/O cost will remain the same and there is no improvement in locality. Therefore, fusion of any loops corresponding to an intermediate node is assumed to cause the resulting intermediate to reside in memory. Alternatively, an intermediate node not fused with its parent (*cut-point*) is assumed to reside in disk.

An arbitrary operation tree with M intermediate nodes theoretically has $O(2^M)$ possible fused sub-trees, but not all of them are legal. If both the children of an intermediate node are fused with it, then the loops corresponding to the summation indices in the given node must be the outermost loops; and it can not be fused with its parent anymore. Thus, either the node itself or one of its children must be a cut-point.

Based on this property, we can restrict the number of top sub-trees to $O(M^2)$. The algorithm to enumerate the fused sub-trees rooted at a given node is shown in Algorithm 1. It proceeds in a bottom-up fashion, constructing all fused sub-trees rooted at a given node from those of its children. Given a node t with two children $left$ and $right$, we can extend a fused sub-tree from either $left$ or $right$ to include the given node. These sub-trees can further be extended to include the given node's parent. Besides, the given node can be considered as a cut-point. In this scenario, all possible pairs of left and right fused sub-trees may form a valid fused sub-tree for the given node. The field $t.TreeSet$ represents the set of fused sub-trees which can be extended to include the parent of t.

4 Loop Structure Enumeration

In this section, we first present an algorithm that can generate a set of loop structures for a fused sub-tree. Then, we present the result that for any loop structure S of the fused sub-tree, we can find a corresponding loop structure S' in the generated set, so that S' can be transformed to S by use of a multi-level tiling strategy.

4.1 Enumeration Algorithm

In the previous section, we showed that a fused sub-tree must be in one of these two forms:

- All contractions form a chain called a *contraction chain*. For instance, Fig. 1 is such an operation tree in which the contraction chain is $T1, T2, T3, B$.
- The contractions form two chains joining at the root node. In this case, the *contraction chain* is connected by these two chains. An example of such an operation tree is shown in Fig. 3, in which the contraction chain is $T1, T2, B, T3, T4$.

Given an operation tree that has n contraction nodes $t_1, t_2, ..., t_n$, let $t_i.indices$ denote all loop indices surrounding the contraction node t_i. First, we create a contraction chain of the operation tree. It corresponds to a sequence of perfectly nested loops. Many different choices exist for the ordering of the fusions within

Algorithm 1. EnumerateFusedSubtrees(t: the root of a subtree) returns $TreeSet$

```
t₁ = the left child of t;   t₂ = the right child of t;   TreeSet = empty
//Only one subtree
if both t₁ and t₂ are input nodes then
  Create a new Tree Tr with Tr.CutpointSet = ∅
  Insert Tr into TreeSet
end if
//Extending subtrees from the child not an input
if t₁ is an input node and t₂ is an intermediate node then
  childSet = t₂.TreeSet
  Create a new Tree Tr with Tr.CutpointSet = {t2}
  Insert Tr into TreeSet
end if
if t₂ is an input node, and t₁ is an intermediate node then
  childSet = t₁.TreeSet
  Create a new Tree Tr with Tr.CutpointSet = {t1}
  Insert Tr into TreeSet
end if
for each subtree st in childSet do
  Create a new Tree Tr with Tr.CutpointSet = st.CutpointSet
  Insert Tr into TreeSet
end for
t.TreeSet = TreeSet
//Entending subtrees from either child, and cutting another child off
if both t and t₂ are intermediate nodes then
  childSet1 = t₁.TreeSet
  for each subtree st in childSet1 do
    Create a new Tree Tr with Tr.CutpointSet = {st.CutpointSet, t2}
    Insert Tr into TreeSet
  end for
  childSet2 = t₂.TreeSet
  for each subtree st in childSet2 do
    Create a new Tree Tr with Tr.CutpointSet = {st.CutpointSet, t1}
    Insert Tr into TreeSet
  end for
  Create a new Tree Tr with Tr.CutpointSet = {t1, t2}
  Insert Tr into TreeSet
  t.TreeSet = TreeSet
  //Merging subtrees from both children, and extending the result
  for each pair of subtrees st1 in childSet1 and st2 in childSet2 do
    Create a new Tree Tr
    Tr.CutpointSet = {st1.CutpointSet, st2.CutpointSet}
    Insert Tr into TreeSet
  end for
end if
```

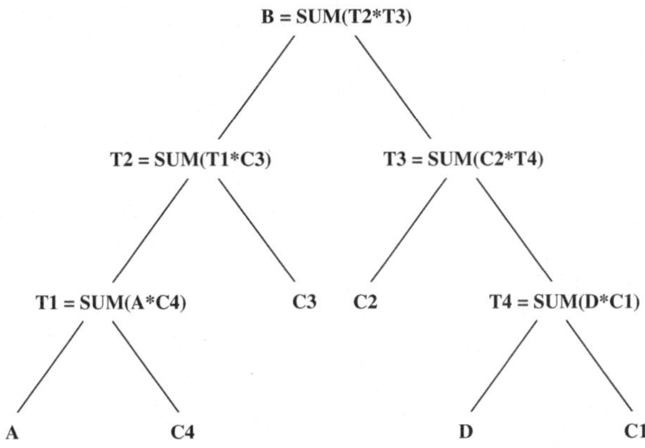

Fig. 3. An operation tree with two chains

this sequence of perfectly nested loop nests. Each of the perfectly nested loops corresponding to a contraction can be considered an independent loop nesting tree. The fusion of sub-trees producing and consuming an intermediate array creates an imperfectly nested loop nest, in which some of the common loops are merged. The process of construction of the loop nesting trees corresponding to a fused sub-tree can be modeled as a paranthesization problem. Consider the sequence of contraction nodes T1, T2, T3, and B in the operation tree shown in Fig. 1. $((T1(T2\ T3))B)$ corresponds to a parenthesization in which the contractions producing T3 and consuming T3 are fused first and the resulting loop nest is fused with the contractions producing T1 and B, in that order. Fig. 4 shows one possible parenthesization for the four-index transform and the corresponding loop nesting tree.

We enumerate all possible parenthesizations of the contraction chain. For each parenthesization, a maximally fused loop structure is created by a recursive construction procedure. We call it *maximally fused* since, in the construction procedure, each intermediate node will have its indices fused as much as possible with its parent. The construction procedure is shown in Algorithm 2. It takes a parenthesization P as input, and generate a corresponding LNT. A parenthesization of a contraction chain with n nodes has $n-1$ pairs of parentheses. Each pair of parentheses includes two elements, left and right element. Each element is either a single contraction node or a parenthesization of a sub-chain within a pair of parentheses.

Fig. 4 illustrates this proceduce for the $((T1(T2\ T3))B)$ parenthesization of the four-index transform.

4.2 Completeness

In this section, we state results that are useful in proving that the set of *maximally fused* loop structures generated by the enumeration algorithm above can represent all loop structures of a fused subtree.

Algorithm 2. Construction(P)

//Given a parenthesization, the algorithm map it to a maximally fused loop structure in LNT

$l = P.left$
$r = P.right$
if l is a parenthesization **then**
  lt = Construction($left$)
else if l is a contraction **then**
  lt = Create a new LNT node
  $lt.indices = l.indices$
  $lt.children = null$
  $lt.contraction = l$ {lt is a leaf, which includes a contraction node in it}
end if
if r is a parenthesization **then**
  rt = Construction($right$)
else if r is a contraction **then**
  rt = Create a new LNT node
  $rt.indices = r.indices$
  $rt.children = null$
  $rt.contraction = r$ {rt is a leaf, which includes a contraction node in it}
end if
$comindices = lt.indices \cap rt.indices$
$lt.indices = lt.indices - comindices$
$rt.indices = rt.indices - comindices$
lnt = Create a new LNT node
$lnt.indices = comindices$
$lnt.children = \{lt, rt\}$
return lnt

Given an arbitrary loop nesting tree lnt, we can map it to a maximal fused loop nesting tree lnt', which is generated by the enumeration algorithm above and can be translated to lnt with proper multi-level tiling strategy. The mapping algorithm consists of two steps:

1. Take lnt as input, and create a parenthesization P of the contraction chain using the generation routine provided in Algorithm 3.
2. Apply the construction procedure in Algorithm 2 on P to generate a maximally fused loop structure lnt'.

Obviously, lnt' is the set of *maximally fused* loop structures generated by the enumeration algorithm. We note that lnt' can be translated to lnt by sinking indices at upper levels down.

Remark 1. For any pair of contraction nodes t_i and t_j, let $common(lnt, t_i, t_j)$ be defined as the loops shared by t_i and t_j in lnt. We have $common(lnt, t_i, t_j) \subseteq common(lnt', t_i, t_j)$.

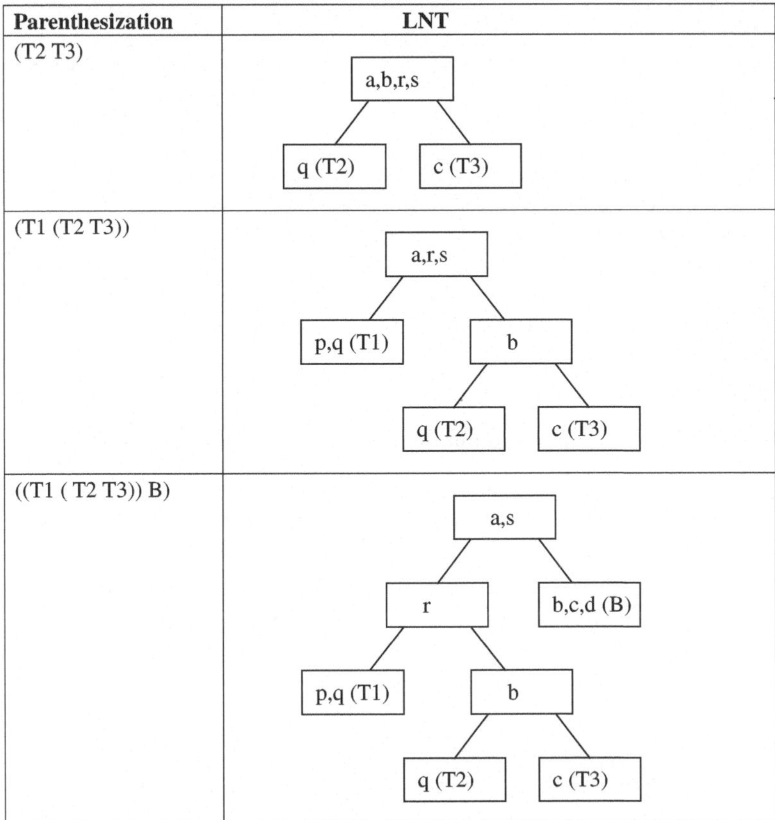

Fig. 4. Construction of a maximally fused loop structure for a particular parenthesization of the four-index transform

Remark 2. If $common(lnt, t_i, t_j) \subset common(lnt', t_i, t_j)$, then we can transform lnt' to form lnt'' by sinking indices down, so that $common(lnt, t_i, t_j) = common(lnt'', t_i, t_j)$

Applying the sinking operation in Remark 2 for each pair of contraction nodes (t_i, t_j), we can transform lnt' to lnt'', which satisfies the condition: $\forall(t_i, t_j), common(lnt, t_i, t_j) = common(lnt'', t_i, t_j)$. After that, if a node r has no indices in $r.indices$, we remove r from lnt'', and put all children of r to its parent. Then, lnt'' is same as lnt.

Using a *multi-level tiling strategy*, a maximally fused loop strcuture can be transformed into an arbitrarily fused loop structure by appropriate choice of tile sizes. *Multi-level tiling* can transform the LNT of a loop structure as follows. Each loop present in the root is split into two components, an inter-tile loop and an intra-tile loop. The intra-tile loop is placed on child nodes of the root. Then the loops present at each of the child nodes, including the intra-tile loops from the root, are again split and intra-tile loops are placed on their respective child nodes.

Algorithm 3. Parenthesize(*lnt*)

```
//Given an LNT, the algorithm map it to a corresponding parenthesization

if lnt.children ≠ null then
  P = null
  for each child c in lnt.children do
    P' = Parenthesize(c)
    if P is null then
      P = P'
    else
      P = new Parenthesization(P, P')
    end if
  end for
else
  P = c.contraction {c is a leaf and includes a contraction node}
end if
return P
```

This process is porformed recursively until leaf nodes are encountered. The loop structure corresponding to the LNT can also be transformed accordingly. Fig. 5 shows the tiling of loop a in the LNT in Fig. 4 and the relationship between different tiles, where $a.range$ represents the range of loop a.

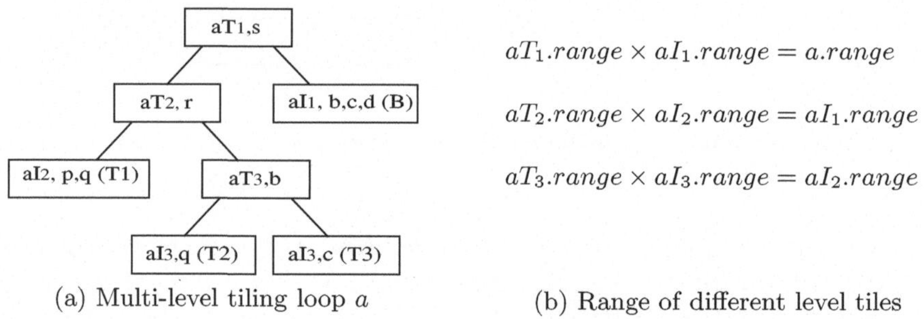

(a) Multi-level tiling loop a (b) Range of different level tiles

Fig. 5. An example of multi-level tiling in LNT

The sinking operation in an LNT can be modeled as a *multi-level tiling* in the loop structure. If we tile a fused loop with a tile size equal to its loop range, it leads to the same result as sinking the loop index from the original node to its children. Let S and S' be loop structures representd by lnt and lnt' respectively. Since we can transform lnt' to lnt by sinking operations, we can also transform S' to S by suitable multi-level tiling. We use an example to show the details of the transformation procedure below.

An arbitrary fully fused loop structure S for the four-index transform is shown in Fig. 6(a), and the corresponding maximally fused loop structure S' may be seen in Fig. 6(b). After we apply multi-level tiling, S' is translated to the form

```
for a
  for r
    for q,s,p
      [t1_{s,q} += A_{p,q,r,s} * C4_{a,p}
    for b,s,q
      [t2_{b,r,s} += t1_{s,q} * C3_{b,q}
  for b,c,r,s
    [t3_{b,c,s} += t2_{b,r,s} * C2_{c,r}
  for b,c,d,s
    [B_{a,b,c,d} += t3_{b,c,s} * C1_{d,s}
```

(a) Arbitrary fused loop structure: S

```
for a,s
  for r
    for q
      for p
        [t1 += A_{p,q,r,s} * C4_{a,p}
      for b
        [t2_b += t1 * C3_{b,q}
    for b,c
      [t3_{b,c} += t2_b * C2_{c,r}
  for b,c,d
    [B_{a,b,c,d} += t3_{b,c} * C1_{d,s}
```

(b) Maximally fused loop structure: S'

Fig. 6. An arbitrary loop structure and the corresponding maximally fused structure

```
for aT1,sT1
  for rT1,aT2,sT2
    for qT1,rT2,aT3,sT3
      for p,qI1,rI2,aI3,sI3
        [t1_{aI,qI,rI,sI} += A_{p,q,r,s} * C4_{a,p}
      for b, qI1,rI2,aI3,sI3
        [t2_{aI,b,rI,sI} += t1_{aI,qI,rI,sI} * C3_{b,q}
    for b, c, rI1, aI2,sI2
      [t3_{aI,b,c,sI} += t2_{aI,b,rI,sI} * C2_{c,r}
  for aI1, b, c, d, sI1
    [B_{a,b,c,d} += t3_{aI,b,c,sI} * C1_{d,s}
```

(a) After inserting intra-tile loops

```
for aT1
  for rT1
    for p,qI1,sI3
      [t1_{aI,qI,rI,sI} += A_{p,q,r,s} * C4_{a,p}
    for b,qI1,sI3
      [t2_{aI,b,rI,sI} += t1_{aI,qI,rI,sI} * C3_{b,q}
  for b,c,rI1,aI2,sI2
    [t3_{aI,b,c,sI} += t2_{aI,b,rI,sI} * C2_{c,r}
  for b,c,d,sI1
    [B_{a,b,c,d} += t3_{aI,b,c,sI} * C1_{d,s}
```

(b) After selecting proper tile counts

Fig. 7. Translate S' to S by multi-level tiling strategy

shown in Fig. 7(a). In addition, if we set ranges of inter-tile loops as shown below, and remove all loops with $range = 1$, S' can be rewritten in the form shown in Fig. 7(b), which is exactly the same as S. The indexing of the intermediate arrays has been shown in a generic fashion.

$$aT_2 = aT_3 = sT_1 = sT_2 = sT_3 = rT_2 = qT_1 = 1; aT_1 = a.range; rI_1 = r.range$$

4.3 Complexity

The total number of loop structures generated by the enumeration algorithm is the same as the number of parenthesizations of the contraction chain. For a contraction chain with n nodes, the number of all possible parenthesizations is called the nth *Catalan Number*. It is exponential in n, and the upper bound is $O(4^n/n^{3/2})$. In contrast, the number of possible loop structures is potentially exponential in the total number of distinct loop indices in the n intermediate nodes, a considerably larger number. The fused operation tree is not very long for most representative computations. In most practical applications, a fused subtree usually has no more than 5 contractions in a single chain. Note that the nth Catalan Number is not very large when n is small. The first six Catalan Numbers are listed here: $1, 1, 2, 5, 14, 42, \ldots$.

5 Experimental Results

The enumeration algorithm discussed in Section 4.1 generates a set of candidates loop structures to be considered for data locality optimization. Without this algorithm, and generalized tiling, the set of loop structures to be evaluated might be too large, precluding their complete evaluation and necessitating the use of heuristics.

We evaluate the effectiveness of our approach using the following tensor contractions from representative computations from the quantum chemistry domain.

1. **Four-index transform (4index):** Introduced in Section 2.
2. **CCSD:** The second and the third computations are from the class of Coupled Cluster (CC) equations [7,15,17] for ab initio electronic structure modeling. The sequence of tensor contraction expressions extracted from this computation is shown as follows:

$$S(j,i,b,a) = \sum_{l,k} (A(l,k,b,a) \times (\sum_d (\sum_c (B(d,c,l,k) \times C(i,c)) \times D(j,d)))$$

3. **CCSDT:** This is a more accurate CC model. A sub-expression from the CCSDT theory is:

$$S(h3,h4,p1,p2) = \sum_{p9,h6,h8} (y\_ooovvv(h8,h6,h4,p9,p1,p2) \times \sum_{h10} \Big(t\_vo(p9,h10) \times \sum_{p7} (t\_vo(p7,h8) \times \sum_{p5} (t\_vo(p5,h6) \times v\_oovv(h10,h3,p7,p5))\Big)\Big)$$

We evaluated the fused subtree corresponding to the entire operation tree without any cut-points. The number of all possible loop structures and the number of candidate loop structures enumerated by our approach are shown in Table 1. It can be seen that a very large fraction of the set of possible loop structures, up to 98%, is pruned away using the approach developed in this paper.

Table 1. Effectiveness of pruning of loop structures

	#Contractions	#Loop structures		Reduction
		Total	Pruned	
4index	4	241	5	98%
CCSD	3	69	2	97%
CCSDT	4	182	5	98%

6 Conclusions

In this paper we addressed the problem of optimizing the disk access cost of tensor contraction expressions by applying loop transformations. We discussed approaches to partitioning of the operation tree into fused sub-trees and generating a small set of maximally-fused loop structures that cover all possible imperfectly nested fused loop structures. The approach was evaluated on a set of computations representative of the targeted quantum chemistry domain and a significant reduction was demonstrated in the number of loop structures to be evaluated.

Acknowledgments. This work is supported in part by the National Science Foundation through awards 0121676, 0121706, 0403342, 0508245, 0509442, 0509467, and 0541409.

References

1. N. Ahmed, N. Mateev, and K. Pingali. Synthesizing transformations for locality enhancement of imperfectly nested loops. In *Proc. of ACM Intl. Conf. on Supercomputing*, 2000.
2. N. Ahmed, N. Mateev, and K. Pingali. Tiling imperfectly-nested loops nests. In *Proc. of SC 2000*, 2000.
3. G. Baumgartner, D.E. Bernholdt, D. Cociorva, R. Harrison, S. Hirata, C. Lam, M. Nooijen, R. Pitzer, J. Ramanujam, and P. Sadayappan. A High-Level Approach to Synthesis of High-Performance Codes for Quantum Chemistry. In *Proc. of SC 2002*, November 2002.
4. D. Cociorva, G. Baumgartner, C. Lam, J. Ramanujam P. Sadayappan, M. Nooijen, D. Bernholdt, and R. Harrison. Space-Time Trade-Off Optimization for a Class of Electronic Structure Calculations. In *Proc. of ACM SIGPLAN PLDI 2002*, pages 177–186, 2002.
5. D. Cociorva, X. Gao, S. Krishnan, G. Baumgartner, C. Lam, P. Sadayappan, and J. Ramanujam. Global Communication Optimization for Tensor Contraction Expressions under Memory Constraints. In *Proc. of IPDPS*, 2003.
6. D. Cociorva, J. Wilkins, G. Baumgartner, P. Sadayappan, J. Ramanujam, M. Nooijen, D. E. Bernholdt, and R. Harrison. Towards Automatic Synthesis of High-Performance Codes for Electronic Structure Calculations: Data Locality Optimization. In *Proc. of the Intl. Conf. on High Performance Computing*, volume 2228, pages 237–248. Springer-Verlag, 2001.
7. T. Crawford and H. F. Schaefer III. An Introduction to Coupled Cluster Theory for Computational Chemists. In K. Lipkowitz and D. Boyd, editor, *Reviews in Computational Chemistry*, volume 14, pages 33–136. John Wiley, 2000.
8. C. Ding and K. Kennedy. Improving effective bandwidth through compiler enhancement of global cache reuse. *J. Parallel Distrib. Comput.*, 64(1):108–134, 2004.
9. G. Gao, R. Olsen, V. Sarkar, and R. Thekkath. Collective Loop Fusion for Array Contraction. In *Proc. of the Fifth LCPC Workshop*, 1992.
10. K. Kennedy. Fast greedy weighted fusion. In *Proc. of ACM Intl. Conf. on Supercomputing*, 2000.

11. K. Kennedy and K. S. McKinley. Maximizing loop parallelism and improving data locality via loop fusion and distribution. In *Proc. of Languages and Compilers for Parallel Computing*, pages 301–320. Springer-Verlag, 1993.
12. S. Krishnan, S. Krishnamoorthy, G. Baumgartner, C. Lam, J. Ramanujam, P. Sadayappan, and V. Choppella. Efficient synthesis of out-of-core algorithms using a nonlinear optimization solver. In *Proc. of IPDPS*, page 34b, 2004.
13. S. Krishnan, S. Krishnamoorthy, G. Baumgartner, C. Lam, J. Ramanujam, P. Sadayappan, and V. Choppella. Efficient synthesis of out-of-core algorithms using a nonlinear optimization solver. *Journal of Parallel and Distributed Computing*, 66(5):659–673, May 2006.
14. C. Lam. *Performance Optimization of a Class of Loops Implementing Multi-Dimensional Integrals.* PhD thesis, The Ohio State University, Columbus, OH, August 1999.
15. T. J. Lee and G. E. Scuseria. Achieving chemical accuracy with coupled cluster theory. In S. R. Langhoff, editor, *Quantum Mechanical Electronic Structure Calculations with Chemical Accuracy*, pages 47–109. Kluwer Academic, 1997.
16. A. W. Lim and M. S. Lam. Maximizing Parallelism and Minimizing Synchronization with Affine Partitions. *Parallel Computing*, 24(3-4):445–475, May 1998.
17. J. M. L. Martin. Benchmark Studies on Small Molecules. In P. v. R. Schleyer, P. R. Schreiner, N. L. Allinger, T. Clark, J. Gasteiger, P. Kollman, and H. F. Schaefer III, editors, *Encyclopedia of Computational Chemistry*, volume 4, pages 115–128. John Wiley, 1998.
18. S. K. Sahoo, S. Krishnamoorthy, R. Panuganti, and P. Sadayappan. Integrated loop optimizations for data locality enhancement of tensor contraction expressions. In *Proc. of Supercomputing (SC 2005)*, 2005.
19. S. Singhai and K. S. McKinley. Loop Fusion for Parallelism and Locality. In *Proc. of Mid-Atlantic States Student Workshop on Programming Languages and Systems*, 1996.
20. Y. Song and Z. Li. New Tiling Techniques to Improve Cache Temporal Locality. In *Proc. of ACM SIGPLAN PLDI*, 1999.

Automatic Measurement of Instruction Cache Capacity

Kamen Yotov, Sandra Jackson, Tyler Steele, Keshav Pingali, and Paul Stodghill

Department of Computer Science,
Cornell University,
Ithaca, NY 14853
kyotov@cs.cornell.edu, {sjj3,ths22}@cornell.edu,
{pingali,stodghil}@cs.cornell.edu

Abstract. There is growing interest in autonomic computing systems that can optimize their own behavior on different platforms without manual intervention. Examples of successful self-optimizing systems are ATLAS, which generates Basic Linear Algebra Subroutine (BLAS) Libraries, and FFTW, which generates FFT libraries.

Self-optimizing systems may need the values of hardware parameters such as the number of registers of various types and the capacities of caches at various levels. For example, ATLAS uses the capacity of the L1 cache and the number of registers in determining the size of cache tiles and register tiles.

We have built a system called X-Ray[1], which uses micro-benchmarks to measure such parameter values automatically. The micro-benchmarks currently implemented in X-Ray can determine the latency of various instructions, the existence of important instructions like fused multiply-add, the number of registers of various kinds, and parameters of the memory hierarchy.

In this paper, we discuss how X-Ray determines the capacity of the instruction cache (I-cache), which is needed for important optimizations such as loop unrolling. We present the micro-benchmark used in X-Ray to measure I-cache capacity, the experimental methodology used to obtain accurate estimates, and experimental results on a large number of current platforms.

1 Introduction

There is growing interest in self-optimizing systems that can optimize their own behavior on different platforms without manual intervention [2,8,5]. These systems are based on the generate-and-test paradigm: instead of writing a program, one implements a program generator that produces a large number of program variants, and determines empirically which variant performs best. To prevent

[1] This work was supported by an IBM Faculty Partnership Award, DARPA grant NBCH30390004, and by NSF grants ACI-0085969, ACI-0090217, ACI-0103723, ACI-0121401, and ACI-0406345.

E. Ayguadé et al. (Eds.): LCPC 2005, LNCS 4339, pp. 230–243, 2007.

a combinatorial explosion in the number of program variants that have to be considered, self-optimizing systems bound the search space by using hardware parameter values such as the number of registers and the capacity of the L1 cache [8,9].

For software to be truly self-optimizing, the values of hardware parameters relevant for software optimization must be determined automatically. It is important to note that these values are not necessarily the same as the values one might find in a hardware manual. For example, loop unrolling in ATLAS is limited by the number of registers on the target architecture. However, most compilers set aside certain registers for holding special values such as the stack or frame pointer, so the number of registers available to the register allocator is usually less than the total number of architected registers. In practice, it is hard to find documentation even for hardware parameter values, let alone for values relevant to software optimization.

To address this need, we have developed a framework called X-Ray, which can be used to implement micro-benchmarks to measure relevant values of hardware parameters automatically. For portability, X-Ray is entirely implemented in ANSI C'89. Currently, X-Ray can determine the latency of various instructions, the existence of important instructions like fused multiply-add, the number of registers of various kinds, and parameters of the memory hierarchy.

In this paper, we describe how X-Ray measures the capacity of the instruction cache (I-cache). Neither well known benchmarks [3,6], nor existing tools [4,7] attempt to measure this parameter.

The I-cache capacity is needed in the implementation of important optimizations like loop unrolling, which is used to reduce loop overhead, to prepare the loop body for scheduling of operations, to improve processor pipeline utilization, to enable register allocation of array values, etc. [1]. If the loop is unrolled too few times, loop overhead can be substantial, and pipeline and register utilization can suffer, lowering performance. On the other hand, if the loop is unrolled too many times, I-cache misses may cause performance to drop. Therefore, compilers need I-cache capacity to estimate how many times a loop should be unrolled.

An example on Intel Itanium 2 is presented in Figure 1. This figure shows the sensitivity of performance to the unrolling of the K loop (KU) of Matrix-Matrix Multiply in ATLAS for two different cache blocking factors (NB). We have verified with hardware counters that the performance drop observed for $KU > 9$ is caused by excessive number of instruction cache misses.

The rest of this paper is organized as follows. In Section 2, we give an overview of the X-Ray framework. The major challenge is to ensure that the C compiler does not restructure the micro-benchmarks thereby polluting the timing results, while enabling performance critical optimizations such as register allocation. In Section 3, we describe the micro-benchmark we use for measuring I-cache capacity. In Section 4, we present experimental results on a number of modern high-performance processors. We also compare I-cache capacity estimates from X-Ray with published values for these architectures. These comparisons show

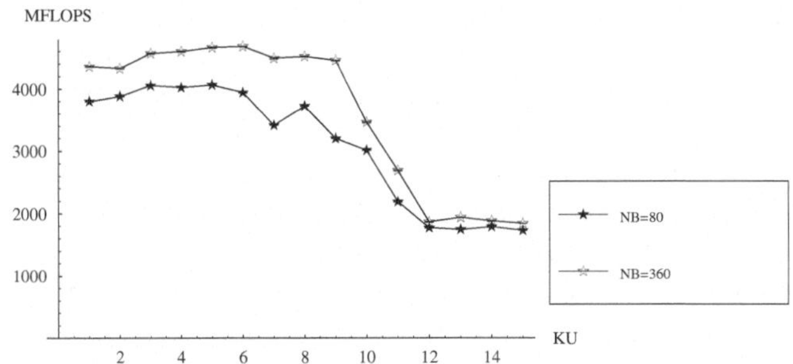

Fig. 1. Sensitivity of performance to K-unrolling on Intel Itaniun 2 in ATLAS

that the estimates of I-cache capacity that X-Ray produces are accurate to within 3% on most architectures.

2 The X-Ray Framework

Hardware parameters are measured by X-Ray *micro-benchmarks.* Figure 2 presents the general structure of a micro-benchmark in the X-Ray framework.

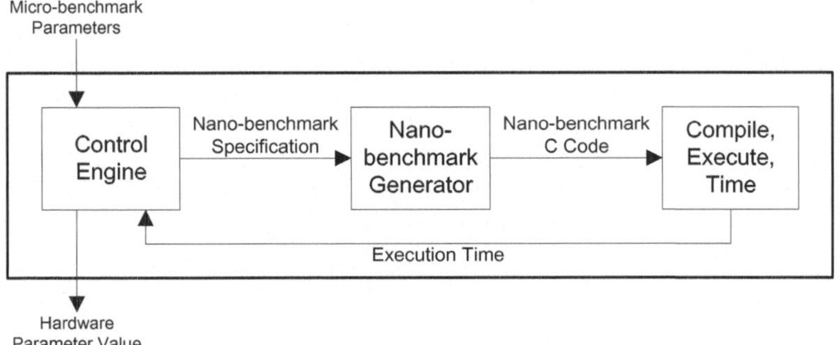

Fig. 2. A micro-benchmark in X-Ray

As an example, consider the measurement of the number of available registers of a particular data type T. One way to determine this value is to perform a number of experiments, all of which perform the same computations but on a different number of variables (N) of type T. When N exceeds the number of available registers for type T, not all variables can be register allocated, and execution time should increase substantially. The number of available registers can be inferred from this cross-over point.

Some general conclusions can be drawn from this example. A micro-benchmark to determine the value of some parameter may need to time a number of different but related programs that we call *nano-benchmarks.* Since there may be no *a priori* bound on the number of required nano-benchmarks, we need a

Nano-benchmark Generator, which can produce *Nano-benchmark C Code* from a high-level *Nano-benchmark Specification.* Finally, generation should happen on-the-fly since the results of one nano-benchmark may determine the nano-benchmark to be executed next.

In X-Ray, the execution of a micro-benchmark is orchestrated by its *Control Engine*, which chooses the nano-benchmarks to execute, the order in which they should be executed, and the appropriate parameters for each one. The Control Engine determines the value of the hardware parameter based on these timing results.

Some micro-benchmarks may also need the results obtained from running other micro-benchmarks. For example, to determine the latency of an instruction in cycles rather than in nanoseconds, the control engine needs to know the cycle time of the processor. This can be specified by the user or it can be measured by another micro-benchmark.

2.1 Nano-benchmarks

Even with access to a high-resolution timer, it is hard to accurately time operations that take only a few CPU cycles to execute. Suppose we want to measure the time required to execute a C statement S. If this time is small compared to the granularity of the timer, we must measure the time required to execute this statement some number of times R_S (dependent on S), and divide that time by R_S. If R_S is too small, the time for execution cannot be measured accurately, whereas if R_S is too big, the experiment will take longer than it needs to.

$$
\begin{array}{l}
R_S \leftarrow 1; \\
\texttt{while (measure}_S\texttt{(}R_S\texttt{)} < t_{min}\texttt{)} \\
\quad R_S \leftarrow R_S \times 2; \\
\texttt{return (measure}_S\texttt{(}R_S\texttt{)} \div R_S\texttt{);}
\end{array}
$$

Fig. 3. Nano-benchmark timing

Figure 3 shows the timing strategy used in X-Ray nano-benchmarks. In this code, $\texttt{measure}_S(R_S)$ measures the time required to execute R_S repetitions of statement S. To determine a reasonable value for R_S, the code in Figure 3 starts by setting R_S to 1, and then doubles it until the experiment runs for at least t_{min} seconds. The value of t_{min} can be specified by the user and defaults to 0.25 seconds in the current implementation.

A simplistic implementation of $\texttt{measure}_S$ is shown in Figure 4(a). This code incurs considerable loop overhead, so we unroll the loop U times (Figure 4(b)).

Another problem is that restructuring compiler optimizations may corrupt the experiment. For example, consider the case when we want to measure the latency of a single addition. In our framework, we would measure the time taken to execute the C statement $p_0 = p_0 + p_1$. It is important to allocate p_0 and p_1 in registers, but it is crucial that the compiler not replace the U statements in the loop body by the statement $p_0 = p_0 + U \times p_1$, since this would prevent the code from timing the original statement correctly.

To solve such problems, we need to generate programs which the compiler can aggressively optimize without disrupting the sequence of operations whose execution time we want to measure. We solve this problem using a `switch` statement on a `volatile` variable v as shown in Figure 4(c). The semantics of C require that v be read from memory; therefore the compiler cannot assume anything about which `case` of the `switch` is selected. Because there is potential control flow to each of the `case` blocks, it is impossible for the compiler to combine or reorder them in any way.

The final problem is that if the compiler is able to deduce that the result of the computations performed in S is not used in the rest of the code, it might perform dead-code elimination and remove all instances of S altogether. To prevent this unwanted optimization, all variables that appear in S are assigned to values read from appropriately typed `volatile` variables in the `initialize` statement; similarly, their final values are copied back to the same `volatile` variables in the `use` statement.

There are cases where we wish to measure the performance of a sequence of different statements $S_1, S_2, \ldots, S_n$. To prevent the compiler from optimizing this sequence, the code generator will give each S_i a different case label, generating code of the form shown in Figure 4(d). In this figure, the number of case labels W is the smallest multiple of n greater than or equal to U.

2.2 Nano-benchmark Generator

The X-Ray nano-benchmark generator accepts as an input a nano-benchmark specification and produces nano-benchmark C code structured as shown in Figures 4(c) and 4(d).

The nano-benchmark specification is a tuple which contains a statement S to be timed and type information for all variables in S. For example, to measure the latency of double-precision floating point ADD operation, we use the nano-benchmark specification $\langle p_1 = p_1 + p_2, \langle p_1, p_2 : \texttt{F64}\rangle\rangle$, which means that we time the statement $p_1 = p_1 + p_2$, where p_1 and p_2 are variables of type double (defined as `F64` in X-Ray). Given this specification, the nano-benchmark generator can produce code as shown in Figure 4(c). Generating code of the form shown in Figure 4(d) is more complex and requires the first element of the tuple to be a function f : $\mathsf{integer} \rightarrow \mathsf{string}$, which computes the code for statement S_i from the case label i.

2.3 Implementing a New Micro-benchmark

Implementing a new micro-benchmark in X-Ray requires:

1. Implementing the nano-benchmarks for all timing experiments. If their code fits the template in Figure 4(d), nano-benchmark specifications are enough;
2. Implementing the micro-benchmark control engine to describe which nano-benchmarks to run, with what parameters, in what order, and how to produce a final result from the external parameters and the timings.

```
measure_S(R) {
   t_s = now();
   i = R;
loop: S;
   if (--i)
      goto loop;
   t_e = now();
   return t_e - t_s;
}
```

(a)

```
measure_S(R) {
   t_s = now();
   i = R / U;
loop:
   S;
   S;
   ...repeat U times...
   S;
   if (--i)
      goto loop;
   t_e = now();
   return t_e - t_s;
}
```

(b)

```
measure_S(R) {
   initialize;
   volatile int v = 0;
   switch (v)
   {
   case 0:
      i = R/U;
      t_s = now();
   loop:
   case 1: S;
   case 2: S;
   ...
   case U: S;
      if (--i)
         goto loop;
      t_e = now();
      if (!v)
         return t_e - t_s;
   }
   use;
}
```

(c)

```
measure_S(R) {
   initialize;
   volatile int v = 0;
   switch (v)
   {
   case 0:
      i = R/U;
      t_s = now();
   loop:
   case 1: S_1;
   case 2: S_2;
   ...
   case i: S_i;
   ...
   case n: S_n;
   case n+1: S_1;
   ...
   case W: S_n;
      if (--i)
         goto loop;
      t_e = now();
      if (!v)
         return t_e - t_s;
   }
   use;
}
```

(d)

Fig. 4. Implementation of $\texttt{measure}_S$

The X-Ray implementation of many useful micro-benchmarks is described in detail in [11,10].

3 Measuring I-Cache Capacity

To estimate I-cache capacity, X-Ray measures the execution time of code sequences of different sizes. These sequences are carefully chosen so that the processor can run them at full speed unless they are too long to fit completely in the I-cache.

More precisely, the X-Ray micro-benchmark generates a sequence of nano-benchmarks. Each nano-benchmark measures the average time needed to execute one statement of a code sequence of specific length N. The micro-benchmark uses these nano-benchmarks to determines the largest value of N for which there is no significant increase in the average execution time per statement. The capacity of the I-cache is declared to be the binary code size for this longest code sequence.

Although this is straight-forward in theory, there are several practical problems we had to address to make this idea work.

3.1 Nano-benchmark

Figure 5 shows the nano-benchmark generated by X-Ray. The basic statements used in the loop body by X-Ray are assignment statements that increment one

```
volatile int v = 0;
volatile int p0 = v, p1 = v, p2 = v, p3 = v, p4 = v;

switch (v)
{
case 0 :
    i = R/N;
    ts = now ();
start :
case 1 : {p1+ = p0; p2+ = p0; p3+ = p0; p4+ = p0; }
case 2 : {p1+ = p0; p2+ = p0; p3+ = p0; p4+ = p0; }
    ...
case N : {p1+ = p0; p2+ = p0; p3+ = p0; p4+ = p0; }
    if(--i)
        goto start;
finish :
    te = now ();
    if(!v)
        return te - ts;
}

v = p0;  v = p1;  v = p2;  v = p3;  v = p4;
```

Fig. 5. Nano-benchmark code generated by X-Ray for measuring I-cache capacity

integer variable with the value of another integer variable. The C compiler is also advised to assign these variables to registers. Therefore, most compilers will map each assignment statement to a single register-to-register integer add instruction since such an instruction is available on all ISAs.

Each case statement in Figure 5 consists of a number of independent assignment statements. The idea is to provide enough instruction level parallelism in each case statement to avoid stalls caused by dependencies. This way we ensure that instructions are dispatched at the highest possible rate by the processor, so the slowdown caused by I-cache misses will be prominent. We have found that using four independent assignment statements per case is adequate on all current architectures.

Therefore, the X-Ray nano-benchmark is parameterized by N, the number of cases in the switch statement, and B, the number of independent assignment statements per case. Not surprisingly, the specification X-Ray uses for its I-cache nano-benchmark is the following.

$$S_{N,B} = \langle [1, N] \mapsto \{p_1+=p_0; p_2+=p_0; \ldots; p_B+=p_0;\}, \langle p_0, p_1, \ldots, p_B : int \rangle\rangle$$

Currently we measure the binary code size of the sequence by using an extension to the C language available in the GCC family of compilers, namely taking the address of a code label. Using this feature, the binary size of the code shown above would be computed by `(char *)&&finish - (char *)&&start`.

We are currently looking into other ways of doing this measurement if a compiler that supports this feature is not available. One possibility is to generate a program listing which includes the generated assembly instructions along with their code addresses and deduce the addresses of the labels of interest by analyzing the listing.

3.2 Micro-benchmark

Figures 7 and 8 show how the average execution time per statement of the nano-benchmark varies as a function of the computed value of binary code size. It can be seen that on many architectures such as the IBM Power 4, there are significant fluctuations in I-cache access time even when loop bodies are small enough to fit comfortably in the I-cache. In particular, access time can increase significantly when the size of the loop body is increased by a small amount, but decreases when the size of the loop body is increased further. This effect is not entirely noise because some part of it is reproducible. Figures 9 and 10 show the distribution of the average access times for various architectures when the loop body is small enough to fit in the I-cache.

Consequently, the micro-benchmark cannot just look for an increase in the statement execution time to determine the capacity of the I-cache; furthermore, performing the measurement for each code size some number of times and using the average time does not always help since some fluctuations occur for different values of code size.

The solution used by X-Ray is to estimate first the mean and standard deviation of the fluctuations in statement execution time when the loop body is

```
μ ← 0;
σ ← 0;
N ← 256;
while (N < 256 + S)
    τ ← time (S_{N,B});
    μ ← μ + τ;
    σ ← σ + τ²;
    N ← N + 1;
μ ← μ ÷ S;
σ ← √((σ − μ² × S) ÷ (S − 1));
while (time (S_{N,B}) < μ + T × σ)
    N ← N × 2;
R ← N;
L ← N ÷ 2;
while (R − L > 1)
    N ← (R + L) ÷ 2;
    if (time (S_{N,B}) ≥ μ + T × σ)
        R ← N;
    else
        L ← N;
return L × B;
```

Fig. 6. Control engine script for I-cache micro-benchmark

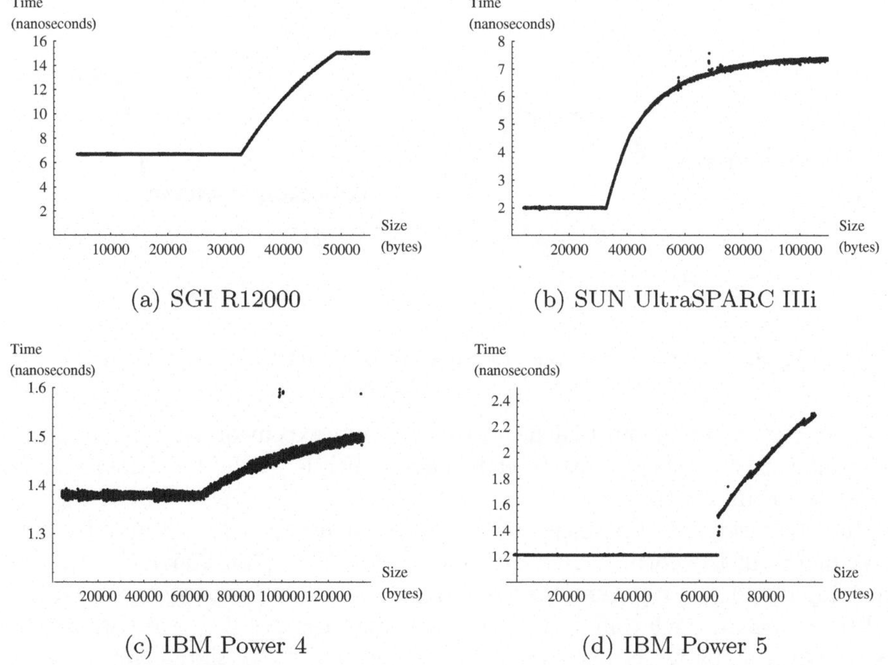

Fig. 7. Execution time per statement on RISC architectures

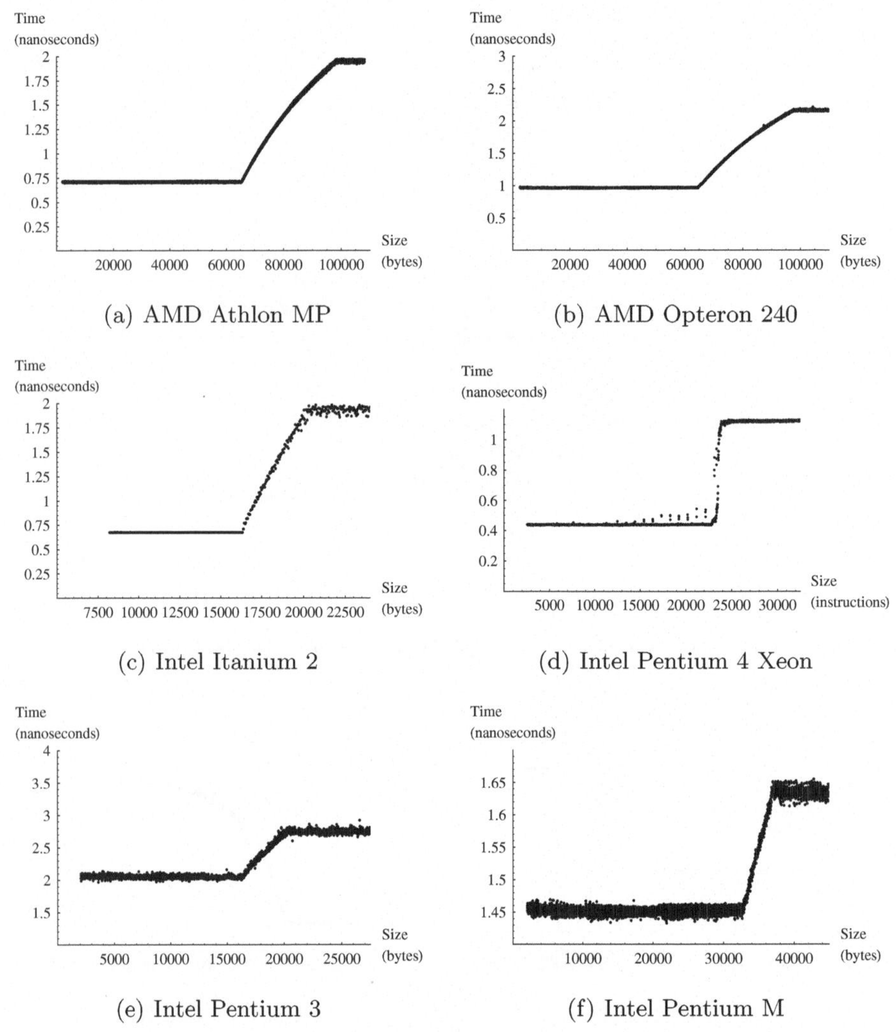

(a) AMD Athlon MP

(b) AMD Opteron 240

(c) Intel Itanium 2

(d) Intel Pentium 4 Xeon

(e) Intel Pentium 3

(f) Intel Pentium M

Fig. 8. Execution time per statement on x86 and EPIC architectures

small enough to fit in the I-cache. An increase in execution time is declared to be significant when the jump exceeds some multiple of the measured standard deviation of the fluctuations.

More precisely, X-Ray measures the statement execution times for nanobenchmarks of the form shown in Figure 5 for $N \in [256, 256 + S - 1]$, where the sample size S is a parameter we currently set to 8. It computes the mean μ and the standard deviation σ of these times, and uses $\mu + T \times \sigma$ as the threshold above which a change in execution time is declared to be significant; currently, we set the parameter T to 2 since this seems to work well in practice.

The sensitivity of Intel Pentium 4 is shown in Figure 8(d). On this architecture we observed that for some values of N, well before the I-cache edge, there are significant, but isolated fluctuations. To avoid confusing these fluctuations with the actual edge, X-Ray applies a smoothing function, which takes the minimum timing in a small neighborhood of N, namely $\left[N - \frac{I}{2}, N + \frac{I}{2}\right]$. I is a parameter of the I-cache micro-benchmark. In our experiments we found that $I = 5$ works well in practice.

These considerations lead to the actual control engine algorithm specified in Figure 6.

This code can be summarized as follows. First, the control engine computes the mean μ and the standard deviation σ of the timings for $N \in [256, 256 + S - 1]$. Then it starts with $N = N_{min} = 256$ and doubles N until timing exceeds the threshold $\mu + T \times \sigma$ for some $N = N_{max}$. After that it performs a binary search in the interval $[N_{max} \div 2, N_{max})$ to find the maximum N, whose timing is below the threshold $\mu + T \times \sigma$. Finally it returns the number of instructions in the sequence, which is $L \times B$. The actual size of the binary code is computed as part of the nano-benchmark (executed for $N = L$) as discussed above.

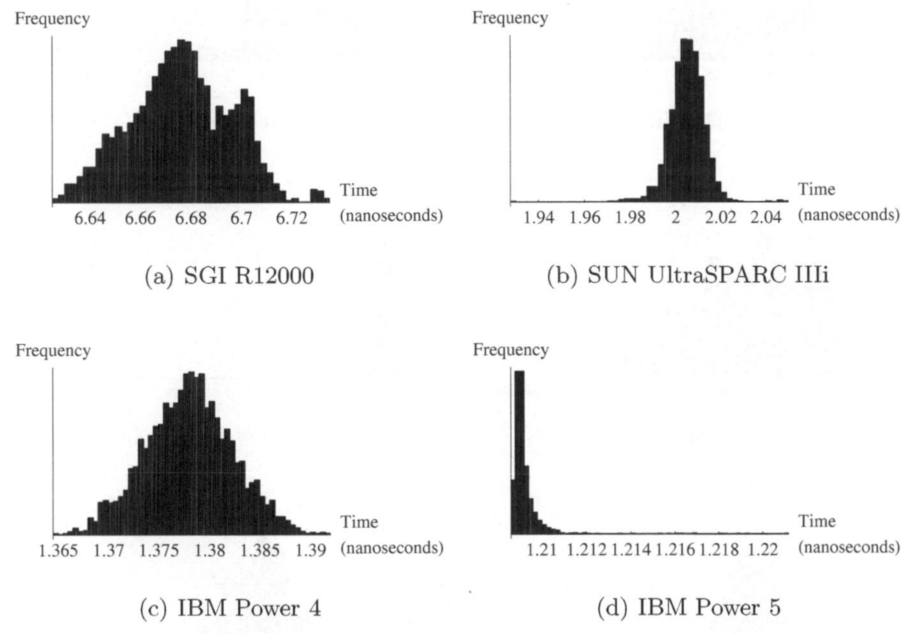

Fig. 9. Hit-time distribution on RISC architectures

4 Experimental Results

We tried the I-cache capacity micro-benchmark, described in Section 3 on a variety of modern architectures. The results obtained on ten of them are presented

Table 1. I-cache capacity experimental results

Architecture	Actual Size	Measured Size	Error	Time (seconds)
SGI R12000	32768 bytes	32108	-2.01%	534
SUN UltraSPARC IIIi	32768 bytes	32768	0.00%	321
IBM Power 4	65536 bytes	64956	-0.89%	350
IBM Power 5	65536 bytes	65016	-0.79%	365
AMD Athlon MP	65536 bytes	65496	-0.06%	904
AMD Opteron 240	65536 bytes	65480	-0.09%	647
Intel Itanium 2	16384 bytes	16352	-0.20%	101
Intel Pentium 4 Xeon	12000 uops	11245	-6.29%	187
Intel Pentium 3	16384 bytes	15940	-2.71%	285
Intel Pentium M	32768 bytes	33040	0.83%	295

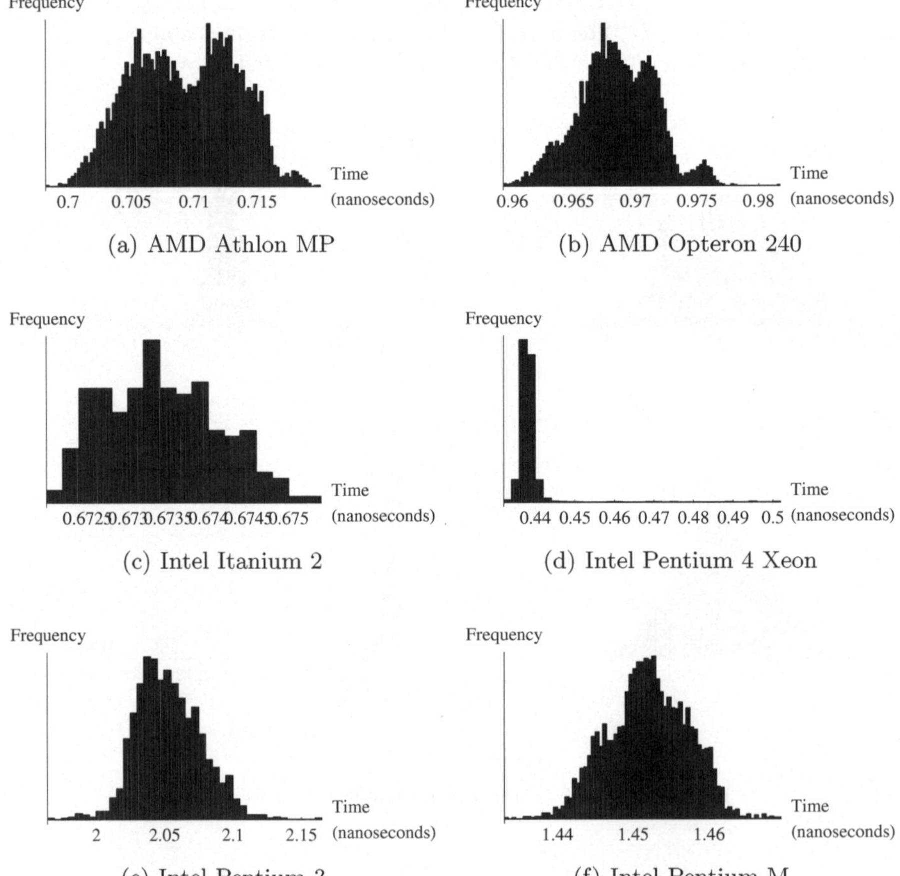

Fig. 10. Hit-time distribution on x86 and EPIC architectures

in Table 1. X-Ray was able to estimate the I-cache capacity within 3% of the actual value, except on the Intel Pentium 4, where the error was about 6%.

All running times are reported for a smoothing interval of $I = 5$. This is only really necessary on the Pentium 4 architecture. No smoothing ($I = 1$) is required for other architectures, which can dramatically decrease runtime (up to five times in this case).

4.1 Intel Pentium 4

The Intel Pentium 4 is an interesting architecture because it translates x86 CISC instructions to RISC-like micro-ops before caching them in its I-cache. Moreover, the I-cache does not have a conventional design but is organized as a trace cache. Because of all this, the information we can determine about the capacity of this cache is limited. The architecture manual reports I-cache size in number of micro-ops, and we have verified that each of our addition statements translates to a single CISC instruction which in turn translates to a single micro-op according to the architecture manual. Therefore X-Ray is able to measure the capacity in micro-ops.

However, this information may not be very useful for self-optimizing software systems because to use it, one needs to consider how many micro-ops each CISC instruction translates to, and to avoid the cases of isolated performance hits visible in Figure 8(d).

5 Conclusions and Future Work

To the best of our knowledge, X-Ray is the first system that can measure I-cache capacity. The micro-benchmark seems to be fairly accurate on all current architectures. The techniques described in this paper for eliminating fluctuations and for smoothing are useful in other contexts as well. For example, we successfully applied them to improve the accuracy of the micro-benchmark for measuring the number of registers in X-Ray.

We are actively developing new micro-benchmarks inside the X-Ray framework. Our current focus includes measuring other parameters of the memory hierarchy such as bandwidth of different levels of the memory hierarchy, as well as determining all bundles of instructions that can be issued in a single CPU cycle at a sustained rate.

X-Ray can be downloaded at `http://iss.cs.cornell.edu/Software/X-Ray.aspx`.

References

1. R. Allan and K. Kennedy. *Optimizing Compilers for Modern Architectures.* Morgan Kaufmann Publishers, 2002.
2. Matteo Frigo and Steven G. Johnson. The design and implementation of FFTW3. *Proceedings of the IEEE*, 93(2), 2005. special issue on "Program Generation, Optimization, and Adaptation".

3. J. L. Hennessy and D. A. Patterson. *Computer Architecture: A Quantitative Approach.* Morgan Kaufmann Publishers, 1990.
4. Larry McVoy and Carl Staelin. lmbench: Portable tools for performance analysis. In *USENIX 1996 Annual Technical Conference, January 22–26, 1996. San Diego, CA*, pages 279–294, Berkeley, CA, USA, January 1996.
5. Markus Püschel, José M. F. Moura, Jeremy Johnson, David Padua, Manuela Veloso, Bryan W. Singer, Jianxin Xiong, Franz Franchetti, Aca Gačić, Yevgen Voronenko, Kang Chen, Robert W. Johnson, and Nick Rizzolo. SPIRAL: Code generation for DSP transforms. *Proceedings of the IEEE*, 93(2), 2005. special issue on "Program Generation, Optimization, and Adaptation".
6. Rafael H. Saavedra and Alan Jay Smith. Measuring cache and TLB performance and their effect of benchmark run. Technical Report CSD-93-767, February 1993.
7. Carl Staelin and Larry McVoy. mhz: Anatomy of a micro-benchmark. In *USENIX 1998 Annual Technical Conference, January 15–18, 1998. New Orleans, Louisiana*, pages 155–166, Berkeley, CA, USA, June 1998.
8. R. Clint Whaley, Antoine Petitet, and Jack J. Dongarra. Automated empirical optimization of software and the ATLAS project. *Parallel Computing*, 27(1–2):3–35, 2001. Also available as University of Tennessee LAPACK Working Note #147, UT-CS-00-448, 2000 (`www.netlib.org/lapack/lawns/lawn147.ps`).
9. Kamen Yotov, Xiaoming Li, Gang Ren, Maria Garzaran, David Padua, Keshav Pingali, and Paul Stodghill. Is search really necessary to generate high-performance BLAS? *Proceedings of the IEEE*, 93(2), 2005. special issue on "Program Generation, Optimization, and Adaptation".
10. Kamen Yotov, Keshav Pingali, and Paul Stodghill. Automatic measurement of memory hierarchy parameters. In *SIGMETRICS'05*, June 2005.
11. Kamen Yotov, Keshav Pingali, and Paul Stodghill. X-ray: A tool for automatic measurement of hardware parameters. In *QEST'05*, September 2005.

Combined ILP and Register Tiling: Analytical Model and Optimization Framework

Lakshminarayanan Renganarayana, U. Ramakrishna, and Sanjay Rajopadhye

Computer Science Department
Colorado State University
{ln,ramakrsn,svr}@cs.colostate.edu

Abstract. Efficient use of multiple pipelined functional units and registers is very important for achieving high performance on modern processors. Instruction Level Parallelism (ILP) and register reuse (through register tiling) are two mechanisms for this, respectively. Program transformations that expose and exploit ILP and register reuse interact with each other in subtle ways. We study the combined problem of optimal ILP and register reuse. We consider the class of uniform dependence, fully permutable, rectangular loop nests. We develop an analytical model of the combined problem and formulate a mathematical optimization problem that chooses the parameters of the ILP-exposing transformation and register tiling so as to minimize the total execution time. We distinguish two cases: when loop permutation can and cannot expose a parallel loop. We show that the combined problem can be reduced to a single integer convex optimization problem for the former case, and to a set of integer convex optimization problems for the latter case, both of which can be solved to global optimality.

1 Introduction

It takes more than a good algorithm to achieve high performance: efficient use of the multiple pipelined functional units and registers are also important. Instruction level parallelism (ILP) allows a sequence of instructions derived from a sequential program to be parallelized for execution on multiple pipelined functional units in modern processors. Exploiting ILP and register reuse is critical for efficient use of execution resources. State-of-the-art compilers perform a variety of program optimizations to expose, enhance and exploit ILP and register reuse.

Loop nests are often the main sources for ILP and register reuse. The traditional approach uses unroll and jam [1] to expose ILP and scalar replacement to expose register reuse. However, this approach has the disadvantage of increased code size and register pressure. Further, it is hard to quantify the interactions [2] between unroll and jam, scalar replacement and software pipelining, the widely used loop scheduling technique [3,4,5].

Loop parallelizing techniques offer many transformations that can expose parallelism. Examples include, loop permutation, loop skewing [1], multi dimensional scheduling [6], etc. In addition, loop tiling [7] can be used enable register

E. Ayguadé et al. (Eds.): LCPC 2005, LNCS 4339, pp. 244–258, 2007.

reuse. We propose to use loop permutation and skewing to expose ILP, followed by tiling to enable register reuse. Our approach does not suffer from increased code size. However, enabling register reuse with tiling requires a register allocator for array variables as compared to the use of scalar register allocator in the scalar replacement approach.

Program transformations that expose ILP and those that enable register reuse interact with each other in subtle ways. For example, loop unrolling and loop skewing will expose ILP but might also increase the number of live values and hence the register pressure. On the other hand, register tiling will enable register reuse but might also limit the amount of ILP with the new order of execution of the tiled program. Quantifying and modeling these interactions between various program transformations is crucial for finding optimal (*w.r.t.* total program execution time) transformations. In this paper we seek to solve the combined problem of choosing the optimal parameters for the ILP exposing (loop skewing) transformation and register tiling. Our contributions are as follows.

- We give an analytical model that quantifies the interaction between the ILP exposing transformation (loop skewing) and register tiling.
- We formulate the optimal ILP and register tiling problem as a mathematical optimization problem. We present a globally optimal solution to this problem by reducing it to a convex optimization problem.
- We distinguish two cases: when loop permutation can and cannot expose a parallel loop. In the former case, we reduce the combined optimization problem to a single integer convex optimization problem. In the later case, when skewing is required to expose ILP, we show that the combined problem can be reduced to a set of integer convex optimization problems.

The solution to our combined problem will produce a loop nest in which the ILP and register reuse are exposed. The scheduling and register allocation phase is an important step in achieving good performance. This phase is beyond the scope of this paper. Our main observation is that this phase can be constructed by adapting well studied techniques like modulo scheduling [4] and register allocation for array variables.

In the next section we give an outline of our solution to the ILP and register tiling problem. In section 3, we define the program, tiling, and execution models and describe the basic building blocks of our analytical model. In section 4, we formulate the mathematical optimization problem that chooses the optimal skew and tile parameters. In section 5, we characterize the condition under which a permutation can expose a parallel loop and present an efficient algorithm to check this condition. In section 6, we characterize the space of valid skewing transformations. In section 7, we show how the optimal tiling problem can be reduced to a convex program and solved efficiently and in section 8, we present the strategy for finding the globally optimal solution to the combined ILP and register tiling problem. In section 9, we illustrate our solution method with an example. In section 10, we present related work and in section 11, we present a discussion and future work. A more detailed version of this paper can be found in the technical report [8].

2 Our Approach to ILP and Register Tiling

Our approach is to use loop skewing to expose ILP, and register tiling to enable register reuse, and software pipelining to expose the ILP so exposed. Since we are using register tiling together with loop skewing, we require that after skewing, the resulting loop nest must admit rectangular tiling.

Software pipeliners look at the innermost loop[1] to find ILP among operations from different iterations of the loop. Hence, if we could transform the loop nest into one in which the inner most loop does not carry any dependences, i.e., all of its iterations can be executed in parallel, then the software pipeliner can find a schedule in which the performance is constrained only by the execution resources as opposed to dependencies. *When sufficient ILP exists and can be exploited, the performance is limited only by the available execution resources – or the execution bandwidth of the machine.* Such a schedule will exploit the maximum possible ILP and have maximum utilization of functional units.

Motivated by the above discussion, we seek a transformation that would transform the given fully permutable loop nest into one

- **(C1):** for which rectangular tiling is valid for any given tile sizes $\boldsymbol{t} = (t_1, \ldots, t_n)$. This validity condition reduces to *non-negativity of all the components of all the dependences*, under the reasonable assumption that the tile size be larger than the dependence lengths, and the iteration space size be larger than the tile size [11].
- **(C2):** in which there is at least one loop which does not carry any dependences (i.e., whose iterations are all parallel). We can always permute this loop to the inner most position, as full permutability (of the transformed loop nest) is necessary for condition (C1) to hold.

There are many classes of transformations that can produce a loop nest that would satisfy the above two conditions. Loop skewing is one such class and we have chosen it for the following reasons. First, for uniform dependence loops, we can always find a skewing transformation that will produce a loop that satisfies (C1) and (C2). Second, loop skewing is conceptually simple and easy to construct, and this allows us to develop an efficient algorithm for finding the optimal skew transformation parameters.

Our solution methodology is as follows. Using the performance model described in Section3, we formulate an optimization problem whose solution yields the skew factor and tile sizes that minimize the overall execution time. We check whether permutation can expose any parallel loop. If so, we permute, expose the parallelism, and then tile for registers. In this case, the combined problem reduces to the problem of finding the optimal tile sizes, which can be reduced to a single integer convex optimization problem. When loop permutation cannot expose a parallel loop, loop skewing is required to expose the ILP. In this case, we need to find the optimal skewing and tile sizes. We find these by solving a set of integer convex optimization problems.

---

[1] The two exceptions are the works of Rong et al. [9] and Ramanujam [10]. See the related work section for details.

3 An Analytical Model

In this section we develop an analytical model that quantifies the interaction between loop skewing and register tiling transformations. A similar model was previously used in the context of tiling for memory hierarchy [12].

3.1 Program and Tiling Model

The programs we consider belongs to the class of fully permutable rectangular loop nests with uniform dependence bodies. Note that this class of programs admit rectangular tiling and are also the class for which software pipelining is usually applied. We consider an n-dimensional loop nest with constant upper and lower bounds. The loop body contains statements with uniform dependences. Let $\mathcal{L} = [L_1, \ldots, L_n]$ be the given n-dimensional loop nest, where each L_i denotes a loop at depth i. Any n-D vector formed by the loop counters of $\mathcal{L}$ is called an iteration vector. Let $D = [d_1, \ldots, d_m]$ be a matrix whose columns are the (n-D) dependence vectors.

To expose ILP we use skewing and permutation. A skewing (transformation) matrix has the form of an upper triangular matrix with all the diagonal entries equal to 1. The non-diagonal entries are determined by the skewing factors. We denote the skewing matrix that we seek by S. Skewing a loop L_i with respect to a loop L_j, by an appropriate factor f, makes the loop L_i carry all the dependences that were originally carried by loop L_j. A permutation transformation that permutes the ith loop with the jth loop can be represented by an identity matrix (of appropriate size) in which the ith and j^{th} rows are interchanged.

We consider *rectangular* (or *orthogonal*) loop tiling: tiling the loop nest with *hyper-rectangles whose boundaries are orthogonal to the canonic axes.* We assume that rectangular loop tiling is valid for the given loop nest [7]. Note that the tiled loops are fully permutable. The *tile graph* is the graph where each node represents a tile and each arc represents a dependency between tiles. In our case, each node of the tile graph represents a hyper-rectangle in the iteration space of size $t_1 \times t_2 \times \cdots \times t_n$. Note that though our iteration space is rectangular, after skewing, we will have hyper-parallelepiped shaped iteration space, and when we tile this with rectangular tiles, we will have some full rectangular tiles and some partial non-rectangular tiles.

It is well known that [13] if the t_i's are large compared to the elements of the dependency vectors, then the dependencies between the tiles are *unit vectors* (or binary combinations thereof, which can be neglected for analysis purposes without loss of generality). In general, the feasible value of each t_i is bounded from below by some constant. For the sake of notational simplicity, in this paper we assume that this is 1.

3.2 Architecture and Execution Model

We use an atomic tile execution model. However, the parallelism available inside the tile is exploited with software pipelining. We first present the architectural parameters used in the execution model and then introduce the functions that model various aspects of the execution time of the transformed loop nest.

Although we do not provide experimental validation of our execution time model in this paper, similar models of execution time have been used by Sarkar [14] (in the IBM XL Fortran compiler) and also by Wolf et al. [15], and they have been thoroughly validated.

We seek an abstraction of the architecture (processor and memory features) that is suitable for use in a cost model for tiling loop programs in our program class. Our model uses the following parameters:

- α – *cost of an iteration*: this is the cost of executing an instance of the loop body (in cycles per iteration). In our case, since the innermost loop is completely parallel, a modulo scheduler can always achieve the resource minimum initiation interval (ResMII) [4], and hence α is equal to ResMII.
- β – the cost (in cycles) for transferring a word from lowest level cache to the registers.
- η – *loop increment and test cost*: this is the cost for incrementing a loop variable and checking its bounds.
- NR – *number of registers available:* depending on the loop body, NR could be either the number of integer or floating point registers.

3.3 Fundamental Measures

Computation volume. *The computation volume,* $\mathsf{TV}(\boldsymbol{t})$*, of a tile is the amount of computation done in a tile.* The computation volume of a tile $\boldsymbol{t} = (t_1, \ldots, t_n)$, is the number of integer points in the n-dimensional hyper-rectangle: $\mathsf{TV}(\boldsymbol{t}) = \prod_{i=1}^{n} t_i$. The tile volume, $\mathsf{TV}(t)$, represents the volume of full tiles. We approximate the volume of partial tiles with that of the full tiles, and hence use $\mathsf{TV}(\boldsymbol{t})$ as the volume for all the tiles.

Load store volume. *The load store volume,* $\mathsf{LS}(\boldsymbol{t}, D)$*, of a tile is the total amount of data that is loaded and stored when the tile is executed.* This quantity is also known as the tile foot-print. The dependences and data reuse patterns determine the load store volume. Our program model restricts dependences to be uniform (constant distance). A tile is compute bound if the amount of data accessed (input/output) during the computation of the tile is at least one dimension less than the computation; otherwise the tile is I/O-bound. It is easy to see that with uniform dependences, the load store volume of I/O-bound tiles is proportional to the tile volume $\mathsf{TV}(\boldsymbol{t})$. The interesting case, where tiling is really useful, is when the tile is compute bound.

For an n-dimensional compute bound tile, the input and output are $O(x^{n-1})$, where, $x = \max_{i=1}^{n} t_i$, where t_i is the tile size along dimension i. We consider the case in which the input and output are of $O(x^{n-1})$, other cases when the input or output is smaller than $O(x^{n-1})$ can be handled easily. Since our tile graph has dependence vectors that correspond to unit vectors, the $O(x^{n-1})$ input/output of a tile directly corresponds to the $(n-1)$ dimensional facets of the tile, and a constant multiple of every facet contributes to the load store volume of a tile. The constant is determined by the dependence distances. There are n pairs of facets, and in rectangular tiling, each of these is potentially involved in a communication. The volume of the ith facet, Δ_i, is given by $\prod_{j=1,j\neq i}^{n} t_j$. Now, the load store volume is $\mathsf{LS}(\boldsymbol{t}, D) = \sum_{i=1}^{n} a_i \Delta_i$, where a_i is a constant that denotes distance along the ith facet that is involved in the communication and is determined by the longest i^{th} dimension component of any dependence vector in the dependence matrix D. Based on the schedule, some facets need not be stored and loaded again. There is at most one such facet, say f, and sharing of f can be captured by excluding it from the load store, i.e., $\mathsf{LS}(\boldsymbol{t}, D) = \sum_{i=1,i\neq f}^{n} a_i \Delta_i$. We can take care of multiple dependences to the same variable by considering the bounding box of the dependences to each variable and using the diagonal of this bounding box as the columns of D.

Number of tiles. *The number of tiles,* $\mathsf{NT}(\boldsymbol{t}, \boldsymbol{N}) = \frac{N_1 \times \cdots \times N_n}{t_1 \times \cdots \times t_n}$, *counts the total number of tiles after a rectangular tiling with tiles of sizes* $\mathbf{t} = (t_1, \ldots, t_n)$, *of the rectangular iteration space of size* $\boldsymbol{N} = (N_1, \ldots, N_n)$. After skewing, the iteration space may no longer be rectangular and counting the number of tiles in this case is complicated. We use the quantity (iteration space volume)/(tile volume), which is a lower bound on the actual number of tiles, as an approximation. Since we start with a rectangular iteration space and skewing is a volume preserving unimodular transformation, the quantity (iteration space volume)/(tile volume) is the same as[2] $\mathsf{NT}(\boldsymbol{t}, \boldsymbol{N})$.

Loop overhead. *The loop overhead of a loop is used to account for the cost of loop termination test and loop variable increment.* It is proportional to the number of times the loop body is executed. An n-dimensional rectangular loop nest after one level of tiling will have $2n$ loops. We call the outer n loops *inter-tile loops* and the inner n loops *intra-tile loops*. The ith inter-tile loop is executed precisely $\frac{N_i}{t_i}$ times for *each* instance of the surrounding loop indices. The total overhead of the n inter-tile loops , $\mathsf{LoInterTile}(\boldsymbol{t}, \boldsymbol{N})$, is $\sum_{i=1}^{n} x_i$, where $x_i = \frac{N_1 \times \ldots \times N_i}{t_1 \times \ldots \times t_i}$. The ith intra-tile loop is executed t_i times. The overhead of the set of n intra-tile loops, $\mathsf{LoIntraTile}(\boldsymbol{t}, \boldsymbol{N})$, is $\sum_{i=n+1}^{2n} y_i$, where $y_i = (t_1 \times \ldots \times t_i) \times \mathsf{NT}(\boldsymbol{t},\boldsymbol{N})$, where $\mathsf{NT}(\boldsymbol{t}, \boldsymbol{N})$ is the total number of tiles and also equal to the number of times the n inter-tile loops surrounding the intra-tile loops will be executed. The total (intra plus inter tile) loop overhead, $\mathsf{LO}(\boldsymbol{t}, \boldsymbol{N}) = \mathsf{LoIntraTile}(\boldsymbol{t}, \boldsymbol{N}) + \mathsf{LoInterTile}(\boldsymbol{t}, \boldsymbol{N})$. Since after skewing the iteration space may not be rectangular, the rectangular tiling might leave some partial and full tiles. Treating partial tiles as full tiles and using the approximation for number tiles, developed above, we can approximate by $\mathsf{LO}(\boldsymbol{t}, \boldsymbol{N})$, the loop overhead of a skewed rectangular loop nest tiled with rectangular tiles.

When we use skewing to expose ILP, the shape of the iteration space, as well as the dependences change. The iteration space becomes a parallelepiped and the transformed dependences are given by SD, where S and D are the skewing and dependence matrices, respectively.

[2] Given that we are tiling for registers, the tile sizes are going to be very small and with small tile sizes, this approximation is better.

4 Optimization Problem Formulation

We now formulate an optimization problem that clearly captures and quantifies the interaction between the skewing and the register tiling transformations. The objective function is the total execution time and the unknowns are the tile sizes ($\boldsymbol{t}$) and the skewing matrix (S).

$$\begin{array}{lc} \text{minimize } \eta \mathsf{LO}(\boldsymbol{t},\boldsymbol{N}) + \mathsf{NT}(\boldsymbol{t},\boldsymbol{N}) \times \max\left(\alpha \times TV(\boldsymbol{t}),\ \beta \times \mathsf{LS}(\boldsymbol{t},\mathsf{bbox}(SD))\right) & \\ \text{s.t.} \qquad \mathsf{LS}(\boldsymbol{t},\mathsf{bbox}(SD)) \leq \mathsf{NR} & (1) \\ \boldsymbol{N} \geq \boldsymbol{t} \geq 1, SD \geq 0, \boldsymbol{t} \in \mathbb{Z}^n, S \in \mathbb{Z}^{n\times n} & \end{array}$$

where, $\boldsymbol{t}$ and S are the variables representing tile sizes and skew matrix, respectively, $\mathsf{NT}(\boldsymbol{t},\boldsymbol{N})$ is the number of tiles, $\mathsf{TV}(\boldsymbol{t})$ is the tile volume, D is the dependence matrix, $\mathsf{LS}(t,\mathsf{bbox}(SD))$ is the load store volume, $\mathsf{LO}(\boldsymbol{t},\boldsymbol{N})$ is the loop overhead, NR is the number of registers available, α,β and η are respectively the cost of an iteration, load store cost, and loop bounds check cost. All vector inequalities in the constraints are component-wise. The first constraint makes sure that the register foot print $\mathsf{LS}(t\ ,\ \mathsf{bbox}(SD))$ fits in the number of available registers, NR, and the second constraint $\boldsymbol{t} \geq 1$ makes sure that the tile sizes are positive and the third constraint $SD \geq 0$ ensures that the skewed loop nest is fully permutable and hence admits a rectangular tiling.

Once we choose a skew transformation S, substituting it in the combined problem gives an optimization problem with $\boldsymbol{t}$ as the only variable. Let $\widehat{D} = \mathsf{bbox}(SD)$. Then the resulting optimization problem is shown below (2). We call (2) the *optimal tiling problem (for a fixed skew).*

$$\begin{array}{ll} \text{minimize } \eta\ \mathsf{LO}(\boldsymbol{t},\boldsymbol{N}) + \mathsf{NT}(\boldsymbol{t},\boldsymbol{N}) \times \max\left(\alpha \mathsf{TV}(\boldsymbol{t}),\ \beta\ \mathsf{LS}(\boldsymbol{t},\ \widehat{D})\right) \\ \text{s.t.} \qquad \mathsf{LS}(\boldsymbol{t}\ ,\ \widehat{D}) \leq \mathsf{NR}, \boldsymbol{N} \geq \boldsymbol{t} \geq 1, \boldsymbol{t} \in \mathbb{Z}^n \end{array}$$

Note that, though $\widehat{D}$ is shown as a parameter to the $\mathsf{LS}(\boldsymbol{t},\widehat{D})$ function, it is here a given constant vector, and not a variable of the optimization problem.

5 Can Permutation Expose a Parallel Loop

We will first introduce some notations (used only in this section) which will make the exposition clear and concise. For any vector x, $x(j)$ represents its j-th component. The *level* of a vector $\mathsf{level}(x)$ is j if $\forall i < j:\ x(i) = 0$ and $x(j) \neq 0$, i.e., $x(j)$ is the first non-zero component of x. A *zero-lead column* is a column vector of the form $(0,0,\ldots,0,c)^T$ for some $c \neq 0$. The j-th *unit vector* e_j is a vector with $e_j(j) = 1$ and $e_j(i) = 0, \forall i \neq j$. A *scaled unit vector*, $\mathsf{suv}(c,j)$ is a vector x of the form $\forall i \neq j:\ x(i) = 0$ and $x(j) = c$ for some non-zero constant c. In other words, $\mathsf{scv}(c,j)$ is an unit vector along j scaled by a non-zero factor c. The dimension of a scaled unit vector is often obvious from the context. An example (of dimension 4) is $\mathsf{suv}(2,3) = (0,0,2,0)$. Note that $\mathsf{level}(\ \mathsf{suv}(c,j)\ ) = j$. $\mathsf{diag}(c_1,c_2,\ldots,c_n)$ constructs a diagonal matrix with $c_1,\ldots,c_n$ as the diagonal entries. A loop is called *parallel* if it does not carry any dependences.

5.1 Existence of a Loop with No Carried Dependences

We seek to characterize a condition under which there exists no permutation of $\mathcal{L}$ with at least one parallel loop. In other words, in every permutation of $\mathcal{L}$, all the loops carry dependences. We seek a characterization based on the dependences. Let us form a dependence (distance vector) matrix $D = [d_1\ d_2\ \dots\ d_m]$ whose columns are the m dependences, $d_1, d_2, \dots, d_m$ present in $\mathcal{L}$'s body. The effect of loop permutation on the dependences is completely captured by permuting the rows of D. In any permutation of $\mathcal{L}$, if there is a dependence d with $\mathsf{level}(d) = j$ then loop l_j, of the permuted loop nest, carries d.

Consider the two dependence matrices:

$$D_1 = \overset{d_1\ d_2\ d_3}{\begin{pmatrix} 1 & 0 & 0 \\ 1 & 0 & 2 \\ 1 & 1 & 0 \end{pmatrix}} \qquad D_2 = \overset{d_1\ d_2\ d_3\ d_4}{\begin{pmatrix} 1 & 0 & 0 & 3 \\ 1 & 0 & 2 & 0 \\ 1 & 1 & 0 & 0 \end{pmatrix}}.$$

In the matrix D_1, the dependence vectors d_2 and d_3 are scaled unit vectors: $d_2 = \mathsf{suv}(1,3)$ and $d_3 = \mathsf{suv}(2,2)$. Now, in this permutation, the dependences d_1, d_2 and d_3 have levels $1, 3$ and 2 respectively and are carried by the loops L_1, L_3 and L_2 respectively. However, we can see that by exchanging rows 1 and 3 of D_1 we can get an innermost loop (row 3 of permuted D_1) with no carried dependences. Now consider matrix D_2 : there exists no permutation of rows of D_2 which can create a parallel loop. What is the structure of the matrix D_2 that induces this property? We seek to characterize this structure in the following discussion leading to Theorem 1.

In any given permutation of the loops, all the n loops will carry dependences if and only if there are (at least) n dependence vectors with levels $1, 2, \dots, n$. If we have dependence vectors of all levels $(1, 2, \dots, n)$ in every permutation of the loops in $\mathcal{L}$, then we can say that there is no permutation that will expose a parallel loop.

Theorem 1: Every permutation of the rows of D will contain n columns with levels $1, 2, \dots, n$ *if and only if* D contains a $n \times n$ sub matrix whose columns can be permuted to form a diagonal matrix, say $\mathsf{diag}(c_1, c_2, \dots, c_n)$, where $c_1, \dots, c_n$ are the scale factors of the n scaled unit vectors.

Proof: ($\Longrightarrow$) Assume that every permutation of the rows of D will contain n columns with levels $1, 2, \dots, n$. Let $x_1, \dots, x_n$ be these n columns with levels $1, 2, \dots, n$ respectively. Given that we have exactly n vectors each having a different level, they all have to be linearly independent. If we show that these n columns are scaled unit vectors, then we can always permute these columns to form a $n \times n$ diagonal sub matrix of D. To show that $x_1, \dots x_n$ are scaled unit vectors we will use proof by contradiction. Let us assume that they are (all) not scaled unit vectors. Note that the vector x_n with level n has to be a scaled unit vector. Let the $n-1$ columns each have one more non-zero entry below their first non-zero entry. Without loss of generality we can assume that this entry is the next immediate entry. Then the matrix looks the matrix M given below.

Algorithm 1. Algorithm to check whether the input loop nest has any parallel loop.

1. **Input**: Dependence matrix D. **Output**: boolean value indicating whether the input loop nest has any parallel loop or not.
2. Pick all the columns of D which are scaled unit vectors. This can be done in $O(nm)$, where, n is the number of rows of D and m, the number of columns. There can be at most m such columns.
3. As we pick the columns in the previous step we can note their levels. Check whether there are n columns each of which is a scaled unit vector for a distinct j, i.e., $\mathsf{suv}(c_j, j)$ for $j = 1 \ldots n$. This can also be done in time $O(nm)$. If there are such n columns return a **true**; return a **false** otherwise.

$$M = \begin{pmatrix} x_{1,1} & 0 & \cdots & 0 & 0 \\ x_{2,1} & x_{2,2} & \cdots & 0 & 0 \\ \vdots & x_{2,2} & \cdots & \vdots & \vdots \\ \vdots & \vdots & \ddots & x_{n-1,n-1} & 0 \\ \cdots & & & x_{n,n-1} & x_{n,n} \end{pmatrix} \Longrightarrow M' = \begin{pmatrix} x_{1,1} & 0 & \cdots & 0 & 0 \\ x_{2,1} & x_{2,2} & \cdots & 0 & 0 \\ \vdots & x_{2,2} & \cdots & \vdots & \vdots \\ \vdots & \vdots & \ddots & x_{n,n-1} & x_{n,n} \\ \cdots & & & x_{n,n-1} & 0 \end{pmatrix}$$

Now we can interchange the last two rows of M to get M' in which there is no dependence of level n and hence loop l_n does not carry any dependence. But this is a contradiction to our assumption that every permutation of the rows of D contains n columns with all the levels. Hence the proof. ◻

Proof: ($\Longleftarrow$) Now we assume that D contains a $n \times n$ sub matrix whose columns can be permuted to form a diagonal matrix say $\mathsf{diag}(c_1, c_2, \ldots, c_n)$. Let C be this $n \times n$ sub matrix of D whose columns can be permuted to form $\mathsf{diag}(c_1, \ldots, c_n)$. We need to show that every permutation of D will contain n column with levels $1, 2, \ldots, n$. It is obvious that after any set of row permutations of a diagonal matrix there exists a set of column permutations that will bring it back to diagonal matrix form. Hence, after any set of permutations of C we can column permute C to make it a diagonal matrix. This diagonal matrix form makes it obvious that the n columns have levels $1, \ldots, n$ respectively. Hence the proof. ◻

Theorem 1 gives us an efficient way to check whether there exists at least one loop no carried dependences – we only need to check whether the dependence matrix D contains $n \times n$ sub matrix whose columns can be permuted to form a diagonal matrix $\mathsf{diag}(c_1, \ldots, c_n)$. This can be done in time linear in the size of the dependence matrix D. The outline of the algorithm is given in Algorithm 1.

6 Space of Valid Skewing Transformations

When loop permutations alone cannot expose a parallel loop, we need to skew the loop nest. We make two observations regarding the skew matrix S that we seek in the combined optimization problem (1). These observations narrow down the search space of S.

- **Only positive skews produce loops that admit rectangular tiling.** We have two constraints: $D \geq 0$ (since our input loop nest admits rectangular tiling) and $SD \geq 0$ (since we require the skewed loop nest to admit rectangular tiling). From Theorem 1, we know that, if the input loop nest does not have any parallel loop, then the dependence matrix D has a $n \times n$ sub matrix whose columns are scaled unit vectors and which can be permuted to form a diagonal matrix, say $M = \mathsf{diag}(c_1, \cdots, c_n)$. Without loss of generality we can assume that that these n columns $c_1, c_2, \ldots, c_n$ have levels $1, 2, \ldots, n$ respectively. At least two of these columns should be made to have the same levels, only then we will have a loop with no carried dependences. Let us view the matrix D as a partitioned as $[M\ N]$, where $M = \mathsf{diag}(c_1, \ldots, c_n)$ is the $n \times n$ diagonal sub matrix and N is the sub matrix that contains rest of the columns of D. We claim that negative skew factors will lead to an invalid transformation by creating negative entries in the sub-matrix M. To see why, let us see what happens when we skew loop L_i with respect to a loop L_j with a negative skew factor $-f$ (cf. Section 3.1 for notation). Such a skew would add to the i-th row of M, the j-th row multiplied by $(-f)$. The new i-th row would have $-f \times c_j$ in its j-th entry. This negative entry is not permitted since we require that all the entries of the transformed matrix (SD) be non-negative. Hence, only positive skew factors are valid, since a zero skew factor is just an identity transformation.
- **Skewing any one loop with respect to just one other loop is sufficient and optimal.** We seek to transform the loop nest so that in the transformed loop nest there is one loop that carries no dependences, i.e., parallel. Given that the input loop nest is fully permutable, after skewing, we can permute this parallel loop to the inner most position to get our desired loop nest. To make any one loop, say L_i, parallel, it is sufficient to skew some other loop, say L_j, with respect to L_i. Also, given that (positive) skewing increases the length of the (positive) dependences, skewing with respect to more than one loop will always produce longer (when compared to skewing w.r.t. to just one loop) dependences. And, the longer the dependences, the larger the bounding box and hence, the greater the load store volume, $\mathsf{LS}(\boldsymbol{t}, \mathsf{bbox}(SD))$. So, skewing with respect to just one other loop is also optimal. By a similar argument, skewing by a factor larger than 1 to parallelize the loop only increases the load store cost and is sub-optimal.

Based on these two observations, we seek to find positive skews of one loop with respect to just one other loop. The number of choices for such skews is $d \times (d-1)$ where, d is the depth of the loop nest. This gives a list of $d(d-1)$ potentially optimal skews. For example, for a loop nest with depth 2 or 3 we will have 2 or 6 choices of skews, respectively.

7 Solving the Optimal Tiling Problem

The optimal tiling problem (2) seeks to choose tile sizes that minimize some criteria and satisfy some constraints. The key insight is that *the variables of this optimization problem, tile sizes, are always positive.* Based on this insight we can directly cast it as an *Integer Geometric Program* (IGP) [16]. Due to space constraints, we do not give the translation of the optimal tiling problem into an IGP. The techniques used to cast the optimal tiling problem as an IGP can be found in the technical report [8].

Geometric programs can be transformed into convex optimization problems using a variable substitution [17] and solved efficiently using polynomial time interior point methods [18]. Integer solutions can be found by using a branch-and-bound algorithm. We use YALMIP [19] – a tool that provides an high level symbolic interface in MATLAB to define and solve IGPs. The number of (tile) variables of our IGPs are related to number of dimensions tiled and hence are often small. In our experience with solving IGPs related to tiling, the integer solutions were found in few (less than ten) iterations of the branch-and-bound algorithm. The (wall clock) running time of this algorithm was just a few seconds, even with the overhead of using the symbolic MATLAB interface.

8 Solving the Combined ILP and Register Tiling Problem

Recall that, according to our solution strategy, we need skewing only when the input loop nest does not contain any parallel loop that can be exposed by permutation. Hence, first we check (using Algorithm 1 discussed in section 5) whether the input loop nest has any parallel loop that can be exposed by permutation. If it does, then just permuting the loop to the inner most position will achieve our goal. This permutation is always valid, since our input loop nest is fully permutable (since rectangular tiling is valid for it). In this case, we just permute the loop and do not skew (i.e., the skew matrix S becomes the identity matrix). Then the combined problem (1) reduces to the optimization problem for finding the optimal tile sizes (for the permuted loop nest), i.e., the optimal tiling problem (c.f. problem (2)) with $S = I$(the identity matrix) and hence $\widehat{D} = \mathsf{bbox}(D)$. This problem can now be directly solved as discussed in section 7. Note that when permutation alone is sufficient, it is globally optimal too, because any skewing will only increase the load store cost and hence the execution time.

When permutation cannot expose a parallel loop, we need skewing to expose ILP. In this case, as shown in Section 6, we have $d(d-1)$ choices for the skewing matrix (where d is the depth of the loop nest). We construct $d(d-1)$ optimal tiling problems (with fixed skewing matrices), one for each choice of the skewing matrix. The optimal skew and tile sizes are obtained by solving these $d(d-1)$ optimal tiling problems (2) and picking the one that has the smallest objective function value (i.e., the minimum execution time).

9 A Complete Example

```
for ( i1 = 1; i1 ≤ N1 ; i1++)
      for ( i2 = 1; i2 ≤ N2; i2++)
            A[i2] = A[i2 −1] + A[i2];
```

Consider the above loop nest and its dependence matrix $D = \begin{pmatrix} 1 & 0 \\ 0 & 1 \end{pmatrix}$. As inidicated by Theorem 1, there exists no permutation of the loops that can expose the parallelism to a software pipeliner. However, the loop has lots of parallelism that can be exposed to a software pipeliner by skewing. We have $d(d-1) = 2$ choices for skewing the loops, viz., skewing `i1` w.r.t to `i2` or vice-versa. But, due the symmetry of D, both skews will have the same effect on the bounding box. Let us consider skewing loop `i2` with respect to `i1`, and then permuting them to make the `i1` loop the innermost. Now, all the dependences are carried by outer loop (`i2`) and the inner loop (`i1`) is completely parallel. A software pipeliner can exploit this parallelism to construct a schedule which is constrained only the available execution resources (and not by the dependence constraints). We then tile this skewed-permuted loop nest to enable register reuse.

To determine the optimal tile sizes, we instantiate the combined optimization problem (1) with the optimal skew (and permute) matrix $S = \begin{pmatrix} 1 & 1 \\ 0 & 1 \end{pmatrix}$, as follows. Now, $\widehat{D} = \mathsf{bbox}(SD) = \begin{pmatrix} 1 \\ 1 \end{pmatrix}$. Instantiating the optimal tiling problem we get

$$\begin{aligned} \text{minimize} \quad & \tfrac{N_1 \times N_2}{t_1 \times t_2} \times \max\left(\alpha \times t_1 \times t_2,\ \beta \times (t_1 + t_2)\right) + \\ & \eta \left(N_1 \times N_2 + \tfrac{N_1 \times N_2}{t_2} + \tfrac{N_1 \times N_2}{t_1 \times t_2} + \tfrac{N_1}{t_1}\right) \\ \text{s.t.} \quad & t_1 + t_2 \le \mathsf{NR}, \boldsymbol{t} \ge 1, \boldsymbol{t} \in \mathbb{Z} \end{aligned} \tag{2}$$

where, α is the cost per iteration and is equal to the II (initiation interval), β is the cost of moving a data item from the lowest level cache to the register and η is the cost of a loop bound check. NR is the number of (floating point) registers in the architecture.

10 Related Work

Unroll and jam. Sarkar [14] addresses the same problem as ours and uses unroll and jam followed by scalar replacement [20] for exposing ILP and register reuse. He formulates the problem as a discrete optimization problem with unroll factors as variables, and proposes an exhaustive search with heuristics to solve it. Our formulation seeks both the skew matrix and the tile sizes, and is solved to global optimality via convex programming. The class of programs considered by Sarkar, loops with affine dependences, is larger than what is considered by ours, loop nests with uniform dependences. However for uniform dependence loop nests, by setting the skew matrix to identity, viewing the tile sizes as unroll factors, and adding the code size constraint, our method can be directly used to solve the problem addressed by Sarkar. In this sense, for this class of loop nests, the problem of solving for optimal unroll factors is a special case of our problem.

Carr and Kennedy [21] propose an algorithm to determine the unroll factors that balance the floating-point and memory access operations. This objective function is different from ours, as well as Sarkar's, viz., minimizing the execution time.

Hierarchical tiling. The work of Carter et al. [22], followed up by Mitchell et al. [23], uses tiling to expose the register reuse as well as ILP. They propose hierarchical tiling as a *hand tuning* technique to better exploit pipelined functional units and registers. Our work is similar to this work in spirit, however, we have proposed a completely *automatic method* to determine the tile sizes and skew factors.

Code generation for register tiling. Jiminez et al. [24] propose a code generation strategy for non-rectangular loop nests tiled for registers. Their strategy uses index set splitting to strip off the partial boundary tiles and the full tiles are completely unrolled. Hence, they assume that unroll and jam followed by scalar promotion is used for exposing ILP and register reuse. Sarkar [14] also proposes a code generation algorithm which takes the unroll factors as input and produces an unrolled loop nest.

Software pipelining of loop nests. Traditionally software pipeliners have only looked at innermost loop nests. Ramanujam [10] proposed a technique where an integer linear programming formulation is used to find a (software) pipelined schedule that exploits the parallelism available in the whole loop nest. However, he did not consider resource constraints. Rong et al. [25] have recently proposed a technique called *single dimension software pipelining for multi-dimensional loops*. Their technique computes the initiation interval and (cache) locality of every loop in the given loop nest and picks the best. They do not consider any ILP exposing transformations like permutation or skewing, and hence, are limited in how ILP can be exploited. On the other hand, our approach, by the virtue of looking at skewing and permutation, will always be able to expose the available ILP. Rong et al. also propose a method for code generation [26] and recently have addressed the register allocation issue [9]. A similar problem in the context of ILP and caches has been addressed by Wolf et al. [15].

11 Discussion and Future Work

We have formulated the combined problem of choosing an ILP-exposing (skewing) transformation and register tiling. We have proposed an efficient way to check whether permutation can expose any parallel loops. We have distinguished two cases: when loop permutation can expose a parallel loop, and when it cannot. For the former case, we have reduced the combined problem to a single convex optimization problem and for the latter case we have reduced the combined problem to a typically small set of convex optimization problems. All these convex optimization problems can be solved efficiently using currently available tools (e.g., YALMIP [19]).

The formulation of the combined problem exposes the fact that the skewing transformation affects the dependences and which in turn affects the overall execution time of transformed loop nest. We see this formulation, and its analysis, as a first step in understanding the structure of this important complex problem. To the best of our knowledge, this is the first formulation and globally optimal solution of this combined problem.

Future work. We are currently working on adapting modulo scheduling techniques [4,5] to schedule the transformed loop nest. Note that the modulo scheduler is guaranteed to find the inner most loop nest parallel. Hence, we do not need any dependence analysis to determine the achievable initiation interval. We are also investigating array register allocation techniques to map all the array values accessed in a tile to registers. Note that from the constraints of the optimal tiling problem, we are guaranteed to have enough registers.

As a future work, we plan to extend the program class. One direction is to extend the work to include iteration spaces with parallelepiped shapes. Another direction is to permit non-uniform (affine) dependences in the loop body.

References

1. Allen, R., Kennedy, K.: Optimizing Compilers for Modern Architectures: A Dependence Based Approach. Morgan Kaufman, San Francisco (2002)
2. Carr, S., Sweany, P.: An experimental evaluation of scalar replacement on scientific benchmarks. Software Practice and Experience **33**(15) (2003) 1419–1445
3. Lam, M.: Software pipelining: an effective scheduling technique for vliw machines. In: PLDI '88: Proceedings of the ACM SIGPLAN 1988 conference on Programming Language design and Implementation, New York, NY, USA, ACM Press (1988) 318–328
4. Rau, B.R.: Iterative modulo scheduling: an algorithm for software pipelining loops. In: MICRO 27: Proceedings of the 27th annual international symposium on Microarchitecture, New York, NY, USA, ACM Press (1994) 63–74
5. Allan, V.H., Jones, R.B., Lee, R.M., Allan, S.J.: Software pipelining. ACM Comput. Surv. **27**(3) (1995) 367–432
6. Darte, A., Robert, Y., Vivien, F.: Scheduling and Automatic Parallelization. Birkhauser Boston (2000)
7. Xue, J.: Loop tiling for parallelism. Kluwer Academic Publishers (2000)
8. Renganarayana, L., Ramakrishna, U., Rajopadhye, S.: Combined ILP and register tiling: Analytical model and optimization framework. Technical Report CS-05-102, Department of Computer Science, Colorado State University (2005) Available from `http://www.cs.colostate.edu/~ln/publications/TR-CS-05-102.pdf`.
9. Rong, H., Douillet, A., Gao, G.R.: Register allocation for software pipelined multidimensional loops. In: PLDI '05: Proceedings of the 2005 ACM SIGPLAN conference on Programming language design and implementation, New York, NY, USA, ACM Press (2005) 154–167
10. Ramanujam, J.: Optimal software pipelining of nested loops. In: IPPS. (1994) 335–342
11. Xue, J.: On tiling as a loop transformation. Parallel Processing Letters **7**(4) (1997) 409–424
12. Renganarayana, L., Rajopadhye, S.: A geometric programming framework for optimal multi-level tiling. In: SC '04: Proceedings of the 2004 ACM/IEEE conference on Supercomputing, Washington, DC, USA, IEEE Computer Society (2004) 18
13. Andonov, R., Balev, S., Rajopadhye, S.V., Yanev, N.: Optimal semi-oblique tiling. IEEE Trans. Parallel Distrib. Syst. **14**(9) (2003) 944–960
14. Sarkar, V.: Optimized unrolling of nested loops. International Journal of Parallel Programming **29**(5) (2001) 545–581

15. Wolf, M.E., Maydan, D.E., Chen, D.K.: Combining loop transformations considering caches and scheduling. In: Proceedings of the 29th Annual International Symposium on Microarchitecture, Paris, IEEE Computer Society TC-MICRO and ACM SIGMICRO (1996) 274–286
16. Duffin, R., Peterson, E., Zener, C.: Geometric Programming – Theory and Applications. John Wiley (1967)
17. Boyd, S., Vandenberghe, L.: Convex Optimization. Cambridge University Press. (Online version available at: `http://www.stanford.edu/~boyd/cvxbook.html`) (2004)
18. Kortanek, K.O., Xu, X., Ye, Y.: An infeasible interior-point algorithm for solving primal and dual geometric programs. Math. Program. **76**(1) (1997) 155–181
19. Löfberg, J.: YALMIP : A toolbox for modeling and optimization in MATLAB. In: Proceedings of the CACSD Conference, Taipei, Taiwan (2004) Available from `http://control.ee.ethz.ch/~joloef/yalmip.php`.
20. Callahan, D., Carr, S., Kennedy, K.: Improving register allocation for subscripted variables. In: PLDI '90: Proceedings of the ACM SIGPLAN 1990 conference on Programming language design and implementation, New York, NY, USA, ACM Press (1990) 53–65
21. Carr, S., Kennedy, K.: Improving the ratio of memory operations to floating-point operations in loops. ACM Trans. Program. Lang. Syst. **16**(6) (1994) 1768–1810
22. Carter, L., Ferrante, J., Hummel, S.F.: Hierarchical tiling for improved superscalar performance. In: Proceedings of the 9th International Symposium on Parallel Processing, Washington, DC, USA, IEEE Computer Society (1995) 239–245
23. Mitchell, N., Högstedt, K., Carter, L., Ferrante, J.: Quantifying the multi-level nature of tiling interactions. International Journal of Parallel Programming **26**(6) (1998) 641–670
24. Jiménez, M., Llabería, J.M., Fernández, A.: Register tiling in nonrectangular iteration spaces. ACM Trans. Program. Lang. Syst. **24**(4) (2002) 409–453
25. Rong, H., Tang, Z., Govindarajan, R., Douillet, A., Gao, G.R.: Single-dimension software pipelining for multi-dimensional loops. In: CGO '04: Proceedings of the international symposium on Code generation and optimization, Washington, DC, USA, IEEE Computer Society (2004)
26. Rong, H., Douillet, A., Govindarajan, R., Gao, G.R.: Code generation for single-dimension software pipelining of multi-dimensional loops. In: CGO '04: Proceedings of the international symposium on Code generation and optimization, Washington, DC, USA, IEEE Computer Society (2004)

Analytic Models and Empirical Search: A Hybrid Approach to Code Optimization

Arkady Epshteyn[1], María Jesús Garzarán[1], Gerald DeJong[1], David Padua[1], Gang Ren[1], Xiaoming Li[1], Kamen Yotov[2], and Keshav Pingali[2]

[1] University of Illinois at Urbana-Champaign, Urbana IL 61801
[2] Cornell University, Ithaca, NY 14853

Abstract. Compilers employ system models, sometimes implicitly, to make code optimization decisions. These models are analytic; they reflect their implementor's understanding and beliefs of the system. While their decisions can be made almost instantaneously, unless the model is perfect their decisions may be flawed. To avoid exercising unique characteristics of a particular machine, such models are necessarily general and conservative. An alternative is to construct an empirical model. Building an empirical model involves extensive search of a parameter space to determine optimal settings. But this search is performed on the actual machine on which the compiler is to be deployed so that, once constructed, its decisions automatically reflect any eccentricities of the target system. Unfortunately, constructing accurate empirical models is expensive and, therefore, their applicability is limited to library generators such as ATLAS and FFTW. Here the high up-front installation cost can amortized over many future uses. In this paper we examine a hybrid approach. Active learning in an Explanation-Based paradigm allows the hybrid system to greatly increase the search range while drastically reducing the search time. Individual search points are analyzed for their information content using an known-imprecise qualitative analytic model. Next-search-points are chosen which have the highest expected information content with respect to refinement of the empirical model being constructed. To evaluate our approach we compare it with a leading analytic model and a leading empirical model. Our results show that the performance of the libraries generated using the hybrid approach is comparable to the performance of libraries generated via extensive search techniques and much better than that of the libraries generated by optimization based solely on an analytic model.

1 Introduction

Application of high-level program transformations such as loop unrolling, array tiling, and software pipelining is critical in optimizing the performance of compiled code. Deciding how to apply these transformations can be exceedingly challenging. These decisions must balance subtle interactions among characteristics of the underlying architecture, the source code, other compilation decisions, and so on. Every optimizing compiler, therefore, embodies a decision procedure either explicitly or implicitly to resolve these choices. Intuitions (confirmed by decision theory) tell us that resolving such difficult choices satisfactorily requires a great deal of information.

Most commonly, this information is supplied explicitly via prior performance models. Such models are extremely efficient, generating solutions almost instantaneously. But

E. Ayguadé et al. (Eds.): LCPC 2005, LNCS 4339, pp. 259–273, 2007.

the information they embody comes entirely from their designer's formal idealization of the process to be optimized. It excludes phenomena that the designer believes to be negligible or too complex to analyze.

By contrast, an empirical approach collects information directly from the system on which the compiler is deployed. This results in first-hand information which can be more accurate than that of a prior performance model. For example, many versions of a loop with different tilings crossed with various loop unrolling amounts might be generated and executed. It then selects the combination with the best measured performance. Unfortunately, searching through combinations of parameter values can be hugely expensive. As a result, this approach cannot service the real-time requests of a compiler as can the prior performance model. But it is well suited to library generation where the high cost of optimal configuration decisions can be paid once. Well-known library generators that employ empirical optimization include FFTW [12], ATLAS [17], PhiPAC [3] and SPIRAL [19].

An alternative decision procedure is an adaptive hybrid which includes only the prior information from the designer which he or she is most confident of. The rest is then filled in empirically. The prior partial model might answer some optimization questions directly but might instead suggest which measurements are likely to be most informative and so guide and limit the empirical searches. The accuracy of this decision procedure is rooted in first-hand measurement of the actual system to be optimized. But it might be efficient enough to make real-time optimization decisions or be automatically re-invoked when necessary to react to changing situations.

The possibility of adaptive models is the motivation and the subject of our current research which we offer as the first tentative steps along a lengthy but, we believe, promising path. We employ an Explanation-Based Learning paradigm [10]. Empirical results are treated as illustrations or manifestations of a deeper pattern to be discovered. They are *explained* in terms of the existing partial model and therefore serve to refine the model and reduce the need for future empirical searches.

To evaluate our adaptive approach we compare it directly with a leading analytic model and a leading empirical optimization approach. Methodologically, these three approaches must be compared on equal footing. They be applied to the same optimization task in as similar a setting as possible. To this end we use the matrix multiplication framework of ATLAS as our experimental platform but without its hand-tuned additions whose influences could be conflated with the behaviors we wish to monitor.

ATLAS produces an optimized Basic Linear Algebra Subroutine (BLAS) library including a module for optimized matrix multiplication. The generated code (referred to in this paper as the mini-MMM code) is compiled and executed to measure its observed performance. ATLAS finds parameter values that maximize the performance of mini-MMM code (in MFLOPs) using a routine that performs a near-exhaustive sampling of a region of the parameter space. It is this module that we replace in our experiments. In one experimental condition it is replaced by a leading analytic model [20], in a second it is replaced by our adaptive system, and in a third the original ATLAS routine is employed. In all three cases the remainder of the MMM generation code is unchanged as are the routines to measure MMM performance.

Our results confirm that the the adaptive approach can perform better than the analytic model and is much more efficient than the empirical approach. The analytic model is based on an architectural idealization that cannot perfectly capture the actual machine to be optimized. On the other hand, the ATLAS routine samples broadly from a large but limited region of the parameter space that, on occasion does not contain the optimal configuration. The adaptive approach only samples those points deemed to be informative given the results of previous samples. This can greatly increase the range of parameter values it entertains, but it only does so when there is an expectation of optimization improvement.

In library installation efficiency is less crucial since cost can be amortized over the lifetime of the machine. But even here there are at least four situations in which efficiency can be important.

1) Adaptation may have to be applied at runtime, in which case an extensive search is not possible, and prior models (when available) may not be accurate enough. This type of search involves measuring the performance of various versions of precompiled code during the sampling phase of the executing, and then using the best version during the (much longer) production phase [11]. Note that runtime searching tailors the optimization system to the requirements of the user not available at library installation time (for instance, small blocking parameter values will be selected if the user only multiplies small matrices).
2) Efficient adaptation can be applied at the time of compilation. [16] describes a compile-time optimization framework that employs empirical search which receives performance feedback from a fast estimator.
3) The space of possible versions can be too large even for once-in-a-life time installation. Empirical search complexity grows exponentially with the number of interacting optimization parameters.
4) An interesting application of library routines is as a benchmark to evaluate alternative machine designs. More efficient adaptation can enable a wider exploration of possible designs.

The paper is organized as follows: we describe the search module of ATLAS in Section 2. The model approach to optimization is discussed in Section 3. Our hybrid approach is presented in Section 4. Finally, experimental results are shown in Section 5.

2 ATLAS

ATLAS is a system that employs empirical search to generate highly-tuned BLAS libraries [17]. In this paper, we focus on the optimization of the matrix-matrix multiplication (MMM) routine. This is the key routine in BLAS since many other kernel operations use it as a primitive. ATLAS contains a generator search module and a multiple implementations search module. The generator search contains a code generator that outputs a kernel based on input parameters. This module searches the inputs that result in the best performing kernel. The multiple implementation module searches among hand-written codes for MMM kernels. ATLAS selects the best-performing kernel out of both modules. ATLAS also records results from previous installations on the target platform and can reduce the installation time by using these instead of the empirical search.

In this work, we focus on the generator search module. The search is used during the installation procedure to find the optimal values of code transformation parameters (amount of tiling, unrolling, etc.). It consists of: (1) generating the versions of matrix multiplication with the parameter values to be tested, (2) compiling and executing them, and (3) selecting the version that perform best.

ATLAS is not a restructuring compiler, but the code generated by ATLAS can be seen as the result of applying a sequence of compiler transformations. We first examine these code transformations (Section 2.1). Then, we explain how ATLAS searches for the most appropriate parameter values of these transformations (Section 2.2).

2.1 Transformations

The code implementing a MMM is shown in Figure 1. Yotov et al [20,21] and Cooper et al [8] found that computing this matrix multiplication using the library generated by ATLAS results in higher performance than that obtained when the naive MMM implementation in Figure 1 is compiled using a general purpose compiler. The reason for this performace gap is that compilers do not apply the appropriate transformations and/or they do not use the correct parameter values for these transformations [8,20,21].

```
for (j = 1; j <= M; j++)
 for (i = 1; i <= N; i++)
  for (k = 1; k <= K; k++)
   C[i][j] = C[i][j] + A[i][k] * B[k][j]
```

Fig. 1. Matrix Multiplication Code

The code generated by ATLAS can be seen as the result of applying well-known compiler transformations to the code in Figure 1. To increase the locality ATLAS uses blocking, while to increase Instruction Level Parallelism (ILP) ATLAS uses pipeline scheduling. Next, we examine these transformations.

- Blocking: This transformation converts matrix multiplication into a sequence of smaller matrix multiplications. Blocking can be accomplished by a loop transformation called tiling, introduced by Wolfe [18]. ATLAS applies blocking at the cache and the register level:
  - Cache Blocking: ATLAS uses blocking to decompose the matrix multiplication of large matrices into the multiplication of smaller sub-blocks. The size of each sub-block is *NB* $\times$ *NB*, where *NB* is an optimization parameter that needs to be chosen so that the working set of the sub-blocks being multiplied fits in the cache [4,7,18]. We call the resulting code mini-MMM.

- Register blocking: The mini-MMM code itself is blocked and then unrolled to optimize the utilization of the registers. The resulting code, that we call micro-MMM, multiplies a column of *MU* elements of matrix *A* by a row of *NU* elements of matrix *B* and stores the result into a $MU \times NU$ sub-matrix of *C*. *MU* and *NU* are optimization parameters that must be chosen so that $MU + NU + MU \times NU$ fit in the registers of the processor [2].

To improve register allocation, ATLAS uses scalar replacement [5]: each element of A, B and C that is accessed in the unrolled micro-MMM code is assigned to a scalar. The array accesses in the micro-MMM code are replaced by these scalar variables. ATLAS expects that the compiler will assign registers to these scalars. Also, ATLAS copies the $NB \times NB$ sub-matrices to consecutive memory locations. This reduces the number of cache and TLB misses. Additional transformations such as loop unrolling and load scheduling applied in ATLAS are described in detail in [17,20,21].

2.2 Search

ATLAS does an almost exhaustive search of the parameter values presented in the previous Section. Since ATLAS searches for several parameters, when searching for one parameter, ATLAS needs to assign values to the other parameters it has not yet optimized. These values are initially assigned based on results obtained from the execution of benchmarks. These benchmarks estimate characteristics of the platform on which ATLAS is being installed, such as cache size and number of registers. After a parameter is optimized, the value that obtains the best performance is used for the search of the subsequent parameters. Parameter values are searched in the same order that appears in our explanation below.

1. L1 cache blocking ($NB \times NB$): ATLAS generates versions of the mini-MMM code with a matrix size $NB \times NB$, where *NB* varies from 16 to the minimum of (80 and $\sqrt{L1\ Size}$), in steps of 4.
2. Register blocking (*MU* and *NU*): ATLAS exhaustively searches for the best values of *MU* and *NU*. All possible combinations of *MU* and *NU* satisfying $MU \times NU + MU + NU + Latency \leq Number\ Of\ Registers$ are tried, and the best performing combination is selected.
3. Loop unrolling, instruction scheduling parameters, etc. are described in [17,20]

More details about ATLAS can be found in [17,20].

3 Model

Yotov et al. [20,21] challenged the notion that empirical optimization is more effective than model-driven optimization by demonstrating that a model-based optimization strategy can calculate near-optimal parameter values without incurring the sampling cost of empirical search. We use Yotov's model as our initial guess of the parameter values. In this Section we summarize it. A further description of the model can be found in [20,21].

The model depends on accurate estimates of machine parameters that include the L1 cache and line size, the number of registers, the latency of the multiply instruction, the existence of a fused multiply-add instruction, and the number of functional units.

1. L1 cache blocking (*NB* $\times$ *NB*): The idea of the model is to compute the value of *NB* that optimizes the use of the L1 data cache. The model is based on the memory access trace of the mini-MMM, and takes into account the loop order, L1 cache and line size, and the LRU replacement strategy of caches. This analysis finds that for a JIK order, the optimal value for *NB* is the maximum value of *NB* that satisfies the inequality below:

$$\left\lceil \frac{NB^2}{L1\ Line\ Size} \right\rceil + 3 * \left\lceil \frac{NB}{L1\ Line\ Size} \right\rceil + 1 \leq \frac{L1\ Size}{L1\ Line\ Size}$$

   Notice that the model in [21] is more accurate that the one just discussed. We started the work reported in this paper before the model was improved and we are using the simpler model from [20]. In any case the value found using the more elaborate model in [21] is close to the value found by the model described above and presented in [20].
2. Register blocking (*MU* and *NU*): To estimate the appropriate values of the register blocking parameters, the model takes into account how the ATLAS generator allocates registers to variables, and the need of *Latency* additional registers to hold the temporary results of the multiplication. With all this, the model picks the maximum values of *MU* and *NU* such that *NU*$\approx$*MU* and *MU*$\times$*NU*+*MU*+*NU*+*Latency* $\leq$ *Number Of Registers*.

This model mimics ATLAS in that it computes a blocking value for the L1 cache. However, sensitivity analysis reported in [20,21] shows that in some machines blocking values that overflow the L1 cache obtain better performance. The conjecture is that, in these machines, the large block size that results in the best performance corresponds to the block size that fits in the L2 cache. Blocking for L2 may result in higher performance than blocking for the L1 cache because in out-of-order processors, which have a deep pipeline, the latency of accessing the L2 cache can usually be hidden without stalling the processor. The rationale is that the processor can continue executing instructions that do not depend on the missed data. A larger block size also increases the opportunity for higher ILP and for the compiler to reorder instructions [6][1].

Given that for some behavioral profiles it may be advantageous to block for the L2 cache, we would like to extend the model from [20,21] to estimate an appropriate L2 blocking parameter value. The inequality above used to compute the L1 cache blocking factor cannot be used to compute the L2 cache blocking factor because it does not take conflict misses into account. Ignoring conflict misses in the L1 cache is safer than

[1] Notice that tiling for L2 may not always be the best choice, because large tiles can result in more time spent in the cleanup code, which can degrade performance for some of the codes calling the MMM library generated by ATLAS [1]. However, it has been shown that in some cases it is necessary to tile for L2 [1], and this is confirmed by our experiments (Figure 5) where the MMM library generated by ATLAS is evaluated in the contex of matrix-matrix multiplication.

ignoring conflict misses in the L2 cache because the difference in latencies between the L1 and L2 caches is much smaller than the difference in latencies between the L2 cache and the main memory.

To compute the L2 blocking factor we use a conservative approach that ensures that *NB*x*NB* blocks of data from all three matrices *A, B*, and *C* fit in the L2 cache. This happens when the combined size of these three blocks ($3 * NB^2$) is equal to the size of the L2 cache.

4 Adaptive Modeling

Our adaptive approach combines the information embedded in the model from Section 3 with feedback information obtained from the execution of versions of the mini-MMM code. Both types of information are used to search for the maximum of the mini-MMM performance function. The approach determines the shape of this function through experimentation. Each experiment consists of generating, compiling, and executing mini-MMM code. The mini-MMM code is generated by ATLAS's code generation module, ensuring that the space of available transformations is the same for ATLAS search and the adaptive approach. The parameter values for transformations, however, are determined by our algorithm. The feedback provided by each experiment (in form of mini-MMM performance) is used to design subsequent experiments to maximize information about the location of performance-maximizing parameter values. Maximizing performance can be done either via a local search (e.g., by performing hill climbing) or by modeling the whole performance function globally via appropriately chosen *regression curves*. Experiments that provide the best feedback about the shape of the regression function are preferred. The location of the maximum in this scenario is determined indirectly from the shape of the regression function. Prior knowledge obtained from the model is used to indicate to the family of regression curves that the maximum performance is going to be located in the neighborhood of the model-predicted values.

In our experiments, we focus on optimizing the cache blocking parameter *(NB)*: This is done by analyzing the general shape of the plot of mini-MMM performance as a function of the cache blocking parameters. Figure 2, for example, shows sampled data

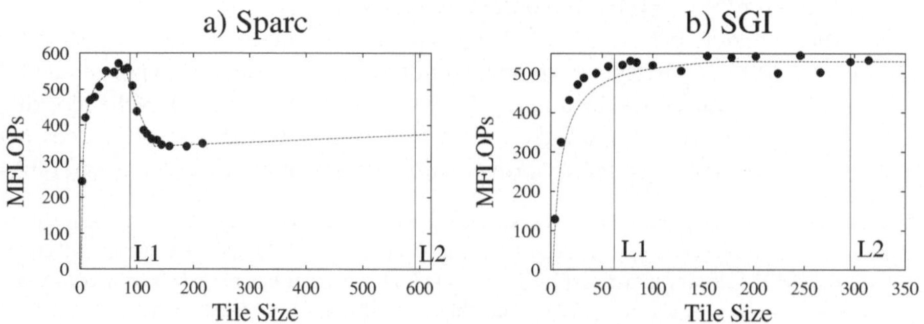

Fig. 2. Performance as a function of cache block size *NB* (complete instruction cache unroll: *KU=NB*)

collected on two different machines. In each plot, the points show the performance of the mini-MMM code (Y-axis) for different values of cache block size (X-axis). As these sampled points are being collected, a regression curve is fitted to the data (this curve is shown in Figure 2 as well). The shape of the curve is adjusted with each newly collected sample point. The best values of the optimization parameters can be determined directly from the location of the maximum point on the regression curve.

Certain characteristics of the shape of the plot can be guessed before any data is collected. For example, we expect the peak in the curve of Figure 2-(a) to coincide with the optimal cache blocking (*NB*) factor predicted by the model. This is the point where the L1 cache is fully utilized. Further increase in the block size results in L1 cache overflow that results in performance degradation. We expect to see a phenomenon similar to this on most of the architectures under consideration. Information about the shape of the performance curve that is available before any data is collected is known as prior information. In statistics, prior information is captured by a probability distribution in the space of optimization parameters. We use the model from Section 3 to construct such a distribution.

Optimization requires a sophisticated algorithm because multiple levels of the cache hierarchy introduce multiple local maxima in the performance function. For example Figure 3 shows the performance obtained by the mini-MMM code as the tile size increases. On Pentium III, the figure shows two distinct peaks, each corresponding to blocking factors for L1 and L2 caches. Our optimization algorithm is described in detail in Section 4.1.

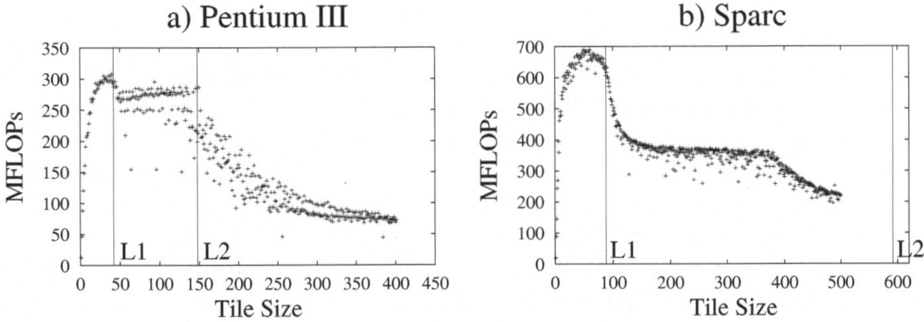

Fig. 3. Complete sampled performance curves on two machines. The vertical lines correspond to the blocking factors for L1 and L2 as predicted by the model.

4.1 Cache Blocking Parameters

The adaptive approach constructs a nonlinear regression curve representing the sampled performance of the mini-MMM code as a function of tile size, with register blocking parameters being held constant. Figure 2 shows examples of such curves fitted to the data collected on the platforms that we evaluate in Section 5.2.

The optimal tile size is calculated directly from the fitted regression function. Thus each point provides global information about the location of the maximum by affecting the shape of the regression curve. A set of regression curves that could fit the data sample is hard-coded and available before any data is collected. In this work, we use a double-peaked family of regression curves, each peak corresponding to a blocking factor for one of the caches.

Our algorithm has two main strategies:

1) The first strategy uses the regression curve available at a given time to identify the next experimental point. That is, it identifies the size of the tile that will be used for the next sample $(tile\ size_{n+1}, performance_{n+1})$. The goal is to sample the point that provides the best feedback about the location of the maxima. This strategy is called Active Sampling.

2) The second computes the curve that "best" fits a set D of experimental points $(tile\ size_1, performance_1)...(tile\ size_n, performance_n)$, taking into account the prior information provided by the model from Section 3. This strategy is done using the Maximum a Posteriori Bayessian Estimate.

Our algorithm consists of a loop that in each iteration applies strategy (1) to generate a sample point and then applies strategy (2) to compute the best fit given all the points selected so far. As the search is conducted, each sample point is determined by generating a mini-MMM program based on the tile size determined by the strategy (1), compiling the program, and measuring the program's execution time.

Maximum a Posteriori Bayessian Estimate. Given a set of experimental points, the second strategy computes a curve that is a good fit to these points and, at the same time, to the model (known as prior). In our case, good fit to the model means that the two peaks of the resulting curve are not too distant from the values predicted by the model. We now describe this strategy more formally.

A typical performance profile is presented in Figure 3-(a). We expect performance to improve until the L1 cache is fully utilized. At that point, it drops off, but begins to improve again as the tile size increases until it reaches the point where L2 cache is fully utilized. The regression curves where the maxima are located at the model-predicted locations are initially favored. As more data is collected, the preference of the system shifts towards the regression curves that fit the data best. This trade-off is governed by the size of the collected sample and is determined by maximum-a-posteriori estimation as follows: let β be one of the curves identified by our algorithm. This curve is defined by the regression parameters w and the separators (l_1, l_2) that correspond to our two peaks (l_1 and l_2). Initially l_1 and l_2 are at the values $L1$ and $L2$ predicted by the model. In successive iterations of our algorithm, the values of l_1 and l_2 are determined in the process of maximizing the formula given below.

Given a set of data points D, the maximum a posteriori Bayesian estimate is used to determine the best curve $\widehat{\beta}$ that maximizes the probability density function $P(\beta|D)$. This density function can be computed via Bayes rule: $P(\beta|D) = P(D|\beta)P(\beta)/P(D)$. $P(\beta)$ is known as the prior and incorporates information from the model. Since any curve β is identified by the regression coefficients w and the peak location parameters

(l_1, l_2), $P(\beta) = P(w, (l_1, l_2)) = P(w|(l_1, l_2))P(l_1, l_2)$. Now, we assume that the curves with peaks at l_1 and l_2 have a uniform prior disttribution, i.e. $P(w|(l_1, l_2))$ is a constant. We also assume that the random variables (l_1, l_2) have a normal distribution centered at $L1$ and $L2$: $P(l_1, l_2) = N(\begin{bmatrix} L1 \\ L2 \end{bmatrix}, \begin{bmatrix} \sigma_1^2 & 0 \\ 0 & \sigma_2^2 \end{bmatrix})$, where σ_1^2 and $\sigma_2^2$are user-controlled parameters representing one's confidence in the model's prediction. The other term of the equation, $P(D|\beta)$ computes the total squared error of the sample with respect to the curve β assuming that the errors are produced by white Gaussian noise:

$$P(D|\beta) = \left(\frac{1}{\sqrt{2\pi\sigma^2}}\right)^n e^{-\sum_{i=1}^{n} (performance_i - \beta(tile\ size_i))^2/(2\sigma^2)}.$$

Notice that $P(l_1, l_2)$ favors the curves that agree with the model, while $P(D|\beta)$ favors the curves β that fit the sample well. As the sample size increases more points contribute to the total squared error and penalize the curves that do not fit the data more heavily, while $P(l_1, l_2)$ remains unchanged. Thus, the system converges to the best regression curve in the limit even if the prior information is inaccurate, but this convergence happens much faster when the model is good.

Active Sampling. The search performs a dual function. First of all, prior knowledge may be inaccurate. Figure 3-(b) shows an example of a peak that does not coincide with any of the predicted blocking factors. Search can verify the tile sizes that fully utilize the caches and adjust them empirically. Second of all, prior knowledge alone does not indicate which cache (L1 or L2) to tile for (see Figure 3-(a)). Search resolves this problem by empirically determining which peak is the dominant one. Moreover, the adaptive search produces a statistical measure of confidence in its estimate that is not available with either pure model or ATLAS search.

The main source of our algorithm's efficiency comes from its ability to select informative sample points intelligently. This process, known as active sampling, represents a major deviation from the philosophy of ATLAS and other empirical optimization engines - the system uses feedback from conducted experiments to adjust its sampling strategy, while ATLAS samples at pre-determined locations.

In doing so, it must take into account conflicting objectives: reducing the time to collect the sample and selecting the most informative points. The first objective directs the system to sample points close to the origin, because the sampling time increases with increasing tile size *NB* due mainly to the significant increase in the amount of time required to compile the program.[2] The second objective is to select the points that provide more information about the location of the peak of the function.

To reconcile these objectives, a heuristic that simulates potential fields is used. It places a negative charge at each sample point to discourage oversampling in the same

[2] With bigger tile sizes, the size of the completely unrolled register loop nest increases, forcing the optimizing compiler to spend more time on instruction scheduling. Increasing the cache block size from 40 to 400 on the SGI machine increases compilation time from 4 seconds to 4 minutes.

region and a positive charge at the origin to encourage less time-consuming data points (since programs generated with smaller values of cache blocking/unrolling take less time to compile). Positive charges encourage sampling in the region around them, negative charges have the opposite effect. The point that minimizes the potential field is selected for sampling. A positive charge is also imposed on regions contributing information about the highest peak. This charge is proportional to the estimated probability that the peak that appears to be the highest actually is the highest.

An example of the heuristic can be seen in Figure 4. The potential field $U(x)$ is a function of the tile size x. Tile sizes with low potentials experience the least amount of repulsive force and the greatest amount of attractive force. The system computes $U(x)$ for every tile size x and chooses the tile size with minimum potential energy for sampling. The potential field is calculated as a sum of contributing factors. Each previously sampled tile size y contributes $\frac{\nu}{(x-y)^2}$ to the potential field at x, creating a repulsive force that increases at tile sizes x close to the sampled point y. The attractive field at the origin contributes $\xi * (x-0)^2$ to the potential field at x, resulting in an attractive force that decreases with increasing tile size. ν and ξ are user-defined constants controlling the strengths of the forces creating the field. The advantage of using this heuristic is its efficiency in combining multiple objectives.

Examples of application of this heuristic are presented in Figure 2. In Figure 2-(a), a two-peaked function is used to fit the data. The first peak (blocking for the L1 cache) is the dominant one. The location of the L1 peak is estimated by the system from the sampled data. The L2 peak is predicted from the intersection of the regression function that fits the data and the location of the L2 blocking factor determined by the prior knowledge. The uncertainty of the estimated regression curve parameters is used to calculate the probability that blocking for the L1 peak yields better performance than blocking for L2. This probability, in turn, forces the sampling heuristic to direct its attention to the points that contribute information about the L1 peak. This, in conjunction with the fact that smaller block sizes correspond to less expensive sample points (in terms of compilation time), prompts the system to direct its attention to the region around the L1 blocking factors.

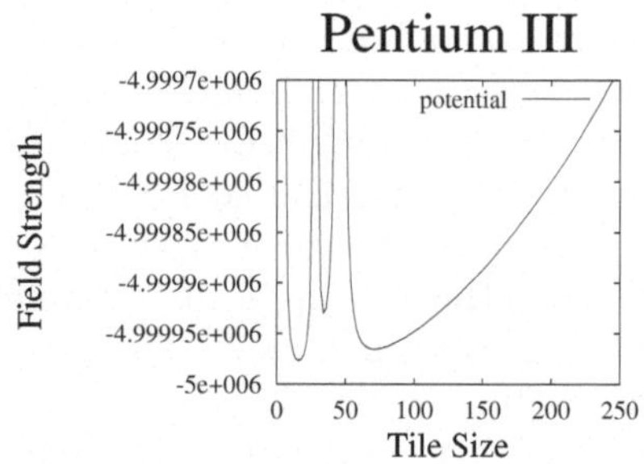

Fig. 4. Potential Field for Active Sampling. The field is constructed based on three sample points. It increases away from the origin and at previously sampled locations.

In Figure 2-(b), a different performance profile results in a different sampling behavior. In this architecture, the optimal cache block size must take advantage of the L2 cache. After the system determines that the dominant peak lies beyond the L1 saturation point, it attempts to collect as much information as possible to ascertain how to take advantage of the L2 cache, even at the expense of incurring a higher sampling cost. It does not make any sense to sample at lower tile sizes if these points do not provide any information about the predicted optimal peak of the model.

5 Experimental Results

In this section, we evaluate the adaptive optimization algorithm. The environmental setup used for our experiments is discussed in Section 5.1 and performance results are shown in Section 5.2. Our experiments demonstrate the feasibility of application of our approach by showing that the adaptive model can achieve performance comparable to (and sometimes exceeding that of) ATLAS and outperform the analytic model, while requiring many fewer experiments than an exhaustive search.

5.1 Environmental Setup

Our experiments were performed on two different architectural platforms: Ultra Sparc III and SGI R12000). Table 1 lists the salient architectural parameters of each platform[3]

The following algorithms were executed on each platform:

1) Model: We use the model from [20] described in Section 3. The model assumes that tiling for the L1 cache is usually optimal.
2) ATLAS search: This is the search strategy using the code generator as described in Section 2. ATLAS assumes that tiling for the L1 cache is optimal for these architectures, and performs a near-exhaustive search of the cache tile space from 16 to the minimum of (80 and $\sqrt{L1\ Cache\ Size}$), in steps of 4.
3) Adaptive: This is the approach we present in this paper, as described in Section 4. The search for the optimal cache blocking parameter values terminates after collecting 20 points.

Table 1. Test Platforms

	Sparc	SGI
CPU	Ultra Sparc III	R12000
Frequency	750 MHz	300 MHz
L1d/L1i Cache	64 KB/32 KB	32 KB/32 KB
L2 Cache	8 MB	2 MB
Memory	4 GB	512 MB
OS	SunOS 5.8	IRIX64 v6.5
ATLAS Compiler	Workshop cc v5.0	MIPSPro cc v7.30
ATLAS Compiler Options	-dalign -fsingle -xO2 -native	-O3 -64 -OPT:Olimit=15000 -TARG:platform=IP30 -LNO:blocking=OFF -LOPT:alias=typed

All of the search strategies are integrated with ATLAS version 3.4.1. Each search strategy optimizes performance by generating versions of code (mini-MMM) with the parameter values under test, compiling and executing them. Once the optimal transformation parameter values are found, a library is generated that uses the discovered values to multiply user-provided matrices. While it is plausible that optimal mini-MMM performance will translate into good performance when multiplying arbitrary matrices, this is not guaranteed. In this Section we generate libraries for multiplying double-precision floating point numbers. For each algorithm and each platform under test, the following measurements are made:

[3] ATLAS compiler and options are the defaults that ATLAS selects in each target platform.

- The amount of time needed to find the optimal parameter values.
- Performance of mini-MMM code generated with the values found to be the optimal.
- Performance of the generated library on a wide range of matrix sizes.

Table 2. Selected Block Size (NB)

	Model	Adaptive	ATLAS
Sparc	88	60	68
SGI	62	170	64

Table 3. Mini-MMM Performance (in MFLOPs)

	Model	Adaptive	ATLAS
Sparc	376.66	851.04	772.33
SGI	499.81	553.15	505.4

Table 4. Time To Complete Search (in minutes)

	Model	Adaptive	ATLAS
Sparc	0:00	3:12	8:59
SGI	0:00	14:02	59:00

5.2 Experimental Results

Table 2 lists the optimal cache block size chosen by each strategy. Table 4 presents the amount of time required for each search strategy to complete. The model performs simple calculations and, therefore, takes a negligible amount of time to complete. The adaptive search, while slower than the model, is three-four times faster than ATLAS search.

The measured performance of each strategy appears in Table 3. As expected, the model is outperformed by ATLAS on these two platforms since the model, while extremely fast, is brittle due to its lack of feedback. ATLAS, on the other hand, requires an extensive sample size to achieve superior performance. The adaptive optimization outperforms both the model and ATLAS after collecting a small sample of points. Its performance gain over ATLAS is most significant on the SGI machine, where it chooses to tile for the L2 cache, not considered for optimization by ATLAS.

On the Sparc machine, while it appears that the adaptive strategy significantly outperforms the model, most of the performance gain is due to the optimal setting of the MU, NU, and $Latency$ parameters which are not considered in this work. The performance gain due to the adaptive search for the optimal NB value is only $\sim$10%. All the reported results for this machine are also affected by the `-native` flag that we are using in the `cc` compiler of the Sparc machine (Table 1) and that is automatically selected by ATLAS. The `-native` flag should direct the compiler to optimize the code for the current machine, but apparently the code generated when using this flag corresponds to that of an older architecture. If instead of `-native` we use the flag `-xarch=v9a` which corresponds to the architecture of the target Sparc machine, we found that the performance results of the code generated by Model were very similar to those in Table 3 for ATLAS or Adaptive.

Figure 5 shows the performance of the libraries generated using the parameters in Table 2 for each of the optimization algorithms under study. Figure 5 shows the performance of each library as the size of the matrices being multiplied increases from 100×100 to 3000×3000. The Figure demonstrates that there is a strong correlation between mini-MMM performance and performance of the final generated library, the metric that the end user of the system is interested in.

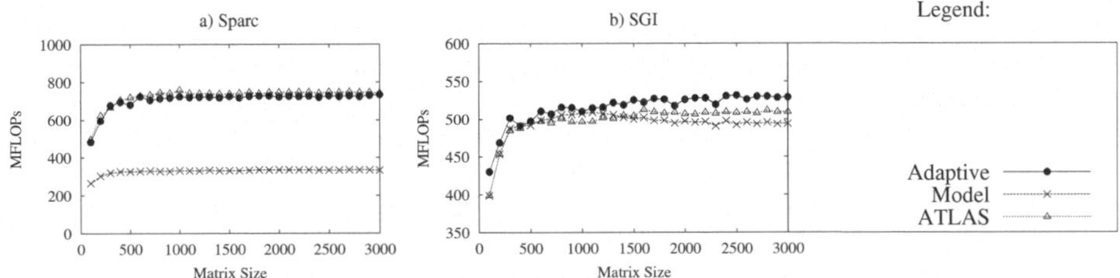

Fig. 5. Library Performance Comparison for ATLAS Search, Model, and Adaptive Search

6 Conclusions and Related Work

Machine learning has been applied to construct adaptive compiler optimizers before. Cooper et. al., for example, use genetic algoithms to search through sequences of optimizing code transformations [9]. Using genetic algorithms (and other machine learning optimization algorithms) can be time-consuming in a large space of possible optimizations.

These techniques have also been extended to search for entire versions of algorithms, as opposed to just code transformations. Li et. al. [13] present a two-phase algorithm for optimizing sorting. The first (offline) phase performs a search to construct a mapping from the parameters of a sorted array (its data entropy and size) to the best-performing sorting algorithm. The second (online) phase uses that mapping to apply the best sorting algorithm to the given array at runtime. A similar framework was applied by Thomas et. al. to optimize parallel matrix multiplication [15].

An important feature which distinguishes our approach to searching is explicit integration of information from the analytic model to guide the search, thereby reducing its time. We believe that adaptive intelligent modeling represents a promising and important direction in code optimization. The defining motivation is to integrate all relevant information into a hybrid model which can both resolve optimization decisions and guide further information collection. The challenge is combining information from different sources that come in radically different forms. In this first proof of concept research, the forms include a general but approximate prior analytical model and empirical measurements of code samples taken directly on the system to be optimized. In our narrow but important test domain of mini-MMM optimization, our adaptive model is much more efficient than the empirical optimization approach. We believe our most significant research contribution is to open a new direction for code optimization. The principle of adaptive intelligent modeling is to actively seek out information that can be used as evidence for refining and restructuring itself so that the optimization decisions are always the best they can be. Our end goal is to expand the applicability of feedback-directed search in the online optimization setting, where both accuracy and speed are crucial.

References

1. ATLAS home page. [Online]. http://math-atlas.sourceforge.net/faq.html#NB80.
2. R. Allan and K. Kennedy. *Optimizing Compilers for Modern Architectures.* Morgan Kaufmann Publishers, 2002.

3. J. Bilmes, K. Asanović, C. Chin, and J. Demmel. Optimizing Matrix Multiply using PHiPAC: a Portable, High-Performance, ANSI C Coding Methodology. In *Proc. of Int. Conf. on Supercomputing*, Vienna, Austria, July 1997.
4. P. Boulet, A. Darte, T. Risset, and Y. Robert. (Pen)-ultimate Tiling? In *INTEGRATION, the VLSI Journal*, volume 17, pages 33–51. 1994.
5. D. Callahan, S. Carr, and K. Kennedy. Improving Register Allocation for Subscripted Variables. In *Proc. of PLDI*, pages 53–65, 1990.
6. S. Carr, C. Ding, and P. Sweany. Improving software pipelining with unroll-and-jam. *Proc. of 29th Hawaii International Conference on System Sciences*, 1996.
7. S. Coleman and K. S. McKinley. Tile Size Selection Using Cache Organization and Data Layout. In *Proc. of PLDI*. ACM Press, June 1995.
8. K. Cooper and T. Waterman. Investigating Adaptive Compilation Using the MIPSPro Compiler. In *Proc. the LACSI Symposium,*, Los Alamos Computer Science Institute, October 2003.
9. K. D. Cooper, D. Subramanian, and L. Torczon. Adaptive optimizing compilers for the 21st century. *The Journal of Supercomputing*, 23(1), 2002.
10. G. DeJong. Explanation-based learning. In A. Tucker, editor, *Computer Science Handbook*, pages 68.1 – 68.18. Chapman & Hall/CRC and ACM, 2nd edition, 2004.
11. P. Diniz and M. Rinard. Dynamic feedback: An effective technique for adaptive computing. *Proc. of PLDI*, 1997.
12. M. Frigo and S. G. Johnson. FFTW: An Adaptive Software Architecture for the FFT. *Proc. IEE Intl. Conf. on Acoustics, Speech, and Signal Processing*, 3:1381–1384, 1998.
13. X. Li, M. J. Garzaran, and D. A. Padua. A dynamically tuned sorting library. In *CGO*, pages 111–124, 2004.
14. C. P. Robert. *The Bayesian Choice*. Springer-Verlag, 1994.
15. N. Thomas, G. Tanase, O. Tkachyshyn, J. Perdue, N. M. Amato, and L. Rauchwerger. A framework for adaptive algorithm selection in stapl. *Proc. ACM SIGPLAN Symp. Prin. Prac. Par. Prog. (PPOPP) (to appear)*, 2005.
16. S. Triantafyllis, M. Vachharajani, N. Vachharajani, and D. August. Compiler optimization-space exploration. *Int. Symp. on CGO*, 2003.
17. R. C. Whaley, A. Petitet, and J. J. Dongarra. Automated Empirical Optimization of Software and the ATLAS Project. *Parallel Computing*, 27(1–2):3–35, 2001.
18. M. Wolfe. Iteration Space Tiling for Memory Hierarchies. In *Third SIAM Conf. on Parallel Processing for Scientific Computing*, December 1987.
19. J. Xiong, J. Johnson, R. Johnson, and D. Padua. SPL: A Language and a Compiler for DSP Algorithms. In *Proc. of PLDI*, pages 298–308, 2001.
20. K. Yotov, X. Li, G. Ren, M. Cibulskis, G. DeJong, M.Garzaran, D. Padua, K. Pengali, P. Stodghill, and P. Wu. A Comparison of Empirical and Model-driven Optimization. *Proc. of PLDI*, pages 63–76, 2003.
21. K. Yotov, X. Li, G. Ren, M. J. Garzarán, D. Padua, K. Pingali, and P. Stodghill. Is Search Really Necessary to Generate a High Performance Blas? *In Proc. of the IEEE, special issue on Program Generation, Optimization, and Platform Adaptation*, 23:358–386, February 2005.

Testing Speculative Work in a Lazy/Eager Parallel Functional Language*

Alberto de la Encina, Ismael Rodríguez, and Fernando Rubio

Facultad Informática. Universidad Complutense de Madrid
C/. Prof. José García Santesmases, E-28040 Madrid. Spain
{albertoe,isrodrig,fernando}@sip.ucm.es

Abstract. Eden is a parallel extension of the functional language Haskell. Eden inherits from Haskell its *laziness*, which allows it to avoid unnecessary computations. However, in order to enable the parallel execution of processes in Eden, this feature must be disabled when new processes are instantiated. Hence, any newly created process can be *speculative*, as it is not known whether the computations it performs will actually be required for the overall computation. Therefore, the performance of a program may be affected by the unneeded speculation. In this paper we present a framework to compare the speculated computations of an Eden program with the computations it actually requires. Thus, the programmer is provided with a profiling tool allowing him to produce better programs where speculative work fits better the actual necessities.

1 Introduction

Parallel programming faces several specific challenges that are not met in sequential programming. The programmer of a sequential program defines a computation in terms of some subcomputations, and the coordination of them is trivially achieved because the order of subcomputations is implicitly given. However, the coordination of subcomputations in parallel programs increases their complexity. In this sense, the *functional* paradigm provides some advantages for the programmer. In particular, parallel functional languages are endowed with useful abstraction mechanisms like function composition and higher-order functions. The higher-order programming level provided by them allows to define the coordination of subcomputations in terms of the same constructions used in the rest of the program, which enables the definition and use of skeletons [2,3,7] to develop simpler parallel programs. Besides, since functional programs do not have *state*, side-effects are eliminated. So, the dependencies between processes are limited to obtaining the arguments needed to execute each function. These features ease the coordination issues and allow to define them in a natural way.

Several parallel functional languages have been proposed (see e.g. [20,7,17,19]). Among them, Eden has the interesting characteristic of requiring relatively low

* Work partially supported by the MCYT project TIC2003-07848-C02-01, the JCCLM project PAC-03-001, and the Marie Curie project MRTN-CT-2003-505121/TAROT.

E. Ayguadé et al. (Eds.): LCPC 2005, LNCS 4339, pp. 274–288, 2007.

programming effort to create programs with acceptable speedups (see [12]). Its main advantage is that it combines high-level constructions to simplify the development of parallel programs, and some controlled low-level constructions to allow increasing the efficiency. Eden extends the (lazy evaluation) functional language Haskell [15] by adding syntactic constructions for defining and instantiating processes. As a Haskell extension, Eden applies the *laziness* for deciding the computations to be executed in each moment. That is, a computation is performed only after it is detected that the result of that computation is required for continuing another computation that is already initiated. Let us note that pure laziness implies *sequential computation.* So, in order to allow parallel computations, Eden creates new processes *eagerly.* Moreover, any newly created process is able to perform computations in parallel before its creator actually demands the result for continuing its execution. This feature, which is necessary for enabling parallelism, may cause that a program performs some computations that turn out to be unneeded. In fact, Eden processes are *speculative*: They perform computations under the assumption that they will actually be needed.

The uncontrolled speculation may be a source of inefficiency in parallel programs. In order to achieve a better use of resources and a higher performance, the programmer should be provided with a measure of the *unnecessary speculation* of a program. In this paper we present a method for comparing the speculative computations and the computations actually needed in an Eden program. Basically, the method consists in comparing the data actually needed by a process and the speculative data evaluated by processes launched by this process.

Unfortunately, making a functional program to show the results of partial computations in some points is not easy. Let us remind that, contrarily to an imperative program, a functional program does not have *state.* Thus, the observation of partial computations cannot be based on observing how some variables change, because variables do not exist in functional environments. Besides, due to the laziness of Eden, the execution of a computation may turn out to be *unnecessary,* but a simple *observation* (e.g., writing a result in the screen or in a file) could create a false demand on such unneeded computation. Hence, observations must be defined in such a way that they produce a (neutral) result that is actually required only in the same situations as if the observations were not introduced. We will address this issue by using and extending *Hood* (*Haskell Object Observation Debugger* [5]). This tool allows a programmer to observe the behavior of a Haskell program by inserting some calls to an *observation function* in the program. The observation function records the value returned by a function in some point of the program, but without creating extra demand. These functions will be the basis of our method to compare the useful speculation and the actual speculation in an Eden program.

The rest of the paper is structured as follows. In the next section we sketch the Eden language. Then, in Section 3 we present the observation constructions of Hood. Next, in Section 4 we present our method to assess the unnecessary speculation in Eden programs. A case study is shown in Section 5, and related work in Section 6. Section 7 contains our conclusions and lines of future work.

2 The Eden Language

Eden [7,13] extends the lazy functional language Haskell [15] by adding syntactic constructs to explicitly define and instantiate processes. It is possible to define a new *process abstraction* `p` by using the following notation that relates the inputs and the outputs of the process: `p = process x -> e` , where variable `x` will be the input of the process, while the behavior of the process will be given by expression `e`. Process abstractions can be compared to functions, the main difference being that the former, when instantiated, are executed in parallel.

Process abstractions are not actual processes. To really create a process, a *process instantiation* is required. This is achieved by using the predefined infix operator `#`. Given a process abstraction and an input parameter, it creates a new process and returns the output of the process. Each time an expression `e1 # e2` is evaluated, the instantiating process will be responsible for evaluating and sending `e2`, while a new process is created to evaluate the application `(e1 e2)`.

Once a process is running, only fully evaluated data objects are communicated. The only exceptions are lists, which are transmitted in a *stream*-like fashion, i.e. element by element. Each list element is first evaluated to full normal form and then transmitted. Concurrent threads trying to access not yet available inputs are temporarily suspended. This is the only way in which Eden processes synchronize. Notice that process creation is explicit, but process communication (and synchronization) is completely implicit.

In contrast to most parallel functional languages, Eden also includes high-level constructions (not shown in the paper) both for developing *reactive* applications and for dynamically establishing direct connections between any pair of processes. This allows handling *low-level* parallel features that cannot be used in conventional functional languages. Thus, Eden provides an intermediate point between very high-level parallel functional languages (whose performance use to be poor), and classical parallel languages (which do not allow using high-level constructions). We do not claim that Eden can obtain optimal speedups, but it can obtain quite *acceptable* speedups with small programming effort (see e.g. [13,12]).

Eden's compiler (see `http://www.mathematik.uni-marburg.de/inf/eden`) has been developed by extending the most efficient Haskell compiler (GHC [14]). Hence, Eden's compiler reuses GHC's capabilities to interact with other programming languages. Thus, Eden can be used as a coordination language, while the sequential computation language can be, for instance, C.

To easily port the compiler to different architectures, the runtime system works on top of a message passing library (the user can choose PVM or MPI).

Eden Skeletons. Process abstractions in Eden are not just annotations, but first class values which can be manipulated by the programmer (passed as parameters, stored in data structures, and so on). This facilitates the definition of skeletons as higher order functions. Next, we illustrate, by using simple examples, how skeletons can be written in Eden. More complex skeletons can be found in [13,18].

The most simple skeleton is map. Given a list of inputs xs and a function f to be applied to each of them, the sequential specification in Haskell is as follows:

```
map f xs  =  [f x | x <- xs]
```

that can be read as *for each element* x *belonging to the list* xs*, apply function* f *to that element.* This can be trivially parallelized in Eden. In order to use a different process for each task, we will use the following approach:

```
map_par f xs =  [pf # x | x <- xs] `using` spine
  where pf = process x -> f x
```

The process abstraction pf wraps the function application (f x). It determines that the input parameter x as well as the result value will be transmitted through channels. The spine strategy (see [21] for details) is used to eagerly evaluate the spine of the process instantiation list. In this way, all processes are immediately created. Otherwise, they would only be created on demand.

Let us remark that it is not necessary to explicitly use constructions for synchronizing the processes. The main process initially sends a task to each of the *worker* processes of the map_par. Afterwards, as soon as any of the workers finishes its assignment, it automatically sends the result to the main process (by using PVM or MPI messages). When the main process has received all the results that it needs, it finishes the computation.

map_par is an essential primitive skeleton used to eagerly create a set of independent processes, but it can be easily improved by reducing the number of processes to be created. In a map_farm the number of processes to be created is fixed (for instance, it can be the number of processors), and tasks are evenly distributed into processes. The implementation firstly distributes the tasks among the processes, producing a list of lists where each inner list is to be executed by an independent process. Then, it applies map_par, and finally it collects the results joining the list of lists of results into a single list of results. Notice that, due to the laziness, these three tasks are not done sequentially, but in interleaving. As soon as any worker computes one of the outputs it is computing, it sends this subresult to the main process, and it goes on computing the next element of the output list. Notice that the communications are asynchronous, so that it is not necessary to wait for acknowledgments from the main process. When the main process has received all the needed results, it finishes the computation. The Eden source code of this skeleton is shown below, where not only the number np of processors but also the distribution and collection functions (unshuffle and shuffle respectively) are also parameters of the skeleton:

```
map_farm np unshuffle shuffle f xs
  = shuffle (map_par (map f) (unshuffle np xs))
```

Different strategies to split the work into the different processes can be used provided that, for every list xs, (shuffle (unshuffle np xs)) == xs.

Let us remark that developing skeletons in Eden is relatively easy. Due to the lack of space, we have only shown the simplest examples, but many others have already been implemented. Details about them can be found in [13].

3 Basic Hood

In this section we show the basic ideas behind Hood. The interested reader is referred to [5,4] for more details about it.

When debugging programs written in an imperative language, the programmer can explore not only the final result of the computation, but also the intermediate values stored in the variables being used by the program. Moreover, it is simple to trace how the value of each variable changes along time.

Let us remark that debugging lazy functional code has two main difficulties. First, lazy functional languages do not contain variables whose value change along time and that can be traced as in imperative languages. Second, introducing observations can modify the order of evaluation, affecting to the overall computation.

Fortunately, Hood allows the programmer to observe something similar to what can be observed in imperative environments. In fact, Hood allows the programmer to observe any intermediate structure appearing in a program. Moreover, we can also observe the evolution in time of the evaluation of the structures under observation.

In order to illustrate what kind of observations can be obtained by using Hood, let us consider an example. It will be complex enough to highlight important aspects of Hood, but also relatively simple to be easily understandable without requiring knowledge about Haskell. Given a natural number, the following Haskell function returns the list of digits of that number:[1]

```
natural :: Int -> [Int]
natural = reverse
          . map ('mod' 10)
          . takeWhile (/= 0)
          . iterate ('div' 10)
```

That is, `natural 3408` returns the list `3:4:0:8:[]`, where `[]` denotes the empty list and : denotes the list constructor. Note that, in order to compute the final result, three intermediate lists where produced in the following order:

```
-- after iterate
3408:340:34:3:0:_
-- after takeWhile
3408:340:34:3:[]
-- after map
8:0:4:3:[]
```

[1] The first line of the definition only provides the type declaration of the function: given an integer it returns a list of integers. The other four lines define the sequence of functions to be applied to obtain the overall effect, being `reverse` the last one to be applied. The higher-order function `iterate` applies infinite times the first function it receives. For instance, applying `iterate (+3) 1` returns the infinite list `1:4:7:10:13:...`

Notice that the first intermediate list is infinite, although only the first five elements are computed. As the rest of the list does not need to be evaluated, it is represented as _ (the underscore char).

By using Hood we can annotate the program in order to obtain the output shown before. In order to do that, we have to use the `observe` combinator that is the core of Hood. The type declaration of this combinator is: `observe :: String -> a -> a` . From the evaluation point of view, `observe` only returns its second value. That is, `observe s a = a`. However, as a side effect, the value associated to `a` will be squirrelled away, using the label `s`, in a file that will be analyzed after the evaluation finishes. It is important to remark that `observe` returns its second parameter in a completely lazy, demand driven manner. That is, the evaluation degree of `a` is not modified by introducing the observation, in the same way that it is not modified when applying the identity function `id`. Thus, as the evaluation degree is not modified, Hood can deal with infinite lists like the one appearing after applying `iterate ('div' 10)`.

If we consider again our previous example, we can observe all of the intermediate structures by introducing three observations as follows:

```
natural :: Int -> [Int]
natural = reverse
            . observe "after map"        . map ('mod' 10)
            . observe "after takeWhile"  . takeWhile (/= 0)
            . observe "after iterate"    . iterate ('div' 10)
```

After executing `natural 3408`, we will obtain the desired result. Hood does not only observe simple structures like those shown before. In fact, it can observe anything appearing in a Haskell program, including functions. For instance,

```
observe "length" length (4:2:5:[])
```

will generate the following observation:

```
-- length
   { \ (_:_:_:[]) -> 3 }
```

That is, we are observing a function that returns the number 3 (without evaluating the concrete elements appearing in the list) when it receives a list with three elements. Let us remark that it is only relevant the number of elements, but not the *concrete* elements. That is, the observation mechanism detects that the laziness of the language will not demand the concrete elements to compute the overall output. As it can be expected, higher-order functions can also be observed, but we do not show it due to lack of space.

4 Testing Speculation by Parallelizing Hood

In this section we present our method to assess the speculation of a parallel Eden program. The method is based on using the observation functionalities provided by Hood in specific points of the program under assessment. Let us recall that the application of `observe` to a term returns only the (partial) evaluation of the term that is actually *required* by other subcomputations in the context where `observe` is invoked. Hence, it gives us the (partial) term that is demanded in the context of the observation. When a process instantiates another process, the former process demands the computation of a term from the latter (from now on, *invoker* and *instantiated* processes, respectively). In order to perform our analysis, we need to consider the evaluation of this term at two different points. On the one hand, the observation of the term required by the invoker (in the context of the invoker) gives us the true necessities of the program at this point. On the other hand, the observation of the term constructed by the instantiated process (in the context of instantiated process) gives us the result of the speculated work performed by the instantiated process. By comparing both values, we can assess the amount of unnecessary speculation performed by the program at this point. In fact, if we obtain not only the final values of the term at both sides but also the order in which each part of the term is calculated, then we can infer not only the amount of unnecessary work but also the relative speeds of both parts. Hence, we can enrich the profiling capabilities of Eden.

4.1 A Simple Example

Let us consider a naïve but illustrative example. The following process generates the (infinite) list of primes greater than or equal to a given input number `n`. The process receives a natural number `n` as input, and produces a (potentially infinite) list of primes `outputs`:

```
pprimes = process n -> outputs
  where outputs = generatePrimes n
generatePrimes x = if (isPrime x) then x : restOfPrimes
                                  else restOfPrimes
  where restOfPrimes = generatePrimes (x+1)
```

The list of primes `outputs` is obtained by calling function `generatePrimes` with parameter `n`. Given any parameter `x`, this function firstly computes the (infinite) list of all the rest of primes, that is, the list of all primes greater than or equal to `x+1` (as we will see below, depending on the necessities of other external computations, only a finite part of the list might be computed). Then, `x` is added at the head of the list if `x` is prime or it is ignored otherwise.

Let us suppose that we are interested in using this process to obtain the shortest list of consecutive primes (greater than or equal to `initialNumber`) such that the multiplication of its elements is greater than or equal to a given minimal threshold `threshold`.[2] For example, given `initialNumber=2` and `threshold=26`, we wish to obtain `[2,3,5]` since $2 * 3 * 5 = 30$. The function `myComputation` performs this task:

[2] A similar functionality will be required in Section 5 to implement the `LinSolv` algorithm. In particular, it will be required to apply the Chinese Remainder Theorem.

```
myComputation initialNumber threshold = take neededNumber primes
  where primes   = pprimes # initialNumber
        products = scanl (*) 1 primes
        neededNumber = length (takeWhile (< threshold) products)
```

Let us explain how function `myComputation` works. The term `primes` represents the list of *all* primes from `initialNumber` on, and it is computed by instanting a new process that executes function `pprimes` with parameter `initial Number`. Fortunately, the rest of expressions used in the context of function `myComputation` will only demand a finite amount of elements of `primes`. Thus, the new process will not compute new primes forever. This is so because when the invoker process finishes the computation of function `myComputation`, the runtime system automatically terminates the instantiated process. The term `products` performs the multiplication of all elements in list `primes` by using function `scanl`. Function `scanl` applies a given binary operator to all the elements in a list. This is done by applying the function to each element in order and cumulating the partial result from each element to the next. An initial cumulated value is given as parameter. Function `scanl` returns a new list where the elements are the cumulated values after each element in the input list is applied. For instance, `scanl (*) 1 [2,3,5]` returns the list `[1,2,6,30]`. The term `neededNumber` computes the number of elements in `products` that are below `threshold`. Since the ith element in `products` provides the multiplication of the first i primes of `primes`, `neededNumber` gives us the number of elements needed in list `primes`. The number `neededNumber` is calculated by taking the list of the elements of `products` below `threshold` and computing its length. Finally, the output of `myComputation` is given by taking `neededNumber` elements from the list `primes`.

Let us remark that the aim of the previous program is not to provide an efficient parallel solution, but to serve as a simple but illustrative basis to develop a first approach to our method. In particular, we will use the previous example to study the speculative work performed by the instantiated process to compute the function `pprimes`. Although this process is devoted to produce an infinite list of numbers, not all of them will be actually required. However, we do not know in advance how many elements of the list will be actually required. We are interested in comparing the amount of primes used by the process that executes the function `myComputation` with the amount of primes computed by the process that runs the function `pprimes`. In fact, all primes calculated by `pprimes` that are higher than the last prime used by `myComputation` are the result of the *unnecessary* speculated work, because these primes are useless for the program necessities. Let us note that a programmer is not likely to properly assess the amount of unnecessary speculative work of this program in advance, because the time required by each process to perform each operation depends on several uncontrollable factors. Actually, both involved processes will race each other to perform their computations. Hence, if their relative speed is unbalanced (in any of both senses) then the overall performance of the program will fall.

Next we show how the previous program can be modified to provide the required information. The modification will be based on introducing observations that will report the computation/use of the list of primes in both processes. First, let us consider the instantiated process. In order to observe the list of primes that is produced by this process, we just need to observe the list that it returns to its invoker. The term to be returned is now replaced by a new expression. It returns the same value to the invoker, but only after any change on the evaluation of `outputs` is properly reported to a log file with a suitable tag (`outsFromProcess`). So, though the introduction of the observation is innocuous for the overall computation, the required profiling information will be obtained:

```
pprimes = process n -> (observe "outsFromProcess" outputs)
  where outputs = generatePrimes n
```

Let us consider the instantiated process. In order to minimize the number of requests between invoker processes and instantiated processes, any value computed by an instantiated process is immediately sent to the invoker in Eden. This means that all primes computed by the instantiated process are locally available for being used by the invoker. However, let us note that the laziness is locally applied in each process in Eden. Hence, the number of primes *obtained* by the invoker (i.e., actually *taken* from those received by the communication channel) perfectly matches its necessities, and no unneeded prime is used. So, by observing the list of primes obtained by the invoker from the instantiated process, we can calculate the true necessities of this process. Any change in this list will be reported in a file with the tag `insFromProcess`:

```
myComputation initialNumber threshold = take neededNumber primes
 where primes = observe "insFromProcess" (pprimes # initialNumber)
       products = scanl (*) 1 primes
       neededNumber = length (takeWhile (< threshold) products)
```

After running the program using 327 and 49472453 as inputs in a two-processors environment, our observations inform us that `outsFromProcess` has 37 entries, while `insFromProcess` has only 4. That is, 33 unnecessary primes where computed by the auxiliary process in our naïve example.

4.2 General Scheme

In the previous example, the speculative work was performed by the instantiated process. However, this could be the other way around: The invoker process instantiates a new process and afterwards produces some values that this new process may or may not need. The values demanded by the instantiated processes are its *parameters*. In this case, the instantiated process takes the values computed by the invoker as long as it needs them, and the speculative work is performed by the invoker process. Let us note that the application of our method to this case is similar to that shown in the previous example. Actually, the method developed in the previous example can be generalized to deal with any scenario where the speculative work of some processes has to be assessed. Next we present a redefinition of the basic Eden constructors. This redefinition performs all the required tracing issues in such a way that the programmer can forget any details concerning observations: He must just instantiate the processes he wants to analyze by calling the functions provided by the new constructors and introducing his function as parameter. Then, the system automatically reports any change on both its input and its output. By applying the new observation constructors to both an invoker and an instantiated process, all the needed information will be properly reported. Thus, if we want to observe the inputs and outputs of a process that computes a given function `f` then, instead of directly using `f`, we will call the following function `processObs` using `f` as parameter:

```
processObs f = process ins -> (observe "outsFromProcess" outs)
          where outs = f ins'
                ins' = observe "insToProcess" ins
```

The previous function defines a process with input `ins`. In order to observe the data that this new process receives from its creator and it actually *requires*, this parameter is observed by the second observation in the previous definition, labelled by `insToProcess`. After function `f` is normally applied to the input, the output `outs` is obtained. The observation of this term (first observation, labelled by `outsFromProcess`) reports the data this process transmits to its creator.

The previous function allows us to observe the treatment of inputs and outputs of the instantiated process. Similarly, we need a new functionality to observe the behavior of the invoker process. Next we redefine the process instantiation operator to include the observation capabilities. The new operator, based on the standard operator `#`, is `##`:

```
p ## actualParameters =
  observe "insFromProcess"
          (p # (observe "outsToProcess" actualParameters))
```

The new operator allows any process to instantiate a new process by using the standard one. Besides, two observations are introduced to report the inputs and outputs that the invoker process exchanges with the new process. Observations labelled by `insFromProcess` report the data that the invoker receives (and actually requires) from the newly instantiated process. Observations labelled by `outsToProcess` report the data that is sent from the invoker to the instantiated process (regardless of whether the instantiated process requires them).

The use of both new constructors leads to the general scheme depicted in Figure 4.2. By combining the new process abstractions `processObs` and `##` we obtain four relevant data. These data provide us with two critical measures concerning the usefulness of the speculation at this point of the program. On the one hand, the difference between `outsFromProcess` and `insFromProcess` gives us how much unnecessary speculative work was done by the new process. On the other hand, the difference between `outsToProcess` and `insToProcess`

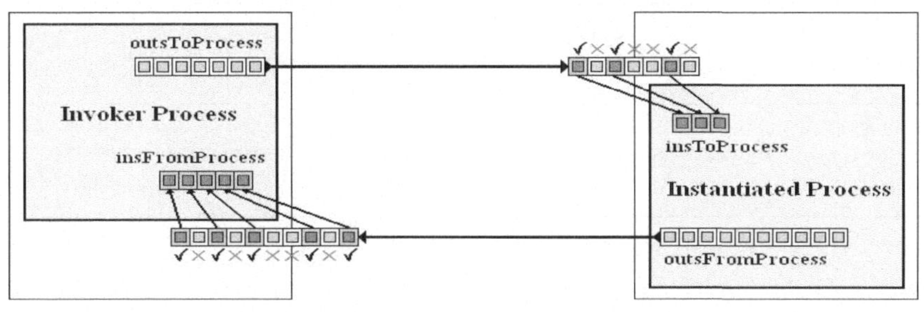

Fig. 1. Invoker and Instantiated Processes

provides us a measure to know how much unnecessary speculative work was performed by the process creating the new instantiation.

Let us note that the definitions of `processObs` and `##` could be trivially extended to include extra parameters representing the strings that want to be used for marking the inputs and outputs of the processes. Moreover, the framework can be easily applied to other general schemes and programming structures in Eden. In particular, all the skeletons defined in the Eden library can be trivially rewritten in terms of the new process abstraction and process instantiation operators. Hence, they inherit the capability to test the amount of speculative work.

5 Case Study: LinSolv

The `linSolv` algorithm finds an exact solution of a linear system of equations of the form $Ax = b$ where $A \in \mathbb{Z}^{n \times n}, b \in \mathbb{Z}^n, n \in \mathbb{N}$. In contrast to more common numerical algorithms, which usually produce an approximate solution over floating point numbers for a given accuracy, the algorithm presented here finds an exact solution and works over arbitrary precision integers.

To find an exact solution for a given system of equations, `linSolv` uses a *multiple homomorphic images* approach [9]. This is a common computer algebra approach and consists of the following three stages: (1) map the input data into several homomorphic images; (2) compute the solution in each of these images; and (3) combine the results of all images to a result in the original domain.

This structure is particularly useful for operations on arbitrary precision integers. In this case the original domain is $\mathbb{Z}$, the set of all integer values, and the homomorphic images are $\mathbb{Z}$ modulo p, written $\mathbb{Z}_p$, with p being a prime number. If the input numbers are very big and each prime number fits into one machine word the basic arithmetic in the homomorphic images is cheap because fixed precision arithmetic can be used. Only in the combination phase, when applying a fold-based Chinese Remainder Algorithm (CRA) (see [10]), expensive arbitrary precision arithmetic has to be used to construct the result values.

Details about the implementation of `linSolv` in Haskell can be found in [12]. In brief, the main part to be parallelized consists in solving each of the homomorphic images, whose basic definition is: `xList = map get_homSol primes`

```
xList_all = map_farm get_homSol primes

xList = filter lucky xList_all
```

Fig. 2. Parallel `linSolv` (Eden speculative version)

```
xList_all = map_rw get_homSol primes

xList = filter lucky xList_all
xList_unlucky = filter (not.lucky) xList_all

(p_needed, p_spec) = splitAt ( 1 + toInt noOfPrimes) primes
primes' = p_needed ++ (additional xList_unlucky p_spec)

additional :: [Integer] -> [Integer] -> [Integer]
additional xs ys = zipWith (\ x y -> y) xs ys
```

Fig. 3. Parallel `linSolv` (Eden conservative version)

where `primes` is an infinite list of primes, and `get_homSol` solves the system modulo a given prime. Thus, the basic parallel structure of the algorithm consists in performing all computations in the homomorphic images in parallel. It uses LU-decomposition followed by forward and backsubstitution to compute the solution `pmx` in the homomorphic image [16]. From a speculation point of view, the main difficulty in the parallelization is that we have to make sure that new results are computed if primes turn out to be "unlucky", i.e. if the determinant of the input matrix A in the homomorphic image generated by this prime number is zero. Let us remark that this is similar to the naïve example we showed in the previous section. However, in this case the task of the processes is not only to create primes, but also to solve a linear system modulo that prime.

Even though the situation now is more complex than in the example of the previous section, our strategy to check how much useless work is done is the same. As we have to solve the linear system modulo several prime numbers, the most obvious parallel scheme is to use a `map_par` scheme as shown in Section 2, so that an independent process is created for each prime. However, as we commented in Section 2, it is better to use a `map_farm` to avoid creating too many processes. So, in our first approach (shown in Figure 2) we just replaced the top level `map` by its parallel counterpart `map_farm`. Unfortunately, when using the `map_farm` version that includes observations, our tools detected a quite big amount of useless work, that reduced considerably the overall speedup.

As a second approach, to avoid the potential waste of resources due to speculation we used a *conservative version* as shown in Figure 3. In this version the prime numbers are divided into those known to be needed (`p_needed`) and those which are only needed if some of the earlier primes are unlucky (`p_spec`). The function `additional` adds for each unlucky prime a new prime number to the task list `primes'`. Note in the definition of `additional` that, due to the demand-driven evaluation, the availability of unlucky primes in `xs` triggers the generation of one result element in `ys`. With this conservative version, the amount of useless

```
xList_all = map_rw get_homSol primes

xList = filter lucky xList_all
```

Fig. 4. Parallel `linSolv` (Eden semi-speculative version)

work was zero. Unfortunately, this does not necessarily implies optimal speedups. The problem is that we had avoided useless work, but at the cost of forcing processes to stop for a while each time they finish a task. So, tough the speedups were better than before, there was still free room for improvement.

Finally, we used a third solution where speculation was restricted but not completely avoided. In this sense, we used a variation of the task farm skeleton as outlined in Section 2. More specifically, we used the replicated workers paradigm. A manager and a set of worker processes are created, and two tasks are initially released to each of the workers. As soon as any worker finishes a task, it sends the result to the manager, and a new task is delivered to the worker. The computation in the manager is demand-driven and triggered by the availability of result values. As soon as the manager has all the needed results it terminates all the worker processes. Notice that in this *semi-speculative version* the workers may be working speculatively on useless tasks, but only when the useful tasks have already been consumed and hence the degree of speculation is tightly limited. More details about the replicated workers skeleton can be found in [8]. Figure 4 shows the Eden code for the semi-speculative version of `linSolv`. The only modification to the sequential code is the use of a parallel replicated workers map (`map_rw`) instead of a sequential map over the infinite list of primes. By using this new version, only a few useless messages where sent. That is, the speculation was actually controlled.

Finally, we illustrate the speedups that can be obtained with Eden, by running the semi-speculative version on a concrete parallel machine. We run the experiments on a 32-node Beowulf cluster consisting of workstations with a 533 MHz Celeron processor, 128 Kb cache and 128 MB of DRAM. The workstations are connected through a 100Mb/s fast Ethernet switch with a latency of 142 μs, measured under PVM 3.4.2. The sequential runtime in this environment was 491.7s. In this environment, an acceptable speedup of 14 is achieved with 16 nodes. For the input data used in these measurements 45 useful and 39 unlucky primes are generated. This leads to a total of 45 top level threads, one for each homomorphic image.

6 Related Work

In addition to Hood, during the last years there have been several proposals for incorporating execution traces to sequential lazy functional languages. In particular, we can highlight the work done with Hat, HsDebug, and the declarative debuggers Freja and Buddha. The approaches followed in each of them are quite different, both from the point of view of the user of the system and from the implementation point of view. From the user point of view, Freja and Buddha are question-answer systems that directs the programmer to the cause of an incorrect value, while Hat allows the user to travel backwards from a value along the redex history leading to it. The interested reader can found a detailed comparison between Freja, Hat and Hood in [1].

Regarding parallel functional profilers, we can highlight GranSim [11] and its derivatives (GranSP and GranCC). GranSim is a GpH [20] simulator. This system provides an accurate and flexible way of studying the dynamic behaviour of GpH programs. It supports extensive tuning of the simulated architecture, having parameters such as number of processors, communication latencies, and others. Additionally, an ideal simulation mode allowing an unlimited number of processors is provided.

Paradise [6] is an adaptation of GranSim to deal with Eden programs. Currently, Eden programers can obtain feedback from Paradise in order to improve the performance of their programs. In this sense, they can detect bottlenecks in the distribution of work. However, it lacks the possibility to check the amount of speculation done by the programs. Thus, the approach presented in this paper constitutes a complement to the profiling capabilities presented in Paradise.

7 Conclusions and Future Work

In this paper we have extended the parallel functional language Eden with capabilities to test how much useless work has been performed in a given execution. Since the core sequential part of Eden uses lazy evaluation while some parallel constructions of it require the use of strict evaluation, we have designed a tool to compare how much data was actually needed (known because of the lazy part of the language) and how much data was actually transmitted (known because of the eager parallel part of the language).

We have rewritten the basic constructions of the language to include facilities for testing the amount of speculative work, and we have also rewritten skeleton libraries so that we can test the amount of speculation of any program written by using skeletons. In fact, we have tested the tool with a concrete case study that consists in solving a linear system of equations.

Currently, our tools only provide textual information about the amount of speculation, and this is the reason why we do not show examples of outputs of the tool in this paper. However, we are working on the implementation of a graphical interface to show not only the amount of speculation, but also the evolution in time of the speculation of the program. This can be done by recording also time-information about the observations. Thus, the implementation of this graphical tool and the application of the framework to a wider set of examples constitute our current lines of work.

References

1. O. Chitil, C. Runciman, and M. Wallace. Freja, Hat and Hood — a comparative evaluation of three systems for tracing and debugging lazy functional programs. In *IFL'00*, LNCS 2011, pages 176–193. Springer-Verlag, 2001.

2. M. Cole. *Algorithmic Skeletons: Structure Management of Parallel Computations.* MIT Press, 1989. Research Monographs in Parallel and Distributed Computing.
3. M. Cole. Bringing skeletons out of the closet: A pragmatic manifesto for skeletal parallel programming. *Parallel Computing*, 30:389–406, 2004.
4. A. Encina, L. Llana, and F. Rubio. Formalizing the debugging process in Haskell. In *International Conference on Theoretical Aspects of Computing, ICTAC'05*, LNCS 3722, pages 211–226. Springer-Verlag, 2005.
5. A. Gill. Debugging Haskell by observing intermediate data structures. In *Proceedings of the 4th Haskell Workshop.* Tech. Rep. University of Nottingham, 2000.
6. F. Hernández, R. Peña, and F. Rubio. From GranSim to Paradise. In *Scottish Functional Programming Workshop, SFP'99*, pages 11–19. Intellect, 2000.
7. U. Klusik, R. Loogen, S. Priebe, and F. Rubio. Implementation skeletons in Eden: Low-effort parallel programming. In *Implementation of Functional Languages, IFL'00*, LNCS 2011, pages 71–88. Springer-Verlag, 2001.
8. U. Klusik, R. Peña, and F. Rubio. Replicated workers in Eden. In *Constructive Methods for Parallel Programming, CMPP'00*, pages 143–164. Nova Science, 2000.
9. M. Lauer. Computing by homomorphic images. In *Computer Algebra — Symbolic and Algebraic Computation*, pages 139–168. Springer-Verlag, 1982.
10. J. D. Lipson. Chinese remainder and interpolation algorithms. In *Symposium on Symbolic and Algebraic Manipulation, SYMSAM'71*, pages 372–391. Academic Press, 1971.
11. H. W. Loidl. Gransim user's guide. Department of Computing Science. University of Glasgow, 1996.
12. H. W. Loidl, F. Rubio, N. Scaife, K. Hammond, S. Horiguchi, U. Klusik, R. Loogen, G. J. Michaelson, R. Peña, Á. J. Rebón Portillo, S. Priebe, and P. W. Trinder. Comparing parallel functional languages: Programming and performance. *Higher-Order and Symbolic Computation*, 16(3):203–251, 2003.
13. R. Loogen, Y. Ortega-Mallén, R. Peña, S. Priebe, and F. Rubio. Parallelism abstractions in Eden. In F. A. Rabhi and S. Gorlatch, editors, *Patterns and Skeletons for Parallel and Distributed Computing*, pages 95–128. Springer-Verlag, 2002.
14. S. L. Peyton Jones. Compiling Haskell by program transformation: A report from the trenches. In *European Symposium on Programming, ESOP'96*, LNCS 1058, pages 18–44. Springer-Verlag, 1996.
15. S. L. Peyton Jones and J. Hughes. Report on the programming language Haskell 98. Technical report, February 1999. `http://www.haskell.org`.
16. W. Press, S. Teukolsky, W. Vetterling, and B. Flannery. *Numerical Recipes in C: The Art of Scientific Computing*, chapter LU Decomposition and Its Applications. Cambridge University Press, 2nd Edition, 1992.
17. R.F. Pointon P.W. Trinder, H.W. Loidl. Parallel and distributed Haskells. *Journal of Functional Programming*, 12(4-5):469–510, 2002.
18. F. Rubio and I. Rodríguez. A parallel framework for computational science. In *International Conference on Computational Science, ICCS'03*, LNCS 2658, pages 1002–1011. Springer-Verlag, 1998.
19. N. Scaife, Horiguchi S., G. Michaelson, and P. Bristow. A parallel SML compiler based on algorithmic skeletons. *J. Functional Programming*, 15(4):615–650, 2005.
20. P. W. Trinder, K. Hammond, J. S. Mattson Jr., A. S. Partridge, and S. L. Peyton Jones. GUM: a portable parallel implementation of Haskell. In *Programming Language Design and Implementation, PLDI'96*, pages 79–88. ACM Press, 1996.
21. P. W. Trinder, K. Hammond, H-W. Loidl, and S. L. Peyton Jones. Algorithm + Strategy = Parallelism. *Journal of Functional Programming*, 8(1):23–60, 1998.

Loop Selection for Thread-Level Speculation

Shengyue Wang, Xiaoru Dai, Kiran S. Yellajyosula,
Antonia Zhai, and Pen-Chung Yew

Department of Computer Science and Engineering
University of Minnesota
Minneapolis, MN 55455, USA
{shengyue, dai, kiran, zhai, yew}@cs.umn.edu

Abstract. Thread-level speculation (TLS) allows potentially dependent threads to speculatively execute in parallel, thus making it easier for the compiler to extract parallel threads. However, the high cost associated with unbalanced load, failed speculation, and inter-thread value communication makes it difficult to obtain the desired performance unless the speculative threads are carefully chosen.

In this paper, we focus on extracting parallel threads from loops in general-purpose applications because loops, with their regular structures and significant coverage on execution time, are ideal candidates for extracting parallel threads. General-purpose applications, however, usually contain a large number of nested loops with unpredictable parallel performance and dynamic behavior, thus making it difficult to decide which set of loops should be parallelized to improve overall program performance. Our proposed loop selection algorithm addresses all these difficulties. We have found that (i) with the aid of profiling information, compiler analyses can achieve a reasonably accurate estimation of the performance of parallel execution, and that (ii) different invocations of a loop may behave differently, and exploiting this dynamic behavior can further improve performance. With a judicious choice of loops, we can improve the overall program performance of SPEC2000 integer benchmarks by as much as 20%.

1 Introduction

Microprocessors that support multiple threads of execution are becoming increasingly common [1, 13, 14]. Yet how to make the most effective use of such processors is still unclear. One attractive method of fully utilizing such resources is to automatically extract parallel threads from existing programs. However, automatic parallelization [4, 10] for general-purpose applications (e.g., compilers, spreadsheets, games, etc.) is difficult because of pointer aliasing, irregular array accesses, and complex control flow. Thread-level speculation (TLS) [3, 6, 9, 11, 16, 22, 24, 26] facilitates the parallelization of such applications by allowing potentially dependent threads to execute in parallel while maintaining the original sequential semantics of the programs through runtime checking. Although researchers have proposed numerous techniques for providing the proper hardware [17, 18, 23, 25] and compiler [27-29] support for improving the efficiency of TLS, how to provide adequate compiler support for decomposing

E. Ayguadé et al. (Eds.): LCPC 2005, LNCS 4339 , pp. 289 – 303, 2007.

sequential programs into parallel threads that can deliver the desired performance has not yet been explored with the proper depth. In this paper, we present a detailed investigation of extracting speculative threads from loops for general-purpose applications.

Loops are attractive candidates for extracting thread-level parallelism, as programs spend significant amounts of time executing instructions within loops, and the regular structure of loops makes it relatively easy to determine (i) the beginning and the end of a thread (i.e., each iteration corresponds to a single thread of execution) and (ii) the inter-thread data dependences. Thus it is not surprising that most previous research on TLS has focused on exploiting loop-level parallelism. However, general-purpose applications typically contain a large number of potentially nested loops, and thus deciding which loops should be parallelized for the best program performance is not always clear. We have found 7800 loops from 11 benchmarks in the SPEC2000 integer benchmarks; among these, *gcc* contains more than 2600 loops. Thus it is necessary to derive a systematic approach to automatically select loops to parallelize for these applications.

It is difficult for a compiler to determine whether a loop can speed up under TLS, as the performance of the loop depends on (i) the characteristics of the underlying hardware, such as thread creation overhead, inter-thread value communication latency, and mis-speculation penalties, and (ii) the characteristics of the parallelized loops, such as the size of iterations, the number of iterations, and the inter-thread data dependence. While detailed profiling information and complex estimations can potentially improve the accuracy of estimation, it is not clear whether these techniques will lead to an overall better selection of loops.

When loops are nested, we can parallelize at only one loop nest level. We say that loop B is nested within loop A when loop B is syntactically nested within loop A or when A invokes a procedure that contains loop B. On average, we observe that the SPEC2000 integer benchmarks have a nesting depth of 8. Figure 1 shows that straightforward solutions that always parallelize the innermost or the outermost loops do not always deliver the desired performance. Therefore a judicious decision must be made to select the proper nest level to parallelize.

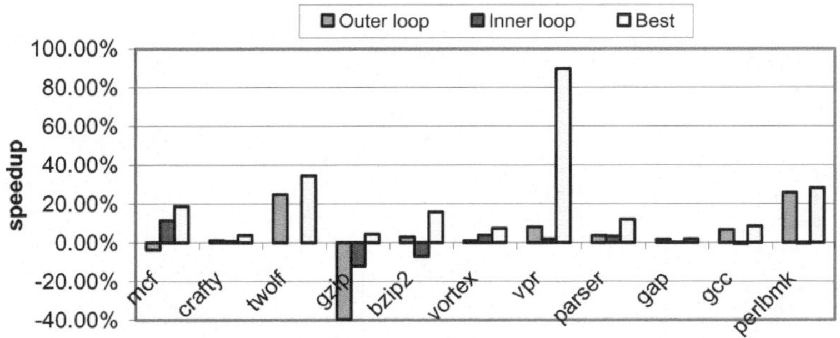

Fig. 1. Performance comparison of simple loop selection techniques

Furthermore, different invocations of the same static loop may have different behaviors. For instance, a parallelized loop may speed up relative to the sequential execution in some invocations but slow down in others. We refer to this behavior as *context sensitivity*. Exploiting this behavior and parallelizing a loop invocation only if that particular invocation is likely to speed up can potentially offer additional performance benefit.

This paper makes the following contributions. First, we propose a loop selection algorithm that decides which loops should be parallelized to improve overall performance for a program with a large number of nested loops. Second, we find that compiler analyses can achieve a reasonably accurate performance prediction of parallel execution. And third, we observe that exploiting dynamic loop behavior can further improve this performance. Overall, by making a judicious choice in selecting loops, we can improve the performance of SPEC2000 integer benchmarks by 20%.

The rest of this paper is organized as follows. In Section 2, we describe a loop selection algorithm that selects the optimal set of loops if the parallel performance of a loop can be accurately predicted. In Section 3, we describe our experimental framework. Three performance estimation techniques are discussed and evaluated in Section 4. We investigate the impact of context sensitivity in Section 5. We discuss related work in Section 6 and present our conclusions in Section 7.

2 Loop Selection Algorithm

In this section, we present a loop selection algorithm that chooses a set of loops to parallelize while maximizing overall program performance. The algorithm takes as input the speedup and coverage of all the loops in a program and outputs an optimal set of loops for parallelization.

2.1 Loop Graph

The main constraint in loop selection is that there should be no nesting relation between any two selected loops. To capture the nesting relation between loops, we construct a directed acyclic graph (DAG) called a *loop graph*. As shown in Figure 2(b),

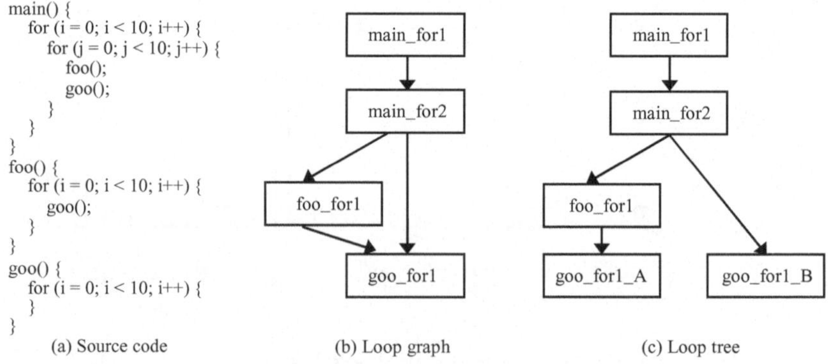

(a) Source code (b) Loop graph (c) Loop tree

Fig. 2. Examples of loop graph and loop tree

each node in the graph represents a static loop in the original program, and a directed edge represents the nesting relation between two loops. Loops could have a direct nesting relation or an indirect nesting relation through procedure calls. In this example, the edge from *main_for1* to *main_for2* indicates direct nesting, while the edge from *main_for2* to *foo_for1* indicates indirect nesting.

A recursive call introduces a cycle in the loop graph that violates the acyclic property. But cycles can be broken if we can identify backward edges. An edge from node s to node t is a backward edge if every path that reaches s from the root passes through t. All backward edges are removed once they are detected. If no backward edge is detected, we arbitrarily select an edge and remove it to break the cycle.

A loop graph, like a call graph, can be constructed through runtime profiling or compiler static inter-procedure analysis. In this study, it is built upon efficiently collected runtime profiles.

2.2 Selection Criterion

We cannot simultaneously select any two loops that have nesting relations. To decide which loop to select, we use a criterion called *benefit* that considers both speedup and coverage of a loop. It is defined as follows:

$$benefit = coverage \times (1 - 1 / speedup) \quad (1)$$

The benefit value indicates the overall performance gain that can be obtained by parallelizing that loop. A loop with a larger benefit value is more likely to be selected. The benefit value is additive, as there is no nesting relationship between the selected loops. The speedup for the whole program can be computed directly from the benefit value as follows:

$$program\ speedup = 1 / (1 - benefit) \quad (2)$$

2.3 Loop Selection Problem

The general loop selection problem can be stated as follows: given a loop graph with benefit value attached to each node, find a set of nodes that maximizes the overall benefits such that there is no path between any two selected nodes.

We transform this loop selection problem into a well-known NP-complete problem, weighted maximum independent set problem [8], by computing the transitive closure of the loop graph. A set of nodes is called an independent set if there is no edge between any two of them.

2.4 Graph Pruning

The general loop selection problem is NP-complete, so that an exhaustive search algorithm only works for a graph with few nodes. For a graph with hundreds or thousands of nodes, which is common for most of the benchmarks that we are studying, a more efficient heuristic has to be used. Because a heuristic-based algorithm only gives a sub-optimal solution, we must use it wisely. By applying a technique called *graph pruning,* we can find a reasonable approximation more efficiently. Graph pruning simplifies the loop graph by eliminating those loops that will not be selected as speculative threads. These would include such loops as: (i) loops that have less than 100 dynamic instructions on average, as they are more appropriate for instruction-level parallelism (ILP); (ii) loops that have no more than 2 iterations on average, as they are more likely to underutilize multiple processor resources; and (iii) loops that are predicted to slow down the program execution if parallelized.

Graph pruning reduces the size of a loop graph by eliminating unsuitable loops. After we delete unnecessary nodes, one single connected graph is split into multiple small disjointed sub-graphs. Then we can apply selection algorithm to each sub-graph independently. It is efficient to use exhaustive searching algorithm for small sub-graphs. For larger sub-graphs, heuristic-based searching algorithm usually gives a reasonable approximation.

2.5 Exhaustive Searching Algorithm

In this simple algorithm, we exhaustively try every set of independent loops to find the one that provides the maximum benefit. For each computed independent loop set, we track all loops that have nesting relations to any loop within this independent set and record them in a vector called a *conflict vector*. By using a conflict vector, it is easy to find a new independent loop to add into the current independent set. After a new loop is added, the conflict vector is updated as well.

An exhaustive searching algorithm gives an accurate solution for the loop selection problem, but is very inefficient. Graph pruning creates smaller sub-graphs that are suitable for exhaustive searching that works efficiently for sub-graphs with fewer than 50 nodes in our experiments.

2.6 Heuristic-Based Searching Algorithm

Even after graph pruning, some sub-graphs are still very big. For those, we use a heuristic-based algorithm. We first sort all the nodes in a sub-graph according to their benefit values. Then we pick one node at a time and add it into the independent set such that the node has the maximal benefit value and it does not conflict with already selected nodes. Similarly to the exhaustive searching algorithm, we maintain a conflict vector for the selected independent set and update it whenever a new node is added.

Although this simple greedy algorithm gives a sub-optimal solution, it can select a set of independent loops from a large graph in polynomial time. In our experiments, the size of sub-graph is less than 200 nodes after graph pruning, so the inaccuracy introduced by this algorithm is negligible.

3 Experimental Framework

We implement the loop selection algorithm in the Code Generation phase of the ORC compiler [2], which is an industrial-strength open-source compiler based on the Pro64 compiler and targeting on Intel's Itanium Processor Family (IPF).

For each selected loop, the compiler inserts special instructions to mark the beginning and the end of parallel loops. Fork instruction is inserted at the beginning of the loop body. We optimize inter-thread value communication using the techniques described in [28, 29]. The compiler synchronizes all inter-thread register dependences and memory dependences with a probability greater than 20%. Both intra-thread control and data speculation are used for more aggressive instruction scheduling so as to increase the overlap between threads.

Our execution-driven simulator is built upon Pin [15]. The configuration of our simulated machine model is listed in Table 1. We simulate four single-issue in-order processors. Each of them has a private L1 data cache, a write buffer, an address buffer, and a communication buffer. The write buffer holds the speculatively modified data within a thread. The address buffer keeps all memory addresses accessed by a speculative thread. The communication buffer stores data forwarded by the previous thread. All four processors share a L2 data cache.

Table 1. Machine configuration

Issue Width	1
L1-D Cache	32K, 2-way, 1 cycle
L2-D Cache	2M, 4-way, 10 cycles
Write Buffer	32K, 2-way, 1 cycle
Address Buffer	32K, 2-way, 1 cycle
Communication Buffer	128 entries, 1 cycle
Communication Delay	10 cycles
Thread Spawning Overhead	10 cycles
Thread Squashing Overhead	10 cycles
Main Memory	50 cycles

Table 2. Benchmark statistics

Program	Number of Loops	Average Loop Iteration Size	Maximal Nest Depth
mcf	51	29,605	4
crafty	420	59,775	10
twolf	899	12,437	7
gzip	178	206,755	6
bzip2	163	109,227	9
vortex	212	45,179	7
vpr	401	1,500	5
parser	532	8,820	10
gap	1,655	53,721	10
gcc	2,619	5,394	10
perlbmk	729	2,826	10

3.1 Benchmarks

We study all the SPEC2000 integer benchmarks except for eon, which is written in C++. The statistics for each benchmark are listed in Table 2. The average loop iteration size is measured by using the *ref* input set and counting dynamic instructions. Most of the benchmarks have a large set of loops with complex loop nesting, which makes it difficult, if not impossible, to select loops without a systematic approach.

3.2 Simulation Methodology

All simulation is performed using the *ref* input set. To save simulation time, we parallelize and simulate each loop once. After applying a selection technique, we directly use the simulation result to calculate the overall program performance. In this way, we avoid simulating the same loop multiple times if it is selected by different techniques.

Moreover, we use a simple sampling method to further speed up the simulation. For each loop, we select the first 50 invocations for simulation. For each invocation, we simulate the first 50 iterations. This simple sampling method allows us to simulate up to 6 billion dynamic instructions while covering all loops.

4 Loop Speedup Estimation

Our goal in loop selection is to maximize the overall program performance, which is represented as the benefit value of the selected loops. In order to calculate the benefit value for each loop, we have to estimate both the coverage and speedup of each loop. Coverage can be estimated using a runtime profile. To estimate speedup, we have to estimate both sequential and parallel execution time.

We assume that each processor executes one instruction per cycle, i.e., each instruction takes one cycle to finish. It is relatively easy to estimate sequential execution time T_{seq} of a loop. We can determine the average size of a thread (average number of instructions executed per iteration) and the average number of parallel threads (average number of times a loop iterates) by using a profile. T_{seq} can be approximated by using equation (3), where S is the average thread size and N is the average number of threads.

$$T_{seq} = S \times N \tag{3}$$

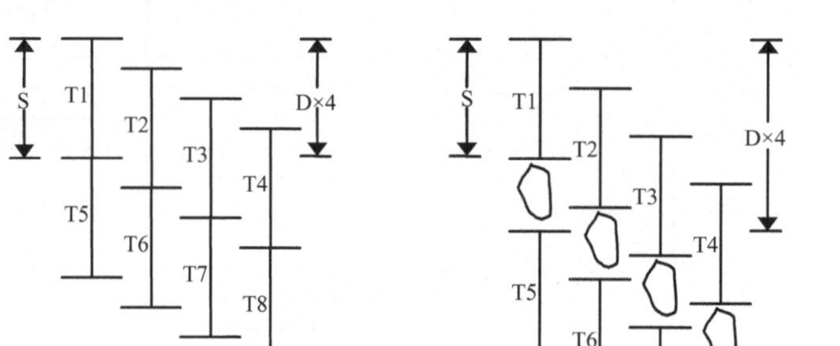

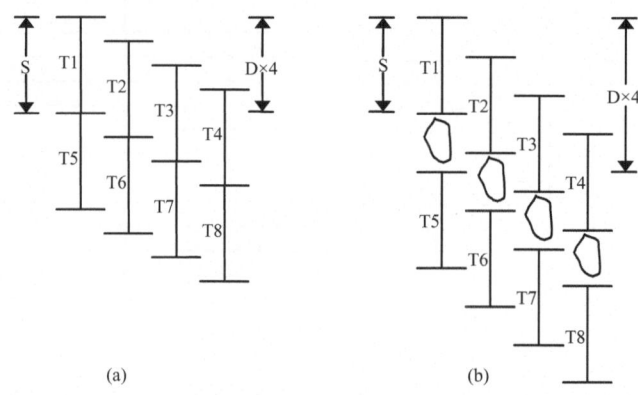

Fig. 3. Impact of delay D assuming 4 processors

On the other hand, the parallel execution time depends on other factors such as the thread creation overhead, the cost of inter-thread value communication, and the cost of mis-speculation. We simplify the calculation by dividing the total parallel execution time T_{par} into two parts: perfect execution time $T_{perfect}$ and mis-speculation time $T_{misspec}$. $T_{perfect}$ is the parallel execution time on p processors assuming that there is no mis-speculation. $T_{misspec}$ is the wasted execution time due to mis-speculation.

$$T_{par} = T_{perfect} + T_{misspec} \tag{4}$$

We also define delay D as the delay between two consecutive threads caused by inter-thread value communication T_{comm} and thread creation overhead O.

$$D = max(T_{comm}, O) \tag{5}$$

Depending on the delay D, we use different equations to estimate $T_{perfect}$. If D S / p, we can have a perfect pipelined execution of threads, as shown in Figure 3(a), and use equation (6) for estimation.

$$T_{perfect} = ((N-1) / p + 1) \times S + ((N-1) \bmod p) \times D \tag{6}$$

If $D > S / p$, delay D causes bubbles in the pipelined execution of threads and has a higher impact on the overall execution time, as shown in Figure 3(b). In this case, we use equation (7) for estimation.

$$T_{perfect} = (N - 1) \times D + S \tag{7}$$

The key to accurately predicting speedup is how to estimate T_{comm} and $T_{misspec}$. T_{comm} is caused by the synchronization of frequently occurring data dependences, while $T_{misspec}$ is caused by the mis-speculation of unlikely occurring data dependences. We describe techniques to estimate $T_{misspec}$ and T_{comm} in the following sections.

4.1 $T_{misspec}$ Estimation

When a mis-speculation is detected, the violating thread will be squashed and all the work done by this thread becomes useless. We use the amount of work thrown away in a mis-speculation to quantify the impact of the mis-speculation on the overall parallel execution. The amount of work wasted depends on when a mis-speculation is detected. For instance, if a thread starts at cycle *c1* and mis-speculation is detected at cycle *c2*, we have *(c2 – c1)* wasted cycles.

In our machine model, a mis-speculation in the current thread is detected at the end of the previous thread, so we could waste *(S – D)* cycles for a mis-speculation. The overall execution time wasted due to mis-speculation is calculated in equation (8), where $P_{misspec}$ is the probability that a thread will violate inter-thread dependences and is obtained through a profile.

$$T_{misspec} = (S - D) \times P_{misspec} \tag{8}$$

4.2 T_{comm} Estimation I

One way to estimate the amount of time that parallel threads spend on value communication is to identify all the instructions that are either the producers or the consumers of inter-thread data dependences and estimate the cost of value communication as the total cost of executing all such instructions.

Although this estimation technique is simple, it assumes that the value required by a consumer instruction is immediately available when it is needed. Unfortunately, this assumption is not always realistic, since it is often the case that the instruction that consumes the value is issued earlier than the instruction that produces the value, as shown in Figure 4(a). Thus the consumer thread T2 has to stall and wait until the producer thread T1 is able to forward it the correct value, as shown in Figure 4(b). The flow of the value between the two threads serializes the parallel execution, so we refer to it as a *critical forwarding path.*

4.3 T_{comm} Estimation II

To take into consideration the impact of the critical forwarding path, we propose estimation technique II. Assuming that *load1*, the consumer instruction in thread T2, is executed at cycle *c2* and that *store1*, the producer instruction in thread T1, is executed at cycle *c1*, the cost of value communication between these two instructions is estimated as *(c1 – c2)*.

If the data dependence does not occur between two consecutive threads but rather has a dependence distance of *d*, the impact on the execution time of a particular thread should be averaged out over the dependence distance. Thus the impact of communicating a value between two threads is estimated as follows:

$$criticalness = (c1 - c2) / d \tag{9}$$

There is one more mission piece if this estimation technique is to be successful, which is how to determine which cycle of a particular instruction should be executed. Since it is not possible to perfectly predict the dynamic execution of a thread, we made a simplification assuming each instruction will take one cycle to execute; thus the start cycle is simply an instruction count of the total number of instructions between the beginning of the thread and the instruction in question. However, due to complex control flows that are inherent to general-purpose applications, there can be multiple execution paths, each with different path length, that reach the same instruction. Thus the start time of a particular instruction is the average path length weighted by path taken probability, as shown in equation (10).

$$c = \Sigma\, p_i \in {}_{all\_paths}(length(p_i) \times prob(p_i)) \tag{10}$$

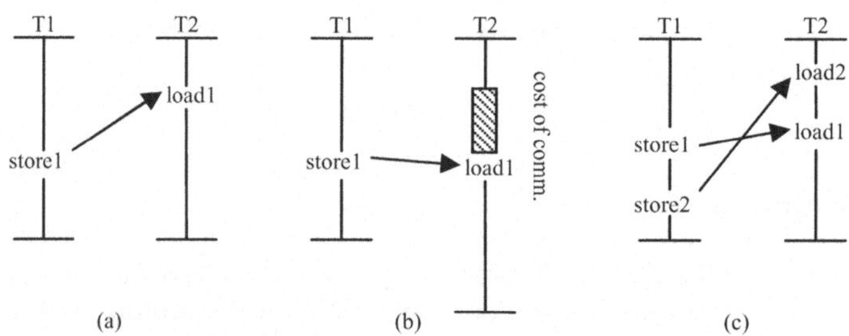

Fig. 4. The data dependence patterns between two speculative threads

For many loops, multiple data dependences exist between two threads, as shown in Figure 4(c). In such cases, the cost of value communication is determined by the most costly one, since the cost of other synchronizations can be hidden.

4.4 T_{comm} Estimation III

Previous work has shown that the compiler can effectively reduce the cost of synchronization through instruction scheduling and that such optimizations are particularly useful for improving the efficiency of communicating register-resident scalars [28, 29]. Unfortunately, the estimation technique described in the previous section does not take such optimization into consideration and tends to overestimate the cost of inter-thread value communication.

It is desirable to find an estimation technique that considers the impact of instruction scheduling on reducing the critical forward path length. Thus, we use a third technique, in which the start time of an instruction is computed from the data dependence graph. When there are multiple paths that can reach an instruction in the data dependence graph, the average start time of this instruction can be measured by equation (11), assuming that the average length of a path p_i that reaches this instruction in the data dependence graph is $length(p_i)$.

$$c = max(length(p_i)) \tag{11}$$

4.5 Evaluation

The three speedup estimation techniques described above have been implemented in our loop selection algorithm and three sets of loops are selected for parallelization respectively. The performance improvement of the parallel execution is evaluated against sequential execution and the results are illustrated in Figure 5. For comparison, we also select loops using speedup value calculated from simulation results and use this perfect estimation as the upper bound.

We make several observations. First, for estimation I, the performance improvement obtained by most benchmarks is close to the perfect performance improvement obtained through simulation. However, for *gzip*, the loops selected using this estimation is completely wrong and results in a 40% performance degradation. Second, the set of loops selected using estimation II is able to achieve only a fraction of the performance obtained by the set of loops selected using simulation results. This estimation technique tends to be conservative in selecting loops. Third, the set of loops

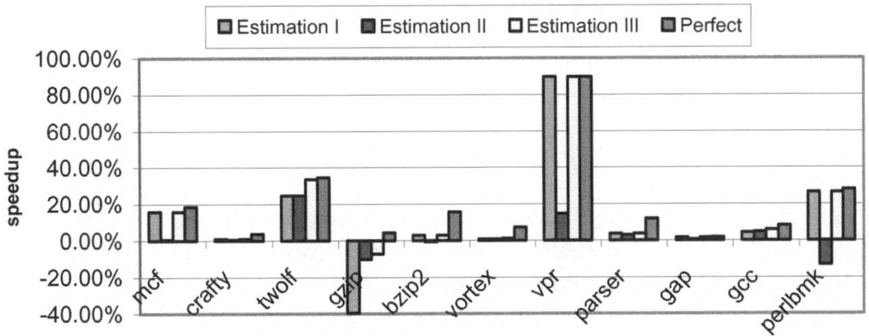

Fig. 5. Performance comparison of different speedup estimation techniques

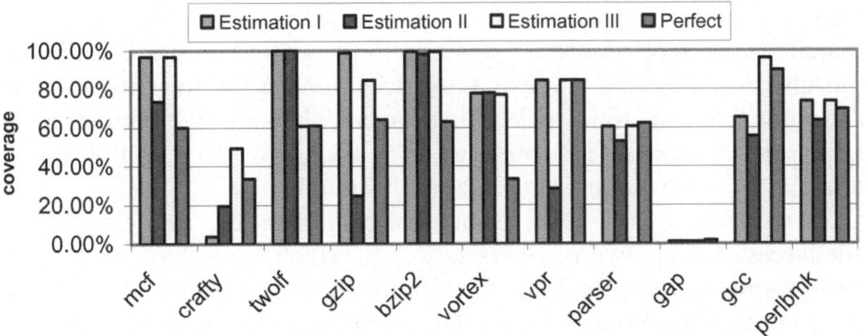

Fig. 6. Coverage comparison of different speedup estimation techniques

selected with estimation III always performs at least as well as the set of loops selected by estimation I and estimation II.

Figure 6 illustrates the coverage of parallel execution on the total execution time. We have found that although the set of loops selected using simulation results demonstrate the most performance improvement, these loops do not always have the large coverage on execution time. In *mcf*, the set of loops selected using estimation III has the similar performance as the set of loops selected using simulation results, however, the coverage of the perfect loop set is significantly smaller. This phenomenon suggests that our estimation method may not be very accurate but is useful in selecting a set of loops that have good performance potential.

5 The Impact of Dynamic Loop Behavior on Loop Selection

Once a loop is selected by our current loop selection algorithm, every invocation of this loop is parallelized. The underlying assumption is that the parallel execution of a loop behaves the same across different invocations. However, some loops exhibit different behaviors when they are invoked multiple times. Different invocations of a loop may differ in the number of iterations, the size of iterations, and the data dependence patterns, and thus demonstrate different parallel execution efficiency. Consequently, it might be desirable to parallelize only certain invocations of a loop. In this section, we address this phenomenon. In particular, we examine whether exploiting such behavior can help us select a better set of loops and improve the overall program performance.

5.1 Calling Context of a Loop

In the loop graph, as described in Section 2, we refer to the path from the root node to a particular loop node as the *calling context* of that loop. It is possible for a particular loop to have several distinct calling contexts, and it is also possible for loops with different calling contexts to behave differently. To study this behavior, we replicate the loop nodes for each distinct calling context. An example is shown in Figure 2(c), where the loop node *goo_for1* has two distinct calling contexts and is thus replicated into *goo_for1_A* and *goo_for1_B*. After the replication, the original loop graph is converted into a tree, which we refer to as the *loop tree*.

We parallelize a loop under a certain calling context if the parallel execution speeds up under that calling context. Loop selection on the loop tree is straightforward. The algorithm is as follows. We first traverse the loop tree bottom-up. For each node in the tree, we evaluate its benefit value as $B_{current}$. We sum up the benefit values if we parallelize its descendants, and refer to this number as $B_{subtree}$. If $B_{current}$ is greater than $B_{subtree}$, we mark this node as a potential candidate for parallelization. We also record the larger of these two numbers as $B_{perfect}$, which is used to calculate $B_{subtree}$ of its parent. Next we traverse the loop tree top-down. Once we have encountered a loop node that is marked as a potential candidate from the previous step, we prune its children. The leaf nodes of the remaining loop tree correspond to the loops that should be parallelized. The accurate solution for selecting loops from a loop tree can be found in polynomial time.

5.2 Dynamic Behavior of a Loop

It is possible for two different invocations of a loop to behave differently even if they have the same calling context. To study this behavior further, we assume an oracle that can perfectly predict the performance of a particular invocation of a loop and parallelize this invocation only when it speeds up. A different set of loops are selected and evaluated assuming that such an oracle is in place.

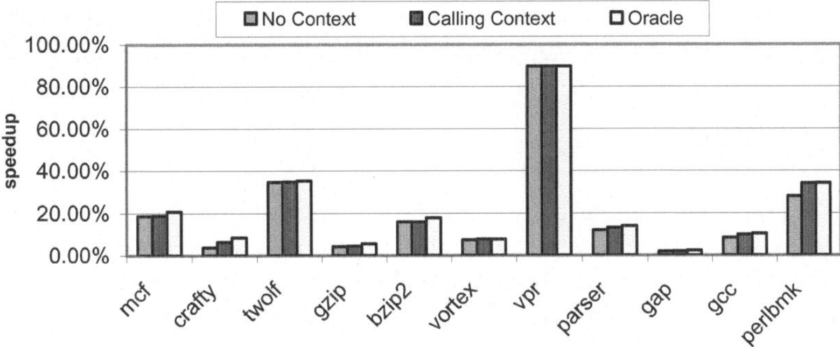

Fig. 7. Performance comparison of loop selection based on different contexts

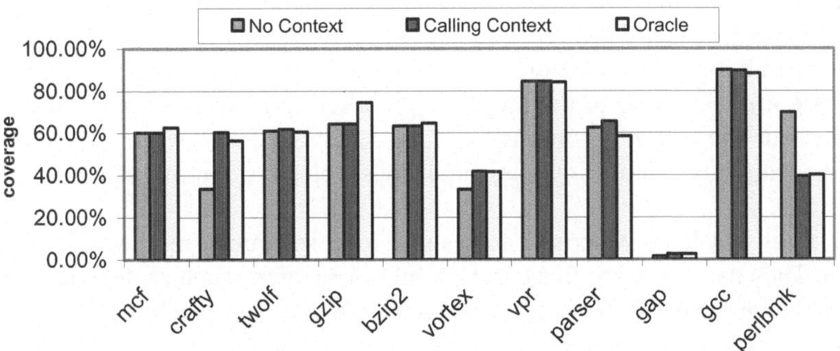

Fig. 8. Coverage comparison of loop selection based on different contexts

5.3 Evaluation

In this section, we evaluate the impact of considering the calling context of a loop (as described in Section 5.1) and the impact of parallelizing only selected invocations of a loop (as described in Section 5.2). The impact of such behavior on overall program performance is shown in Figure 7. We have observed that by differentiating loops with different calling contexts, some benchmarks are able to obtain better program performance. Among them, *crafty* has an additional speed up of 2% and *perlbmk* speeds up by 7%. The performance of *mcf*, *crafty,* and *bzip2* improves an additional 2% by having an oracle that parallelizes only invocations of loops that speed up. Thus, we found that the dynamic behavior of loops has performance impact for some benchmarks. We believe that a dynamic or static loop selection strategy that can predict whether a particular invocation of a loop speeds up can help us achieve additional performance improvement.

Figure 8 shows the coverage for the selected loops. For some benchmarks, such as *perlbmk*, we observe that the overall program performance improves although the coverage of parallelized loops decreases when we take context information into consideration. Close examination reveals that *perlbmk* contains a loop that only speeds up under certain circumstances, and by parallelizing only such invocations, we can achieve better performance. For some other benchmarks, such as *crafty* and *vortex*, the coverage of parallel loops increased due to the selection of a different set of loops.

6 Related Work

Colohan et al. [7] have empirically studied the impact of thread size on the performance of loops, and derived several techniques to determine the unrolling factor of each loop. Their goal is to find the optimal thread size for parallel execution. Our estimation techniques can be employed to determine the candidate loops to unroll. They also propose a runtime system to measure the performance and select loops dynamically.

Oplinger et al. [19] have proposed and evaluated a static loop selection algorithm in their study of the potential of TLS. In their algorithm, they select the best loops in each level of a dynamic loop nest as possible candidates to be parallelized and compute the frequency with which each loop is selected as the best loop. Then they select loops for parallelization based on the computed frequencies. Their concept of a dynamic loop nest is similar to the loop tree proposed in this paper, but is used only to guide the heuristic in context-insensitive loop selection. Their performance estimation is obtained directly from simulation and does not consider the effect of compiler optimization.

Chen et al. [5] have proposed a dynamic loop selection framework for the Java program. They use hardware to extract useful information (such as dependence timing and speculative state requirements) and then estimate the speedup for a loop. Their technique is similar to the runtime system proposed by Colohan et. al. [7] and can only select loops within a simple loop nest. Considering the global loop nesting relations and selecting loops globally introduces significant overhead for a runtime system.

Several papers [12, 21] have studied thread generation techniques that extract speculative parallel threads from consecutive basic blocks. Threads generated using these techniques are fine-grained and usually contain neither procedure calls nor inner loops. These thread generation techniques can complement loop-based threads by exploiting parallelism in the non-loop potion of the program or in loops that are not selected for parallel execution by our algorithm.

Prabhu et al. [20] manually parallelize several SPEC2000 applications using techniques beyond the capabilities of current parallelizing compilers. However, only a few loops are evaluated due to the time-consuming and error-prone nature of this process.

7 Conclusions

Loops, with their regular structures and significant coverage on execution time, are ideal candidates for extracting parallel threads. However, typical general-purpose applications contain a large number of nested loops with complex control flow and ambiguous data dependences. Without an effective loop selection algorithm, determining which loops to parallelize can be a daunting task. In this paper, we propose a loop selection algorithm that takes the coverage and speedup achieved by each loop as inputs and produces the set of loops that should be parallelized to maximize program performance as the output. One of the key components of this algorithm is the ability to accurately estimate the speedup that can be achieved when a particular loop is parallelized. This paper evaluates three different estimation techniques and finds that with the aid of profiling information, compiler analyses are able to come up with reasonably accurate estimates that allow us to select a set of loops to achieve good overall program performance. Furthermore, we have observed that some loops behave differently across different invocations. By exploiting this behavior and parallelizing only invocations of a loop when it actually speeds up, we can potentially achieve better overall program performance for some benchmarks.

References

1. Intel Pentium Processor Extreme Edition. http://www.intel.com/products/processor/pentiumXE/prodbrief.pdf.
2. Open Research Compiler for Itanium Processor Family. http://ipf-orc.sourceforge.net/.
3. Akkary, H. and Driscoll, M., A Dynamic Multithreading Processor. in Proceedings of Micro-31, (December 1998).
4. Blume, B., Eigenmann, R., Faigin, K., Grout, J., Hoeflinger, J., Padua, D., Petersen, P., Pottenger, B., Rauchwerger, L., Tu, P. and Weatherford, S., Polaris: Improving the Effectiveness of Parallelizing Compilers. in Proceedings of the 7th LCPC, (1994).
5. Chen, M. and Olukotun, K., TEST: A Tracer for Extracting Speculative Threads. in Proceedings of 2003 International Symposium on CGO, (March 2003).
6. Cintra, M.H., Martínez, J.F. and Torrellas, J., Architectural support for scalable speculative parallelization in shared-memory multiprocessors. in Proceedings of the ISCA, (2000).
7. Colohan, C.B., Zhai, A., G., S.J. and Mowry, T.C., The Impact of Thread Size and Selection on the Performance of Thread-Level Speculation. in progress.
8. Du, D.Z. and Pardalos, P.M., Handbook of Combinatorial Optimization. Kluwer Academic Publishers., 1999.
9. Gopal, S., Vijaykumar, T., Smith, J. and Sohi, G., Speculative Versioning Cache. in Proceedings of the 4th HPCA, (February 1998).
10. Hall, M.W., Anderson, J.M., Amarasinghe, S.P., Murphy, B.R., Liao, S.-W., Bugnion, E. and Lam, M.S., Maximizing Multiprocessor Performance with the SUIF Compiler. IEEE Computer, 1999 (12).
11. Hammond, L., Willey, M. and Olukotun, K., Data Speculation Support for A Chip Multiprocessor. in Proceedings of ASPLOS-8, (October 1998).
12. Johnson, T.A., Eigenmann, R. and Vijaykumar, T.N., Min-Cut Program Decomposition for Thread-Level Speculation. in Proceedings of PLDI, (2004).

13. Kalla, R., Sinharoy;, B. and Tendler, J.M., IBM Power5 Chip: a Dual-Core Multithreaded Processor. IEEE MICRO, 2004 (2).
14. Kongetira, P., Aingaran, K. and Olukotun, K., Niagara: A 32-Way Multithreaded Sparc Processor. IEEE MICRO, 2005 (2).
15. Luk, C.-K., Cohn, R., Muth, R., Patil, H., Klauser, A., Lowney, G., Wallace, S., Reddi, V.J. and Hazelwood, K., Pin: Building Customized Program Analysis Tools with Dynamic Instrumentation. in Proceedings of the ACM Intl. Conf. on Programming Language Design and Implementation, (June 2005).
16. Marcuello, P. and Gonzlez, A., Clustered Speculative Multithreaded Processors. in Proceedings of MICRO-32, (November 1999).
17. Moshovos, A.I., Breach, S.E., Vijaykumar, T. and Sohi, G.S., Dynamic Speculation and Synchronization of Data Dependences. in the proceedings of the 24th ISCA, (June 1997).
18. Olukotun, K., Hammond, L. and Willey, M., Improving the Performance of Speculatively Parallel Applications on the Hydra CMP. in Proceedings of the ACM Int. Conf. on Supercomputing, (June 1999).
19. Oplinger, J., Heine, D. and Lam, M.S., In Search of Speculative Thread-Level Parallelism. in Proceedings of PACT, (October 1999).
20. Prabhu, M. and Olukotun, K., Exposing Speculative Thread Parallelism in SPEC2000. in Proceedings of the 9th ACM Symposium on Principles and Practice of Parallel Programming, (2005).
21. Quinones, C.G., Madriles, C., Sanchez, J., Marcuello, P., González, A. and Tullsen, D.M., Mitosis Compiler: An Infrastructure for Speculative Threading Based on Pre-Computation Slices. in Proceedings of the ACM Intl. Conf. on Programming Language Design and Implementation, (June 2005).
22. Rauchwerger, L. and Padua, D.A., The LRPD Test: Speculative RunTime Parallelization of Loops with Privatization and Reduction Parallelization. IEEE Transactions on Parallel Distributed Systems, 1999 (2). 160-180.
23. Renau, J., Tuck, J., Liu, W., Ceze, L., Strauss, K. and Torrellas, J., Tasking with Out-of-Order Spawn in TLS Chip Multiprocessors: Microarchitecture and Compilation. in Proceeding of the 19th ACM International Conference on Supercomputing, (2005).
24. Sohi, G.S., Breach, S.E. and Vijaykumar, T.N., Multiscalar Processors. in Proceedings of the 22nd ISCA, (June 1995).
25. Steffan, J.G., Colohan, C.B., Zhai, A. and Mowry, T.C., Improving Value Communication for Thread-Level Speculation. in Proceedings of the 8th HPCA, (February 2002).
26. Tsai, J.-Y., Huang, J., Amlo, C., Lilja, D. and Yew, P.-C., The Superthreaded Processor Architecture. IEEE Transactions on Computers, 1999 (9).
27. Vijaykumar, T.N. and Sohi, G.S., Task Selection for a Multiscalar Processor. in Proceeding of the 31st International Symposium on Microarchitecture, (December 1998).
28. Zhai, A., Colohan, C.B., Steffan, J.G. and Mowry, T.C., Compiler Optimization of Memory-Resident Value Communication Between Speculative Threads. in Proceedings of 2004 International Symposium on CGO, (March 2004).
29. Zhai, A., Colohan, C.B., Steffan, J.G. and Mowry, T.C., Compiler Optimization of Scalar Value Communication Between Speculative Threads. in Proceedings of the 10th ASPLOS, (October 2002).

Software Thread Level Speculation for the Java Language and Virtual Machine Environment

Christopher J.F. Pickett and Clark Verbrugge

School of Computer Science, McGill University
Montréal, Québec, Canada H3A 2A7
{cpicke,clump}@sable.mcgill.ca

Abstract. Thread level speculation (TLS) has shown great promise as a strategy for fine to medium grain automatic parallelisation, and in a hardware context techniques to ensure correct TLS behaviour are now well established. Software and virtual machine TLS designs, however, require adherence to high level language semantics, and this can impose many additional constraints on TLS behaviour, as well as open up new opportunities to exploit language-specific information. We present a detailed design for a Java-specific, software TLS system that operates at the bytecode level, and fully addresses the problems and requirements imposed by the Java language and VM environment. Using SableSpMT, our research TLS framework, we provide experimental data on the corresponding costs and benefits; we find that exceptions, GC, and dynamic class loading have only a small impact, but that concurrency, native methods, and memory model concerns do play an important role, as does an appropriate, language-specific runtime TLS support system. Full consideration of language and execution semantics is critical to correct and efficient execution of high level TLS designs, and our work here provides a baseline for future Java or Java virtual machine implementations.

1 Introduction

Thread level speculation (TLS), also known as speculative multithreading (SpMT), is a technique for automatic program parallelisation that has been investigated from a hardware perspective for several years, and current systems are capable of showing good speedups in simulation based studies [1,2]. As a hardware problem, the issues of ensuring correctness under speculative execution have been well defined, and different rollback or synchronization approaches are sufficient to guarantee overall correct program behaviour. Software approaches to TLS, however, need to take into account the full source language semantics and behaviour to ensure correct and efficient execution, and in general this is not trivially ensured by low level hardware mechanisms.

In this paper we provide a detailed description of the requirements and performance impact of various high level aspects of Java TLS execution. We consider the full Java semantics, including all bytecode instructions, garbage collection (GC), synchronization, exceptions, native methods, dynamic class loading, and the new Java memory model [3]. These requirements are often dismissed or ignored in existing Java TLS work [1,4,5,6,7,8], but in fact are crucial to correct execution and can significantly affect performance.

E. Ayguadé et al. (Eds.): LCPC 2005, LNCS 4339, pp. 304–318, 2007.

Language and VM level speculation also produce design constraints due to efficiency concerns; for instance, Java programs tend to have frequent heap accesses, object allocations, and method calls. Our runtime TLS support system accomodates this behaviour, and we evaluate the relative importance of dependence buffering, stack buffering, return value prediction, speculative allocation, and priority queueing.

General purpose software and intermediate, VM level implementations of TLS are difficult goals, but have significant potential advantages, including the use of high level program information and the ability to run on existing multiprocessor hardware. Previously we used SableSpMT, our Java TLS analysis framework, to characterize both thread parallelism and overhead in software speculation [9]; our work here is complementary and aims to provide a thorough Java TLS design and an understanding of the requirements and relative impact of high level language semantics.

2 Related Work

Thread level speculation has been the subject of hardware investigations for over a decade, and a variety of general purpose machines have been proposed and simulated (reviewed in [2]). These have also been tailored to specific speculation strategies; *loop level* speculation focusses on loop iterations, whereas *method level* speculation or *speculative method level parallelism* (SMLP) speculates over method calls. SMLP has been identified as particularly appropriate for Java, given the relatively high density of method calls in Java programs, and simulation studies have shown quite good potential speedup [4]. The impact of frequent method calls was further explored and optimised by Hu *et al.* in their study of return value prediction [5].

Most current hardware designs could in fact be classified as hybrid hardware/software approaches since they rely to various extents on software assistance. Most commonly, compiler or runtime processing is required to help identify threads and insert appropriate TLS directives for the hardware [6,10]. Jrpm makes further use of several code optimisations that reduce variable dependencies [1], and other recent designs such as STAMPede [2] and Mitosis [11] are based to a large degree on cooperative compiler and software help.

Speculative hardware, even with software support, largely obviates the consideration of high level language semantics: correct machine code execution implies correct program behaviour. Pure software architectures based on C or FORTRAN also have relatively straightforward mappings to speculative execution, and thus designs such as Softspec [12], thread pipelining for C [7], and others [13,14] do not require a deep consideration of language semantics.

For Java stronger guarantees must be provided. In the context of designing JVM rollback for debugging purposes some similar semantic issues have been considered [15], but much less so for Java TLS. As part of their software thread partitioning strategy, Chen and Olukotun do discuss Java exceptions, GC, and synchronization requirements [1]. However, they do not consider class loading, native methods, or copying GC behaviour, and nor does their handling of speculative synchronization by simply ignoring it correctly enforce Java semantics. Pure Java source studies, such as the partially or fully hand-done examinations by Yoshizoe *et al.* [8] and Kazi [7], focus on small execution traces in a limited environment or rely on human input respectively. In the former case the environment is too constrained for Java language issues to arise. In the latter, exceptions, polymorphism, and GC are discussed, though not analysed, and assumptions about ahead-of-time whole program availability are contrary to Java's dynamic linking model. Differences and omissions such as these make it difficult to compare Java studies, and leave important practical implementation questions open; our work here is meant to help rectify this situation.

3 Background and System Overview

In our design for Java TLS we employ *speculative method level parallelism* (SMLP), as depicted in Figure 1. SMLP uses method callsites as fork points: the parent thread enters the method body, and the child thread begins execution at the first instruction past the callsite. When the parent returns from the call, then if there are no violations the child thread is committed and non-speculative execution continues where speculation stopped, otherwise the parent re-executes the child's body.

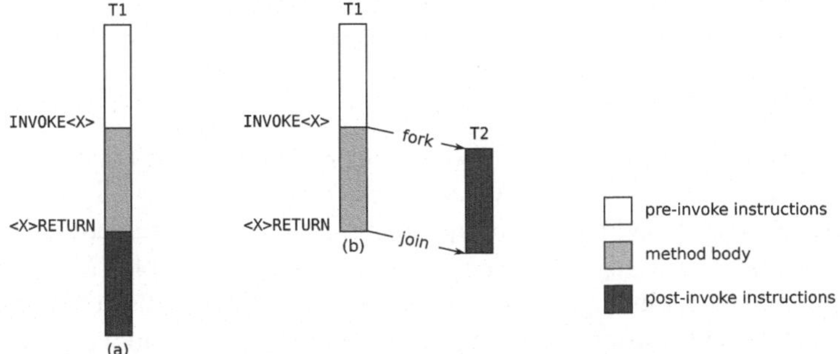

Fig. 1. (a) *Sequential execution of Java bytecode.* The target method of an `INVOKE<X>` instruction executes before the instructions following the return point. (b) *Speculative execution of Java bytecode under speculative method level parallelism (SMLP).* Upon reaching a method callsite, the non-speculative *parent* thread `T1` forks a speculative *child* thread `T2`. If the method is non-void, a predicted return value is pushed on `T2`'s Java operand stack. `T2` then continues past the return point in parallel with the execution of the method body, buffering main memory accesses. When `T1` returns from the call, it joins `T2`. If the actual return value matches the predicted return value, and there are no dependence violations between buffered reads and post-invoke values, `T2`'s buffered writes are committed and non-speculative execution jumps ahead to where `T2` left off, yielding speedup. If there *are* dependence violations or the prediction is incorrect, `T2` is simply aborted.

An overview of the SableSpMT analysis framework [9] and Java TLS execution environment is shown in Figure 2. SableSpMT is an extension of the "switch" bytecode interpreter in SableVM [16], a Free / open source software Java virtual machine. Static analysis with Soot [17] occurs ahead-of-time, and SableSpMT uses the results to prepare special speculative *code arrays* for Java methods from their non-speculative equivalents in SableVM; code arrays are generated from Java bytecode, and are contiguous sequences of word-sized instructions and instruction operands representing method

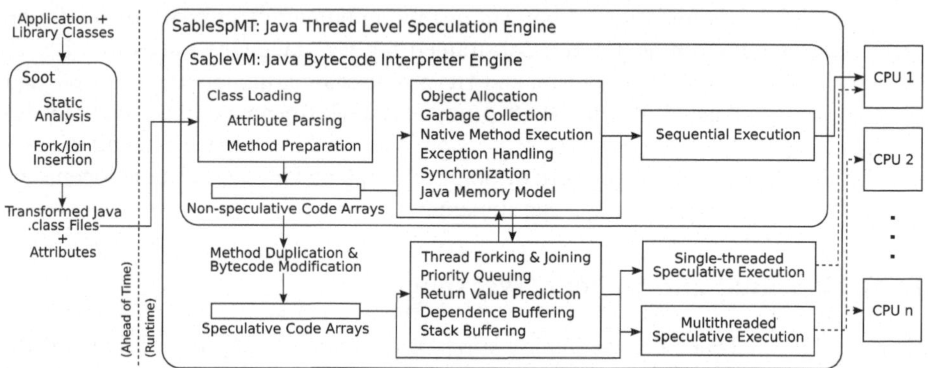

Fig. 2. *The SableSpMT thread level speculation execution environment.* SableSpMT is an extension of SableVM. Soot is used to transform, analyse, and attach attributes to `.class` files in an ahead-of-time step. SableVM reads in these classes during class loading, parsing attributes and preparing method bodies. Sequential execution depends only the non-speculative code arrays, and interacts with normal JVM support components. Speculative execution requires preparation of special speculative code arrays, and depends on additional TLS support components. SableSpMT's single-threaded execution mode shares processors with non-speculative execution, whereas the multithreaded mode splits single non-speculative threads across multiple processors.

bodies. SableSpMT forks and joins child threads at runtime, and these depend on the speculative code arrays for safe out-of-order execution. Various TLS runtime support facilities are needed, including priority queueing, return value prediction, dependence buffering, and stack buffering. SableSpMT also interacts with SableVM's own runtime support components, including a semi-space copying garbage collector, native method execution, exception handling, synchronization, and the Java memory model. Outside of thread forking and joining, speculation has negligible impact on and is largely invisible to normal multithreaded VM execution, with speculative threads running only on free processors.

4 Java TLS Design

We now describe the main Java TLS structures in our design for SMLP at the Java virtual machine level. These can be broadly classified into speculative method preparation components, speculative runtime support components, and speculative execution modes.

4.1 Speculative Method Preparation

In order to prepare method bodies for TLS, classfile attributes are parsed for static analysis info, fork and join points are inserted, and bytecode instructions are modified. The final stages of preparation occur when a method is invoked for the first time. Once primed for speculation, a child thread can be forked at any callsite within the method body. Furthermore, speculation can continue across method boundaries as long as the methods being invoked or returned to have been similarly prepared.

Static Analysis and Attribute Parsing. An advantage to language level TLS is the ability to use high level program information. In our case we incorporate information from the Soot compiler analysis framework [17], and include two analyses for improved return value prediction [18]. The results are encoded using Soot's attribute generation framework, and parsed by SableVM during class loading. During method preparation, the analysis data are associated with callsites for use by the return value prediction component.

Fork and Join Insertion. The SableSpMT TLS engine needs the ability to fork and join child threads. We introduce new `SPMT_FORK` and `SPMT_JOIN` instructions that provide this functionality. Under SMLP threads are forked and joined immediately before and after method invocations, and so these instructions are inserted around every `INVOKE<X>` instruction.

Table 1. *Java bytecode instructions modified to support speculation.* Each instruction is marked according to its behaviours that require special attention during speculative execution. These behaviours are marked "once", "maybe", or "yes" according to their probabilities of occurring within the instruction. "Forces stop" indicates whether the instruction may force termination of a speculative child thread, but does not necessarily imply abortion and failure. Not shown are branch instructions; these are trivially fixed to support jumping to the right `pc`.

<table>
<tr><th>instruction</th><th>reads global</th><th>writes global</th><th>locks object</th><th>unlocks object</th><th>allocates object</th><th>throws exception</th><th>enters native code</th><th>loads class(es)</th><th>orders memory</th><th>forces stop</th></tr>
<tr><td>GETFIELD</td><td>yes</td><td></td><td></td><td></td><td></td><td>maybe</td><td></td><td>once</td><td>maybe</td><td>maybe</td></tr>
<tr><td>GETSTATIC</td><td>yes</td><td></td><td></td><td></td><td></td><td></td><td></td><td>once</td><td>maybe</td><td>maybe</td></tr>
<tr><td><X>ALOAD</td><td>yes</td><td></td><td></td><td></td><td></td><td>maybe</td><td></td><td></td><td></td><td>maybe</td></tr>
<tr><td>PUTFIELD</td><td></td><td>yes</td><td></td><td></td><td></td><td>maybe</td><td></td><td>once</td><td>maybe</td><td>maybe</td></tr>
<tr><td>PUTSTATIC</td><td></td><td>yes</td><td></td><td></td><td></td><td></td><td></td><td>once</td><td>maybe</td><td>maybe</td></tr>
<tr><td><X>ASTORE</td><td></td><td>yes</td><td></td><td></td><td></td><td>maybe</td><td></td><td></td><td></td><td>maybe</td></tr>
<tr><td>(I|L)(DIV|REM)</td><td></td><td></td><td></td><td></td><td></td><td>maybe</td><td></td><td></td><td></td><td>maybe</td></tr>
<tr><td>ARRAYLENGTH</td><td></td><td></td><td></td><td></td><td></td><td>maybe</td><td></td><td></td><td></td><td>maybe</td></tr>
<tr><td>CHECKCAST</td><td></td><td></td><td></td><td></td><td></td><td>maybe</td><td></td><td>once</td><td></td><td>maybe</td></tr>
<tr><td>ATHROW</td><td></td><td></td><td></td><td></td><td></td><td>yes</td><td></td><td></td><td></td><td>yes</td></tr>
<tr><td>INSTANCEOF</td><td></td><td></td><td></td><td></td><td></td><td></td><td></td><td>once</td><td></td><td>maybe</td></tr>
<tr><td>RET</td><td></td><td></td><td></td><td></td><td></td><td></td><td></td><td></td><td></td><td>maybe</td></tr>
<tr><td>MONITORENTER</td><td>yes</td><td>yes</td><td>yes</td><td></td><td></td><td>maybe</td><td></td><td></td><td>yes</td><td>yes</td></tr>
<tr><td>MONITOREXIT</td><td>yes</td><td>yes</td><td></td><td>yes</td><td></td><td>maybe</td><td></td><td></td><td>yes</td><td>yes</td></tr>
<tr><td>INVOKE<X></td><td>maybe</td><td>maybe</td><td>maybe</td><td></td><td></td><td>maybe</td><td>maybe</td><td>once</td><td>maybe</td><td>maybe</td></tr>
<tr><td><X>RETURN</td><td>maybe</td><td>maybe</td><td></td><td>maybe</td><td></td><td>maybe</td><td>maybe</td><td>once</td><td>maybe</td><td>maybe</td></tr>
<tr><td>NEW</td><td></td><td>yes</td><td></td><td></td><td>yes</td><td>maybe</td><td></td><td>once</td><td></td><td>maybe</td></tr>
<tr><td>NEWARRAY</td><td></td><td>yes</td><td></td><td></td><td>yes</td><td>maybe</td><td></td><td></td><td></td><td>maybe</td></tr>
<tr><td>ANEWARRAY</td><td></td><td>yes</td><td></td><td></td><td>yes</td><td>maybe</td><td></td><td>once</td><td></td><td>maybe</td></tr>
<tr><td>MULTIANEWARRAY</td><td></td><td>yes</td><td></td><td></td><td>yes</td><td>maybe</td><td></td><td>once</td><td></td><td>maybe</td></tr>
<tr><td>LDC_STRING</td><td></td><td></td><td></td><td></td><td>once</td><td></td><td></td><td></td><td></td><td>once</td></tr>
</table>

Bytecode Instruction Modification. The majority of Java's 201 bytecode instructions can be used verbatim for speculative execution; however, roughly 25% need modification to protect against potentially dangerous behaviours, as shown in Table 1. If these instructions were modified in place, the overhead of extra runtime conditionals would impact on the speed of non-speculative execution. Instead, modification takes place in a duplicate copy of the code array created especially for speculative execution. Indeed, the only significant change to non-speculative bytecode is the insertion of fork and join points. Problematic operations include:

- *Global memory access.* Reads from and writes to main memory require buffering, and so the `<X>A(LOAD|STORE)` and `(GET|PUT)(FIELD|STATIC)` instructions are modified to read and write their data using a dependence buffer, as described in Section 4.2. If final or volatile field access flags are set, these instructions may also require a memory barrier, as described in Section 5, in which case speculation must also stop.
- *Exceptions.* In unsafe situations, many instructions must throw exceptions to ensure the safety of bytecode execution, including `(I|L)(DIV|REM)` that throw ArithmeticExceptions upon division by zero, and others that throw NullPointerExceptions, ArrayIndexOutOfBoundsExceptions, and ClassCastExceptions. Application or library code may also throw explicit exceptions using `ATHROW`. In both cases, speculation rolls back to the beginning of the instruction and stops immediately; however, the decision to abort or commit is deferred until the parent joins the child. Exceptions must also be handled safely if thrown by non-speculative parent threads with speculative children, as discussed in Section 5.
- *Detecting object references.* The `INSTANCEOF` instruction computes type assignability between a pre-specified class and an object reference on the stack. Normally, bytecode verification promises that the stack value is always a valid reference to the start of an object instance on the heap, but speculative execution cannot depend on this guarantee. Accordingly, speculation must stop if the reference does not lie within heap bounds, or if it does not point to an object header; currently we insert a magic word into all object headers, although a bitmap of heap words to object headers would be more accurate and space-efficient.
- *Subroutines.* `JSR` (jump to subroutine) is always safe to execute because the target address is hardcoded into the code array. However, the return address used by its partner `RET` is read from a local variable, and must point to a valid instruction. Furthermore, for a given subroutine, if the `JSR` occurs speculatively and the `RET` non-speculatively, or vice versa, the return address must be adjusted to use the right code array. Thus a modified *non-speculative* `RET` is also needed.
- *Synchronization.* The `INVOKE<X>` and `<X>RETURN` instructions may lock and unlock object monitors, and `MONITOR(ENTER|EXIT)` will always lock or unlock object monitors; they furthermore require memory barriers and are strongly ordering. These instructions are also marked as reading from and writing to global variables, as lockwords are stored in object headers. Speculative locking and unlocking is not currently supported, and always forces children to stop.
- *Method entry.* Speculatively, `INVOKE<X>` are prevented from entering unprepared methods and triggering class loading and method preparation. Furthermore, at non-static callsites, the receiver is checked to be a valid object instance, the target is checked to have the right stack effect, and the type of the target's class is checked for assignability to the receiver's type. Invokes are also prevented from entering native code or attempting to execute abstract methods.
- *Method exit.* After the synchronization check, the `<X>RETURN` instructions require three additional safety operations: 1) potential buffering of the non-speculative

stack frame from the parent thread, as described in Section 4.2; 2) verifying that the caller is not executing a *preparation sequence*, a special group of instructions used in SableVM to replace slow instructions with faster versions [16]; and 3) ensuring that speculation does not leave bytecode execution entirely, which would mean Java thread death, VM death, or a return to native code.
- *Object allocation*. Barring an exception being thrown or GC being triggered, the `NEW` and `((MULTI|)A|)NEWARRAY` instructions are safe to execute. The `LDC_STRING` specialisation of `LDC` allocates a constant `String` object upon its first execution, the address of which is patched into both non-speculative and speculative code arrays, and forces speculation to stop only once. Allocation and GC are discussed in greater detail in Section 5.

4.2 Speculative Runtime Support

In addition to preparing method bodies for speculative execution, the speculation engine provides various support components that interact with bytecode and allow for child thread startup, queueing, execution, and death to take place while ensuring correct execution through appropriate dependence buffering.

Thread Forking. Speculative child threads are forked by non-speculative parents and also by speculative children at `SPMT_FORK` instructions. Speculating at every fork point is not necessarily optimal, and in the context of SMLP various heuristics for optimising fork decisions have been investigated [6]. SableSpMT permits relatively arbitrary fork heuristics; however, we limit ourselves to a simple “always fork” strategy in this paper as a more generally useful baseline measurement.

Having made the decision to fork a child, several steps are required. First, those variables of the parent thread environment (`JNIEnv`) that can be accessed speculatively are copied to a child `JNIEnv` struct; in this fashion, the child assumes the identity of its parent. Second, a child stack buffer is initialized and the parent stack frame is copied to the child, giving it an execution context. Third, a dependence buffer is initialized; this protects main memory from speculative execution, and allows for child validation upon joining. Fourth, the operand stack height of the child is adjusted to account for the stack effect of the invoke following the fork point, and the `pc` of the child is set to the first instruction past the invoke. Fifth, a return value is predicted for non-void methods; technically, any arbitrary value can be used as a “prediction”, although the chance of speculation success is greatly reduced by doing so.

Priority Queueing. In the default multithreaded speculative execution mode, children are enqueued at fork points on a global $O(1)$ concurrent priority queue. Priorities 0–10 are computed as $\min(l \times r/1000, 10)$, where l is the average bytecode sequence length and r is the success rate; higher priority threads are those that are expected to do more useful work. The queue consists of an array of doubly-linked lists, one for each priority, and supports `enqueue`, `dequeue`, and `delete` operations. Helper OS threads compete to dequeue and run children on separate processors. The queue is globally synchronized using spinlocks, which works well for a small number of priorities and processors, as found by Shavit *et al.* in their study of scalable concurrent priority queues [19].

Return Value Prediction. Speculative children forked at non-void callsites need their operand stack height adjusted to account for the return value, and must be aborted if an incorrect value is used. Accurate return value prediction (RVP) can significantly improve the performance of Java SMLP [5], and we previously reported on our aggressive RVP implementation in SableSpMT [20], the use of two compiler analyses for extracting further accuracy [18], and the integration of RVP analysis into our framework [9].

Return value predictors are associated with individual callsites, and can use context, memoization, and hybrid strategies, amongst others. The attributes generated by the compiler analyses are parsed during method preparation, and can be used to relax predictor correctness requirements and reduce memory consumption.

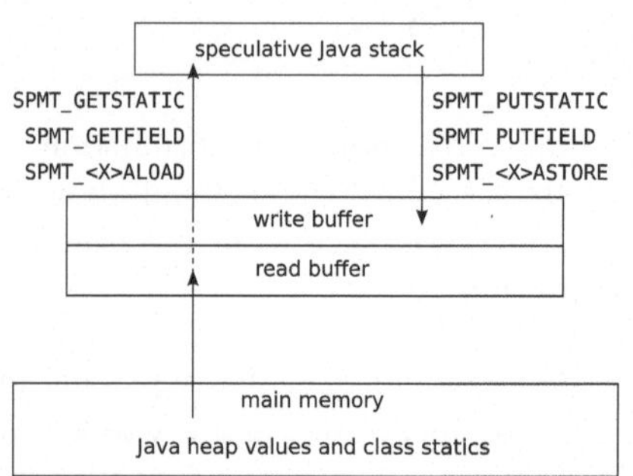

Fig. 3. *Dependence buffering.* When a speculative global read instruction is executed, first the write buffer is searched, and if it does not contain the address of the desired value then the read buffer is searched. If the value address is still not found, the value at that address is loaded from main memory. When a speculative global write instruction is executed, the write buffer is searched, and if no entry is found a new mapping is created.

Fig. 4. *Stack buffering. f1* through *f6* are stack frames corresponding to Java methods. A speculative child is forked at *f4* in the parent, and in turn a second-generation grandchild thread is forked at *f5* in the child. Stack frames are buffered on forking, and additionally when children return from methods; *f2* in the grandchild is buffered from the non-speculative parent, as its immediate ancestor never descended below *f3*.

Dependence Buffering. Most TLS designs propose a mechanism for buffering reads from and writes to main memory by speculative threads in order to prevent against potential dependence violations. In Java, main memory consists of object instances and arrays on the garbage-collected heap, and static fields in class loader memory.

In hardware, dependence buffers can be built as table based structures similar to caches [2], and we propose a similar design for software TLS, as shown in Figure 3. Buffer objects are attached to speculative threads on startup, and are implemented using open addressing hashtables; values are stored using the value address as a key, and fast lookup is provided by double hashing. A backing linked list allows for fast iteration during validation and committal.

Stack Buffering. As well as heap and static data, speculative threads may also access local variables and data stored on the Java operand stack. It follows that stack accesses must be buffered to protect the parent stack in the event of failure, as shown in Figure 4. The simplest mechanism for doing so is to copy stack frames from parent threads to separate child stacks both on forking children and on exiting methods speculatively. Additionally, children must create new stack frames for any methods they enter.

Pointers to child threads are stored one per stack frame, and this allows for convenient *out-of-order* thread spawning [21] where each parent can have multiple immediate children, exposing additional parallelism. When nested speculation is combined with out-of-order spawning it leads to a tree of children for a single fork point.

Thread Joining. Upon reaching some termination condition, a speculative child will stop execution and leave its entire state ready for joining by its parent. The child may stop of its own accord if it attempts some illegal behaviour as summarized in Table 1, if it reaches an *elder sibling*, that is, a speculative child forked earlier on by the same parent at a lower stack frame, or if it reaches a pre-defined speculative sequence length limit. The parent may also signal the child to stop if it reaches the join point associated with the child's fork point, or if it reaches the child's forking frame at the top of the VM exception handler loop.

The join process involves verifying the safety of child execution and committing results. First, a full memory barrier is issued, and the child is then validated according to four tests: 1) the predicted return value is checked against the actual return value for non-void methods, according to the safety constraints of static analyses [18]; 2) the parent is checked for not having had its root set garbage-collected since forking the child; 3) the dependence buffers are checked for overflow or corruption; and 4) values in the read dependence buffer are checked against main memory for violations.

If the child passes all four tests, then the speculation is safe; all values in the write buffer are flushed to main memory, buffered stack frames entered by the child are copied to the parent, and non-speculative execution resumes with the `pc` and operand stack size set as the child left them. Otherwise, execution continues non-speculatively at the first instruction past the `SPMT_JOIN`. Regardless of success or failure, the child's memory is recycled for use at future fork points. Note that buffer commits may result in a reordering of the speculative thread's write operations, which must in turn respect the requirements imposed by the new Java memory model, as discussed in Section 5.

4.3 Speculative Execution

SableSpMT supports two speculative execution modes, a single-threaded mode where bytecode interpretation alternates between non-speculative and speculative execution in a single thread, and a truly multithreaded mode that depends on multiple processors for parallelisation. Both modes allow for non-speculative Java threads to coexist with the speculative system.

The single-threaded mode has previously been described as appropriate for debugging, testing, porting, and limit analyses [9]. In the multithreaded mode, children are assigned priorities at fork points based on speculation histories, and enqueued on the $O(1)$ priority queue. A minimal amount of initialization is done to limit the impact of fork overhead on non-speculative threads. There is a pool of helper OS threads running, one per free processor, and these dequeue and execute children according to priority.

If the parent thread joins a child that it previously enqueued, and that child did not get removed by a helper OS thread, the child is deleted by simply unlinking it from the list for that priority, and its memory is recycled. Otherwise, if the child has started, the parent signals it to stop, and then begins the usual validation procedure.

5 Java Language Considerations

Several traps await the unsuspecting implementor that tries to enhance a JVM to support thread level speculation. These traps are actually core features of the Java language — object allocation, garbage collection, native method execution, exception handling, synchronization, and the Java memory model — and a Java TLS implementation must handle them all safely in order to be considered fully general. The impact of these features is measured in Section 6.

Object Allocation. Object allocation occurs frequently in many Java programs, and permitting speculative allocation significantly increases maximum child thread lengths. Additionally, it is unnecessary to buffer accesses to objects allocated speculatively. Speculative threads can either allocate without synchronization from a thread-local heap, or compete with non-speculative threads to acquire a global heap mutex. Speculation must stop if the object to be allocated has a non-trivial finalizer, i.e. not `Object.finalize()`, for it would be incorrect to finalize objects allocated by aborted children. Allocation also forces speculation to stop if either GC or an OutOfMemoryError would be triggered as a result. Object references only become visible to non-speculative Java threads upon successful thread validation and committal; aborted children will have their allocated objects reclaimed in the next collection.

Garbage Collection. All objects in Java are allocated on the garbage-collected Java heap. SableVM uses a stop-the-world semi-space copying collector by default [16], and every object reference changes upon every collection; thus, any speculative thread started before GC must be invalidated after GC. Threads are invalidated if the collection count of the parent thread increases between the fork and join points. The default collector in SableVM is invoked relatively infrequently, and we find that GC is responsible for a negligible amount of speculative invalidations. Other GC algorithms are trickier to negotiate with, and may require either pinning of speculatively accessed objects or updating of dependence buffer entries.

Native Methods. Java provides access to native code through the Java Native Interface (JNI), and native methods are used in class libraries, application code, and the VM itself for low-level operations such as thread management, timing, and I/O. Speculation must stop upon encountering native methods, as these cannot be executed in a buffered environment without significant further analysis. However, non-speculative threads can safely execute native code while their speculative children execute pure bytecode continuations.

Exceptions. Implicit or explicit exceptions simply force speculation to stop. Speculative exception handling is not supported in SableSpMT for three reasons: 1) exceptions are rarely encountered, even for "exception-heavy" applications like `jack` [20]; 2) writing a speculative exception handler is somewhat complicated; and 3) exceptions in speculative threads are often the result of incorrect computation, and thus further progress is likely to be wasted effort.

Non-speculatively, if exceptions are thrown out of a method in search of an appropriate exception handler, any speculative children encountered as stack frames are popped must be aborted. In order to guarantee a maximum of one child per stack frame, children *must* be aborted at the *top* of the VM exception handler loop, before jumping to the handler `pc`. This prevents speculative children from being forked inside either `catch` or `finally` blocks while another speculative child is executing in the same stack frame.

Synchronization. Object access is synchronized either explicitly by the `MONITORENTER` and `MONITOREXIT` instructions, or implicitly via synchronized method entry and exit. Speculative synchronization is unsafe without explicit support [22], and must force children to stop; somewhat surprisingly, synchronization has been unsafely ignored by Java TLS studies in the past [1,5]. Non-speculatively, synchronization always remains safe, and it is even possible to fork and join speculative threads inside critical sections.

The Java Memory Model. The new Java memory model (JMM) [3] imposes constraints on multithreaded execution; these constraints can be satisfied by inserting memory barriers [23]. Speculative execution can only continue past a memory barrier if the dependence buffer records an exact interleaving of memory accesses and the relevant barrier operations; that we reuse entries for value addresses already in the buffer and do not record memory barriers precludes doing so in our current implementation.

The orderings required for various API calls, including non-speculative thread creation and joining, are provided by our design due to their implementations as native methods, which already force speculation to stop. For object synchronization several rules apply; most critically, a memory barrier is required before unlock operations to guarantee that writes in the critical section are visible to future threads entering the same monitor. By disabling speculative locking entirely we provide a much stronger guarantee than required; future work on speculative locking will need a finer grained approach.

Loads and stores of volatile fields also require memory barriers, to ensure interprocessor visibility between operations. Similarly, the loads and stores of final fields require barriers, except that on `x86` and `x86_64` these are no-ops [23]. However, speculatively, we must stop on final field stores, which appear only in constructors, to ensure that a final field is not used before the object reference has been made visible, a situation that is made possible by reordering writes during commit operations. Our conservative solution is to stop speculation on all volatile loads and stores and also all final stores.

6 Experimental Analysis

In this section we employ the SableSpMT framework to analyse the impact of both speculation support components and Java language features on TLS execution. All experiments were performed on a 1.8 GHz 4-way SMP AMD Opteron machine running Linux 2.6.7, with all free processors running speculative threads. We use the SPECjvm98 benchmark suite at size 100 (S100), and a speculative child thread is forked at every callsite. Nested speculation is disabled, but out-of-order spawning does take place. Although `raytrace` is technically not part of SPECjvm98 and therefore excluded from geometric means, we include results for purposes of comparison; it is the single-threaded equivalent of `mtrt`.

Table 2. Child thread termination

termination reason	comp	db	jack	javac	jess	mpeg	mtrt	rt
class resolution and loading	2.14K	1.76K	94.8K	487K	3.80K	14.7K	4.79K	5.64K
failed object allocation	1	3	23	17	39	0	28	40
invalid object reference	563	553K	342K	280K	431K	485	407K	278K
finals and volatiles	842	1.45M	2.17M	1.11M	1.95M	888	115K	68.8K
synchronization	4.30K	26.8M	6.95M	17.0M	4.89M	10.4K	658K	351K
unsafe method entry or exit	2.66K	1.55K	16.0K	622K	2.62K	1.65K	3.60K	3.00K
implicit non-ATHROW exception	989K	828K	9.57K	572K	78.6K	2.00K	31.2K	20.8K
explicit ATHROW exception	0	0	187K	82	0	0	0	0
native code entry	332	28.2K	1.02M	1.02M	2.63M	527K	259K	260K
elder sibling reached	1.24M	3.81M	5.06M	16.1M	5.62M	14.1M	4.03M	4.23M
deleted from queue	348K	686	559K	3.13M	2.55M	4.48M	34.2M	1.57M
signalled by parent	202M	92.6M	20.1M	42.1M	56.3M	80.8M	122M	124M
TOTAL CHILD COUNT	204M	127M	36.5M	82.4M	74.5M	99.9M	162M	131M

In Table 2, total counts are given for all child thread termination reasons. In all cases, the majority of children are signalled by their parent thread to stop speculation. Significant numbers of child threads are deleted from the queue, and elder siblings are frequently reached. We looked at the average thread lengths for speculative children, and found them to be quite short, typically in the 0–10 instruction range. These data all indicate that threads are being forked too frequently, and are consistent with the general understanding of Java application behaviour: there are many short leaf method calls and the call graph is very dense [24]. Inlining methods will change the call graph structure, and it has previously been argued that inlined Java SMLP execution benefits from coarser granularity [5]. Introducing inlining into our system and exploring fork heuristics are therefore part of future work.

Outside of these categories, it is clear that synchronization and the memory barrier requirements for finals and volatiles are important; enabling speculative locking and recording barrier operations would allow threads to progress further. Native methods can also be important, but are much harder to treat. The other safety considerations of the Java language do not impact significantly on speculative execution; even speculative exceptions are responsible for a minority of thread terminations.

Data on the number of speculative thread successes and failures, as well as a breakdown of failure reasons, are given in Table 3. Failures due to GC, buffer overflows and exceptions are quite rare, and the majority of failures typically come from incorrect return value prediction. This again emphasizes the importance of accurate RVP in Java SMLP, and the weak impact of exceptions and GC. Dependence violation counts are not insignificant, and reusing predictors from the RVP framework for generalised load

Table 3. Child thread success and failure

join status	comp	db	jack	javac	jess	mpeg	mtrt	rt
exception in parent	0	0	386K	23.4K	0	0	0	0
incorrect prediction	18.0M	22.7M	2.80M	11.3M	5.80M	7.73M	4.85M	3.72M
garbage collection	4	20	119	206	470	0	90	68
buffer overflow	0	0	0	10	0	0	0	0
dependence violation	1.60M	1.44K	160K	1.53M	342K	14.7M	4.14M	4.00M
TOTAL FAILED	19.6M	22.7M	3.34M	12.9M	6.14M	22.4M	9.00M	7.72M
TOTAL PASSED	184M	103M	32.6M	66.4M	65.8M	73.0M	119M	122M

value prediction should help to lower them. In general, failures are much less common than successes, the geometric mean failure rate being 12% of all speculations. While this is encouraging, many threads are quite short due to an abundance of method calls and therefore forked children, and the high overheads imposed by thread startup. Thus it is likely the case that had they progressed a lot further, more violations would have occurred.

Table 4. *Impact of TLS support components on application speedup.* The priority queue was disabled by only enqueueing threads if a processor was free, return value prediction was disabled by always predicting zero, and the remaining components were disabled by forcing premature thread termination upon attempting to use them.

experiment	comp	db	jack	javac	jess	mpeg	mtrt	rt	mean
forced failure baseline	1297s	931s	293s	641s	665s	669s	1017s	1530s	722s
no priority queueing	0.94x	1.22x	1.35x	1.32x	1.58x	0.97x	1.68x	2.05x	1.27x
no return value prediction	1.03x	1.17x	1.28x	1.24x	1.44x	1.03x	1.72x	1.70x	1.25x
no dependence buffering	1.04x	1.22x	1.12x	1.05x	1.16x	1.02x	0.95x	0.97x	1.08x
no object allocation	0.95x	1.30x	1.39x	1.26x	1.55x	0.98x	1.13x	1.23x	1.21x
no method entry and exit	0.94x	1.02x	0.97x	0.98x	1.02x	0.95x	0.79x	0.91x	0.95x
full runtime TLS support	1.06x	1.27x	1.39x	1.37x	1.64x	1.01x	1.82x	2.08x	1.34x

Table 4 shows the impact of individual support components on Java TLS execution. Currently, thread overheads preclude actual speedup, and run times are within one order of magnitude [9]. This is competitive with hardware simulations providing full architectural and program execution detail [25], but we are also optimistic about techniques for achieving real speedup. In order to factor out the effects of fork and join overhead, we use a baseline execution time where speculation occurs as normal, but failure is automatically induced at every join point, calculating a mean relative speedup of 1.34x.

We note first of all that `compress` and `mpegaudio` are resilient to parallelisation, likely due to our current, naïve thread forking strategies. In some cases, disabling components can even lead to slight speedup. This phenomenon occurs if overhead costs outweigh component benefits; for example, disabling return value prediction can mitigate the cost of committing many short threads. In general, we can provide a partial ordering of support components by importance: the priority queue is least important; method entry and exit, or stack buffering, and dependence buffering are most important; return value prediction and speculative object allocation lie somewhere in-between.

7 Conclusions and Future Work

Language and software based thread level speculation requires non-trivial consideration of the language semantics, and Java in particular imposes some strong TLS design constraints. Here we have defined a complete system for Java TLS, taking into account various aspects of high level language and virtual machine behavioural requirements. Our implementation work and experimental analysis of Java-specific behaviour show that while most of these concerns do not result in a significant impact on TLS performance, conservatively correct treatment of certain aspects can reduce potential speedup, most notably synchronization. Part of our future work is thus to investigate different forms of speculative locking [22] within a Java-specific context.

Our design focuses on defining correct Java semantics in the presence of TLS, and demonstrating the associated cost. However, as with any speculative system, performance and TLS overhead are also major concerns, and efforts to improve speedup in many fashions are worthwhile, as suggested by previous profiling results [9]. We are confident that overhead can be greatly reduced in our prototype implementation, through optimisation of individual components, greater use of high level program information, and employment of general and Java-specific heuristics for making forking decisions and assigning thread priorities. Further speedup is also expected by allowing speculative children to spawn speculative children, and by supporting load value prediction, both increasing the potential parallelism. Longer term future work includes an implementation of TLS within the IBM Testarossa JIT and J9 VM, where we hope to incorporate and measure these and other improvements, and research JIT-specific TLS problems and opportunities.

Acknowledgements

This research was funded by the IBM Centre for Advanced Studies in Toronto, NSERC, FQRNT, and McGill University.

References

1. Chen, M.K., Olukotun, K.: The Jrpm system for dynamically parallelizing Java programs. In: ISCA. (2003) 434–446
2. Steffan, J.G., Colohan, C., Zhai, A., Mowry, T.C.: The STAMPede approach to thread-level speculation. TOCS **23**(3) (2005) 253–300
3. Manson, J., Pugh, W., Adve, S.V.: The Java memory model. In: POPL. (2005) 378–391
4. Chen, M.K., Olukotun, K.: Exploiting method-level parallelism in single-threaded Java programs. In: PACT. (1998) 176–184
5. Hu, S., Bhargava, R., John, L.K.: The role of return value prediction in exploiting speculative method-level parallelism. JILP **5** (2003)
6. Whaley, J., Kozyrakis, C.: Heuristics for profile-driven method-level speculative parallelization. In: ICPP. (2005) 147–156
7. Kazi, I.H.: A Dynamically Adaptive Parallelization Model Based on Speculative Multithreading. PhD thesis, University of Minnesota (2000)

8. Yoshizoe, K., Matsumoto, T., Hiraki, K.: Speculative parallel execution on JVM. In: 1st UK Workshop on Java for High Performance Network Computing. (1998)
9. Pickett, C.J.F., Verbrugge, C.: SableSpMT: A software framework for analysing speculative multithreading in Java. In: PASTE. (2005) 59–66
10. Bhowmik, A., Franklin, M.: A general compiler framework for speculative multithreading. In: SPAA. (2002) 99–108
11. Quiñones, C.G., Madriles, C., Sánchez, J., Marcuello, P., González, A., Tullsen, D.M.: Mitosis compiler: An infrastructure for speculative threading based on pre-computation slices. In: PLDI. (2005) 269–279
12. Bruening, D., Devabhaktuni, S., Amarasinghe, S.: Softspec: Software-based speculative parallelism. In: FDDO-3. (2000)
13. Rundberg, P., Stenström, P.: An all-software thread-level data dependence speculation system for multiprocessors. JILP **3** (2001)
14. Cintra, M., Llanos, D.R.: Toward efficient and robust software speculative parallelization on multiprocessors. In: PPoPP. (2003) 13–24
15. Cook, J.J.: Reverse execution of Java bytecode. The Computer Journal **45**(6) (2002) 608–619
16. Gagnon, E.M.: A Portable Research Framework for the Execution of Java Bytecode. PhD thesis, McGill University (2002) `http://www.sablevm.org`.
17. Vallée-Rai, R.: Soot: A Java bytecode optimization framework. Master's thesis, McGill University (2000) `http://www.sable.mcgill.ca/soot/`.
18. Pickett, C.J.F., Verbrugge, C.: Compiler analyses for improved return value prediction. Technical Report SABLE-TR-2004-6, Sable Research Group, McGill University (2004)
19. Shavit, N., Zemach, A.: Scalable concurrent priority queue algorithms. In: PODC. (1999) 113–122
20. Pickett, C.J.F., Verbrugge, C.: Return value prediction in a Java virtual machine. In: VPW2. (2004) 40–47
21. Renau, J., Tuck, J., Liu, W., Ceze, L., Strauss, K., Torrellas, J.: Tasking with out-of-order spawn in TLS chip multiprocessors: Microarchitecture and compilation. In: ICS. (2005) 179–188
22. Martínez, J.F., Torrellas, J.: Speculative synchronization: Applying thread-level speculation to explicitly parallel applications. In: ASPLOS. (2002) 18–29
23. Lea, D.: The JSR-133 cookbook for compiler writers. `http://gee.cs.oswego.edu/dl/jmm/cookbook.html` (2005)
24. Dufour, B., Driesen, K., Hendren, L., Verbrugge, C.: Dynamic metrics for Java. In: OOPSLA. (2003) 149–168
25. Krishnan, V., Torrellas, J.: A direct-execution framework for fast and accurate simulation of superscalar processors. In: PACT. (1998) 286–293

Lightweight Monitoring of the Progress of Remotely Executing Computations

Shuo Yang, Ali R. Butt, Y. Charlie Hu, and Samuel P. Midkiff

School of Electrical and Computer Engineering
Purdue University, West Lafayette IN 47907, USA
{yang22,butta,ychu,smidkiff}@purdue.edu

Abstract. The increased popularity of grid systems and cycle sharing across organizations requires scalable systems that provide facilities to locate resources, to be fair in the use of those resources, and to monitor jobs executing on remote systems. This paper presents a novel and lightweight approach to monitoring the progress and correctness of a parallel computation on a remote, and potentially fraudulent, host system. We describe a monitoring system that uses a sequence of program counter values to monitor program progress, and compiler techniques that automatically generate the monitoring code. This approach improves on earlier work by omitting the need to duplicate computation, which both simplifies and reduces the overhead of monitoring. Our approach allows dynamic and accountable cycle-sharing across the Internet. Experimental results show that the overhead of our system is negligible and our monitoring approach is scalable.

1 Introduction

Computational workloads for academic groups, small businesses and consumers are characterized by long periods of little or no processing punctuated by periods of intense computational needs. It has been observed that computational resource demands can be "smoothed out" across sub-groups by aggregating large numbers of resources and users together. Computational resources across the world naturally experience different levels of demand at any given time because of their distribution. Computational resources are perishable, thus failing to use cycles, bandwidth and disk space does not create additional resources to be used in the future. However, if resources that would otherwise go unused could be provided to other users with the promise of sufficient compensation to cover the overhead of providing the resources, along with a small profit, then these resources would yield some value to the provider.

The major value of computational resources to their owner is the knowledge that they are available when needed. The major cost of sharing unneeded cycles is the legal and administrative overheads involved in allowing others access to the resources. Allowing compensation for these administrative overheads would dramatically increase the quantity, and decrease the cost, of available cycles. Both the decreased cost and the ease of accessing cycles increase the number of applications that can exploit these resources and increase the number of users that can access them. Academics and research laboratories would have access to a vast array of machines for running simulations, benchmarking programs, and running scientific applications; small businesses

E. Ayguadé et al. (Eds.): LCPC 2005, LNCS 4339, pp. 319–333, 2007.

would have machines available for data-mining sales, accounting and forecasting; and consumers would have machines available to perform computationally intensive, but low-economic value activities such as games and digitally processing home movies. Elimination of these overheads would allow automatic intermediation between consumers and providers of resources, allowing shared resources to blend seamlessly with locally owned resources.

Current cycle sharing systems take two approaches to minimizing these overheads. The first approach relies on volunteers providing cycles to a trusted job provider [1,2,3] with no desire for real compensation. These projects have allowed large computations, which would be infeasible on committed hardware, to be performed using surplus cycles on thousands of machines world-wide, and show the value of exploiting surplus cycles. By having volunteers provide the machines and absorb the local administrative overhead of enabling the application to run, by having a single trusted application, and by avoiding compensation issues, these projects avoid the difficulties that a more general approach must tackle. Although this model performs well in its targeted application domain, it clearly cannot be generalized to support cycle sharing for applications that do not inspire similar levels of generosity.

The second approach is typified by centrally managed systems like Condor [4] and LoadLeveler [5] that have been developed to allow resources to be aggregated within permanent or ad-hoc organizations. Centralized administration of resources allows a trusted entity – the system administrators – to verify and track the trustworthiness of users given access to the resources, *and* it allows users to deal with a known, trusted entity. Although this model has allowed organizations to share unused cycles internally, it does not work well for sharing cycles across organizations.

Four technical challenges must be overcome to allow the exploitation of the massive amounts of computational resources that are going unused. Solutions to the first three of these have been developed by other projects. The first challenge is how to discover resources to be used, and how to compensate the providers of the resources and punish cheaters [6,7,8]. The second challenge is how to enable a *submitter* machine to generate executables compatible with the *host* platform in a heterogeneous system [9,10]. The third challenge is how to protect the *host* machine, i.e. the machine executing the job, from hostile binaries [11,12].

In this paper, we discuss a solution to the fourth technical challenge, the problem of allowing the *submitter* machine, i.e. the machine submitting a job, to know its job is being faithfully executed. This capability is necessary for widespread cycle sharing, both to allow submitters of jobs to have confidence that their jobs are making progress towards completion, and to allow submitters of jobs to incrementally compensate the system hosting the job, thereby bounding the risk of the host. In this paper, we assume that host nodes may act *fraudulently*, but not maliciously. That is, a host node may take actions to gain compensation for which it is not entitled, but it will not take actions that harm the submitter but which do not benefit the host. We make the following contributions to monitoring the progress of remote jobs:

- We present a novel, lightweight technique to remotely monitor the incremental progress of a program that is executing in an untrusted environment. This technique has a lower overhead than any previous technique known to the authors.

- We present experimental data showing the overhead of this system is less than 2.1% on the remote system executing the program, and is negligible on the submitter system that is monitoring the application's progress.
- We present a monitoring technique that uses characteristics of the currently executing binary to generate and encode progress information, and is impervious to replay attacks.
- We show how the relatively uniform distribution of system and library calls can be used to guide the placement of the monitoring code, allowing simple compiler algorithms to be used to generate the monitoring code. We present experimental data that validates this approach.

The rest of the paper is organized as follows. Section 2 presents our novel *binary file location beacon (BLB)* approach to remote job monitoring for native binary executable programs. Section 3 presents the implementation of our general BLB approach to target MPI programs. Section 4 presents the experimental results showing the effectiveness of the system. Finally, Section 5 discusses the related work and Section 6 concludes the paper.

2 Monitoring Progress and Correctness with Beacons

In this section, we present a light-weight technique based on *binary file location beacons (BLB)* for monitoring the progress of remotely executing programs.

We assume a generic Internet cycle sharing system where each participating node can submit jobs (i.e. be a *submitter* node) or host jobs (i.e. be a *host* node). In this paper, we focus on remote job monitoring, with other components, such as resource location and credit management, being beyond the scope of this paper.

2.1 Key Idea

Before the *submitter* node submits a computational job to the *host* node for execution, it passes the program to our tool which transforms the original program into a pair of programs, one that executes on the host machine (*H-code*) and one that executes on the submitter machine (*S-code*). The H-code is the original program augmented with *beacons* and auxiliary code that send information about the program to the submitter machine. The S-code uses this information to track the progress, and verify the execution of, the program. Figure 1 shows an example of the runtime architecture of a remote job monitoring system.

The basic idea of this paper is to use place *location beacons (L-beacons)* along the control flow graph (CFG) of a program to track the fine-grained remote job progress information. However, a L-beacon based tracking mechanism is vulnerable to a replay attack. For example, Miller et al. [13] describes how to use existing tools to replace, on-the-fly, a process with another process. Thus, if a valid L-beacon value stream of a previous execution is captured, the attacker can replace the process of the later computation with a process that emits the captured L-beacon value sequence to cheat the submitter.

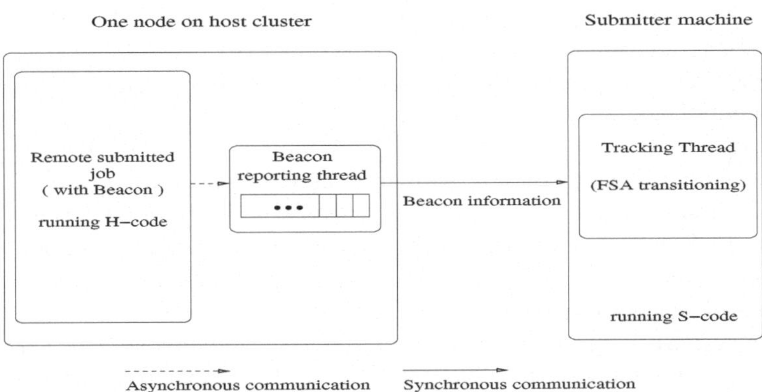

Fig. 1. The run time monitoring system for MPI programs: displaying only one tracking thread and the corresponding process it monitors

The contribution of this paper is on how to use the location beacons to monitor remote program execution. Specifically, the key idea of this paper is that by *making the value transmitted by location beacons reflect the structure of the program and by partially randomizing their placement, we can defeat replay attacks.* We call this technique *binary file location beacons*, or *BLB*-based remote monitoring for binary applications.

In our BLB-based remote job monitoring, the submitter constructs a finite state automaton (FSA) that tracks the progress of the remote job executing on the host machine. BLBs are placed along control flow graph (CFG) edges of a program and used to identify the current location of the program during its execution. At runtime, a BLB invokes a function f that stores the beacon value in a buffer, with the buffer sent to the submitter program at predetermined intervals. The value placed in the buffer is the value of the program counter at the BLB site, more precisely, it is the program counter of the instruction immediately following the call to f. By using the program counter value, the beacon value is intimately tied to the layout of the binary code generated for the program.

Our beacon insertion technique works as follows. The original program is scanned for candidate beacon insertion points, i.e., the entries to computationally significant regions. Computationally significant regions can be identified by the programmer or can be identified via an analytical cost model (see [14] for details). In this paper, we use a variant of the former approach, but instead of having the programmer explicitly identify candidate insertion points, we make use of the observation that system and library calls tend to be relatively uniformly distributed across programs, and tend to not appear within the inner loops of high performance programs. By using system and library call sites as candidate sites for placing BLBs, we do not need to use analytical models within the compiler to locate candidate sites.

2.2 Possible Attacks

Each BLB inserted will attempt to add a beacon value, which is a program counter (PC) value, into the BLB buffer to be sent to the host. An attack on our monitoring system needs to emit a stream of valid BLB values to be communicated to the submitter machine. There are two ways of doing this. The first is to capture a valid stream of beacon values from a previous correct execution of the program, and then replay this stream on future requests to execute the program. We prevent this attack by not always inserting beacons at the same locations when generating a program. At each potential BLB insertion site B, a beacon is actually inserted with probability P_B. If $P_B = 0$, no beacon is ever inserted at this site, if $P_B = 1$ a beacon is always inserted at this site. For $0 < P_B < 1$ a beacon may be inserted. By setting the values of P_B to be non-zero and less than one, each version of the program generated by our compiler will likely have a different set of beacons inserted and consequently a different set of valid beacon values. Because the values of P_B can be different at different candidate sites B the placement of beacons can be made more or less likely, depending on the hotness of a program region. In any case, attempts to replay the old beacon values will fail, with a high probability, because the replayed set of beacons will likely contain invalid beacon values. Because the binaries for programs used in high performance computing are usually orders of magnitude smaller than the data they operate on, shipping a (possibly) new binary with each execution imposes only a small overhead.

The second form of attack is for the host to analyze the binary and to extract the set of BLB call sites and the reachability information between BLB call sites necessary to construct the FSA. With this information a host can reconstruct the FSA and generate a valid sequence of BLB values. Two approaches can be used to prevent this attack. The first is to use code obfuscation to hide the control flow structure of the program, and consequently make it very difficult to determine the reachability information necessary to construct the FSA. A moderate use of jump tables to implement branches, and a moderate use of jump tables for function dispatch in code not on the critical path, should be sufficient to thwart program analysis tools. We note that simply compiling programs at high optimization levels performs a high degree of code obfuscation, and that is the technique we use now. Explicit code obfuscations techniques, such as the one described in [15] to enhance the difficulty of reverse-engineering, can be applied to our approach to further enhance the security of the system.

We note that attacks predicated on changing the binary must simultaneously preserve two structural properties of the program. First, the reachability of beacons from other beacons must be unchanged. Failing to do this will cause the host to run the risk that sequences of beacons not possible in the original program will be sent to the submitter. Second, the location of the code (explained in detail in the next section) that obtains the PC cannot be changed, since this will cause sequences of beacons sent to the submitter to contain values that are not possible in the original program.

Finally, we note that our goal is not to construct an unbreakable system, but rather to construct a system where the cost of breaking it is as high as the benefit.

3 Implementation Details

In the previous section we introduced a general BLB-based technique applicable to any binary executable program. In this section, we present a concrete implementation using

BLBs in MPI message passing programs. We choose MPI programs because MPI is the most popular programming model for high performance computing. Moreover, MPI programs are able to work on more diversified platforms, including SMP and distributed memory systems, than any other programming model.

3.1 Program Counters of MPI Calls as BLB Values

As described in Section 2, BLBs provide fine-grained location information about an executing program. The compiler in the monitoring system generates host code by inserting hard-coded beacon instructions at significant points in the program. Because beacon instructions that are inserted in the host code take time to execute and therefore add to the overhead of the program, the selection of locations to insert BLBs must account for the tradeoff between the granularity of monitoring and the program overhead. Thus locations chosen to insert beacon instructions should be: (i) where the overhead of executing the beacon instructions is affordable, and (ii) easily identified by a compiler as an efficient place to locate a binary location beacon.

In an MPI program, interprocess communication and synchronization are achieved by calling MPI library functions. Therefore, locations of interprocess communication and synchronization points, i.e., the MPI calls in the program, naturally satisfy the above two criteria because (i) the cost of a beacon instruction is insignificant compared to the interprocess communication or synchronization cost plus the cost of the computation performed since the last beacon, and (ii) a compiler front-end can trivially identify MPI calls.

The code in Figure 2 shows our implementation to obtain PC values to be used as BLB values. `GetPC()` is an instruction that obtains the PC value of the next instruction (the invocation of the `mpi_send` call) in a C program targeting an Intel IA32 processor running FreeBSD. Function `getPC()` returns the address that is placed on the stack frame when it is invoked, i.e. the PC of the instruction immediately after the invocation of `getPC()`. Adding the C expression `pc = getPC()` immediately before an MPI call returns the address where the MPI operation is invoked, i.e., the PC value at the MPI operation call site. We have implemented the same functionality for Fortran. The only difference between the C and Fortran implementations is how the value is returned by the respective `getPC()` functions because of the different function calling conventions.

For different machine architectures, a slightly different function needs to be provided. AMD64 family processors have the same calling convention and stack layout as the Intel IA32 architecture, and the above method to get the program counter value is valid. For architectures that allow more aggressive use of registers during code generation (e.g. the PowerPC architecture), slightly different code is generated because the return address from a function call is saved into a dedicated register instead of onto the stack. Therefore the `getPC()` function for these architectures returns the value held in the dedicated register instead of returning the value on the stack frame. For 64-bit Intel Itanium architecture, the cost of `getPC()` can be reduced by utilizing its "register stack frames" architecture, which enables `getPC()` to avoid accesses to the stack frames in main memory.

```
main(){
    ...
    mpi_send(...);
    ...
}
```

(a) *An MPI call in original code*

```
int pc;
main(){
    ...
    pc = getPC();
    mpi_send(...);
    ...
}
...
int getPC(){
    asm("mov 4(%ebp), %eax");
}
```

(b) *PC values returned by getPC() as BLB*

Fig. 2. Obtaining the program counter of an MPI call in a C program on IA32

3.2 FSA Constructed with Program Counters of MPI Calls

We now present the method used to construct a finite state automaton (FSA) to track legal sequences of BLB values. Each process in the host system executing the submitted program runs the same MPI executable, and their FSAs are identical.

The FSA construction algorithm is presented in [14]. This algorithm projects a complete program control flow graph onto a program control flow graph containing only nodes that are annotated with beacons. A node n_i in the new graph can reach a node n_j in the new graph if and only if n_i could reach n_j in the original graph. Using this algorithm, we construct an FSA where states in the FSA represent nodes in the new control flow graph. After compiling the code into a binary executable, we use a disassembler (`objdump()` in our case) to get the addresses of the MPI calls that are identified as beacon sites, map them onto the corresponding states in the FSA, and use the addresses as the state labels in the FSA. The address of the call to `mpi_init()` corresponds to the initial state of the FSA, and the address of the call to `mpi_finalize()` corresponds to the final state of the FSA. The transition symbol α driving a transition toward a specific state (also labeled α) is the address of the corresponding node in the binary executable.

Figure 3 shows an MPI program fragment, the corresponding H-code and the resulting FSA. In this example, we treat each MPI call as a beacon site (i.e. all P_B = 1). As shown in Figure 3(b), the compiler identifies each MPI call and inserts a call to `getPC()` immediately before the MPI call. The compiler also inserts a call to `deposit_beacon()`, which puts the BLB value into the beacon buffer, after each MPI call identified as a BLB. After the FSA is constructed, and after the transformed code is compiled, the BLB values are mapped onto the states and transition symbols in the FSA, as shown in in Figure 3(c).

3.3 Runtime System of Monitoring MPI Programs

We now discuss the details of how the `deposit_beacon()` call places the BLB value generated by `getPC()` into a beacon buffer, and how the sequence of values placed into the buffer is transmitted to the submitter machine and used to monitor the progress of the program. Figure 1 shows a *tracking thread* on the submitter and the corresponding process that it monitors in the host cluster.

```
main(){
    ...
    mpi_irecv(...);
    ...
    if(...)
        mpi_send(...);
    ...
    mpi_wait();
    ...
}
```

(a) *A piece of pseudo code of MPI program*

```
main(){
    ...
    pc = getPC();
    mpi_irecv(...);// @0x804a641 in the executable
    deposit_beacon(pc);
    ...
    if(...){
        pc = getPC();
        mpi_send(...);// @0x804a679 in the executable
        deposit_beacon(pc);
    }
    ...
    pc = getPC();
    mpi_wait(); // @0x804a69b in the executable
    deposit_beacon(pc);
    ...
}
```

(b) *Generated host code*

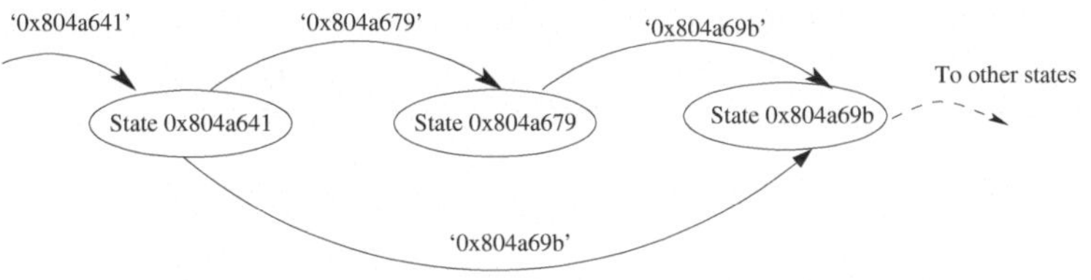

(c) Part of FSA corresponding to above program: transition symbols on the edges correspond to the unique program counter emitted by the inserted beacon instructions

Fig. 3. An example of program counter based FSA

At the beginning of the computation on the host, the H-code performs an initialization procedure. Each MPI process allocates a beacon buffer where the BLB values generated by this process are inserted. A beacon buffer in our current implementation can hold up to 1500 beacon values. Each process also creates a separate *reporting thread*. The reporting thread on each process builds a TCP socket that connects to the monitoring S-code program running on the submitter. During the computation, the main computation thread on each process takes beacon values returned by invocations of the `getPC()` function and, via a call to `deposit_beacon()`, places the beacon value into the beacon buffer. This is shown in Figure 3(b). Periodically the reporting thread on each process sends the contents of its buffer to the submitter, and then clears the buffer to allow more beacon values to be deposited. The *pthread* mutex and condition variables are used to synchronize access to the beacon buffer by the main computation and the reporting thread.

The reporting thread on a process sends the values in the beacon buffer back to the submitter using a *paced* transmission scheme. The paced transmission scheme works as follows. The reporting thread sleeps for an interval, which is set by the submitter when the program is submitted to the host. When this interval passes, the reporting thread wakes up to send the values in the beacon buffer. If the buffer is filled before the interval expires, the reporting thread is woken up and immediately sends the buffer to the submitter node. When the reporting thread finishes sending the buffer, it sleeps for another interval. Thus, the cross-network data transfer procedure is asynchronous to the main computation of the program.

We now discuss the submitter machine actions. The submitter machine creates a dedicated thread (the *tracking thread*) for each MPI process executing on the host machine. Each tracking thread maintains an FSA, and the current state of the FSA is initialized to be the *initial* state, i.e. a state corresponding to an `mpi_init` call. Over time, the tracking thread receives buffers from its corresponding *reporting thread*, via the already established socket. Each beacon value in the buffer is processed by comparing it to states adjacent to the current state, which are found by performing a lookup in the FSA's transition table. If the beacon value does not match a valid transition from the current state, it is an illegal transition and the appropriate action is taken. Buffers continue to be received, and beacon values in the buffers continue to be processed, until the submitter receives the final state beacon value.

Finally we note that the monitoring runtime system can be configured with different setups. For example, the submitter can only build a connection to a single host process (e.g., the master node) and by receiving and tracking the single node's BLB values, the submitter can track the progress of the remote computation. Our system has sufficiently low overhead when tracking all host processes that we have not investigated this strategy further.

4 Experimental Results

In this section, we present performance results showing the overhead and effectiveness of our system.

4.1 Experimental Platform

Our experiments were run on a submitter/host pair located at the University of Illinois at Urbana-Champaign and Purdue University. The submitter machine, located at UIUC, is a uniprocessor with an Intel 3GHz Xeon processor, 512KB cache and 1GB main memory running the Linux 2.4.20 kernel. It is connected to the Internet through the campus network. The host machine is a cluster located at Purdue with 8 computational nodes, each of which has an Intel Pentium IV processor with 512KB cache, 512MB main memory, and runs FreeBSD 4.7. The nodes within the cluster are interconnected by a FastEthernet. The nodes in the cluster share a single file system, and the MPICH 1.2.5 library is installed on the cluster. Programs were hand-transformed using the approach described in Section 3.

4.2 NAS Parallel Benchmark Kernels

The NAS Parallel Benchmarks(NPB) [16] version 3.2 is a set of benchmarks developed to evaluate the performance of highly parallel computational resources. These benchmarks consist of five parallel kernels and three simulated applications. From these kernels and applications, we selected four kernels representing totally different types of computation and communication patterns to evaluate our approach.

- EP (an embarrassingly parallel kernel) represents computations without significant interprocessor communication. EP provides an estimate of the upper achievable limits for floating point performance.
- IS (a large integer sort kernel) performs a sorting operation that is important in particle method codes. IS tests both integer computation and communication performance.
- MG (a simplified multigrid kernel) performs the 3D V-cycle multigrid algorithm which solves the discrete Poisson problem with periodic boundary conditions. MG represents highly structured long distance communication and tests both short and long distance data communication.
- CG (a conjugate gradient kernel) performs the computation of the smallest eigenvalue of a large, sparse, symmetric positive definite matrix. CG represents irregular long distance communication and unstructured matrix vector multiplication, which is typical of unstructured grid computations.

In our measurements, the inter-transmission intervals of the beacon reporting thread is set to 2 seconds, which represents a highly aggressive monitoring scenario. In an actual system, the inter-transmission interval would be tens of seconds or minutes. Also, we generate beacon information for each MPI call in the program, reflecting the case of $P_B = 1$ described in Section 2, which is the most expensive version of the H-code to monitor. Therefore, our experiment provides an upper bound on the performance overhead and network traffic incurred by using our monitoring system.

4.3 Run Time Computation Overhead

We first evaluate the scalability of our system by measuring the system performance overhead with computations running on different numbers of processors. To evaluate this, we run each of the above benchmarks with problem size-B inputs on 2, 4 and 8 processors of our cluster. We measure the time to run the original benchmarks on our cluster, which reflects the scenario of remote job execution without monitoring. These form our baseline numbers. We then run the manually transformed submitter code and host code of the same benchmarks on the submitter/host pair, which reflects the scenario of a remote job submission with monitoring. Figure 4 shows the overhead of job executions, using beacons for monitoring, over the corresponding un-monitored baseline job execution times. Our experimental results show that the maximum performance overhead is under 2.1%. We notice that the overhead does not monotonically increase with an increasing number of processors, and now explain why. Both the base line number (the computation time without monitoring) and the number of beacon calls under monitoring (the number of the MPI function calls per process at run time) decrease when the number of processes increases. There is, however, no explicit relationship between these two decreasing values. As well, our monitoring system introduces additional synchronization overhead by adding a single *reporting thread* to each process. But this synchronization overhead is always one extra thread (the *reporting thread*) per process no matter how many processes the MPI code runs on.

Next we evaluate the relationship between the problem size of a monitored computation and the monitoring overhead. A problem with size-C input represents a larger

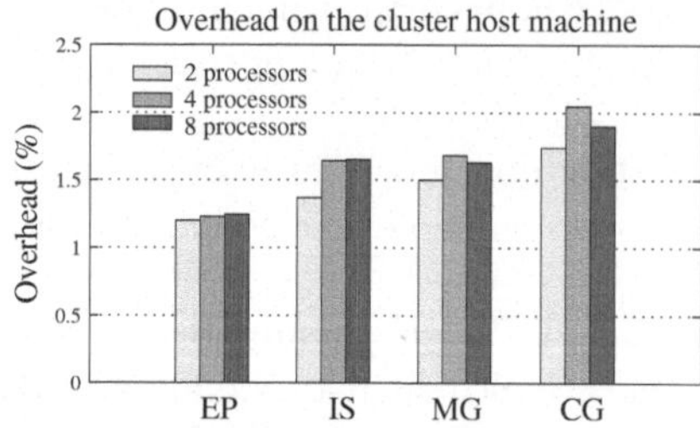

Fig. 4. Host Side Overhead with Different Number of Processors (Problem Size-B)

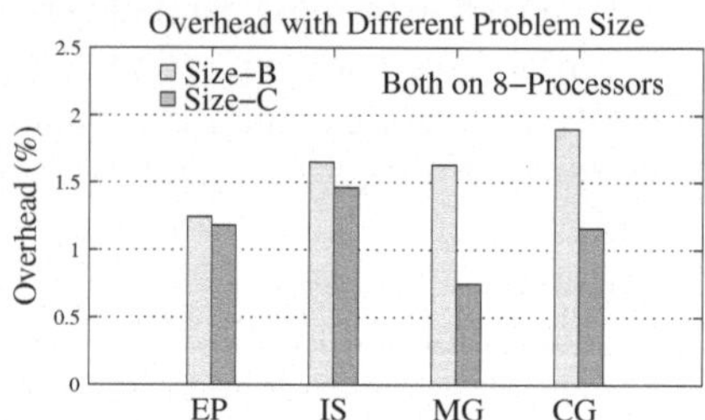

Fig. 5. Host Side Overhead with Different Problem Sizes

problem size than the problem with size-B input. For example, for MG problem size-B uses a 256 by 256 by 256 matrix as the input data set, and problem size-C uses a 512 by 512 by 512 matrix as the input data set. Figure 5 shows that the overhead to monitor a larger computation (in this case, size-C) is always smaller than that to monitor a smaller computation (in this case, size-B). This is because the number of MPI calls in problem size-B and in problem size-C runs of each benchmark are similar. Therefore the cost of depositing BLBs into the buffer and transferring them across the network (the overhead on the host machine) for both problem sizes are similar. However, the total computation time for problem size-C is greater than that for problem size-B, thus the overhead is lower for problem size-C.

Finally, we evaluate the submitter node CPU usage to monitor a remote job. As the submitter code only performs FSA transitioning, it uses a small fraction of the CPU. We use the system `time` facility to measure the computational resources used by the verification process on the submitter. This is an imperfect evaluation because this ratio changes according to two factors: (1) the submitter's hardware, and (2) the submitter's workload while monitoring a remote job, which affects the resources available to perform the monitoring. We believe, however, that the numbers give a feel for the low overheads, and small amount of resources required to perform the monitoring. Table 1 shows the ratio of the sum of the user CPU time and the system CPU time to the wall clock time (elapsed real time) during the S-code execution.

As the results in Table 1 show, monitoring a computation with a larger problem size always takes a smaller percentage of the submitter's CPU resources than monitoring a computation with a smaller problem size. This is because the amount of beacon information processed by the submitter for problem size-B and problem size-C is same for each benchmark, while the monitoring time, i.e., the computation time on the host for problem size-C is significantly longer than that for problem size-B. These numbers were measured while one author logged into the submitter machine and launched two emacs processes, one *vi* process, and one *Mozilla* web browser process, which mimics a 'realistic' working scenario of a job submitter.

4.4 Network Bandwidth Overhead

Since network resources are finite, it is necessary to limit the amount of data sent from the host to the submitter node. We evaluate the network traffic generated by our system

Table 1. CPU Usage of Monitoring Computation with Different Problem Size Code on Submitter: 8-processors on the host in both cases

	Size-B	Size-C
EP	0.06%	0.02%
IS	0.07%	0.02%
MG	0.15%	0.03%
CG	0.17%	0.07%

Table 2. Average network traffic (total traffic / execution time) in for different problem sizes

	Size-B (8 procs)	Size-C (8 procs)
EP	4.2 bytes/sec	1.0 bytes/sec
IS	101.5 bytes/sec	23.2 byte/sec
MG	21.2K bytes/sec	1.5K bytes/sec
CG	21.9K bytes/sec	7.9K bytes/sec

by measuring the number of bytes sent from the host machine to the submitter machine. In our experimental setup, each working process in the host cluster builds a TCP connection to the monitoring program (S-code, which creates tracking threads for all remote working processes) running on the submitter machine. In a real monitoring system setup, the submitter could choose to track a subset of the processes. Therefore, our experimental results reflect the upper bound of network traffic in a monitoring system.

In our experiment, we measured the average network traffic incurred by different benchmarks with problem size-B and problem size-C running on 8 processors. Table 2 shows the result of the above measurement, i.e. the total bytes of BLB values divided by the job execution time for each experiment. The results show that the larger the problem size , the smaller the average amount of network traffic the monitoring system incurs per unit time. The EP (embarrassingly parallel) kernel causes nearly zero traffic because this benchmark represents the type of computation without interprocessor communication. The BLB traffic is non-zero for EP because the benchmark uses several `mpi_reduce()` calls to get the computation result at the end of the benchmark. IS is the integer sorting benchmark and it uses a small amount of interprocessor communication to exchange the single elements at the boundaries of sub-arrays. MG and CG are typical numerical computations representing different communication patterns. These numbers show that the network traffic caused by our monitoring system is within the dial-up bandwidth.

4.5 Beacon Distribution over Time

Our BLB based MPI program tracking approach leverages the observation that MPI calls are relatively uniformly distributed across most programs. This property enables the *incremental* progress tracking by the submitter. To verify this observation, we measure the number of beacon packets received by the submitter, i.e., the number of TCP send operations on the host machine, across the execution (monitoring) time. Figure 6 shows the number of packets received in a single *tracking thread*, which reflects the beacon temporal distribution over execution time during computations of problem size-C for a single computation process in the host cluster in our experiment. Each bin in Figure 6 represents a two seconds interval. Figure 6 shows that with the exception of EP, the beacon buffer packets sent by the host machine in our benchmarks are relatively uniformly distributed across the program execution time. EP is an embarrassingly

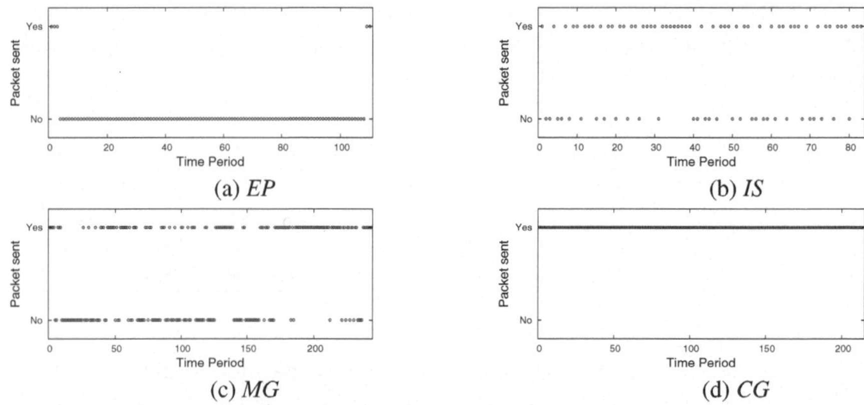

(a) *EP* (b) *IS*

(c) *MG* (d) *CG*

Fig. 6. Beacon packets sent by the host machine distributed during the execution (problem size-C) period: each bin representing a 2-second interval; 'yes' meaning there is BLB packet sent to receiver at that interval, 'no' meaning no BLB packet sent at that interval

parallel program and has no communication (because no data dependencies exist) during the main computation. For EP style programs, the submitter may choose to insert BLBs via an analytical cost model, as mentioned in Section 2.1 and described in [14], to get a relatively uniform BLB distribution. (We chose not to use that approach in this paper for the EP benchmark to keep our experimental conditions consistent.) We conclude that our approach of using MPI calls to place beacon calls gives good incremental progress information for most MPI programs.

5 Related Work

With the increasing popularity of grid systems and cycle sharing, efficient protection against malicious machines has become an important research topic. Sarmenta discusses a spot checking mechanism to catch malicious machines (saboteurs) [17]. The central manager randomly assigns some computations, whose results are known to the central manager, to volunteer machines. By comparing the known results with the results sent by the volunteer machines, malicious volunteers can be caught efficiently. Du et al. [18] proposed a Merkle (Hash) tree based technique to detect cheating nodes when embarrassingly parallel computations are being performed. By verifying a subset of leaves in the Merkle tree, a central job manager can grant the correctness of all the results in the tree. Both of above techniques ensure the integrity of participant machines by checking a subset of *independent computations* completed by the participant machines. Our approach differs in that it monitors the integrity of all parts of an application execution. Moreover, our approach monitors the progress of the application and enables partial payments or detection of errors before a long running application finishes. We note that monitoring the progress of an execution is stricter than only checking that a remote machine has faithfully executed the program. Monitoring the progress of execution requires *incremental* confirmation of faithful execution. This is important for long running jobs so that the submitter machine does not have to wait for the job to finish to know the job's progress.

Hofmeyr et al. [19] uses sequences of system calls to detect intrusions. They built a profile of normal system call behavior for a process of interest, treating deviations from this profile as anomalies. Chen and Wagner [20] designed the MOPS system based on the formal model of a program and of a security property, which uses a finite state automaton to describe security rule of a process. Both of these techniques analyze system call sequences to achieve anomaly detection. Our approach differs from theirs in that the beacons in our monitoring system are not limited to system calls (e.g. the implementation example in this paper uses MPI function calls as beacons). Moreover, the purpose of our approach is to monitor the remote job progress instead of assuring the security of a local machine.

Our previous monitoring system [14] provides an approach to monitoring remote computations running Java bytecode. The submitter constructs an FSA to track the progress of the program, and it duplicates a portion of the computation (R-beacon) to prevent replay attacks. The BLB approach presented in this paper differs from it in that the BLB approach obviates the need for recomputation beacons (R-beacon), which are the main component of network traffic and computational burden on the submitter side incurred by the monitoring system. The BLB approach also makes the beacon location identification much easier for the compiler.

Program monitoring is also employed in the Globus project for providing better quality of service [21]. This monitoring is either achieved indirectly by determining the resource utilization of the program, or by modifying the program to insert explicit calls to the Globus API. The motivation of our work is different in that we are using the monitoring to determine if we are receiving a resource as promised, and we do not need any special APIs in the host system, increasing the portability of our approach.

6 Conclusion

We have described a solution for monitoring the progress and correctness of a remote job. We show that the overhead of performing this monitoring is small. Although we describe our approach in the context of the MPI programming model, it is applicable to any binary. It is beneficial to both resource providers and resource consumers by limiting their risks. This technique, combined with our work, and the work of others, in resource discovery, sandboxed execution and automatic credit systems, opens the way for exploiting idle cycles across the Internet in a dynamic, ad-hoc fashion.

Acknowledgment

We thank Josep Torrellas for giving us access to his machines at UIUC to perform remote job submission and monitoring experiments. This work was supported in part by NSF CAREER award grant ACI-0238379 and NSF grants CCR-0313026 and CCR-0313033.

References

1. Genome@home: Genome at home. (http://www.stanford.edu/group/pandegroup/genome/index.html (December 16, 2004))
2. SETI@home: Search for extraterrestrial intelligence at home. (http://setiathome.ssl.berkeley.edu/index.html (December 16, 2004))
3. David, A.P.: BOINC:A System for Public-Resource Computing and Storage. In: Proc. 5th IEEE/ACM International Workshop on Grid Computing. (2004)
4. Litzkow, M., Livny, M., Mutka, M.: Condor - A Hunter of Idle Workstations. In: Proc. 8th International Conference on Distributed Computing Systems (ICDCS 1988). (1988)
5. Kannan, S., Roberts, M., Mayes, P., Brelsford, D., Skovira, J.F.: Workload Management with LoadLeveler. IBM International Technical Support Organization (2001) http://www.ibm.com/redbooks (Dec. 17, 2004), publication number SG24-6038-00.
6. Butt, A.R., Fang, X., Hu, Y.C., Midkiff, S.: Java, Peer-to-Peer, and Accountability: Building Blocks for Distributed Cycle Sharing. In: Proc. of VM'04. (2004)
7. Castro, M., Druschel, P., Hu, Y.C., Rowstron, A.: Exploiting Network Proximity in Distributed Hash Tables. In: International Workshop on Future Directions in Distributed Computing. (2002)
8. Lo, V., Zappala, D., Zhou, D., Liu, Y., Zhao, S.: Cluster Computing on the Fly: P2P Scheduling of Idle Cycles in the Internet . In: Proc. of IPTPS'04. (2004)
9. Minchew, C.H., Tai, K.C.: Experience with Porting the Portable C Compiler. In: ACM 82: Proceedings of the ACM '82 conference, New York, NY, USA (1982)
10. PARISC-Linux: The PARISC-Linux Cross Compiler HOWTO. (http://www.baldric.uwo.ca/HOWTO/PARISC-Linux-XC-HOWTO.html (March 16, 2005))
11. Barham, P., Dragovic, B., Fraser, K., Hand, S., Harris, T., Ho, A., Neugebauer, R., Pratt, I., Warfield, A.: Xen and the Art of Virtualization. In: Proc. of SOSP'03. (2003)
12. Kamp, P.H., N.M.Watson, R.: Jails: Confining the Omnipotent Root. In: Proceedings of SANE 2000 Conference. (2000)
13. Miller, B.P., Christodorescu, M., Iverson, R., Kosar, T., Mirgorodskii, A., Popovici, F.: Playing Inside the Black Box: Using Dynamic Instrumentation to Create Security Holes. In: Proceedings of 2nd Los Alamos Computer Science Institute Symposium. (2001)
14. Yang, S., Butt, A.R., Hu, Y.C., Midkiff, S.P.: Trust but Verify: Monitoring Remotely Executing Programs for Progress and Correctness. In: Proc. of PPOPP'05. (2005)
15. Linn, C., Debray, S.: Obfuscation of Executable Code to Improve Resistance to Static Disassembly. In: Proc. of CCS'03. (2003)
16. Bailey, D., Barszcz, E., Barton, J., Browning, D., Carter, R., Dagum, L., Fatoohi, R., Fineberg, S., P.Frederickson, Lasinski, T., Schreiber, R., Simon, H., Venkatakrishnan, V., Weeratunga, S.: The NAS Parallel Benchmarks. Technical Report NAS Technical Report RNR-94-007, NASA Ames Center (1994)
17. Sarmenta, L.F.: Sabotage Tolerance Mechanism for Volunteer Computing Systems. In: CCGrid'01. (2001)
18. Du, W., Jia, J., Mangal, M., Murugesan, M.: Uncheatable Grid Computing. In: Proceedings of the 24th International Conference on Distributed Computing Systems (ICDCS'04). (2004)
19. Hofmeyr, S.A., Forrest, S., Somayaji, A.: Intrusion detection using sequences of system calls. Journal of Computer Security **6** (1998)
20. Chen, H., Wagner, D.: MOPS: an Infrastructure for Examining Security Properties of Software. In: Proc. of CCS' 02. (2002)
21. Foster, I., Roy, A., Sander, V.: A Quality of Service Architecture that Combines Resource Reservation and Application Adaptation. In: Proc. 8th International Workshop on Quality of Service. (2000)

Using Platform-Specific Performance Counters for Dynamic Compilation

Florian Schneider and Thomas R. Gross

Laboratory for Software Technology
Department of Computer Science
ETH Zürich
Zürich, Switzerland

Abstract. Hardware performance counters provide information about events in the hardware platform (e.g., cache misses, pipeline stalls), in contrast to profiles that capture program properties (e.g., execution frequencies for basic blocks, methods, function calls). As platform architectures become more complex and also more diverse, it is important for a compiler to exploit platform-specific information. A dynamic (JIT) compiler is in the unique position to run on the same platform as the target application, but in practice, exploiting the wealth of information available through performance counters is far from easy. If a JIT compiler is to use performance counter information, this information must be fine-grained (e.g., attributing cache misses to a single load instruction) and must be obtainable without undue overhead. We present a runtime+compiler framework to tie hardware performance counter information to a dynamic compiler and argue that the overhead is low and fine-grained. As parallel architectures or multi-core architectures proliferate, performance issues will play a crucial role in all compilation engines, and our paper reports on a modular approach to make such counter information available to the compiler.

1 Introduction

The combination of VM and JIT compiler is now the most common execution platform for programs written in object-oriented languages. Unlike the classic ahead-of-time compilation model, the JIT compiler is able to take immediate advantage of dynamic information. There are two kinds of information that such a compiler may use: *profiles*, i.e. measurements of program properties (e.g., number of method invocations) and measurements of platform-specific properties, such as number of cache misses, TLB misses, branch prediction failures). The latter must be obtained from the performance measurement unit of the execution platform, and this paper details how this information can be provided to and used by a compiler for a high-level language like Java.

Many compilers for high-performance linear algebra computing already use information from the execution platform for cache optimization: For example, blocking is a common technique to reduce cache misses in matrix computations, but using it effectively requires that the characteristics of the memory hierarchy

E. Ayguadé et al. (Eds.): LCPC 2005, LNCS 4339, pp. 334–346, 2007.

be considered [14]. Another example is inter-variable padding [18], which can be used to reduce conflict misses, but requires a precise knowledge about the application's memory access patterns. For programs in the domain of scientific computing these access patterns can often be obtained exactly or can be approximated by an analytical model. Still, the design of performance monitoring units is still the subject of current research [15].

On the other hand, object-oriented programs have many properties that are difficult to determine at compile-time (e.g., memory access patterns, synchronization patterns). As multi-core and parallel architectures proliferate, attention to performance for object-oriented programs increases the need to use platform-specific information to generate efficient code. Most modern CPUs (like the Pentium 4 (P4), Itanium, PowerPC) offer the ability to deliver information about performance-related events to the OS or the application, yet most previous JIT compilers focussed only on using program properties to guide optimizations [6]. Preliminary studies (without full compiler support) have however demonstrated that platform-specific metrics can also improve the performance of object-oriented programs[2].

To be useful for an optimizing JIT compiler the collected information must be accurate enough and cheap to obtain at run-time. Since modelling memory access patterns analytically for pointer-intensive code (typically found in OO programs) is not feasible at the moment, the use of hardware performance monitors presents a viable way of getting detailed information about memory hierarchy performance aspects. This paper presents a general infrastructure to feed hardware performance monitor information into a JIT compiler at run-time.

2 Requirements

Our basic assumption is that the object-oriented program executes on some VM and that this VM provides a JIT compiler (possibly offering different optimization levels). A module that makes information from the hardware performance monitors available in a JIT compiler must meet a couple of requirements:

- The runtime+compiler infrastructure should be flexible enough to allow obtaining different execution metrics. The exact group of events that can be monitored depends on the specific hardware performance counters that are available, but the interface between compiler and performance monitoring unit should attempt to hide machine-specific details where possible.
- The overhead to obtain the monitor's information should be low, and the executed applications should not be perturbed by the measurements.
- Processing the information should be done in a separate module, to keep the need for changes to VM and/or the compiler to a minimum.
- The information must be accurate enough to be useful for online optimizations in a JIT compiler. Often the granularity of a method or even a basic block is too coarse to allow the compiler to infer what instruction/operation is responsible for some event (e.g., cache misses).

– The platform should work for "general" VMs. We don't want to change the core VM code too much. Otherwise the effort to port it to another VM would be prohibitively large.

Of course, any compiler that uses platform-specific information may also use profile information, e.g., to decide where and when to exploit the results obtained from the performance measurement unit. We will not dwell on this aspect in this paper.

3 Related Work

There are two areas of prior work that we concentrate on in this paper: techniques to provide platform-specific information in a form that the compiler can exploit and specific optimizations in a compiler that are influenced by this information. While there exists a fair bit of prior work regarding profiling (e.g., discussion of types of profiles, algorithms to select the best place to insert code to maintain counters, choice of sampling intervals), it is not central to the topic of this paper, and so is not covered here.

3.1 Data Gathering Techniques

Profiling to obtain execution frequencies and profile-guided optimizations have been applied in ahead-of-time compilers (see, e.g., [17,8]) and JIT compilers [6,20]. Here we focus on related work that uses hardware-specific information for optimizations.

Ammons et al. [5] use hardware performance counters together with path profiling. They use code instrumentation to associate hardware metrics (like cache misses) to basic blocks and execution paths in the program. The reported overhead of flow and context sensitive profiling is between 60 and 80%. This overhead is acceptable when doing off-line performance analysis.

Trace-driven simulation of the memory hierarchy can be used for analyzing data locality and identifying bottlenecks [11,10]. The results depend on how precise the simulation reflects the real platform. One disadvantage of precise simulation is that the slowdown can be several orders of magnitude [23].

Vera et al. [24] use an analytical model to approximate the behavior of the CPU and memory hierarchy. They use cache miss equations to describe the behavior of loop-oriented code. Their approach is mainly targetted at scientific compuations which exhibit regular access patterns.

In recent years OO applications have been analyzed using profiles and hardware support. Hauswirth et al. [12] analyze Java programs and their interaction with the VM, the OS and the hardware using *vertical profiling*. They distinguish different execution layers in a system: application, libraries, VM, OS and hardware. To analyze the performance of these layers they introduce "software performance monitors". These monitors capture performance characteristics of the different subsystems. The results are correlated with data from the hardware performance counters to find out how different metrics influence each other.

Georges et al. [9] present an off-line technique for analyzing the performance behavior of individual methods. Since instrumenting every method would be too expensive, they identify method-level phases by measuring the execution time spent in each method. In a second step, only those methods that consitute an execution phase are instrumented. The hardware performance counters are read at the method prologue and at the epilogue. Finally, the profiling results are mapped back to the Java source code. The approach has a low overhead because only those methods selected by the phase analysis are instrumented. It uses the hardware performance counters in normal counting mode, not in event-based sampling mode like we do.

3.2 Optimizations

Cache optimizations reduce the gap between memory and processor speeds. Loop-tiling, loop-skewing, and blocking [25] can increase data locality in scientific, array-oriented programs. To obtain maximal performance, cache parameters must be considered when choosing the block size [14].

Software-controlled prefetching [16] hides the memory latency by overlapping memory access with other operations. It is mainly used for scientific applications which are array-oriented and have regular iteration patterns that can be determined statically.

OO programs require a different approach because they usually use pointers heavily and do not exhibit the regular structure of scientific applications. Adl-Tabatabai et al. [2] use hardware performance monitors of the Itanium 2 processor to inject prefetch instructions into Java programs. Their approach relies on the fact that objects that are accessed consecutively often have a constant delta between their addresses. A "meta-data graph" captures references between classes that exhibit a large number of long-latency misses and the corresponding deltas. The prefetching uses this graph to ensure the right data is available in the cache. They achieve a speedup of 14% for the SPEC JBB2000 benchmark [21]. Software prefetching is very effective on Itanium because it has only in-order execution and lacks the hardware-based prefetching of the P4.

Huang et al. [13] implemented a technique called online object reordering that reorders objects at garbage collection time. They identify "hot" fields by gathering access statistics using code instrumentation. The garbage collector then copies the object referenced by hot fields together with their parent object to increase spatial locality.

4 Implementation Platform

This section presents background of the hardware and software platform that we used for our implementation.

4.1 Hardware Performance Monitors

The P4 offers a large variety of performance events for counting [1]. Two modes of operation are supported:

- Normal counting: The performance counters are configured to count events detected by the CPU's event detectors. A tool can read those counter values after program execution and report the total number of events. This mode can be used to obtain numbers like the cache miss rate, total execution cycles, and so on. One application would be to evaluate the effect of program transformations.
- Sampling-based counting: Whenever a certain number of events has occurred, the CPU samples its register contents. This way it is possible to locate the sources of an event. The P4 supports precise event-based sampling, so it reports both the exact instruction where the sampled event happened and the register contents at that point.

  To keep the overhead of sampling low, the CPU stores a certain number of samples in a buffer provided by the OS. The CPU generates a performance monitor interrupt when this buffer is filled up to a "high-water" mark. The interrupt service routine of the OS copies the samples to a more permanent location.

  This mechanism makes it possible to obtain data address profiles with the P4. The instruction pointer (IP) together with the other registers' contents can be used to calculate the data address of an event (e.g., cache miss). A data memory address of an event can be computed by decoding the instruction that caused the event and using the values of the registers to calculate its address operand.

Previous CPUs could only measure an approximate location for sampled events because of a super-scalar design and out-of-order execution. The P4 and other newer architectures (e.g. Itanium) have the capability to localize the event precisely (precise event-based sampling). Sprunt [19] wrote a detailed overview of the P4's hardware performance monitoring capabilities.

4.2 Jikes RVM

Our implementation is done with the IBM Jikes RVM (version 2.3.3) [4,3], a high performance Java virtual machine written mostly in Java. It includes an adaptive optimization system [6]. First, every method is compiled with a simple and quick baseline compiler. Only methods that are executed frequently enough are recompiled and optimized further.

5 Runtime+compiler Platform Issues

Our extension allows the VM to monitor the performance of a running application using the CPU's hardware performance monitors. In a dynamic compilation environment like the Jikes VM the compiler can then react and use this information to dynamically recompile and optimize parts of the program. We extended the abyss&brink tools [7] to configure and access the P4 performance counters. The tools consist of a kernel module and a user-level program to gather statistics about the program that is being measured.

The kernel module initializes the hardware performance monitors and provides the sampling interrupt handler that copies the samples from the kernel buffer into a more permanent buffer supplied by the application (in our case the Java VM). The P4 hardware supports precise event-based sampling for only a subset of events. The most important of those are:

- L1 and L2 load misses,
- DTLB misses, and
- branch mispredictions.

At the moment the type of event that is monitored is specified as a command-line parameter.

We modified the Linux kernel and the kernel module to be able to monitor individual processes. Otherwise the results would be disturbed by other processes running at the same time.

The monitoring infrastructure consists of three parts:

1. Loadable kernel module: The kernel module offers the functions to access the performance counter hardware. It is implemented as a device driver, and the application communicates with it via IOCTL calls. The kernel module hides the platform-specific details from the JVM. It also provides the interrupt handler that is called by the sampling hardware when the CPU buffer for the samples is full. When this happens the samples are copied into a more permanent location. At the moment we allocate a 4MB shared memory buffer for this purpose.
2. Native shared library (C): Since we cannot call device drivers directly from Java or from the Jikes RVM we use a native library to provide an interface and call it via the Java Native Interface (JNI). The library gives access to the shared buffer where all the collected samples are stored.
3. Collector thread (Java): We use a separate Java thread that polls the device driver via the library interface whether there are any new samples. The polling interval is set to 1-10ms depending on the size of the sample buffer. Each sample is converted into a Java object by the collector thread and handed to the VM for further processing.

Figure 1 shows how the samples get from the CPU to the JVM. Buffering the samples in user space makes the JVM independent of any platform idiosynchracies as those are handled by the kernel device driver.

On the P4 platform one sample has a size of 36 bytes. It contains the instruction pointer (IP) where the sampled event occurred and all the values of the registers at this point in the program. Figure 2 shows the structure of one sample. The CPU writes those values directly into the buffer provided by the kernel module. To be able to use these raw data for optimization we need to recover some higher-level information for each sample. The JIT compiler keeps a sorted table of all methods' start/end addresses that were compiled so far. From the IP we can quickly find out the method and the bytecode instruction where the event happened by performing a binary search. When the adaptive optimization system recompiles a method this method table must be updated.

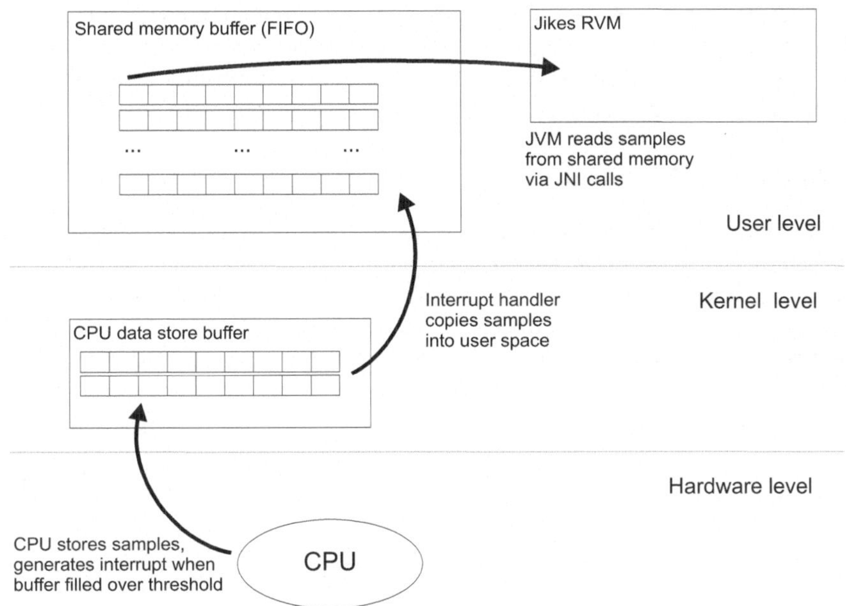

Fig. 1. Getting the samples from the CPU to the JVM

The bytecode instruction tells us the operation and the type of the object that caused the event. With the bytecode instruction we can produce a human readable output that contains the Java statement and the source line number for the event. When we encounter an event caused by a heap access we determine the actual type of the responsible object by scanning backward in memory starting at the calculated data address until we find the object header [2].

EAX	EBX	ECX	EDX	ESI	EDI	EBP	ESP	EIP

Fig. 2. One sample (total 36 bytes) contains the instruction pointer (EIP) and all register contents

6 Evaluation

6.1 Measurements

The measurements are carried out on a 3.0 GHz P4 processor running the Linux kernel version 2.4.26. This processor has a 1MB L2-cache and a 64K L1 cache and 1024 MB of main memory. One cache line has a width of 64 bytes. For each data point we ran the benchmark three times and reported the average. As a VM we ran Jikes RVM 2.3.3 with the configuration "FastAdaptiveGenCopy", which includes the adaptive optimization system [6] and a generational garbage collector.

For our experiments we set the system to measure cache misses. The sampling interval should be large enough to keep the overhead low, but not too large. Otherwise the collected data won't be meaningful. A sampling interval between 1000 and 10000 events proved to be most suitable for our benchmark programs.

6.2 Sampling Overhead

Table 1 compares the performance of the system with and without sampling enabled. For this measurement we sampled every 10000 and every 1000 events. (columns s=10000 resp. s=1000). For the SPEC JVM98 [22] and the SPEC JBB2000 [21] benchmarks we observed an overhead between 0.1% and 2% (average 1.6%) for a sampling interval s of 10000. For s = 1000 the overhead is between 0.1% and 5% (average 2.1%).

Table 1. Overhead of collecting sample data with two different sampling intervals s=1000 and s=10000

program	orig	s=10000	s=1000
javac	7.18	1.02	1.02
raytrace	4.04	1.02	1.02
jess	2.93	1.01	1.00
jack	2.73	1.00	1.03
db	10.49	1.01	1.03
compress	6.5	1.01	1.02
mpegaudio	6.54	1.02	1.00
jbb	6209.67	1.02	1.05
average		1.016	1.021

To analyze the influence of the sampling interval on the overall performance we studied the JBB benchmark in more detail. Figure 3 shows the correlation between the sampling interval and the performance as measured by the *specJBB* score. The interrupt rate of the HPM hardware grows linearly with decreasing sampling interval size. The overall performance drops even more at high interrupt rates; the resulting context switches for each invocation of the interrupt service routine consume further CPU time. From the observed execution times we can estimate the cost of processing one sample with $< 1\mu s$ (=3000 CPU cycles on a 3 GHz P4).

6.3 Distribution of Cache Misses

The precise event-based sampling of the P4 allows us to measure the distribution of cache misses over the load instructions in the program. We use a sampling interval of 1000 events for L2 misses and 10000 events for L1 misses.

For *db*, *javac*, and *specJBB* we measure the frequency of L1- and L2-misses. Figure 4 shows the histogram of the 100 most contributing load instructions for L1 cache misses. These loads produce 37% of the L1 misses in *javac*, 98%

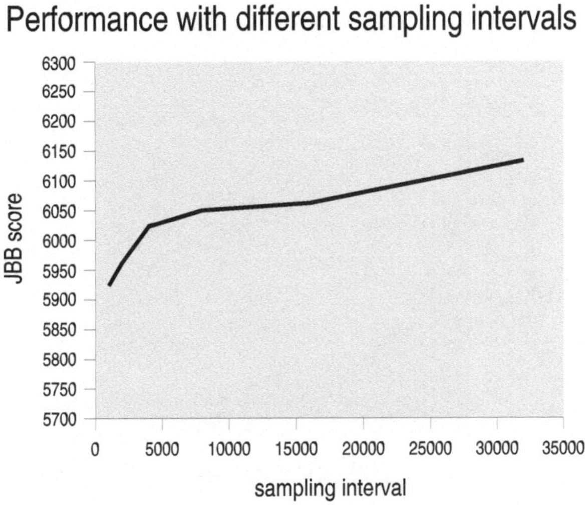

Fig. 3. Performance with different sampling intervals

in *db*, and 55% in *specJBB*. The picture is different for long latency L2 cache misses. Figure 5 shows the same information for L2 misses. There, the 100 most contributing load instructions are responsible for 74%, 99% and 85% of the events. For *db* the distribution of L1 and L2 misses is quite similar – there are very few "hot" loads. In *javac* and *specJBB*, on the other hand, the L1 misses are generally distributed over the whole program, whereas the L2 misses are more localized. (except for one instruction in *specJBB* that produces the majority of the L1 misses). This suggests that if we focus optimizations on these cache misses, or "hot" spots, we can achieve a large impact.

7 Concluding Remarks

Using platform-specific information about a program's execution in a dynamic compiler is attractive; the result of the platform's performance measurement unit can be mapped to source-language constructs that are relevant for the compiler. A necessary condition (to be satisfied by the platform's architect) is that the monitoring unit can accurately capture the processor state related to an event. Fortunately, newer processors provide this capability.

A JIT compiler is in a good position to exploit this information, since we have shown that the overhead of gathering and processing the information about hardware-specific events can be kept low.

To demonstrate the practicality of this approach, we implemented a module to tie the Jikes VM to the execution monitoring unit of the P4. As an example application we showed that the compiler can use this mechanism to identify individual load instructions that are responsible for a high percentage of the

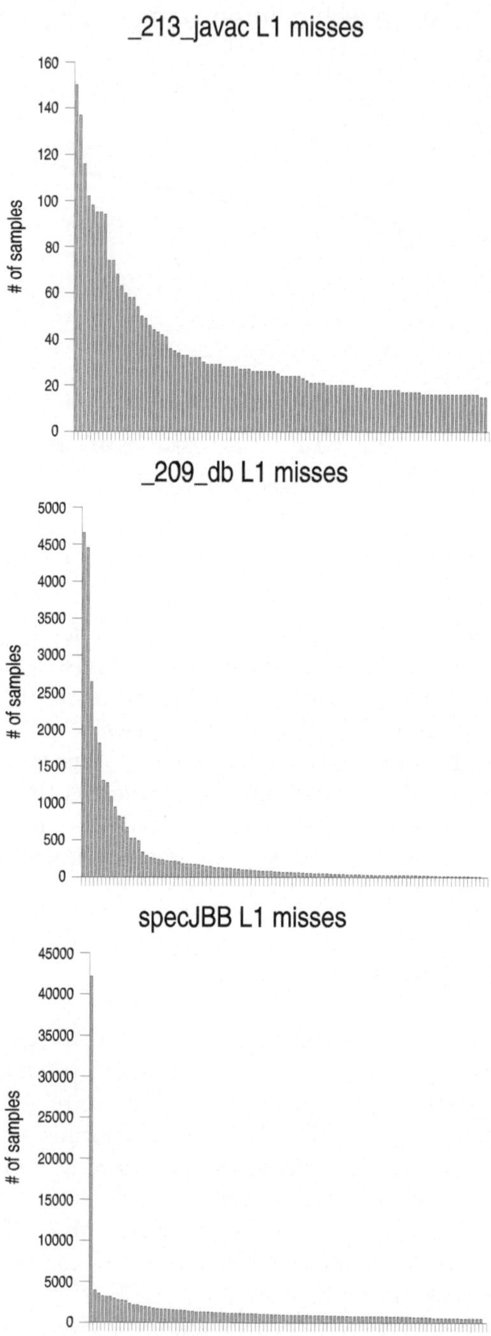

Fig. 4. Histograms of L1 cache misses (100 most contributing load instructions)

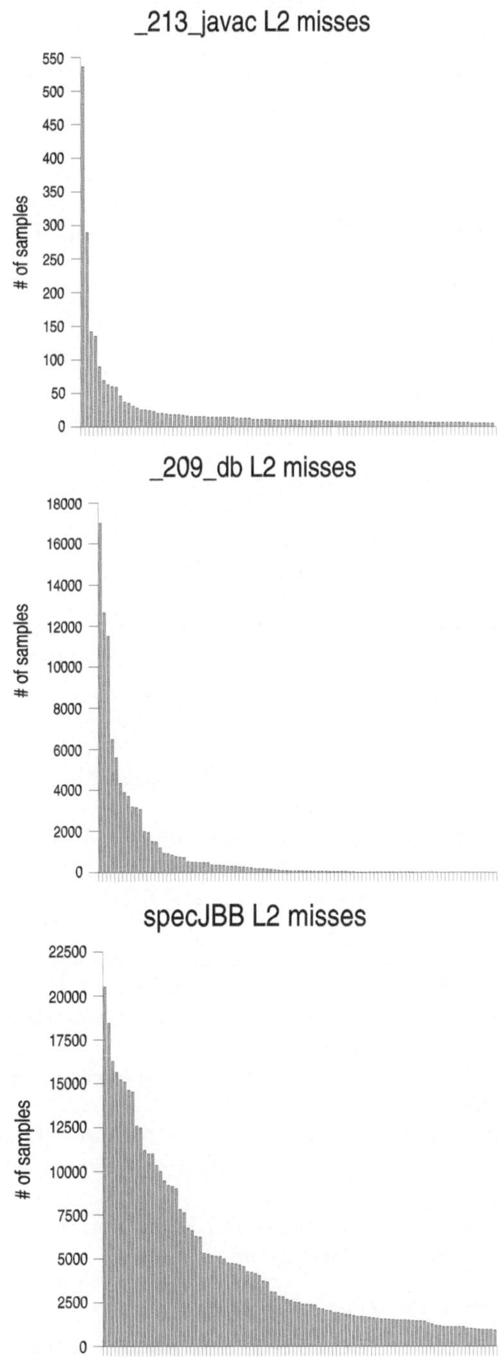

Fig. 5. Histograms of L2 cache misses (100 most contributing load instructions)

cache misses. This information allows feedback-driven optimization that does not solely rely on high-level information like method execution frequencies, but is directly guided by information about performance critical hardware events.

Acknowledgments

We thank Lukas Löhrer and Flavio Pellanda for their help and their contributions to the implementation.

References

1. IA-32 Intel Architecture Software Developer's Manual, Volume 3: System Programming Guide. 2005.
2. A.-R. Adl-Tabatabai, R. L. Hudson, M. J. Serrano, and S. Subramoney. Prefetch injection based on hardware monitoring and object metadata. In *Proc. of the ACM SIGPLAN 2004 Conf. on Programming language design and implementation*, pages 267–276, New York, NY, USA, 2004. ACM Press.
3. B. Alpern, C. R. Attanasio, J. J. Barton, A. Cocchi, S. F. Hummel, D. L. ber, T. Ngo, M. F. Mergen, J. C. Shepherd, and S. Smith. Implementing jalapeno in java. In *Conference on Object-Oriented*, pages 314–324, 1999.
4. B. Alpern, D. Attanasio, J. Barton, M. Burke, P. Cheng, J.-D. Choi, A. Cocchi, S. Fink, D. Grove, M. Hind, S. F. Hummel, D. Lieber, V. Litvinov, T. on Ngo, M. Mergen, V. Sarkar, M. Serrano, J. Shepherd, S. Smith, V. C. Sreedhar, H. rini Srinivasan, and J. Whaley. The Jalapeno virtual machine. *IBM Systems Journal, Java Performance Issue*, 39(1), 2000.
5. G. Ammons, T. Ball, and J. R. Larus. Exploiting hardware performance counters with flow and context sensitive profiling. In *Proc. of the ACM SIGPLAN 1997 conference on Programming language design and implementation*, pages 85–96, New York, NY, USA, 1997. ACM Press.
6. M. Arnold, S. Fink, D. Grove, M. Hind, and P. F. Sweeney. Adaptive optimization in the jalapeo jvm. In *Proc. of the 15th ACM SIGPLAN conference on Object-oriented programming, systems, languages, and applications*, pages 47–65, New York, NY, USA, 2000. ACM Press.
7. Brink & Abyss. http://www.eg.bucknell.edu/ bsprunt/emon/brink_abyss/brink_abyss.shtm.
8. P. P. Chang, S. A. Mahlke, and W. W. Hwu. Using profile information to assist classic code optimizations. *Software Practice and Experience*, 21(12):1301–1321, Dec 1991.
9. A. Georges, D. Buytaert, L. Eeckhout, and K. D. Bosschere. Method-level phase behavior in java workloads. In *Proc. of the 19th annual ACM SIGPLAN Conference on Object-oriented programming, systems, languages, and applications*, pages 270–287, New York, NY, USA, 2004. ACM Press.
10. A. J. Goldberg and J. L. Hennessy. Performance debugging shared memory multiprocessor programs with mtool. In *Supercomputing '91: Proc. of the 1991 ACM/IEEE conference on Supercomputing*, pages 481–490, New York, NY, USA, 1991. ACM Press.

11. S. R. Goldschmidt and J. L. Hennessy. The accuracy of trace-driven simulations of multiprocessors. In *Proc. of the 1993 ACM SIGMETRICS conference on Measurement and modeling of computer systems*, pages 146–157, New York, NY, USA, 1993. ACM Press.
12. M. Hauswirth, P. F. Sweeney, A. Diwan, and M. Hind. Vertical profiling: understanding the behavior of object-priented applications. In *Proc. of the 19th annual ACM SIGPLAN Conference on Object-oriented programming, systems, languages, and applications*, pages 251–269, New York, NY, USA, 2004. ACM Press.
13. X. Huang, S. M. Blackburn, K. S. McKinley, J. E. B. Moss, Z. Wang, and P. Cheng. The garbage collection advantage: improving program locality. In *Proc. of the 19th annual ACM SIGPLAN Conference on Object-oriented programming, systems, languages, and applications*, pages 69–80, New York, NY, USA, 2004. ACM Press.
14. M. S. Lam, E. E. Rothberg, and M. E. Wolf. The cache performance and optimizations of block algorithms. In *4th International Conference on Architectural Support for Programming Languages and Operating Systems*, pages 63–74, Santa Clara, CA, Apr. 1991.
15. Lubeck, O. et al. WS6: Hardware Performance Monitor Design and Functionality, Los Alamos Computer Science Institute Symposium 2005. Web archive http://lacsi.rice.edu/workshops/hpca11, Feb 12-16 2005, San Francisco, 2005.
16. T. C. Mowry, M. S. Lam, and A. Gupta. Design and evaluation of a compiler algorithm for prefetching. In *Proc. of the 5th international conf. on Architectural support for programming languages and operating systems*, pages 62–73, New York, NY, USA, 1992. ACM Press.
17. K. Pettis and R. Hansen. Profile guided code positioning. In *Proc. ACM SIGPLAN'90 Conf. on Prog. Language Design and Implementation*, pages 16–27, White Plains, N.Y., June 1990. ACM.
18. G. Rivera and C.-W. Tseng. Data transformations for eliminating conflict misses. In *Proc. of the ACM SIGPLAN 1998 Conf. on Programming language design and implementation*, pages 38–49, New York, NY, USA, 1998. ACM Press.
19. B. Sprunt. Pentium 4 performance monitoring features. In *IEEE Micro*, pages 72–82, July–August 2002.
20. T. Suganuma, T. Yasue, M. Kawahito, H. Komatsu, and T. Nakatani. A dynamic optimization framework for a Java just-in-time compiler. In *Conf. on Object-Oriented Programming, Systems, Languages & Applications (OOPSLA '01)*, pages 180–194, 2001.
21. The Standard Performance Evaluation Corporation. SPEC JBB2000 Benchmark. http://www.spec.org/jbb2000/.
22. The Standard Performance Evaluation Corporation. SPEC JVM98 Benchmarks. http://www.spec.org/osg/jvm98, 1996.
23. R. A. Uhlig and T. N. Mudge. Trace-driven memory simulation: a survey. *ACM Comput. Surv.*, 29(2):128–170, 1997.
24. X. Vera, N. Bermudo, J. Llosa, and A. González. A fast and accurate framework to analyze and optimize cache memory behavior. *ACM Trans. Program. Lang. Syst.*, 26(2):263–300, 2004.
25. M. E. Wolf and M. S. Lam. A data locality optimizing algorithm. In *Proc. of the ACM SIGPLAN '91 Conference on Programming Language Design and Implementation*, volume 26, pages 30–44, Toronto, Ontario, Canada, June 1991.

A Domain-Specific Interpreter for Parallelizing a Large Mixed-Language Visualisation Application

Karen Osmond, Olav Beckmann, Anthony J. Field, and Paul H.J. Kelly

Department of Computing, Imperial College London,
180 Queen's Gate, London SW7 2AZ, United Kingdom
p.kelly@imperial.ac.uk

Abstract. We describe a technique for performing domain-specific optimisation based on the formation of an execution plan from calls made to a domain-specific library. The idea is to interpose a proxy layer between the application and the library that delays execution of the library code and, in so doing, captures a recipe for the computation required. This creates the opportunity for a "domain-specific interpreter" to analyse the recipe and generate an optimised execution plan. We demonstrate the idea by showing how it can be used to implement coarse grained tiling and parallelisation optimisations in MayaVi, a 44,000-line visualisation application written in Python and VTK, with no change to the MayaVi code base. We present a generic mechanism for interposing a domain-specific interpreter in Python applications, together with experimental results demonstrating the technique's effectiveness in the context of MayaVi. For certain visualisation problems, in particular the rendering of isosurfaces in an unstructured mesh fluid flow simulation, we demonstrate significant speedups from coarse grained tiling, and from both SMP and distributed-memory parallelisation.

1 Introduction

Key objectives in engineering high-quality software are the need for high performance and protecting existing investment. The work we present in this paper illustrates how the use of domain-specific libraries can make it difficult to bridge these requirements. We propose domain-specific interpreters as a design pattern for addressing this problem. We show an example of a domain-specific interpreter implemented in Python and demonstrate that this can be used to achieve transparent parallelisation of large-scale visualisation tasks.

Software systems are being built from increasingly large and complex domain-specific libraries. Using such domain-specific libraries (DSLs) often dominates and constrains the way a software system is built just as much as a programming language. To illustrate the increasing size and complexity of DSLs, consider the following three examples:

– The Legacy BLAS 1, 2 and 3 libraries [1] are very successful libraries, domain-specific to dense linear algebra, with a total number of around 150 functions.

E. Ayguadé et al. (Eds.): LCPC 2005, LNCS 4339, pp. 347–361, 2007.

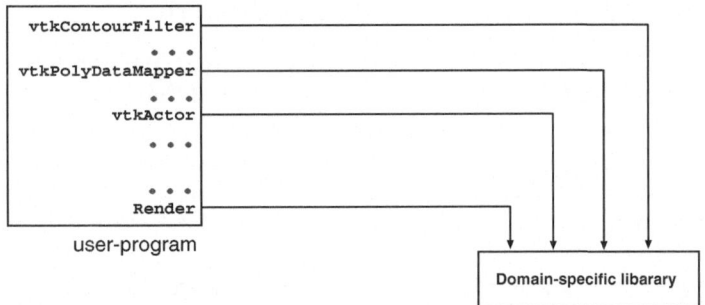

(a) User program is processed by a standard compiler or interpreter. DSL code is mixed with other code. No domain-specific optimisation is performed.

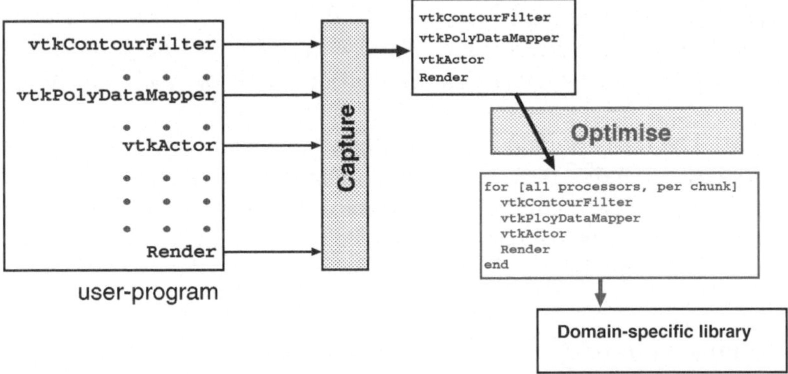

(b) User program is compiled or interpreted by an unmodified language compiler or interpreter. All calls to the DSL are captured and recorded in an execution plan. Domain-specific optimisations are applied to the execution plan before it is executed.

Fig. 1. Domain-specific library use: (a) typical use and (b) domain-specific interpreter

- MPI is a slightly later, but equally successful library which is domain-specific to message-passing communication. MPI-1 [2] included over 100 functions, MPI-2 over 200 functions.
- VTK (Visualisation Toolkit) [3, 4] is a large C++ visualisation library. The total number of classes and methods is hard to count; the user's guide is 325 pages long, and additional documentation is found in a 500-page book.

Using domain-specific libraries and abstractions often introduces domain-specific semantics into a software system in a manner similar to a programming language. The problem is that the base-language compilers or interpreters have no knowledge of these domain-specific semantics, and in particular, of domain-specific optimisations that might be possible. Furthermore, calls to DSLs are typically mixed with other, non-domain-specific code, which might make it hard for a conventional compiler to infer the exact sequence of calls that will be made to the DSL. This is illustrated in Figure 1(a).

1.1 Domain-Specific Interpreter Design Pattern

We propose a "domain-specific interpreter" as a design pattern for overcoming the problem described above. The idea is illustrated in Figure 1(b): The application program is still processed by a standard compiler or interpreter. However, calls to the DSL are captured by a proxy layer which records an execution plan consisting of the operations to be performed. We then have the opportunity to apply restructuring optimisations to the execution plan before it is executed.

Applicability. The applicability of domain-specific interpreters depends on being able to capture reliably all calls that are made to the DSL, and, on having accurate data-flow information available. The latter means knowing whether the data which is processed by the DSL can also be modified by the intervening non-domain-specific code, and being able to derive an accurate data-flow graph by inspection of the execution plan. As discussed in Section 3, both these requirements are met for visualisation applications built on VTK and Python.

Profitability. The likely benefit of using a domain-specific interpreter depends on whether we have domain-specific semantic information available, and on whether opportunities for cross-component optimisation exist. For our case-study, the optimisations we discuss are parallelisation and a form of tiling. Semantic information is, for the time being, supplied by hand.

1.2 Visualisation of Large Scientific Datasets

Visualising large scientific datasets is a computationally expensive operation, which typically involves processing a "visualisation pipeline" of domain-specific data analysis and rendering components: before the rendering step various feature extraction or data filtering computations may be executed, such as isosurface calculation, interpolation of a regular mesh or flow-lines integration. Modular visualisation environments (MVEs), such as the Python/VTK-based open-source MayaVi tool [5, 6, 4], present end-users with an interface for assembling such components. This effectively defines a high-level graphical programming language for visualisation pipelines. Such a dynamic-assembly architecture forms the core of many software frameworks, and is essential for their flexibility. As discussed in Section 1, it unfortunately also presents a barrier to conventional compile-time optimisation.

We describe the implementation of a domain-specific interpreter that allows us to apply restructuring optimisations, specifically parallelisation, to visualisation pipelines specified from MayaVi. Our approach requires no changes to the MayaVi code. We achieve this by intercepting DSL calls at the Python-VTK binding interface. This allows us to build up a "visualisation plan" of the underlying VTK routines applied to the dataset without actually executing those routines. We partition the dataset off-line using a tool such as METIS [7], and then apply the captured visualisation plan in parallel on each partition where that is consistent with the semantics of the data analysis components.

The work described in this paper was motivated by the visualisation requirements of ocean current simulations using adaptive, unstructured (*i.e.* tetrahedral) meshes. Even small runs generate multi-gigabyte datasets. Each stage of such a visualisation pipeline can be a computationally very expensive operation which is typically applied to the entire dataset. This can lead to very significant delays before any visual feedback is offered to an application scientist who is trying to compose and parameterise a visualisation pipeline.

1.3 Contributions

The main contributions of this paper are as follows.

- We present our experience of performing cross-component optimisation in a challenging, dynamic, multi-language context.
- We present a domain-specific interpreter which intercepts DSL calls at the Python/C++ interface, and we show how this allows a data-flow graph for the required computation to be extracted at runtime while avoiding many complex dependence issues (Section 3).
- We discuss how applying visualisation pipelines one partition at a time, even on a uniprocessor, can lead to performance improvements. We refer to this optimisation as "coarse grained tiling"[1] (Section 4).
- We present parallelisation strategies for visualisation pipelines captured by the domain-specific interpreter, for both shared- and distributed-memory architectures (Sections 5–6).
- We present results from performance experiments that show encouraging speedups for coarse grained tiling and both types of parallelisation (Sections 5–6).

This paper builds on our earlier work [8] where we restructured the MayaVi source code by hand to improve response time. Apart from changing the MayaVi source code, this earlier work also did not achieve parallelisation.

The remainder of this paper is structured as follows. In Section 2, we place this work in the context of ongoing research into optimisation techniques for dynamically composed assemblies of high-level software components. In Section 3, we present an implementation of the domain-specific interpreter pattern in Python for optimising the use of VTK. In Section 4, we present results for the coarse grained tiling optimisation mentioned above. In Section 5 we discuss parallelisation of visualisation pipelines for shared memory, and in Section 6, we discuss parallelisation for distributed memory platforms. Section 7 concludes and describes our plans for future work.

---

[1] This is not tiling in the classical sense of non-linear transformations of loops over dense arrays — however, it does represent a re-ordering of the iteration space over a large dataset.

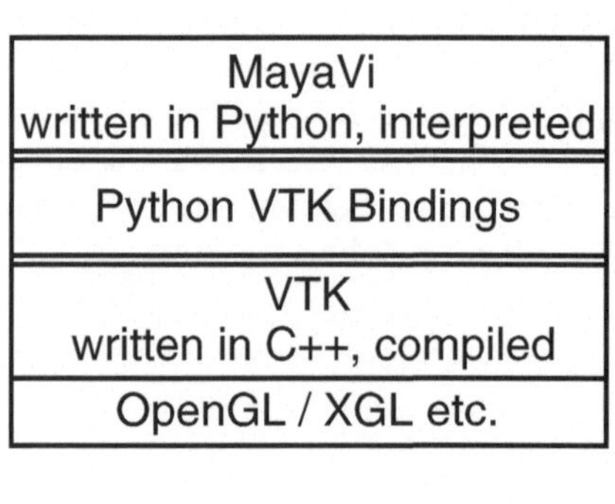

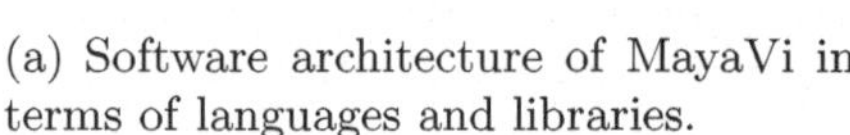

(a) Software architecture of MayaVi in terms of languages and libraries.

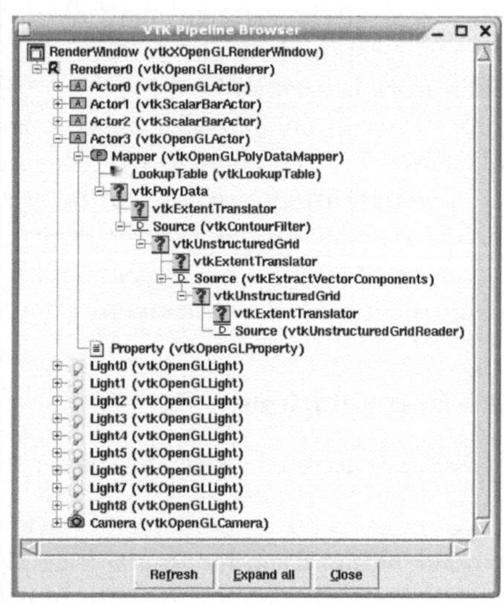

(b) VTK visualisation pipeline in MayaVi's pipeline browser for the visualisation in Figure 3.

Fig. 2. MayaVi software architecture (a) and pipeline browser (b)

2 Background and Related Work

Modular visualisation environments (MVEs) present end-users with a GUI representing an analysis and rendering pipeline [9]. MayaVi is one of many MVEs implementing this general model. Other examples from image processing include Adobe Photoshop or the Gimp, via its scripting mechanism. The MVE architecture offers the potential to integrate visualisation with simulation and computational steering [10,11] and this is finding broader application in the Grid [12,13]. To make MVEs work interactively on very large datasets, execution needs to be demand-driven, starting from a volume-of-interest (VOI) control, which specifies the 3-dimensional region where high resolution is required [14].

However, this paper is not about visualisation itself, but rather about the performance optimisation challenge raised by MVE-like software structures: how can we extend optimising and restructuring compiler technologies to operate on dynamically-composed assemblies of high-level components? This issue is part of a wider programme of research into cross-component optimisation issues: our DESO (delayed evaluation, self-optimising) parallel linear algebra library [15,16] uses carefully constructed metadata to perform cross-component parallel data placement optimisation at runtime, and the DÉSORMI project has resulted in a generalised framework for deploying runtime optimisation and instrumentation in Java programs [17]. Optimising component-based applications is also one of the research challenges addressed by the Grid effort [18].

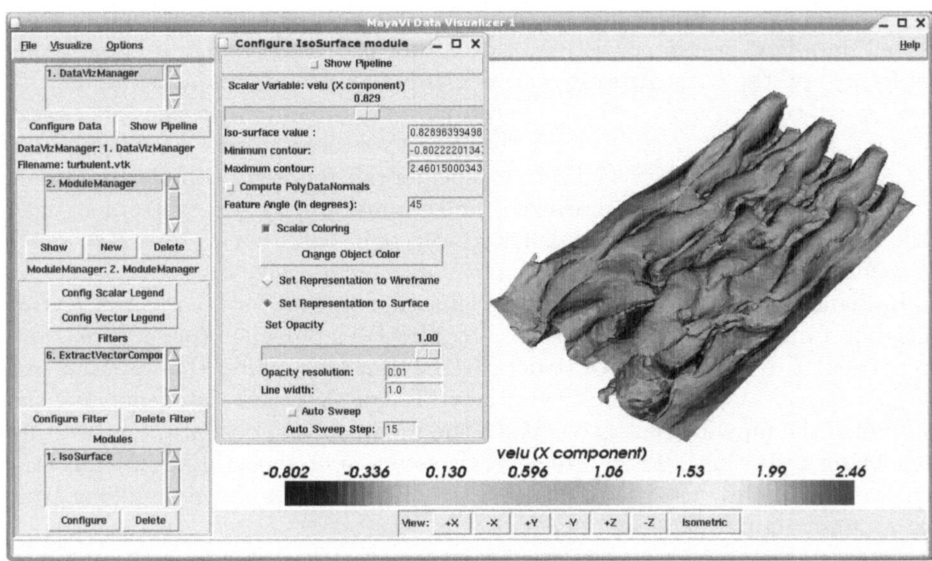

Fig. 3. MayaVi screenshot, showing the main MayaVi GUI, the GUI for configuring a specific visualisation module (IsoSurface) and the render window, showing an isosurface of the x component of the velocity vectors in a turbulent flow simulation

2.1 MayaVi's Modular Visualisation Environment Architecture

In Figure 2(a), we illustrate the software architecture of MayaVi in terms of programming languages and libraries used: MayaVi is written in the interpreted language Python. The core of VTK [3, 4] is written in C++ and is compiled; however, VTK has a complete set of bindings for Python, Tcl/Tk and Java. VTK in turn uses different graphics libraries such as OpenGL for 3D rendering.

2.2 Object-Oriented Visualisation in VTK

The VTK design distinguishes between the *graphics model*, an object-oriented representation of 3D computer graphics and the *visualisation model*, which is essentially a model of data-flow.

The VTK graphics model is described in detail in [4]. The key concepts that are relevant to this paper are the following. A RenderWindow represents a window on the display. A Renderer is an object that is responsible for rendering a region of such a window. Actors are objects that are rendered within the scene. In Figure 3, we show an isosurface visualisation of a turbulent flow. Such an isosurface corresponds to one Actor. Actors consist of Mappers, representing geometric structure (in the case of the isosurface in Figure 3, this is a set of polygons), Properties, representing colour, texture etc., and Transforms, which are 4×4 matrices that describe the usual transformations on homogeneous coordinates used in 3D computer graphics.

The VTK visualisation pipeline is an object-oriented representation of a directed data-flow graph, consisting of data and processes, which are operations performed on the data. Process objects can be *sources*, representing inputs, *filters*, which can be many-to-many operations on data, and *mappers*, representing outputs from the data-flow graph that are then used by the graphics model for rendering. The VTK visualisation pipeline can represent complex data-flow graphs, including graphs with cycles (time-stamps are used to control looping). The VTK design provides for data-flow graphs to be executed in either a *demand-driven* or a *data-driven* manner.

In Figure 2(b), we show the VTK visualisation pipeline for the isosurface visualisation from Figure 3, as represented by MayaVi's pipeline browser tool. Note in particular the source (vtkUnstructuredGridReader), a filter that extracts one of the components of the velocity vector (vtkExtractVectorComponents) and the output of the pipeline that is passed to the mapper (vtkPolyData, representing a polygon collection). There are several instances of the vtkExtentTranslator process: this can be used to calculate a structured extent (*i.e.* a bounding box) for an unstructured dataset.

3 A Domain-Specific Interpreter for VTK in Python

In Section 1, we outlined our proposal for a domain-specific interpreter as a means of overcoming barriers to restructuring optimisation in the use of domain-specific libraries. In this section, we present an implementation of this design pattern in Python, using VTK as a domain-specific library.

The key observation is that when a MayaVi visualisation is rendered, the data flow happens entirely on the C++ side of the Python/VTK interface. This implies that all nodes in the data flow graph have to be created via calls through the VTK Python bindings. Therefore, we are able to capture an accurate representation of the visualisation pipeline, which represents the data-flow graph of the computation to be performed, if we intercept calls made through this interface.

When visualisation is "forced", *i.e.* when an image has to be rendered, we can perform optimisations on this pipeline before it is executed. The next four sections explain how this is done.

3.1 Building the Proxy Layer

We rename the original `vtkpython.py` file which implements VTK's Python bindings to `vtkpython_real.py`. We implement a new file `vtkpython.py`, which is shown in Listing 1.1. This file dynamically creates a new, initially empty class definition for every class in the original `vtkpython` interface. The key point is that these empty classes are all derived from a new class `ProxyObject`; thus, the absence of methods in the dynamically created empty classes means that all method calls will be deferred to the superclass.

Listing 1.1. Implementation of a proxy layer for intercepting calls through the VTK Python binding interface

```
import os
if ("new_vtk" in os.environ): # Control the DS interpreter via the environment
  import vtkpython_real # Import the original VTK Python bindings
  from parallel import proxyObject
  from parallel import setPartitionInfo
  from parallel import setParameters
  from parallel import setScalar
  for className in dir(vtkpython_real): # For all classes in vtkpython_real
    # Create a class with the same name and no methods (yet),
    # derived from "ProxyObject".
    exec "class " + className + "(proxyObject): pass"
else:
  # default behaviour: fall-through to the original VTK Python bindings
  from vtkpython_real import *
```

Listing 1.2. A sample portion of a visualisation plan or recipe

```
['construct', 'vtkConeSource', 'vtkConeSource_913']
['callMeth', 'vtkConeSource_913', 'return_926', 'SetRadius', '0.2']
['callMeth', 'vtkConeSource_913', 'return_927', 'GetOutput', '']
['callMeth', 'vtkTransformFilter_918', 'return_928', 'SetInput', "self.ids['return_927']"]
['callMeth', 'vtkTransformFilter_918', 'return_929', 'GetTransform', '']
['callMeth', 'return_929', 'return_930', 'Identity', '']
```

3.2 Creating Skeleton Classes

MayaVi uses a dynamic lookup of method signatures in Python VTK classes as well as `__doc__` strings to create some GUI components on the fly, including for example the Pipeline Browser tool shown in Figure 2(b). We have to make sure therefore that the interface of the classes in the proxy layer matches the original VTK Python classes in terms of method signatures and `__doc__` strings. This is done by adding skeleton methods and `__doc__` strings on the fly following a dynamic lookup of class interfaces (using Python's built-in reflection mechanism). This adds a few seconds to program startup time when the tool is launched.

The only action performed by the skeleton methods is to call the `proxyCall` method from the `proxyObject` superclass, passing the name of the class, the name of the method and the list of actual parameters as arguments (more on this below).

3.3 Representing Execution Plans

We have implemented a Python data structure called `Code` which holds the information representing one call through the Python VTK interface. A `CodeList`

Listing 1.3. Code which creates an entry in the visualisation plan.

```
def proxyCall(self, callName, callArgs): # Add an entry to a recipe

  # Check whether we have reached a "force point"
  if(globals()["codeList"].numPartitions > 0 and callName == "Render"):
    return forcePointReached()

  result = proxyObject_return() # Create an identifier for the result
  code = Code(result,self,callName,callArgs)
         # Construct "Code" object which represents one method call
  globals()["codeList"].add(code) # Add to the visualisation plan
```

Listing 1.4. Code snippet of recipe application for a method call

```
def callMeth(self, objId, retId, methName, argString):
  object = self.ids[objId]
  retobj = None
  retobj = eval('object.' + methName + '(' + argString + ')')
  self.ids[retId] = retobj
  return retId
```

maintains the whole visualisation plan (or “recipe”). A symbol table for looking up identifiers is also maintained.

Listing 1.2 gives an example of what a part of a recipe may look like. The first item in the list is always `callMeth` or `construct` and signifies whether the recipe component is a constructor or an ordinary method call. If it is a constructor, the following items give the name of the class of the object to be constructed, the name of the identifier for the returned object, and (optionally) any arguments. If it is an ordinary method call, the following items give the object the method is to be called on, the name of the identifier for the returned object or value, the name of the method to be called and finally, the argument list. In the argument list, any names of identifiers for objects are converted into the a symbol table lookup of the form `self.ids[identifier]`.

Listing 1.3 shows part of the implementation of the `proxyCall` method, which creates entries in the visualisation plan, and which is called for every method invocation, via the skeleton methods in the proxy layer.

3.4 Forcing Execution

Listing 1.3 shows that when we call `Render`, we reach a force point, *i.e.* we force evaluation of the visualisation plan.

Listing 1.4 gives a code snippet (slightly simplified for clarity) of the function which applies a method call when a visualisation plan is executed. Again, the symbol table `ids` is used to map names of identifiers to real objects.

In Sections 4–6, we now present the performance benefits that accrue from applying two kinds of optimisation (coarse grained tiling and parallelisation) to a VTK execution plan.

4 Coarse Grained Tiling of Visualisation Pipelines

Our case study is an ocean circulation model developed by our collaborators in the Department of Earth Science and Engineering at Imperial College. The datasets that result from such simulations are multi-gigabyte unstructured tetrahedral meshes. We use the METIS tool [7] to partition these datasets. The results presented in this paper are for a sample dataset representing a fluid flow around a heated sphere. This dataset is 16MB in size, and we have used a 2-,4-,8- and 16-way partitioning of this dataset. Note that VTK does have a built-in mechanism for handling partitioned datasets ("parallel unstructured grid storage format"); however, for the unmodified MayaVi, using such a dataset does not change the way the data is processed — the partitions are simply 'glued together' after loading from disk, resulting in a single monolithic dataset.

The first optimisation we study is coarse grained tiling. By coarse grained tiling, we mean that we apply the visualisation plan to one partition of the dataset at a time, rather than following the default behaviour where the partitions would be merged to form one monolithic dataset which is then processed. Note that this has strong similarities with classical tiling optimisations in that we are effectively restructuring the execution order (iteration space).

Experimental Setup. The MayaVi GUI has the capability of being run from a Python script, and this was of immense benefit for performance evaluation. Python's built-in `time` module was used to take wall-clock time measurements. Each test was repeated three times (error bars are shown in all graphs). Two hardware platforms were used in testing:

- Intel Pentium 4 2.8GHz with hyperthreading (one physical processor), cache size 512KB, 1GB physical memory. We used this architecture both as a uniprocessor and in a cluster of four such processors.
- Athlon MP 1600+, cache size 256KB, 1GB physical memory. We used this architecture both as a uniprocessor and as a 2-way SMP.

In each case, the benchmarks were applied to a version of MayaVi that uses the unmodified Python/VTK library and to "MayaVi+DSI", the version that uses our domain-specific interpreter for Python/VTK.

Use Case. The following usage scenario was used for evaluation: The dataset is loaded, and the IsoSurface module added to the visualisation pipeline. The contour value is changed seven times (0.00, 0.15, 0.30, 0.45, 0.60, 0.75 and 0.90), and the time taken for each change is recorded. When calculating an IsoSurface, the number of polygons generated, as well as computation time, varies widely with contour value.

Results for Coarse Grained Tiling. Table 1 includes results for the coarse grained tiling optimisation on uniprocessors. This indicates that in some cases, we can achieve a speedup of nearly a factor of 3 by this optimisation. Calculating isosurfaces partition-wise appears to be significantly cheaper than performing that calculation on the whole dataset in one operation, due to the nature of the VTK data structures involved.

5 Shared-Memory Parallelisation

It is apparently a simple extension of coarse grained tiling to spawn one Python thread per partition. Unfortunately, with this basic approach, the threads always run sequentially due to Python's Global Interpreter Lock (GIL), which prevents Python threads from running simultaneously. Any C code called from within the Python program is subject to this same limitation. To allow C code called from the VTK Python interface to be run in parallel, this lock must be explicitly claimed and dropped from within the C code.

Python wrapper classes for VTK are generated by a special-purpose C program (`vtkWrapPython.c`). Adding code to deal with the GIL within the wrapper generator requires minimal modification (2 lines): At every point that a VTK wrapped function is called, the function call is surrounded by code to drop and reclaim the lock. However, since not all of VTK is thread-safe, it is necessary to restrict parallel operation to certain parts of VTK only. In particular, no operations on the shared Renderer and RenderWindow occur in parallel.

Table 1 shows results for SMP parallelisation using the method outlined above on a dual-processor machine. This shows very encouraging results: a maximum speedup of around 6 for parallel execution of the visualisation pipeline over 16 partitions. We spawn one thread per partition, rather than per processor, these results show the combined effects of coarse grained tiling and SMP parallelisation. This explains the superlinear speedup which is seen for some IsoSurface values. Our data indicate that on a 2-way SMP, a significant part of the overall speedup is already obtained by coarse grained tiling alone.

Some readers may wonder where the "parallel loop" for our parallelisation is. The answer is that this is in the domain-specific interpreter. It is the task of this interpreter to execute the recipe that has been captured. This is done by applying the entire recipe, which could be a multi-stage computation, to each partition separately.

6 Distributed Memory Parallelisation

To allow for an easier implementation of distributed processing, a Python library called 'Pyro' was used, which provides Java RMI-like features. Pyro allows any pickleable[2] object to be transferred across the network. A class which needs to be

[2] A 'pickleable' object is one which can be serialised using Python's built-in 'pickle' module.

Table 1. IsoSurface Benchmark on Dual Athlon 1600+ SMP with 256 KB L2 cache and 1GB physical RAM (above) and cluster of four Pentium 4 2.8 GHz HT with 512 KB L2 cache and 1 GB physical RAM (below). Results for the Tiling columns only use one processor in both cases.

Athlon 1600+ SMP

	2 Partitions					4 Partitions					8 Partitions					16 Partitions				
	Base	Tiling		SMP		Base	Tiling		SMP		Base	Tiling		SMP		Base	Tiling		SMP	
IsoSurface	Time	Time	S'up	Time	S'up	Time	Time	S'up	Time	S'up	Time	Time	S'up	Time	S'up	Time	Time	S'up	Time	S'up
0	4.73	5.12	0.92	4.9	0.97	3.32	3.96	0.84	3.63	0.92	3.16	5.21	0.61	4.92	0.64	3.01	3.84	0.78	2.53	1.19
0.15	1.62	0.88	1.84	0.67	2.43	1.41	0.92	1.53	0.79	1.79	1.48	0.92	1.62	0.71	2.08	1.43	0.94	1.53	0.74	1.94
0.3	1.77	1.66	1.07	1.02	1.74	1.64	1.58	1.04	1.06	1.55	1.67	1.35	1.24	1	1.67	1.74	1.33	1.31	1	1.74
0.45	3.65	3.49	1.04	2.13	1.71	3.21	2.83	1.13	1.82	1.76	3.22	1.72	1.87	1.34	2.41	3.36	1.61	2.09	1.22	2.76
0.6	7.7	6.91	1.11	4.78	1.61	6.98	5.42	1.29	3.6	1.94	7.46	3.27	2.28	2.65	2.81	7.28	2.6	2.8	1.84	3.96
0.75	15.44	13.48	1.14	10.71	1.44	15.56	11	1.41	8.07	1.93	15.06	6.89	2.18	5.77	2.61	15.27	4.45	3.43	2.9	5.27
0.9	27.5	22.53	1.22	19.47	1.41	24.78	20.48	1.21	16.82	1.47	25.92	12.55	2.07	10.88	2.38	25.24	6.58	3.83	4	6.31

Pentium 4 2.8 GHz Cluster

	2 Partitions					4 Partitions					8 Partitions					16 Partitions				
	Base	Tiling		Parallel		Base	Tiling		Parallel		Base	Tiling		Parallel		Base	Tiling		Parallel	
IsoSurface	Time	Time	S'up	Time	S'up	Time	Time	S'up	Time	S'up	Time	Time	S'up	Time	S'up	Time	Time	S'up	Time	S'up
0	4.91	4.56	1.08	6.6	0.74	3.55	2.96	1.2	4.18	0.85	3.23	3.28	0.99	4.18	0.77	3.14	3.29	0.95	1.9	1.65
0.15	0.65	0.73	0.89	0.83	0.78	0.65	0.67	0.97	0.64	1.01	0.66	0.65	1.02	0.57	1.16	0.68	0.66	1.03	0.6	1.12
0.3	1.33	1.47	0.9	1.32	1.01	1.25	1.29	0.97	0.92	1.36	1.27	1.02	1.24	0.81	1.57	1.32	0.97	1.36	0.72	1.82
0.45	2.64	3.21	0.82	2.31	1.14	2.35	2.38	0.99	1.23	1.91	2.37	1.27	1.86	1.11	2.13	2.45	1.23	2	1.01	2.43
0.6	5.35	5.9	0.91	4.3	1.24	5.02	4.5	1.12	2.57	1.95	5.08	2.41	2.1	2.01	2.53	5.18	2.12	2.45	1.45	3.57
0.75	10.82	10.54	1.03	8.69	1.24	10.43	8.64	1.21	5.66	1.84	10.49	4.79	2.19	4.14	2.53	10.6	3.77	2.81	2.11	5.03
0.9	18.28	17.24	1.06	14.39	1.27	18.6	14.72	1.26	10.21	1.82	16.92	8.48	2	7.38	2.29	17.04	5.83	2.92	2.79	6.1

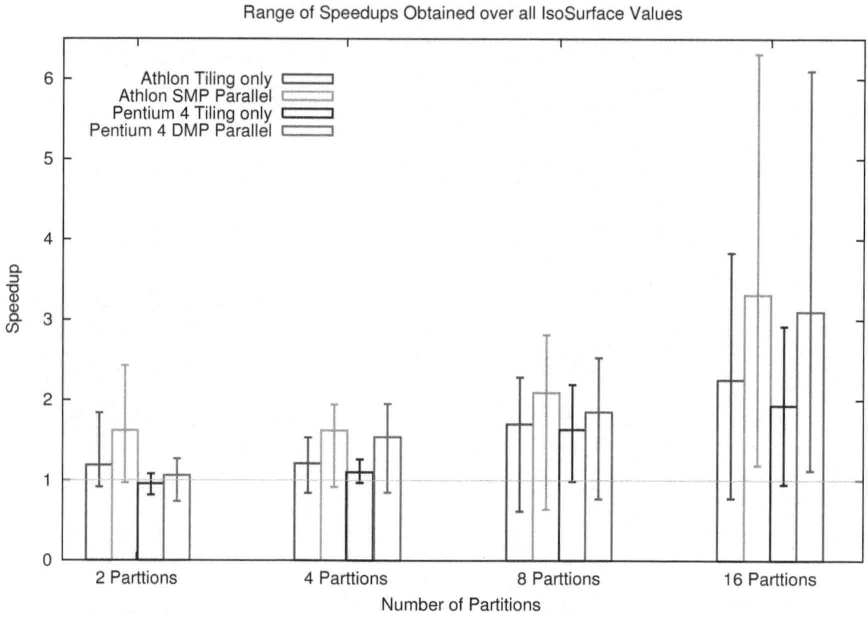

Range of Speedups Obtained over all IsoSurface Values

Athlon Tiling only
Athlon SMP Parallel
Pentium 4 Tiling only
Pentium 4 DMP Parallel

Speedup

2 Parttions 4 Parttions 8 Parttions 16 Parttions

Number of Partitions

Fig. 4. Summary of speedups obtained through our optimisations: For each experiment, we show for all degrees of partitioning the average, smallest and largest speedup obtained over all IsoSurface values in our use case. The details for these figures are contained in Table 1.

remotely accessible is subclassed from `Pyro.core.ObjBase`. In addition, there is a `Pyro.core.SynchronizedObjBase` class, which automatically synchronises remote access to the class methods.

Unfortunately, VTK pipeline components and data objects are not pickleable, and, as such, cannot be transferred using Pyro. Data objects may, however, be read and written to temporary files using VTK's data reading and writing classes, and these files are written by servers and read by clients to transfer input and output data. MayaVi includes some pickling capabilities for VTK pipeline components, although it is not complete enough as not all attributes are pickled. Therefore, in order to propagate the pipeline structure, the client needs to cache and transfer all calls and arguments needed to recreate the visualisation pipeline.

A limitation of the data transfer implementation is that files are not explicitly transferred between server and client, but rather to a shared file system. A direct transfer between local disks would be more flexible and may give better performance.

Table 1, as well as Figure 4 show the performance of our distributed memory parallelisation scheme. This shows that the speedup obtained from distributed memory parallelisation for most calculations (in particular, the slowest ones) exceeds the benefit of coarse grained tiling on a uniprocessor. The key overhead involved with distributed memory parallelisation is the saving and loading of resultant data (the implementation of returning results involves the server writing VTK data to a file, which the client then has to read in). So, it is indeed expected that the performance gains will be best when the decrease in computation time can outweigh this overhead (this, in turn, is smallest when the computation results are small).

In Figure 4, we summarise our experimental results. Since the computation time in our use case varies greatly with the IsoSurface value, we show speedups as box-and-whisker plots, giving the average, minimum and maximum speedup over all IsoSurface values. This shows that coarse grained tiling is almost always beneficial: we obtain a speedup of around a factor 2 for larger numbers of partitions on both architectures. Furthermore, for the computationally more expensive operations, combining coarse grained tiling with parallelisation can lead to significant performance improvements (up to a factor 6 for both a dual-processor Athlon SMP and a 4-processor Pentium 4 cluster).

7 Conclusions and Future Work

We have presented an overview of a project which is aimed at applying traditional restructuring compiler optimisations in the highly dynamic context of modular visualisation environments. The challenge is that a computationally expensive pipeline of operations is constructed by the user via interactions with the GUI and then executed. Our approach is based on intercepting the construction of the visualisation pipeline, assembling a visualisation plan, on which we can then perform optimisations such as coarse grained tiling before it is executed. The MayaVi modular visualisation environment enabled us to capture reliably the construction of the visualisation pipeline by intercepting all calls that pass through the Python/C++ VTK interface. We have presented results for coarse grained tiling on a uniprocessor, as well as shared- and distributed-memory parallelisation.

We are currently exploring how we can build on the infrastructure we have described.

- *Using VTK Streaming Constructs.* As stated in Section 2.2, VTK itself provides various constructs for data streaming and parallel execution using MPI that could be exploited from within our framework; we are planning to investigate this.
- *Interaction with the Underlying Simulation.* We are interested in investigating the possibility of pushing the scope for cross-component restructuring optimisations further back into the simulation software that generates the datasets which are visualised by MVEs such as MayaVi. In particular, we are interested in extending demand-driven data generation into the simulation model: if a higher level of detail is required for a small VOI of the dataset, how much of the simulation has to be re-run?

We see this work as part of a wider programme of research into optimising component-based scientific software frameworks.

References

1. BLAST Forum: Basic linear algebra subprograms technical forum standard. (2001) Available via www.netlib.org/blas/blas-forum.
2. Message Passing Interface Forum: MPI: A Message Passing Interface Standard. University of Tenessee, Knoxville, Tenessee. (1995) Version 1.1.
3. Kitware, Inc.: The VTK User's Guide: VTK 4.2. (2003)
4. Schroeder, W., Martin, K., Lorensen, B.: The Visualization Toolkit: An Object-Oriented Approach To 3D Graphics. 3rd edn. Kitware, Inc. (2002)
5. Ramachandran, P.: MayaVi: A free tool for CFD data visualization. In: 4th Annual CFD Symposium, Aeronautical Society of India. (2001) mayavi.sourceforge.net.
6. van Rossum, G., Fred L. Drake, J.: An Introduction to Python. Network Theory Ltd (2003)
7. Karypis, G., Kumar, V.: Multilevel algorithms for multi-constraint graph partitioning. In: Supercomputing '98, IEEE Computer Society (1998) 1–13
8. Beckmann, O., Field, A.J., Gorman, G., Huff, A., Hull, M., Kelly, P.H.J.: Overcoming barriers to restructuring in a modular visualisation environment. In Cox, A., Subhlok, J., eds.: LCR '04: Languages, Compilers and Runtime Support for Scalable Systems. (2004) ACM Digital Library.
9. Cameron, G.: Modular visualization environments: Past, present, and future. Computer Graphics **29** (1995) 3–4
10. Parker, S.G., Johnson, C.R.: SCIRun: A scientific programming environment for computational steering. In: Proceedings of Supercomputing 1995. (1995)
11. Wright, H., Brodlie, K., Brown, M.: The dataflow visualization pipeline as a problem solving environment. In: Virtual Environments and Scientific Visualization '96. Springer-Verlag, Vienna, Austria (1996) 267–276
12. Johnson, C.R., Parker, S.G., Weinstein, D.: Large-Scale Computational Science Applications Using the SCIRun Problem Solving Environment. In: ISC 2000: International Supercomputer Conference, Mannheim, Germany (2000)
13. Foster, I., Vöckler, J., Wilde, M., Zhao, Y.: Chimera: A virtual data system for representing, querying, and automating data derivation. In: 14th International Conference on Scientific and Statistical Database Management (SSDBM'02). (2002)
14. Cignoni, P., Montani, C., Scopigno, R.: MagicSphere: An insight tool for 3D data visualization. Computer Graphics Forum **13** (1994) C/317–C/328
15. Beckmann, O., Kelly, P.H.J.: Efficient interprocedural data placement optimisation in a parallel library. In: LCR98: Languages, Compilers and Run-time Systems for Scalable Computers. Number 1511 in LNCS, Springer-Verlag (1998) 123–138
16. Liniker, P., Beckmann, O., Kelly, P.H.J.: Delayed evaluation self-optimising software components as a programming model. In: Euro-Par 2002: Proceedings of the 8th International Euro-Par Conference. Number 2400 in LNCS (2002) 666–673
17. Yeung, K.C., Kelly, P.H.J.: Optimising Java RMI programs by communication restructuring. In: Proceedings of the ACM/IFIP/USENIX International Middleware Conference 2003, Rio De Janeiro, Brazil, 16–20 June 2003. LNCS (2003)
18. Furmento, N., Mayer, A., McGough, S., Newhouse, S., Field, T., Darlington, J.: Optimisation of component-based applications within a grid environment. In: Supercomputing 2001. (2001)

Compiler Control Power Saving Scheme for Multi Core Processors

Jun Shirako[1], Naoto Oshiyama[1], Yasutaka Wada[1], Hiroaki Shikano[2], Keiji Kimura[1,2], and Hironori Kasahara[1,2]

[1] Dept. of Computer Science
[2] Advanced Chip Multiprocessor Research Institute
Waseda University
3-4-1 Ohkubo, Shinjuku-ku, Tokyo, 169-8555, Japan
{shirako,oshiyama,yasutaka,shikano,kimura,kasahara}@oscar.elec.waseda.ac.jp

Abstract. With the increase of transistors integrated onto a chip, multi core processor architectures have attracted much attention to achieve high effective performance, shorten development period and reduce the power consumption. To this end, the compiler for a multi core processor is expected not only to parallelize program effectively, but also to control the voltage and clock frequency of processors and storages carefully inside an application program. This paper proposes a compilation scheme for reduction of power consumption under the multigrain parallel processing environment that controls Voltage/Frequency and power supply of each processor core on a chip. In the evaluation, the OSCAR compiler with the proposed scheme achieves 60.7 percent energy savings for SPEC CFP95 applu without performance degradation on 4 processors, and 45.4 percent energy savings for SPEC CFP95 tomcatv with real-time deadline constraint on 4 processors, and 46.5 percent energy savings for SPEC CFP95 swim with the deadline constraint on 4 processors.

1 Introduction

According to the increase of transistors integrated onto a chip, a chip multiprocessor architecture, or multicore architecture, that can achieve higher performance and save the power consumption is collecting much attention as future processors. To realize efficient parallel processing on multiprocessor systems, cache and local memory optimization to cope with memory wall problems and minimization of data transfer among processors using DMAC (Direct Memory Access Controller), in addition to the extraction of parallelism from an application program. For the exploitation of parallelism for multiprocessors, there have been a large number of researches in the areas of loop parallelizing compilers [1,2,3]. However, the loop parallelization techniques are almost matured and new generation of parallelization techniques like multi-grain parallelization are required to attain further speedup. There are a few compilers trying to exploit multiple levels of parallelism, for example, NANOS compiler[4] extracts the multi-level parallelism including the coarse grain task parallelism by using

E. Ayguadé et al. (Eds.): LCPC 2005, LNCS 4339, pp. 362–376, 2007.

extended OpenMP API and OSCAR multigrain parallelizing compiler [5,6,7] extracts coarse grain task parallelism among loops, subroutines and basic blocks and near fine grain parallelism among statements inside a basic block, in addition to the loop parallelism. Also, OSCAR compiler realizes the automatic determination of parallelism of each part of a program and the number of required processors to process the program part efficiently with the global cache memory optimization over different loops.

This required number of processors determination scheme determines the suitable number of processors to execute each part of a program and stops the unnecessary processors to minimize processing overhead and reduce power consumption by shutting off power supply for idle processors.

For the power saving techniques, various methods have been proposed. Adaptive Processing[8] estimates the workload of computing resources using counters for cache misses and instruction queues and powers off unnecessary resources. Online Methods for Voltage and Frequency Control [9] settles on the fitting voltage and frequency for each domain of processors using instruction issue queue occupancies as feedback signals. As the compiler algorithm for CPU energy reduction, compiler-directed DVS(dynamic voltage scaling)[10] is known. This method gets the relations between frequency and execution time for each part of a program by profiling. It solves minimization problem of total energy consumption and determines the suitable frequency for each part.

This paper proposes a static compiler control scheme of power saving for a multi core processor without profiling, which realizes

- power supply cutoff for unnecessary processors
- voltage/frequency(V/F) control of each task or of each processor in an application program under the constraints of the minimum time execution or the satisfaction of real-time deadline

2 Multigrain Parallel Processing

The proposed power saving scheme is mainly used with the coarse grain task parallelization in the multigrain parallel processing. This section describes the overview of the coarse grain task parallel processing.

2.1 Generating Macro-tasks [5,6,7][11,12]

In multigrain parallelization, a program is decomposed into three kinds of coarse grain tasks, or macro-tasks, such as block of pseudo assignment statements(BPA) repetition block(RB), subroutine block(SB)[7]. Macro-tasks can be hierarchically defined inside each un-parallelizable repetition block, or sequential loop, and a subroutine block as shown in Figure 1. Repeating the macro-task generation hierarchically, the source program is decomposed into the nested macro-tasks as in Figure 1.

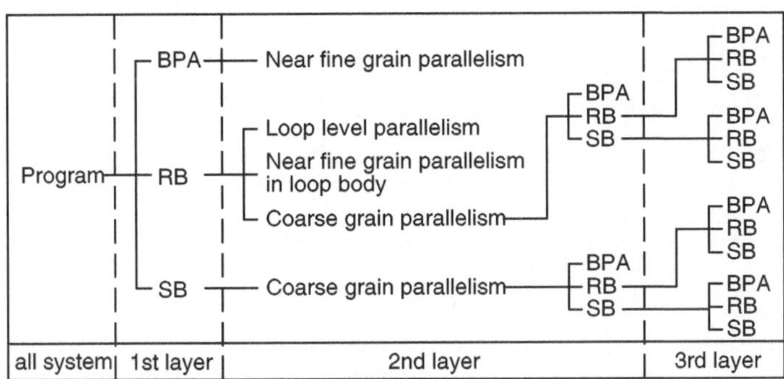

Fig. 1. Hierarchical Macro Task Definition

2.2 Extraction of Coarse Grain Task Parallelism

After generation of macro-tasks, the data dependency and the control flow among macro-tasks are analyzed in each nested layer, and hierarchical macro flow graphs(MFG) representing control flow and data dependencies among macro-tasks are generated [5,6,7]. Then, to extract coarse grain task parallelism among macro-tasks, Earliest Executable Condition analysis [5,6,7] which analyzes control dependencies and data dependencies among macro-tasks simultaneously is applied to each Macro flow graph. Earliest Executable Conditions are the conditions on which macro-task may begin its execution earliest. By this analysis, a macro-task graph(MTG)[5,6,7] is generated for each macro flow graph. Macro-task graph represents coarse grain parallelism among macro-tasks.

2.3 Processor Groups and Processor Elements

To execute hierarchical macro-task graphs efficiently, the compiler groups processors hierarchically. This grouping of processor elements(PEs) into Processor Groups(PGs) is performed logically, and macro-tasks are assigned to processor groups in each layer.

Figure 2 shows an example of a hierarchical processor groups. For execution of a macro-task graph in the 1st nest level, or 1st layer, the 8 processors are grouped into 2 processor groups each of which has 4 processor elements. This is represented as (2PGs, 4PEs). The macro-task graph in the 1st nest level is processed by the 2PGs. For each macro-task graph in the 2nd nest level, 4 processors are available. In the Figure 2, the grouping of (4PGs, 1PE) is chosen for the left PG and (2PGs, 2PEs) is chosen for the right PG.

2.4 Automatic Determination Scheme of Parallelizing Layer

In order to improve the performance of multigrain parallel processing, it is necessary to schedule the tasks on the macro-task graph with the extracted parallelism to processors the grouped processor layer. OSCAR compiler with the automatic parallelized layer determination scheme [11,13] estimates the parallelism

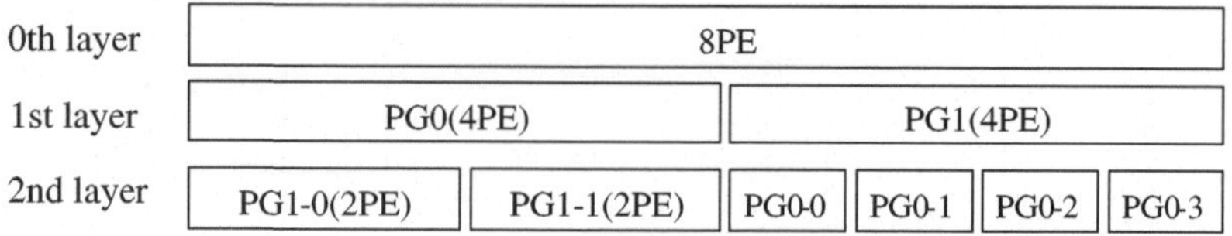

Fig. 2. Hierarchical definition of processor groups and processor elements

of each macro-task graph and determine the suitable (PGs, PEs) grouping. This scheme determines the suitable number of processors executing each macro-task, considering trade-off between parallelization and scheduling and data transfer overhead. Therefore, OSCAR compiler doesn't assign tasks to the excessive processors to reduce parallel processing overhead.

2.5 Macro-task Scheduling

In the coarse grain task parallel processing, a macro-task in the macro-task graph is assigned to a processor group. At this time, static scheduling or dynamic scheduling is chosen for each macro-task graph.

If a macro-task graph has only data dependencies and is deterministic, the static scheduling is selected. In this case, the compiler schedules macro-tasks to processer groups. The static scheduling is effective since it can minimize data transfer and synchronization overhead without runtime scheduling overhead.

If a macro-task graph is un-deterministic by conditional branches among coarse grain tasks, the dynamic scheduling is selected to handle the runtime uncertainties. The dynamic scheduling routines are generated by the compiler and inserted into a parallelized program code to minimize scheduling overhead.

This paper proposes the power saving static scheduling scheme for the determinable macro-task graphs.

In the following sections, MT represents macro-task, MTG is macro-task graph, PG is processor group, PE is processor element, BPA is block of pseudo assignment statements, RB is repetition block and SB is subroutine block.

3 Compiler Control Power Saving Scheme

The multigrain parallel processing can take full advantage of multi level parallelism in a program. However, there isn't always enough parallelism in all part of a program for available resources. In such a case, shutting off the power supply to the idle processors, to which tasks are not assigned, can reduce power consumption. Also, execution at lower voltage and frequency may reduce the total energy consumption in real time processing with the deadline constraint. The proposed scheme realizes the following two modes of power reduction. The first is the fastest execution mode that doesn't apply the power saving scheme to the

Table 1. The rate of frequency, voltage, dynamic energy and static power

state	FULL	MID	LOW	OFF
frequency	1	1/2	1/4	0
voltage	1	0.87	0.71	0
dynamic energy	1	3/4	1/2	0
static power	1	1	1	0

critical path of a program to guarantee the fastest processing speed. The second is real-time processing mode with deadline constraint that minimizes the total energy consumption within the given deadline.

3.1 Target Model for the Proposed Power Saving Scheme

In this paper, it is supposed that the target multi core processors have the following functions with the hardware supports like OSCAR multi core processor shown in Figure 3. The OSCAR(Optimally Scheduled Advanced Multiprocessor) architecture has been proposed to support optimization of multigrain parallelizing compiler [14,5,6], especially static and dynamic task scheduling [15,14,16]. In the OSCAR architecture, simple processor cores having local and/or distributed shared memory both of which are double mapped to the global address space so that can be accessed by remote processor cores DTC(Data Transfer Controller), or DMAC, are connected by interconnection network like multiple busses or cross bar switches to control shared memory(CSM) [15,14,16,17]. In addition to the traditional OSCAR architecture, in this paper, the following power control functions are supported.

- The frequency for each processor can be changed in several levels individually.
- The voltage can be changed with the frequency.
- Each processor can be powered on and off individually.

There are a lot of approaches for voltage and frequency(V/F) control. The proposed power saving scheme assumes frequency changes discretely, and the optimal voltage is fixed for each frequency. Table 1 shows an example of the combinations of voltage, dynamic energy and static power at each frequency, which supposes FULL is 400MHz, MID is 200MHz and LOW is 100MHz at 90nm technology. For the table, dynamic energy rate for each frequency is the rate of energy consumption to the energy consumption at FULL. The power supply is shut off completely at OFF, then the static power becomes 0. These parameters and the number of frequency states can be changed, according to architectures and technology. This scheme also considers the state transition overhead that is given for each state.

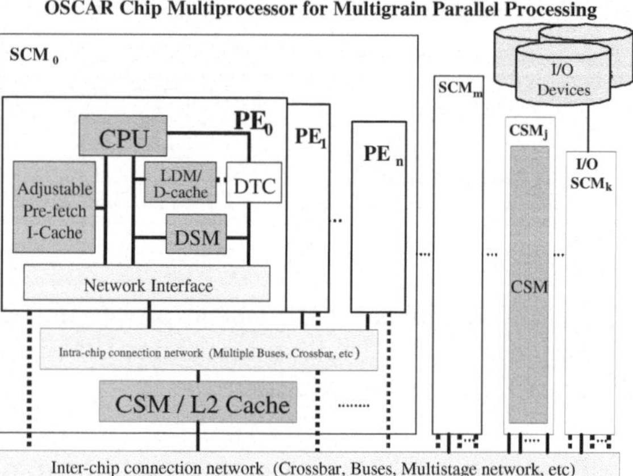

Fig. 3. OSCAR architecture(Chip multiprocessor)

3.2 Target MTG for the Proposed Control Scheme

OSCAR compiler selects dynamic scheduling or static scheduling for each MTG, as to whether there is runtime uncertainty like conditional branches in the MTG. The proposed scheme can be only applied to static scheduled MTGs. However, separating the parts without branches from dynamic scheduled MTG, this scheme is applied for the static scheduling parts of MTGs. In the static scheduling at the compile time, execution cost and consumed energy of each MT is estimated. The cost and energy at each frequency level like "FULL" and "MID" can be calculated using the previously prepared parameter table for each target multicore processor of each instruction cost embedded in the compiler.

3.3 Deadline Constraint of Target MTG

The proposed scheme determines suitable voltage and frequency for each MT on a MTG based on the result of static task assignment. In other words, the proposed power saving scheme is applied for the static task schedule like Figure 4 generated by static task scheduling algorithms to minimize processing time including data transfer overhead, such as CP/DT/MISF, DT/CP, ETF/CP, which have been used for a long time in OSCAR compiler. Figure 4 shows MTs 1, 2 and 5 are assigned to PG0, MTs 3 and 6 are assigned to PG1, MTs 4, 7 and 8 are assigned to PG2 by the static scheduling algorithms. The best schedule is chosen among different schedules generated by the different heuristic scheduling algorithms. In Figure 4, edges among tasks show data dependence.

First, the following is defined for MT_i, in order to estimate the execution time of the target MTG to which the proposed scheme is applied.

T_i : execution time of MT_i after V/F control

T_{start_i} : start time of MT_i

T_{finish_i} : finish time of MT_i

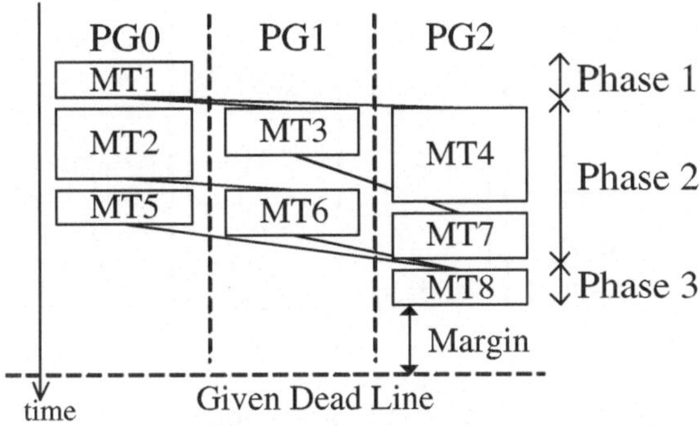

Fig. 4. static scheduled MTG

At the beginning of the proposed scheme, T_i is not yet fixed. The start time of the target MTG is set to 0. If MT_i is the first macro-task executed by a PG and has no data dependent predecessor. T_{start_i} and T_{finish_i} are represented as shown below.

$T_{start_i} = 0$

$T_{finish_i} = T_{start_i} + T_i = T_i$

For instance, the MT_1 is the entry node of MTG, so it is the first and has no data dependent predecessor. Then, $T_{start_1} = 0$, $T_{finish_1} = T_1$. In other case, the previous macro-task which is assigned to the same PG as MT_i is represented as MT_j. The data dependent predecessors of MT_i are defined as $\{MT_k, MT_l, ...\}$. Then, MT_i starts when MT_j, MT_k, MT_l, ... finish.

$T_{start_i} = max(T_{finish_j}, T_{finish_k}, T_{finish_l}, ...)$

$T_{finish_i} = T_{start_i} + T_i$

In Figure 4, MT_2 and MT_3 start execution immediately after the time MT_1 is finished. So, the start time is represented as $T_{start_2} = T_{start_3} = T_{finish_1} = T_1$, the finish time is $T_{finish_2} = T_{start_2} + T_2 = T_1 + T_2$, $T_{finish_3} = T_{start_3} + T_3 = T_1 + T_3$. MT_6 is started after MT_2 and MT_3, then $T_{start_6} = max(T_{finish_2}, T_{finish_3}) = max(T_2 + T_1, T_3 + T_1)$. In addition, the common term of the arguments in max may be put out of max. Then, $T_{start_6} = max(T_2+T_1, T_3+T_1) = max(T_2, T_3)+T_1$. As the same way, the finish time of MT_8 which is the exit node is represented as $T_{finish_8} = T_1 + T_8 + max(T_2 + T_5, T_6 + max(T_2, T_3), T_7 + max(T_3, T_4))$.

The exit node is generally represented by

$T_{finish_{exit}} = T_m + T_n + ... + max_1(...) + max_2(...) + ...$

The start time of the entry node is 0, therefore $T_{finish_{exit}}$ expresses the execution time of the target MTG, defined as T_{MTG}. The given deadline for the target MTG is defined as $T_{MTG\_deadline}$. Then, the next condition should be satisfied.

$T_{MTG} \leq T_{MTG\_deadline}$

The proposed scheme determines suitable clock frequency for MT_i to satisfy the condition.

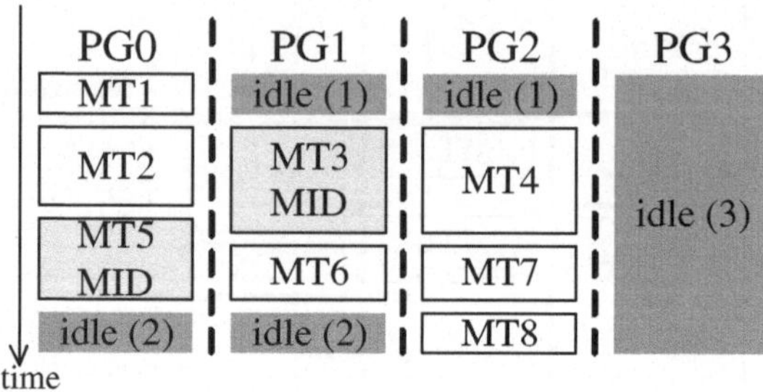

Fig. 5. Result of FV control

3.4 Voltage / Frequency Control

This paragraph describes how to determine the voltage and frequency to execute each MT using next conditions. The execution time of MT_i is T_i, the execution time of target MTG is T_{MTG}, the real-time deadline of the terget MTG is $T_{MTG\_deadline}$, then

$T_{MTG} = T_m + T_n + ... + max_1 + max_2 + ...$ - - - (a)

$T_{MTG} \leq T_{MTG\_deadline}$ - - - (b)

For sake of simplicity, the MTs corresponding to each term of the expression (a) such as T_m, T_n, ..., max_1, max_2, ... are called Phase. Each term represents the different part of T_{MTG}. Therefore, the different Phase is not executed in parallel on any account as shown in Figure 4. The following parameters for $Phase_i$ at frequency F_n are defined.

$T_{sched_i}(F_n)$: scheduling length at F_n

$Energy_i(F_n)$: energy consumption at F_n

$T_{sched_i}(F_n)$ represents the execution time when the whole $Phase_i$ is processed at F_n. $T_{sched_i}(FULL)$ is the minimum value of the term in the expression (a). $Energy_i(F_n)$ expresses the total energy consumption as $Phase_i$ is excuted at F_n.

Here, it is considered to change frequency from F_n to F_m. The scheduling length is increased from $T_{sched_i}(F_n)$ to $T_{sched_i}(F_m)$. The energy is decreased from $Energy_i(F_n)$ to $Energy_i(F_m)$. Using these values, $Gain_i(F_m)$ is defined as

$$Gain_i(F_m) = -\frac{Energy_i(F_m) - Energy_i(F_n)}{T_{sched_i}(F_m) - T_{sched_i}(F_n)}$$

$Gain_i(F_m)$ represents reduction rate of energy on scheduling length when F_n is changed into F_m. Therefore, if the increases of scheduling length are same, the more energy consumption can be prevented by prioritizing $Phase_i$ with larger $Gain_i(F_m)$.

Next, to estimate the margin of the target MTG, the minimum value of T_{MTG} is calculated. This is equal to the summation of $T_{sched_i}(FULL)$. Then, using this minimum value and $T_{MTG\_deadline}$, the margin T_{MTG_margin} is defined as

$$T_{MTG\_margin} = T_{MTG\_deadline} - \sum T_{sched_i}(FULL)$$

As the target MTG must finish in minimum execution time, $T_{MTG\_margin} = 0$, then each Phase has to be executed at FULL. When $T_{MTG\_margin} > 0$, the proposed scheme turns down the voltage and frequency of each Phase, according to

Table 2. Power and frequency transition overhead

dynamic power	220[mW]
static power	2.2[mW]
overhead(FULL - MID - LOW)	0.1[ms]
overhead({FULL, MID, LOW} - OFF)	0.2[ms]

$Gain_i(F_m)$. If Phase has a single MT, the frequency of MT is the same as the Phase. If Phase includes some MTs and corresponds to max term, the proposed scheme also defines Phases for each argument of max, then determines clock frequency to execute these Phases. The algorithm to determine frequency for each Phase is described below. The initial value of each frequency is FULL.

Step.1 Determining each frequency of Phase

Step.1.1 selecting target Phase

This step considers only a Phase whose frequency isn't fixed. F_n is represented as current frequency and F_m is defined as one step lower than F_n, then $Phase_i$ having the maximum $Gain_i(F_m)$ is selected as the target Phase. goto **Step.1.2**

Step.1.2 determining effectiveness for target Phase

For target Phase, the conditions to change the frequency from F_n to F_m is as follows.

1. Including the frequency transition overhead, the target Phase can finish at F_m within the T_{MTG_margin}.
2. The energy at F_m with overhead is lower than the energy at F_n.

If both conditions are satisfied,
then the frequency of target Phase is changed to F_m. goto **Step.1.3**
else the frequency of target Phase is confirmed as F_n. goto **Step.1.4**

Step.1.3 updating the margin of MTG

The required time to execute the target Phase at F_m is calculated, then the required time is subtracted from T_{MTG_margin}. If F_m is the lowest frequency, the frequency of target Phase is confirmed as F_m. goto **Step.1.4**

Step.1.4 determining exit

The conditions to exit are as follows.

1. The frequency of all Phase is confirmed.
2. T_{MTG_margin} is 0.

If either of these conditions is satisfied,
then goto **Step.2**
else goto **Step.1.1**

The remained margin is given $Phase_i$ which satisfies next conditions, if T_{MTG_margin} is not 0 at the end.

- The frequency is not the lowest.
- $Gain_i(F_m)$ is the maximum.

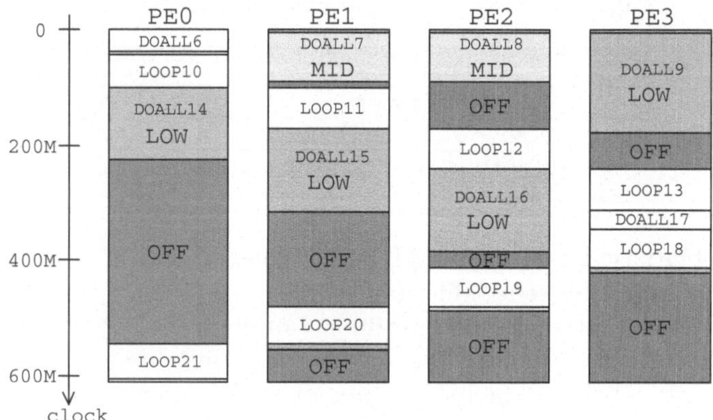

Fig. 6. FV control of applu(4proc.)

Step.2 Voltage/frequency control within each Phase

In the proposed scheme, the following algorithm is applied to each Phase.

Step.2.1 classifying Phases

If Phase includes only a single MT,

then the frequency of the MT is the same as Phase. **exit**

else goto **Step.2.2**

Step.2.2 Voltage/frequency control of max term

Phase includes some MTs and corresponds to max term, the proposed scheme calculates the executing time of this Phase at the already determined frequency in **Step.1**. Then, the calculated execution time is defined as $T_{max_i\_deadline}$.

$max_i = max(arg_{i\_1}, arg_{i\_2}, ...) \leq T_{max_i\_deadline}$

$arg_{i\_j} = T_{i\_j\_m} + T_{i\_j\_n} + ... + max_{i\_j\_1} + max_{i\_j\_2} + ...$

Therefore, arg_{i_j} should meet the next condition.

$T_{i\_j\_m} + T_{i\_j\_n} ... + max_{i\_j\_1} + max_{i\_j\_2} ... \leq T_{max_i\_deadline}$ - - - (c)

The MTs corresponding to each term in the expression (c) are also considered as Phase, then **Step.1** is applied to determine the frequency of each Phase. At this time, the execution time of each arg_{i_j} at FULL frequency is calculated. Then each arg_{i_j} is applied **Step.1** in descending order of the execution time, or ascending order of the margin. Some Phases in different args may include the same macro-tasks in common. However, once the frequency of a macro-task has been determined, the frequency isn't changed.

Applying **Step.1** and **Step.2** recursively, the suitable frequency of all MTs are determined.

3.5 Power Supply Control

This paragraph explains power supply control to reduce unnecessary energy consumption including static leak current by idle processors. The cases where the idle time occurs in a MTG are,

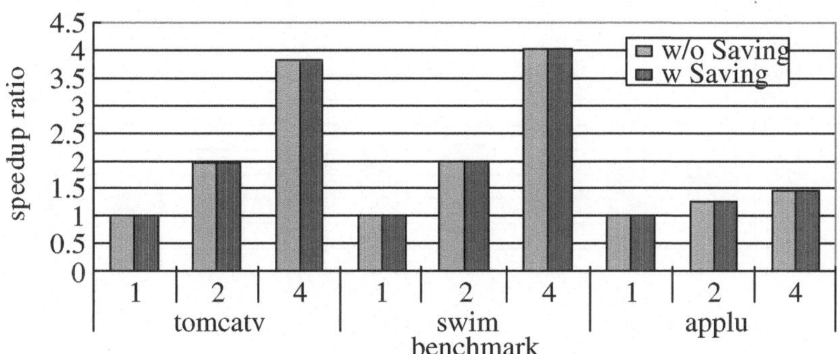

Fig. 7. Speedup in fastest execution mode

1. before MT with data dependency is executed,
2. after all MTs in a PG are finished,
3. the idle time created by the determination scheme of parallelizing layer, which is described in paragraph 2.4.

The gray parts of Figure 5 are the idle in each case. Here, the PG3 is the processor group determined as unnecessary. In the idle time which meets the next conditions, the power of the processor is turned off.

- The idle time is longer than the frequency transition overhead.
- The energy becomes lower by power-off.

3.6 Applying Power Saving Scheme to Inner MTG

If a MT_i includes a MTG_i inside, it may be more effective to control each MT_{i_j} in MTG_i than to process the whole MT_i at the same clock frequency. Therefore, the deadline for MTG_i is defined as $T_{MTG_i\_deadline}$, which is given by T_i. Then, MTG_i is applied the proposed power saving control described in paragraph 3.4 and 3.5. Comparing both case to execute the whole MT_i at the same frequency and case to apply the power saving control to MTG_i, the more effective one is selected.

4 Performance Evaluation

This section describes the performance of OSCAR multigrain parallelizing compiler with the proposed power saving scheme. The evaluation are performed by using the static scheduler in the compiler. For this evaluation, the parameters for frequencies, voltages, dynamic energies, and static powers shown in Table 1 are used. In this paper, only energy for processors was evaluated. The state transition overhead with frequency, dynamic and static power is shown in Table 2. The dynamic power at FULL frequency is measured by using Wattch[18]. Cooperative Voltage Scaling[19] is vebered to determine the parameters like the

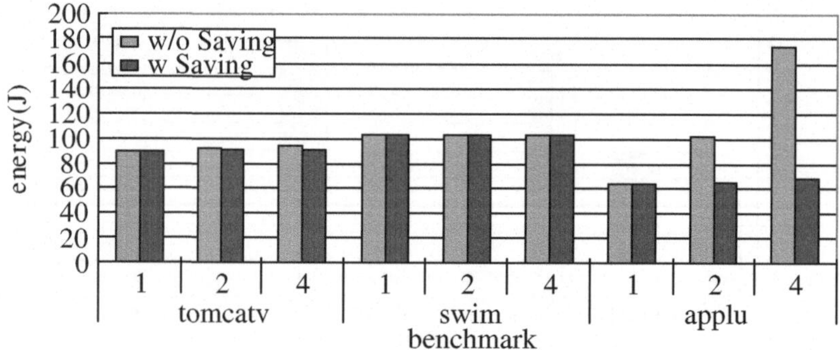

Fig. 8. Energy in fastest execution mode

transition overhead, attribute of voltage/frequency and dynamic power at MID and LOW frequency. Application programs, such as applu, tomcatv and swim from SPEC95 CFP, are used in the evaluation. For applu, inline expansion and loop aligned decomposition for the data localization[12] are applied. Also, the main loop in applu is divided into the static part without conditional branch and the dynamic part with branches, in order to apply the proposed scheme.

4.1 Performance in the Fastest Execution Mode

Figure 7 shows the speedup ratio of each program, and Figure 8 shows the total energy consumption for 1, 2 and 4 processors in the fastest execution mode. In these graphs, the left bars represents the results of OSCAR compiler without the proposed power saving scheme, the right bars show the results of OSCAR compiler using the proposed scheme. As shown in Figure 7, there is no performance degradation by using the power saving scheme in the fastest execution mode, while the energy consumption is reduced as shown in Figure 8. The proposed scheme reduced the consumed energy by 36.3 %(from 102[J] down to 65.0[J]) for 2 processors, 60.7 %(from 174[J] down to 68.4[J]) for 4 processors in SPEC95 applu, 1.56 %(from 92.1[J] down to 90.6[J]) for 2 processors, 4.64 %(from 95.0[J] down to 90.6[J]) for 4 processors in tomcatv.

The reason why the proposed scheme can not reduce the energy consumption in tomcatv and swim is that the both application programs have large parallelism and the all processors must execute in "FULL" mode to attain the minimum execution time. The parallel execution time of these programs with 4 processors is about one quarter of sequential execution time. Therefore, though the power consumption is quadrupled by using 4 processors, the total energy consumption is almost equal to the energy of sequential execution.

On the other hand, there is a certain amount of idle time in applu. Therefore, the following controls were made. Figure 6 shows the main loop to which the power saving scheme is applied for 4 processors. The DOALL6, LOOP10-13, DOALL17, LOOP18-21, DOALL22 had no margin, then their frequencies were set to FULL. MID or LOW was chosen for other MTs according to each margin of task. Furthermore, the proposed scheme shut off the power supply in the idle times.

4.2 Performance in Real-Time Processing with Deadline Constraints

Next, the evaluation results of real-time execution mode with the deadline constraint are described. Figure 9 shows the speedup ratio and Figure 10 shows the total energy consumption with the real-time deadline that was set to equal to the sequential execution time. The speedup ratio could be kept almost 1, as shown in Figure 9. This means the proposed scheme could satisfy the deadline constraints, or the sequential processing time.

Figure 10 shows that the saved power for real-time processing mode were 37.8 %(from 102[J] down to 63.3[J]) for 2 processors, 62.2 %(from 174[J] down to 65.8[J]) for 4 processors in applu, 21.6 %(from 92.1[J] down to 72.2[J]) for 2 processors, 45.4 %(from 95.0[J] down to 51.9[J]) for 4 processors in tomcatv, and

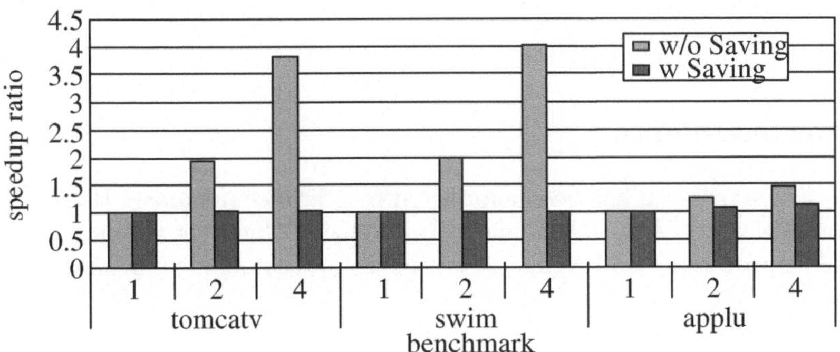

Fig. 9. Speedup in deadline mode

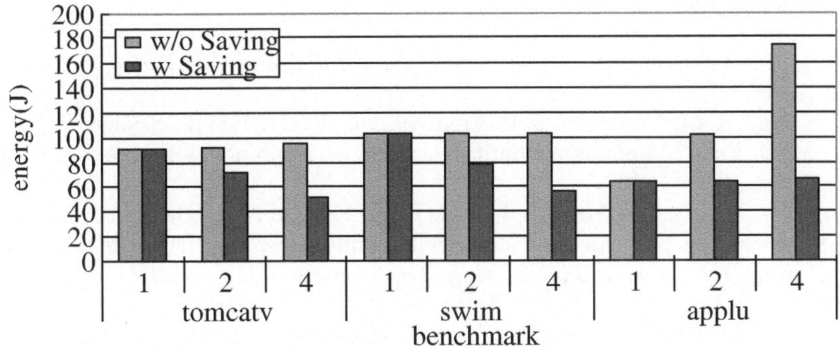

Fig. 10. Energy in deadline mode

23.7 %(from 103[J] down to 78.7[J]) for 2 processors, 46.5 %(from 103[J] down to 55.2[J]) for 4 processors in swim.

These results shows the proposed scheme could realize large power reduction for programs with large parallelism under the real-time execution mode.

5 Conclusions

This paper has proposed compiler control power saving scheme for multi core processors. The proposed scheme can be applied for both the fastest parallel executing mode and the real-time execution mode with deadline constraint. The scheme gives us good effective performance and low energy consumption for the both modes.

The evaluation using OSCAR multigrain parallelizing compiler has shown the proposed scheme gave 60.7 percent energy savings for SPEC CFP95 applu using 4 processors without the performance degradation, and 45.4 percent energy savings for SPEC CFP95 tomcatv using 4 processors with real-time deadline constraint, or the sequential processing time, and 46.5 percent energy savings for SPEC CFP95 swim using 4 processors with the deadline constraint.

The detailed evaluation using an actual multi core processor and the implement of the dynamic scheduling are the future works.

Acknowledgments

A part of this research has been supported by NEDO "Advanced Heterogeneous Multiprocessor", STARC "Automatic Parallelizing Compiler Cooperative Single Chip Multiprocessor" and NEDO "Multi core processors for real time consumer electronics".

References

1. M.Wolfe. High performance compilers for parallel computing. *Addison-Wesley Publishing Company*, 1996.
2. R. Eigenmann, J. Hoeflinger, and D. Padua. On the automatic parallelization of the perfect benchmarks. *IEEE Trans. on parallel and distributed systems*, 9(1), Jan. 1998.
3. M. W. Hall, J. M. Anderson, S. P. Amarasinghe, B. R. Murphy, S. Liao, E. Bugnion, and M. S. Lam. Maximizing multiprocessor performance with the suif compiler. *IEEE Computer*, 1996.
4. Marc Gonzalez, Xavier Martorell, Jose Oliver, Eduard Ayguade, and Jesus Labarta. Code generation and run-time support for multi-level parallelism exploitation. In *Proc. of the 8th International Workshop on Compilers for Parallel Computing*, Jan. 2000.
5. H. Honda, M. Iwata, and H. Kasahara. Coarse grain parallelism detection scheme of a fortran program. *Trans. of IEICE*, J73-D-1(12):951–960, Dec. 1990.
6. H.Kasahara et al. A multi-grain parallelizing compilation scheme on oscar. *Proc. 4th Workshop on Language and Compilers for Parallel Computing*, 1991.

7. Hironori Kasahara. Advanced automatic parallelizing compiler technology. *IPSJ MAGANIE*, Apr 2003.
8. David H. Albonesi et al. Dynamically tuning processor resources with adaptive processing. In *IEEE Computer*, Dec. 2003.
9. Q. Wu, P. Juang, M. Martonosi, and D. W. Clark. Formal online methods for voltage/frequency control in multiple clock domain microprocessors. In *Eleventh International Conference on Architectural Support for Programming Languages and Operating Systems*, Oct. 2004.
10. Chung-Hsing Hsu and Ulrich Kremer. The design, implementation, and evaluation of a compiler algorithm for cpu energy reduction. In *The ACM SIGPLAN Conference on Programming Language Design and Implementation*, Jun. 2003.
11. M. Obata, J. Shirako, H. Kaminaga, K. Ishizaka, and H. Kasahara. Hierarchical parallelism control for multigrain parallel processing. In *Proc. of 15th International Workshop on Languages and Compilers for Parallel Computing*, Aug. 2002.
12. K. Ishizaka, T. Miyamoto, M. obata J. Shirako, K. kimura, and H. Kasahara. Performance of oscar multigrain parallelizing compiler on smp servers. In *Proc. of 17th International Workshop on Languages and Compilers for Parallel Computing*, Sep. 2004.
13. Jun shirako, Kouhei Nagasawa, Kazuhisa Ishizaka, Motoki Obata, and Hironori Kasahara. Selective inline expansion for improvement of multi grain parallelism. *PDCN2004*, Feb. 2004.
14. H. Kasahara, H. Honda, M. Iwata, and M. Hirota. A compilation scheme for macro-dataflow computation on hierarchical multiprocessor system. *Proc. Int Conf. on Parallel Processing*, 1990.
15. H. Kasahara, S. Narita, and S. Hashimoto. Architecture of oscar. *Trans of IEICE*, J71-D(8), Aug. 1988.
16. H. Kasahara, H. Honda, and S. Narita. Parallel processing of near fine grain tasks using static scheduling on oscar. *Proceedings of Supercomputing '90*, Nov. 1990.
17. K. Kimura, W. Ogata, M. Okamoto, and H. Kasahara. Near fine grain parallel processing on single chip multiprocessors. *Trans. of IPSJ*, 40(5), May. 1999.
18. David Brooks, Vivek Tiwari, and Margaret Martonosi. Wattch: A framework for architectural-level power analysis and optimizations. In *Proc. of the 27th ISCA*, Jun. 2000.
19. Hiroshi Kawaguchi, Youngsoo Shin, and Takayasu Sakurai. uitron-lp: Power-conscious real-time os based on cooperative voltage scaling for multimedia applications. In *IEEE Transactions on multimedia*, Feb. 2005.

Code Transformations for One-Pass Analysis

Xiaogang Li and Gagan Agrawal

Department of Computer Science and Engineering
Ohio State University, Columbus OH 43210
{xgli,agrawal}@cse.ohio-state.edu

Abstract. With the growing popularity of streaming data model, processing queries over streaming data has become an important topic. Streaming data has received attention in a number of communities, including data mining, theoretical computer science, networking, and grid computing. We believe that streaming data processing involves challenges for compilers, which have not been addressed so far. Particularly, the following two questions are important:

- How do we transform queries so that they can be correctly executed with a single pass on streaming data ?
- How do we determine when a query, possibly after certain transformations, can be correctly executed with only a single pass on the dataset.

In this paper, we address these questions in the context of XML query language, XQuery. Because of XQuery's single assignment nature and special constructs for dealing with sequences, the above questions can be answered more easily than for a general imperative language. However, we believe our work also forms the basis for addressing these questions for more general languages.

1 Introduction

Increasingly, a number of applications across computer sciences and other science and engineering disciplines rely on, or can potentially benefit from, analysis and monitoring of *data streams*. In the stream model of processing, data arrives continuously and needs to be processed in *real-time*, i.e., the processing rate must match the arrival rate. There are two trends contributing to the emergence of this model. First, scientific simulations and increasing numbers of high precision data collection instruments (e.g. sensors attached to satellites and medical imaging modalities) are generating data continuously, and at a high rate. The second is the rapid improvements in the technologies for Wide Area Networking (WAN), as evidenced, for example, by the National Light Rail (NLR) proposal and the interconnectivity between the TeraGrid and Extensible Terascale Facility (ETF) sites. As a result, often the data can be transmitted faster than it can be stored or accessed from disks within a cluster.

Realizing the challenges posed by the applications that require real-time analysis of data streams, a number of computer science research communities have initiated efforts. In the theoretical computer science or data mining algorithms research area, work has been done on developing new data analysis or data mining algorithms that require only a single pass on the entire data [17]. At the same time, database systems community has been developing architectures and query processing systems targeting continuous data streams [4].

E. Ayguadé et al. (Eds.): LCPC 2005, LNCS 4339, pp. 377–396, 2007.

We believe that streaming data processing involves challenges for compilers, which have not been addressed so far. Particularly, the following two questions are important:

- How do we transform queries so that they can be correctly executed with a single pass on streaming data ?
- How do we determine when a query, possibly after certain transformations, can be correctly executed with only a single pass on the dataset.

In this paper, we address these questions in the context of XML query language, XQuery. XML is a flexible exchange format that has gained popularity for representing many classes of data, including structured documents, heterogeneous and semi-structured records, data from scientific experiments and simulations, digitized images, among others. As a result, querying XML documents has received much attention. To query and process XML data streams, XQuery designed by W3C [7] can be an ideal language, because of its declarative nature and powerful features. XQuery is a high-level language like SQL, but it also supports more advanced and complex features such as types and recursive functions. XQuery allows user-defined functions, which are often key for specifying the type of processing that is required for streaming data.

In this paper, we make the following contributions. In many cases, direct translation of a XQuery query requires multiple passes on the data, whereas the query can be transformed to correctly execute with only a single pass. We present techniques for enabling such transformations. We model the dependencies in the query using a representation we refer to as the *stream data flow graph*. We apply a series of high-level transformations, including *horizontal* and *vertical* fusion. These techniques enable a larger number of queries to be evaluated correctly on streaming data, and efficiently on any large dataset. Moreover, based on our stream data flow graph, we present a methodology to determine if a query can be evaluated correctly in a single pass. This enables us to avoid generating a query evaluation plan that is going to fail, and instead, a user can be given feedback sooner.

Our transformations are implemented as part of a XQuery compilation system. Our experiments with eight queries show that our techniques are able to transform them for single-pass execution, whereas naive execution is very expensive.

The rest of the paper is organized as follows. A motivating application is described in Section 2.3. The overall problem is described in Section 3. Our analysis, including the stream data flow graph, horizontal and vertical fusion techniques, and the analysis to determine if the query can be executed correctly on streaming data are presented in Section 4. Experimental evaluation is presented in Section 5. We compare our work with related research efforts in Section 6 and conclude in Section 7.

2 Background: XML, XML Schemas, and XQuery

This section gives background on XML, XML Schemas, and XQuery.

2.1 XML and XML Schemas

XML provided a simple and general facility which is useful for data interchange. Though the initial development of XML was mostly for representing structured and

```
< student >
 < firstname > Darin < / firstname >
 < lastname > Sundstrom < /lastname >
 <DOB > 1974-01-06 < / DOB >
 < GPA > 3.73 < / GPA >
< / student >
...
```

(a) XML example

```
   Schema Declaration
< xs:element name=st udent" >
 < xs:complexType >
   < xs:sequence >
        < xs:element name="lastname" type="xs:string"/ >
        < xs:element name="firstname" type="xs:string"/ >
        < xs:element name="DOB" type="xs:date"/>
        < xs:element name= "GPA" type="xs:float"/ >
   < /xs:sequence >
 < /xs:complexType >
< /xs:element >
```

(b) XML Schema

Fig. 1. XML and XML Schema

semi-structured data on the web, XML is rapidly emerging as a general medium for exchanging information between organizations. XML and related technologies form the core of the web-services model [13] and the Open Grid Services Architecture (OGSA) [15].

XML models data as a tree of *elements*. Arbitrary depth and width is allowed in such a tree, which facilitates storage of deeply nested data structures, as well as large collections of records or structures. Each element contains *character data* and can have *attributes* composed of *name-value* pairs. An XML document represents elements, attributes, character data, and the relationship between them by simply using angle brackets.

Applications that operate on XML data often need guarantees on the structure and content of data. XML Schema proposals [5,6] give facilities for describing the structure and constraining the contents of XML documents. The example in Figure (a) shows an XML document containing records of students. The XML Schema describing the XML document is shown in Figure (b). For each student tuple in the XML file, it contains two string elements to specify the last and first names, one date element to specify the date of birth, and one element of float type for the student's GPA.

2.2 XML Query Language: XQuery

As stated previously, XQuery is a language recently developed by the World Wide Web Consortium (W3C). It is designed to be a language in which queries are concise and easily understood, and to be flexible enough to query a broad spectrum of information sources, including both databases and documents.

XQuery is a functional language. The basic building block is an *expression*. Several types of expressions are possible. The two types of expressions important for our discussion are:

- FLWR expressions, which support iteration and binding of variables to intermediate results. FLWR stands for the keywords *for*, *let*, *where*, and *return*.
- Unordered expressions, which use the keyword *unordered*. The unordered expression takes any sequence of items as its argument, and returns the same sequence of items in a nondeterministic order.

```
unordered(
  for $d in document("depts.xml")//deptno
    let $e := document("emps.xml")//emp[deptno = $d]
        where count($e) >= 10
    return
      <big-dept>
        {
          $d,
          <headcount> { count($e) } </headcount>,
          <avgsal> {avg($e/salary)} </avgsal>
        }
      </big-dept>
)
```

Fig. 2. An Example Using XQuery's FLWR and Unordered Expressions

We illustrate the XQuery language and the *for*, *let*, *where*, and *return* expressions by an example, shown in Figure 2. In this example, two XML documents, *depts.xml* and *emps.xml* are processed to create a new document, which lists all departments with ten or more employees, and also lists the average salary of employees in each such department.

In XQuery, a *for* clause contains one or more variables, each with an associated expression. The simplest form of *for* expression, such as the one used in the example here, contains only one variable and an associated expression. The evaluation of the expression typically results in a sequence. The *for* clause results in a loop being executed, in which the variable is bound to each item from the resulting sequence in turn. In our example, the sequence of distinct department numbers is created from the document *depts.xml*, and the loop iterates over each distinct department number.

A *let* clause also contains one or more variables, each with an associated expression. However, each variable is bound to the result of the associated expression, without iteration. In our example, the *let* expression results in the variable $e being bound to the set or sequence of employees that belong to the department $d. The subsequent operations on \$e apply to such sequence. For example, $count(\$e)$ determines the length of this sequence.

A *where* clause serves as a filter for the tuples of variable bindings generated by the *for* and *let* clauses. The expression is evaluated once for each of these tuples. If the resulting value is true, the tuple is retained, otherwise, it is discarded. A *return* clause is used to create an XML record after processing one iteration of the *for* loop. The details of the syntax are not important for our presentation.

The last key-word we explain is *unordered*. By enclosing the *for* loop inside the *unordered* expression, we are not enforcing any order on the execution of the iterations in the *for* loop, and in generation of the results. Without the use of *unordered*, the departments need to be processed in the order in which they occur in the document *depts.xml*. However, when *unordered* is used, the system is allowed to choose the order in which they are processed, or even process the query in parallel.

2.3 A Motivating Application

We now describe an application we refer to as *satellite data processing* [9]. We show how it can be expressed in XQuery, and the issues involved in transforming and executing it correctly on streaming data.

This application involves processing the data collected continuously from satellites and creating composite images. A satellite orbiting the Earth collects data as a sequence of pixels. Each pixel is characterized by the spatial coordinate (the latitude and longitude) and a time coordinate. The satellite contains sensors for five different bands. Thus, each pixel captured by the satellite stores the latitude, longitude, time, and 16-bit measurements for each of the 5 bands.

The typical computation on this satellite data is as follows. A portion of Earth is specified through latitudes and longitudes of end points. For any point on the Earth within the specified area, all available pixels (corresponding to different time values) are scanned and an application dependent output value is computed. To produce such a value, the application will perform computation on the input bands to produce one output value for each input value, and then the multiple output values for the same point on the planet are combined by a reduction operation. For instance, the Normalized Difference Vegetation Index (ndvi) is computed based on bands one and two, and correlates to the "greenness" of the position at the surface of the Earth. Combining multiple ndvi values consists of execution a max operation over all of them, or finding the "greenest" value for that particular position.

XQuery specification of such processing is shown in Figure 3. The code iterates over the two-dimensional space for which the output is desired. Since the order in which the points are processed is not important, we use the directive *unordered*. Within an iteration of the nested for loop, the *let* statement is used to create a sequence of all pixels that correspond to the those spatial coordinates. The desired result involves finding the pixel with the best NDVI value. In XQuery, such reduction can only be computed recursively.

The computations performed to obtain the output value of a given spatial coordinate are often associative and commutative. In such cases, these computations can be performed correctly on streaming data. When a pixel is received, we can find the spatial coordinate it corresponds to, and update the output value for that spatial coordinate.

```
unordered(
  for $i in ($minx to $maxx)
    for $j in ($miny to $maxy)
      let $p := /stream/data/pixel
          where(( $p/x = $i) and ($p/y = $j ))
      return
        <pixel>
          <latitude> {$i} </latitude>
          <longitude> {$j} </longitude>
          <summary> {accumulate($p)} </summary>
        </pixel>
)

declare function accumulate ($p)
    as double
{
  let $inp := $p[1]
  let $NVDI := ( ($inp/band1 - $inp/band0) div
          ($inp/band1 + $inp/band0)+1) * 512
  return
    if( fn:empty($p) )
    then 0
    else { fn:max($NVDI, accumulate(fn:subsequence($p,2))) }
}
```

Fig. 3. Satellite Data Processing Expressed in XQuery

However, direct translation of the XQuery specification, as we had shown in Figure 3, will require multiple scans on the entire dataset. It is clearly desirable that the streaming XQuery processor can transform the query to execute it correctly with only a single pass on the entire dataset. Thus, we have the following challenges:

1. How can we systematically and correctly transform a given XQuery query so that it can be executed on streaming data, when possible ?
2. How can we determine if a given XQuery query, possibly after our transformations, can be executed correctly with only a single pass on the entire dataset ?

We address the above two challenges in the rest of this paper.

3 Preliminaries

This section describes our data and evaluation model. We introduce the notion of *progressive blocking operators*, and describe the overall problem.

3.1 Evaluation Model

We assume that the length of the incoming XML stream exceeds our capability of storing it. We only investigate the possibility of obtaining exact query results in a single pass. Approximate processing of queries using a single pass on streaming data has been extensively studied by many researchers, and we do not consider this possibility here. We limit the number of input streams to be one. Also, we assume that duplicate-preserving is always used for XPath expressions in the query.

When an incoming tuple is available, it is fetched for evaluation and a series of internal computations are performed. As a result of this computation, an output tuple may be dispatched. A limited amount of memory is available for internal buffering, which is much smaller than the entire length of the data stream.

The internal computations can be viewed as a series of linked operators. Each operator receives input from its parent(s), performs an operation on the input, and sends the output tuples to its children. An operator could be a *pipeline operator* or a *blocking operator*.

Pipeline Operator: A pipeline operator can immediately dispatch the output tuple after processing one input tuple. In our system, assume that the input of the operator f is

$$Input(f) = [x_1, x_2, \ldots, x_n]$$

and the output stream is

$$Output(f) = [y_1, y_2, \ldots, y_k]$$

A pipeline operator f has the property:

$$y_i = g(x_{h(i)}, b)$$

where, h is monotonically increasing and b is a bounded size buffered synopsis of $x_1, x_2, \ldots, x_{h(i)-1}$. An example of a pipeline operator is the selection operation.

Blocking Operator: A blocking operator must receive all its input before generating the output. Using the above notation for input and output, for a blocking operator we have

$$[y_1, y_2, ...y_k] = g(x_1, x_2, ..., x_n)$$

An example of a blocking operator is the sort operation.

For our analysis, we introduce a special type of a blocking operator, which we refer to as the *progressive blocking operator*. This is based on the observation that not all blocking operators require buffering of the entire input before generating the output. If the following two conditions hold true, a blocking operator is a progressive blocking operator.

$$|Output(f)| \ll |Input(f)| \quad (1)$$

$$g(x_1, x_2, ..., x_n) = g_1(g(x_1, x2, ..., x_{n-1}), x_n) \quad (2)$$

In such cases, the operator can be evaluated as follows. At each step, we only need to buffer the temporary results and can discard the input. This is because the Equation 2 ensures that the input is no longer necessary for the later computations. Equation 1 ensures that temporary results can actually be buffered in our evaluation model. An example of such an operator is the count operation.

3.2 Problem Overview

The analysis we perform in this paper is based on the following key observation. In a system with limited memory, a query cannot be evaluated using a single pass on the entire data stream to obtain an exact answer if the following conditions holds true:

- A blocking operator with unbounded input is involved in the query, or
- A progressive blocking operator with unbounded input is involved and its output is used by another pipeline or progressive blocking operator.

The first condition is straight-forward. Let us consider the second condition. When the final output of a progressive blocking operator f_1 is referred by another operator f_2, which is either a pipeline or a progressive blocking operator, f_2 must wait until the computation of f_1 finishes. This blocks the pipeline or progressive blocking computation f_2 defines. Queries that satisfy this propriety are referred to as *correlated aggregates* [16], which in most cases can only be evaluated approximately with a single pass.

The dependence between blocking operators and pipeline or progressive blocking operators that prevents a query from being evaluated in a single pass can either be a control dependence or a data dependence. The following query, referred to as the `Query 1`, is an example where data dependence between operators is involved. Here, `pixel` contains two elements, `x` and `y`.

```
Query 1:
let $b = count(stream/pixel[x>0])
  for $i in stream/pixel
     return $i/x idvi $b
```

4 High-Level Analysis

This section describes the high-level analysis done in our system. Our goal is to correctly transform the query so that it can be processed in a single pass, when it is possible, and also to recognize when single pass analysis is not possible. Initially, we give an overview of our overall framework.

4.1 Overview

As we had discussed in the previous section, there are two cases in which a query cannot be processed in a single pass. The first one involves a blocking operator with unbounded input. The second one involves a progressive blocking operator with unbounded input whose output is used by another pipeline or progressive blocking operator. The first case is simple to detect. Therefore, for our analysis in this section, we assume that we only have pipelined or progressive blocking operators in our query, i.e., we do not have a blocking operator which cannot be evaluated progressively.

Figure 4 shows the key phases in our system. First, we construct the stream data flow graph representing the data dependence information for the query. Then, we apply a series of high-level transformations to prune and merge the stream data flow graph.

Such techniques not only simplify the later analyses, but most importantly, they can rewrite some queries to enable single pass processing. After pruning the graph, a *single pass analysis* algorithm will be applied to the resulting data flow graph to check if single pass evaluation is possible. If the answer is no, further processing will not be performed. Otherwise, we apply low-level transformations and our code generation algorithm, and efficient single pass execution code is generated.

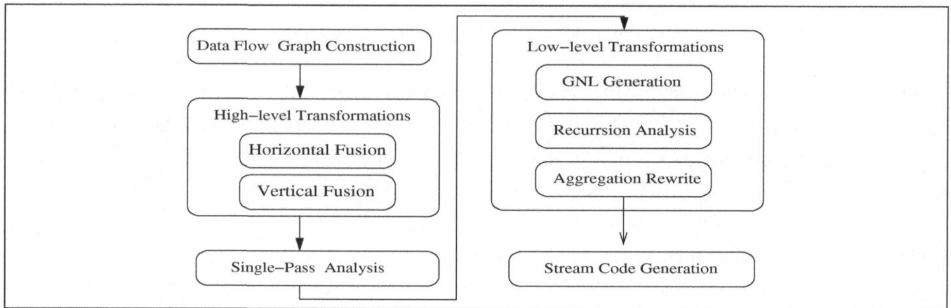

Fig. 4. Overview of the Framework

4.2 Stream Data Flow Graph

We introduce the stream data flow graph to represent dependence information and enable high-level analysis and optimizations on XQuery.

Definition 1. *A stream data flow graph is a directed graph in which each node represents a variable in the original query and the directed edges $e = (v_1, v_2)$ implies that v_2 is dependent on v_1.*

We introduce nodes for the variables defined in the original query, such as those defined in *Let* and *For* clauses, as well as for output value of a function or an XPath expression that is not explicitly defined in the original query. We distinguish between nodes that represent a sequence, and nodes which represent *atomic* values. This is because dependence relationships between sequences and atomic values are of particular importance. We represent nodes of sequence type (of unbounded length) with rectangles and nodes of atomic type (or sequences of bounded length) with circles.

The stream data flow graph for the `Query 1` described in the previous section is shown in Figure 5. $S1$ is the implicit variable that represents the XPath expression `stream/pixel[x>0]`. Similarly, $S2$ is used to represent `stream/pixel`. The output of the aggregate function `count()` is represented by $v1$. Here i in the for clause is treated as an atom variable to represent each item in the binding sequence.

Lemma 1. *The stream data flow graph for a valid XQuery query is acyclic.*

Proof: The proof directly follows from the single assignment feature of XQuery [7]. Assume there is a cycle, then one of the following conditions must hold true: 1) a variable v is defined more than once, or 2) a variable v is referred to without definition.

Neither of the above are allowed in a valid XQuery query. □

We distinguish between two types of dependence relationship among the nodes.

Definition 2. *Given two variables* v_1,v_2, *we say that* v_2 *is* aggregate dependent *on* v_1 *if: 1)* v_2 *is dependent on* v_1, *and 2)* v_1 *is a sequence variable,* v_2 *is an atomic variable, and moreover,* v_2 *is not used as the iterator variable for any* for *expression. In such a case, we denote* $v_1 \succ v_2$.

Aggregate dependence typically exists between a progressive blocking operator and its output.

Definition 3. *Given two variables* v_1,v_2, *we say that* v_2 *is flow dependent on* v_1 *if: 1)* v_2 *is dependent on* v_1, *and 2)* v_2 *is not aggregate dependent on* v_1. *In such a case, we denote* $v_1 \rightarrow v_2$.

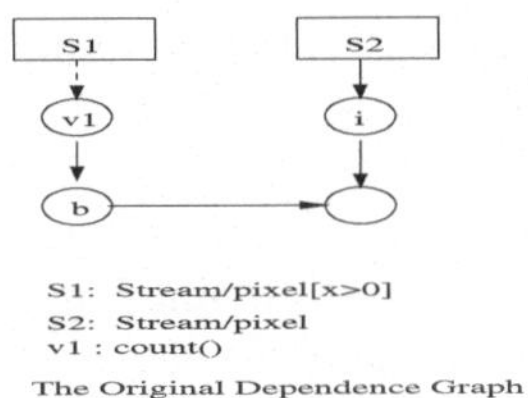

Fig. 5. Example of Stream Data Flow Graph

Let us reconsider the Figure 5. We have used dashed arrows to represent aggregate dependence, and solid arrows for flow dependence.

4.3 High-Level Transformations

Let us consider a stream data flow graph. If this graph contains multiple rectangle nodes, the corresponding query cannot be evaluated in a single pass, if we strictly follow the original syntax and do not allow pipelined execution. This is because each rectangle node represents a sequence that may have an infinite length, which cannot be buffered in the main memory.

However, by applying our query transformation and graph pruning techniques, including horizontal and vertical fusion, many queries can still be evaluated in a single pass.

Graph Pruning with Horizontal Fusion. Consider a query that involves multiple traversals of a data stream. If these traversals share a common prefix in their corresponding XPath expressions, we can merge these traversal into one, and could enable processing in a single pass.

As an example, we consider the following query:

```
Query 2:
let $b = count(stream/pixel[x>0])
     return sum(stream/pixel/y) idvi $b
```

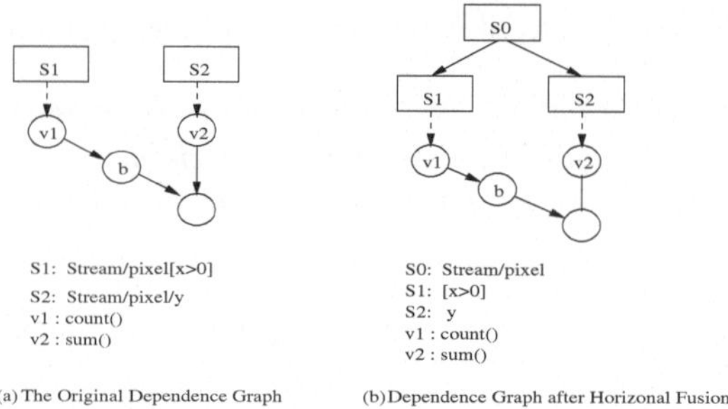

Fig. 6. Example of Horizontal Fusion

The original query involves two traversals of the entire stream, and cannot be processed directly without buffering the stream. However, since the two XPath expressions share a common prefix `stream/pixel`, the computation of `count` and `sum` can be carried out in a single traversal of `stream/pixel`.

To fuse multiple traversals together, we first generate a new node representing their common prefix. Then, for each original sequence node representing the traversal, the label will be changed to the subexpression obtained by removing the common prefix. A new edge will be added linking this node to the new node. If the subexpression obtained after removing the common prefix is empty, the corresponding node is deleted, and its children have an edge from the parent node.

The stream data flow graph for the `Query 2` after horizontal fusion is shown in Figure 6. In this example, a new sequence node $S0$ is generated corresponding to the common prefix `/stream/pixel`. The label of the two original sequence node are changed to the remaining XPath expressions, which are $[x > 0]$ and $/y$, respectively. Each new node is linked to $S0$.

Sometimes horizontal fusion in a query may lead to incorrect results, because of inter-dependence among the traversal of sequences. As an example, consider the `Query 1`. The data flow graph after horizontal fusion is shown in Figure 7. When we combine the traversal to compute count and the final output together, in each iteration, the output will be computed using partial result of $b, which is not correct. In our method, we just apply horizontal fusion irrespective of such inter-dependence. Later, during single pass analysis, such dependence will be detected and the query will be eliminated from further processing.

For nested queries with pre-defined iteration space, which are common in many scientific data processing applications, horizontal fusion can be applied after *unrolling*. Unrolling is a commonly used technique in traditional compilers. Consider the following simple query:

```
unordered(
  for $i in (1 to 2)
    let $b: =//stream/pixel[x=$i]
       return count($b))
```

By unrolling the first *for* expression, we can generate the following intermediate query:

```
unordered(
   let $b1: =//stream/pixel[x=1]
   let $b2: =//stream/pixel[x=2]
      return count($b1), count($b2)
```

Since the XPath expressions generated after unrolling share the same common prefix, horizontal fusion can be applied to all the sequence node corresponding to the different iterations.

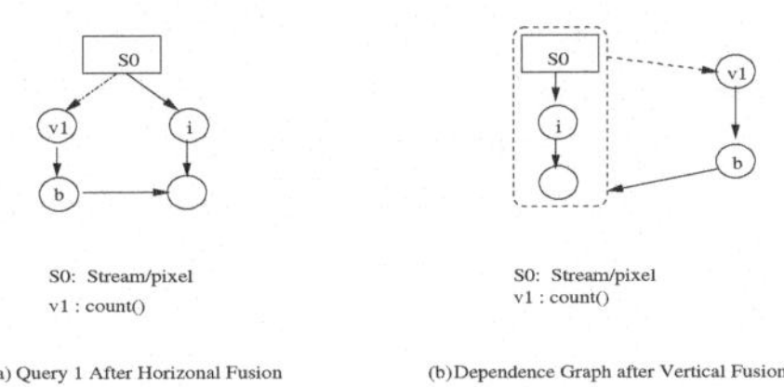

Fig. 7. Horizontal and Vertical Fusion for Query 1

Graph Pruning with Vertical Fusion. The stream data flow graph can be further pruned using a technique called vertical fusion. Vertical fusion exploits the benefits of the pipelined processing, which can remove unnecessary buffering and simplify the data flow graph.

Consider the following example.

```
Query 3:
let $b: = for $i in  stream/pixel[x>0]
   return $i
for $j in $b/y
   return $j
   where $j = count($b)
```

In this query, b contains all tuples from the original stream with a positive value of the x coordinate. In a pipelined fashion, we can further process each tuple in b as soon as it is available without buffering the entire sequence of b, which is required for unbounded streams.

As described in 3.2, we only need to check dependence between a progressive blocking operator and a pipeline operator, while dependence among pipeline operators can be ignored. In vertical fusion, we try to merge multiple pipeline operations on each traversal path into a single cluster in the stream data flow graph. The cluster obtained after fusion is referred to as a *super-node*. A super-node is represented in the data flow graph with a dashed box enclosing all the merged nodes. By doing so, the pipeline operation and the progressive blocking operations can be separated, and the number of isolated nodes in the data flow graph is reduced. This significantly simplifies later analysis on their dependence relationships.

Our algorithm does a top-down traversal from each root node, following only the flow dependence edges. For each node visited during the traversal, it will be fused with the current super-node, if it is not already in another super-node. Note that not all sequence nodes can be merged by vertical fusion. If a sequence B is flow dependent on both the sequence node A and the sequence node C, which normally occurs when B is the result of a join between A and C, we will merge B with either A or C, but not both of them.

The details of the algorithm are shown in Figure 9. R is the set of the nodes in the graph that do not have an incoming edge. N denotes the set of nodes that have been inserted in any super-node. $\bar{N}$ denotes the compliment of N, i.e., the nodes in the graph that are not in the set N. The algorithm picks a sequence node s_i. It follows the flow dependence edges (denoted as $\rightarrow$) to find nodes that can be fused into a super-node with s_i. These nodes are put in the set M. Any node that has already been fused into a super-node, (i.e., is not in $\bar{N}$) is not inserted in M.

The data flow graph for the `Query 1` after vertical fusion is shown in Figure 7(b). The data flow graph for the `Query 3` after vertical fusion is shown in Figure 8 (b).

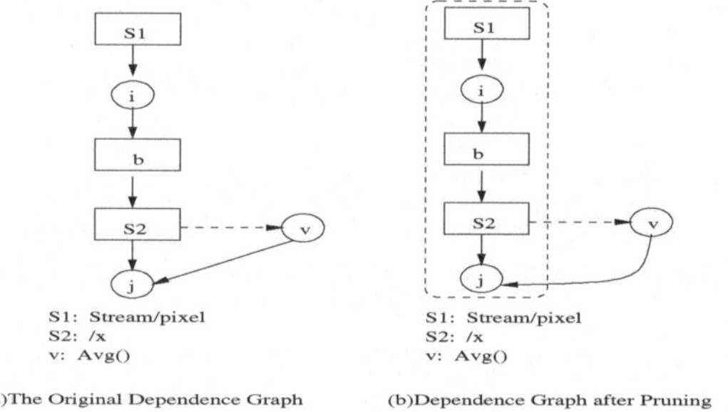

Fig. 8. Example of Vertical Fusion (Query 3)

Vertical fusion simplifies the stream data flow graph for further analysis and optimization. After vertical fusion, most of the queries that can be processed in a single pass will have only one rectangle node in their data flow graph.

4.4 Single Pass Analysis

After horizontal and vertical fusion, analyzing whether a query can be evaluated in a single pass becomes simpler. *For our discussion here, we treat all nodes in a super-node after vertical fusion as a single sequence node.* With this, any stream data flow graph that contains more than one sequence node cannot be evaluated in a single pass. This is because each such node represents one traversal of a sequence of length $\theta(\mathcal{N})$. If two sequence nodes are not fused with vertical fusion to apply pipelined execution, two traversals must be used. Thus, we have the following theorem.

Theorem 1. *If a query Q with dependence graph $G = (V, E)$ contains more than one sequence node after vertical fusion, Q may not be evaluated correctly in a single pass.*

However, for queries whose stream data flow graph contains only one sequence node, a single pass evaluation may still not be possible. Two types of dependence relationship may prevent the query from being executed in a single pass. Examples of these two cases are shown in Figure 10.

Vertical_Fusion
Input: 1) data flow graph G =(V ,E)
  2) root set R

$N = \oslash$
foreach node $s_i \in R$ {
  if s_i is a sequence node
    $M = \{s_i\}$
  do {
    $N = N \cup M$
    Let $T = \{v | \exists x, (x \in M) \wedge (x \rightarrow v)\}$
    $M = M \cup (T \cap \bar{N})$
  } until $(T \cap \bar{N} == \oslash)$
  fuse M into super-node
}
end

Fig. 9. Algorithm for Vertical Fusion

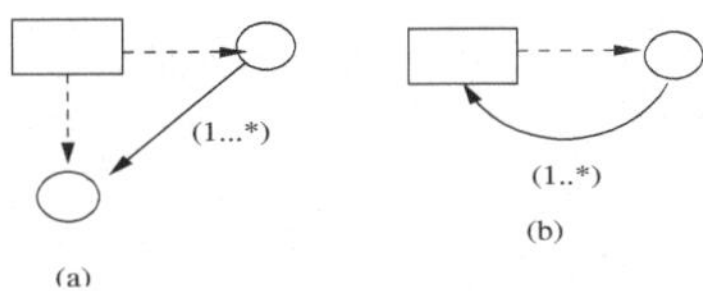

Fig. 10. Stream Data Flow Graphs that Require Multiple Traversals

Theorem 2. *Let S be the set of atomic nodes that are aggregate dependent on any sequence node in a stream data flow graph G. For any given two elements $s_1 \in S$ and $s_2 \in S$, if there is a path between s_1 and s_2, the query may not be evaluated correctly in a single pass.*

Proof: For each $s_i \in S$, s_i can only be computed after the sequence V_i it depends on is fully scanned. Assume there is a path from s_1 to s_2, then the value of s_2 must be computed using s_1. Thus, the scan of V_2 must follow the scan of V_2. This implies that the query cannot be processed with a single pass. □

In addition to the condition associated with the Theorem 2, there is another condition we need to check for.

Lemma 2. *If a stream data flow graph G contains a cycle, it is formed after horizontal or vertical fusion.*

Proof: From lemma 1 there is no cycle in the original stream data flow graph. Therefore, the cycle must be formed by either horizontal fusion or vertical fusion. □

Theorem 3. *If there is a cycle in a stream data flow graph G, the corresponding query may not be evaluated correctly using a single pass.*

Proof: From the lemma above, the cycle is formed after horizontal or vertical fusion. If the cycle is formed right after horizontal fusion of s_1 and s_2, there must be a path between s_1 and s_2, which implies dependence of s_2 on s_1. In this case, horizontal fusion will generate incorrect results, and single pass evaluation is impossible.

If the cycle is formed after vertical fusion, a super-node must be involved in the cycle. Assume the cycle is $v_1, v_2, \ldots, v_k, v_1$, and v_i is a super-node. Then, it is true that v_{i+1} is aggregate dependent on the node v_i, otherwise, v_{i+1} will be fused with v_i during vertical fusion. Thus, the value of v_{i+1} can only be valid after the pipelined execution of v_i is completed. Because a cycle exists, the pipelined execution of v_i also requires the value of v_{i+1}. As a result, pipelined execution of v_i is not possible, and the query cannot be evaluated in a single pass. □

After vertical fusion, stream data flow graphs for both `Query 1` and `Query 3` contain cycles, and therefore, these queries cannot be executed with a single pass.

If the conditions corresponding to any of the above three theorems hold true for a query, we cannot further process the query using a single pass and ensure correct results. If the original graph has n vertex, the conditions corresponding to Theorems 1, 2, and 3 can be applied in $O(n)$, $O(n^2)$, and $O(n)$ time, respectively.

The next theorem shows that if the conditions corresponding to the Theorems 1, 2, and 3 all hold false, the query can be processed correctly in a single pass.

Theorem 4. *If the results of a progressive blocking operator with an unbounded input are referred to by a pipeline operator or a progressive blocking operator with unbounded input, then for the stream data flow graph $G = (V, E)$, at least one of the following three conditions holds true:*

1. *There are multiple sequence nodes.*
2. *There is a cycle involved.*
3. *$\exists$ sequence node $s \in V$, $\exists$ atomic nodes $a_1 \in V$,$a_2 \in V$, a_1 and a_2 are aggregate dependent on s, and there is a path from a_1 to a_2.*

Proof: Assume that the progressive blocking operation is represented in G with a sequence node s and an atomic node a, such that a is aggregate dependent on s. Assume that there is no other sequence node in G, otherwise the first condition holds true.

If the value of a is referred to by another progressive blocking operator to compute a', since s is the only sequence node in V, a' must be aggregate dependent on s. Because a' uses the value of a, there must be a path $a, v_1, \ldots, v_k, a'$, $a \rightarrow v_1, \ldots, v_k \rightarrow a'$. Therefore, the third condition holds true.

Now, suppose the value of a is referred by a pipeline operator. Then, there must be a super-node in the graph, and there is a path $a, v_1, \ldots, v_k, s$, such that $a \rightarrow v_1, \ldots, v_k \rightarrow s$. Since a is aggregate dependent on s, there will be a cycle $a, v_1, \ldots, v_k, s, a$ in the graph. Then, the second condition holds true. □

Finally, it should be noted that like all static analyses, our analysis is conservative in nature. There could be cases where a query can be processed in a single pass, but our analysis will determine that it cannot be. We consider the following example:

```
let $p: =  stream/pixel/x
 for $i in $p
   where $i <= max($p)
   return $i
```

This query has a *redundant predicate* [3]. Though the predicate always returns true and does not impact the results from the query, it introduces a cycle in our graph, and disallows processing with a single pass. Our analysis can be extended to recognize and remove such redundant predicates, but we do not expect them to arise frequently in real situations.

XMark Query 1

Size	Ours	Qizx	Saxon	Galax
1.16M	0.76	1.03	2.46	4.65
5.75M	2.26	3.2	5.57	24.59
30M	9.98	11.23	MO	173.85
120M	13.97	MO	MO	*
240M	27.59	MO	MO	*

XMark Query 5

Size	Ours	Qizx	Saxon	Galax
1.16M	0.74	1.09	2.46	4.93
5.75M	2.30	3.35	5.55	25.26
30M	10.02	13.9	MO	174.08
120M	13.95	MO	MO	*
240M	27.87	MO	MO	*

XMark Query 6

Size	Ours	Qizx	Saxon	Galax
1.16M	0.73	1.07	2.42	4.75
5.75M	2.26	3.21	5.39	24.96
30M	9.94	13.68	MO	215.64
120M	13.87	MO	MO	*
240M	27.81	MO	MO	*

XMark Query 7

Size	Ours	Qizx	Saxon	Galax
1.16M	0.74	1.13	2.44	6.6
5.75M	2.28	3.45	5.53	47.79
30M	9.95	13.96	MO	MO
120M	13.70	MO	MO	MO
240M	27.44	MO	MO	MO

XMark Query 20

Size	Ours	Qizx	Saxon	Galax
1.16M	0.78	1.32	2.57	5.15
5.75M	2.31	3.59	5.93	26.38
30M	10.00	15.77	MO	190.22
120M	14.16	MO	MO	*
240M	27.81	MO	MO	*

Satellite Processing

Size	Ours	Qizx	Saxon	Galax
0.05M	0.28	5.88	3.08	72.03
0.10M	0.33	20.48	4.45	136.7
0.66M	0.48	945.5	18.76	944.4
10.6M	3.47	*	MO	MO
100M	28.31	MO	MO	MO

Virtual Microscope

Size	Ours	Qizx	Saxon	Galax
0.05M	0.28	47.51	2.01	18.97
0.10M	0.32	*	2.47	38.98
0.66M	0.44	*	7.66	300.18
2.70M	1.54	*	24.56	MO
10.6M	3.29	*	MO	MO
100M	27.88	*	MO	MO

Karp Frequent Item

Size	Ours	Qizx	Saxon	Galax
0.05M	0.26	*	4.71	25.09
0.10M	0.32	*	10.66	122.63
0.66M	0.61	*	554.07	MO
2.70M	1.80	*	8302.7	MO
10.6M	5.61	*	MO	MO
100M	29.41	*	MO	MO

***: Unable to produce result after 24 hours MO: Out of memory**

Fig. 11. Experiments Results for XMark Queries and Real Streaming Applications (All Execution Times in Seconds)

5 Experimental Results

Our transformations have been implemented as part of a XQuery compilation system that is based on the open source SAX parser[1]. In this section, we demonstrate that many XQuery queries can be transformed to achieve single-pass execution, whereas their naive execution results in much more expensive processing. For this purpose, we took 8 XQuery queries, and compared our implementation with other well known

[1] http://www.saxproject.org

XQuery processors which are publically available. Specifically, we use Galax (Version 0.3.1) [11], Saxon (Version 8.0) [19] and Qizx/Open (Version 0.4/_p1) [1]. All these query processors are implemented using a SAX Parser, which we believe makes the comparison reasonable.

We used two sets of queries for our experiments. The first set comprised the queries 1, 5, 6, 7, and 20 from the XMark benchmark set [25]. These five queries were chosen because each of them could be processed in a single pass either directly, or after our transformations. We use datasets of different sizes, which were generated by the XMark data generator using factors 0.01, 0.05, 0.25, 1, and 2, respectively. The second set comprised three real applications which involve streaming data. Satellite data processing was described earlier in Section 2. Virtual microscope is an application to support interactive viewing and processing of digitized data arising from tissue specimens [12]. Frequent element counting is a well known data mining problem, here we use the one-pass algorithm by Karp *et al.* to find a superset of frequent items in a data stream [18]. Each of these three applications uses recursive functions to perform aggregations. After applying our techniques and optimizations, including analysis of recursive functions, aggregate rewriting, and horizontal and vertical fusion, each of these could be processed correctly using only a single pass on the entire data stream. We generated synthetic datasets of varying sizes to evaluate performance on these applications.

The results of our experiments are shown in Figure 11. Our experiments were conducted on a 933 MHz Pentium III workstation, with 256 MB of RAM, and running Linux version 7.1, with JDK V1.4.0. Each of the systems we compared was executed on this same environment. In the tables in Figure 11, `Ours` denotes our basic framework. Because we use compiled Java byte code, the running time shown in the tables excludes the compilation time for other XQuery systems. All available options for fast execution and optimization are turned on for each system. Specifically, for Galax, we disable sorting and duplicate removal on Path expressions, and set the option of projection to be on.

The results show that we consistently outperform other systems. For XMark queries with small datasets, Qizx is often quite close, but our system is at least 25% faster. There are at least two reasons for this. First, our static analysis based technique produced operations only on elements that are referred in the query. Second, we generate imperative code directly, which is more efficient compared with interpreted execution used by other engines.

For XMark queries with larger datasets, either our system was significantly faster, or other systems had a memory overflow. It should be noted that none of the other systems have been designed to deal with large datasets and/or streaming data. They often require in-memory processing. For example, Saxon builds a DOM tree after retrieving all data in memory, and therefore, cannot process large datasets or streaming data.

For the three real streaming applications, our implementation outperforms other systems by at least one order of magnitude, and often, much more. None of the other systems was able to execute these applications with only a single pass on the data, whereas, our techniques and transformations enabled such execution.

6 Related Work

Our work is related to the large body of research in the area of loop transformations. Many loop transformations, such as loop fusion [27] or data-centric transformations [21] can often help in executing a code with a single-pass or fewer passes on the input data. However, we are not aware of any previous work on systematically transforming and analyzing code for single pass analysis on streaming data.

Language and compiler support for streaming data has been considered by the StreamIt effort at MIT [26]. There work also does not consider analysis and transformation to enable single-pass analysis.

There have been many research efforts on efficient evaluation of XPath expressions over streaming data. Because of the regularity of XPath expressions, automaton based approaches are most popular when predicates are not present [2,10,8]. To deal with predicates and other features, such as closures where buffering of certain elements is necessary, transducers have been used in XSQ [24] and SPEX [23].

Compared with XPath, XQuery is more expressive, and therefore, involves additional challenges. Currently, there is limited work on processing XQuery queries over streaming data. Transducer networks have also been used to handle a subset of XQuery, in which only join and node creation operations are investigated [22]. Without query transformations and rewriting, their techniques will not work on streaming data when the queries are not strictly written to execute on streaming data. In Flux [20], an intermediate representation (IR) extends XQuery with new constructs for event-based processing. XQuery is translated into this event-based IR and the buffer size is optimized by analyzing the DTD as well as the query syntax. Fusion of *for* expressions has been discussed in Flux, but algorithms to systemically perform such optimizations are not provided. In comparison, we present systematic and powerful techniques for optimizing and transforming queries that are not specifically written for single-pass processing. For code generation based on SAX events, we use a similar approach to enable efficient buffering. As we stated earlier, our additional contribution in code generation is handling user-defined aggregations with the use of GNLs. The BEA/XQRL processor [14] supports pipelined processing of streams by implementing the iterator model at the expression level. However, query optimizations specially designed for XML streams are limited in this system, and large documents cannot be processed.

Algebraic approach for deciding whether a SQL-like query can be evaluated with a single pass on continuous streams has been proposed recently by Babu and Widom [3]. Their approach cannot handle user-defined aggregates and computations described with binary expressions, which are both frequently used in XQuery. Unlike SQL, developing an algebra to handle complete XQuery is hard. As an example, user defined functions allowed as part of XQuery can be very hard to model through such an algebra, and we are not aware of any existing effort which is able to do this.

7 Conclusions

Our work has been driven by growing popularity of the streaming data model. We have considered the following two questions. First, how do we transform queries so that they can be correctly executed with a single pass on streaming data. Second, how do we determine when a query, possibly after certain transformations, can be correctly executed with only a single pass on the dataset.

We have addressed these questions in the context of XML query language, XQuery. However, we believe our work also forms the basis for addressing these questions for more general languages.

References

1. Qizx/open: An open source implementation of xml query in java. http://www.xfra.net/qizxopen/.
2. Mehmet Altinel and Michael J. Franklin. Efficient Filtering of XML Documents for Selective Dissemination of Information. In *Proceedings of the 26th International Conference on Very Large Data Bases*, pages 53–64, 2000.
3. Arvind Arasu, Brian Babcock, Shivnath Babu, Jon McAlister, and Jennifer Widom. Characterizing Memory Requirements for Queries over Continuous Data Streams. *ACM Transactions on Database Systems*, 29(1):162–194, 2004.
4. B. Babcock, S. Babu, M. Datar, R. Motwani, and J. Widom. Models and Issues in Data Stream Systems. In *Proceedings of the 2002 ACM Symposium on Principles of Database Systems (PODS 2002) (Invited Paper)*. ACM Press, June 2002.
5. D. Beech, S. Lawrence, M. Maloney, N. Mendelsohn, and H. Thompson. XML Schema part 1: Structures, W3C working draft. Available at http://www.w3.org/TR/1999/xmlschema-1, May 1999.
6. P. Biron and A. Malhotra. XML Schema part 2: Datatypes, W3C working draft. Available at http://www.w3.org/TR/1999/xmlschema-2, May 1999.
7. S. Boag, D. Chamberlin, M. F. Fernandez, D. Florescu, J. Robie, and J. Simeon. XQuery 1.0: An XML Query Language. W3C Working Draft, available from http://www.w3.org/TR/xquery/, November 2002.
8. C. Y. Chan, P. Felber, M. Garofalakis, and R. Rastogi. Efficient Filtering of XML documents with XPath Expressions. *VLDB Journal: Very Large Data Bases*, 11(4):354–379, December 2002.
9. Chialin Chang, Bongki Moon, Anurag Acharya, Carter Shock, Alan Sussman, and Joel Saltz. Titan: A high performance remote-sensing database. In *Proceedings of the 1997 International Conference on Data Engineering*, pages 375–384. IEEE Computer Society Press, April 1997.
10. Y. Diao, P. Fischer, and M. J. Franklin. Y. Filter: Efficient and Scalable filtering of XML Documents. In *Proceedings of the 18th International Conference of Data Engineering*, 2002.
11. Mary F. Fernandez, Jérôme Siméon, Byron Choi, Amélie Marian, and Gargi Sur. Implementing Xquery 1.0: The Galax experience. In *VLDB 2003: Proceedings of 29th International Conference on Very Large Data Bases, September 9–12, 2003, Berlin, Germany*, pages 1077–1080, 2003.
12. R. Ferreira, B. Moon, J. Humphries, A. Sussman, J. Saltz, R. Miller, and A. Demarzo. The Virtual Microscope. In *Proceedings of the 1997 AMIA Annual Fall Symposium*, pages 449–453. American Medical Informatics Association, Hanley and Belfus, Inc., October 1997. Also available as University of Maryland Technical Report CS-TR-3777 and UMIACS-TR-97-35.
13. Chris Ferris and Joel Farrell. What are Web Services. *Communications of the ACM (CACM)*, pages 31–35, June 2003.

14. Daniela Florescu, Chris Hillery, Donald Kossmann, Paul Lucas, Fabio Riccardi, Till Westmann, Michael J. Carey, Arvind Sundararajan, and Geetika Agrawal. The BEA/XQRL Streaming XQuery Processor. In *VLDB 2003: Proceedings of 29th International Conference on Very Large Data Bases, September 9–12, 2003, Berlin, Germany*, pages 997–1008, 2003.
15. Ian Foster, Carl Kesselman, Jeffrey M. Nick, and Steven Tuecke. The Physiology of the Grid: An Open Grid Services Architecture for Distributed Systems Integration. In *Open Grid Service Infrastructure Working Group, Global Grid Forum*, June 2002.
16. Johannes Gehrke, Flip Korn, and Divesh Srivastava. On Computing Correlated Aggregates over Continual Data Streams. In *Proceedings of the 2001 ACM SIGMOD international conference on Management of data*, pages 13–24, 2001.
17. S. Guha, N. Mishra, R. Motwani, and L. O'Callaghan. Clustering Data Streams. In *Proceedings of 2000 Annual IEEE Symp. on Foundations of Computer Science (FOCS)*, pages 359–366. ACM Press, 2000.
18. Richard M. Karp, Scott Shenker, and Christos H. Papadimitriou. A simple algorithm for finding frequent elements in streams and bags. *ACM Trans. Database Syst.*, 28(1):51–55, 2003.
19. Michael H. Kay. Saxon: The xslt and xquery processor. http://saxon.sourceforge.net/.
20. C. Koch, S. Scherzinger, N. Schweikardt, and B. Stegmaier. Schema-based Scheduling of Event Processors and Buffer Minimization for Queries on Structured Data Streams. In *Proceedings of the 30th International Conference on Very Large Data Bases*, 2004.
21. Induprakas Kodukula, Nawaaz Ahmed, and Keshav Pingali. Data-centric multi-level blocking. In *Proceedings of the SIGPLAN '97 Conference on Programming Language Design and Implementation*, pages 346–357, June 1997.
22. B. Ludascher, P. Mukhopadhayn, and Y. Papakonstantinou. A Transducer-Based XML Query Processor. In *Proceedings of the 28th International Conference on Very Large Data Bases*, 2002.
23. D. Olteanu, T. Kiesling, and F. Bry. An Evaluation of Regular Path Expressions with Qualifiers against XML Streams. In *Proceedings of ICDE 2003, Psoter Session*, 2003.
24. Feng Peng and Sudarshan S. Chawathe. XPath Queries on Streaming Data. In *Proceedings of the 2003 ACM SIGMOD international conference on on Management of data*, pages 431–442, 2003.
25. A. R. Schmidt, F. Waas, M. L. Kersten, M. J. Carey, I. Manolescu, and R.Busse. Xmark: A benchmark for xml data management. In *Proceedings of the 28th International Conference on Very Large Data Bases (VLDB)*, pages 974–985, 2002.
26. William Thies, Michal Karczmarek, and Saman Amarasinghe. StreamIt: A Language for Streaming Applications. In *Proceedings of Conference on Compiler Construction (CC)*, April 2002.
27. Michael Wolfe. *High Performance Compilers for Parallel Computing*. Addison-Wesley, 1995.

Scalable Array SSA and Array Data Flow Analysis*

Silvius Rus, Guobin He, and Lawrence Rauchwerger

Parasol Lab, Department of Computer Science, Texas A&M University
{silviusr,guobinh,rwerger}@cs.tamu.edu

Abstract. Static Single Assignment (SSA) has become the intermediate program representation of choice in most modern compilers because it enables efficient data flow analysis of scalars and thus leads to better scalar optimizations. Unfortunately not much progress has been achieved in applying the same techniques to array data flow analysis, a very important and potentially powerful technology. In this paper we propose to improve the applicability of previous efforts in array SSA through the use of a symbolic memory access descriptor that can aggregate the accesses to the elements of an array over large, interprocedural program contexts. We then show the power of our new representation by using it to implement a basic data flow algorithm, reaching definitions. Finally we apply this analysis to array constant propagation and show performance improvement (speedups) for benchmark codes.

1 Introduction

Important compiler optimization or enabling transformations such as constant propagation, loop invariant motion, expansion/privatization depend on the power of data flow analysis. The Static Single Assignment (SSA) [9] program representation has been widely used to explicitly represent the flow between definitions and uses in a program.

SSA relies on assigning each definition a unique name and ensuring that any use may be reached by a single definition. The corresponding unique name appears at the use site and offers a direct link from the use to its corresponding and unique definition. When multiple control flow edges carrying different definitions meet before a use, a special ϕ node is inserted at the merge point. Merge nodes are the only statements allowed to be reached directly by multiple definitions.

Classic SSA is limited to scalar variables and ignores control dependence relations. Gated SSA [1] introduced control dependence information in the ϕ nodes. This helps selecting, for a conditional use, its precise definition point when the condition of the definition is implied by that of the use [26]. The first extensions to array variables ignored array indices and treated each array definition as possibly killing all previous definitions. This approach was very limited in

* This research supported in part by NSF Grants EIA-0103742, ACR-0081510, ACR-0113971, CCR-0113974, ACI-0326350, and by the DOE.

E. Ayguadé et al. (Eds.): LCPC 2005, LNCS 4339, pp. 397–412, 2007.

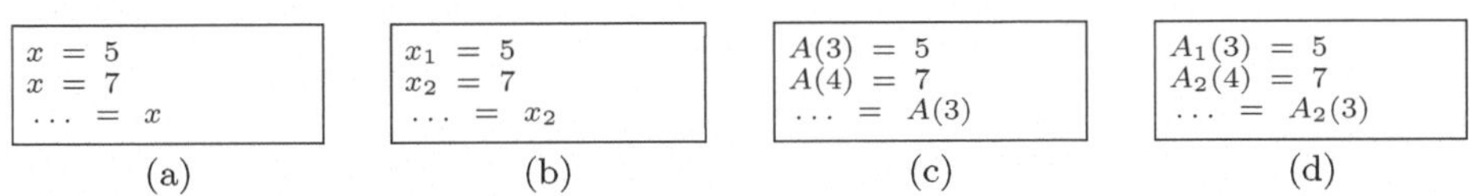

$x = 5$
$x = 7$
$\ldots = x$
(a)
$x_1 = 5$
$x_2 = 7$
$\ldots = x_2$
(b)
$A(3) = 5$
$A(4) = 7$
$\ldots = A(3)$
(c)
$A_1(3) = 5$
$A_2(4) = 7$
$\ldots = A_2(3)$
(d)

Fig. 1. (a) Scalar code, (b) scalar SSA form, (c) array code and (d) improper use of scalar SSA form for arrays

functionality. Array SSA was proposed by [15,23] to match definitions and uses of partial array regions. However, their approach of representing data flow relations between individual array elements makes it difficult to complete the data flow analysis at compile time and requires potentially high overhead run-time evaluation.

We propose an *Array SSA* representation of the program that accurately represents the *use-def* relations between array regions and accounts for control dependence relations. We use the *USR* symbolic representation of array regions previously introduced as RT_LMAD [22] which can represent uniformly and symbolically memory location sets. We present a reaching definition algorithm based on Array SSA that distinguishes between array subregions and is control accurate. The algorithm is used to implement array constant propagation, for which we present whole application improvement. Although the Array SSA form that we present in this paper only applies to structured programs without recursive calls, it can be generalized to any programs with an acyclic Control Dependence Graph (except for self-loops).

2 Region Array SSA Form

Static Single Assignment (SSA) is a program representation that presents the flow of values explicitly. In Fig. 1(a), it is not clear to the compiler which of the two values, 5 or 7, will be used in the last statement because they are represented by the same name, x. By numbering each static definition and matching them with the corresponding uses, the use-def chains become explicit. In Fig. 1(b) it is clear that the value used is x_2 (7) and not x_1 (5).

Unfortunately, such a simple construction cannot be built for arrays the same way as for scalars. Fig. 1(d) shows a failed attempt to apply the same reasoning to the code in Fig. 1(c). Based on SSA numbers, we would draw the conclusion that the value used in the last statement is that defined by A_2, which would be wrong. The fundamental reason why we cannot extend scalar SSA form to arrays directly is that an array definition generally does not kill all previous definitions to the same array variable, unlike in the case of scalar variables. In Fig. 1(c), the second definition does not kill the first one. In order to represent the flow of values stored in arrays, the SSA representation must account for individual array elements rather than treating the whole array as a scalar.

Element-wise Array SSA was proposed as a solution by [23]. Essentially, for every array there is a corresponding *@ array*, which stores, at every program

```
Do i=1,3
  A1(i)=0
Enddo
Do i=1,3
  A2(i+3)=1
EndDo
@A3 = MAX(@A1,@A2)
```

(a)

```
Element-wise Array SSA:
@A3 = [(A1,1),(A1,2),(A1,3),(A2,1),(A2,2),(A2,3)]
```

```
Simplified version (no iteration vectors):
@A3 = [A1,A1,A1,A2,A2,A2]
```

```
Proposed: aggregated array regions
A3 <- A1 = [1:3]
A3 <- A2 = [4:6]
```

(b)

Fig. 2. Illustration of our proposed Array data flow representation based on array regions. (a) Sample code in the Array SSA form proposed by [15] (not all gates shown for simplicity). (b) Data flow relations: (top) element wise, with operation level accuracy as proposed by [15], (center) element wise, with reduced accuracy and (bottom) as proposed by us: region wise, using aggregated array regions.

point and for every array element, the location of the corresponding reaching definition under the form of an iteration vector. The computation of *@ arrays* consists of lexicografic *MAX* operations on iteration vectors, because they must contain the *reaching definition*, or in other words the last (lexicografically maximum) definition before a given point in the program. Although there are methods to reduce the number of *MAX* operation for certain cases, in general they cannot be eliminated. This led to limited applicability for compile-time analysis and potentially high overhead for derived run-time analysis, because the *MAX* operation must be performed for each element.

We propose a new Region Array SSA representation. Rather than storing the exact iteration vector of the reaching definition for each array location, we just store the SSA name of the reaching definition. Although our representation is not as precise as [23], it did not affect the effectiveness of our associated optimization techniques. This simplification allowed us to employ a different representation of *@ arrays* as aggregated array regions. Fig. 2 depicts the relation between element-wise Array SSA and our Region Array SSA. Rather than storing for each array element its reaching definition, we store, for each use-def relation such as $A_3 \leftarrow A_1$, the array region on which values defined at A_1 reach A_3.

We use the USR [22] representation for array regions, which can represent uniformly arbitrarily complex regions. Our resulting Region Array SSA representation has an important advantage over [15]: We can analyze many complex patterns using symbolic array region analysis (essentially symbolic set operations), whereas the previous Array SSA representation often fails to compute element-wise MAX operations symbolically because it lacks a symbolic aggregated representation.

We will now present the USR representation for array regions, describe the structure of Region Array SSA, and then illustrate its use in an algorithm that computes reaching definitions for arrays.

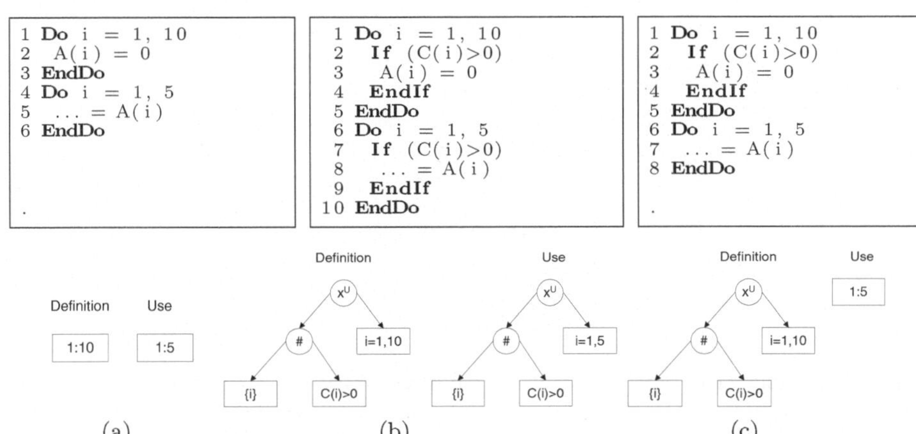

Fig. 3. Constant propagation scenarios: (a) symbolically comparable linear reference pattern, (b) symbolically comparable nonlinear reference pattern and (c) nonlinear reference pattern that require a run time test

2.1 Array Region Representation: The USR

In the example in Fig. 3(a), we can safely propagate constant value 0 from the definition at site 2 to the use at site 5 because the array region *used*, [1:5], is included in the array region *defined* above, [1:10]. In the example in Fig. 3(b), we could not represent the array regions as intervals because the memory references are guarded by an array of conditionals. However, we can represent the array regions as *expressions on intervals*, in which the operators represent predication # and union $\otimes^{\cup}$ across an iteration space. This symbolic representation allows us to compare the *defined* and *used* regions even though their shapes are not linear. In the example in Fig. 3(c), a static decision cannot be made. The needed values of the predicate array C(:) may only be known at run time. We can still perform constant propagation on array A optimistically and validate the transformation dynamically, in the presence of the actual values of the predicate array. Although the profitability of such a transformation in this particular example is debatable due to the possibly high cost of checking the values of C(:) at run time, in many cases such costs can be reduced by partial aggregation and amortized through hoisting and memoization.

The *Uniform Set of References* (**USR**) previously introduced in [22] formalizes the *expressions on intervals* shown in Fig. 3. It is a general, symbolic and analytical representation for memory reference sets in a program. It can represent the aggregation of scalar and array memory references at any hierarchical level (on the loop and subprogram call graph) in a program. It can represent the control flow (predicates), inter-procedural issues (call sites, array reshaping, type overlaps) and recurrences. The simplest form of a USR is the Linear Memory Access Descriptor (LMAD) [19], a symbolic representation of memory

$$
\begin{aligned}
\Sigma = \{&\cap, \cup, -, (,), \#, \otimes^{\cup}, \otimes^{\cap}, \bowtie, \\
&LMADs, Gate, Recurrence, CallSite\} \\
N = \{&USR\},\ \ S = USR \\
P = \{&USR \to LMADs | (USR) \\
&USR \to USR \cap USR \\
&USR \to USR \cup USR \\
&USR \to USR - USR \\
&USR \to Gate\#USR \\
&USR \to \otimes^{\cup}_{Recurrence} USR \\
&USR \to \otimes^{\cap}_{Recurrence} USR \\
&USR \to USR \bowtie CallSite\}
\end{aligned}
$$

Fig. 4. USR formal definition. $\cap$, $\cup$, $-$ are elementary set operations: intersection, union, difference. $Gate\#USR$ represents reference set USR predicated by condition $Gate$. $\otimes^{\cup}_{i=1,n} USR(i)$ represents the union of reference sets $USR(i)$ across the iteration space $i = 1 : n$. In this paper we also use the equivalent set algebra notation $\bigcup_{i=1}^{n} USR(i)$. $USR(formals) \bowtie Call\ Site$ represents the image of the generic reference set $USR(formals)$ instantiated at a particular call site.

reference sets accessed through linear index functions. It may have multiple dimensions, and all its components may be symbolic expressions. Throughout this paper we will use the simpler interval notation for unit-stride single dimensional LMADs. For the loop in Fig. 3(a), the array subregion *defined* by the first loop can be represented as an LMAD, [1:10], and the array subregion *used* in the second loop can also be represented as another LMAD, [1:5].

The USR is stored as an abstract syntax tree with respect to the language presented in Fig. 4 and can be thought of as symbolic expressions on sets of memory locations. When memory references are expressed as linear functions, USRs consist of a single leaf, i.e., a list of LMADs. When the analysis process encounters a nonlinear reference pattern or when it performs an operation (such as set difference) whose result cannot be represented as a list of LMADs, we add internal nodes that record accurately the operations that could not be performed.

2.2 Array SSA Definition and Construction

Region Array SSA Nodes

In scalar SSA, pseudo statements ϕ are inserted at control flow merge points. These pseudo statements show which scalar definitions are combined. [1] refines the SSA pseudo statements in three categories, depending on the type of merge point: γ for merging two forward control flow edges, μ for merging a loop-back arc with the incoming edge at the loop header, and η to account for the possibility of zero-trip loops. The array SSA form proposed in [23] presents the need for additional ϕ nodes after each assignment that does not kill the whole array. These extensions, while necessary, are not sufficient to represent array data flow efficiently because they do not represent array indices.

In order to provide a useful form of Array SSA, it is necessary to incorporate array region information into the representation. Region Array SSA gates differ

```
A(1)=0
If (x > 0)
   A(2)=1
EndIf

Do i = 3, 10
   A(i)=3
   ···=A(···)
   A(i+8)=4
EndDo

···=A(1)
···=A(5)
If (x > 0)
  ···=A(2)
EndIf
```

(a)

```
     A0 :  [A0, ∅] = Undefined
1    A1 :  A1(1)=0
     A2 :  [A2, {1}] = δ(A0, [A1, {1}])
2             If (x>0)
     A3 :     [A3, ∅] = π([A2, (x > 0)])
3    A4 :     A4[2] = 0
     A5 :     [A5, {2}] = δ(A3, [A4, {2}])
4             EndIf
     A6 :  [A6, {1} ∪ (x > 0)#{2}] =
               γ(A0, [A2, {1}], [A5, (x > 0)#{2})
5             Do i = 3, 10
     A7 :     [A7, [3 : i + 2] ∪ [11 : i + 8]] =
                 μ(A6, (i = 3, 10), [A9, [3 : i − 1]], [A11, [11 : i + 7]])
6    A8 :     A8(i) = 1
     A9 :     [A9, {i}] = δ(A7, [A8, {i}])
7                ···=A9(···)
8    A10 :    A10(i + 8) = 1
     A11 :    [A11, {i, i + 8}] = δ(A7, [A9, {i}], [A10, {i + 8}])
9             EndDo
     A12 :    [A12, {1} ∪ (x > 0)#{2} ∪ [3 : 18]] =
                     η(A0, [A6, {1} ∪ (x > 0)#{2}], [A7, [3 : 18]]
10            ···=A12(1)
11            ···=A12(5)
12            If (x>0)
      A13 :   [A13, ∅] = π(A12, (x > 0))
13               ···=A13(2)
14            Endif
```

(b)

Fig. 5. (a) Sample code and (b) Array SSA form

from those in scalar SSA in that they represent, at each merge point, the array subregion (as a USR) corresponding to every ϕ function argument.

$$[A_n, \Re_n] = \phi(A_0, [A_1, \Re_1^n], [A_2, \Re_2^n], \ldots, [A_m, \Re_m^n]) \tag{1}$$

$$where\ \Re_n = \bigcup_{k=1}^{m} \Re_k^n\ and\ \Re_i^n \cap \Re_j^n = \emptyset, \forall\ 1 \le i, j \le m, i \ne j \tag{2}$$

Equation 1 shows the general form of a ϕ node in Region Array SSA. $\Re_k^n$ is the array region (as USR) that carries values from definition A_k to the site of the ϕ node. Since $\Re_k^n$ are mutually disjoint, they provide a basic way to find the definition site for the values stored within a specific array region at a particular program context. Given a set $\Re_{Use(A_n)}$ of memory locations read right after A_n, equation 1 tells us that $\Re_{Use(A_n)} \cap \Re_k^n$ was defined by A_k. The free term A_0 is used to report locations undefined within the program block that contains the ϕ node. Let us note that two array regions can be disjoint because they represent different locations but also because they are controlled by contradictory predicates.

Essentially, our ϕ nodes translate basic data flow relations to USR comparisons. These USR comparisons can be performed symbolically at compile time in many practical cases.

Our node placement scheme is essentially the same as in [23]. In addition to ϕ nodes at control flow merge points, we add a ϕ node after each array definition. These new nodes are named δ. They merge the effect of the immediately previous definition with that of all other previous definitions. Each node corresponds to a structured block of code. In the example in Fig. 5, A_2 corresponds to statement 1, A_6 to statements 1 to 4, A_{11} to statements 6 to 8, and A_{12} to statements 1 to 9. In general, a δ node corresponds to the maximal structured block that ends with the previous statement.

Accounting for Partial Kills: δ Nodes

In the example in Fig. 5, the array use A(1) at statement 10 could only have been defined at statement 1. Between statement 1 and statement 10 there are two blocks, an *If* and a *Do*. We would like to have a mechanism that could quickly tell us not to search for a reaching definition in any of those blocks. We need SSA nodes that can summarize the array definitions in these two blocks. Such summary nodes could tell us that the range of locations defined from statement 2 to statement 9 does not include A(1).

The function of a δ node is to aggregate the effect of disjoint structured blocks of code. [1] Fig. 6(a) shows the way we build δ gates for straight line code. Since the USR representation contains built-in predication, expansion by a recurrence space and translation across subprogram boundaries, the δ functions become a powerful mechanism for computing accurate use-def relations.

Returning to our example, the reaching definition of the use at line 10 can be found by following the use-def chain $\{A_{12}, A_6, A_2, A_1\}$. A use of $A_{12}(20)$ is found undefined using a single USR intersection, by following trace $\{A_{12}, A_0\}$.

Definitions in Loops: μ Nodes

The semantics of μ for Array SSA is different than those for scalar SSA. Any scalar assignment kills all previous ones (from a different statement or previous iteration). In Array SSA, different locations in an array may be defined by various statements in various iterations, and still be visible at the end of the loop. In the code in Fig. 5(a), Array A is used at statement 7 in a loop. In case we are only interested in its reaching definitions from within the same iteration of the loop (as is the case in array privatization), we can apply the same reasoning as above, and use the δ gates in the loop body. However, if we are interested in all the reaching definitions from previous iterations as well as from before the loop, we need additional information. The μ node serves this purpose.

$$[A_n, \Re_n] = \mu(A_0, (i = 1, p), [A_1, \Re_1^n], \ldots, [A_m, \Re_m^n]) \quad (3)$$

The arguments in the μ statement at each loop header are all the δ definitions within the loop that are at the immediately inner block nesting level (Fig. 6(c)), and in the order in which they appear in the loop body. Sets $\Re_k^n$ are functions of the loop index i. They represent the sets of memory locations defined in some iteration $j < i$ by definition A_k and not killed before reaching the beginning of iteration i. For any array element defined by A_k in some iteration $j < i$, in order to reach iteration i, it must not be killed by other definitions to the same

[1] A δ function at the end of a *Do* block is written as η, and at the end of an *If* block as γ to preserve the syntax of the conventional GSA form. A δ function after a subroutine call is marked as θ, and summarizes the effect of the subroutine call on the array.

element. There are two kinds of definitions that will kill it: definitions ($Kill_s$) that will kill it within the same iteration j and definitions ($Kill_a$) that will kill it at iterations from $j+1$ to $i-1$.

$$\Re_k^n(i) = \bigcup_{j=1}^{i-1} \left[\Re_k(j) - \left(Kill_s(j) \cup \bigcup_{l=j+1}^{i-1} Kill_a(l) \right) \right] \tag{4}$$

$$where\ Kill_s = \bigcup_{h=k+1}^{m} \Re_h,\ and\ Kill_a = \bigcup_{h=1}^{m} \Re_h$$

This representation gives us powerful closed forms for array region definitions across the loop. We avoid fixed point iteration methods by hiding the complexity of computing closed forms in USR operations. The USR simplification process will attempt to reduce these expressions to LMADs. However, even when that is not possible, the USR can be used in compile-time symbolic comparisons(as in Fig. 3(b)), or to generate efficient run-time assertions (as in Fig. 3(c)) that can be used for run-time optimization and speculative execution.

The reaching definition for the array use $A_{12}(5)$ at statement 11 (Fig. 5(b)) is found inside the loop using δ gates. We use the μ gate to narrow down the block that defined A(5). We intersect the use region $\{5\}$ with $\Re_9^7(i=11) = [3:10]$, and $\Re_{11}^7(i=11) = [11:18]$. We substituted $i \leftarrow 11$, because the *use* happens after the last iteration. The use-def chain is $\{A_{12}, A_7, A_9\}$.

Representation of Control: π Nodes

Array element $A_{13}(2)$ is conditionally used at statement 13. Based on its range, it could have been defined only by statement 3. In order to prove that it *was* defined at statement 3, we need to have a way to associate the predicate of the use with the predicate of the definition. We create fake definition nodes π to guard the entry to control dependence regions associated with *Then* and *Else* branches: $[A_n, \emptyset] = \pi(A_0, cond)$. This type of gate does not have a correspondent in classic scalar SSA, but in the Program Dependence Web [1]. Their advantage is that they lead to more accurate use-def chains. Their disadvantage is that they create a new SSA name in a context that may contain no array definitions. Such a fake definition A_{13} placed between statement 12 and 13 will force the reaching definition search to collect the conditional $x > 1$ on its way to the possible reaching definition at line 2. This conditional is crucial when the search reaches the γ statement that defines A_6, which contains the same condition. The use-def chain is $\{A_{13}, A_{12}, A_6, A_5, A_4\}$.

Array SSA Construction

Fig. 6 presents the way we create δ, η, γ, μ, and π gates for various program constructs. The associated array regions are built in a bottom-up traversal of the Control Dependence Graph intraprocedurally, and the Call Graph interprocedurally. At each block level (loop body, *then* branch, *else* branch, subprogram body), we process sub-blocks in program order.

$A(R_1) = \ldots$
$A(R_2) = \ldots$
$A(R_n) = \ldots$

(a) Straight line code.

$[A_0, \emptyset] = \mathit{Undefined}$
$A_1(R_1) = \ldots$
$[A_2, R_1] = \delta(A_0, [A_1, R_1])$
$A_3(R_2) = \ldots$
$[A_4, R_1 \cup R_2] = \delta(A_0, [A_2, R_1 - R_2], [A_3, R_2])$
$A_{2n-1}(R_n) = \ldots$
$[A_{2n}, \bigcup_{i=1}^{n} R_i] =$
$\quad \delta(A_0, [A_{2n-2}, \bigcup_{i=1}^{n-1} R_i - R_n], [A_{2n-1}, R_n])$

$A(R_x) = \ldots$
If (cond)
$\quad A(R_y) = \ldots$
EndIf

(b) If block.

$[A_0, \emptyset] = \mathit{Undefined}$
$A_1(R_x) = \ldots$
$[A_2, R_x] = \delta(A_0, [A_1, R_x])$
If (cond)
$\quad [A_3, \emptyset] = \pi(A_2, \mathit{cond})$
$\quad A_4(R_y) = \ldots$
$\quad [A_5, R_y] = \delta(A_3, [A_4, R_y])$
EndIf
$[A_6, R_x \cup \mathit{cond}\#R_y] =$
$\quad \gamma(A_0, [A_2, R_x - \mathit{cond}\#R_y], [A_5, \mathit{cond}\#R_y])$

Do i=1,n
$\quad A(R_x(i)) = \ldots$
$\quad A(R_y(i)) = \ldots$
EndDo

(c) Do block. $\Re_k^5(i)$ = definitions from A_k not killed upon entry to iteration i (Equation 4).

$[A_0, \emptyset] = \mathit{Undefined}$
Do i=1,n
$\quad [A_5, \Re_2^5(i) \cup \Re_4^5(i)] =$
$\quad\quad \mu(A_0, (i = 1, n), [A_2, \Re_2^5(i)], [A_4, \Re_4^5(i)])$
$\quad A_1(R_x(i)) = \ldots$
$\quad [A_2, R_x(i)] = \delta(A_5, [A_1, R_x])$
$\quad A_3(R_y(i)) = \ldots$
$\quad [A_4, R_x(i) \cup R_y(i)] =$
$\quad\quad \delta(A_5, [A_2, R_x(i) - R_y(i)], [A_3, R_y(i)])$
EndDo
$[A_6, \bigcup_{i=1}^{n} \Re_2^5(i) \cup \Re_4^5(i)] =$
$\quad \eta([A_0, \emptyset], [A_5, \bigcup_{i=1}^{n} \Re_2^5(i) \cup \Re_4^5(i)])$

Fig. 6. Region Array SSA transformation: original code on the left, Region Array SSA code on the right

2.3 Reaching Definitions

Finding the reaching definitions for a given use is required to implement a number of optimizations: constant propagation, array privatization etc. We present here a general algorithm based on Array SSA that finds, for a given SSA name and array region, all the reaching definitions and the corresponding subregions. These subregions can then be used to implement particular optimizations such as constant propagation. Any such optimization can be performed either at compile time, when associated USR comparison can be solved symbolically, or at run-time, when USR comparisons depend on input values.

For each array use $\Re_{Use(A_u)}$ of an SSA name A_u, and for a given block, we want to compute its reaching definition set, $\{[A_1, \Re_1^{RD}], [A_2, \Re_2^{RD}], \ldots, [A_n, \Re_n^{RD}], [\bot, \Re_0^{RD}]\}$, in which $\Re_k^{RD}$ specifies the region of this use defined by A_k and not killed by any other definition before it reaches A_u. $\Re_0^{RD}$ is the region undefined within the given block. Restricting the search to different blocks produces different reaching definition sets. For instance, for a use within a loop, we may be interested in reaching definitions from the same iteration of the loop (block = loop body) as is the case in array privatization. We can also be interested in

```
Algorithm Search(A_u, ℜ_use, GivenBlock)
If A_u ∉ GivenBlock or ℜ_use = ∅ Then Return
Switch definition site(A_u)
 Case original statement:
   ℜ_u^RD = ℜ_u ∩ ℜ_use
 Case δ, γ, η, θ: [A_u, ℜ_u] = φ(A_0, [A_1, ℜ_1^u], ...)
   ForEach [A_k, ℜ_k^u]
     Call Search(A_k, ℜ_use ∩ ℜ_k^u, GivenBlock)
   Call Search(A_0, ℜ_use − ℜ_n, GivenBlock)
 Case μ: [A_u, ℜ_u(i)] = μ(A_0, (i = 1, p), [A_1, ℜ_1^u(i)], ...)
   ForEach [A_k, ℜ_k^u(i)]
     Call Search(A_k, ℜ_use(i) ∩ ℜ_k^u(i), Block(A_k))
   Call Search(A_0, ⊗^∪_{i=1,p}(ℜ_use(i) − ℜ_u(i)), GivenBlock)
 Case π(A_0, cond)
   Call Search(A_0, cond#ℜ_use, GivenBlock)
EndIf
```

Fig. 7. Recursive algorithm to find reaching definitions. A_u is an SSA name and $\Re_{use}$ is an array region. Array regions $\Re$ are represented as USRs. They are built using USR operations such as $\cap$, $-$, $\#$, $\otimes^{\cup}$.

```
Sub ssor              Sub jacld(A)        Sub blts(A)
...                   Do i=1, n, 1        Do i=1, n, 1
Call jacld(A)          A(1,i)=0            Do m=1, 5, 1
Call blts(A)          EndDo                 V(1,i)=V(1,i)+A(m,i)*V(1+m,i)
...                   End                  EndDo
End                                       EndDo
.                     .                   End
```

Fig. 8. Example from benchmark code Applu (SPEC)

definitions from all previous iterations of the loop (block = whole loop) or for a whole subroutine (block = routine body). Fig. 7 presents the algorithm for computing reaching definitions. The algorithm is invoked as *Search(*A_u*,* $\Re_{Use(A_u)}$*, GivenBlock)*. $\Re_{use}$ is the region whose definition sites we are searching for, A_u is the SSA name of array A at the point at which it is used, and *GivenBlock* is the block that the search is restricted to. The set of memory locations containing undefined data is computed as: $\Re_{use} - \bigcup_{i=1}^{n} \Re_i^{RD}$.

In case the SSA name given as input corresponds to an original statement, the reaching definition set is computed directly by intersecting the region of the definition with the region of the use. If the definition is a δ, γ, η, θ, we perform two operations. First, we find the reaching definitions corresponding to each argument of the ϕ function. Second, we continue the search outside the current block for the region containing undefined values. As shown, the algorithm would make repeated calls with the same arguments to search for undefined memory locations. The actual implementation avoids repetitious work, but we omitted the details here for clarity.

When A_u is inside a loop within the given block, the search will eventually reach the μ node at the loop header. At this point, we first compare $\Re_{use}$ to the arguments of the μ function to find reaching definition from previous iterations of the loop. Second, we continue the search before the loop for the region undefined within the loop. When the definition site of A_u is a π node, we simply predicate

$\mathfrak{R}_{use}$ and continue the search. The search paths presented in Section 2.2 were obtained using this algorithm.

3 Application: Array Constant Propagation

3.1 Array Constant Collection

We present an *Array Constant Propagation* optimization technique based on our Array SSA form. Often programmers encode constants in array variables to set invariant or initial arguments to an algorithm. Analogous to scalar constant propagation, if these constants get propagated, the code may be simplified which may result in (1) speedup or (2) simplification of control and data flow which enable other optimizing transformations, such as dependence analysis.

We define a *constant region* as the array subregion that contains constant values at a particular use point. We define *array constants* are either (1) integer constants, (2) literal floating point constants, or (3) an expression f(v) which is assigned to an array variable in a loop nest. We name this last class of constants *expression constants.* They are parameterized by the iteration vector of their definition loop nest. Presently, our framework can only propagate expression constants when (1) their definition indexing formula is a linear combination of the iteration vector described by a nonsingular matrix with constant terms and (2) they are used in another loop nest based on linear subscripts (similar to [28]).

In Array SSA, the reaching definitions of an array use can be computed by calling algorithm *Search* (Fig. 7). Based on reaching definition set of the use, the constant regions can be computed by simply uniting the regions of the reaching definitions corresponding to assignments of the same constant. To do interprocedural constant propagation, we (1) propagate constant regions into routines at call sites, and (2) compute constant regions for routines and propagate them out at call sites. We iterate over the call graph until there are no changes.

We define a *value tuple* $[\mathfrak{R}, Val]$ as the array subregion $\mathfrak{R}$ where each element stores a copy of Val. $\mathfrak{R}$ is expressed as a USR and Val is an array constant. A *value set* is a set of value tuples. We define the following operations on value sets. *Filter* (Equation 5) restricts the value tuple subregions to a given array region. *Intersection* (Equation 6) and *union* (Equation 7) intersect and unite, respectively, subregions across tuples with the same value.

$$Filter(VS, R) = \bigcup_{VT_i \in VS} [\mathfrak{R}(VT_i) \cap R, Val(VT_i)] \tag{5}$$

$$VS_1 \cap VS_2 = \{VT \mid \exists\, VT_i \in VS_1, VT_j \in VS_2, s.t. \quad Val(VT) = Val(VT_i) = Val(VT_j) \; and \; \mathfrak{R}(VT) = \mathfrak{R}(VT_i) \cap \mathfrak{R}(VT_j)\} \tag{6}$$

$$VS_1 \cup VS_2 = \{VT \mid \exists\, VT_i \in VS_1, VT_j \in VS_2, s.t. \quad Val(VT) = Val(VT_i) = Val(VT_j) \; and \; \mathfrak{R}(VT) = \mathfrak{R}(VT_i) \cup \mathfrak{R}(VT_j)\} \tag{7}$$

Fig. 9 shows the algorithm that collects array constants reaching the definition point of SSA name A_k. The algorithm collects constants either directly from the

```
Algorithm Collect(A_n) → VS(A_n)
 VS(A_n)=∅
 Switch (DefinitionSite(A_n))
  Case assignment statement: // A_n(index) = value
   VS(A_n) = [{index}, value]
  Case μ or δ gate: //[A_n, ℜ_n] = φ(A_before, ..., [A_1, ℜ_1^n], ..., [A_m, ℜ_m^n])
   VS(A_n) = ⋃_{k=1}^n Filter(Collect(A_k), ℜ_k^n)
   If (DefinitionSite(A_n) = μ(i = 1, p) gate ) Then
    VS(A_n)=⋃_{i=1}^p VS(A_n)(i)
   EndIf
 EndSwitch
 Return VS(A_n)
End
```

Fig. 9. Array Constant Collection Algorithm

right hand side of assignment statements, or by merging constant value sets corresponding to δ arguments. For loops, constant value sets collected within an iteration are expanded across the whole iteration space. In order to collect all the constants from a routine (needed for interprocedural propagation), we invoke this algorithm with the last SSA name in the routine and its body.

3.2 Propagating and Substituting Constants

A subroutine may have multiple value sets for an array at its entry. Suppose these value sets are VS_1, $\cdots$, VS_m, then $VS_1 \cap \cdots \cap VS_m$ is the *incoming value set* for the whole subroutine. The incoming value set can be increased by subroutine cloning. Let us assume that for an array use A_u, its reaching definitions are $\{[A_0, \Re_0], [A_1, \Re_1], [A_2, \Re_2], \ldots [A_n, \Re_n]\}$. Its value sets for this use are $Filter(VS(A_i), \Re_i)$, where $VS(A_0)$ is the incoming value set for A_u's subroutine. In general, $VS(A_u) = \bigcup_{i=0}^{n} Filter(VS(A_i), \Re_i)$.

The whole program is traversed in topological order of its call graph. Within a subroutine, statements are visited in lexicographic order. We compute the value set for each *use* encountered. Interprocedural translation of *constant regions* and *expression constants* is performed at routine boundaries as needed. For example, in Fig 8, during the first traversal of the program, the outcoming set of subroutine *jacld* is collected and translated into subroutine *ssor* at call site *call jacld*. In the next traversal, the value set of A at callsite *call blts* is computed and translated into the incoming value set of subroutine *blts*.

When multiple value sets reach a single small loop, we unroll the loop completely if possible, to permit propagation of the various different constants corresponding to the value sets. Constant propagation is followed by aggressive dead code elimination based on simplified control and data dependences.

4 Implementation and Experimental Results

We implemented (1) Array SSA construction, (2) the reaching definition algorithm and (3) array constant collection in the Polaris research compiler [2].

Table 1. Constant propagation results. (a) Experimental setup and (b) Speedup.

Machine	Processor	Speed
Intel PC	Pentium 4	2.8 GHz
HP9000/R390	PA-8200	200 MHz
SGI Origin 3800	MIPS R14000	500 MHz
IBM Regatta P690	PowerR4	1.3 GHz

(a)

Program	Intel	HP	IBM	SGI
QCD2	14.0%	17.4%	12.8%	15.5%
173.applu	20.0%	4.6%	16.4%	10.5%
048.ora	1.5%	22.8%	11.9%	20.6%
107.mgrid	12.5%	8.9%	6.4%	12.8%

(b)

Propagation was done by hand. We applied constant propagation to four benchmark codes 173.applu, 048.ora, 107.mgrid (from SPEC) and QCD2 (from PERFECT). The speedups were measured on four different machines (Table 1). The codes were compiled using the native compiler of each machine at *O3* optimization level (*O4* on the Regatta). 107.mgrid and QCD2 were compiled with *O2* on SGI because the codes compiled with *O3* did not validate).

In subroutine OBSERV in QCD2, which takes around 22% execution time, the whole array *epsilo* is initialized with 0 and then six of its elements are reassigned with 1 and -1. The array is used in loop nest OBSERV_do2, where much of the loop body is executed only when *epsilo* takes value 1 or -1. Moreover, the values of *epsilo* are used in computation in the innermost loop body. From the value set, we discover that the use is all defined with constant 0, 1 and -1. We unrolled the loop OBSERV_do2, substituted the array elements with their corresponding values, eliminated *If* branches and dead assignments and removed more than 30% of the floating-point multiplications. Additionally, array *ptr* is used in loops HIT_do1 and HIT_do2 after it is initialized with constants in a DATA statement. In subroutine SYSLOP, called from within these two loops, the iteration count of a *While* loop is determined by the values in *ptr*. After propagation, the loop we can fully unroll the loop and eliminate several *If* branches.

In 173.applu, a portion of arrays *a, b, c, d* is assigned with constant 0.0 in loop JACLD_do1 and JACU_do1. These arrays are only used in BLTS_do1 and BUTS_do1 (Fig. 8), which account for 40% of the execution time. We find that the uses in BLTS_do1 and BUTS_do1 are defined as constant 0.0 in JACLD_do1 and JACU_do1. Loops BLTS_do111* and BUTS_do111* are unrolled. After unrolling and substitution, 35% of the multiplications are eliminated.

In 048.ora, array *i1* is initialized with value 6 and then some of its elements are reassigned with constant -2 and -4 before it is used in subroutine ABC, which takes 95% of the execution time. The subroutine body is a *While* loop, which is unrolled after propagating *i1*. Array *a1* is used in ABC after a portion of it is assigned with floating-point constant values.

107.mgrid was used as a motivating example by previous papers on array constant propagation [29,23]. Array elements A(1) and C(3) are assigned with constant 0.0 at the beginning of the program. They are used in subroutines *RESID* and *PSINV*, which account for 80% of the execution time. After constant propagation, the uses of A(1) and C(3) in multiplications are eliminated.

5 Related Work

Array Data Flow. There has been extensive research on array dataflow, most of it based on reference set summaries: regular sections (rows, columns or points) [4] linear constraint sets [25,11,10,3,27,17,20,16,21,14,13,8,18,6,29,22], and triplet based [12]. Most of these approaches approximate nonlinear references with linear ones [16,8]. Nonlinear references are handled as uninterpreted function symbols in [21], using symbolic aggregation operators in [22] and based on nonlinear recurrence analysis in [13]. [7] presents a generic way to find approximative solutions to dataflow problems involving unknowns such as the iteration count of a while statement, but limited to intraprocedural contexts. Conditionals are handled only by some approaches (most relevant are [27,16,12,18,22]).

Array SSA and its use in constant propagation and parallelization. In the Array SSA form introduced by [15,23], each array assignment is associated a reference descriptor that stores, for each array element, the iteration in which the reaching definition was executed. Since an array definition may not kill all its old values, a merge function ϕ is inserted after each array definition to distinguish between newly defined and old values. This Array SSA form extends data flow analysis to array element level and treats each array element as a scalar. However, their representation lacks an aggregated descriptor for memory location sets. This makes it is generally impossible to to do array data flow analysis when arrays are defined and used collectively in loops. Constant propagation based on this Array SSA can only propagate constants from array definitions to uses when their subscripts are all constant. [6,5] independently introduced Array SSA forms for explicitly parallel programs. Their focus is on concurrent execution semantics, e.g. they introduce π gates to account for the out-of-order execution of parallel sections in the same parallel block. Although [5] mentions the benefits of using reference aggregation they do not implement it.

Array constant propagation can be done without using Array SSA [29,24]. However, we believe that our Array SSA form makes it easier to formulate and solve data flow problems in a uniform way.

Table 2. Comparison of our proposed Region SSA against Element-wise Array SSA [23], Distr. Array SSA [5], Fuzzy Dataflow [7], and Predicated Dataflow [18]. Nonlinear = able to solve problems involving nonlinear references.

	Region SSA	**[23]**	**[5]**	**[7]**	**[18]**
SSA Form	Yes	Yes	Yes	No	No
Aggregated	Yes	No	No	Yes	Yes
Interprocedural	Yes	No	No	No	Yes
Accuracy	Statement	Operation	Operation x Thread	Operation	Statement
Nonlinear	Yes	No	No	Yes	No

Table 2 presents a comparison of some of the most relevant related work to Region SSA. The table shows that Region SSA is the only representation of data flow that is explicit (uses SSA numbering), is aggregated, and can be computed efficiently at both compile-time and run-time even in the presence of nonlinear memory reference patterns. The precision of Region SSA is not as good as that of the other two SSA representations because we lack iteration vector information. However, iteration vectors would become very complex in interprocedural contexts (they must include call stack information), whereas USRs represent arbitrarily large interprocedural program contexts in a scalable way.

6 Conclusions and Future Work

We introduced a region based Array SSA providing accurate, interprocedural, control-sensitive *use-def* information at array region level. Furthermore, when the data flow problems cannot be completely solved statically we can continue the process dynamically with minimal overhead. We used Array SSA to write a compact *Reaching Definitions* algorithm that breaks up an array use region into subregions corresponding to the actual definitions that reach it. The implementation of array constant propagation shows that our representation is powerful and easy to use.

References

1. R. A. Ballance, A. B. Maccabe, and K. J. Ottenstein. The Program Dependence Web: A representation supporting control-, data-, and demand-driven interpretation of imperative languages. In *ACM PLDI*, White Plains, NY, 1990.
2. W. Blume, *et. al.* Advanced Program Restructuring for High-Performance Computers with Polaris. *IEEE Computer*, 29(12):78–82, December 1996.
3. M. Burke. An interval-based approach to exhaustive and incremental interprocedural data-flow analysis. *ACM TOPLAS.*, 12(3):341–395, 1990.
4. D. Callahan and K. Kennedy. Analysis of interprocedural side effects in a parallel programming environment. In *Supercomputing: 1st Int. Conf.*, LNCS **297**, pp. 138–171, Athens, Greece, 1987.
5. D. R. Chakrabarti and P. Banerjee. Static single assignment form for message-passing programs. *Int. J. of Parallel Programming*, 29(2):139–184, 2001.
6. J.-F. Collard. Array SSA for explicitly parallel programs. In *Euro-Par*, 1999.
7. J.-F. Collard, D. Barthou, and P. Feautrier. Fuzzy array dataflow analysis. In *PPOPP '95*, pp. 92–101, New York, NY, USA, 1995. ACM Press.
8. B. Creusillet and F. Irigoin. Exact vs. approximate array region analyses. In *LCPC*, LNCS **1239**, pp. 86–100, San Jose, CA, 1996.
9. R. Cytron, *et al* An efficient method of computing static single assignment form. In *16th ACM POPL*, pp. 25–35, Austin, TX., Jan. 1989.
10. P. Feautrier. Dataflow analysis of array and scalar references. *Int. J. of Parallel Programming*, 20(1):23–54, 1991.
11. T. Gross and P. Steenkiste. Structured dataflow analysis for arrays and its use in an optimizing compilers. *Software: Practice & Experience*, 20(2):133–155, 1990.
12. J. Gu, Z. Li, and G. Lee. Symbolic array dataflow analysis for array privatization and program parallelization. In *Supercomputing '95*, pp. 47. ACM Press, 1995.

13. M. R. Haghighat and C. D. Polychronopoulos. Symbolic analysis for parallelizing compilers. *ACM TOPLAS*, 18(4):477–518, 1996.
14. M. H. Hall, S. P. Amarasinghe, B. R. Murphy, S.-W. Liao, and M. S. Lam. Detecting coarse-grain parallelism using an interprocedural parallelizing compiler. In *Supercomputing '95*, pp. 49, 1995.
15. K. Knobe and V. Sarkar. Array SSA form and its use in parallelization. In *ACM POPL*, pp. 107–120, 1998.
16. V. Maslov. Lazy array data-flow dependence analysis. In *ACM POPL*, pp. 311–325, Portland, OR, Jan. 1994.
17. D. E. Maydan, S. P. Amarasinghe, and M. S. Lam. Array data-flow analysis and its use in array privatization. In *ACM POPL*, pp. 2–15, Charleston, SC, Jan. 1993.
18. S. Moon, M. W. Hall, and B. R. Murphy. Predicated array data-flow analysis for run-time parallelization. *ACM ICS*, pp. 204–211, Melbourne, Australia, 1988.
19. Y. Paek, J. Hoeflinger, and D. Padua. Efficient and precise array access analysis. *ACM TOPLAS*, 24(1):65–109, 2002.
20. W. Pugh and D. Wonnacott. An exact method for analysis of value-based array data dependences. In *LCPC 1993*, LNCS **768**, pp. 546–566, Portland, OR.
21. W. Pugh and D. Wonnacott. Nonlinear array dependence analysis. UMIACS-TR-94-123, Univ. of Maryland, College Park, MD, USA, 1994.
22. S. Rus, J. Hoeflinger, and L. Rauchwerger. Hybrid analysis: static & dynamic memory reference analysis. *Int. J. of Parallel Programming*, 31(3):251–283, 2003.
23. V. Sarkar and K. Knobe. Enabling sparse constant propagation of array elements via array ssa form. In *SAS*, pp. 33–56, 1998.
24. N. Schwartz. Sparse constant propagation via memory classification analysis. TR1999-782, Dept. of Compute Science, Courant Institute, NYU, March, 1999.
25. R. Triolet, F. Irigoin, and P. Feautrier. Direct parallelization of Call statements. In *ACM '86 Symp. on Comp. Constr.*, pp. 175–185, Palo Alto, CA., June 1986.
26. P. Tu and D. Padua. Gated SSA–based demand-driven symbolic analysis for parallelizing compilers. In *9th ACM ICS*, Barcelona, Spain, pp. 414–423, July 1995.
27. P. Tu and D. A. Padua. Automatic array privatization. In *LCPC*, LNCS **768** Portland, OR, 1993.
28. P. Vanbroekhoven, G. Janssens, M. Bruynooghe, H. Corporaal, and F. Catthoor. Advanced copy propagation for arrays. In *LCTES '03*, pp. 24–33, New York, 2003.
29. D. Wonnacott. Extending scalar optimizations for arrays. In *LCPC '00*, LNCS **2017**, pp. 97–111.

Interprocedural Symbolic Range Propagation for Optimizing Compilers*

Hansang Bae and Rudolf Eigenmann

School of Electrical and Computer Engineering
Purdue University, West Lafayette, IN 47907
{baeh,eigenman}@purdue.edu

Abstract. We have designed and implemented an interprocedural algorithm to analyze symbolic value ranges that can be assumed by variables at any given point in a program. Our algorithm contrasts with related work on interprocedural value range analysis in that it extends the ability to handle symbolic range expressions. It builds on our previous work of intraprocedural symbolic range analysis. We have evaluated our algorithm using 11 Perfect Benchmarks and 10 SPEC floating-point benchmarks of the CPU 95 and CPU 2000 suites. We have measured the ability to perform test elision, dead code elimination, and detect data dependences. We have also evaluated the algorithm's ability to help detect zero-trip loops for induction variable substitution and subscript ranges for array reductions.

1 Introduction

The motivation for the present work is the pursuit of the long-term goal of developing higher-level programming languages. At the same time, we aim to increase the power of the present generation of optimizing compilers. One thrust towards these goals is to strengthen the capabilities of compilers to reason about and manipulate program sections in symbolic terms. Developing an algorithm for interprocedural range propagation is a small step in this direction. By knowing the value range that a variable may assume at any given program point, compiler techniques can make more informed optimization decisions. We have developed and used such techniques in the past for our Polaris parallelizing compiler [2,13,4]. Knowing symbolic value ranges has become key to detecting data dependences, privatizing variables, substituting induction variables, and parallelizing reduction operations. Polaris' Range Test [5] makes use of advanced symbolic expression manipulation capabilities, which exploit knowledge about possible value ranges of program variables. The privatization pass [17] is able to analyze and comprehend the meaning of certain compute patterns. The induction variable and reduction recognition passes [15] exploit value range information to prove zero-trip loops and to narrow array subscript ranges, respectively.

* This work is supported in part by the National Science Foundation under Grants No. 0103582-EIA, and 0429535-CCF.

E. Ayguadé et al. (Eds.): LCPC 2005, LNCS 4339, pp. 413–424, 2007.

```
X = 1                 X = [-INF,INF]
IF (X.LE.N) THEN      X = [1,1]
  X = 2*X             X = [1,1]
ELSE                  X = [2,2]
  X = X+2             X = [MAX(1,1+N),1]
ENDIF                 X = [MAX(3,3+N),3]
...                   X = [2,3]
```

Fig. 1. Intraprocedural symbolic range propagation

In all these cases, value range information significantly boosts Polaris' ability to detect parallelism. Currently, Polaris uses only *intraprocedural* range analysis. It operates in concert with interprocedural expression propagation and forward substitution, which we consider the best alternative to the new techniques and reference point for the evaluation section. In Section 4 we will explain why we have chosen this reference point over other related contributions. Briefly, related work either focuses on interprocedural expression propagation [11], where no range representation is used, or restricts the bounds of ranges to simple expressions [14]. A number of approaches have also considered range information in the context of pointer analysis for C-type languages.

2 Interprocedural Symbolic Range Propagation (ISRP)

Our framework for interprocedural analysis follows the classical fixed-point approach based on abstract interpretation, and it uses existing intraprocedural range analysis techniques as the source of range information to propagate. During the analysis, ISRP collects symbolic range information within a subroutine and generates interprocedural ranges at every important program point – at subroutine returns and at call sites. Next, it propagates the collected data towards the leaves of the call graph. This is similar to the jump function approach [9]; we use terms in that approach to present our algorithm[1]. We also apply procedure-cloning to enhance the accuracy of the analysis in every calling context. Before introducing our algorithm in detail, we briefly review our existing framework for intraprocedural symbolic range analysis.

The goal of symbolic range propagation [3] is to collect a valid set of symbolic value ranges for each variable at every program point. The collected ranges can be used for advanced compiler analyses such as data dependence testing, dead code elimination, and program verification – the main application of the analysis in the current Polaris compiler is a nonlinear symbolic data dependence test [5]. Figure 1 gives an example of the value ranges for program variable X, valid before each statement, as analyzed by the existing intraprocedural analysis

[1] In contrast to [9], our jump function is defined for the value ranges of all variables of a statement, not for a single variable.

technique. To derive this information, ranges defined by individual statements are intersected along the control flow. At control flow merge points, unions of ranges are computed. The ranges so analyzed supply the source of candidate interprocedural symbolic ranges for ISRP.

In presenting the ISRP algorithm, we make use of the following terms.

Definition 1. *A* symbolic range *is a mapping from a variable to its value range, V = [LB,UB], where LB is the lower bound and the UB is the upper bound. All variables contained in the expressions {V,LB,UB} belong to the scope of the subroutine enclosing the program point being analyzed. If either LB or UB is infinite, we call it an* open range, *otherwise it is a* closed range.

Definition 2. *An* interprocedural (symbolic) range *is a symbolic range that is gathered from information in one subroutine and inserted at relevant points in another subroutine – either at the subroutine entry or after a call statement.*

Definition 3. *For a caller P, a callee Q, and a call site S that calls Q in P, the* jump function *at S is the set of known symbolic ranges before S, expressed in terms of input variables to Q (actual parameters and global variables).*

Definition 4. *The return jump function at Q is the set of known symbolic ranges at the end of Q, expressed in terms of return variables to P (return parameters, reference parameters and global variables).*

Without loss of generality we use only integer type and logical type. The existing, intraprocedural framework did not allow logical type, but we added it to make our analysis more general. If the type of *V* is logical, *LB* should be equal to *UB*. Notice, that the jump functions express symbolic ranges in terms of variable names in the present subroutine. In order to create interprocedural ranges, these names may need to be changed to those used in the target subroutine. This also applies for the return jump functions.

Figure 2 gives a high-level description of our algorithm. It uses the following functions:

`Compute_Jump_Functions()`

This routine produces intraprocedural value ranges that are valid at each program point in a subroutine. The source of information are ranges as analyzed by the intraprocedural range analysis algorithms plus the inserted interprocedural ranges (at the beginning of the subroutine and after each call statement). At each call statement, the interprocedural ranges collected from Get_Backward_Interprocedural_Ranges are intersected with ranges that exist before the call site. However, when a certain variable is modified in the callee or its descendants in the call graph, the previous range for that variable is discarded. Note that the resulting jump functions, as per Definition 3 are expressed in terms of variables in the current subroutine. In order to create interprocedural ranges, renaming of actual to formal parameters will need to be performed (by Get_Forward_Interprocedural_Ranges()).

```
Propagate_Interprocedural_Ranges()
{
  Initialize_Call_Graph()
  while (there is any change in interprocedural ranges) {
    foreach Subroutine (reverse topologically) {
      Get_Backward_Interprocedural_Ranges()
      Compute_Jump_Functions()
      Compute_Return_Jump_Functions()
    }
    Get_Forward_Interprocedural_Ranges()
  }
}
```

Fig. 2. Algorithm for interprocedural symbolic range propagation

`Compute_Return_Jump_Functions()`
This routine generates value ranges as per Definition 4 at the return point of the current subroutine. Information at multiple return points is merged – for simplicity, we just take unions.

`Get_Forward_Interprocedural_Ranges()`
This routine creates the interprocedural symbolic value ranges valid at the entry point of each subroutine – this is done by applying jump functions to each subroutine, appropriately converting actual parameters to formal parameters. In addition, this step performs procedure-cloning for different calling contexts.

`Get_Backward_Interprocedural_Ranges()`
This routine propagates interprocedural symbolic value ranges backward from all callees to the current subroutine. It uses information from return jump functions in the callees. If a value range contains a formal parameter of the callee, it is mapped to the corresponding actual parameter. Note that the algorithm performs this step reverse topologically. Hence, intraprocedural analysis for each callee has already been done, including the generation of return jump functions. For leaves in the call graph, this subroutine performs no action. This reverse order is for speeding up a single iterative step; in-order traversal would converge to the same solution, eventually.

In summary, the algorithm computes the interprocedural symbolic ranges propagated backward from callees' contexts and ranges propagated forward from callers' contexts until it reaches a fixed point. Each iteration performs range analysis within a subroutine, selects valid symbolic ranges across subroutine boundaries, and feeds those new data into the intraprocedural range analysis for the next iterative step.

The example illustrated in Figure 3 shows a simple program with three program units and two subroutine calls, and interprocedural symbolic range propagation on that program. The goal of the analysis is to compute Interprocedural

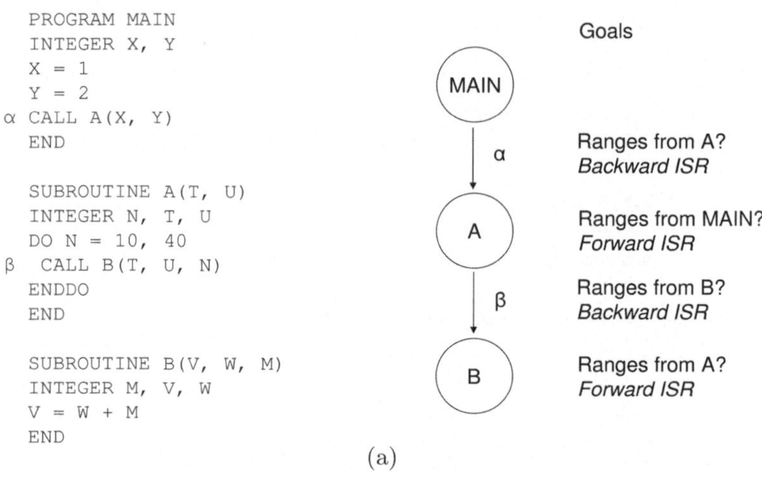
PROGRAM MAIN
INTEGER X, Y
X = 1
Y = 2
α CALL A(X, Y)
END
SUBROUTINE A(T, U)
INTEGER N, T, U
DO N = 10, 40
β CALL B(T, U, N)
ENDDO
END
SUBROUTINE B(V, W, M)
INTEGER M, V, W
V = W + M
END
Goals
MAIN
α
Ranges from A?
Backward ISR
A
Ranges from MAIN?
Forward ISR
β
Ranges from B?
Backward ISR
B
Ranges from A?
Forward ISR
(a)

Subroutine	Forward ISR	Return Jump	Callsite	Jump	Backward ISR
1st iteration					
B	-	V=[W+M,W+M]	-	-	-
A	-	ϕ	β	N=[10,40]	T=[U+N,U+N]
MAIN	-	-	α	X=[1,1],Y=[2,2]	ϕ
A	T=[1,1],U=[2,2]	-	β	-	T=[U+N,U+N]
B	M=[10,40]	-	-	-	-
2nd iteration					
B	M=[10,40]	V=[W+M,W+M],M=[10,40]	-	-	-
A	T=[1,1],U=[2,2]	U=[2,2]	β	N=[10,40],U=[2,2]	T=[U+N,U+N],N=[10,40]
MAIN	-	-	α	X=[1,1],Y=[2,2]	Y=[2,2]
A	T=[1,1],U=[2,2]	-	β	-	T=[U+N,U+N],N=[10,40]
B	M=[10,40],W=[2,2]	-	-	-	-
3rd iteration					
B	M=[10,40],W=[2,2]	V=[W+M,W+M],M=[10,40] W=[2,2]	-	-	-
A	T=[1,1],U=[2,2]	U=[2,2]	β	N=[10,40],U=[2,2]	T=[U+N,U+N],N=[10,40] U=[2,2]
MAIN	-	-	α	X=[1,1],Y=[2,2]	Y=[2,2]
A	T=[1,1],U=[2,2]	-	β	-	T=[U+N,U+N],N=[10,40] U=[2,2]
B	M=[10,40],W=[2,2]	-	-	-	-

(b)

Fig. 3. Interprocedural symbolic range propagation on an example code. (a) An example program with three program units and two call sites. The goal is to compute backward/forward Interprocedural Symbolic Ranges (ISRs) at the entry to each subroutine and at the call sites. (b) Step-by-step process of ISRP on the code. Each row is completed in a single step by the algorithm in Figure 2.

Symbolic Ranges (ISR) that are valid at the entry to each subroutine and after the call sites. In other words, the analysis collects forward ISR at the entry of each subroutine and backward ISR for each call site as shown in Figure 3(a). Figure 3(b) presents step-by-step process of ISRP on the code example. Each column shows the result after performing each step in the algorithm in Figure 2. For example, during the first iteration, the analysis computes return jump function for B ($V = [W + M, W + M]$), backward ISR for β ($T = [U + N, U + N]$), jump function for β ($N = [10, 40]$), return jump function for A (ϕ), backward ISR for α (ϕ), and jump function for α ($X = [1, 1], Y = [2, 2]$) successively. Then it finally computes forward ISRs for A and B, which come directly from

Table 1. Benchmark suite

Code	Size	Subroutines	Call sites	Code	Size	Subroutines	Call sites
ARC2D	4650	36	100	applu	3868	13	26
BDNA	4843	38	162	apsi	7361	66	328
DYFESM	8446	57	204	fpppp	2784	13	52
FLO52Q	2324	27	86	hydro2d	4292	39	200
MDG	1430	12	42	mgrid	484	11	46
MIGRATION	3455	23	110	su2cor	2332	26	242
OCEAN	3198	34	490	swim	429	6	10
QCD2	2816	30	166	tomcatv	190	1	0
SPEC77	4870	39	232	turb3d	2101	19	206
TRACK	4628	29	106	wupwise	2184	22	284
TRFD	580	4	20	*Total*	67265	545	3112

the jump functions for α and β after converting actual parameters into formal parameters. The resulting forward ISRs have changed since the start of the iteration, which triggers next iteration and the analysis continues with a new set of initial information. The analysis finally stops after third iteration where the starting forward ISRs are identical to the resulting forward ISRs.

3 Experiments

We have measured the effectiveness of the presented interprocedural symbolic range propagation algorithm on several aspects of optimizing compilers – data dependence analysis, test elision with dead code elimination, and other optimizations for automatic parallelization. We implemented our analysis in the Polaris parallelizing compiler and our reference point, to which we refer as *Base*, is the performance of the current version of Polaris with full optimization. That includes intraprocedural symbolic range propagation, interprocedural expression propagation with forward substitution, automatic partial inlining, and procedure cloning. The existing constant propagation pass also removes unreachable code sections due to control flows resolved at compile time. We switched this function off and implemented a stand-alone pass that can interface with the range information.

Another feature of our ISRP implementation is a substitution pass that substitutes a variable with its corresponding symbolic expression. This capability builds the interface with existing compiler passes that do not have the ability to query range information. For this substitution, we used simple decision heuristics to avoid unwanted chains of forward substitutions generating large expressions (a drawback of the current constant propagation and forward substitution technique). For example, replacing a variable with a known numeric value is always preferred, whereas replacing loop variables (indices, bounds) with complex expressions is not.

Table 2. The number of test elision and dead code elimination

Codes	Base	ISRP	Codes	Base	ISRP
ARC2D	4	5	applu	4	4
BDNA	15	15	apsi	1	18
DYFESM	18	26	fpppp	12	7
FLO52Q	2	5	hydro2d	9	9
MDG	0	1	mgrid	0	0
MIGRATION	4	6	su2cor	7	8
OCEAN	67	72	swim	0	0
QCD2	0	3	tomcatv	0	0
SPEC77	3	3	turb3d	5	15
TRACK	4	10	wupwise	19	27
TRFD	2	8	*Total*	176	242

3.1 Benchmark Suite

We selected 21 scientific engineering codes from the Perfect Benchmarks, SPEC CPU95 floating point, and SPEC CPU2000 floating point suites. This set of codes includes most of the Fortran 77 codes in each benchmark suite except for some codes that fail to compile (for reasons other than ISRP). Table 1 shows the feature of each benchmark, such as code size, number of subroutines or function calls, and number of call sites. Our algorithm converts all function calls to subroutine calls as a preliminary step.

3.2 Test Elision and Dead Code Elimination

Test elision and dead code elimination are optimizations that can benefit from static analysis such as constant propagation and range propagation. As more information about conditions is known, the compiler may prove that the test condition is always true or always false and thus eliminate one branch. We measured how the interprocedural range information affects the compile-time resolution of branches and corresponding dead code elimination.

Table 2 presents the number of successfully resolved branches with the Base method and with ISRP. For a fair comparison, we only counted one instance of cloned procedures. The results show that the number of statically resolved branches with ISRP is greater than or equal to that with Base for all benchmark codes except for `fpppp`. `Fpppp` contains a pattern that benefits from repeated information propagation and dead code elimination, which is performed by the Base technique but not by ISRP. The type of information to be propagated is simple, however, and done equally well by both techniques.

Overall, Table 2 shows that ISRP provides more accurate static information than Base and (except for the minor case in `fpppp`) subsumes the Base techniques.

Table 3. The number of data dependence arcs

Codes	Base	ISRP	Codes	Base	ISRP
ARC2D	801	459	applu	677	677
BDNA	1124	1081	apsi	11395	8222
DYFESM	1388	1108	fpppp	22064	20006
FLO52Q	263	279	hydro2d	110	66
MDG	1120	908	mgrid	83	19
MIGRATION	7180	6219	su2cor	10915	8712
OCEAN	433	370	swim	0	0
QCD2	17257	3579	tomcatv	45	45
SPEC77	2392	1652	turb3d	371	342
TRACK	2003	1781	wupwise	2013	1071
TRFD	93	40	*Total*	81727	56636

3.3 Data Dependence Analysis

Data dependence analysis is of obvious importance in optimizing compilers. We counted the number of dependence arcs in each benchmark code with Base and with ISRP to see how effective ISRP is in breaking data dependence arcs.

Table 3 shows the resulting numbers for each benchmark code. ISRP reduced the number of dependence arcs up to 79% for all benchmark codes except for `FLO52Q`. The increased number in `FLO52Q` is due to limitations of our simple forward substitution heuristics. Those variables were marked as private variables with Base whereas they carry cross-iteration dependences with ISRP. Another observation is that the total number of dependence pairs to disprove is increased for some codes and decreased for other codes – numbers are not presented here. Limited forward substitution accounts for the former case and better test elision accounts for the latter case. However, in both cases, the number of data dependence arcs decreased for most codes. This shows that limited forward substitution is not a significant factor to achieve accuracy in the data dependence analysis.

3.4 Detecting Zero-Trip Loops and Array Bounds

Our parallelizing compiler additionally makes use of the collected range information when making decisions in several parallelization passes. One such case is the induction variable substitution pass, which tries to decide if a loop is a zero-trip loop. Not knowing that a loop is non-zero-trip may prevent the substitution of an induction variable with its closed form [15]. The Polaris compiler inserts a runtime test in this case. ISRP can potentially eliminate this runtime overhead.

Another pass benefiting from range analysis is the reduction parallelization technique. In absence of accurate information about index ranges used by an array reduction pattern, the compiler must consider the entire array a potential reduction variable. This conservative measure cost significant runtime overhead. Again, ISRP has the potential to reduce this cost.

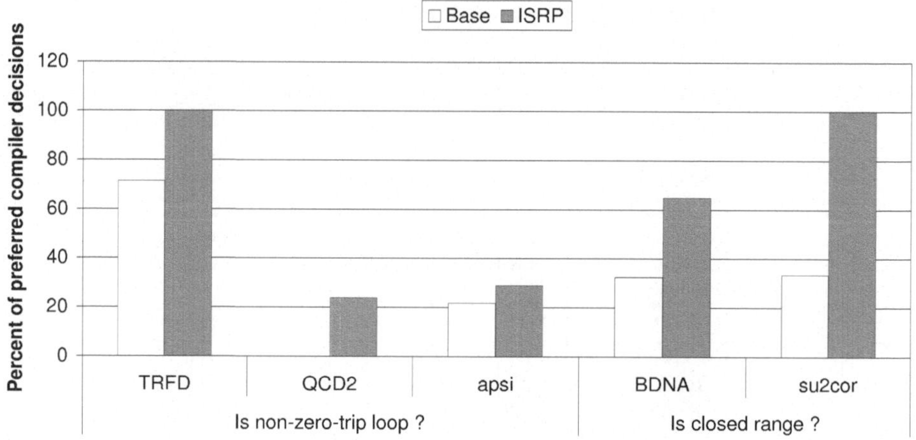

Fig. 4. Compiler's decisions for relevant questions with ISRP. If a loop is a non-zero-trip loop, the induction variable substitution pass can safely transform the code. If there is a closed subscript range for an array reduction, the compiler generates more efficient code for the reduction.

Figure 4 shows the percentage of preferred compiler's decisions in those passes with Base and with ISRP. In the benchmarks not listed here, we did not find any significant differences. ISRP substantially increased the number of desirable decisions for the codes in Figure 4. The compiler could answer all the questions in favor of each optimization for `TRFD` and `su2cor`. In `TRFD`, a significant code section was statically parallelized with ISRP whereas Base relied on a run-time test.

4 Related Work

Range analysis in imperative programming languages has been addressed in several contexts over the last few decades, most of them stemming from a formal foundation – *Abstract Interpretation*[6,7]. One of the major concerns of early work was how to make the analysis reach a fixed point at reasonable speed in the presence of loop-like program structures, and widening and narrowing[6] were then introduced to guarantee termination of the analysis. The demand for whole program analysis has also emerged and interprocedural analysis has become a key enabler of compiler optimizations in many contexts. The importance and effectiveness of range analysis or symbolic analysis have also been addressed in several contributions.

Havlak's work[11] served as an infrastructure for interprocedural symbolic analysis in the Parascope compilation system[1]. He divided a symbolic interprocedural analysis problem into four sub-problems, depending on if the analysis propagates symbolic values for variables or predicates, and if the information is passed to or returned from the callee. Two of the problems, returned values and passed predicates (linear equalities) were evaluated in his work. Our approach differs in two important regards. First, Havlak's work focuses on symbolic expression propagation, as opposed to value ranges. Second, our work is more general in that it can give solutions to all the four sub-problems. Before and after a call site, each symbolic value range with the same lower bound and the upper bound gives a set of passed expressions and returned expressions. Symbolic lower bounds and upper bounds can be used to infer a valid relationship between two expressions or variables. Including this work, interprocedural symbolic analysis was also applied in analyzing array accesses [8,10] to be used for interprocedural parallelization and other optimizations. Although analyzing array subscripts is a major application of our framework, ISRP has more flexibility that enables many other potential optimizations.

Patterson[14] adopted value range propagation to statically predict if a certain branch is taken or not. The range representation used in his work carries the probability that a variable has a certain lower bound, an upper bound, and a stride. Because the analysis is intended for a single optimization, static branch prediction, he limited the complexity of the problem so that the analysis can trade-off accuracy and efficiency. For example, the interprocedural analysis only concerns about propagation through parameter mappings, and symbolic expressions for the value ranges can have at most one variable, which greatly simplifies the problem. Our analysis is intended for general use in several compiler optimizations and considers arbitrary symbolic expressions.

There are also efforts that adopt range analysis in the C language because of its applicability for non-numerical programs. While tackling issues that arise in C-type languages (primarily pointer analysis) these approaches have not shown or claimed progress for high-performance computing applications. The work by Verbrugge et. al.[18] expressed range analysis as Generalized Constant Propagation (GCP) and implemented it in the McCAT optimizing/parallelizing compiler[12]. They used the concept of an invocation graph that maintains context-sensitive information, and also utilized points-to information and read/write sets to minimize the loss of information during interprocedural analysis. They also introduced "stepping", which is a variation of widening and narrowing, to guarantee finite fixed-point iterations. The use of the invocation graph is similar to procedure cloning in that it maintains context-sensitive special information for each invocation of a function. One limitation of their work is that it only handles non-symbolic ranges.

Rugina's work[16] on symbolic bounds analysis took a different approach to achieve a similar goal. He did not adopt conventional concepts such as abstract interpretation and fixed-point algorithm. Instead, he set up a system of constraints within a region of interest and introduced a way of reducing the constraint system to a linear program under an assumption that the positivity of each coefficient is known. A framework for interprocedural analysis was also introduced, which describes mapping and unmapping actions at call sites. To avoid fixed-point iteration for recursive calls, he introduced a method of building a system of recursive constraints. The idea of not doing fixed-point iteration is an outstanding feature compared with other related work. This feature may improve the efficiency of the analysis but it left unclear how to compare the accuracy of this technique with that of a conventional fixed-point technique, such as ours.

The most recent work by Yong and Horwitz[19] also adopted range analysis to compute a safe approximation of the set of memory locations that may be accessed by each pointer dereference. To simplify the problem, they treated all memory accesses as pointer dereferences even for a scalar variable. Their work focused on language-specific challenges such as pointer arithmetic and type mismatch due to union and casting, introducing advanced range description methods that embed type information. Like other conventional techniques, they adopted the concept of widening and narrowing for convergence but their interprocedural analysis does not handle context-sensitive information and symbolic ranges.

5 Conclusion

We have designed and implemented an interprocedural symbolic range analysis technique and have shown that the resulting compiler pass substantially enhances the accuracy of other optimizations. The reference point we have chosen in our evaluation of 21 science/engineering benchmarks is the combination of interprocedural expression propagation, intraprocedural symbolic range analysis, forward substitution, and automatic partial inlining, as currently implemented in the Polaris parallelizing compiler. We believe this to be the best state-of-the-art symbolic range analysis framework for high-performance computing applications, among related contributions.

ISRP is an enabling technique for other optimizations. We can expect substantial performance improvement once we enhance existing optimization passes to take advantage of the new information. As is, we have already found 14 more parallel loops in our benchmark codes.

Advanced program analysis comes at the cost of longer compilation time. We have measured up to 150% increased compilation time in all but two cases. Such increase seems acceptable, given the benefits and ever-increasing processor speeds. It is known that symbolic range analysis has exponential worst-case complexity [3], which explains substantial increases in compilation time in two of our codes – `OCEAN` and `TRACK`, which have a large number of call sites. In ongoing work we are considering optimizations of the algorithm to improve such behavior.

References

1. V. Balasundaram, K. Kennedy, U. Kremer, K. McKinley, and J. Subhlok. The parascope editor: an interactive parallel programming tool. In *Supercomputing '89: Proceedings of the 1989 ACM/IEEE conference on Supercomputing*, pages 540–550, New York, NY, USA, 1989. ACM Press.
2. W. Blume, R. Doallo, R. Eigenmann, J. Grout, J. Hoeflinger, T. Lawrence, J. Lee, D. Padua, Y. Paek, B. Pottenger, L. Rauchwerger, and P. Tu. Parallel programming with Polaris. *IEEE Computer*, 29(12):78–82, December 1996.
3. William Blume and Rudolf Eigenmann. Symbolic range propagation. In *Proceedings of the 9th International Parallel Processing Symposium*, pages 357–363, Santa Barbara, CA, April 1995.

4. William Blume and Rudolf Eigenmann. Demand-driven, Symbolic Range Propagation. *Lecture Notes in Computer Science, 1033: Languages and Compilers for Parallel Computing*, pages 141–160, 1996.
5. William Blume and Rudolf Eigenmann. Nonlinear and symbolic data dependence testing. *IEEE Transactions on Parallel and Distributed Systems*, 9(12):1180–1194, December 1998.
6. Patrick Cousot and Radhia Cousot. Static determination of dynamic properties of programs. In *Proceedings of the 2nd Internatioal Symposium on Programming*, pages 106–130, April 1976.
7. Patrick Cousot and Rhadia Cousot. Abstract interpretation: A unified lattice model for static analysis of programs by construction or approximation of fixpoints. In *Proceedings of 4th ACM Symposium*, pages 238–252, 1977.
8. Béatrice Creusillet and Francois Irigoin. Interprocedural Array Region Analyses. In *Eighth International Workshop on Languages and Compilers for Parallel Computing (LCPC'95)*, pages 4–1 to 4–15, August 1995.
9. Dan Grove and Linda Torczon. Interprocedural constant propagation: A study of jump function implementations. In *SIGPLAN Conference on Programming Language Design and Implementation*, pages 90–99, 1993.
10. Mary W. Hall, Brian R. Murphy, Saman P. Amarasinghe, Shih-Wei Liao, and Monica S. Lam. Interprocedural analysis for parallelization. In *LCPC '95: Proceedings of the 8th International Workshop on Languages and Compilers for Parallel Computing*, pages 61–80, London, UK, 1996. Springer-Verlag.
11. Paul Havlak. *Interprocedural Symbolic Analysis*. PhD thesis, Dept. of Computer Science, Rice University, May 1994.
12. Laurie J. Hendren, C. Donawa, Maryam Emami, Guang R. Gao, Justiani, and B. Sridharan. Designing the mccat compiler based on a family of structured intermediate representations. In *Proceedings of the 5th International Workshop on Languages and Compilers for Parallel Computing*, pages 406–420, London, UK, 1993. Springer-Verlag.
13. Seuing-Jai Min, Seon Wook Kim, Michael Voss, Sang-Ik Lee, and Rudolf Eigenmann. Portable compilers for OpenMP. In *OpenMP Shared-Memory Parallel Programming*, Lecture Notes in Computer Science #2104, pages 11–19, Springer Verlag, Heidelberg, Germany, July 2001.
14. Jason R. C. Patterson. Accurate static branch prediction by value range propagation. In *Proceedings of the conference on Programming language design and implementation*, pages 67–78. ACM Press, 1995.
15. William M. Pottenger and Rudolf Eigenmann. Idiom recognition in the polaris parallelizing compiler. In *Proceedings of the 9th International Conference on Supercomputing*, pages 444–448, 1995.
16. Radu Rugina and Martin C. Rinard. Symbolic bounds analysis of pointers, array indices, and accessed memory regions. In *Proceedings of the SIGPLAN Conference on Programming Language Design and Implementation*, pages 182–195, Vancouver, Canada, June 2000.
17. Peng Tu and David Padua. Array privatization for shared and distributed memory machines (extended abstract). *SIGPLAN Not.*, 28(1):64–67, 1993.
18. Clark Verbrugge, Phong Co, and Laurie J. Hendren. Generalized constant propagation: A study in c. In *Proceedings of the Internatioal Conference on Compiler Construction*, pages 74–90, April 1996.
19. Suan Hsi Yong and Susan Horwitz. Pointer-range analysis. In *Proceedings of the 11th International Static Analysis Symposium (SAS '04)*, page 16 pages, August 2004.

Parallelization of Utility Programs Based on Behavior Phase Analysis

Xipeng Shen and Chen Ding

Computer Science Department, University of Rochester,
Rochester, NY, USA 14627
{xshen,cding}@cs.rochester.edu

Abstract. With the fast development of multi-core processors, automatic parallelization becomes increasingly important. In this work, we focus on the parallelization of utility programs, a class of commonly used applications including compilers, transcoding utilities, file compressions, and databases. They take a series of requests as inputs and serve them one by one. Their high input dependence poses a challenge to parallelization.

We use active profiling to find behavior phase boundaries and then automatically detect run-time dependences through profiling. Using a unified framework, we manually parallelize programs at phase boundaries. We show that for two programs, the technique enables parallelization at large granularity, which may span many loops and subroutines. The parallelized programs show significant speedup on multi-processor machines.

1 Introduction

Nowadays due to the increasing complexity, it is difficult to improve the speed of high-performance uniprocessors. Chip multiprocessors is becoming the key of the next generation personal computers. But many applications, especially those running on past personal computers, are sequential programs and require parallelization to benefit from multiple cores.

In this paper, we describe a novel coarse-grain parallelization technique focused on a class of commonly used programs. *Utility programs* are a class of dynamic programs whose behavior strongly depends on their input. The examples include compilers, interpreters, compressions, transcoding utilities and databases. The applications all provide some sort of service: they accept, or can be configured to accept, a sequence of requests, and each request is processed more-or-less independently of the others. Because their behavior depend heavily on the input, utility applications display much less regular behavior than typical scientific programs. Many of them invoke many recursive function calls.

Our parallelization is based on behavior-based phase analysis. Here we define behavior as the operations of a program, which changes from input to input. A *behavior phase* is a unit of the recurring behavior in any execution. It may have plenty of loops and function calls. We use active profiling and pattern recognition techniques to detect phases [7]. Each instance of the top-level phase is the processing of a request. For example, the compilation of a function is a phase instance in GCC, and the parsing

E. Ayguadé et al. (Eds.): LCPC 2005, LNCS 4339, pp. 425–432, 2007.

of a sentence is a phase instance in Parser. The key observation is that the phases in utility programs coincide with program service periods and thus its *memory usage periods*. Operations inside a phase instance may have complex dependences but different phase instances are usually independent or can be made independent. Therefore, phase boundaries are good places to parallelize utility programs.

Phase-level parallelization has three steps. First, we automatically employ behavior-based phase analysis to find phases and mark them in the program source code through debugging tools [7]. Secondly, we discover the run-time data dependences among phase instances through profiling. Finally, we parallelize the program under a unified framework. The last step is currently semi-automatic, and the correctness requires the verification of a programmer. The step can potentially be automated with run-time system support, which automatically detects dependence violations and recovers when necessary. We have applied phase-level parallelization on two programs, Gzip and Parser and obtained up to 12.6 times speedup on a 16-processor machine.

There have been many efforts on automatic parallelization. Dynamic parallelization was pioneered more than a decade ago [5,10]. Many recent papers studied thread-level speculation with hardware support ([2] contains a classification of various schemes). Most of those methods exploit loop-level parallelism, especially in low-level loops. Ortega et al. manually find parallelism in coarse loops for SPECInt benchmarks, which they call distant parallelism [4]. Our technique exploits parallelism at phase granularity for utility programs with some user support. It is orthogonal to fine-grain parallelism techniques.

2 Parallelization Techniques

2.1 Phase Detection

Phase detection is to find the boundaries of recurring behavior patterns in a program. We use a two-step technique to detect phases in utility programs. Active profiling uses a sequence of identical requests to induce behavior that is both representative of normal usage and sufficiently regular to identify outermost phases. It then uses different real requests to capture common sub-phases and to verify the representativeness of the constructed input. The phase boundaries are determined through statistic analysis on the dynamic basic block trace of the execution and are marked in the program code (see [7] for details.)

Phases have a hierarchical structure. In this study, we make use of the outermost phases only. We use process-based parallelization, where each phase instance is executed by a child process. If phase instances are small, a process can execute a group of phase instances at a time.

2.2 Phase-Dependence Detection

Phase-dependence detection is to find run-time data dependences between phase instances during profiling runs. Similar to loop-dependence analysis[1], there are three kinds of phase-dependences: *flow dependence*, *antidependence*, and *output dependence*.

A flow dependence happens when a phase instance stores a value into a memory location and a later phase instance reads the value. An antidependence happens when a phase instance reads from and a later one writes to the same location. Finally, an output dependence happens when two phase instances write to the same memory location. Since process-based parallelization creates a separate address space for different phase instances, we can ignore anti- and output dependences. In comparison, thread-based parallelization must deal with them explicitly.

```
NODE* xlevel (NODE * expr) { /* function definition */
   if (++xltrace < TDEPTH){...} /* read and write xltrace */
   --xltrace;} /* read and write xltrace */
```
(a) False dependence due to implicit initialization

```
char*buf;
...
buf[i] = 0; /* both load and store operations due to byte operations*/
```
(b) Addressing false dependence

```
*u = *t; /* load value of *t */
...
("t" is freed and "deletable" is allocated)
deletable[i][j] = FALSE; /* store operation*/
(deletable is freed)
...
```
(c) Allocator false dependence

```
for (sym = getelement(array,i);...){... } /* load "array" element*/
setelement (array, i, sym); /* store "array" element */
```
(d) Real phase dependence

Fig. 1. Example code of LI and Parser from the SPEC CPU2000 benchmark suite showing removable flow dependences. Each case contains a load from and a store to the same memory location. The dependence flows from the store in each phase instance to the load of the next phase instance.

Most flow dependences among phases are removable. Here "removable" means that the flow dependence can be safely ignored in process-based parallelization. We divide the removable flow dependences into three classes, give examples for each class, and describes the detection of these dependences as well as possible run-time support to guarantee correctness. As examples, Figure 1 shows fragments of the code of LI and Parser in the SPEC CPU2000 benchmark suite. Figure 1 (a) shows the first class of removable dependence, which are caused by *implicit initialization*. In this case, the variables are reset to their initial value at the end of each phase instance. In the example, the global variable *xltrace* is a stack pointer. It increments by 1 when evaluating an expression and the evaluation function may call itself to evaluate subexpressions. It decrements by 1 after the evaluation. It is always equal to -1, its initial value, at the beginning and the end of each phase instance. Such objects can be automatically detected by checking the consistency of their values at the beginning of every phase. If their values are always the same, the variables are likely to belong to this class. In the runtime system, the value of those variables may be checked dynamically, and the parallel process may be rolled back when the value is unexpected.

Figure 1 (b) shows the second class of removable dependences, *addressing dependences*. In this class, the source code has no loading operations but the binary code has because of addressing. In the example code, there is a write of a byte. The code is compiled into the following assembly code on a Digital Alpha machine, which does not have a byte write operation.

```
lda    s4, -28416(gp) /* load array base address */
addq   s4, s0, s4     /* shift to the target array element */
ldq_u  v0, 0(s4)      /* load a quadword from the current element */
mskbl  v0, s4, v0     /* set the target byte to 0 by masking */
stq_u  v0, 0(s4)      /* store the new quadword to the array */
```

Our dependence detection finds a flow dependence between instruction "stq_u v0, 0(s4)" and "ldq_u v0,0(s4)" when more than one phase instances execute that statement. It is removable dependence since the loading operation is purely for the store operation and the value of the loaded location has no effects on the program's execution.

Finally, flow dependences may happen when memory is reused across phase instances by a dynamic memory allocator. Figure 1 (c) shows an example. The two objects $*t$ and *deletable* are independent and have exclusive live periods. They are allocated to the same memory region by the memory allocator. Process-based parallelization can ignore all these three classes of flow dependences because it uses separate address spaces for processes.

Figure 1 (d) shows a real phase-dependence. An earlier phase instance fills *array* with some calculation results, which are loaded in a later phase instance. For correctness, the parallelization must protect such objects to avoid the violation of the dependence.

We develop an automatic tool to trace memory accesses in profiling runs, detect different kinds of dependences, and then find the corresponding source code. The tool cannot detect all possible dependences in a program but it can help the parallelization process by finding the likely parallel regions in the program. The tool first instruments the binary code of a program to monitor memory accesses for dependence detection through instrumentor ATOM [8] and then finds and displays the source code related to phase-level flow dependences that are not removable. Trace-level dependence tracking has been used extensively for studying the limit of parallelism (an early example is give by Kumar [3]) and for easing the job of debugging.

The effect of profiling depends on the coverage, that is, the portion of phase-level dependences that we find through profiling. Multiple training runs help to improve the coverage. Utility programs take a series of requests as an input; thus one execution contains the process of many different requests. This leads to good coverage even with a single input.

2.3 Program Transformation

Our parallelization is process based. Thread-based parallelization is an alternative. Processes have their own address space and are thus more independent than threads. Utility programs often have just a small number of phase-level flow dependences, since phase instances coincide with the memory usage period of a program. For example, variable *optind* is the only flow dependence that is not removable in benchmark Gzip and requires code movement. There are other global data structures shared by phase instances, but they can be privatized since they introduce no flow dependences. In thread-based parallelization, multiple threads share the address space and must deal with antidependences and output dependences explicitly. In our study, we use process-based parallelization.

Many utility programs have a common high level structure; they first read requests and then process them one by one. We design a unified framework for their parallelization, which is shown in our technical report [6] for lack of space.

There are two strategies for parallelization. One is to let programmers know the phase structure and the detected dependences so the programmer may parallelize the program when possible. The manual effort is simplified by the automatic tools, which suggest parallel regions that have good efficiency and scalability. The other strategy is run-time dependence detection and phase-level speculation. All objects are put into a protected region so speculation can be canceled when it fails. To improve efficiency and scalability, we can give special treatment to the dependences detected in the profiling runs. The operating system can monitor the accesses to those objects and roll back later processes only when the dependences on those objects are violated or an earlier process writes to the other objects in the protected region. This strategy requires less manual work but requires the support of operating system. It has extra overhead. We use the first strategy in this work and are in the process of developing the second strategy.

3 Evaluation

We apply phase-level parallelization on Parser and Gzip in Spec CPU2000 suite. We first discuss the issues in the parallelization of each benchmark, then report the performance of the parallelized programs.

3.1 Parser

Parser is a natural language (English) parsing program. It takes a series of sentences as its input and parses them one by one. The detected phase boundary is before the parsing of a sentence. The dependence detector reports 208 dependences in which 6 are distinct flow dependences. Figure 2 shows part of the report. Among the six, the first two are removable addressing dependences. The next two are implicit initialization removable dependences: the store statement for *lookup_list* traverses the list to free the list elements and *mn_free_list* is freed at the end of each phase instance. The rest two dependences are not easily removable. They include four global variables as array *user_variable*, *unknown_word_defined*, *use_unknown_word* and *echo_on*. The last three variables are elements of array *user_variable*. They are a set of global boolean variables, used to configure the parsing environment. For example, variable *echo_on* determines whether to output the original sentence or not. As the program comes across a command sentence like "!echo" in the input file, it turns on the boolean value of *echo_on*. The command sentences are part of the input file. In our parallelization, we let the root process handle those command sentences first and then create child processes to parse every other sentence with the corresponding environment configuration.

Dep. type	Operation	File	Line	Source code
addressing	store	analyze-linkage.c	659	patch_array[i].used = FALSE;
	load	analyze-linkage.c	659	patch_array[i].used = FALSE;
addressing	store	and.c	540	if (*s == '*') *u = *t;
	load	and.c	540	if (*s == '*') *u = *t;
initialization	store	read-dict.c	763	lookup_list = n;
	load	read-dict.c	760	while(lookup_list != NULL) {
initialization	load	fast-match.c	59	mn_free_list = m;
	store	fast-match.c	44	if (mn_free_list != NULL) {
real dep.	store	main.c	620	(∗(user_variable[i].p)) = !!(∗(user_variable[i].p));
	load	main.c	1557	if (!(unknown_word_defined && use_unknown_word)) {
real dep.	store	main.c	674	∗(user_variable[j].p) = !(∗(user_variable[j].p));
	load	main.c	1573	if (echo_on) printf("%c ", mc);

Fig. 2. The partial report of dependences in Parser. Each pair of rows show the two lines of code causing a phase-level flow dependence.

3.2 Gzip

Gzip is a popular data compression program (the Gzip used in the experiment is configured as the GNU compression program instead of the SPEC CPU2000 default version). It takes a series of files as the input and compresses them one by one. It has only one phase-level flow dependence, variable *optind*, which counts the number of input files. It increases by one in each phase instance. Automatically our analysis tool finds the boundary of file processing as the phase boundary. The dependence detection finds the flow dependence. After applying the unified framework for transformation, the only remaining work is to move the counter increment operation from child processes to the root process to resolve the dependence.

3.3 Methodology

We measure the performance on two multi-processor machines, whose configurations are shown in Table 1.

We use "gcc -O3" for compilation. The Gzip has only one input file as its test input. We duplicate the file multiple times as the regular input for profiling. The ref input of Gzip contains too few files to measure the effectiveness. We create 105 files by duplicating all ref inputs 20 times each. The regular input for Parser is a file containing

Table 1. Machine configurations

CPU Number	4	16
CPU Type	Intel Xeon	Sunfire Sparc V9
CPU Speed	2.0GHz	1.2GHz
L1 cache	512K	64K

six identical English sentences. We use the test input for the dependence profiling of Parser and the ref input for evaluation.

3.4 Speedup

Figure 3 (a) and (b) show the speedup curves of the parallelized programs on Intel Xeon and Sunfire multi-processor machines. The x-axis is logarithmic. We experiment up to 8 processes on the 4-CPU Intel machine. When the number of process is smaller than the number of processors, the speedup increases significantly and reaches the peak when the process number is equal to the processor number. Gzip achieves 1.6 times speedup and Parser achieves 2.0.

On the 16-CPU Sunfire machine, Parser shows 12.6 times speedup with 16 processes. Gzip shows 2.4 times speedup. The limited speedup of Gzip is due to the saturation of file I/O.

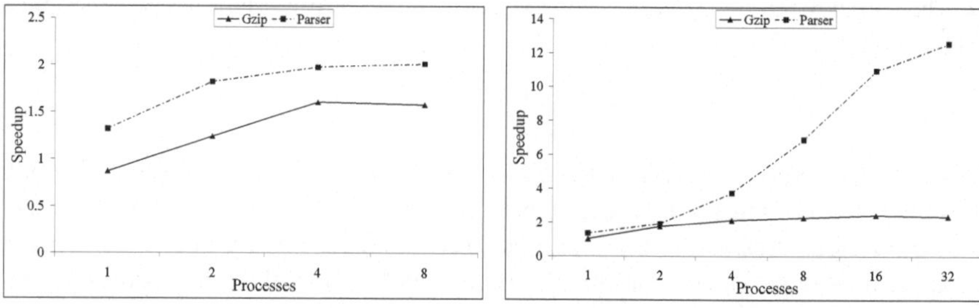

(a) Speedup on an Intel Xeon machine (b) Speedup on a Sunfire Sparc V9 machine

Fig. 3. Speedup of parallelized programs on multiple-processor machines

4 Related Work

There have been many efforts on automatic parallelization. The most related work is the study from software aspects. Those efforts roughly include two classes: task and data based parallelization.

Previous parallelization techniques are based on static compiler or run-time techniques. The former tries to find the parallelism opportunities in program loops through static dependence analysis in compilers and then applies privatization and reduction parallelization [1,9].) Static techniques work well for programs with regular, statically analyzable access patterns. Run-time parallelization can reveal and exploit input dependent and dynamic parallelism in loop nests [5,10]. In comparison, this work uses profiling to parallelize programs at phase boundaries and exploit parallelism that may span many loops and subroutines.

Another class of parallelization is based on Thread-level Speculation (TLS) hardware. TLS hardware provides support for speculative threads and dynamical roll back given the violation of dependences. This work partially relies on programmer knowledge but requires no special hardware support.

5 Conclusions

In this work, we propose a phase-level parallelization technique for parallelizing utility programs. It finds phase boundaries by active profiling, identifies common phase-level dependences by training, handles anti- and output dependences through process-based parallelization, classifies removable flow dependences, and relies on programmer support to handle remaining flow dependences and ensure the correctness of the transformation. Unlike previous work, this technique helps to parallelize a program in coarse granularity, which may span many loops and subroutines. Our preliminary experiments show significant speedups for two non-trivial utility programs on multi-processor machines.

References

1. R. Allen and K. Kennedy. *Optimizing Compilers for Modern Architectures: A Dependence-based Approach.* Morgan Kaufmann Publishers, October 2001.
2. M. J. Garzaran, M. Prvulovic, J. M. Llaberia, V. Vinals, L. Rauchwerger, and J. Torrellas. Tradeoffs in buffering memory state for thread-level speculation in multiprocessors. In *Proceedings of International Symposium on High-Performance Computer Architecture*, 2003.
3. M. Kumar. Measuring parallelism in computation-intensive scientific/engineering applications. *IEEE Transactions on Computers*, 37, 1988.
4. D. Ortega, Ivan Martel, Eduard Ayguade, Mateo Valero, and Venkata Krishnan. Quantifying the benefits of specint distant parallelism in simultaneous multi-threading architectures. In *Proceeding of the Eighth International Conference on Parallel Architectures and Compilation Techniques*, Newport Beach, California, October 1999.
5. L. Rauchwerger and D. Padua. The LRPD test: Speculative run-time parallelization of loops with privatization and reduction parallelization. In *Proceedings of ACM SIGPLAN Conference on Programming Language Design and Implementation*, La Jolla, CA, June 1995.
6. X. Shen and C. Ding. Parallelization of utility programs based on behavior phase analysis. Technical Report TR 876, Department of Computer Science, University of Rochester, September 2005.
7. X. Shen, C. Ding, S. Dwarkadas, and M. L. Scott. Characterizing phases in service-oriented applications. Technical Report TR 848, Department of Computer Science, University of Rochester, November 2004.
8. A. Srivastava and A. Eustace. ATOM: A system for building customized program analysis tools. In *Proceedings of ACM SIGPLAN Conference on Programming Language Design and Implementation*, Orlando, Florida, June 1994.
9. M. Wolfe. *Optimizing Compilers for Supercomputers.* The MIT Press, 1989.
10. C. Q. Zhu and P. C. Yew. A scheme to enforce data dependence on large multiprocessor systems. *IEEE Transactions on Software Engineering*, 13(6), 1987.

A Systematic Approach to Model-Guided Empirical Search for Memory Hierarchy Optimization*

Chun Chen, Jacqueline Chame, Mary Hall, and Kristina Lerman

University of Southern California/Information Sciences Institute
4676 Admiralty Way, Suite 1001, Marina del Rey, CA 90292
{chunchen,jchame,mhall,lerman}@isi.edu

Abstract. The goal of this work is a systematic approach to compiler optimization for simultaneously optimizing across multiple levels of the memory hierarchy. Our approach combines compiler models and heuristics with guided empirical search to take advantage of their complementary strengths. The models and heuristics limit the search to a small number of candidate implementations, and the empirical results provide accurate feedback information to the compiler. In previous work, we propose a compiler algorithm for deriving a set of parameterized solutions, followed by a model-guided empirical search to determine the best integer parameter values and select the best overall solution. This paper focuses on formalizing the process of deriving parameter values, which is a *multi-variable* optimization problem, and considers the role of AI search techniques in deriving a systematic framework for the search.

1 Introduction

Since the development of the earliest optimizing compilers, it has been well understood that compiler optimization is a challenging problem with a variety of tradeoffs. As architectures and applications become increasingly complex, statically predicting the impact of individual compiler optimizations and the aggregate impact of a collection of optimizations is becoming increasingly difficult.

Currently, optimization of high-end computing applications is done manually in an ad-hoc manner. A recent strategy to address this complexity and improve performance employs *empirical optimization*, to systematically evaluate a collection of automatically-generated *code variants* and *parameter values* [7,3]. Code variants, in this context, are alternative but equivalent implementations of the same computation. For a particular variant, there may additionally be optimization parameters such as unroll factors and tile sizes. Rather than estimating performance through analysis, implementation variants are actually *executed on the target architecture* with representative input data sets across different parameter values so that performance can be measured and compared. However a recent paper [8] showed that the model-driven approach on Matrix Multiply can

* This work has been supported by NSF grants ACI-0204040 and CSR-0509517.

E. Ayguadé et al. (Eds.): LCPC 2005, LNCS 4339, pp. 433–440, 2007.

yield comparable performance with ATLAS [7], suggesting that the compiler-derived model may be able to limit the search space.

In a previous paper, we demonstrated that combining the strengths of models with empirical search can yield better performance than either ATLAS or hand-coded BLAS [1]. For memory hierarchy optimization, finding a set of variants and parameters that result in high performance is difficult because of the complex tradeoffs among memory hierarchy levels. In addition, the search space is difficult to model analytically since performance can vary dramatically with problem size and optimization parameters. Empirical results can help the compiler tune the accuracy of its models and select the best candidate implementations. A purely empirical approach is not practical in general because the search space of possible variants and their parameters is prohibitively large. A compiler's understanding of the impact of code transformations on performance can be used to limit the search space and rule out the vast majority of inferior implementations.

This paper explores the parameter search in an effort to develop a systematic and generalizable approach that goes beyond our memory hierarchy optimization strategy. Realizing that many compiler optimizations require some sort of heuristic-based search, we consider the suitability of AI search techniques. Although compiler researchers have begun to apply elements of AI to their work [2,5,6], no principled methodology yet exists. We believe a formal framework will enable compiler developers and application programmers to move away from ad-hoc approaches toward a principled process of design.

The remainder of the paper is organized as follows. Section 2 illustrates the problem of optimizing for multiple levels of the memory hierarchy and describes our framework. Section 3 formalizes the search problem as a multi-variable optimization problem. Finally, Section 4 concludes the paper.

2 Guided Empirical Search for the Memory Hierarchy

Achieving high performance on today's architectures with deep memory hierarchies requires considering the overall performance impact of individual optimizations. In [1] we proposed an approach for simultaneously optimizing across all levels of the memory hierarchy using a combination of compiler analysis, architecture models and a guided empirical search for optimization parameters.

Figures 1 (a) and (b) show the original matrix multiply and a parameterized code variant derived by applying several optimizations (loop interchanging, unrolling, tiling, data copying and data prefetching). The optimized code variant in (b) has a set of parameters $\{U_I, U_J, T_I, T_J, T_K, P_{P,K}\}$ where U_I and U_J are unroll factors, T_I, T_J, T_K are tile sizes and $P_{P,K}$ is the prefetch distance of array `P` in loop `K`. We executed this optimized code variant on an SGI Octane R10000 using five distinct parameter sets (details in [1]). The best performance was achieved using a set of parameters that did not result in either the lowest cache miss ratios, or the lowest number of memory accesses or the best TLB behavior. Instead, the best performance was achieved by exploiting reuse at all

```
DO K = 1,N
  DO J = 1,N
    DO I = 1,N
      C[I,J] += A[I,K]*B[K,J]
```

(a) Original Matrix Multiply

```
new P[TK,TJ]
new Q[TI,TK]
DO KK = 1,N,TK
  DO JJ = 1,N,TJ
    copy B[KK..KK+TK-1,JJ..JJ+TJ-1] to P
    DO II = 1,N,TI
      copy A[II..II+TI-1,KK..KK+TK-1] to Q
      DO J = JJ,min(JJ+TJ-1,N),UJ
        DO I = II,min(II+TI-1,N),UI
          load C[I..I+UI-1,J..J+UJ-1] into registers
          DO K = KK,min(KK+TK-1,N)
            prefetch P's
            multiply Q's and P's to registers
          store C[I..I+UI-1,J..J+UJ-1]
```

(b) Optimized Matrix Multiply

Fig. 1. Matrix Multiply

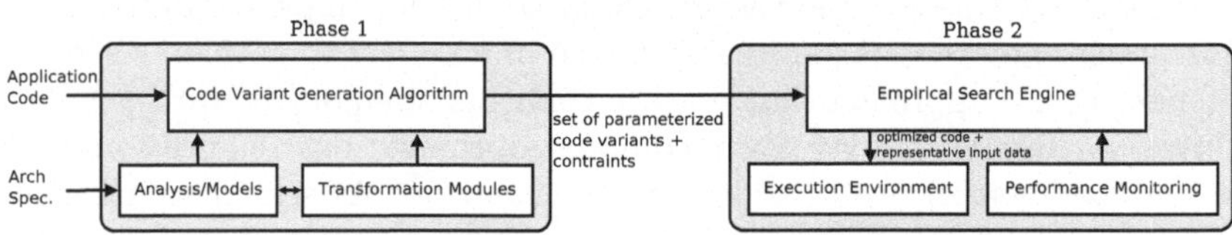

Fig. 2. Optimization framework

levels of the memory hierarchy, trading off best performance at any particular level for locality at all levels.

The remainder of this section presents a summary of our framework, which is organized into two main phases (Figure 2). In the first phase the compiler generates a set of parameterized code variants. The second phase is a search among parameter values for each code variant, guided by models and heuristics.

Phase 1: Generate Parameterized Variants using Models. The code generation algorithm systematically applies individual transformations based on analysis and models (the details of the algorithm can be found in [1]). The compiler uses dependence analysis to determine the legality of code transformations, locality analysis to evaluate data reuse and select specific locality optimizations, register reuse analysis to estimate register pressure, etc. The models include register, cache and TLB models and also incorporate various heuristics for those optimizations. Along with each code variant, the compiler generates a set of constraints for the optimization parameters, which are used in the second phase to guide and prune the search. Table 1 shows the code transformations and parameters used by the algorithm. The fourth column indicates whether a transformation results in more than one code variant. For example, for loop permutation the algorithm may generate multiple code variants, each with a different loop order, if it cannot decide which order is best statically. Other transformations, such as loop tiling, do not increase the number of variants, but result in code variants with unbound parameters, as illustrated in the table's last column.

Table 1. Transformation variants and parameters

Transformations	Definition	Goal	Variants	Parameters
Loop permutation	Change loop order	Enable U&J, tiling Reduce TLB misses	Different loop orders	-
Unroll and Jam	Unroll outer loops, fuse inner loops	Reuse in registers	-	Unroll factors
Scalar replacement	Replace array accesses with scalar variables			
Tiling	Divide iteration space into tiles	Reuse in cache	-	Tile sizes
Data copying (w/tiling)	Copy subarray into contiguous memory space	Avoid conflict misses and TLB thrashing	Yes/no on specific data structures	-
Prefetching	Prefetch data into cache	Hide memory latency	-	Prefetch distances

Phase 2: Search for Parameter Values. In this phase, a guided empirical search performs a series of experiments to derive parameter values for each code variant. In addition, code transformations that depend on parameter values are applied during this phase. The resulting code variants are then compiled and executed on the target machine. The search engine uses metrics collected by performance monitoring tools to evaluate the quality of a code variant with a given set of parameter values.

In [1] we use compiler domain knowledge about specific optimizations to search the parameter space efficiently. In the next section we discuss how to approach the search for parameter values systematically and explore this problem in a broader context.

3 Systematically Searching the Parameter Space

The goal of this section is to provide insight into a systematic solution to Phase 2, searching for integer parameter values of code variants to select the best variant and parameter set. Before discussing search techniques, we describe aspects of the search that can be captured by search algorithms to expedite the search and lead to high-quality solutions. We use the memory hierarchy optimization problem to make the discussion more concrete. The search for a set of parameter values leading to the best performance can be expressed as a function of several features, which are specified by the compiler:

$$Search = \{Parameters,\ Constraints,\ Dependence,\ Ordering,\ Starting\ Points\}$$

Set of parameters. In the case of memory hierarchy optimization, let us assume we are optimizing a single n-deep loop nest.[1] Then the following set of parameters is associated with each variant:

[1] Without loss of generality, if the code has multiple loop nests, each nest will have such a set of parameters associated with them. For simplicity we treat them independently in this discussion.

- $U_{L1}, \ldots, U_{Ln}$: *unroll factors* for each loop in an n-deep loop nest.
- $T_{L1}, \ldots, T_{Ln}$: *tile sizes* for each loop in an n-deep loop nest.
- $P_{A1,L1}, \ldots, P_{A1,Ln}, \ldots, P_{Am,Ln}$: *prefetch distances* for arrays $A1$ through Am within the loop nest.

Set of constraints on integer values. Phase 1 provides a set of constraints for each unbound parameter of a code variant.[2] For example, when unroll-and-jam is applied to multiple loops the unroll factors should be such that reuse is maximized while satisfying the register capacity constraints. In general, a constraint on unroll factors due to register capacity can be expressed as $\sum_{i=1}^{M} a_{i1} * U_1 * a_{i2} * U_2 * \ldots * a_n * U_{in} \leq R$, where a_{ij} are constants, M is the number of array references in the loop nest and R is register file size. Similarly, tile sizes should be such that the tile footprint fits in cache, and a constraint on tile sizes can be expressed as an inequality involving the product of the tile sizes of each loop. These constraints prune off uninteresting portions of the search space, and keep the search focused on the area of the search space most likely to achieve the best results.

Dependence between parameters. Parameters that appear on a same constraint are considered interdependent and are evaluated as a set. Unroll factors of multiple loops may appear in a same constraint due to register capacity, and are considered interdependent. Similarly, tile sizes of multiple loops may appear in one or more constraints related to cache capacity. Unroll factors and tile sizes are considered independent from each other, based on the knowledge that reuse in registers and caches are complementary as long as the unroll factor of each loop in the original loop nest does not exceed the tile size of that same loop.

Ordering of parameter selection. In general, optimization parameters may be inter-related, and the order in which they are evaluated may impact the search results. Compiler domain knowledge can be used to determine a search ordering for parameters that are considered independent. In memory hierarchy optimization the benefits from unroll-and-jam and scalar replacement are typically much higher than those of tiling and copying: reuse in registers reduces the *number* of memory operations, while reuse in cache reduces only the *latency* seen by the processor. Similarly, tiling reduces number of accesses to memory, while prefetching hides the memory latency. Therefore, the search for unroll factors precedes the search for tile sizes, which in turn precedes selecting prefetch distances. Since prefetching may displace data from the cache, tiling parameters may need to be adjusted after prefetch parameters are determined.

3.1 A Systematic Search Space

Given the previous discussion, a systematic approach could search for parameter values using the specified ordering of parameters, and within the specified constrained range. Although much of the search space has been pruned away, there still remains a fairly large number of points to search.

---

[2] Parameters that are set to their default values at Phase 1 indicate that an optimization should not be performed. The default values for unroll factors, tile sizes and prefetch distances are 1, 1, and 0, respectively.

In the following we discuss how to incorporate domain knowledge in a systematic search for parameter values, using the parameter space of the code variant shown in Figure 1(b) as an example.[3]

Figure 3 shows a tree representation of the parameter space of the code variant in Figure 1(b). The parameters of this code variant are the unroll factors U_I, U_J and U_K, the tile sizes T_I, T_J and T_K, and the prefetch distance of array P in loop K, $P_{P,K}$. The evaluation function is measured execution time. Each tree level, except the root, corresponds to a set of interdependent parameters. In this example the second level corresponds to unroll factors, the third level to tile sizes and the fourth level to the prefetch distance $P_{P,K}$. On a given level, each node corresponds to a set of integer values for the parameters associated with that level. For example, each node at the second level corresponds to a set $\{U_I$, U_J, $U_K\}$ where $1 \leq U_I, U_J, UK \leq R$, and R is the number of registers available. Hence each node is a partial set of parameters for the code variant. Selecting a set of parameters corresponds to finding a path, from root to a leaf node, such that the performance of the variant with the complete set of parameter values in this path is maximized.

This tree representation incorporates some of the compiler's domain knowledge discussed in the previous section.

Dependence: In Figure 3 each node in the second level represents a set of interdependent unroll factors and each node in the third level represents a set of tile sizes. Unroll factors and tile sizes are considered independent from each other and are represented as different levels of the tree.

Ordering: The search tree has three levels, with parameters that have greatest impact on performance at the highest levels. Thus the compiler's domain knowledge about the effect of optimizations on performance is captured by the order implied by the levels. Therefore the search for unroll factors is performed before selecting tile sizes, which is performed before selecting prefetch distances. If prefetching is found to be profitable the tree representation allows the search to backtrack to a previous solution. For example, the search can explore solutions with a larger tile size for the loop in which prefetches are inserted, to increase the amount of latency that can be covered so that prefetches are effective.

Pruning the parameter space: Constraints derived at Phase 1 are used to prune the search. In Figure 3 all second-level nodes $< U_I = R, U_J \geq 2, \ldots >$ violate the constraint $U_I * U_J * U_K \leq R$. Therefore all subtrees rooted at these nodes can be pruned. In addition, known properties of optimizations are used to guide and prune the search. For example, the amount of reuse exposed by unroll-and-jam increases with the unroll factors, until there are no more registers available and register spilling occurs. Hence when a set of unroll factors $U =<$

[3] Additional domain knowledge for guiding the search is the subject of future work, which may include: providing a direction for the search (upward, downward) based on estimated upper and lower bounds for a parameter; providing a step size for traversing a given range (such as tile sizes should be a multiple of the cache line size); exploiting characteristics of transformations (such as reuse increases monotonically with each unroll factor).

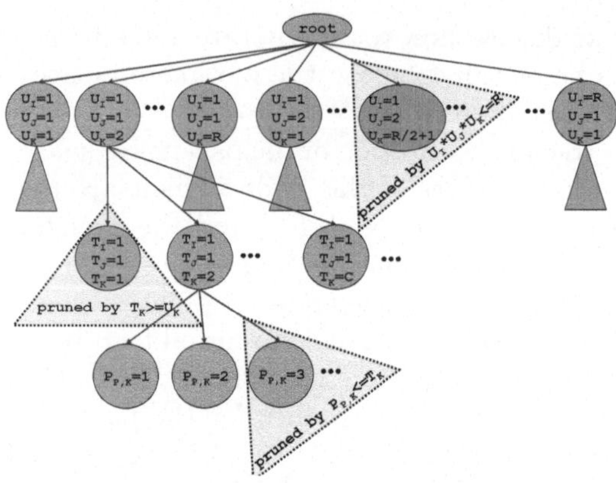

Fig. 3. Parameter space

$U_1, U_2, \ldots, U_n >$ results in a decrease in performance due to register spilling, all sets $V =< V_1, V_2, \ldots, V_n >$ such that $V_i \geq U_i$ can be pruned.

Starting points: At present, we use models to suggest a starting point for parameter values, based on the model's estimate of the optimal solution, and provide stopping criteria by estimating bounds for the performance of the optimized code variants.

3.2 AI Search Techniques

A multi-variable optimization problem, such as the one we are considering, can be cast as a search problem. The field of Artificial Intelligence (AI) has developed various search techniques for solving complex, multi-parameter optimization problems, which are characterized by very large and rough parameter landscapes. Search starts at some point in the parameter search space and progresses until a solution (a maximum in the objective function, such as performance) is found. Exhaustive algorithms, such as depth-first and breadth-first for searching trees, that evaluate every point in the parameter search space cannot be applied in practice due to the size of the search space. Methods such as hill climbing often fail due to roughness of landscape (that is, the existence of many local maxima). To address these issues, random and heuristic search algorithms have been developed [4].

Random search algorithms explore small neighborhoods of the search space at different points throughout the parameter space, keeping track of the quality of the solutions found. Typically, the search is terminated after some time when only a small portion of the search space has been explored. The resulting solution, while rarely the best, is often a good enough solution. Random algorithms such as GSAT have been shown to successfully solve hard optimization problems.

Heuristic search introduces a function that evaluates the quality of the solution. The main differences between random and heuristic search techniques are how the parameter space is explored and how the quality of a solution is evaluated. Heuristic hill climbing only explores a local neighborhood of current solution for better solution. In effect, the search is guided to a local maximum. Simulated annealing and genetic algorithms typically choose a new solution at random, thus avoiding being stuck in local maxima. Simulated annealing in particular first samples many points in the parameter space randomly, then settles down for finer local search in the best neighborhood. Best-first search algorithms, on the other hand, choose a new point in the path to the best solution based on a heuristic, or an evaluation function. A* algorithm is a best first algorithm that includes the cost of getting to the current point in the parameter space in its evaluation function. Backtracking, or returning to a previous best solution, can be implemented to continue exploration of profitable paths while avoiding getting stuck in dead ends.

In future work, we plan to evaluate this set of AI search techniques to identify the contribution of domain knowledge to speeding up the search process, and compare the resulting code quality when search time is constrained.

4 Conclusion

This paper shows how the problem of optimizing for multiple levels of the memory hierarchy can be recast as a multi-variable optimization problem. We formalized our approach as an AI search problem and identified search algorithms suitable for our optimization problem. We feel this work is an important first step in a general strategy for developing a principled approach to solving complex multi-variable optimization problems in a compiler, such as managing locality and communication in parallel codes.

References

1. C. Chen, J. Chame, and M. W. Hall. Combining models and guided empirical search to optimize for multiple levels of the memory hierarchy. In *Proc. of the International Symposium on Code Generation and Optimization*, Mar. 2005.
2. K. D. Cooper, P. J. Schielke, and D. Subramanian. Optimizing for reduced code space using genetic algorithms. In *Proc. of the Workshop on Languages, Compilers, and Tools for Embedded Systems*, May 1999.
3. M. Frigo. A fast Fourier transform compiler. In *Proc. of the Conference on Programming Language Design and Implementation*, May 1999.
4. N. J. Nilsson. *Artificial Intelligence: A New Synthesis.* Morgan Kaufman, San Francisco, CA, 1998.
5. M. Stephenson, S. Amarasinghe, M. Rinard, and U. O'Reilly. Meta optimization: Improving compiler heuristics with machine learning. In *Proc. of the Conference on Programming Language Design and Implementation*, June 2003.
6. X. Vera, J. Abella, A. González, and J. Llosa. Optimizing program locality through CMEs and GAs. In *Proc. of the International Conference on Parallel Architectures and Compilation Techniques*, Sept. 2003.
7. R. C. Whaley, A. Petitet, and J. J. Dongarra. Automated empirical optimization of software and the ATLAS project. *Parallel Computing*, 27(1–2):3–35, Jan. 2001.
8. K. Yotov, X. Li, G. Ren, M. Garzaran, D. Padua, K. Pingali, and P. Stodghill. Is search really necessary to generate high-performance BLAS? *Proceedings of the IEEE*, 93(2):358–386, Feb. 2005.

An Efficient Approach for Self-scheduling Parallel Loops on Multiprogrammed Parallel Computers

Arun Kejariwal[1], Alexandru Nicolau[1], and Constantine D. Polychronopoulos[2]

[1] Center for Embedded Computer Systems
University of California at Irvine
Irvine, CA 92697, USA
arun_kejariwal@computer.org, nicolau@cecs.uci.edu
http://www.cecs.uci.edu/

[2] Center for Supercomputing Research and Development
University of Illinois at Urbana-Champaign
Urbana, IL 61801, USA
cdp@csrd.uiuc.edu
http://www.csrd.uiuc.edu/

Abstract. Clusters and grids have increasingly become standard platforms for high performance computing as they provide extremely high execution rates with great cost effectiveness. Such systems are designed to support concurrent execution of multiple jobs. It calls for multiprogrammed scheduling of the different jobs for effective system utilization and for keeping average response times low. Although a significant amount of work has been done in scheduling parallel jobs on multiprocessor systems, the problem of scheduling parallel tasks of an individual job on a multiprogrammed parallel system has not been given enough attention so far. In this paper, we present a dynamic scheduling technique for scheduling iterations of a DOALL loop (of a single application) to achieve load balance between a given set of processors. Experimental results show the effectiveness of our approach.

1 Introduction

Although multiprogramming allows to better service multiple users, it also greatly complicates the scheduling process. This can be attributed to the space-time sharing of processors by the different jobs and the trade-off between the different performance metrics. Several techniques have been proposed for job scheduling with different objectives such as minimizing average mean response time, minimizing makespan, minimizing the tardiness [1,2]. Similarly, the impact of other parameters such as knowledge of job service demands, variability of job parallelism, preemption of jobs on performance of scheduling policies has also been investigated [3]. However, from the standpoint of performance of an individual job, the impact of the dynamics of a multiprogrammed system on the scheduling of parallel tasks of a single job has not been given enough attention.

E. Ayguadé et al. (Eds.): LCPC 2005, LNCS 4339, pp. 441–449, 2007.

One of the critical problems to be addressed in this context is how to efficiently allocate the parallel tasks amongst a given set of processors so as to distribute the computational load as evenly as possible, in order to minimize the maximum completion time.

In this paper, we address the problem of minimizing the maximum completion time of DOALL [4] loops. We model the problem as a task allocation problem wherein at any scheduling step, given a set of idle processors, one or more iterations are allocated to each processor. The key consideration in task allocation is the selection of the task size, i.e., the number of iterations constituting a task. While a small task size incurs significant scheduling overhead, a large task size results in load imbalance. Thus, the task allocation problem naturally reduces to determining the optimal task size in order to minimize the total execution time. Several static scheduling schemes have been proposed for the above, however, these do not perform well in a multiprogramming environment. Similarly, several dynamic scheduling schemes have been proposed to perform task allocation on the "on-the-fly" wherein one or more iterations are assigned to a processor whenever it becomes available. However, run-time scheduling overhead becomes a critical factor in the context of dynamic scheduling and can potentially account for a significant portion of the total execution time [5]. Thus, the idea is to avoid the use of the operating system in order to minimize the scheduling overhead, by instrumenting the code corresponding to the parallel loop such that the processors perform scheduling by themselves at run-time. *Self-scheduling* [6] exemplifies this philosophy where task size is determined by the processors themselves rather then by the operating system or a global control unit.

Several self-scheduling techniques have been proposed for scheduling parallel loops [7]. The computation of the task size (or chunk size) at any scheduling step (from hereon, we shall use the term *chunk size*, instead of task size, for literary consistency) in each is based on the number of remaining iterations. It assumes the availability of a "fixed" number of processors. However, the latter is not valid in context of multiprogramming. This can potentially give rise to "gaps" in processor availability, i.e., a processor may not be continuously available to the same job. For example, in Figure 1 processor P_2 is not available for $t \in (750, 850)$. The effect of varying number of processors and the presence of *gaps* on self-scheduling is not well understood. In this paper, we propose a novel scheduling technique, referred to as *Gap-Aware Self-Scheduling* (GAS), to capture the effect of presence of *gaps* in processors availability on self-scheduling. At each scheduling step, GAS computes the chunk size based on the number of remaining iterations and *gaps* in processor availability. We show that gap-aware computation of chunk size helps achieve load balance between the different processors.

The rest of the paper is organized as follows. In the next section, we present the motivation behind this work. In Section 3, we present our approach for dynamic scheduling of parallel loops on multiprogrammed parallel processor systems. Experimental setup and results are presented in Section 4.

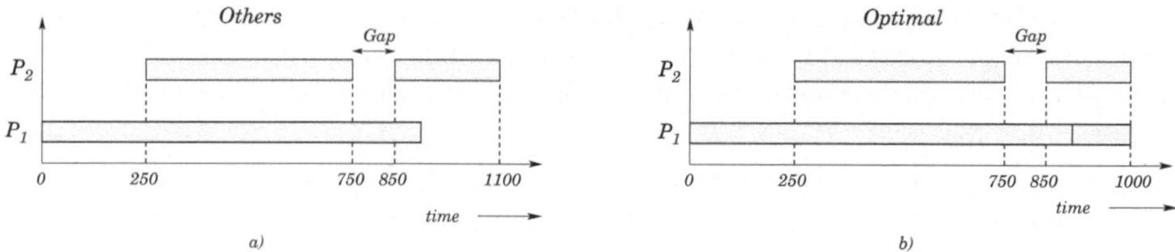

Fig. 1. a) Schedule obtained from the existing techniques; b) Optimal Schedule

2 Motivation

Though it is fairly intuitive that gaps reduce the degree of parallel execution, the impact of gaps on load balance between the processors is not obvious. In this work, we study the latter. From hereon, we shall consider only those gaps which can potentially result in load imbalance. Conditions for the existence of such gaps are discussed in detail in [8]. We argue that it is important to account for such gaps during the scheduling of parallel tasks — iterations of a (nested) parallel loop in our case.

For example, consider the schedules shown in Figure 1, where the length of a block represents the size of a chunk allocated to a processor at a given scheduling step. For simplicity, we assume that each iteration takes a unit amount of time. In Figure 1(a), we note that 250 iterations are allocated to processor P_2 at $t = 850$ regardless of the gap for $t \in (750, 850)$. Clearly, this results in uneven finishing times. On the other hand, the optimal schedule is shown in Figure 1(b) where the 250 iterations are distributed amongst the two processors to yield even finishing times. From above, we learn that it is critical to modulate the chunk size in presence of gaps in order to achieve better load balance.

3 The Approach

In this section we present the algorithm for our approach — *Gap-Aware Self-Scheduling* (GAS). Although several models have been proposed for work queues, viz., global, local and hybrid, in context of self-scheduling, we adopt the model proposed by Polychronopoulos and Kuck in [9] owing to its simplicity. Note that model selection per se is orthogonal to the concerns we address in this paper. The algorithm is designed for non-preemptive scheduling, whereby a chunk, once assigned to a processor may not be removed until it has finished execution. The design of our approach is guided by the following: a) how to capture the effects of gaps in processor availability; b) how to select $W_{\min}$, i.e., the minimum workload per chunk; and c) how to minimize the synchronization overhead between the processors. The rest of the section describes the different phases of our scheduling algorithm.

3.1 Determining the Gap Factor

As illustrated in Section 2, gaps in processor availability play a critical role in load balancing and directly relate to the efficiency of a dynamic scheduling scheme. In order to capture the effects of gaps on the performance of a self-schedule, we define a *displacement factor*, denoted by α, for online modulation of the chunk size. Let t_{last} denote the finishing time of the most recently completed chunk (on any processor) and let t_{first} denote the earliest finishing time of any chunk under execution (on any processor). At a given time instant t, the *displacement factor* is computed as follows:

$$\alpha(t) = \begin{cases} \frac{t - t_{\text{last}}}{t_{\text{first}} - t_{\text{last}}} & \exists \text{ a gap at time } t \\ 0 & \text{otherwise} \end{cases} \tag{1}$$

Intuitively, the *displacement factor* is a measure of the length of a gap w.r.t. the earliest finishing time of all the currently active processors. Arguably, one could potentially use α as the modulation factor. However, from Equation 1 we observe that when $t = t_{\text{last}}$, $\alpha = 0$. Thus, in this case the chunk size is reduced to zero. Consequently, α in itself cannot be used for chunk size modulation. In order to alleviate the problem, we define a *gap factor* as a function of α, denoted by $\beta(\alpha)$, and is computed as follows:

$$\beta(\alpha) = a\alpha^2 + b\alpha + c \tag{2}$$

Let us now revisit Equation 1 to study the behavior of α as $t \to t_{\text{first}}$ (by definition, $t \neq t_{\text{first}}$) as it is required to derive the boundary conditions for β.

$$\lim_{t \to t_{\text{first}}} \frac{t - t_{\text{last}}}{t_{\text{first}} - t_{\text{last}}} = 1 \quad \Rightarrow \alpha(t \to t_{\text{first}}) = 1 \tag{3}$$

From Equation 2, we deduce that when $\alpha = 0$, $\beta = 1$ and when $\alpha \to 1$ (refer to Equation 3), $\beta \to 1$. Note that the above conditions are compliant with the existence conditions of a gap [8] which form the very basis of online chunk size modulation. To summarize,

$$\beta = 1, \text{ when } \alpha = 0 \text{ and } \alpha = 1$$

Further, we assume that $\beta = 0.5$ when $\alpha = 0.5$. Solving for a, b and c using the above conditions yields the following:

$$\beta = 2\alpha(\alpha - 1) + 1 \tag{4}$$

3.2 Determining the Chunk Size

Markatos and LeBlanc showed that load imbalance is the prime factor governing the efficiency of a self-schedule [10]. The extent of load imbalance introduced depends on the amount of workload allocated relative to the amount of remaining workload. At any point in time, the amount of workload assigned to each processor[1] should be chosen such that the remaining workload is "sufficient" to balance the workload evenly, i.e., the difference in finishing times of the processors (at the end of the schedule) is minimal. With the above goal, we now derive the expression for the chunk size, denoted by Λ. In general, at any given time instant t in a self-schedule, the chunk size is defined as a multivariate function f, as given below:

$$\Lambda(t) = f(W_R(t), P, (t_{\text{first}} - t), \beta, W_{\text{min}}) \tag{5}$$

where $W_R(t)$ denotes the number of remaining iterations at time t and W_{min} denotes the minimum chunk size. In the rest of this subsection, we follow a step-by-step approach to derive the expression for chunk size.

A modified form of Λ (w.r.t. the one proposed in *guided self-scheduling* by Polychronopoulos and Kuck [9]) is given by:[2]

$$\Lambda(t) = \left\lceil \frac{W_R(t)}{1.5P} \right\rceil \tag{6}$$

However, the chunk size as defined above can potentially increase the scheduling overhead as illustrated by the following example.

Example 1. *Consider a (coalesced) parallel loop with 3000 iterations with identical workloads and a system of two processors P_1 and P_2, where P_1 is available at $t = 0$ and P_2 is available at $t = 200$ in case a) and at $t = 900$ in case b). For simplicity of exposition, we assume that there do not exist gaps in processor availability.*

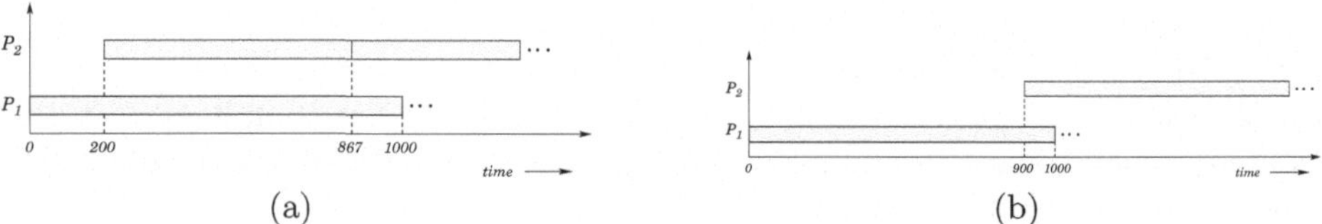

Fig. 2. Example partial schedules

Consider the partial self-schedule shown in Figure 2(a). From the figure, we observe that at $t = 200$, P_2 is assigned only 667 iterations. This implies that P_2 would finish before P_1 finishes and would result in "early" rescheduling of P_2. Clearly, this incurs additional scheduling overhead without any increase in parallel execution. In order to alleviate the above, we propose to "delay" the rescheduling of P_2 by allocating 800 iterations at time $t = 200$. In such cases, we argue to allocate $(t_{first} - t)$ number of iterations. This minimizes the number of allocation points without loss in parallel execution.

[1] Recall that multiple processors may be available at the same time.

[2] For derivation of Equation 6, the reader is referred to [8].

However, as $t \rightarrow t_{first}$ *the above strategy may result in allocation of small chunks which adversely affects the performance of a self-schedule [9]. For example, consider the partial schedule shown in Figure 2(b), where* P_2 *is available at time* $t = 900$*. In this case, we assign* 667 *iterations to* P_2 *instead of* 100 $(= t_{first} - t)$ *iterations so as to minimize the number of allocations, thereby reducing the scheduling overhead.*

Based on the discussion of Example 1 we refine the expression for computation of chunk size (given in Equation 6) to balance the trade-off between maximizing parallel execution and minimizing scheduling overhead. For this, we introduce a new parammeter called *lag*, as defined below:

$$lag(t) = \begin{cases} t_{\text{first}} - t & \exists \text{ a gap at time } t \\ 0 & \text{otherwise} \end{cases} \tag{7}$$

The modified expression for chunk size is given as follows:

$$\Lambda(t) = \max\left(lag(t), \left\lceil \frac{W_R(t)}{1.5P} \right\rceil\right) \tag{8}$$

Equation 8 implicitly assumes that for all t in a self-schedule $t_{\text{first}} - t < W_R$. It is easy to see that the same is valid for $P \geq 2$ as at any scheduling step less than half of the remaining number of iterations are allocated. Next, we incorporate the effect of existence of gaps in processor availability in the expression for chunk size.

$$\Lambda(t) = \max\left(lag(t), \left\lceil \frac{\beta\, W_R(t)}{1.5P} \right\rceil\right) \tag{9}$$

The exponential decrease of chunk size during self-scheduling results in scheduling of individual iterations towards the end of the schedule. The latter incurs high scheduling overhead. In order to alleviate this the chunk size is restricted to a pre-defined quantum, denoted by $W_{\min}$ (for further details the reader is referred to [9]). We further refine the expression of chunk size to capture $W_{\min}$ and is given as follows:

$$\boxed{\Lambda(t) = \max\left(W_{\min}, \max\left(lag(t), \left\lceil \frac{\beta\, W_R(t)}{1.5P} \right\rceil\right)\right)} \tag{10}$$

The parameter $W_{\min}$ is application and input data dependent. The selection of an appropriate value for $W_{\min}$ is critical for the existing self-scheduling schemes. While a small value of $W_{\min}$ may result in scheduling of individual iterations (irrespective of their workload) at the end which may incur significant synchronization overhead, whereas a large value of $W_{\min}$ may lead to load imbalance. A formal description of the algorithm for GAS is presented as Algorithm 1.

The discussion in this subsection so far has been based on the assumption that iterations have equal workloads (or execution times). However, the workload

Algorithm 1. Gap-Aware Self-Scheduling

Input : A N-dimensional iteration space Γ and P processors. Note that at any given time instant, all the processors may be available.

Output : A near-optimal dynamic schedule of Γ w.r.t. load balance amongst the different processors and schedule length.

```
repeat
  /* Self-schedule the remaining iterations at time t */
  p_f ← 0
  Compute lag(t) using Equation 7
  Compute the gap factor β(t) using Equation 4
  Compute the chunk size Λ(t) using Equation 10
  for each available processor do
    Compute index range for each processor
    Assign the corresponding iterations to the processor
    p_f ← p_f + 1
  end for

  /* Update the remaining workload */
  W ← W − Λ(t) × p_f
until W > 0
```

of individual iterations may differ from each other when there are conditional statements in the loop; even otherwise, their workloads may differ due to system variations such as data access latency, network interference and operating system. Even in such cases, our gap-driven chunk size modulation approach is still applicable. A detailed discussion of this beyond the scope of this paper.

4 Experiments

We implemented a simulator to compare the performance of GAS with the "upper algorithm" of the *adaptive self-tuning scheduling* scheme [11] (referred to as HLS in the rest of the paper). For our experiments, we extracted kernels (parallel nested loops) from LAMMPS [12] (a classical molecular dynamics code designed to simulate systems at the atomic and molecular level) and DAKOTA [13] (a design analysis kit for optimization and terascale applications). The execution time of the loops was determined via profiling. A random generator was used for dynamic processor allocation; random numbers are generated using a uniform distribution. The simulator supports uneven start times of the processors. Further, it also accounts for the synchronization overhead. Processors are assumed to access the shared variables, in our case loop indexes, using appropriate synchronization primitives. A maximum of 2000 processors was assumed

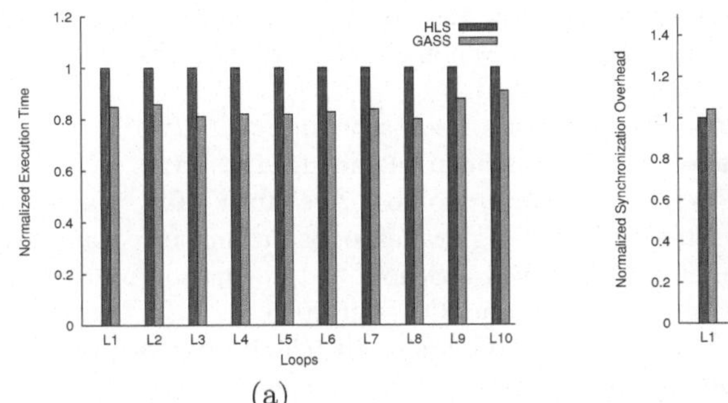

(a)

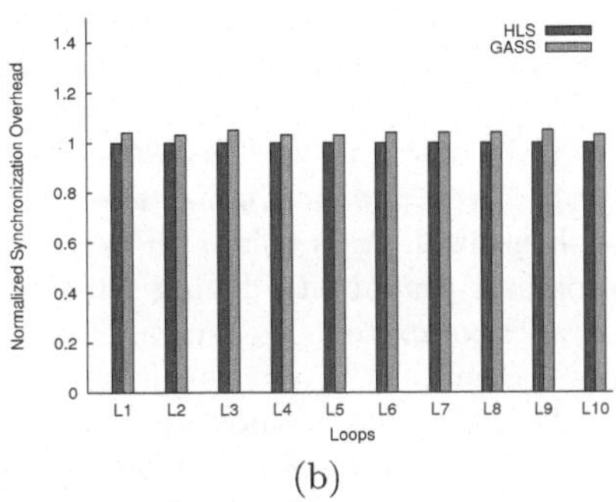

(b)

Fig. 3. a) Performance comparison; b) Synchronization overhead

as commonly found in clusters and grids. Recall that at any given scheduling step, the number of processors available is *not* fixed. The loops were dynamically scheduled using Algorithm 1.

Figure 3(a) presents a performance comparison between HLS and GAS. The execution times were computed as an average of execution times of 10 simulation runs with different processor availability configurations. From the figure, we note that our approach achieves a speedup of 10–15%. As explained earlier, the speed up can be attributed to the better load balance between the different processors which facilitates higher degree of parallel execution. In addition, it enables better processor utilization.

From Figure 3(b) we observe that the GAS incurs 3% (on an average) synchronization overhead. It can be attributed to the overhead incurred in online update of the expected workload of the remaining iterations. However, the performance gain obtained by online chunk size modulation outweighs the synchronization overhead.

References

1. R. W. Conway, W. L. Maxwell, and L. W. Miller. *Theory of scheduling.* Addison-Wesley, Reading, MA, 1967.
2. D. G. Feitelson. A survey of scheduling in multiprogrammed parallel systems. Technical Report RC 19790(87657), IBM T. J. Watson Research Center, February 1995.
3. S. Majumdar, D. L. Eager, and R. B. Bunt. Scheduling in multiprogrammed parallel systems. In *Proceedings of the 1988 ACM SIGMETRICS conference on Measurement and modeling of computer systems*, pages 104–113, Santa Fe, NM, 1988.
4. S. Lundstrom and G. Barnes. A controllable MIMD architectures. In *Proceedings of the 1980 International Conference on Parallel Processing*, St. Charles, IL, August 1980.
5. C. P. Kruskal and A. Weiss. Allocating independent subtasks on parallel processors. *IEEE Transactions on Software Engineering*, 11(10):1001–1016, 1985.

6. B. J. Smith. Architecture and applications of the HEP multiprocessor computer system. In *Proceedings of SPIE - Real-Time Signal Processing IV*, pages 241–248, 1981.
7. A. Kejariwal and A. Nicolau. Reading list of self-scheduling of parallel loops. http://www.ics.uci.edu/~akejariw/SelfScheduleReadingList.pdf.
8. A. Kejariwal, A. Nicolau, and C. D. Polychronopoulos. Accounting for "Gaps" in processor availability during self-scheduling of parallel loops on multiprogrammed parallel computers. Technical Report TR-05-14, School of Information and Computer Science, University of California at Irvine, October 2005.
9. C. D. Polychronopoulos and D. J. Kuck. Guided self-scheduling: A practical scheduling scheme for parallel supercomputers. *IEEE Transactions on Computers*, 36(12):1425–1439, 1987.
10. E. Markatos and T. LeBlanc. Using processor affinity in loop scheduling on shared-memory multiprocessors. *IEEE Transactions on Parallel and Distributed Systems*, 5(4):379–400, April 1994.
11. Y. Zhang, M. Burcea, V. Cheng, R. Ho, and M. Voss. An adaptive OpenMP loop scheduler for hyperthreaded SMPs. In *Proceedings of the 17th International Conference for Parallel and Distributed Computing Systems*, San Francisco, CA, 2004.
12. LAMMPS. http://www.cs.sandia.gov/~sjplimp/lammps.html.
13. DAKOTA. http://endo.sandia.gov/DAKOTA/software.html.

Dynamic Compilation for Reducing Energy Consumption of I/O-Intensive Applications*

Seung Woo Son[1], Guangyu Chen[1], Mahmut Kandemir[1], and Alok Choudhary[2]

[1] Pennsylvania State University, University Park PA 16802, USA
{sson,gchen,kandemir}@cse.psu.edu
[2] Northwestern University, Evanston IL 60208, USA
choudhar@ece.northwestern.edu

Abstract. Tera-scale high-performance computing has enabled scientists to tackle very large and computationally challenging scientific problems, making the advancement of scientific discovery at a faster pace. However, as computing scales to levels never seen before, it also becomes extremely data intensive, I/O intensive, and energy consuming. Amongst these, I/O is becoming a major bottleneck, impeding the expected pace of scientific discovery and analysis of data. Furthermore, the applications are becoming increasingly dynamic in terms of their computation patterns as well as data access patterns to cope with larger problems and data sizes. Due to the complexities of systems and applications and their high energy consumptions, it is, therefore, very important to address research issues and develop dynamic techniques at the level of run-time systems and compilers to scale I/O in the right proportions. This paper presents the details of a dynamic compilation framework developed specifically for I/O-intensive large-scale applications. Our dynamic compilation framework includes a set of powerful I/O optimizations designed to minimize execution cycles and energy consumption, and generates results that are competitive with hand-optimized codes in terms of energy consumption.

1 Introduction and Motivation

Tera-scale high-performance computing has enabled scientists to tackle very large and computationally challenging problems, such as those found in the scientific computing domain. This in turn helps advancement of scientific discovery at a faster pace. However, as computing scales to levels never seen before, it also becomes extremely data intensive, I/O intensive, and energy consuming. Thus, I/O is becoming a major bottleneck, slowing the expected pace of scientific discovery and analysis of data. This high I/O intensiveness also means that a significant portion of the energy consumption during the execution of high-performance applications occurs in the I/O systems. Furthermore, to cope with larger problems and data sizes, models and applications are being designed to be dynamic in nature. That is, the applications are becoming increasingly dynamic [8,9] in terms of their computation patterns and data access patterns (e.g., changing smaller structured mesh based designs to dynamic adaptive mesh refinement techniques for algorithm scalability, or dynamically analyzing the data to determine interesting features

* This work is supported by NSF grants #0444158, #0406340, #0093082 and a grant from GSRC.

E. Ayguadé et al. (Eds.): LCPC 2005, LNCS 4339, pp. 450–457, 2007.

or events to steer computation, etc.). Due to the complexities of systems and applications, it is, therefore, very important to address research issues and develop techniques at the level of run-time systems and compilers to scale I/O in the right proportions. If such techniques are not developed, users will be overwhelmed with I/O bottlenecks since the complexities of large-scale systems do not lend to manual optimizations.

Consider a typical scientific exploration process that involves large-scale simulations. It usually has several phases including simulation runs, post-processing, and analysis. The simulation phase consists of intensive computations that generate large quantities of data. The data need to be saved quickly as they are generated so that the computation is not slowed down because of I/O bottlenecks. In some cases, the simulation can benefit from dynamic steering (which means dynamically changing I/O access patterns), by quickly analyzing intermediate results. A subsequent phase usually requires the post-processing of the simulation data. This may include transformation of the data from one format (storage layout) to another, summarization of the data, reorganization of the data at run-time to facilitate future use efficiently and most effectively. In this phase, a large volume of data has to be read efficiently, and a large volume of data may be generated as well. In the next phase, the analysis phase, relevant subsets of the data need to be selected and analyzed based on the properties of the data (that is, the processing and access patterns are data dependent and dynamic). The analysis phase may require methods that discover specific patterns and relationships in the data as well as capturing inter-relationships between the different datasets. Clearly, the complexities of various phases and steps are tremendous, and all these phases involve energy-consuming operations. Data read/write, processing, organization and flow are major components and represent a major bottleneck today and for the future. An important impact of this I/O intensiveness of large-scale applications is the increased energy consumption on the I/O system. Frequent accesses to parallel disks, for example, can be responsible from a significant fraction of overall power budget, as noted by several prior studies such as [1,2].

As a result of high-level dynamic changes in the application behavior and/or data layout, two important entities also change: *data access pattern* (i.e., how the datasets are accessed – direction of access, volume of access, frequency of access, etc) and *I/O performance* (e.g., the time spent in I/O activities and energy consumption on the disk subsystem). A data-intensive application can benefit a lot if these changes in its I/O access pattern and I/O performance can be captured and feedback to a *dynamic compiler* that can re-compile the application to take the best advantage of the changing behavior and to improve the time/energy spent in I/O.

This paper explores dynamic compilation for I/O-intensive applications. Specifically, we present an infrastructure that contains a *dynamic optimizing compiler/linker*, a *high-level I/O library* (called HLL), a *mini database system* (a *metadata manager*), and a *layout manager* that together manage a parallel, hierarchical storage system The framework provides I/O-optimized access to datasets regardless of the type of the media they currently reside on, what their storage layouts are, or where the media is located. Where/how the datasets are stored and in what type of media they are stored are hidden from the user. This allows the user applications to access a dataset the same way regardless of its current location and storage layout. The compiler, the HLL, the mini database, and the layout manager cooperate to maintain this uniform storage system view. While the dynamic compilation framework discussed in this paper can be used for optimizing both performance and power/energy, in this paper we focus exclusively on energy reduction on the I/O system.

The rest of this paper is organized as follows. Section 2 discusses the major components of our system at a high-level. Since the main focus of this paper is the dynamic compiler, Section 3 focuses on the compiler alone and discusses the suite of I/O optimizations it employs. Finally, Section 4 concludes the paper with a summary of our major contributions.

2 Dynamic Compilation Infrastructure

Figure 1 illustrates the major components of our dynamic compilation framework for I/O-intensive parallel applications. The storage system is assumed to be a parallel, hierarchical storage architecture that has typically a disk-based layer such as NAS (Network Attached Storage) [10] or SAN (Storage Area Network). We also assume that there is a tertiary storage (tape system) that serves as the next level in the storage hierarchy. In this storage architecture, the most critical issue is to schedule and coordinate accesses to data, and manage the data-flow between the different components. We assume that this storage system is used by parallel applications.

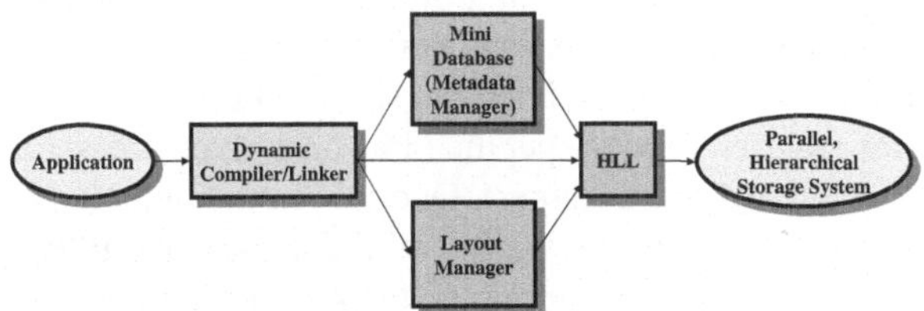

Fig. 1. High-level view of the dynamic compilation approach

The main goal of the dynamic compilation support discussed in this paper is to identify and implement various I/O optimizations dynamically using the features provided in the HLL. The HLL's capabilities include an interface that facilities the propagation of I/O access patterns and hints for run-time optimizations. Furthermore, to take advantage of the past access patterns from the application, the HLL makes use of a mini database (called the metadata manager) that maintains information about the I/O access patterns as well as relationships among datasets. This is akin to the locality concept in memories. For example, spatial locality says that data items that are close in data space tend to be accessed together and this locality is determined using the addresses of data items. Our approach identifies and takes advantage of so-called dataset locality, which indicates which datasets tend to be accessed together. The metadata stored in the mini database contains such information, and is periodically updated during the course of execution. The goal of the mini database is to learn and store access patterns at various levels and maintain I/O performance statistics. It does not perform I/O in our implementation. Since the proposed analyses for dynamic compilation are oriented towards exploiting the I/O optimizations supported by the HLL, we first explain the HLL and briefly discuss its functionality and user interface.

The HLL allows an application to access data located in the storage hierarchy via a simple interface expressed in terms of datasets (and arbitrary rectilinear regions of datasets). The main difference between the HLL and the previous array-oriented run-time I/O libraries (e.g., Passion [5,6] and Panda [12]) is that the HLL maintains the same abstraction (dataset name) across an entire storage hierarchy, and that it accommodates storage hierarchy-specific dynamic I/O optimizations.

The routines in the HLL can be divided into four major groups based on their functionality: Initialization/Finalization Routines, Data Access Routines, Data Movement Routines, and Hint-Related Routines/Queries. Each routine takes a processor id as one of its input parameters, and is invoked by each participating processor. This enables the HLL to see the global picture (which includes the I/O access pattern of each processor) in its entirety. Initialization/finalization routines are used to initialize the library buffers and metadata structures (in the mini database), and finalize them when all the work is done. Data access routines manage the data flow between storage devices and memory. An arbitrary rectilinear portion of a dataset can be read or written using these routines. Using a read routine, for example, the HLL can bring a rectangular portion of a dataset from tape (or disk) to memory. Data movement routines are used to transfer data between storage devices other than memory. These provide a powerful abstraction by expressing the data movement between any storage device pair as a simple copy operation; moreover, these routines work on arbitrary rectilinear portions of datasets. All these routines also have their asynchronous counterparts that return the control to the application code immediately (but perform the specified operation at the background). Hint-related routines are used to pass specific hints on a given dataset to the HLL (hints and queries are not discussed in this paper). Queries, on the other hand, are used by the HLL to extract specific information from the mini database about the datasets such as their current locations in the storage hierarchy, the sizes of their subfiles, etc.

The HLL contains a large set of I/O optimizations (implemented as library routines) that can be incorporated into the application in an on-demand fashion using dynamic linking. However, if a desired I/O optimization (for the best I/O performance and energy savings) is not available in the HLL, the proposed dynamic compiler (that will be described shortly) generates the optimized version by making use of the already available routines (in the HLL).

3 Details of the Dynamic Compilation Framework

Our dynamic compiler has four major components as depicted in Figure 2: (1) dynamic compiler; (2) dynamic linker; (3) performance tracer; and (4) steering unit. The performance tracer is responsible from collecting both I/O access pattern information and performance/energy statistics. The I/O access pattern information includes access directions for data arrays (e.g., row-wise vs. column-wise accesses), whether the dataset is accessed in the read-write mode or mostly in the read-only mode, which datasets are accessed with temporal affinity, how frequently the datasets are accessed, and similar information that indicates how different datasets are manipulated by the application.

Table 1. An illustration of performance optimization rules incorporated for data access strategies for efficient I/O. The "Invoked if" column lists the conditions under which the corresponding optimization is invoked by the dynamic compiler.

Optimization	Brief Explanation	Invoked if
Collective I/O (CIO)	Distributing the I/O requests of different processors processor among them so that each accesses as many consecutive data as possible it involves some extra communication between processors.	Access pattern of the data is different from its storage pattern, and multiple processors are use to access the data.
Subfiling (SUB)	Dividing large array into subarrays to reduce transfer latency between different levels of the storage hierarchy	A small subregion of a file is accessed. with high temporal locality.

The performance statistics include the number of accesses to different storage units (e.g., tapes, disks), misses in disk/file caches, and the time spent in I/O and the energy consumption in different storage elements.

After collecting this information from the metadata manager, the performance tracer passes it to the steering unit (note that the performance analyzer collects only application-specific data from the metadata manager, which keeps metadata for different entities and applications). The main responsibility of the steering unit is to decide whether any dynamic linking and/or compilation needs to be performed, and if so, select the most appropriate libraries and/or optimizations to be invoked . While different triggering criteria can be used for determining whether dynamic compilation/linking is necessary at a particular point during execution, in this work we use a data structure centered approach as explained in rest of this section. As shown in Figure 2, our dynamic compiler and linker are invoked by the steering unit.

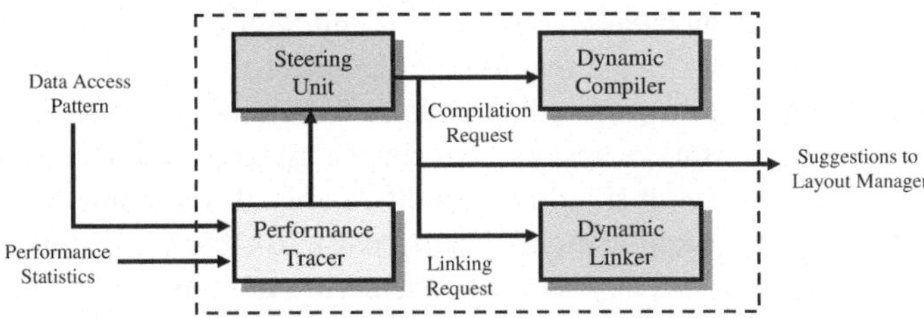

Fig. 2. Components of the dynamic compilation framework

Table 1 lists the I/O optimizations currently supported by our dynamic compilation framework. The second column briefly describes each optimization, and the third column gives the condition(s) under which each optimization is to be invoked dynamically at run-time.

In collective I/O, small disk requests are merged into fewer larger requests to minimize the number of times the disks are accessed. While it can be used for both read and write operations, we describe it here only for the read operations. In two-phase I/O [6], a client-side collective I/O implementation, the processors first communicate with each other so that each processor knows the total data that need to be read from the disk system. In the second step, they decide what data each processor needs to read so that the number of disk accesses is minimized. In the next step, the processors perform disk accesses (in parallel). In the last step, they engage in interprocessor communication so that each data item is transferred to its original requester. It needs to be noted that collective I/O, where applicable, can be beneficial from the energy consumption viewpoint since it can reduce the number of disk accesses. While it is true that it also causes some extra interprocessor data communication, the energy incurred by these communications is normally very small compared to the energy gains achieved on the disk system.

Our dynamic compilation analysis for collective I/O has four components: (1) Determining I/O access pattern to the data; (2) Determining storage pattern (layout) of the data; (3) Comparing access and storage patterns to decide whether to apply collective I/O or not; and (4) Modifying the code dynamically if necessary. The access pattern information is obtained from the performance tracer, which keeps track of the dynamic I/O access patterns. The storage pattern indicates how the data is stored in the storage system, and is maintained by our metadata manager. If these two patterns do not match collective I/O is expected to be useful and can reduce energy consumption, and the steering unit either links the appropriate library routine (in the HLL) that implements collective I/O (if such a library routine is available), or dynamically recompiles the application code (that is, the application code is compiled to implement collective I/O using the existing I/O support provided by the HLL). This dynamic compilation is confined to the relevant part(s) of the code, that is, typically the loop nest (or a set of related loop nests) that accesses the data in question. Therefore, the energy spent during dynamic compilation is not expected to be excessive.

It is also possible that the steering unit may decide a "storage layout (pattern) change" for the dataset in question. This may be required in cases where the desired modification to the application code may not preserve the original semantics of the application (hence, it is not legal). In such cases, the steering unit advises the layout manager (see Figures 1 and Figure 2) to change the storage layout of the data. It should be noted that the layout manager can receive such requests from multiple applications running concurrently on the same storage system, and since a given dataset can be accessed by multiple applications, its layout should be modified only if it is going to be beneficial globally (i.e., from multiple applications' perspective). In other words, the steering unit of our framework just makes a suggestion (considering only one application), and the layout manager is free to obey it or not. In this paper, however, we do not evaluate the behavior of layout optimizer.

It should be emphasized that applying I/O optimizations such as collective I/O in a dynamic compilation/linking based setting brings some unique benefits. For example, in many cases, the data access patterns cannot be extracted statically. Consequently, a static compiler either cannot apply collective I/O (as it does not know the access pattern) or can apply it conservatively, which means reduced energy savings. Also, in some cases, the same data can be shared by multiple applications. It is possible that, between two successive accesses by the same application to the same dataset, the layout of data could be modified. In such a case, we need to change the I/O access strategy of the application on-the-fly to take advantage of the new storage layout. Dynamic compilation and linking allow us adapt the I/O access behavior to the current status (layout, location) of the data.

The second optimization for which we discuss the necessary dynamic compilation support in this paper is subfiling [11]. In many I/O-intensive applications such as terrain imaging, document imaging, and visualization, although the datasets manipulated are very large, at a given time, only small portions (regions of interest) of the datasets are used. Unfortunately, most current solutions to large-scale data movement across the storage hierarchies proposed by hierarchical storage management systems [7,3,4] retrieve the entire file that contains the dataset in question. This increases latency enormously, and also wastes significant bandwidth. In addition, this also increases the energy consumption significantly. For example, to satisfy a program request of 50 KB of data, they retrieve, say, an entire 8 GB file from tape to disk. In fact, this limitation forces the application programmers/users to break their datasets into small, individually addressable objects, thereby cluttering the storage space and making file management very difficult. In addition, this process is very time consuming and error-prone. Instead, subfiling moves a minimum amount of data between storage devices when satisfying a given program's I/O requirements. This is achieved by breaking up the large datasets into uniform, small-sized chunks, each of which is stored as a subfile in the storage hierarchy. As mentioned above, if we do not employ any subfiling, a large file needs to be transferred from tape to disk. This increases both access latency and energy consumption. Therefore, subfiling is expected to bring energy benefits in both tape and disk accesses (though in this paper we focus only on the disk energy benefits). Then, an important job of the dynamic compilation framework is to determine the optimal chunk size and restructure the code on-the-fly based on it. Our approach achieves this by exploiting the data access pattern information. Specifically, the data access pattern information gives us the type and volume of data reuse. For example, if the accesses are localized (clustered) in small regions of the dataset, the chunk size should be kept small; otherwise, we can use a large chunk size. It should also be observed that using subfiling in conjunction with dynamic compilation brings an important advantage over the static compilation-directed subfiling. If we do not use dynamic compilation, then we are forced to select a specific chunk size (most probably based on the profile data), generate code customized for that size, and use that size throughout the execution. In comparison, with the dynamic compilation support, we can change the chunk size during the course of execution, thus better adapting to the dynamic changes in the I/O access patterns.

While dynamic compilation has the potential for improving the performance of I/O-intensive applications and reducing their energy consumptions, it also comes with its own costs that need to be accounted for. Therefore, our dynamic compilation framework should be selective in applying I/O optimizations. However, an overly selective compiler will not work well either as it can miss lots of optimization opportunities. Our approach maintains cost information within the metadata manager. This cost information consists of the time/energy overhead incurred for each I/O optimization for the last couple of invocations. When the next time the same I/O optimization is needed, the steering unit obtains this cost information from the metadata manager (through the performance tracer) quickly, and uses it in deciding whether the optimization in question should really be applied. A similar cost-benefit tradeoff is also carried out by the layout manager with one major difference. Unlike the dynamic compiler (which modifies the generated code), the layout manager modifies the storage layout of the data. And, since a given dataset can be manipulated by different applications in different fashions, the changes to its layout should be performed with extreme care. A further argument for this is the fact that a typical layout change in the storage system can be much more expensive (in terms of the number of execution cycles it takes and energy consumption) than a typical dynamic code restructuring at run-time.

4 Concluding Remarks

This paper has presented the structure and operation of a dynamic compilation infrastructure that specifically targets I/O-intensive scientific applications. Focusing on the energy benefits of dynamic compilation in this application domain, we have described dynamic compilation framework that employs a suite of I/O optimizations, so that it allows I/O-intensive applications to optimize energy savings.

References

1. J. Chase, D. Anderson, P. Thackar, A. Vahdat, and R. Boyle, "Managing Energy and Server Resources in Hosting Centers," In *Proc. of the 18th Symposium on Operating Systems Principles*, pages 103-116, October 2001.
2. J. Chase and R. Doyle, "Balance of Power: Energy Management for Server Clusters," In *Proc. of the 8th Workshop on Hot Topics in Operating Systems*, page 165, May 2001.
3. L. T. Chen, R. Drach, M. Keating, S. Louis, D. Rotem, and A. Shoshani, "Efficient Organization and Access of Multi-Dimensional Datasets on Tertiary Storage Systems," *Information Systems Journal* 20(2): 155–183, 1995.
4. L. T. Chen, R. Drach, M. Keating, S. Louis, D. Rotem, and A. Shoshani, "Optimizing Tertiary Storage Organization and Access for Spatio-Temporal Datasets," In *Proc. of the NASA Goddard Conference on Mass Storage Systems*, 1995.
5. A. Choudhary, R. Thakur, R. Bordawekar, S. More, and S. Kutipidi, "PASSION: Optimized Parallel I/O," *IEEE Computer*, June 1996.
6. A. Choudhary, R. Bordawekar, M. Harry, R. Krishnaiyer, R. Ponnusamy, T. Singh, and R. Thakur, "PASSION: Parallel and Scalable Software for Input-Output," *NPAC Technical Report SCCS-636*, Syracuse, NY, September 1994.
7. R. A. Coyne, H. Hulen, and R. Watson, "The High-Performance Storage System," In *Proc. of Supercomputing*, Portland, OR, November 1993.
8. F. Darema, "Dynamic Data Driven Applications Systems: A New Paradigm for Application Simulations and Measurements," In *International Conference on Computational Science*, pages 662–669, 2004.
9. F. Darema, "Dynamic Data Driven Applications Systems: New Capabilities for Application Simulations and Measurements," In *International Conference on Computational Science*, pages 610–615, 2005.
10. G. Gibson and R. Van Meter, "Network Attached Storage Architecture," *Communications of the ACM*, 43(11). November 2000.
11. G. Memik, M. Kandemir, A. Choudhary, "APRIL: A Run-Time Library for Tape Resident Data," In *Proc. of the NASA Goddard Conference on Mass Storage Systems and Technologies*, Baltimore, MD, April 2000.
12. K. E. Seamons, Y. Chen, P. Jones, J. Jozwiak, and M. Winslett, "Server-Directed Collective I/O in Panda," In *Proc. of Supercomputing*, San Diego, CA, December 1995.

Supporting SELL for High-Performance Computing

Bjarne Stroustrup and Gabriel Dos Reis

Department of Computer Science
Texas A&M University
College Station, TX 77843-3112

Abstract. We briefly introduce the notion of *Semantically Enhanced Library Languages*, SELL, as a practical and economical alternative to special-purpose programming languages for high-performance computing. Then we describe the *Pivot* infrastructure for program analysis and transformation that is our main tool for supporting SELL. Finally, we outline how the IPR (The Pivot's *Internal Program Representation*) can be used to represent central notions of high-performance computing, such as parallelizable array operations. Our focus is on a broad exposition of ideas, rather than technical details[1].

1 Languages and Libraries

For ease of programming, portability, and acceptable performance, we design and implement special-purpose programming languages for high-performance computing [15]. Alternatively, we can use a *Semantically Enhanced Library Language.* A SELL is a language created by extending a programming language (usually a popular general-purpose programming language) with a library providing the desired added functionality and then using a tool to provide the desired semantic guarantees needed to reach a goal (often a higher level semantics, absence of certain kinds of errors, or library-specific optimizations) [12]. This paper focuses on a tool, *The Pivot*, being developed to support SELLs in ISO C++ [11,5] and its application to High-Performance Computing.

2 A Brief Overview of the Pivot

The Pivot is a general framework for the analysis and transformation of C++ programs. It is designed to handle the complete ISO C++, especially more advanced uses of templates and including some proposed C++0x features. It is compiler independent. The central part of the Pivot is a fully typed abstract syntax tree called IPR (*Internal Program Representation*).

[1] This is the "cut" or "abbreviated" version of this paper. For a full version, see `http://www.research.att.com/~bs/papers.html`

E. Ayguadé et al. (Eds.): LCPC 2005, LNCS 4339, pp. 458–465, 2007.

There are lots of (more than 20) tools for static analysis and transformation of C++ programs, e.g. [7,2,8,6]. However, few — if any — handle all of ISO Standard C++, most are specialized to particular forms of analysis or transformation, and few will work well in combination with other tools. We are particularly interested in advanced uses of templates as used in generic programming, template meta-programming, and experimental uses of libraries as the basis of language extension. For that, we need a representation that deals with types as first-class citizens and allows analysis and transformation based on their properties. In the C++ community, this is discussed under the heading of *concepts* and is likely to receive significant language support in the next ISO C++ standard (C++0x) [13,9,14,3]. We use the word concept to a designate collection of properties that describes usage of values and types. From the point of view of support for HPC — and for the provision of special-purpose facilities in general — a concept can be seen as a way of specifying new types with associated semantics without the modification of compilers or new syntax. That done, the SELL approach then uses the concepts as a hook for semantic properties beyond what C++ offers.

This paper is an overview and will not go into details of concepts, the Pivot, the IPR, or our initial uses.

2.1 System Organization

To get IPR from a program, we need a compiler. Only a compiler "knows" enough about a C++ program to represent it completely with syntactic and type information in a useful form. In particular, a simple parser doesn't understand types well enough to do a credible general job. We interface to a compiler in some appropriate and minimally invasive fashion. A compiler-specific IPR generator produces IPR on a per-translation-unit basis. Applications interface to "code" through the IPR interface. So as not to run the compiler all the time and to be able to store and merge translation units without compiler intervention, we can produce a persistent form of IPR called XPR (*eXternal Program Representation*).

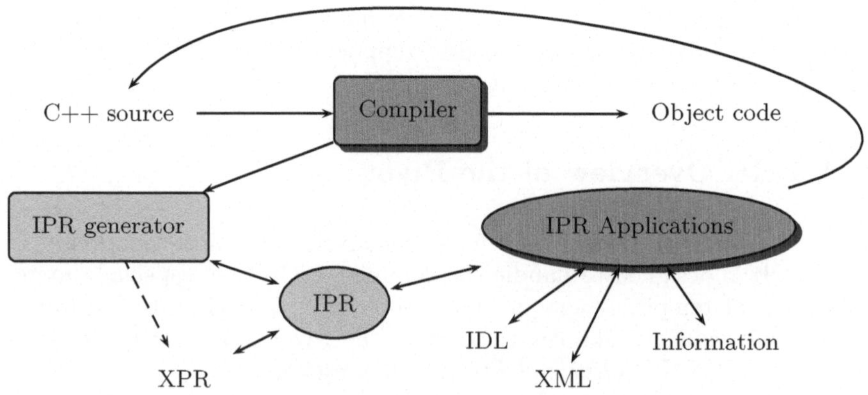

Fig. 1. An overview of *The Pivot* infrastructure

From a compiler, we generate IPR containing fully typed abstract syntax trees. In particular, every use of a function name and operator is resolved to its proper declaration, all scope resolution is done, and all implicit calls of constructors and destructors are known. We have IPR generators from GCC and EDG, so that the Pivot is not compiler specific. The reason for preserving compiler independence is to maximize the portability of IPR-based tools. A tool that is built directly on a compiler's internal interface cannot easily be ported to another compiler. In fact, the interfaces to current C++ compilers' data structures for syntax and type information differ dramatically and most are de facto inaccessible for technical, commercial, or political reasons.

Early versions of this system (and its precursors) have been used to write pretty printers, generate XML for C++ source, CORBA IDL from C++ classes, and distributed programs using C++ source augmented with a library defining modularity.

The XPR is a compact and human readable ASCII representation of IPR. XPR can be used as a transfer format between two different runs of the Pivot or two different implementations of the IPR. The library implementing the IPR is elegant, compact, and efficient. It is just 2,500 lines of C++ to cope with all of C++, unify types (and literals and anything else we might want to unify), and manage memory.

2.2 IPR Principles

The IPR is compact, completely typed (every entity has a type, even types), representation with an interface consisting of abstract classes. The IPR has a unified representation so that its memory consumption is minimal. For example there will be only one node representing the type `int` and only one node representing the integer value `42` in a program that uses those two entities. This minimalism (in time and space) is key to its use for large systems — million line programs are no longer rare.

The IPR does its own memory management so users do not have to keep track of created objects. It is arguably optimal in the number of indirections needed to access a given piece of information. The IPR is minimal in that it holds only information directly present in the C++ source. IPR can be annotated by the user and flow graphs can be generated. However, that's considered jobs for IPR applications rather than something belonging to the core framework itself. In particular, traversal of C++ code represented as IPR can be done in several ways, including "ordinary graph traversal code", visitors [4], iterators [10,11], or tools such as Rose [7]. The needs of the application — rather than the IPR — determines what traversal method is most suitable.

The IPR can represent both correct and incorrect (incomplete) C++ code and both individual translation units and merged units (such as a complete program). It is therefore suitable for both analysis of individual separately-compiled units and whole-program analysis.

The IPR represents ISO C++ code. That implies that it can trivially be extended to represent C code and common C++ dialects. However, since the initial aim of the Pivot is to look into high-level type-based and concept-based transformation, there is no immediate desire to extend it to cope with other languages with significantly different semantics, such as Fortran or Java.

User programs can annotate IPR nodes. An annotation is a (name,value) pair optionally attached to an IPR node by a Pivot application for its own uses. An annotation does not affect the way the IPR functions. The IPR "remembers" the C++ source locations of its nodes, so that a tool can refer back to the original source code.

3 High-Level Program Representation for HPC

Type systems have been introduced in programming primarily for correctness and efficiency. For example, if we know at translation time that an operation involving read and write accesses is alias free, we can exploit that for generating efficient code. Some programming languages, notably FORTRAN, are designed to allow the compiler to assume the absence of aliases. Other general-purpose programming languages, such as C or C++, allow only a restricted set of type-based aliasing. For example a pointer of type `void*` can be used to access any kind to data, but a pointer of type `int*` cannot be effectively used to access data of type `double`.

A typeful programming discipline can help make programs both correct and efficient. Abstract representation of programs naturally enables symbolic manipulation. Here, we present an approach to correctness and performance based on IPR. We will use the notion of *parallelizable vector* operation as a running example.

Why C++? For the SELL approach we need a widely-used general-purpose language for our "host language". For type transformation and high-level work, we need a language that provides a flexible type system that can be used in a type-safe manner. For high-performance computing, we need a language that can efficiently use hardware resources and is available on high-end computers. For wide use, we need a non-proprietary and operating system neutral language.

3.1 A Notion of Parallelizable

Consider the classic operation

```
z = a * x + y;
```

where `a` is scalar; `x`, `y` and `z` denotes vectors, and the operations `*` and `+` are component-wise. It can be parallelized if we know that the destination `z` does not overlap with the sources `x` and `y` in a way that displays non-trivial data dependencies. That happens, for example, if we know no vector element has its address taken. For exposition purpose, we will simplify the notion of Parallelizable to a collection of types whose objects support the operation `[]` (subscription) but not `&` (address-of) on its elements. For instance, in the generic function

```
template<Parallelizable T>
void f(const T& v)
{
    double a = v[2];     // #1: OK
    double* p = &v[2];   // #2: NOT OK.
}
```

line `#1` is valid but line `#2` is an error because it uses a forbidden operation. We generalized the standard notation `template<typename T>` which reads "for all T", to `template<Parallelizable T>` meaning "for all `T` such that `T` is is `Parallelizable`".

Concepts will almost certainly be part of C++0x. However, using IPR we can handle concepts without waiting for the C++ standards committee to decide on the technical details, see Section 3.3.

A programmer might use `Parallelizable` to constrain the use of a vector:

```
vector<double> v(10000);
// ...
f(v);  // f will use v as an Parallelizable (only)
```

Here we now know that `f()` will not use `&` on `v` even though the standard library vector actually allows that operation. We can use `f()` with its no-alias guarantee for any type that supports subscripting. For example we might use a STAPL [1] `pvector`:

```
pvector<double> vd(100000);
// ...
f(vd);
```

The concept checking allows no assumptions about types uses beyond what the concept actually specifies (here, a `Paralleizable` provides `[]`). In particular, no hierarchical ordering or run-time mechanisms are required.

Note that when defined in this way, `Parallelizable` requires no modification to C++0x or to any compiler. Furthermore, the use of `Parallelizable` is most likely to be composable with other facilities introduced as concepts – even if the facilities were developed in isolation.

Below, we will briefly present a high-level representation of C++ programs that support concept-based analysis and transformations.

3.2 Concepts in the IPR

A translation unit is represented as a graph with a distinguished root for the sequence of top-level declarations. In IPR, every entity in a C++ program is viewed as an expression possessing some type. So, types have types, which are called concepts. This becomes more useful, and maybe clearer, for a type variable as we find them in template parameter lists.

In Fig. 2, we have drawn a view of the representation of the declaration `Parallelizable T`. The declaration of the template-parameter `T` has type `Parallelizable`. If we knew about the syntax and semantics of `Parallelizable`,

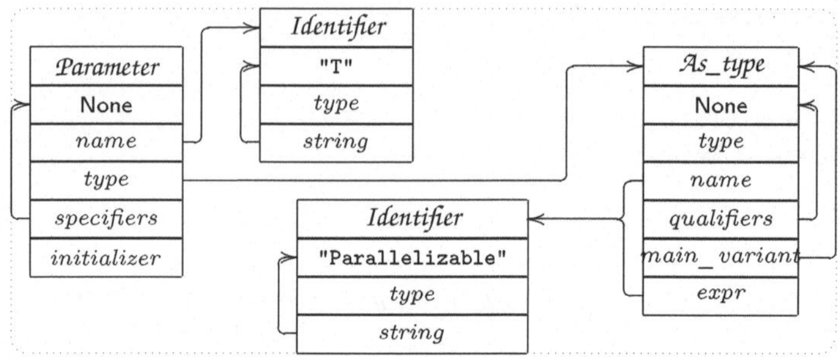

Fig. 2. IPR model `Parallelizable T`

that knowledge would be represented by a node referred to by the `type` field of the node with the identifier `"Parallelizable"`.

Note how `Parallelizable` fits into the IPR framework without modification or special rules. `Parallelizable` is simply a (deliberately trivial) example of what can be done with concepts in general.

Concepts are the basis for checking usage of types in templates, just like ordinary types serve to check uses of values in functions. Concept checking is done at two sites: (a) at template use site; and (b) at template definition site. If concept checking succeeds at both sites, then it is guaranteed that template arguments are used (only) according to the semantics expressed in the concepts. In the particular case of `Parallelizable`, it means that no vector has its address taken, and consequently parallelization transformations can be safely applied.

3.3 Getting Concepts into the IPR

How do we get concepts into our program? C++0x will most likely provide a way of specifying and checking concepts. That will provide a convenient handle for all concepts and for all SELL type-based analysis and transformation. For example:

```
concept Parallelizable<typename T> {
    // operations required by any Parallelizable type
    // only required operations will be accepted
    // for an object of a Parallelizable type
};
```

Once, this concept is part of the program, the Pivot (or similar tool) can operate based on its understanding of `Parallelizable`. Note that this "understaning" can be extra-linguistic based on the tool builders knowledge of the semantics of the library of which `Parallelizable` is part.

However, what do we do if we don't have a C++0x compiler that directly supports concepts? After all, C++0x won't be fully specified for another couple of years. We could rely on annotations, pragmas, language extensions, etc., but that has serious implications and costs. In particular, our programs almost certainly will not be composable with extensions defined and implemented by another group. The obvious alternative is to rely on convention: Traditionally, C++ programmers name template parameters to indicate their intended use. For example:

```
template<class Parallelizable>
void f(const Parallelizable& v)
{
    // operate on v according to Parallelizable rules
}
```

A Pivot application (tool) can easily recognize the type name Parallelizable and connect it to the definition of the concept Parallelizable as defined by the tool. From the point of view SELL and the Pivot, C++0x concepts is a significant convenience that provides a major advantage in notation and checking. However, it is only a (major) convenience because a Pivot-based tool can manipulate the IPR directly. For example, we could take code using the C++ standard library `accumulate`

```
template<class InputIterator, class T>
T accumulate(InputIterator first, InputIterator last,
             const T& init);
```

and transform every use into its equivalent parallel STAPL p-algorithm if (and only if) the STAPL requirements for its arguments are met. That is, the transformation takes place iff in addition to being an `InputIterator` the argument tyoe is a `BidirectionalIterator` or a `RandomAccessIterator`. This general approach to semantics-based transformation applies to all C++ standard algorithms described in terms of "abstract sequences".

The concept-based techniques rely critically on the use of templates, so that we can type template paraments with concepts to get a handle on their semantic properties. So, what do we do with code that doesn't use templates? Given an abstract syntax tree that represents a function declaration, we can transform it into a templated version and concept-check it. Consequently, we can check and transform a whole program as if it was fully templated.

4 Conclusion

The SELL, *Semantically Enhanced Library Language*, approach to supporting special-purpose languages can yield extension that are composable and portable. We presented our main tool for supporting the "semantic part" of that approach, *The Pivot*. The Pivot provides a general framework for analysis and transformation of C++ programs with an emphasis on high-level and type sensitive approaches. Our semantics-based analysis and transformation do not require modification to a host language and is minimally invasive to tool chains. It relies on a high-level program representation, the IPR, with emphasis on types and concepts. Using the IPR we can perform analysis and transformation for high-performance computing (as well as other forms of computing) that traditionally required special-purpose languages or ownership of a specialized compiler and related tool chain.

References

1. Ping An, Alin Jula, Silvius Rus, Steven Saunders, Tim Smith, Gabriel Tanase, Nathan Thomas, Nancy Amato, and Lawrence Rauchwerger. STAPL: An Adaptive, Generic Parallel C++ Library. In *Proceeedings of the International Workshop on Languages and Compilers for Parallel Computation (LCPC)*, pp. 193–208, Cumberland Falls, Kentucky, August 2001.
2. O. Bagge, K. Kalleberg, M. Haveraaen, and E. Visser. Design of the CodeBoost transformation system for domain-specific optimisation of C++ programs. In Dave Binkley and Paolo Tonella, editors, *Third International Workshop on Source Code Analysis and Manipulation (SCAM 2003)*, pp. 65–75, Amsterdam, The Netherlands, September 2003. IEEE Computer Society Press.
3. Gabriel Dos Reis and Bjarne Stroustrup. Specifying C++ concepts. *Conference Record of POPL '06: The 33th ACM SIGPLAN-SIGACT Symposium on Principles of Programming Languages*, pp. 295–308, Charleston (South Carolina), USA, January 2006.
4. Erich Gamma, Richard Helm, Ralph Johson, and John Vlissides. *Design Patterns.* Addison-Wesley, 1994.
5. International Organization for Standards. *International Standard ISO/IEC 14882. Programming Languages — C++*, 2nd edition, 2003.
6. Georges C. Necula, Scott McPeak, Shree Prakash Rahul, and Westley Weimer. CIL: Intermediate Language and Tools for Analysis and Tranformations of C Programs. In *Proceedings of the 11th International Conference on Compiler Construction*, volume 2304 of *Lecture Notes in Computer Science*, pp. 219–228. Springer-Verlag, 2002. `http://manju.cs.berkeley.edu/cil/`.
7. M. Schordan and D. Quinlan. A Source-to-Source Architecture for User-Defined Optimizations. In *Proceeding of Joint Modular Languages Conference (JMLC'03)*, volume 2789 of *Lecture Notes in Computer Science*, pp. 214–223. Springer-Verlag, 2003.
8. S. Schupp, D. Gregor, D. Musser, and S.-M. Liu. Semantic and behavioral library transformations. *Information and Software Technology*, 44(13):797–810, 2002.
9. Jeremy Siek, Douglas Gregor, Ronald Garcia, Jeremiah Willcock, Jaakko Järvi, and Andrew Lumsdaine. Concept for C++0x. Technical Report N1758=05-0018, ISO/IEC SC22/JTC1/WG21, January 2005.
10. Alexander Stepanov and Meng Lee. The Standard Template Library. Technical Report N0482=94-0095, ISO/IEC SC22/JTC1/WG21, May 1994.
11. Bjarne Stroustrup. *The C++ Programming Language.* Addison-Wesley, special edition, 2000.
12. Bjarne Stroustrup. A rationale for semantically enhanced library languages. In *Proceedings of LCSD'05*, October 2005.
13. Bjarne Stroustrup and Gabriel Dos Reis. Concepts — Design choices for template argument checking. Technical Report N1522, ISO/IEC SC22/JTC1/WG21, September 2003.
14. Bjarne Stroustrup and Gabriel Dos Reis. A Concept Design (rev.1). Technical Report N1782=05-0042, ISO/IEC SC22/JTC1/WG21, April 2005.
15. Gregory V. Wilson and Paul Lu, editors. *Parallel Programming using C++.* Scientific and Engineering Computation. MIT Press, 1996.

Compiler Supports and Optimizations for PAC VLIW DSP Processors

Yung-Chia Lin, Chung-Lin Tang, Chung-Ju Wu, Ming-Yu Hung, Yi-Ping You, Ya-Chiao Moo, Sheng-Yuan Chen, and Jenq-Kuen Lee

Department of Computer Science
National Tsing-Hua University
Hsinchu 300, Taiwan

Abstract. PAC DSP is a novel VLIW DSP processor exceedingly utilized with port-restricted, distinct partitioned register file structures in addition to the heterogeneous clustered datapath architecture to attain low power consumption and reduced die size; however, these architectural features lend new challenges to the compiler construction. This paper[1] describes our employment of the Open Research Compiler (ORC) infrastructure on PAC DSP architectures and the specific compilation design. Preliminary results indicated that our compiler development for PAC DSP is effective for the architecture and the evaluation is useful for the refinement of the architecture. Our experiences in designing the compiler support for heterogeneous VLIW DSP processors with irregular resource constraints may benefit the similar architectures.

1 Introduction

While high-end embedded processor and DSP design nowadays is moving towards exploiting intensively instruction level parallelism (ILP) and incorporating many advanced application specific features, the complexity of compilers for these advanced processors grows into immensity, which demands more long-term development efforts and extremely larger man power than before. ORC [1] is an open-source compiler infrastructure released from Intel, which incorporates most of the optimization techniques of industry strength so far and is capable of generating codes with good performance on its original IA-64 target by utilizing numbers of EPIC/VLIW architectural advantages.

In this paper, we study the issue of supporting ORC infrastructures for VLIW DSP processors. We present our experiences in the development of code generation support and preliminary register allocator design for a novel 32-bit VLIW DSP processor designed with several new architectural features, such as distinct partitioned register files with significant port restriction [2]. The target processor, named as Parallel Architecture Core (PAC) DSP [3], is being developed from

[1] The work was supported in part by NSC under grant no. 94-2220-E-007-019 and 94-2220-E-007-020, by Ministry of Economic Affairs under grant no. 94-EC-17-A-01-S1-034, and by MOE research excellent project under grant no. 94-2752-E-007-004-PAE in Taiwan.

E. Ayguadé et al. (Eds.): LCPC 2005, LNCS 4339, pp. 466–474, 2007.

scratch by SOC Technology Center at Industrial Technology Research Institute in Taiwan with several joint efforts of academic research works [4, 5]. PAC DSP is natively designed to meet the high-performance computing requirement of multimedia and the low power consumption demand of mobile system. Beside fundamental compilation support, the architecture evaluation with compilers advantages the development of PAC DSP in the early design stage since several tuning iterations may be needed between architecture and software designs by co-exploration, to attain the finest result with satisfactory in the end. The preliminary experiments showed that the effectiveness of our developed register allocation policies in the compiler framework to support the specific register file organizations in PAC architectures. Our experience may benefit the architecture designers and compiler developers who are interested in similar heterogeneous clustered VLIW architectures with port-restricted, distinct partitioned register file structures.

The remainder of this paper is organized as follows. Section 2 introduces the PAC DSP architecture and the compilation issues on it. The development of compilers for PAC DSP, including specific register allocator design for the architecture, is presented in Section 3. Experimental results of the early stage evaluation are then showed in Section 4. Finally, Section 5 concludes this paper.

2 An Insight into PAC DSP Architectures

PAC DSP is a 32bit, fixed-point, VLIW digital signal processor, constructed as a heterogeneous five-way issue VLIW architecture, comprised of two integer ALUs (I-unit), two memory load/store units (M-unit), and the program sequence control unit/scalar unit (B-unit). The M- and I- units are organized in pairs, and each pair contains exactly one M-unit and one I-unit to form a cluster arrangement with associated register files, logically appropriate for the complete data stream processing. The scalability of the cluster design in PAC DSP may allow the processor to easily involve more clusters than the current two. The B-unit with its own register file is placed separatedly from data stream processing clusters, capable of simple load/store and address arithmetic in addition to the operations of control flow instructions. The overall architecture is illustrated in Fig. 1.

As shown in Fig. 1, registers in PAC DSP are organized into four distinct partitioned register files and placed as cluster structures, to reduce wire connections between functional units and registers so that chip area and power consumption may be decreased. The A, AC, and R register files are private registers, directly attached to and only accessible by the M-, I-, and B-unit, respectively; D register files are shared within a cluster and can be used to communicate across clusters; only the B-unit, being able to access all D registers, is capable of executing cross-copy operations to move data between clusters. The internal of the D register file is further designed to utilize the instructional port switching technology in order that reducing more wire connections between the shared functional units. The technology, being referred to the name as '*ping-pong*

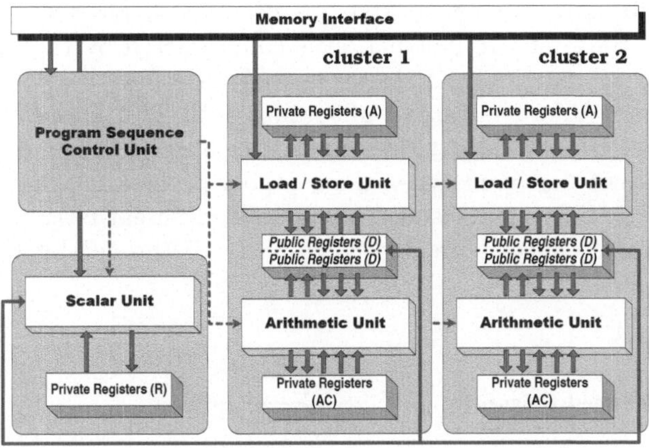

Fig. 1. The PAC DSP architecture illustration

register file structure', means dividing one register file into two banks, and each bank can only be accessed mutual-exclusively by one functional unit at the same time. The instruction bundle encoding contains the information of which bank to be accessed for each functional unit so that the hardware can do port switching between register file banks and functional units, to attain the purpose of data sharing within a cluster. The advantage of such a '*ping-pong register file structure*' design is believed to consume less power due to its reduced read/write ports [7] while retaining an effective way of data communication capability.

PAC DSP architectures introduce more interference between valid code generation, instruction scheduling, and register allocation than typical VLIW architectures. One of the most significant issues is caused by the '*ping-pong register file structure*', given that accesses from two different FUs to the same D register bank are mutually exclusive in a cycle. In addition, each FU in the PAC DSP has different set of instructions that could be executed and each instruction has its own register access constraints. All of these irregular designs make that conventional instruction scheduling policies and register allocation strategies are seldom applicable to the code generation for the PAC DSP architecture. For example, the short code sequence in Fig. 2: moves two constants into two virtual registers, TN1 and TN2 and then takes an arithmetic operation on them. While observing the first two instructions, these two can be scheduled in parallel only if TN1 and TN2 are assigned registers from distinct D register bank; if both are assigned to the same D register bank, they can only be scheduled and issued sequentially. But '*ping-pong register file structure*' affects more than limiting the parallelism in the instruction scheduling. While further observing the third instruction, the instance becomes complicated. Since the last instruction in the code sequence refers TN1 and TN2, which are the results of the first two instructions, TN1 and TN2 must be in the register access range of the last instruction. Referring to the Fig. 2, without considering other hazards, there must be a copy instruction insertion before the last instruction if allocating TN1 and TN2 to different D register banks for parallelizing the first two instruction. Therefore, the advantage of parallelizing the first two instruction is counteracted by the insertion of the additional copy instruction and the generated code may be worse because the code size is larger than the case of allocating both TN1 and TN2 to the same D register bank. But allocating the same D register bank will always raise the register pressure of that bank when the compiler process the register allocation, and spilling from different register file will make different cost in the PAC DSP architecture, these cause more unpredictability of the combined effects of all code generation issues.

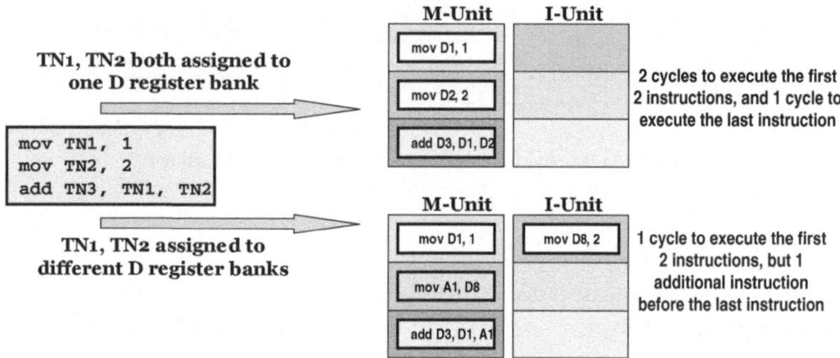

Fig. 2. The Illustration of interference caused by Ping-Pong register file structures

Vector Dot Product

$X = (A, B)$

$Y = (7,8)$

$Z = 6 + X \bullet Y$

mov TN1, 6
mov TN2, .A
lw TN3, [TN2]
mov TN4, 7
mul TN5, TN3, TN4
add TN6, TN1, TN5
mov TN7, .B
lw TN8, [TN7]
mov TN9, 8
mul TN10, TN8, TN9
add TN11, TN6, TN10
mov TN12, .Z
sw TN11, [TN12]

Exploiting Parallelism in Two Clusters as Usual

B-Unit	M-Unit	I-Unit	M-Unit	I-Unit
	mov A0, .A	mov AC0, 6	mov A8, .B	mov AC8, 8
	lw D0, [A0]	mov AC1, 7	lw D17, [A8]	
		mul D1, D0, AC1		mul D18, D17, AC8
copy D3, D18	mov A1, .Z	add D2, AC0, D1		
	add D4, D2, D3			
	sw D4, [A1]			

Utilizing Ping-pong Registers (1 more instruction, but may turn-off 1 I-Unit)

B-Unit	M-Unit	I-Unit	M-Unit	I-Unit
mov R0, 6	mov A0, .A	mov AC0, 7	mov A8, .B	
copy D1, R0	lw D0, [A0]	mov AC1, 8	lw D17, [A8]	
copy D8, D17	mov A1, .Z	mul D2, D0, AC0		
	add A2, D1, D2	mul D9, D8, AC1		
	add D10, A2, D9			
	sw D10, [A1]			

Fig. 3. An example of generating optimal scheduled codes across clusters

Another critical subject of how the register allocation interferences with both the instruction scheduling and the code generation is issued by the implementation of data communication across clusters in the PAC DSP architecture. The current version of PAC DSP require the code to explicitly issue a cross-cluster copy instruction to complete the data communication between clusters. Although the cross-cluster copy instruction is designed to be issued by the B-unit without occupying a slot in the clusters, the additional instruction insertion introduces additional data-dependency and data available latency for any code which is scheduled and distributed into two clusters. Fig. 3 gives an illustration of the two possible scheduling of code distributed on the two clusters (considering only major constraints for easier understanding), which both have their own benefit. As a result, it seems that the compiler for PAC DSP needs a well cluster usage to avoid the penalty of cross-cluster communication disadvantaging the parallelism of two clusters. The complication and non-determinism with the interference of all these issues make more challenges to construct a good compiler for the PAC DSP architecture.

3 Compiler Supports for PAC DSP Processors

In this section, we describe our development works of applying compiler supports for the PAC DSP architecture based on the ORC infrastructure. The preliminary employment from original IA-64 to PAC DSP includes the new implementation of machine description tables and the essential supports for PAC DSP code generation. Some optimization phases such as LNO (Loop-Nest Optimizer) and EBO (Extended Block Optimizer) are also initially ported and individually tested. Till now, our development of compiler support for PAC DSP is still an on-going effort. In this paper, we focus on the studies of supporting basic ORC infrastructures for PAC VLIW DSP processors in register allocation as follows.

With PAC's highly-partitioned register file design, the phase-interaction between register allocation and instruction scheduling becomes a critical problem, elevating this classical phase ordering issue in compiler code generation. Our current proposed solution to this problem, is to add a new instruction scheduling phase before register allocation/assignment by *simulated annealing* (SA). The design is extended from Leupers' work [8] and our initial implementation [6], by using a hybrid instruction scheduling/cluster assignment algorithm to iteratively approach the near-optimal result. The algorithm roughly operates by first generating a random cluster partitioning of instructions; a modified List-Scheduler (LS) then schedules the partitioned instructions, inserting/managing cross cluster communications along the way.

The following iterations then make a random change to the partitioning state, and re-run the LS to schedule again. The LS returns the obtained schedule length of the instructions as the 'energy' value used in an usual simulated annealing optimization process, representing an evaluation of the current partitioning state. Depending on that improvement is gained or not, the random change may be retained or discarded. This process is iterated until the energy/evaluation falls to be under some thresholds, where we are confident that the obtained optimization state is of sufficient quality.

Adapting this simulated annealing solution for the PAC DSP involves changes in the formulation of optimized state: our search is for register file assignments in the chosen schematic placement (as the search space) for virtual registers, instead of the original bi-partitioning of the instructions. The above algorithm in Fig. 4 is the high-level simulated annealing algorithm. It controls the scheduler, which does fine-grain sequencing of operations, and returns the schedule length

Hybrid Instruction Scheduling/Register File Assignment by Simulated Annealing

```
   Input:  n operations to be scheduled
  Output:  Schedule of the n instructions and a register file assignment (RFA) map:
           VR: set of all virtual registers, RF: set of register files
           RFA_map = {(v1, f1), (v2, f2), ...} vi ∈ VR, fi ∈ RF
1. Choose a schematic register file placement(e.g. 1 cluster, 2 clusters, ...).
2. Make initial register file assignments: randomly assign each
   virtual register to any of the wanted register files, and record in RFA_map.
3. Given RFA_map, run PAC_Scheduler,
   and set sched_len to the computed total schedule length in cycles.
4. Set initial values for:
       threshold: threshold value for the simulated annealing process.
       energy: initial energy, larger than threshold.
       p_test: a probability test value p_test (0 < p_test < 1).
5. Repeat the following steps while energy > threshold:
   5a. Make change in RFA_map:
       randomly choose a virtual register, and assign it to a different register file.
       optionally change the schematic register file placement.
   5b. With the new RFA assignment change, run PAC_Scheduler again,
       and set new_sched_len to the new count of total schedule length.
   5c. Adjust energy, sched_len, and RFA_map by the following rules:
       If new_sched_len < sched_len then
         decrease energy, set sched_len to new_sched_len,
         and keep the new RFA changes made in step 5a.
       If new_sched_len ≥ sched_len, get random number 0 ≤ R ≤ 1:
         If R > p_test then
           decrease energy, set sched_len to new_sched_len,
           and keep the changes made in step 5a.
         If R ≤ p_test then
           increase energy and revert changes made in step 5a.
6. Optionally choose another schematic register file placement,
   and repeat steps 2–5 to select the better results.
7. Retain the final schedule and RFA_map as the output results.
```

Fig. 4. The high-level simulated annealing algorithm

The *PAC_Scheduler* Algorithm

```
  Input:  ReadyList of operations to be scheduled
          RFA_map, in the form of a function RegisterFile : VR → RF
 Output:  Schedule of the n instructions, and the schedule length
While ReadyList is not empty:
   Select operation Op from ReadyList
   Find earliest cycle Cycle we can schedule Op
   While Op is not scheduled:
       Examine available resources in Cycle, and:
       For each register operand oi of Op:
         If no resources available to access RegisterFile(oi):
           Enumerate possible copy sequences to transfer oi to an accessible register file
           For each copy sequence cpseq
             If cpseq is schedulable in prior cycles:
               Feasible(cpseq) = true
       If for each register operand oi of Op we have resources to access RegisterFile(oi),
       or we have some c such that Feasible(c):
         Schedule Op into Cycle, advance ReadyList
         Break from inner loop
       else
         Increment Cycle
Return length of schedule
```

Fig. 5. The scheduler/evaluation algorithm

as the evaluation of the current optimization state. The two optional procedures in the algorithm could let the compiler dynamically control the iterative scale and limit the register file usage to coordinate with other optimizations; they may also improve the overall register allocation speed.

Fig. 5 illustrates more details of the scheduler algorithms. In general, the overall operation of the algorithm is to proceed through the state space, making changes according to the feedback obtained from the LS. The assignment of register files will improve progressively throughout the SA iterations, with respect to the schedulable length of the instructions. A final register allocator is then run to allocate and assign hardware registers, which is guided by the register file assignments (RFA_map).

4 Experimental Results

Preliminary experiments were done with the DSPstone benchmarks [9]. Since the PAC DSP compiler is still in progress, we only evaluated some stable optimization combinations for early stage performance evaluations our designs. All benchmark programs are compiled with three types of option combinations and disabling all other optimizations; they are the traditional-approach-based register allocation (TRA), the traditional-approach-based register allocation plus LNO and EBO (LNO+EBO), and the register allocation using the simulated-annealing approach (SARA), respectively. The TRA, which is a modification of the original ORC register allocation that assumes PAC DSP has only one unified register file containing all registers and inserts necessary codes to make register allocation result executable, is treated as the base reference in the comparison. Fig. 6 compares the speedup of DSP benchmarks on the later two options, LNO+EBO and SARA, with the numbers of -O0 (with the traditional approach based register allocation). As shown in Fig. 6, the performance gain for PAC DSP varies widely across different benchmarks with the average 1.78 speedup for LNO+EBO and the average 1.58 speedup for SARA. Though the integrated test of LNO+EBO plus SARA has not yet stable enough to exhibit the overall advantage, the results shows that our approaches in LNO, EBO, and register allocation could achieve significant performance improvement for code compilation in most cases. Also, the simulated-annealing approach gives a locally exhaustive exploration on how the register usage affects PAC DSP and investigate the flaws of the architecture. Currently, there is a fateful hazard among any data that has dependency across different functional units and needs 3 cycle delay slots. This hazard makes a contradictive impact on exploiting ILP on all functional units because the increase of ILP will often introduce more hazards, causing some of the benchmark codes, like *biquad_one_section*, less affected by our optimizations. By our evaluations, several suggestions have also been proposed to the DSP design team, to enhance the architecture support for better compiler code generation. The revision process is on-going for the next generation of PAC DSP.

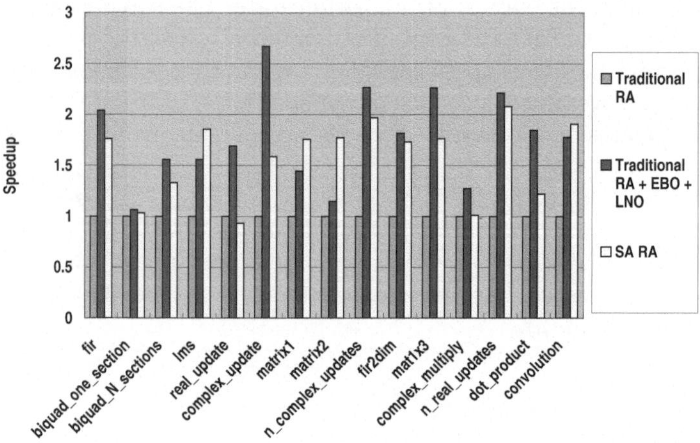

Fig. 6. The Speedup comparison while activating various optimization options

5 Conclusion

In this paper we present the compiler development for a novel high-end DSP processor, PAC DSP, which comes with a clustered architecture design and distinct partitioned register files. We demonstrated the viability of our approaches based on ORC infrastructure to PAC DSP via several preliminary experiments which are done with the PAC DSP prototype. Since some drawbacks of the first generation of PAC DSP architecture were revealed by the evaluation, we are currently referring to the experiences and reforming the development of compilers for the next generation of PAC DSP architecture, which will further extend our current works.

References

1. Roy Ju, Sun Chan, and Chengyong Wu: Open Research Compiler for the Itanium Family. Tutorial at the 34th Annual Int'l Symposium on Microarchitecture, Dec. 2001
2. Tay-Jyi Lin, Chen-Chia Lee, Chih-Wei Liu, and Chein-Wei Jen: A Novel Register Organization for VLIW Digital Signal Processors. Proceedings of 2005 IEEE International Symposium on VLSI Design, Automation, and Test, pages 335–338, 2005
3. David Chang and Max Baron: Taiwan's Roadmap to Leadership in Design. Microprocessor Report, In-Stat/MDR, Dec. 2004. http://www.mdronline.com/mpr/archive/mpr_2004.html
4. Tay-Jyi Lin, Chin-Chi Chang. Chen-Chia Lee, and Chein-Wei Jen: An Efficient VLIW DSP Architecture for Baseband Processing. Proceedings of the 21th International Conference on Computer Design, 2003

5. Tay-Jyi Lin, Chie-Min Chao, Chia-Hsien Liu, Pi-Chen Hsiao, Shin-Kai Chen, Li-Chun Lin, Chih-Wei Liu, Chein-Wei Jen: Computer architecture: A unified processor architecture for RISC & VLIW DSP. Proceedings of the 15th ACM Great Lakes symposium on VLSI, April 2005
6. Cheng-Wei Chen, Chung-Lin Tang, Yung-Chia Lin, and Jenq-Kuen Lee: ORC2DSP: Compiler Infrastructure Supports for VLIW DSP Processors. Proceedings of 2005 IEEE International Symposium on VLSI Design, Automation, and Test, pages 224-227, 2005
7. S. Rixner, W. J. Dally, B. Khailany, P. Mattson, U. J. Kapasi, and J. D. Owens: Register organization for media processing. International Symposium on High Performance Computer Architecture (HPCA), pp.375-386, 2000
8. R. Leupers: Instruction scheduling for clustered VLIW DSPs. In Proc. Int'l Conference on Parallel Architecture and Compilation Techniques, pages 291–300, Oct. 2000
9. V. Zivojnovic, J. Martinez, C. Schläger and H. Meyr: DSPstone: A DSP-Oriented Benchmarking Methodology. Proc. of ICSPAT, Dallas, 1994

Author Index

Lecture Notes in Computer Science

For information about Vols. 1–4264

please contact your bookseller or Springer

Vol. 4377: M. Abe (Ed.), Topics in Cryptology – CT-RSA 2007. XI, 403 pages. 2006.

Vol. 4369: M. Umeda, A. Wolf, O. Bartenstein, U. Geske, D. Seipel, O. Takata (Eds.), Declarative Programming for Knowledge Management. X, 229 pages. 2006. (Sublibrary LNAI).

Vol. 4361: H.J. Hoogeboom, G. Păun, G. Rozenberg, A. Salomaa (Eds.), Membrane Computing. IX, 555 pages. 2006.

Vol. 4357: L. Buttyán, V. Gligor, D. Westhoff (Eds.), Security and Privacy in Ad-hoc and Sensor Neworks. X, 193 pages. 2006.

Vol. 4355: J. Julliand, O. Kouchnarenko (Eds.), B 2007: Formal Specification and Development in B. XIII, 293 pages. 2006.

Vol. 4353: T. Schwentick, D. Suciu (Eds.), Database Theory – ICDT 2007. XI, 419 pages. 2006.

Vol. 4348: S.T. Taft, R.A. Duff, R.L. Brukardt, E. Ploedereder, P. Leroy (Eds.), Ada 2005 Reference Manual. XXII, 765 pages. 2006.

Vol. 4347: J. Lopez (Ed.), Critical Information Infrastructures Security. X, 286 pages. 2006.

Vol. 4345: N. Maglaveras, I. Chouvarda, V. Koutkias, R. Brause (Eds.), Biological and Medical Data Analysis. XIII, 496 pages. 2006. (Sublibrary LNBI).

Vol. 4344: V. Gruhn, F. Oquendo (Eds.), Software Architecture. X, 245 pages. 2006.

Vol. 4342: H. de Swart, E. Orłowska, G. Schmidt, M. Roubens (Eds.), Theory and Application of Relational Structures as Knowledge Instruments II. X, 373 pages. 2006. (Sublibrary LNAI).

Vol. 4341: P.Q. Nguyen (Ed.), Progress in Cryptology - VIETCRYPT 2006. XI, 385 pages. 2006.

Vol. 4339: E. Ayguadé, G. Baumgartner, J. Ramanujam, P. Sadayappan (Eds.), Languages and Compilers for Parallel Computing. XI, 476 pages. 2006.

Vol. 4338: P. Kalra, S. Peleg (Eds.), Computer Vision, Graphics and Image Processing. XV, 965 pages. 2006.

Vol. 4337: S. Arun-Kumar, N. Garg (Eds.), FSTTCS 2006: Foundations of Software Technology and Theoretical Computer Science. XIII, 430 pages. 2006.

Vol. 4333: U. Reimer, D. Karagiannis (Eds.), Practical Aspects of Knowledge Management. XII, 338 pages. 2006. (Sublibrary LNAI).

Vol. 4332: A. Bagchi, V. Atluri (Eds.), Information Systems Security. XV, 382 pages. 2006.

Vol. 4331: G. Min, B. Di Martino, L.T. Yang, M. Guo, G. Ruenger (Eds.), Frontiers of High Performance Computing and Networking – ISPA 2006 Workshops. XXXVII, 1141 pages. 2006.

Vol. 4330: M. Guo, L.T. Yang, B. Di Martino, H.P. Zima, J. Dongarra, F. Tang (Eds.), Parallel and Distributed Processing and Applications. XVIII, 953 pages. 2006.

Vol. 4329: R. Barua, T. Lange (Eds.), Progress in Cryptology - INDOCRYPT 2006. X, 454 pages. 2006.

Vol. 4328: D. Penkler, M. Reitenspiess, F. Tam (Eds.), Service Availability. X, 289 pages. 2006.

Vol. 4327: M. Baldoni, U. Endriss (Eds.), Declarative Agent Languages and Technologies IV. VIII, 257 pages. 2006. (Sublibrary LNAI).

Vol. 4326: S. Göbel, R. Malkewitz, I. Iurgel (Eds.), Technologies for Interactive Digital Storytelling and Entertainment. X, 384 pages. 2006.

Vol. 4325: J. Cao, I. Stojmenovic, X. Jia, S.K. Das (Eds.), Mobile Ad-hoc and Sensor Networks. XIX, 887 pages. 2006.

Vol. 4320: R. Gotzhein, R. Reed (Eds.), System Analysis and Modeling: Language Profiles. X, 229 pages. 2006.

Vol. 4319: L.-W. Chang, W.-N. Lie (Eds.), Advances in Image and Video Technology. XXVI, 1347 pages. 2006.

Vol. 4318: H. Lipmaa, M. Yung, D. Lin (Eds.), Information Security and Cryptology. XI, 305 pages. 2006.

Vol. 4317: S.K. Madria, K.T. Claypool, R. Kannan, P. Uppuluri, M.M. Gore (Eds.), Distributed Computing and Internet Technology. XIX, 466 pages. 2006.

Vol. 4316: M.M. Dalkilic, S. Kim, J. Yang (Eds.), Data Mining and Bioinformatics. VIII, 197 pages. 2006. (Sublibrary LNBI).

Vol. 4313: T. Margaria, B. Steffen (Eds.), Leveraging Applications of Formal Methods. IX, 197 pages. 2006.

Vol. 4312: S. Sugimoto, J. Hunter, A. Rauber, A. Morishima (Eds.), Digital Libraries: Achievements, Challenges and Opportunities. XVIII, 571 pages. 2006.

Vol. 4311: K. Cho, P. Jacquet (Eds.), Technologies for Advanced Heterogeneous Networks II. XI, 253 pages. 2006.

Vol. 4309: P. Inverardi, M. Jazayeri (Eds.), Software Engineering Education in the Modern Age. VIII, 207 pages. 2006.

Vol. 4308: S. Chaudhuri, S.R. Das, H.S. Paul, S. Tirthapura (Eds.), Distributed Computing and Networking. XIX, 608 pages. 2006.

Vol. 4307: P. Ning, S. Qing, N. Li (Eds.), Information and Communications Security. XIV, 558 pages. 2006.

Vol. 4306: Y. Avrithis, Y. Kompatsiaris, S. Staab, N.E. O'Connor (Eds.), Semantic Multimedia. XII, 241 pages. 2006.

Vol. 4305: A.A. Shvartsman (Ed.), Principles of Distributed Systems. XIII, 441 pages. 2006.

Vol. 4304: A. Sattar, B.-h. Kang (Eds.), AI 2006: Advances in Artificial Intelligence. XXVII, 1303 pages. 2006. (Sublibrary LNAI).

Vol. 4303: A. Hoffmann, B.-h. Kang, D. Richards, S. Tsumoto (Eds.), Advances in Knowledge Acquisition and Management. XI, 259 pages. 2006. (Sublibrary LNAI).

Vol. 4302: J. Domingo-Ferrer, L. Franconi (Eds.), Privacy in Statistical Databases. XI, 383 pages. 2006.

Vol. 4301: D. Pointcheval, Y. Mu, K. Chen (Eds.), Cryptology and Network Security. XIII, 381 pages. 2006.

Vol. 4300: Y.Q. Shi (Ed.), Transactions on Data Hiding and Multimedia Security I. IX, 139 pages. 2006.

Vol. 4299: S. Renals, S. Bengio, J.G. Fiscus (Eds.), Machine Learning for Multimodal Interaction. XII, 470 pages. 2006.

Vol. 4297: Y. Robert, M. Parashar, R. Badrinath, V.K. Prasanna (Eds.), High Performance Computing - HiPC 2006. XXIV, 642 pages. 2006.

Vol. 4296: M.S. Rhee, B. Lee (Eds.), Information Security and Cryptology – ICISC 2006. XIII, 358 pages. 2006.

Vol. 4295: J.D. Carswell, T. Tezuka (Eds.), Web and Wireless Geographical Information Systems. XI, 269 pages. 2006.

Vol. 4294: A. Dan, W. Lamersdorf (Eds.), Service-Oriented Computing – ICSOC 2006. XIX, 653 pages. 2006.

Vol. 4293: A. Gelbukh, C.A. Reyes-Garcia (Eds.), MICAI 2006: Advances in Artificial Intelligence. XXVIII, 1232 pages. 2006. (Sublibrary LNAI).

Vol. 4292: G. Bebis, R. Boyle, B. Parvin, D. Koracin, P. Remagnino, A. Nefian, G. Meenakshisundaram, V. Pascucci, J. Zara, J. Molineros, H. Theisel, T. Malzbender (Eds.), Advances in Visual Computing, Part II. XXXII, 906 pages. 2006.

Vol. 4291: G. Bebis, R. Boyle, B. Parvin, D. Koracin, P. Remagnino, A. Nefian, G. Meenakshisundaram, V. Pascucci, J. Zara, J. Molineros, H. Theisel, T. Malzbender (Eds.), Advances in Visual Computing, Part I. XXXI, 916 pages. 2006.

Vol. 4290: M. van Steen, M. Henning (Eds.), Middleware 2006. XIII, 425 pages. 2006.

Vol. 4289: M. Ackermann, B. Berendt, M. Grobelnik, A. Hotho, D. Mladenič, G. Semeraro, M. Spiliopoulou, G. Stumme, V. Svatek, M. van Someren (Eds.), Semantics, Web and Mining. X, 197 pages. 2006. (Sublibrary LNAI).

Vol. 4288: T. Asano (Ed.), Algorithms and Computation. XX, 766 pages. 2006.

Vol. 4287: C. Mao, T. Yokomori (Eds.), DNA Computing. XII, 440 pages. 2006.

Vol. 4286: P. Spirakis, M. Mavronicolas, S. Kontogiannis (Eds.), Internet and Network Economics. XI, 401 pages. 2006.

Vol. 4285: Y. Matsumoto, R. Sproat, K.-F. Wong, M. Zhang (Eds.), Computer Processing of Oriental Languages. XVII, 544 pages. 2006. (Sublibrary LNAI).

Vol. 4284: X. Lai, K. Chen (Eds.), Advances in Cryptology – ASIACRYPT 2006. XIV, 468 pages. 2006.

Vol. 4283: Y.Q. Shi, B. Jeon (Eds.), Digital Watermarking. XII, 474 pages. 2006.

Vol. 4282: Z. Pan, A. Cheok, M. Haller, R.W.H. Lau, H. Saito, R. Liang (Eds.), Advances in Artificial Reality and Tele-Existence. XXIII, 1347 pages. 2006.

Vol. 4281: K. Barkaoui, A. Cavalcanti, A. Cerone (Eds.), Theoretical Aspects of Computing - ICTAC 2006. XV, 371 pages. 2006.

Vol. 4280: A.K. Datta, M. Gradinariu (Eds.), Stabilization, Safety, and Security of Distributed Systems. XVII, 590 pages. 2006.

Vol. 4279: N. Kobayashi (Ed.), Programming Languages and Systems. XI, 423 pages. 2006.

Vol. 4278: R. Meersman, Z. Tari, P. Herrero (Eds.), On the Move to Meaningful Internet Systems 2006: OTM 2006 Workshops, Part II. XLV, 1004 pages. 2006.

Vol. 4277: R. Meersman, Z. Tari, P. Herrero (Eds.), On the Move to Meaningful Internet Systems 2006: OTM 2006 Workshops, Part I. XLV, 1009 pages. 2006.

Vol. 4276: R. Meersman, Z. Tari (Eds.), On the Move to Meaningful Internet Systems 2006: CoopIS, DOA, GADA, and ODBASE, Part II. XXXII, 752 pages. 2006.

Vol. 4275: R. Meersman, Z. Tari (Eds.), On the Move to Meaningful Internet Systems 2006: CoopIS, DOA, GADA, and ODBASE, Part I. XXXI, 1115 pages. 2006.

Vol. 4274: Q. Huo, B. Ma, E.-S. Chng, H. Li (Eds.), Chinese Spoken Language Processing. XXIV, 805 pages. 2006. (Sublibrary LNAI).

Vol. 4273: I. Cruz, S. Decker, D. Allemang, C. Preist, D. Schwabe, P. Mika, M. Uschold, L. Aroyo (Eds.), The Semantic Web - ISWC 2006. XXIV, 1001 pages. 2006.

Vol. 4272: P. Havinga, M. Lijding, N. Meratnia, M. Wegdam (Eds.), Smart Sensing and Context. XI, 267 pages. 2006.

Vol. 4271: F.V. Fomin (Ed.), Graph-Theoretic Concepts in Computer Science. XIII, 358 pages. 2006.

Vol. 4270: H. Zha, Z. Pan, H. Thwaites, A.C. Addison, M. Forte (Eds.), Interactive Technologies and Sociotechnical Systems. XVI, 547 pages. 2006.

Vol. 4269: R. State, S. van der Meer, D. O'Sullivan, T. Pfeifer (Eds.), Large Scale Management of Distributed Systems. XIII, 282 pages. 2006.

Vol. 4268: G. Parr, D. Malone, M. Ó Foghlú (Eds.), Autonomic Principles of IP Operations and Management. XIII, 237 pages. 2006.

Vol. 4267: A. Helmy, B. Jennings, L. Murphy, T. Pfeifer (Eds.), Autonomic Management of Mobile Multimedia Services. XIII, 257 pages. 2006.

Vol. 4266: H. Yoshiura, K. Sakurai, K. Rannenberg, Y. Murayama, S. Kawamura (Eds.), Advances in Information and Computer Security. XIII, 438 pages. 2006.

Vol. 4265: L. Todorovski, N. Lavrač, K.P. Jantke (Eds.), Discovery Science. XIV, 384 pages. 2006. (Sublibrary LNAI).